The Boundaries of Freedom

The Boundaries of Freedom brings together, for the first time in English, a group of key scholars whose work is helping to reconceive the social and cultural history of Brazilian slavery. Brazil was the largest and most enduring slave society in the Americas, with nearly five million enslaved Africans brought forcibly to its shores over four-and-a-half centuries. Slavery was integral to every aspect of its history. This book introduces English-language readers to a paradigm-shifting renaissance in Brazilian scholarship that has upended long-standing assumptions about slavery's relation to law, property, sexuality, and family; reconceived understandings of slave economies; and explored issues of agency, autonomy, identity, and freedom. These vibrant debates are explored in fifteen essays that emphasize the centrality of slavery, abolition, and Black subjectivity in the forging of modern Brazil and place the Brazilian experience in dialogue with the afterlives of slavery worldwide. This title is also available as Open Access on Cambridge Core.

Brodwyn Fischer is Professor of Latin American History at the University of Chicago. Her book *A Poverty of Rights* received awards from the Social Science History Association, the Urban Studies Association, the Brazilian Studies Association, and the Conference on Latin American History. She is also coeditor of *Cities from Scratch: Poverty and Informality in Urban Latin America* and the author of essays on the histories of law, race, informality, and inequality in urban Brazil.

Keila Grinberg is Professor of Latin American and Atlantic History at the University of Pittsburgh. She is a specialist on slavery and race in the Atlantic world. Her book *A Black Jurist in a Slave Society* was a finalist for the 2020 Frederick Douglass Prize.

T0371261

Afro-Latin America

Series editors

George Reid Andrews, *University of Pittsburgh*
Alejandro de la Fuente, *Harvard University*

This series reflects the coming of age of the new, multidisciplinary field of Afro-Latin American Studies, which centers on the histories, cultures, and experiences of people of African descent in Latin America. The series aims to showcase scholarship produced by different disciplines, including history, political science, sociology, ethnomusicology, anthropology, religious studies, art, law, and cultural studies. It covers the full temporal span of the African Diaspora in Latin America, from the early colonial period to the present, and includes continental Latin America, the Caribbean, and other key areas in the region where Africans and their descendants have made a significant impact.

A full list of titles published in the series can be found at:
www.cambridge.org/afro-latin-america

The Boundaries of Freedom

Slavery, Abolition, and the Making of Modern Brazil

Edited by

BRODWYN FISCHER

University of Chicago

KEILA GRINBERG

University of Pittsburgh

CAMBRIDGE
UNIVERSITY PRESS

CAMBRIDGE
UNIVERSITY PRESS

Shaftesbury Road, Cambridge CB2 8EA, United Kingdom

One Liberty Plaza, 20th Floor, New York, NY 10006, USA

477 Williamstown Road, Port Melbourne, VIC 3207, Australia

314–321, 3rd Floor, Plot 3, Splendor Forum, Jasola District Centre,
New Delhi – 110025, India

103 Penang Road, #05–06/07, Visioncrest Commercial, Singapore 238467

Cambridge University Press is part of Cambridge University Press & Assessment.

It furthers the University's mission by disseminating knowledge in the pursuit of
education, learning, and research at the highest international levels of excellence.

www.cambridge.org
Information on this title: www.cambridge.org/9781009287975
DOI: 10.1017/9781009287968

First published 2023
Reissued as Open Access, 2023

A catalogue record for this publication is available from the British Library.

ISBN 978-1-108-83153-6 Hardback
ISBN 978-1-009-28797-5 Paperback

Contents

Contents

Figures

Tables

This title is part of the Cambridge University Press *Flip it Open* Open Access Books program and has been "flipped" from a traditional book to an Open Access book through the program.

Flip it Open sells books through regular channels, treating them at the outset in the same way as any other book; they are part of our library collections for Cambridge Core, and sell as hardbacks and ebooks. The one crucial difference is that we make an upfront commitment that when each of these books meets a set revenue threshold we make them available to everyone Open Access via Cambridge Core.

This paperback edition has been released as part of our Open Access commitment and we would like to use this as an opportunity to thank the libraries and other buyers who have helped us flip this and the other titles in the program to Open Access.

To see the full list of libraries that we know have contributed to *Flip it Open*, as well as the other titles in the program please visit www.cambridge.org/fio-acknowledgements

Acknowledgments

This collection owes its greatest debt to the generations of scholars who have collectively reimagined the history of Brazilian slavery, abolition, and freedom over the past half-century. The work here only exists in dialogue with this immensely rich body of scholarship. We owe thanks as well to the Brazilian public institutions that have made deep historical work possible by supporting universities, archives, libraries, museums, and the students, scholars and artists who occupy them. The Brazilian National Council for Scientific and Technological Development (CNPq), the Brazilian Coordination for the Improvement of Higher Education Personnel (CAPES), the Carlos Chagas Foundation in the State of Rio de Janeiro (FAPERJ), and the São Paulo Research Foundation (FAPESP) have directly supported much of the research for this volume. At a time when faith in the public value of historical research is under grave threat, it has never been more important to recognize the enormous social and intellectual impacts of such investment.

We also owe thanks to a number of people and organizations in the United States. The Tinker Foundation sponsored Keila Grinberg's visiting professorship at the University of Chicago. The Tinker Foundation and the University of Chicago's Center for Latin American Studies, Franke Institute for the Humanities, and Center for the Study of Race, Politics and Culture funded the two workshops that incubated *The Boundaries of Freedom* from idea to text. Natalie Arsenault, Jamie Gentry, and Claudia Giribaldi made our meetings possible with their generosity, warmth, and expert organizational skills.

The discussions at those two conferences involved a far wider circle than is represented in these pages. Felipe Azevedo e Souza, Dain Borges,

Mariana Candido, Sidney Chalhoub, Roquinaldo Ferreira, Israel Ozanam, and Martha Santos were an integral part of the initial discussions, and we are very grateful for their impact on the work published here. Paulina Alberto, Peter Beattie, Dain Borges, Sherwin Bryant, Caitlin Fitz, Thomas Holt, Emilio Kourí, Kate Masur, Agnes Lugo-Ortiz, Julie Saville, and Tara Zahra all offered generous comments on our draft articles. Amy Dru Stanley, Larissa Brewer García, César Braga Pinto, and many others offered precious feedback.

We are grateful also to George Reid Andrews and Alejandro de la Fuente for finding a home for this work in their Afro-Latin American series, as well as to Cecilia Cancellaro, Ruth Boyes, and everyone else at Cambridge University Press who worked to bring this project to completion. We are grateful as well to Sofía Kourí for editing the footnotes and bibliography, to Tanya Izzard for the index, and to Wade Guyitt for copy editing.

The coeditors would like to extend thanks to all of the volume's contributors and also to our families, who have been more than patient with our periodic absences, late nights, and postponed conversations. Finally, we wish to express our deep sadness at the untimely passing of Ricardo Salles in November of 2021. A key contributor to this volume, Ricardo was among the most preeminent historians of his generation. His essential work on slavery, abolition, agrarian economies and the Paraguayan War left an indelible mark on our field, and his friendship and collaboration enriched our personal and professional lives. Ricardo's influence infuses this volume, and we pay tribute to his life work.

INTRODUCTION

Slavery and Freedom in Nineteenth-Century Brazil

Brodwyn Fischer and Keila Grinberg

There was sun, abundant sun, on that 1888 Sunday when the Senate
approved the abolition decree and the Princess-Regent signed it. We all
went to the streets ... [W]e all breathed happiness, everything was ecstasy.
Truly, it was the only day of public delirium that I can remember.[1]

With these words, Brazilian novelist Joaquim Maria Machado de Assis
described May 13, 1888, the day that ended legalized slavery in his country.
Brazil was the last nation in the Western hemisphere to abolish slavery; it had
also been the largest and the most enduring slave society in the Americas. For
more than 350 years, from the arrival of the first enslaved Africans in the
early sixteenth century until abolition, slavery shaped Brazilian history
across nearly every region of its continental geography. Over those centuries,
nearly five million enslaved Africans arrived in Brazil, more than 45 percent
of the total number of persons forcibly brought to the Americas.[2] In the years
that followed that sunny May 13 of abolition, Machado de Assis himself
would be witness to the brevity of its joy and to the immense challenges of
Brazilian freedom. The scale of those challenges was such that, a scant decade
after abolition, Machado de Assis' friend Joaquim Nabuco would write:
"Slavery will long remain Brazil's defining national feature."[3] Well over

---

[1] Joaquim Maria Machado de Assis, *Gazeta de Notícias*, May 14, 1893.
[2] According to the most recent available estimates in the Slave Voyages Database, 4,864,373
enslaved captives disembarked in Brazil, out of a total of 10,538,225 who disembarked
across the Americas (including the Caribbean). This amounts to 46.2 percent. Website
database accessed on July 24, 2020: www.slavevoyages.org/assessment/estimates.
[3] Joaquim Nabuco was a historian, diplomat, politician, and abolitionist who played a key
role in Brazil's antislavery campaign and was perhaps Brazil's most important abolitionist
voice in the transatlantic circuit. When the Brazilian Empire gave way to the Republic in

a century later, the power of those words persists: slavery and its legacies remain Brazil's most formative elements.

SLAVERY AND RACE RELATIONS IN HEMISPHERIC CONVERSATION

There is no question that the marks of slavery are still vivid in Brazilian society. Long before the term "afterlives of slavery" became current in the North Atlantic, generations of Brazilian historians wrote prolifically and creatively on the profound and lasting impact of African slavery (and its many forms of violence) on every dimension of Brazilian life.[4]

These legacies have been explored from multiple angles and through many discrete histories.[5] Some scholars have opted to study flight, revolt, and the formation of maroon communities (*quilombos*), emphasizing issues of agency, resistance, and resilient forms of cultural-political self-determination and historical memory. Others have emphasized the ways in which enslaved persons and their descendants forged spaces of humanity, solidarity, and voice within institutions such as the family and religious brotherhoods. Afro-descendant cultural and artistic production is so central to Brazilian cultural history writ large as to be inseparable. Polemic multigenerational debates have focused on the role of slavery in the history of the Brazilian economy and of Brazilian capitalism, focusing especially on plantations, mining, the domestic agricultural economy, and the slave trade itself. Ever since Joaquim Nabuco first linked slavery to Brazil's character as an independent nation, scholars have explored slavery's formative influence on Brazilian state-building and institutional life, with particular influence on the law, the military, the political dynamics of the Brazilian Empire, and the contested dimensions and boundaries of civil, political, and social citizenship. At the other end of the spectrum, historians have long explored slavery's deep imprint on Brazil's intimate and material cultures and on the ways in which Brazilians remember their

---

1889, Nabuco went into bitter and nostalgic exile, which greatly colored the work from which this quotation is taken (J. Nabuco, *Minha formação*).

[4] Saidiya Hartman coined the term "afterlife of slavery" in *Lose Your Mother*, with specific reference to slavery's power to structure political, social, institutional, cultural, and social violence and inequality in the contemporary world. The term has since entered general academic usage as a way of describing slavery's enduring influence, especially through racialized forms of violence, inequality, and injustice.

[5] For overviews of the Brazilian field in English, see J. Hébrard, "Slavery in Brazil." See also H. Klein and F. Luna, *Slavery in Brazil*; R. Slenes, "Brazil"; H. Klein and J. Reis, "Slavery in Brazil"; S. Schwartz, *Slaves, Peasants and Rebels*, pp. 1–38.

past. The range of additional topics is seemingly endless: slavery's influence on Portuguese imperial politics and on Brazil's international and borderland politics; slavery's role in shaping Indigenous history; slavery's place in Brazil's urban evolution; slavery's influence over public health and medicine. Throughout, scholars have explored the histories of slavery, manumission, and fragile freedom in order to understand the Brazilian histories of race and color, as well as the enduring ways in which they have structured both Brazilian inequality and Brazilian national life. This dense and sophisticated historiography continues to develop theoretically and methodologically and occupies a central place in Brazil's broader intellectual sphere.

The transnational and comparative study of slavery has deeply influenced the evolution of this diverse field, which has in turn shaped debates about the meaning of race and the nature of racial inequality in Brazil and across the Americas in the twentieth century. Brazilians and US travelers, journalists, intellectuals, artists, and statespeople have thought comparatively about slavery and race relations since at least the mid-nineteenth century. But the transnational historiography really began in the 1930s, when the publication of Gilberto Freyre's *Casa Grande e Senzala* sparked an intense debate about the comparative history of slavery in the Americas.[6]

Many have misread Freyre's complex and multifaceted analysis, equating it with the notion of "racial democracy." The term itself has deep and diverse origins within and outside of Brazil, and Freyre only began to use it after World War II.[7] Even then, he employed it sparsely and ambiguously; while Freyre was willing to promote "ethnic and social" and later "racial" democracy as Brazil's most salient and original contribution to world civilization, he deployed the idea to describe not liberal egalitarianism (which he openly despised) but rather racial fluidity and sociocultural, sexual, and affective connection within a structure of racial and patriarchal hierarchy. Although Freyre was raised by a traditional family in post-abolition Recife, his eclectic analysis was also deeply rooted in his experience as a student at Baylor and Columbia between 1918 and 1923, and it reflected intense engagement with overtly racist strains of US southern historiography as well as the better-known influence of Franz Boas (with whom he never studied closely).[8]

---

[6] G. Freyre, *The Masters* (first published in Portuguese in 1933).

[7] On the evolution of the term "racial democracy" in Brazil, see A. S. Guimarães, "Democracia racial" and "A democracia racial revisitada." On the idea of racial democracy in the Americas, see P. Alberto and J. Hoffnung-Garskof, "Racial Democracy."

[8] On Freyre's experience in the United States, see M. Pallares Burke, *Gilberto Freyre*; M. Pallares Burke and P. Burke, *Gilberto Freyre*.

All the same, Freyre did formulate an enduring and deeply influential historical account of Brazilian civilization that emphasized the formative (if subordinate) influence of enslaved Africans on Brazil's sociocultural, material, and intimate life. Frank Tannenbaum's *Slave and Citizen* (1947) systematized the legal and religious dimensions of Freyre's argument and expanded it to a trans-American comparison, arguing that Brazilian and Latin American institutions had created a moderate slave regime that favored manumission, recognized the spiritual humanity of enslaved persons, and promoted pacific relations between masters and slaves.[9]

Tannenbaum's perspective, amplified in North America by Stanley Elkins, was highly criticized almost from its inception.[10] Ironically, some of the earliest empirical contestations sprung from a UNESCO-sponsored social science research initiative inspired by Brazil's supposed racial harmony.[11] These critiques merged with a wave of Marxist historical scholarship that, following Brazilian historian Caio Prado Junior and Eric Williams, emphasized slavery's capitalist logic and profound brutality.[12] In the 1960s, Brazilian scholars such as Florestan Fernandes, Fernando Henrique Cardoso, Octavio Ianni, and Emilia Viotti da Costa explicitly countered both Freyre and Tannenbaum's portrayals of Brazilian slavery and race relations, producing studies that focused on the intrinsic violence of the slave system and became fundamental to the academic contestation of what had by then become the full-blown myth of racial democracy.[13] In subsequent years, Carl Degler would produce the first comprehensive historical comparison of race relations in Brazil and the United States, calling into question Tannenbaum's optimistic views of the benign nature of Brazilian slavery and racism and helping to consolidate the comparative historiography.[14]

In 1988, the centennial anniversary of Brazilian abolition, the English-language scholarship on comparative slavery was still significantly shaped

---

[9] F. Tannenbaum, *Slave and Citizen*. For an analysis of the impact of Frank Tannenbaum's work on Gilberto Freyre, see A. S. Guimarães, "A democracia," and A. de la Fuente, "From Slaves to Citizens." For comprehensive comparative analyses of American slaveries, see R. Marquese and R. Salles, eds., *Escravidão e capitalismo*; H. Klein, "A experiência."

[10] S. Elkins, *Slavery*.

[11] C. Wagley, *Race and Class*; L. Costa Pinto, *O negro*; T. de Azevedo, *As elites*; R. Bastide and F. Fernandes, *Relações raciais*; M. Chor Maio, "O projeto." For analysis of the UNESCO project, see A. S. Guimarães, "Preconceito de cor" and "Baianos e paulistas."

[12] C. Prado Júnior, *Formação do Brasil*; E. Williams, *Capitalism and Slavery*.

[13] See F. Fernandes, *A integração*. A number of other important works emerged in this period, including F. Cardoso, *Capitalismo e escravidão*; O. Ianni, *As metamorfoses*; and E. Viotti da Costa, *Da senzala*.

[14] C. Degler, *Neither Black nor White*.

by the debates that had begun with Tannenbaum. In Brazil, however, the anniversary helped to accelerate and consolidate a transformative wave of new scholarship on race and slavery that had begun to take root in the 1970s. Heavily impacted by Brazil's Black movement, in conversation with new and innovative social histories of slavery in the United States and the Caribbean, and influenced by new methods of economic, socio-cultural, and legal history, Brazilian scholars complicated and questioned many of the paradigms that had been most central to both the Tannenbaum debates and Marxist and revisionist analyses of race and slavery.[15]

This scholarship, and especially its sociocultural strain, first acquired broad visibility in the English-speaking world with the publication of *The Abolition of Slavery and the Aftermath of Emancipation in Brazil* (Duke University Press, 1988).[16] In five linked essays, Rebecca Scott, Seymour Drescher, Hebe Maria Mattos de Castro (now Hebe Mattos), George Reid Andrews, and Robert Levine explored abolition, rural freedom, urban industrialization, millenarian rebellion, and Brazil's place in the comparative history of Atlantic slavery. Their work was especially notable for its rejection of once-hegemonic arguments about elite control, the passivity or irrational violence of the enslaved, and an abolition process driven by the modernizing force of agrarian capitalism. The collection also problematized the very notion of freedom: Rebecca Scott's opening salvo challenged historians to embrace new sources and interpretive methodologies in order to deepen their understandings of the complex geographical and social configurations of slavery and emancipation, the intricate interplay of dependency and resistance in the post-abolition period, and the legal and institutional dimensions of unequal citizenship.

---

[15] In the context of the centennial anniversary of Brazilian abolition, several books were published, such as H. Mattos, *Ao sul*; S. Lara, *Campos da violência*; J. Reis, ed., *Escravidão e invenção*; J. Reis and E. Silva, *Negociação e conflito*. The *Revista Brasileira de História*, the most prestigious history journal in Brazil, published a special issue that became a fundamental reference on the theme (8:16, 1988), organized by Silvia Lara with articles by Eric Foner, Katia Mattoso, João José Reis, Sidney Chalhoub, Luiz Carlos Soares, Maria Helena Machado, Horácio Gutierrez, and Robert Slenes. Also in 1988, Portuguese translations were published of S. Schwartz's *Sugar Plantations* and R. Scott's *Slave Emancipation in Cuba*. On Brazil's Black movement, see P. Alberto, *Terms of Inclusion*; F. Gomes and P. Domingues, eds., *Experiências da emancipação*; A. Pereira and V. Alberti, *Histórias do movimento*; M. Hanchard, *Orpheus and Power*.

[16] This book was first published as a *Hispanic American Historical Review* special issue in 1988 (68:3).

When *Abolition* was published, a new generation of Brazilian scholars, immersed in their country's exhilarating political transformations, was already rising to Scott's challenges. Historians such as Celia Azevedo, Sidney Chalhoub, Maria Helena Machado, Marcus Carvalho, Silvia Lara, Hebe Mattos, and João José Reis forged new paths in slavery's sociocultural history, even as others built on foundational works by foreign scholars such as Philip Curtin, Warren Dean, Peter Eisenberg, Mary Karasch, Katia Mattoso, Nancy Naro, Stuart Schwartz, Robert Slenes, Stanley Stein, and Scott herself to propose new demographic, legal, economic, and political paradigms.[17] Since then, in what has become a remarkable collective project, hundreds of researchers have systematically revised Brazilian interpretations of nearly every dimension of slavery, emancipation, and post-abolition, with a particularly revelatory impact on our understanding of everyday violence, resistance, agency, family, race, manumission, the slave trade, law, and citizenship. This body of scholarship is deeply rooted in the archives, intensely engaged with transnational historiographies, and unusually imaginative in its engagement of nontraditional sources of individual and collective experience. Slavery and abolition has arguably become the most dynamic historical subfield in Brazil and has provoked wide-ranging reevaluations of slavery's modern legacies and afterlives.

This transformation has had a significant impact on the English-language historiography of Brazil. Many Brazilian historians who came of age in the 1980s have spent extended periods in the United States and Europe, and several publish regularly in English. Their students – now leading scholars in their own right – often conduct portions of their training and postdoctoral work in the North Atlantic and collaborate closely with colleagues around the globe. Foreign Brazilianists build their scholarship in conversation with Brazilian innovations, and many – perhaps most notably Herbert Klein, Robert Slenes, and Barbara Weinstein – have provided vital syntheses of recent scholarship for English-speaking Atlantic World scholars.[18]

---

[17] C. Azevedo, *Onda negra*; S. Chalhoub, *Visões da liberdade*; M. H. Machado, *O plano*; M. Carvalho, "Hegemony and Rebellion"; H. Mattos, *Ao sul*; J. Reis and E. Silva, *Negociação*; S. Lara, *Campos da violência*; P. Curtin, *The Atlantic Slave Trade*; S. Stein, *Vassouras*; W. Dean, *Rio Claro*; P. Eisenberg, *The Sugar Industry*; M. Karasch, *Slave Life*; K. Mattoso, *To Be a Slave*; N. Naro. "The 1848 Praieira Revolt"; R. Slenes, "The Demography and Economics"; S. Schwartz, *Sugar Plantations*; R. Scott, *Slave Emancipation*.

[18] See H. Klein and F. Luna, *Slavery in Brazil*; H. Klein and J. Reis, "Slavery in Brazil"; R. Slenes, "Brazil"; B. Weinstein, "Postcolonial Brazil."

Still, Brazilian scholarship remains considerably less accessible to outsiders than that of the Anglo, Hispanic, or Francophone Atlantics. Ironically, this is partially due to the sheer enormity and magnetism of the Brazilian historical field. Like their counterparts in the United States, Brazilian historians often structure their work around deep national intellectual traditions and internal scholarly debates, which can render their findings opaque for outsiders. Linguistically accurate translations often fail to convey historical and historiographical context or to fully expose the stakes of Brazilian scholarly debates. Brazilian authors generally publish their work individually or as the "Brazilian contribution" to collective projects organized around transatlantic themes. There are very few publications that allow English-language readers to directly experience the range, richness, and methodological sophistication of the Brazilian conversation – to grasp, in short, that there is a complex, multifaceted Brazilian school of slavery and abolition studies. As a partial consequence, Brazil is consistently underrepresented in English-language debates about Atlantic slavery and abolition, both as a site of experience and as a source of interpretation. Brazil was by far the most numerically important destination for enslaved Africans, but the United States and the British Caribbean wield far more influence on the transnational historiography.

This volume emerged in response to this paradox, and thus it is in part a work of translation – not only of words, from Portuguese to English, but also of experiences, memories, and understandings of slavery and post-abolition that are at once deeply familiar and surprisingly alien to scholars of other histories of captivity and freedom. Our authors research and write in both Brazil and the United States and approach this work of translation from multiple transnational perspectives. We do not aim to provide a survey of Brazil's multisecular experience as a slave society, nor do we claim to represent every dimension of Brazil's broad scholarly field. We intend, rather, to spark transnational debate about a few of the strongest currents in Brazil's contemporary historiography. This collection offers multifaceted histories of Brazilian slavery's final surge and prolonged abolition over the course of the nineteenth century, written with a particular sensibility to the long afterlives of captivity and to the constrained and precarious freedoms they engendered. We highlight, above all, the contributions of the sociocultural, legal, and economic historians who have sought answers to broad historical and theoretical questions in the everyday lives of enslaved Brazilians and their descendants.

CHRONOLOGIES OF SLAVERY AND FREEDOM

The chapters that follow assume some familiarity with the basic contours of Brazilian slavery, emancipation, and abolition. Our work of translation thus begins with a brief overview of Brazil's final eight decades of captivity.

When did Brazilian abolition begin? The notion that the abolition process spanned Brazil's entire nineteenth century might seem to fly in the face of economic and demographic realities. Brazil's independence from Portugal, in 1822, occurred in the initial stages of a nineteenth-century coffee boom that transformed the Brazilian Southeast and dramatically accelerated commerce in enslaved Africans.[19] All told, more than 1,800,000 enslaved Africans arrived on Brazilian shores between 1801 and 1850; together, they comprised more than a third of the total number of laborers forcibly brought to Brazil.[20] In this context, Independent Brazil, like the United States, was conceived as a slave-holding nation.

Yet that history can obscure emancipation's deep roots in Brazilian soil. In stark contrast with the United States, newly independent Brazil had the largest freed African and free Afro-descendant population in the Americas. Due in part to comparatively high rates of manumission (the highest in the Americas, peaking at around 4 percent per year), that number continued to grow over the course of the nineteenth century. Even with the mass expansion of the slave trade before 1850, the rate of population increase among free Blacks was greater than that among the enslaved. By 1850, the number of free Afro-descendants had surpassed the number of enslaved persons. By the time of the 1872 census, free Afro-Brazilians comprised the largest single sector of the Brazilian population: out of a total of 9.5 million inhabitants, 4,200,000 (or 43 percent) were free people of African descent, in contrast with 1.5 million enslaved people and 3.7 million whites. While many of these manumissions were complex and incomplete, leading to something far short of full freedom, they cumulatively forged a world in which enslavement and African descent were not coterminous.[21]

Just as importantly, the political process that would eventually lead to the abolition of slavery in 1888 began at least eight decades earlier, when

---

[19] R. Marquese, "Capitalism, Slavery."

[20] These estimates are from the *Slave Voyages Database*, for all known transatlantic slave arrivals in Brazil (www.slavevoyages.org). For discussion, see H. Klein and F. Luna, *Slavery in Brazil*.

[21] H. Klein and F. Luna, *Slavery in Brazil*, pp. 78, 253–254.

the Napoleonic invasion of the Iberian Peninsula drove the Portuguese royal family and thousands of their courtiers across the Atlantic to Rio de Janeiro in 1807–1808. The Court relied on British protection to flee and was obliged in return to open Brazilian ports to British commerce and acknowledge the need to adopt "the most effective means to achieve the gradual abolition of the slave trade in the full extension of its dominions."[22] In practice, neither the treaty nor British patrols of the Brazilian coast contained the traffic in enslaved Africans. Yet the Congress of Vienna reinforced the European commitment to ending the slave traffic: Britain and Portugal both signed the treaty prohibiting the trade north of the equator, provoking protest from traffickers based in Rio de Janeiro and Bahia.

Brazilian independence inaugurated a new chapter in this process. Founding father José Bonifácio de Andrada e Silva argued, in the 1823 Constitutional Assembly, for the need to "abolish the slave trade, improve conditions for those now in captivity, and promote their gradual emancipation."[23] Many enslaved people eagerly wielded the political language of the Age of Revolutions, demanding liberty and citizenship.[24] Yet the Brazilian elite considered slave traffic essential for the development of the coffee economy, which was already emerging as Brazil's economic motor, and had no intention of loosening the hierarchical power structures born of slavery. Britain conditioned its recognition of independent Brazil on a commitment to end the slave trade, and the Brazilian Parliament was forced to cede ground: on November 7, 1831, they formally banned the slave trade and barred the entry of enslaved Africans onto Brazilian territory.[25] Yet elite commitment to slavery was stronger than the rule of formal law: despite an initial surge in enforcement and recurrent English attempts to contain "piracy," at least 700,000 enslaved Africans were illegally brought to Brazilian shores in the 1830s and 1840s.[26] When Brazilian authorities intercepted such Africans, their freedom was radically circumscribed: they were classified

---

[22] Treaty of Friendship and Alliance between Great Britain and Portugal, signed at Rio de Janeiro, February 19, 1810, *Oxford Public International Law*, 61 CTS 41–1. https://opil.ouplaw.com/view/10.1093/law:oht/law-oht-61-CTS-41-1.regGroup.1/law-oht-61-CTS-41-1.

[23] J. B. De Andrade e Silva, *Representação à assemblea*.

[24] K. Schultz, *Tropical Versailles*.

[25] Law of November 7 1831. Brasil, *Coleção de Leis do Império do Brasil – 1831*, vol. 1, p. 182. Available at www2.camara.leg.br/legin/fed/lei_sn/1824-1899/lei-37659-7-novembro-1831-564776-publicacaooriginal-88704-pl.html.

[26] *Slave Voyages Database*, estimates of all slaves disembarked in Brazil from 1831 to 1850.

as "liberated Africans," legally free but nonetheless obligated to work for local authorities or specially designated masters. It took more than fourteen years for most of them to attain autonomy and freedom, and often they were forced to labor far beyond the legal limit and could only (and only exceptionally) attain their freedom in the courts.[27]

The complicity of Brazilian authorities in the illegal slave traffic led to escalating tensions with Great Britain. In 1845, the British Parliament approved the Aberdeen Bill, legalizing the seizure of any Brazilian ship involved in the slave traffic, regardless of circumstances and even in Brazilian territorial waters. In 1850, under British threat, Brazil passed Law 581, which extinguished the trade in enslaved Africans and authorized the confiscation of recently arrived Africans, even if it did not criminalize those who purchased the illegally enslaved. Although there are records of slave cargoes landing in Brazil as late as 1856, and although the vast majority of those illegally involved in the "infamous commerce" escaped sanction, the 1850 law in the end succeeded in definitively ending the trade.[28]

The 1850 law unleashed profound changes in Brazil's demography, as well as in its political, social, and economic life. Above all, the cessation of the Atlantic trade provoked an acceleration of domestic slave trafficking; in the economically stagnant Brazilian Northeast, legions of enslaved people were sold against their will to fuel the labor demands of the rapidly expanding coffee plantations in the Brazilian Southeast.[29] The end of the Atlantic traffic also resulted in scarcity and rapid inflation in the value of slave property, which in turn led to a rapid concentration of slaveholding. Before 1850, slave purchase had been widely accessible among the free population, including freedpeople and poor laborers; when the Atlantic slave trade ended, slaveholding became increasingly the privilege of large landholders who were well integrated in the export economy.[30]

In the 1850s and 1860s, the number of enslaved people who openly sought their own liberty grew substantially. This was especially true in the Paraíba Valley, site of Brazil's largest coffee plantations.[31] In that region, before 1850, at least half of the enslaved labor force had been born in Africa. Ten years later, the figure was only 20 percent. This rapid

[27] B. Mamigonian, "Conflicts."
[28] J. Rodrigues, *Infame comércio*; B. Mamigonian, *Africanos livres*.
[29] R. Graham, "Another Middle Passage?"
[30] Z. Frank, *Dutra's World*; R. Salles, *E o vale*.
[31] On the historiography of plantations in the Paraíba Valley, see R. Marquese and R. Salles, "Slavery in Nineteenth Century Brazil."

transformation cannot be explained by natural reproduction alone; it resulted as well from the importation of Brazilian-born slaves from regions such as Pernambuco and Maranhão, where erratic fluctuations and general decline in the sugar and cotton economies forced many slaveholders into dire economic straits. These men and women, violently torn from their families, arrived in the Paraíba Valley with long-established expectations about the contours of enslavement; the rupture in these norms intensified both individual and collective resistance, which little by little subverted the traditional equilibria of the Brazilian slave regime.[32] Revolted by the possible loss of customary rights and by deteriorating living conditions, many enslaved people began to openly struggle against their masters. Some resisted physically, injuring or even murdering their overseers or owners; others fled; many more did everything within their power to achieve manumission.[33] One result was the acceleration and politicization of civil freedom suits, which became especially frequent in the 1860s as slave resistance converged with activism among abolitionist lawyers.[34]

The end of the Civil War abolished US slavery in 1865, and Cuba's Moret law liberated newborns and the elderly in 1870, definitively isolating Brazil in the international arena. At the same time, the end of the Paraguayan War (1864–1870) added urgency to the problem of Brazilian emancipation.[35] In the Paraguayan War, as in the United States during the struggles for Independence and the Civil War, thousands of enslaved people were either "donated" to the army by their masters or joined the nation's fighting forces in hopes of gaining their liberty. At the same time, the African ancestry of many forced recruits awoke the fears of scientific racists, who worried that slavery was condemning Brazil to degenerate inferiority. No less significantly, the Paraguayan War's carnage, in combination with the wrenching horrors of the US Civil War, convinced many Brazilian politicians that gradual emancipation was preferable to violent conflict over the issue of slavery.

In 1867, a governmental commission elaborated a gradual emancipation project that entered into prolonged legislative discussion in 1871. Predictably, the proposal provoked fierce conflict in Congress, where pro-emancipation members of the Liberal party were only an outspoken

---

[32] H. Mattos, "The Madness."
[33] H. Mattos, *Das cores*; F. Gomes, *Histórias de quilombolas.*
[34] S. Chalhoub, *Visões*; K. Grinberg, "Manumission, Gender, and the Law."
[35] V. Izecksohn, *Slavery and War.*

minority. Liberal and Conservative representatives from the southeastern coffee provinces of Rio de Janeiro, Minas Gerais, and São Paulo – and especially those from the most prosperous and fertile micro-regions – opposed the project. Nonetheless, after four months of debate, amidst escalating tension between proslavery and emancipationist legislators and agile patronage politicking by the Baron of Rio Branco, the congress approved the Free Womb Law on September 28, 1871.[36] As the name indicates, the law's principal provision liberated all children of enslaved mothers born after the date upon which the law went into effect. The masters themselves could decide the fate of newborns born to enslaved mothers, choosing either to release them to "freedom" at the age of eight (in which case owners would receive a government indemnity) or to retain the children's services until the age of twenty-one years before releasing them without recompense. The Free Womb Law also created an Emancipation Fund to free an annual quota of slaves and made it mandatory for owners to matriculate their slaves in a governmental registry. That registry was a crucial escalation of the Brazilian state's power to regulate slavery, both because it established for the first time a record of who was legally enslaved and because it served to facilitate tax collection on enslaved property. Finally, the Free Womb Law formally recognized enslaved people's right to accumulate savings, whether from gift or inheritance or through independent paid work that a master permitted a slave to perform on the side. A slave could use those funds for whatever he or she saw fit, including self-purchase, without the master's intervention or impediment.

Historians still debate the practical efficacy of the 1871 law; despite its profound implications for governance and the future of captive labor, slavocrats did their best to undermine it, and abolitionists did not consider it adequate. Yet regardless of its practical implications, the Free Womb Law had a critical symbolic function, both because it limited seigneurial authority by recognizing the legal rights of enslaved persons and because it placed the Imperial government at the forefront of the emancipation process. As former minister of justice José Tomás Nabuco de Araújo Filho affirmed, "no one would ever again be born a slave."[37] If the

---

[36] The Free Womb Law (Law 2040), September 28, 1871, translated in S. Peabody and K. Grinberg, *Slavery, Freedom, and the Law*, pp. 158–161. For a succinct summary of the 1871 law, see J. Mendonça, "Legislação emancipacionista." On the approval of the Free Womb Law, see R. Salles, *E o vale*, chapter 2. On the politics of the same, see J. Needell, *The Sacred Cause*, pp. 44–45. See also C. Cowling, *Conceiving Freedom*.

[37] Speech by José Tomás Nabuco de Araújo Filho in the Câmara dos Deputados, September 26, 1871, in J. Nabuco, *Um estadista*, v. II, p. 845.

African traffic had finally ended, and all Brazilians would henceforth be born free, Brazilian slavery's days were numbered.

After nearly a decade of abolitionist advocacy in Brazil's courtrooms, the 1880s witnessed both a deepening crisis within the Brazilian Empire and the growth, diversification, and institutionalization of the Brazilian abolitionist movement. In 1880, abolitionists founded the Sociedade Brasileira contra a Escravidão (Brazilian Anti-Slavery Society); that same year, monarchist abolitionist leaders such as Joaquim Nabuco and André Rebouças joined with abolitionist Republicans such as José do Patrocínio and João Clapp to found the landmark newspaper *O Abolicionista*. From that point forward, abolitionist societies and papers proliferated, and abolitionist happenings were organized in theaters and clubs in Rio and throughout urban Brazil. Newspapers, demonstrations, and emancipation funds gained impressive ground in provinces outside of the southeastern coffee regions, many of which had already sold most slaves of prime working age south. In combination with enslaved people's own efforts at self-purchase (which were in many regions the most important route to freedom), and with accelerating open resistance among the enslaved, these movements succeeded in at least conditionally manumitting the vast majority of captives before 1888. In Ceará and Amazonas, all slaves were emancipated by 1884.

Emancipationist societies had called for reforms in the institution of slavery since the 1860s, but many post-1880 associations went far further, demanding immediate abolition. Similarly, while insurrections, maroon settlements, flight, and instances of violent resistance were recurrent throughout slavery's long history, they intensified in the 1870s and especially the 1880s.[38] During this period, slave resistance – and, as in the United States, slave flight – gained particularly strong support and legitimacy in Brazilian cities, some of which became important nodes in trajectories of escape that echoed the US underground railway.

Both the importance and the challenges of this growing abolitionist movement emerged especially clearly in 1885, when the Brazilian Parliament approved a new law regarding slave emancipation. The so-called Sexagenarian Law liberated all slaves over sixty years of age, but it also imposed restrictions, requiring freedpersons to perform three years of "free" labor and to remain in their county of residence for five years. It

---

[38] In Brazil, advocates of slavery's end can be divided into two general groups: the emancipationists, who favored a slow and gradual emancipation process; and the abolitionists, who favored the immediate abolition of slavery. See A. Alonso, *The Last Abolition*.

also (like the US Fugitive Slave Act of 1850) threatened prison time for anyone who assisted escaped slaves. The 1885 law was the last legal act related to slave emancipation before abolition, but it was also widely perceived as a conservative attempt to slow abolitionist momentum.[39] Historians such as Robert Conrad and Emilia Viotti da Costa concluded in the 1960s and 1970s that it had few practical effects because relatively few slaves were of such advanced age (and few among them were still able to perform productive labor). Yet recent scholarship has shown that the Sexagenarian Law in fact contributed to the manumission of many enslaved people because it – like the Free Womb Law – required the liberation of all slaves who had not been matriculated in a state registry by their owners.[40]

In 1887, rural slave flights intensified, and fugitives established extensive networks in smaller cities of Brazil's southeastern coffee heartland such as Santos in São Paulo and Campos in Rio de Janeiro. In the wake of a serious crisis in military–state relations in the late 1880s, officers and soldiers of the Imperial Army, charged with capturing fugitive slaves, increasingly refused to do so.[41] The Baron of Cotegipe, the conservative head of the Imperial cabinet, ordered that the enslaved fugitives and those who came to their aid – including students from Rio's Military Academy (Escola Militar) – be subdued. Over the course of 1887, conflicts brewed between the Cotegipe Cabinet and positivist and abolitionist military officials, many of whom advocated for the replacement of the monarchical regime with a republic. The panorama was one of complete uncertainty: slave revolts, proslavery forces that attempted to contain them, abolitionist civil disobedience, republican rallies, and the insubordination of the army left the monarchy in a very difficult situation. And to top it off, the

---

[39] On the actions of conservative influence on the law's enforcement, see J. Needell, *The Sacred Cause*, pp. 157–167; J. Mendonça, *Legislação emancipacionista*.
[40] R. Conrad, *The Destruction*; E. Viotti da Costa, *Da senzala*. On the recent scholarship of the Sexagenarian Law, see J. Mendonça, *Entre a mão*.
[41] The military crisis centered on the role of the Brazilian military in national politics and was aggravated by abolitionist pressure as well as the positivist and republican sympathies of many young officers; though a May 1887 crisis that nearly led to the fall of Cotegipe's cabinet was averted, the crisis set the stage for army resistance to accelerating calls to contain mass flights on São Paulo plantations. In October 1887, a group of military officers from Rio's newly formed Clube Militar requested that the army should no longer be called on to capture individuals who were "peacefully fleeing the horrors of servitude." The petition was widely publicized, demonstrating military dissatisfaction with an increasingly unpopular role. For an account of the "military question" and army resistance, see J. Needell, *The Sacred Cause*, pp. 178–181, 184; see also R. Conrad, *The Destruction*, p. 251; M. H. Machado, *O plano*, pp. 149–152.

emperor's declining health transformed the crisis of the Cotegipe Cabinet into a crisis of the monarchy itself. As rumors spread that Emperor Dom Pedro II was headed to Europe for treatment, criticism grew regarding a possible "Third Reign" of the Brazilian Empire, headed by Princess Isabel, who in June 1887 had rushed back from a European tour to temporarily take her father's place as head of government.

By this time, regions outside of Brazil's coffee lands held relatively few slaves; only coffee growers in Minas Gerais, São Paulo, and Rio de Janeiro continued to defend slavery and demand gradual indemnity for any "property" they might be forced to manumit. The situation became grave enough to threaten the coffee harvest; in the face of such imminent loss, even São Paulo's conservative planters began to argue for immediate abolition in hopes of accelerating European immigration and facilitating the creation of a free rural labor force. Rio de Janeiro's slavocrats became increasingly isolated in their defense of slavery as the parliamentary majority shifted to favor immediate abolition without indemnity as the only solution for the rural crisis.

The pressure on Princess Isabel was enormous. All indications pointed toward Pedro II's death abroad, though he would in fact live for three more years. Princess Isabel was neither popular nor politically adept. Despite a personal commitment to abolitionism, she hesitated to place it at the center of her governing agenda. It was only at the beginning of 1888 – in the wake of a strategically timed papal encyclical partially engineered by Nabuco, growing frustration with the Cotegipe Cabinet, and urban riots in Rio – that the princess publicly embraced the abolition- ist cause, famously organizing Carnival dances soliciting donations for the enslaved.[42]

With Princess Isabel's abolitionist turn, Cotegipe's Cabinet – in direct conflict with the military and lacking moral force – could not stand. In March 1888, Isabel substituted Cotegipe's so-called politics of the cudgel with the more moderate conservatism of João Alfredo, a politician with long experience in debates about the future of slavery. The new cabinet took office on the assumption that, in order to avoid even greater social convulsions, there was no alternative but to propose slavery's extinction.

On May 3, 1888, an abolition bill was proposed to Brazil's Parliament. The Black abolitionist André Rebouças crafted the initial draft to include elements of what he termed "rural democracy," which among other things

---

[42] J. Needell, *The Sacred Cause*, pp. 193–198; A. Alonso, *The Last Abolition*, pp. 318–320; K. Grinberg and M. Muaze, *O 15 de Novembro*, pp. 103–108.

posited land reform as a crucial component of meaningful abolition. Yet the government forwarded to the legislature only those provisions that mandated the unconditional abolition of slavery without indemnity. Ten days later, ruling in her father's absence, Princess Isabel sanctioned the Lei Áurea, or Golden Law, a model of terse concision: "From this date forward, slavery is extinguished in Brazil. All contrary provisions are revoked."[43]

The Lei Áurea formally freed somewhere near 600,000 individuals, approximately 5 percent of Brazil's population. Yet the law did nothing to promote their access to property and the full rights of citizenship; on the contrary, by designating freedpersons as Brazilians indistinguishable from those who had never been enslaved, the Imperial government paradoxically ensured that the dispossessions of slavery would continue to structure the social and economic realities of post-abolition society. In Brazil, as in the United States, full equality would remain a distant mirage for the vast majority of Afro-descendants.

AGENCY, SCALE, AND METHOD

The essays that follow explore this history, emphasizing approaches that have shaped Brazil's social, cultural, and legal historiography of slavery and its afterlives for the past four decades. This loose historiographical tradition emerged in specific geographic and thematic terrains and shares a distinctive set of intellectual and methodological commitments.

To begin to understand this school of thought, it is useful to return to an old question. Who abolished slavery? The query evokes an influential polemic unleashed fifteen years ago by Portuguese historian João Pedro Marques, whose strident call to downplay the causal significance of enslaved people's resistance in destroying the institution of slavery breathed revisionist life into a nearly fifty-year cycle of North Atlantic debates about slave agency.[44] By Marques' reading, the notion that slave

---

[43] "The Aurea Law," translated in S. Peabody and K. Grinberg, *Slavery, Freedom, and the Law*, pp. 165–166.

[44] J. Marques, "Terão os escravos." For English speakers, the debate was brought home in S. Drescher and P. Emmer, eds., *Who Abolished Slavery?* Marques' arguments especially recall Eugene Genovesie's *Roll, Jordan, Roll*. For a history of agency debates and introduction to their recent iterations – which are specifically concerned with the liberal origins of agency and presentist readings of the link between agency and resistance, see W. Johnson, "On Agency," as well as R. Follett et. al., "Slavery's Ghost." For a different strain in contemporary agency debates, see S. Hartman, *Scenes of Subjection*.

rebellion and resistance led directly to abolition was doubly flawed. First, enslaved rebels rarely articulated their struggles in abolitionist terms; they rebelled against the conditions of their own captivity, not the system of slavery as such. Their conscious agency, by this line of reading, did not lead directly to slavery's demise. Secondly, Marques argued that specific historical instances of large-scale rebellion could rarely be linked empirically to the advancement of the abolitionist cause: paradoxically, they often led instead to slavery's re-entrenchment. Marques thus reasoned that it would be absurd to argue that enslaved people were themselves fundamental to slavery's dissolution.

While Marques offered a useful corrective to facile narratives in which every action taken by a slave is read as a form of resistance and all Afro-descendants are understood as advocates of radical equality, his readings of agency and abolition also exposed an excessively narrow and teleological perspective. Many scholars have emphasized the constraining power of slavery's violence and called into question the ahistorical equation of enslaved agency and contemporary liberal visions of individual freedom without ignoring the deeper meanings of the histories that enslaved peoples made.[45] Others have argued for the primacy of political dynamics in the abolition process, while also recognizing the symbiotic interdependence of high politics and Afro-Brazilian mobilization.[46] Marques often mistook archival silence for quiescence and lack of stated intention for lack of causal impact, and he did not engage half a century of dense methodological debates about the sinuous interactions of structure, politics, ideas, and quotidian agency in shaping historical change.

North American historians of slavery such as Ira Berlin and Manisha Sinha have argued forcefully for a subtler and more holistic vision of historical causality, demonstrating both the depth of antislavery ideology among North America's enslaved peoples and the cumulative impact of a full spectrum of resistance practices that took place over a century or more.[47] Together, slave resistance and imaginaries of humanity and freedom were crucial not only to the direct contestation of slavery but also to the delegitimization that contributed greatly to its destruction. Similar perspectives have animated Brazilian debates about abolition, agency, and causality, laying bare tensions between renewed structuralist explanations of abolition (which echo arguments first advanced in the 1960s) and the

---

[45] R. Marquese, "Estrutura e agência"; R. Soares, "Nem arrancada."
[46] See J. Needell, *The Sacred Cause.*
[47] I. Berlin, *The Long Emancipation*; M. Sinha, *The Slave's Cause.*

social histories of slave agency and resistance that came to dominate Brazilian historiography after 1988.[48]

The historiography in this volume does not respond directly to Marques' query; to ask "who abolished slavery" is to accept the false premises that abolition has a singular lineage and that it is necessary to choose from among mutually exclusive causal forces. Yet the polemic is important, because it places in sharp relief a vision of the temporality, content, and impact of Brazilian abolition that has emerged from four decades of socio-cultural and legal historiography. Our authors, rooted in that school, envision slavery and freedom as a spectrum rather than a dichotomy; they understand abolition less as specific event than as a multisecular historical process, rooted in the early nineteenth century and in some sense still ongoing. We are interested not only in the actions that led directly to the Lei Áurea but also in the shifting meanings of slavery and freedom, as well as the ways in which captivity shaped myriad economic, social, cultural, and political forms that long outlasted formal bondage. And we trace not only the actors who intentionally and directly contributed to the abolition-ist cause but also those who shaped slavery's demise by transforming the nature of the institution and widely varying structures that undergirded it. Like any other complex historical process, Brazilian abolition should not be understood as a linear or teleological progression, a straight march that ended in legal emancipation after a pitched struggle between clearly delineated camps. On the contrary, every step forward came with disjunctive steps back: freedpeople became slaveowners, and slaves reinforced their owners' authority even as they loosened their own constrictions; emancipa-tionists ceded ground to nationalists who saw slave labor as key to economic development; the elimination of legal Atlantic trade changed meaning in the face of illicit trafficking, re-enslavement, and hardening forms of racialization; and enforced dependency kept step with the quickening pace of manumission.[49] Abolition itself was a milestone in that rutted route to freedom, but formal emancipation was gutted by new forms of political restriction, dispossession, and racialized governance.

This historical vision has emerged from careful methodological scaling, whereby broad temporal and theoretical perspectives are juxtaposed with the microhistory of lived experience. At these junctures, we begin to

---

[48] J. Needell, "Brazilian Abolitionism"; R. Marquese and R. Salles, "Slavery in Nineteenth Century Brazil"; M. H. Machado and C. Castilho, eds., *Tornando-se livre*; R. Salles, "A abolição."

[49] S. Chalhoub, *A força*; B. Mamigonian, *Africanos livres*.

perceive the ways in which structures are inhabited and transformed into elements of a dynamic and contingent historical process. One of the major contributions of Brazil's historiography of slavery over the last half-century has been its systematic engagement with archives, especially the judicial archives of the Roman or civil law tradition, which are generally far richer in detail and testimony than their common-law equivalents. Unlike some of their counterparts in the North Atlantic, Brazilian slaves and freedpersons rarely left intentionally written testimonies. But legal records – read against the grain and imaginatively cross-referenced with newspapers, church and civil registries, economic records, diplomatic correspondence, and inherited oral histories and cultural forms – have allowed historians of Brazil to develop a dense vision of slavery's everyday life in remarkably varied contexts. In unearthing the trajectories, interactions, and experiences of individuals and families, we can come to understand the range of ways in which slaves, freedpersons, free citizens, and slaveholders constantly renegotiated the meaning and limits of slavery and freedom. In aggregate, those microhistories help us understand the ways in which Brazil's nineteenth-century Afro-descendant population was united not only by the experience of bondage and hard-won manumission but also by the precariousness of freedom and impotence of formal citizenship.[50] This close-up view allows us to glimpse the complex social and political relationships that undergird larger-scale historical processes of transformation and persistence.

THEMATIC RANGE

The chapters that follow engage intensely with these issues of agency, structure, and scale, across varied thematic terrains. In many cases, our authors reimagine classic motifs in Brazilian social thought, a tradition itself deeply entwined with slavery and its legacies. This is especially apparent in relation to Gilberto Freyre. Perhaps the most internationally (in)famous of Brazil's twentieth-century social thinkers, Freyre became well-known both

---

[50] The concept of the "precariousness of freedom" was coined by Henrique Espada Lima and amplified by Sidney Chalhoub; it has been employed both to highlight the contingencies of African and Afro-descendant liberty in the nineteenth century and to stress the tenuous post-abolition position of Afro-descendants. The concept seeks an equilibrium between recognizing the possibilities of freedom and acknowledging the reality of phenomena such as illegal enslavement, illicit re-enslavement, and forms of racism and coercion that long outlived legal slavery. H. Lima, "Sob o domínio"; S. Chalhoub, "The Precariousness of Freedom."

inside and outside Brazil for his idealized vision of Brazil's colonial past, in which the sugar plantation emerged as the cradle of what came to be known as "racial democracy," where the violence and hierarchy of slavery was mediated – and maintained – by the relational fabric of paternalism and through dense (if often forced and violent) sexual and sociocultural exchanges. Our authors are deeply critical of the notion of racial democracy, and none share Freyre's reverence for hierarchy or his normalizing detachment from slavery's violence. Yet many of our chapters emphasize the structuring force and enduring legacy of relational and patrimonial power, or they reexamine questions that first emerged in Freyre's earliest work. How did family structures and sexual relationships, slave and free, shape Brazilian slavery, emancipation, and freedom? What is the role of emotion, affection, and intimate violence in organizing, reinforcing, or eroding slavocratic and seigneurial authority? How did the informal relationships of dependency, favor, and kinship, so fundamental to Brazil's slave order, structure or vacate "freedom" and delimit the possibilities of equality after abolition? Such questions have been central not only to Brazil's historiography of slavery but also to broader Brazilian accounts of culture, state formation, and nation-building. In reopening these debates, while discarding the neo-patriarchal sensibilities that begat them, these essays intervene in discussions about Brazil's persistent inequalities, incomplete citizenships, and patrimonial forms of governance that have long outlasted slavery's formal bonds.

Readers will find many other classic debates reimagined here: the impact of shifting forms of capitalist agriculture on the intimate worlds of slavery; the influence of Afro-descendant culture – and especially Black music – on Brazil's racial and cultural formation; the history of Brazilian racism and racial ideologies; the politics of formal abolition; the ways in which the economies and politics of Brazilian slavery intersected with the transnational currents of the Atlantic world. Yet these chapters also pursue lines of inquiry that have emerged since the 1980s as significantly autonomous spheres of debate. How were the experiences of slavery, manumission, and freedom shaped by individual and collective subjectivities? How did slavery and its afterlives constrain the development of Brazilian citizenship and curtail the hegemony of Brazilian law? What historical meanings could Brazilian freedom attain, given that it was conceptualized and actualized in a terrain of slavery?

As is true in the broader Atlantic world, questions of gendered and racialized subjectivities have become increasingly central in Brazil. Gendered analysis has deep roots in the study of race and slavery in

Brazil, extending at least to Ruth Landes' *City of Women* (1947) and evident even in Gilberto Freyre's misogynistic but keen attention to women's racialized roles in patriarchal society. Research on gender, race, and slavery gained significant ground in the 1980s with a wave of innovative research on the lives of enslaved women and female slaveholders that starkly mapped the intersectional unfreedoms of urban Brazil.[51] In recent decades, Brazilian research has continued to document the lives of women under slavery, but it has also accompanied the broader Atlantic field in seeking to understand how gender and sexuality shaped slavery, freedom, and their afterlives.[52] Many of our authors contribute to this transnational project, placing the gendered dimensions of violence, relational power, labor, and the struggle for freedom at the center of the histories of slavery and abolition.

Many of the essays collected here also foreground Afro-descendant subjectivities, with particular emphasis on the need to historicize racial identities, document the quotidian practices of racism, and apprehend the enduring stigma and violence of slavery. Our authors understand racial democracy as an ideological construct and reject the normative notion that post-abolition inequalities were shaped by class rather than race. At the same time, they are also wary of ahistorical scripts of racial subjectivity, especially those grounded in the experiences of legally enforced segregation and explicit racial violence that characterized the Jim Crow South or South Africa. Instead, these essays emphasize the ways in which Brazil's particular trajectories of slavery and freedom – culminating in a racial order in which formal equality and limited forms of racial fluidity and mobility cloaked the persistence of brutal, violent hierarchies – led to distinctive forms of racism and racial consciousness. Brazilian Afro-descendants, slave and free, confronted the paradoxical coexistence of formal equality and radical subjugation in myriad ways, according to the

---

[51] See, for example, M. Silva Dias, *Power and Everyday Life*; S. Graham, *House and Street* and *Caetana Says No*; Mary Karasch, *Slave Life*.

[52] For the Atlantic world, prominent recent examples include Saidiya Hartman, Thavolia Glymph, Stephanie Camp, Tera Hunter, Marisa Fuentes, Katherine McKitrick, and Stephanie E. Jones-Rogers. For examples of the very recent scholarship, see the double special issues of *Slavery & Abolition* (28:2, 2017) and the *Women's History Review* (27:6, 2018), "Mothering Slaves: Motherhood, Childlessness and the Care of Children in Atlantic Slave Societies," edited by M. H. Machado, D. Paton, C. Cowling, and E. West. On gender and slavery in Brazil after Silva Dias, Lauderdale Graham, and Karasch, see C. Cowling, *Conceiving Freedom*; O. Otovo, *Progressive Mothers*; C. Roth, "From Free Womb"; F. Gomes, G. Xavier, and J. Farias, eds., *Black Women in Brazil*; M. Ariza, "Mães libertas."

degrees of freedom and autonomy they eked out from widely varying circumstances. Our chapters explore a broad range of quotidian experience of race and racism, from the domestic worlds of wet nurses and recalcitrant house-servants to the combative trenches of political journalism to the national and transnational milieu of statespeople, engineers, and artists. In so doing, they illuminate the infrastructure of Brazil's enduring racial inequalities, even as they allow us also to better apprehend alternate logics of Afro-descendant politics, survival strategies, and "self-making."[53]

Many of the most distinctive dimensions of Brazil's Black subjectivities grew from the country's deeply paradoxical relationship with political liberalism. From its inception, Brazil's constitution (1824) formulated political citizenship as the universal prerogative of independent free men, regardless of race. Yet that formal commitment to color-blind male citizenship coexisted with racialized political practices and political cultures in which virtually every adult male noncitizen was Black or Indigenous and every Afro-descendant citizen was disproportionately vulnerable to informal but systemic denigration and exclusion. In this sense, Brazilian Afro-descendants faced in the nineteenth century a dilemma that has become endemic across the globe in the twentieth: what did the struggle for Black political equality look like when the legal foundations for racially unequal citizenship were no longer clearly visible?[54]

Brazil's nineteenth-century citizenship dilemmas are related to another classic preoccupation of Brazilian social thought, taken up here in a new key: the paradoxes of a modernization process that is at once liberal and slavocratic. The contradictions of this process expressed themselves in Brazil's institutional, legal, political, and diplomatic structures, which integrated patrimonial practices and liberal forms; they were also evident in Brazil's Imperial iteration of "second slavery," which concomitantly embraced global capitalism and fomented the expansion of forced labor.[55] In this context, several unresolvable tensions emerged in

---

[53] This use of "self-making" is drawn from S. Hartman, *Scenes of Subjection*.

[54] Brazilian debates on this issue have tended to focus on the racist dimensions of "racial silence," in ways that speak to Eduardo Bonilla-Silva's conception of "color-blind racism." See E. Bonilla-Silva, *Racism without Racists*. See also K. Grinberg, *A Black Jurist*.

[55] On patrimonialism and the political structure of the Brazilian Empire and First Republic, see R. Faoro, *Os donos do poder*; W. dos Santos, *Ordem burguesa*; J. Murillo de Carvalho, *A construção*, *Teatro de sombras*, and "Federalismo e centralização"; R. Graham, *Patronage and Politics*. On "second slavery" in Brazil, see R. Marquese and D. Tomich, "O vale do Paraíba."

particular relief, even beyond the flagrant incongruity of a regime where the equality and liberty of a few were built on the civil and political negation of the many. The imperative to expand the supply of enslaved labor for the booming coffee economy grew ever more challenging as Brazil was forced – as the price of entry to an international system dominated by the British – to accept a formal ban on the Atlantic slave trade. Domestic pressure to flout the ban clashed with the perceived need to construct a modern state, founded in institutionalized power and the rule of law, a project that was also undermined by the private spheres of authority inherent to the slave system. Forced to choose between slavery and the rule of law, Brazil's governing classes chose to tolerate illegal forms of captivity on a massive scale, first by accepting the lawless continuation of the Atlantic slave trade and then by maintaining illegal captives in bondage and turning a blind eye to the illegal enslavement of freedpersons and free-born Afro-descendants. In this way, many of our chapters argue, tolerated illegality became a fundamental component of Brazil's nineteenth-century national formation, with significant implications for the legitimacy of the nation's property regimes, the hegemony of legal and judicial authority, and the construction of a doxa of impunity among the powerful.

As is true in most studies of Atlantic slavery and abolition, it has become nearly impossible to study the meaning of bondage in Brazil without considering also the significations of freedom. It no longer makes sense to conceive of a sharp transition from slave to free labor in Brazil, as if the two had not coexisted in the decades before abolition. Likewise, oppositional understandings of slavery and freedom have given way to relational analyses, a trend that has also eroded dualistic conceptions of adjacent categories such as public and private or rural and urban. In this conception, our authors especially emphasize the limitations inherent in understanding freedom only through the lenses of formal manumission or emancipation, arguing that freedom was embodied also in familial integrity, access to property or employment, and various forms of social and physical mobility – education, movement to rural or urban localities less dominated by patriarchal logics, the forging of autonomous spheres of politics, culture, and community. At the same time, moving beyond oppositional analyses also requires us to acknowledge the persistence and continuity of myriad unfreedoms. After abolition, Brazilian society remained hierarchical, patriarchal, unequal, and deeply racist; the slavery that had marked Brazil throughout the Brazilian colony and empire lived on in the normative inequity of the Brazilian Republic.

It is worth noting that there are important limitations to our thematic
and geographic range. Our authors engage with important recent contributions to the economic history of slavery, the history of Brazilian capitalism, and the high politics of abolition and free labor, but those
historiographical schools are not our central focus.[56] Similarly, although
we place considerable and unusual emphasis on the important northeastern state of Pernambuco, and although our essays do touch on Bahia and
on Brazil's southern frontier regions, many of our authors follow the
Brazilian historiography in emphasizing Rio de Janeiro and São Paulo.
Minas Gerais and Amazonia – areas central to our understanding of the
interaction of regional specificities and larger historical processes in
Brazil's nineteenth century – are especially important omissions.[57] We
also do not include any essays focused on the impact of Brazilian practices
of slavery and emancipation in Africa or in the Atlantic world.[58] While we
regret these absences, we hope that readers will appreciate our choice to
emphasize the depth of the sociocultural and legal historiography we do
cover, and that the references in this volume will allow readers to explore
these other schools of thought with the attention they deserve.

A SLAVE SOCIETY AFTER SLAVERY: FRAMEWORKS AND CHAPTERS

The idea that slavery's legacies are integral to Brazil's history as a "free"
nation has deep roots. In August 1883, Joaquim Nabuco, living in self-
imposed exile in London, articulated the abolitionist position on slavery's
inheritance, planting the seeds for generations of reflection. *O abolicionismo*,
at once Brazil's most internationally influential abolitionist tract and
a foundational portrait of Brazilian national character, minced no words in
portraying Brazil as a slave society internally corroded by its most formative
institution.[59] Brazilian slavery, Nabuco argued, was illegitimate, immoral,

[56] Examples of recent historiography on the economic history of Brazilian slavery and capitalism are R. Marquese and R. Salles, "Slavery in Nineteenth Century Brazil"; M. Ferraro,
"Capitalism, slavery"; and M. Muaze and R. Salles, eds., *A segunda escravidão*. Recent
works on the high politics of abolition include J. Needell, *The Sacred Cause*; A. Alonso, *The
Last Abolition*; R. Salles, "Resistência escrava"; C. Santos, "O ativismo político."
[57] About slavery in Minas Gerais, see L. Cota, "Ave, libertas"; N. Wicks, "Pathways to
Freedom." On the Amazon, see F. Gomes, ed., *Nas terras*; J. Bezerra Neto, "Por todos os
meios"; O. de la Torre, *The People of the River*.
[58] See J. Rodrigues, *De costa a costa*; R. Ferreira, *Cross-Cultural Exchange*; L. Marques, *The
United States*.
[59] J. Nabuco, *O abolicionismo*. The tract utilizes repetition as a rhetorical strategy; the
arguments summarized here can be found at multiple points in the text. For the most

and a shameful stain on Brazil's international image. It had created a *mestiço* (mixed-race) national population that bore the enduring cultural and biological mark of Africa, which Nabuco portrayed in deeply racist terms.[60] But, above all, slavery was a sin against the *patria* – against a mythical national whole, composed of slaves but also of freedmen and slaveowners, all of whom suffered the perversions and deformations of an encompassing slave society. So long as slavery endured, Brazil would not follow the normative tracks of economic progress: its natural environment would be devastated, its property monopolized by unproductive overlords, its human capital stunted, its capacity to modernize, industrialize, and develop consumer markets hopelessly weakened.[61] The slaveholding class would render the Brazilian state patrimonial and parasitic, making a mockery of liberal ideals and the rule of law; the masses of poor laborers, rural and urban, would fail to develop as a free political class. Brazil's moral fabric would rot, as there would be no incentive for honest work or redemptive education or religion. Slavery would vilify the souls of *senhores* (masters) and degrade the enslaved; its "secretions" would channel their way into every cell of the national body.[62]

Wherever it existed, in short, Nabuco argued that slavery had been "a wind of destruction" that spared nothing and no one.[63] And the very qualities that rendered Brazilian slavery more malleable than its extinct US counterpart only amplified its symbiotic corrosiveness: in the absence of a "fixed division of classes," freedpeople became masters, complicit in the ills that had brutalized them; slaveowners were the lovers, parents, siblings, and even children of the enslaved, hopelessly entwining familial sentiments and mercenary logics. The fact that blackness and slavery

---

succinct and comprehensive summary, see chapter XI, "A influência da escravidão sobre a nacionalidade," especially pp. 114–116.

[60] Nabuco's tract was in many ways emblematic of the racist precepts that infiltrated even the heights of abolitionist thought: Nabuco wrote of racial mixture as the "first vengeance" (137) of an enslaved African race characterized by "retarded mental development, barbarous instincts, and crude superstitions" (144); he advocated European immigration and whitening (233) and warned his compatriots that the importation of Chinese labor would reproduce the errors of slavery (137). Just as consequentially, in writing for an international audience, Nabuco generally portrayed enslaved men and women as passive and degraded victims, significant mainly for their impact on a broader mestiço nationality.

[61] On the environmental dimensions of slavery, see J. Nabuco, *O abolicionismo*, ch. 14, especially p. 148; this dimension of Nabuco's work is analyzed in depth in J. Pádua, *Um sopro*, pp. 272–280. The argument would be taken up by many subsequent analysts, including W. Dean, *With Broadax*.

[62] J. Nabuco, *O abolicionismo*, p. 173.   [63] J. Nabuco, *O abolicionismo*, p. 168.

were never entirely coterminous only rendered the Brazilian system more *hábil* (agile) and its impact more enduring and perverse.[64] Indeed, slavery had penetrated the Brazilian organism so thoroughly that formal abolition would only be the beginning: it was only "after the slaves and the *senhores* are liberated from the yoke that incapacitates both for a free life, that we will be able to embark on a serious program of reform." And that reform would not and could not take place "to the applause of multitudes in a public plaza"; to create "a strong, intelligent, patriotic and free people," reforms would have to be made "day by day, night by night, in the shadows, anonymously, in the intimacy of our lives, in the glow of family, with no recompense other than an invigorated conscience, moralized and disciplined, at once virile and humane."[65]

Many of Nabuco's argumentative threads extended to form the warp and woof of twentieth-century debates about Brazil's national formation: his arguments about slavery's detrimental impact on the development and modernization of the Brazilian economy and class relations; his assertions about slavery's decisive role in the development of latifundia and destructive environmental practices; his articulation of slavery's influence on the development of patronage and patrimonial state practices; and his condemnation of slavery's corruption of the rule of law.[66] Stripped of its moral critique, Nabuco's evocation of the intimate bonds that undergirded slavery inspired Gilberto Freyre's patriarchal vision of Brazilian civilization.[67] Yet, morally amplified, his vision of slavery's destitution and disenfranchisement of the enslaved also found continuity in Florestan Fernandes' searing analysis of Brazilian post-abolition society.[68]

Nabuco's prescience about some of slavery's enduring legacies – from its centrality to private life to its capacity to shape international relations, from its ability to create complicity across the color and class spectrum to its potential to corrode the institutions and ideals of liberal modernity – has significantly shaped contemporary debates and is also manifest in this collection. Ricardo Salles and Mariana Muaze's account (Chapter 3) of the intersection of coffee capitalism and family formation echoes Nabuco's occasional glimmers of optimism, documenting the ways in

[64] J. Nabuco, *O abolicionismo*, pp. 174–176.
[65] J. Nabuco, *O abolicionismo*, pp. 251–252.
[66] S. Buarque de Holanda, *Raízes do Brasil*; C. Prado Júnior, *Formação do Brasil*; R. Faoro, *Os donos*; C. Furtado, *Formação econômica*; J. Pádua, *Um sopro*; W. Dean, *With Broadax*.
[67] G. Freyre, *Casa grande* and *Sobrados*.
[68] R. Bastide and F. Fernandes, *Brancos e negros*; F. Fernandes, *O negro*.

which the formation of "agrarian empires" could – despite overwhelming brutalities and inequalities – open and even require spaces that allowed enslaved people to create and sustain the networks of community and kinship that undergirded Black life during and after slavery. In a darker vein, Marcus Carvalho's analysis of the illegal slave trade in Pernambuco (Chapter 2) argues that the economic logics of slave commerce could not be separated from the traumatic experience of child slavery nor the complicity of regional planter clans – and that the political and affective echoes of such trauma and collusion were palpable long after the last enslaved children disembarked. In a similar key, Beatriz Mamigonian and Keila Grinberg (Chapter 1) document slavery's foundational role in the development of Brazilian law and citizenship. In showing how nineteenth-century judges, juries, and superior courts undermined freedom by refusing to convict defendants of the crime of illegal enslavement, Mamigonian and Grinberg substantiate the degree to which Brazilian law and Brazilian citizenship were corroded at their inception, despite the activism of the many lawyers and prosecutors who attempted to use the courts as vehicles of freedom.

Especially haunting, 130 years after abolition, are the ways in which the essays collected here echo Nabuco's arguments about Brazilian slavery's flexibility, capilarity, and power to survive its own legal extinction. Brodwyn Fischer's Chapter 7 shows how Recife remained a "slave city" long after most enslaved people had been emancipated; for Anísia, Guilherme, and Esperança – the people whose histories Fischer's chapter traces – the possibilities of urban mobility and freedom were strictly curtailed by economic decadence, private authority, and the networks of recognition and relational power that slavery had inscribed on the urban form. Sueann Caulfield's account (Chapter 14) of the tangled politics of intimacy and complicity that allowed Brazilian families to perpetuate slavery's inequalities also gives vivid expression to Nabuco's foreshadowing, illustrating how the ambiguous and informal recognition that was granted as a "favor" to the mixed-race children of elite Brazilian families ensured the persistence of patriarchy and paternalism even as it allowed for limited social mobility. Wlamyra Albuquerque's portrait of Teodoro Sampaio (Chapter 10) captures the pathos of the free Black experience in the decades surrounding abolition more arrestingly still. By documenting the intersection of legal freedom and ascendant racism and the wrenching ideological and personal compromises that conditioned movement from slavery to freedom and from obscurity to the highest reaches of Brazil's professional classes, Albuquerque revisits Nabuco's notion of complicity.

But she does so with a searing awareness of the sociocultural circumstances that rendered such complicity unavoidable and the cruel blockades that blunted its efficacy as an instrument of true equality.

On the issue of slavery's legacies, Nabuco was also a touchstone for Black activist Abdias do Nascimento (1914–2011), who cited Nabuco's words in the 1968 preface to *O Negro Revoltado*: "So long as the Nation remains unaware that it is indispensable to adapt to liberty every apparatus of its organism that slavery has appropriated, slavery will endure, even when there are no longer a single slave."[69] Yet Nascimento's admiration for Nabuco was tempered by incisive critique, two elements of which have been especially important in shaping Brazilian studies of slavery and abolition in the past half-century. The first involved a sharp rebuke of white "advocates" and men of letters who claimed to speak for the Afro-descendant masses, both under slavery and beyond it.[70] Nascimento's criticism was selective – he reserved particular scorn for L. A. da Costa Pinto and Gilberto Freyre, but he cited Nabuco frequently and greatly admired contemporary allies such as Florestan Fernandes.[71] All the same, Nascimento crafted a forceful argument for Black people's agency in the struggle against slavery, and he demanded equal voice for Black intellectuals as part and parcel of freedom. Nascimento also skillfully eviscerated the unity that Nabuco implied among the Brazilian people, shattering the myth of a national family in which the enslaved and the enslavers were united in both the degradation and guilt of slavery and the arduous task of post-abolition nation-building.

On all of these counts, Nascimento asserted Black subjectivity as a fundamental right and Black suffering as a unique and outrageous burden: Afro-descendants were actors in their own history, and both slavery and post-abolition destitution and prejudice had caused them deep harm that demanded recognition and recompense. Slavery in Brazil had penetrated every cell of Brazil's national body, and its legacies were

---

[69] A. do Nascimento, *O negro revoltado*, p. 21.
[70] See for example A. do Nascimento, *O genocídio*, p. 137.
[71] On L. A. Costa Pinto, see A. do Nascimento, *O negro revoltado*, pp. 16–17; on Freyre, see A. do Nascimento, *O genocídio*, pp. 42–45; on Fernandes, see A. do Nascimento, *O genocídio*, pp. 40, 46, 82, 136, and *O negro revoltado*, p. 17. Nascimento maintained uncharacteristic silence with regard to Nabuco's complicity in the construction of Brazilian paradigms of cultural and racial mixture, even quoting Nabuco as a capstone to his withering assessment of Pierre Verger's "paternalistic" "domestication" of Afro-descendant culture: "Who can say that the Black race does not have the right to protest before the world and history against Brazil's behavior?" (A. do Nascimento, *O genocídio*, p. 122).

indeed felt by all. But it had marked Black bodies, families, and destinies in specifically devastating ways, and those harms had been perpetuated by practices and institutions that extended to Nascimento's lifetime. Though he did not use her language, Nascimento was arguing – in essence – that Brazilian slavery had what Saidiya Hartman would later term "after-lives," which perpetuated its racially specific devastation and would not disappear without the wholesale recognition of Black voices and Black subjectivities.

Nascimento, like Nabuco, was an activist as well as an intellectual, and while his aim to upturn Brazil's worst racial inequities remains out of reach, a remarkable number of his initiatives became policy in Brazil between the 1980s and the 2010s: the breaking of racial silence (rhetoric-ally, politically, culturally, and through the inclusion of racial statistics in national surveys); the creation of educational curricula focused on the Brazilian Black experience; the recognition of Afro-Brazilian culture and the associations that practice and promote it; and affirmative action in public education and employment.[72] Since the 1970s, historians and other social scientists have pursued Nascimento's intellectual aims with similar energy. Brazilian historiography still does not adequately reflect Afro-descendants' historical role in Brazil; the Black experience, articulated by Black scholars, still does not occupy its rightful space in the academic world. But Black intellectuals and activists have played a crucial role in constructing the historiography of slavery, abolition, and post-abolition, and the field as a whole has embraced the challenges of documenting Black subjectivities; recognizing Afro-descendant resistance to slavery and Black agency in the social and intellectual struggles of abolition and its after-maths; and understanding the specific historical impact of slavery and its afterlives on Brazilian Afro-descendants.[73]

The essays collected here emerge from that movement. As noted, many of our authors work within Nabuco's tradition, interrogating the ways in which slavery and abolition shaped institutions and historical processes at the heart of Brazil's national history; family, law, gender, urbanity, rural property and labor relations, diplomacy, art, and music. In undertaking such analysis, however, they depart from earlier generations in striving to comprehend those processes through the lens of Afro-descendant experi-ence and in arguing that slavery's legacies are separable neither from the

---

[72] A. do Nascimento, *O genocídio*, pp. 137–141.
[73] F. Gomes and P. Domingues, *Da nitidez*; G. Xavier (org.), *Histórias da escravidão*; G. Xavier (org.), *Intelectuais negras*.

afterlives that have extended its abuses and inequities to our own times nor from the practices of resistance and contestation that continue to anchor Black struggle.

The analytical consequences of foregrounding Afro-descendant experience and agency within broader historical phenomena emerge clearly in Keila Grinberg's Chapter 5, about the origins of the Paraguayan War. Grinberg's argument centers on the ways in which conflicts over free soil contributed to the diplomatic tensions that preceded the war. Yet she makes her case with a deep awareness that those tensions were created by real people living on the borderlands of Brazil and Uruguay in an era of precarious enslavement and precarious freedom: kidnapping and illegal slave-trading would never have become matters of diplomatic tension if people such as Rufina and Juan Rosa had not risked everything to denounce criminals such as Laurindo José da Costa and the legions of complicit officials who made his actions possible. In obscuring the role of free-soil conflicts in sparking the Paraguayan War, historians – beginning with Nabuco himself – have not only underplayed the historical impact of Black agency; they have also obscured slavery's central place in one of Brazil's most impactful experiences of national formation.

On a more intimate scale, other contributors build on questions of women's experience of enslavement and racial formation that were equally fundamental to Nascimento's thought, drawing our attention to specifically Afro-descendant experiences of gender formation and precarious freedom.[74] Mariana Muaze, in Chapter 4, travels to racial democracy's darkest heart. By examining what forced wet-nursing meant to enslaved women whose own motherhood was silenced by the sustenance and affection they provided to the children of their owners, Muaze reveals the violence and dispossession that undergirded the "slavocratic habitus," and in so doing she undermines any remaining Nabuquian notion that all Brazilians were united in enduring the tragedy of slavery. Maria Helena Machado performs similar labor at the intersection of gender and freedom struggles in Chapter 6, unveiling the logics of an enslaved woman's canny dislocations, pursued according to the conflicting imperatives of family reunification and escape. Machado's exploration of Ovídia and the two Benedictas also brings alive the continuities in women's lives under slavery and freedom, which foreshadowed the specific afterlives of female bondage.

---

[74] In A. do Nacimento's *O genocídio*, chapter 3 focuses on the sexual exploitation of Black women.

Nascimento's influence emerges even more directly when our chapters turn to questions of agency, voice, and resistance. On occasion, this involves giving voice to forgotten and heroic articulations of Black politics. In analyzing Felipe Neri Collaço's pathbreaking journalism, Celso Castilho and Rafaella Valença de Andrade Galvão (Chapter 9) capture the defiant radical edge of Black racial thinking on the eve of abolition. In Chapter 11, meanwhile, Ana Flávia Magalhães Pinto shows the coevolution of class and racial consciousness among people of color in Rio de Janeiro, as well as the deep Brazilian roots of Black educational initiatives and the early entwinement of racial and working-class solidarity. Yet even in those moments, our authors are deeply aware of the countercurrents that have worked across the decades to silence Black voices and suppress the practice and possibility of Black politics. Castilho and Galvão note the racist suppression of Collaço's demands for equality, showing vividly how elite men used Brazil's public sphere to racially degrade and punish those who deviated from the script of racial silence; Magalhães Pinto demonstrates the racial marginalization of Black actors across the political spectrum.

That kind of analytical subtlety – the determination to work in the borderlands that Nabuco and Nascimento both inhabited, to trace the historical roots of Black politics and agency without losing sight of the legacies and afterlives of slavery – may well be the most enduring mark of the historiographical tradition represented in this volume. It is certainly a guiding thread for Robson Martins and Flávio Gomes in their analysis of land and labor relations in the emancipation-era Brazilian Southeast (Chapter 8). Martins and Gomes painstakingly reconstruct the multiple ideals of autonomy, freedom, and family that animated freedpeople's quotidian choices about land and labor, even as they demonstrate how local potentates used tropes of racialized disorder to delegitimize those choices and actively limited freedpeoples' capacity to engage in commerce, move freely, and dispose of arable land as they pleased. Martha Abreu (Chapter 15) captures a similar complex duality: her comparative biographical analysis of Eduardo das Neves and Bert Williams highlights their shared liminality, demonstrating how Black musicians and performing artists created opportunities for cultural expression, artistic advancement, and racial affirmation within transnational cultural circuits that also required them to maneuver within racially oppressive norms and scripts. Daryle Williams (Chapter 13) offers the most optimistic and counterintuitive iteration of this strain of scholarship: rather than focusing on Black agency in a context of oppression, Williams instead demonstrates that freedpeople's understandings of emancipation and its meanings were powerful enough to penetrate the consciousness of a white immigrant artist like Modesto Brocos y Gómez. By reinterpreting the iconic *Redemption of Ham* as a celebration of the possibilities created by Black women, Williams shows the power of an historical method that affirms the historical significance of Black agency through painstaking analysis of Afro-descendant world-making in the murky and ever-shifting landscape of Brazilian post-emancipation.

Williams' elegant optimism is not the dominant spirit in these pages. We wrote these chapters at a sober juncture in the historiography of slavery, post-abolition, and race relations. In Brazil, as in the broader diasporic world, a deep strain of Afro-pessimism has emerged, aiming both to give the lie to triumphal narratives of post-racialism and to call attention to the violent politics of whiteness that have emerged in response to Afro-descendant claims to equality. In this sense, Hebe Mattos' analysis of André Rebouças' tortured transnational engagement with racism and racial subjectivity (Chapter 12) serves as an epigraph for a generation of scholarship that has invested enormous hope in the history of Black freedom. In portraying an iconic Afro-descendant leader whose rupturing of the ethic of racial silence stemmed not from liberty but rather from disillusionment and despair, Mattos' chapter serves as an enduring reminder that the afterlife of hope has often been far more fragile than the afterlives of bondage in the history of modern Brazil.

PART I

LAW, PRECARITY, AND AFFECTIVE ECONOMIES DURING BRAZIL'S SLAVE EMPIRE

The Crime of Illegal Enslavement and the Precariousness of Freedom in Nineteenth-Century Brazil

Beatriz G. Mamigonian and Keila Grinberg*

In April 1849, in the southern Brazilian city of Porto Alegre, public prosecutor Antonio Pedro Francisco Pinho filed charges against Manoel Pereira Tavares de Mello e Albuquerque for the crime of reducing to slavery the *parda* Porfíria and her two sons, Lino and Leopoldino, aged eight and four respectively.[1] The case, in the form of a "*sumário crime*" (summary criminal procedure), was based on Article 179 of the Brazilian Criminal Code, which punished with three to nine years of imprisonment and a fine those found guilty of "reducing to slavery a free person who is in possession of his liberty."[2] Slavery in Brazil coexisted with a sizable free population of African descent, a result of historically high rates of manumission. After independence from Portugal in 1822, the constitution

---

* Translated by Kristin McGuire. A previous version of this text was published in French in *Brésil(s), Sciences humaines et sociales*, 11 (May 2017), and a preliminary version was presented by Beatriz Mamigonian and Mariana Armond Dias Paes at the seminar "Legislating and Litigating in the Campaign Against Modern Slavery: Theory Meets Practice" at the University of Michigan Law School in December 2014. The authors thank Mariana Armond Dias Paes for her collaboration, sharing of documents, and valuable critique. They also thank Gabriela Barretto de Sá, Ariana Moreira Espíndola, and Maysa Espíndola Souza for their work collecting and transcribing primary documents, as well as Rebecca J. Scott, Jean Hébrard, and Leonardo Barbosa for early discussions of the topics discussed here and for their input on versions of this chapter.
[1] "Pardo" was a racial classification that stood between "Branco" (White) and "Preto" (Black) in nineteenth-century Brazil, applying to people of mixed race, either enslaved or free. Public Archives of the State of Rio Grande do Sul (APERS), Acervo Judiciário, Comarca de Porto Alegre, Sub-Fundo 2a Vara Cível e Crime, Ano 1849, processo n. 3618, réu Manoel José Tavares de Mello e Albuquerque, vítimas Porfíria (parda), Lino e Leopoldino.
[2] Brazil. Law of December 16, 1830. Manda executar o Código Criminal do Império. *Coleção de Leis do Império do Brasil – 1830*, v. 1, p. 1, p. 142.

deemed all free and freed people born in Brazil, regardless of color, Brazilian citizens.[3] Years later, lawmakers sought to protect free people from enslavement by targeting the practice in the Criminal Code of 1830. As the case of Porfíria and her two sons demonstrates, the enforcement of the measure evoked legal and political challenges.

In many ways, the case of Porfíria and her two sons can be seen as a manumission transaction gone wrong. Some time before the criminal case was filed, the three had been the objects of a transaction between Albuquerque and their former master, Joaquim Álvares de Oliveira. Oliveira had received two enslaved persons in exchange for Porfíria and her sons; Albuquerque apparently wanted to marry the woman to his brick foreman in order to keep him at his job. In her testimony, Porfíria alleged that Oliveira had given her a letter of manumission at the time of the exchange, and this was confirmed by one of the witnesses. The defendant Albuquerque, however, denied this allegation, presenting documents to show that Porfíria's manumission was conditional on the payment of a certain sum by her future husband. Witnesses for the case were questioned to clarify Porfíria's status and condition, and she conceded under questioning that she had all along been "under the dominion and captivity" of Albuquerque until she fled for fear of being sold.[4] In filing a criminal case, the judge deemed her free and a victim of illegal enslavement.

The case of Porfíria was by no means exceptional. In the catalog of nineteenth-century criminal cases related to slavery held in the Public Archives of Rio Grande do Sul, sixty-eight cases relate to accusations of "reducing a free person to slavery" based on Article 179 of the Criminal Code.[5] The uncertainty of Porfíria's status was not unique either, and a sizable number of the criminal proceedings as well as many civil actions involved disputes over the status of the person in question. Significant archival documentation exists on the enslavement of free people. And yet, although historians have recently drawn some attention to the subject, it nonetheless remains a neglected topic in the study of Brazilian criminal justice in the nineteenth century.[6]

---

[3] Even though basic civil rights were granted to all Brazilian citizens, there were many restrictions on freedpeople's political rights; they could not, for example, serve as candidates or participate in second-round elections. See K. Grinberg, *A Black Jurist in a Slave Society*, chapter 3.

[4] G. Sá, *O crime.*   [5] B. Pessi and G. Souza e Silva, eds., *Documentos.*

[6] J. Freitas, "Slavery and Social Life"; S. Chalhoub, "The Precariousness of Freedom" and *A Força da escravidão*; K. Grinberg, "Re-enslavement, Rights and Justice"; G. Sá, *O crime.*

Some of the most innovative works in the field of Atlantic slavery in recent years focus on the frontiers of enslavement. First, attention was given to geographic frontiers. Since colonial times, even before abolition appeared on the horizon, individuals who sought freedom made use of frontiers; they served native Indians as well as enslaved Africans and their descendants. The benefits of entering foreign territory could compensate for the risky journey, because it was a way to put oneself far from the reach and grip of masters and local authorities. The transit of people through frontiers not only gave rise to a transnational runaway movement but also created, from at least the early eighteenth century forward, an array of diplomatic incidents, given that requests for repatriation were exchanged and limits had to be negotiated.[7] During the Independence Wars and the movement for slave emancipation in the Americas, however, the transit of slaves through frontiers gained a new status: state formation meant the creation of elaborate legal and diplomatic protocols to guarantee free soil and slave soil. The Brazilian Empire was one of the most powerful American states forged in part to defend slavery.[8]

Besides geographic frontiers, historians have lately turned their attention to the conceptual frontiers of enslavement – that is, to the changes in what was considered legal and legitimate bondage. Studies of legal cases have made it clear that, in different places and in varying circumstances, the illegal enslavement of certain groups was questioned long before the nineteenth-century movement for the abolition of the slave trade and slavery in the Americas.[9] A closer analysis of freedom lawsuits in Brazil has allowed historians to identify the circumstances that favored or allowed (re)enslavement and to consider the relationship of enslavement to the physical and social vulnerability of its victims, as well as the institutional response to particular cases.

Working within this historiographical framework, with the intention of furthering the discussion about the precariousness of freedom in nineteenth-century Brazil, we will consider here how cases that involved the enslavement of free people were criminalized and brought to court in

---

[7] F. Gomes, "A 'Safe Haven'"; F. Gomes and R. Acevedo Marin, "Reconfigurações coloniais"; M. Almeida and S. Ortelli, "Atravesando fronteras"; J. Landers, "Spanish Sanctuary"; A. Ferrer, "Haiti, Free Soil, and Antislavery"; R. Scott and J. Hébrard, *Freedom Papers*.

[8] K. Grinberg, "Fronteiras, escravidão e Liberdade."

[9] S. Peabody and K. Grinberg, *Free Soil*; S. Lara, "O espírito"; F. Pinheiro, "Em defesa da liberdade"; M. Candido, *An African Slaving Port*.

Brazil throughout the nineteenth century. The cases give an overview of the patterns of enslavement and the varying applications of Article 179 of the Criminal Code. We have divided the cases into three groups, according to the circumstances of enslavement: Africans who were brought illegally after the 1831 ban on the Atlantic trade (along with their descendants); freedpersons who lived in vulnerable conditions; and, lastly, free people of African descent or freedpersons who were kidnapped and/or sold as slaves. Although the number of potential victims of enslavement from illegal trafficking or from ploys of re-enslavement was much greater than the number of people subjected to abductions, these latter cases were brought to justice more often. The most notorious of these were cases involving free people who were physically abducted on the border with Uruguay and sold as slaves in Rio Grande do Sul. Our hypothesis is that the distorted relationship among the number of occurrences, the number of cases filed, and their outcomes points to political choices that influenced the application of Article 179 of the Criminal Code and the law of November 7, 1831, that prohibited the Atlantic slave trade.

THE CRIMINAL CODE OF 1830 AND THE CRIME OF REDUCING A FREE PERSON TO SLAVERY

The Brazilian Criminal Code of 1830 was seen at the time as an important step toward the modernization of criminal law. Codification was a crucial initiative for a newly independent country that aspired to position itself within the so-called civilized nations. The deputies and senators responsible for drafting the Code took into consideration two bills prepared by José Clemente Pereira and Bernardo Pereira de Vasconcelos, elements of civil codes and statutes from other countries, and debates held in Parliament in 1830.[10]

The bill presented by Deputy Bernardo Pereira de Vasconcelos included an article against the enslavement of the "free man, who is in possession of his freedom," proposing a sentence of imprisonment with forced labor for a period of five to twenty years.[11] This was something new, as the Philippine Code, the Portuguese legislation in force in Brazil during the

---

[10] M. Dantas, "Dos statutes" and "Introdução."

[11] "Art. 152 Reducing to slavery the free man who is in possession of his freedom will be punished with the penalty of the galleys for five to twenty years. And if the unjust captivity has been of longer duration, the penalty will always exceed a third of that plus the corresponding fine." B. Pereira de Vasconcellos, "Projeto do Código Criminal," p. 101.

colonial period, did not have a specific provision for the crime of enslaving free people. Indeed, the opposite was the case: legislation at the time allowed for the possibility of holding individuals in captivity if a master wished to revoke manumission granted to former slaves or questioned whether they should live as free people. These cases were regulated by the Philippine Ordinances under the heading "Of Gifts and Manumission That Can Be Revoked Because of Ingratitude," which applied to freedpersons.[12] Interestingly, here, re-enslavement was not only legally possible but also based on the premise that enslavement was the natural condition of Africans and their descendants, rendering their freedom always temporary and questionable. All the same, this heading of the Philippine Ordinances applied only to those who had been enslaved, not to just anyone.[13]

Although the Philippine Ordinances sanctioned these instances of re-enslavement, even prior to 1830 there were cases of enslavement of free people that were considered illegal. At least three situations could lead to this: the enslavement of the descendants of Indigenous people (in many cases, the children of Indigenous mothers and Africans or descendants of African fathers), which had been illegal since 1680;[14] the enslavement of children who were born free, meaning the sons and daughters (who often did not even know they were free) of free women; and disregard for the charters (*alvarás*) of 1761 and 1773, which prohibited bringing enslaved Africans into the Kingdom of Portugal. Although this last prohibition referred specifically to the Kingdom, there are indications that it was enforced in the African colonies as well.[15] These three types of offenses led to judicial inquiries. In her analysis of cases of re-enslavement in the cities of Mariana (Minas Gerais, Brazil) and Lisbon from 1720 to 1819, Fernanda Domingos Pinheiro found fifty-four cases that addressed illegal captivity in Mariana alone.[16] In contrast with the prosecutions against illegal enslavement after 1830, however, these earlier instances were civil cases, not criminal. Although it was possible for someone to contest their

---

[12] C. Mendes de Almeida, "Código Filipino," Book IV, Heading 63.

[13] A. Russell-Wood, *Escravos e libertos*, p. 48; S. Lara, *Fragmentos setecentistas*; E. Paiva, "Revendications de droits."

[14] In 1680, the Portuguese Crown promulgated a decree, based on a previous decision in 1609, establishing the illegality of the enslavement of natives. The order was reiterated in 1755, when the so-called Law of Liberty reinforced the full freedom of the natives, considering them vassals of the king of Portugal as any others. Portugal, "Lei de 6 de junho de 1755."

[15] L. Silva, "Esperança de liberdade"; C. N. Silva and K. Grinberg, "Soil Free from Slaves."

[16] F. D. Pinheiro, "Em defesa da liberdade."

illegal enslavement through freedom suits, the practice of enslavement itself was not considered a punishable crime. Thus, before 1830, the only consequence for a slaveholder was the loss of his or her alleged property.

By the time the Criminal Code of the Brazilian Empire was being discussed, the context had changed radically: the lines between slavery and freedom were being redrawn as the country prepared for the abolition of the slave trade. Theoretically, as newly enslaved Africans could no longer be brought into the country, new slaves would come only from natural reproduction. Article 7 in Vasconcelos' bill was intended to guarantee the freedom of those who were born free, and we cannot assume that it was meant to protect the newly arrived Africans from enslavement.[17]

It is interesting to note that the final version of the article reverses the premise of earlier legislation, which presumed that enslavement was the natural state of Afro-descendants in Brazil. By making it a crime against individual liberty "to reduce to slavery a free person who is in possession of his freedom"[18] – and thus placing such an action in the same category as undue arrest[19] – the bill treated enslavement not only as an illegal act but as a violation of the fundamental rights of personhood, which were as inherent in Afro-descendant people as they were in anyone else.

According to Monica Dantas, Vasconcelos probably drew inspiration from the Livingston Code, the Criminal Code proposed in Louisiana in the 1820s.[20] Indeed, Article 452 of the Louisiana Code states: "If the offense be committed against a free person for the purpose of detaining or

---

[17] Newly arrived Africans were generically termed "barbarians" by the members of this same legislature when discussing the law on leasing labor: "Art. 7: The contract maintained by the present law cannot be celebrated, under any pretext whatsoever, with the barbarian Africans, except for those who currently exist in Brazil." Brazil, "Law of September 13, 1830."

[18] "Art. 179. To reduce a free person to slavery who is in possession of his freedom. Penalties – imprisonment for three to nine years and a fine, corresponding to a third of the time; however, the time of imprisonment will never be less than one third of the time of unjust captivity." Brazil, "Law of December 16, 1830."

[19] The crime of enslaving free persons was listed among the "private crimes" in the Criminal Code and was treated as a "crime of public action" in the Code of Criminal Procedure of 1832 (Article 31, par. 1). As a crime that should be judged according to regular criminal procedures, it was technically the jury, presided over by the judge, who had to decide whether to incriminate the defendant and initiate proceedings. The jury was made up of citizens who were classified as "electors" (citizens born free with higher incomes than mere "voters"), and the judge was a civil servant trained in law and appointed by the emperor. J. R. L. Lopes, *O direito*, pp. 268–269.

[20] Monica Dantas has linked the crime of insurrection (Articles 113 to 115 of the Brazilian Criminal Code) to the legislation of certain states in the United States, including Virginia and South Carolina, suggesting that the connection came from Brazilian legislators

disposing of him as a slave, knowing such person to be free, the punishment shall be a fine of not less than five hundred dollars nor more than five thousand dollars, and imprisonment at hard labor, not less than two nor more than four years."[21]

There is, however, a significant difference in wording between the two Codes. In the proposed Louisiana Code, enslavement was illegal if the perpetrator was aware of the freedom of his victim (which, in a way, always allowed for the defense to claim that the act was based on ignorance of someone's status), even in cases when the person was living under someone's dominion. In the Brazilian case, the situation was different. First, it did not matter whether or not the perpetrator had information about the victim's freedom. Second, enslavement was only criminalized if the victim was living as a free person. The terminology here is particularly important, since it defined the circumstances of the crime and made the assertion of the "possession of freedom" central to legal arguments in lawsuits about enslavement in Brazil. The possession of freedom was the condition that separated illegal from legal enslavement and would serve throughout the nineteenth century to determine whether captives could claim legal protection.

THE PROHIBITION OF TRAFFICKING AFRICANS AND THE EXPANSION OF ILLEGAL ENSLAVEMENT

The law of November 7, 1831, which aimed to abolish the international slave trade to Brazil, referred to Article 179 of the Criminal Code for prosecution of those accused of trafficking. In other words, legislators chose to charge those involved in the financing, the transportation, and the arrival of Africans, as well as those who purchased newly arrived Africans, with the crime of reducing a free person to slavery.[22] This interpretation of the law extended the protection afforded by the provisions of Article 179 to newly arrived Africans, whose "possession of

reading a French copy of the penal code prepared for Louisiana in the 1820s by Edward Livingston (1833), which was never instated. See M. Dantas, "Introdução."

[21] E. Livingston, *A System of Penal Law*, book II, title 19, section II, article 452.

[22] "Importers of slaves in Brazil will incur the corporal punishment of article one hundred and seventy-nine of the Criminal Code, imposed on those who reduce to slavery free persons, and pay a fine of two hundred thousand reis per head of each of the imported slaves, in addition to paying the costs of re-export to any part of Africa; re-export, which the Government will make effective as soon as possible, working with the African authorities to grant them asylum. The offenders will answer each one for himself, and for all." Brazil, "Law of November 7, 1831."

freedom" at the time of enslavement was impossible to determine. A decree of April 1832 regulated the procedures, specifying that traffickers should be tried in criminal court, while the status of Africans should be addressed as a civil matter.[23] This asymmetrical treatment of criminals and victims often led to confusion because the focus on a victim's status (which, as a general rule, was uncertain) tended to divert attention away from the circumstances of the crime and to minimize the possibilities of punishment.

The law of 1831 became known in Brazil as legislation "para inglês ver" (for the English to see), an expression that, while highlighting British pressure to abolish the slave trade, came to imply in popular usage that the Brazilian government had never intended to apply it. In the last decade, however, research has shown that the uses and meanings of this law varied widely in the nearly sixty years between its adoption in 1831 and the abolition of slavery in 1888.[24] Despite attempts by the Brazilian government to enforce the law, particularly between 1831 and 1834, the smuggling of enslaved Africans resumed and slowly increased in volume, giving political strength to groups advocating amnesty and impunity for those involved. Between the early 1830s and the passage of the second law abolishing the slave trade in 1850, at least 780,000 Africans were smuggled into the country and held illegally in captivity, a status which was then extended to their children.[25]

Rio Grande do Sul, although not the site of frequent clandestine landings, was nonetheless an area with significant illegal enslavement. Most likely, the labor supply for the *charqueadas* (dried meat plants), the cattle ranches, and the towns was met through the internal slave trade between provinces. Tracing the actions of the authorities responsible for repressing the illegal trade and the enslavement of free persons in the province brings to light contradictions and variations that existed throughout the country: repression and collusion coexisted with compliance with guidelines from Rio de Janeiro as well as with attempts to challenge those same guidelines in the courts.

A slave landing on the coast of Tramandaí, in Rio Grande do Sul in April 1852, is a good example of varying legal strategies involving

---

[23] Brazil, "Decree of April 12, 1832."
[24] K. Grinberg and B. Mamigonian, "Para Inglês Ver?"; K. Grinberg, "Slavery, Manumission and the Law"; E. Azevedo, *O direito dos escravos*; B. Mamigonian, "O estado nacional" and *Africanos livres*; S. Chalhoub, *A força da escravidão*.
[25] M. Florentino, *Em costas negras*; T. Parron, *A política da escravidão*; B. Mamigonian, *Africanos livres*.

"illegal" Africans, strategies in which slaveowners and authorities col-
luded in order to deflect prosecutorial attempts to enforce the regulations. After having crossed the Atlantic, the ship ran aground in the town
of Conceição do Arroio, a district of Santo Antônio da Patrulha, in the
province of Rio Grande do Sul. Hundreds of Africans – later estimated
between 200 and 500 – were quickly unloaded from the ship. Provincial
authorities tried to capture the Africans, but most were claimed by
coastal residents, and many were then sent "up the mountains."[26]
Twenty Africans who were taken into custody by the authorities were
emancipated in July and handed over to the Santa Casa de Misericordia
in Porto Alegre to fulfill their obligation to provide services as "liberated
Africans."[27] They had been seized separately, in small groups. Three
African boys found in Lombas (a town in the Viamão district) as part of
a mission ordered by the vice-president of the province on April 27 were
most likely among this group. Authorities rescued the three newly
arrived Africans and also arrested Nicolau dos Santos Guterres and
José Geraldo de Godoy, who owned the lands where the boys were
found.[28]

Historians, long focused on the fate of enslaved people and assuming
that the 1831 law was only *para inglês ver*, have rarely examined the
repressive actions of the local authorities or judicial responses to criminal
accusations involving illegal enslavement. The cases concerning the
Africans who arrived in Tramandaí in 1852 illustrate some of the contradictory measures enacted against such suspects. The two owners of the
lands where the three African boys were found, when interrogated by the
acting chief of police, claimed that they were unaware of the landing on
the Tramandaí coast and that they did not know the people who brought
the Africans to the area and offered them for sale. The two did not claim
possession or ownership over the Africans, and the authorities did not ask
them about how the captives had been acquired. The witnesses who were

---

[26] P. R. S. Moreira, "Boçais e malungos"; V. P. Oliveira, *De Manoel Congo*; D. Barcellos
et al., *Comunidade negra*.
[27] "Liberated Africans" is a legal category that defined enslaved Africans who were found on
slave ships caught by authorities from countries such as Britain, Portugal, Spain, the USA,
and Brazil during the repression of the illegal slave trade. Although these individuals were
legally considered free, their fates were decided by international commissions and local
authorities. Most of them went through a long process before being granted autonomy
and freedom. In Brazil, for example, liberated Africans had to work for at least fourteen.
B. G. Mamigonian, *Africanos livres*.
[28] APERS, Fundo Comarca de Porto Alegre, Vara Cível e Crime, processo 3511, 1852.
Digitalized and transcribed by Gabriela Barretto de Sá.

called to testify could not appear, and the few who spoke about the case said little, simply confirming that the Africans were found on the defendants' lands. Although the prosecutor characterized the accused men's actions as a crime against "art. 179 of the Criminal Code, pursuant to the Law of November 7, 1831," within ten days the interim judge and police chief, Antonio Ladislau de Figueiredo Rocha, dismissed the case for lack of evidence and ordered the two defendants' release.[29]

Ten years later, the rescue of Manoel Congo, another African man who had landed in Tramandaí, again placed in question the willingness of the Imperial justice system to punish those involved in illegal enslavement. According to Manoel Congo's account from 1861, someone captured him after the landing, kept him in hiding, and sold him "up the mountains" after a few months. Aware that he was free, he fled from his first master and headed to the Santa Casa of Porto Alegre. But on the way he encountered Captain José Joaquim de Paula, who dissuaded him from going to the authorities, promising him lands in exchange for his labor. Yet a complaint brought against Paula many years later, when Manoel was discovered and rescued from Paula's property in São Leopoldo, made clear that this promise had been a deception. Not only had been Manoel been baptized as a slave despite one vicar's refusal to cooperate, but around 1854, in an attempt to forge documents that would legitimize Manoel Congo's enslavement, Paula had falsified a document attesting that he (Paula) had purchased Manuel from another supposed "owner," promising Manoel freedom after eight years of labor.[30] Seized in 1861, Manoel was sent to the Santa Casa de Misericórdia in Porto Alegre where, according to the records, he worked as a "liberated African." Paula, in turn, was accused of an offense against Articles 167 and 265 of the Criminal Code, which addressed deceit and the use of falsified documentation to exploit a person. In addition to not being accused of the crime of reducing a free person to slavery, Paula was able to appeal his eventual conviction on charges of deceit, which suggests that he may have gone unpunished, despite the fact that the case had garnered significant publicity.[31]

During the preliminary police inquiry, Deputy Gaspar Silveira Martins addressed the Provincial Assembly to criticize the police chief's handling

[29] APERS, Fundo Comarca de Porto Alegre, Vara Cível e Crime, file n. 3511, 1852, p. 31.
[30] V. Oliveira, *De Manoel Congo*, pp. 39–43, 75–78.
[31] APERS, Fundo Comarca de Porto Alegre, Vara Cível e Crime, processo 3511, 1852, p. 111v.

of the case, specifically alleging that the chief had not ordered the arrest of José Joaquim de Paula or insisted on obtaining evidence to corroborate Paula's version of the facts. Martins' fellow assembly members, however, defended the provincial authorities, based largely on their belief in Captain Paula's good faith. The principle of good faith was used regularly to exculpate those who owned Africans illegally. Silveira Martins responded by proposing to shift the burden of proof from the enslaved to the enslaver: Paula should prove that he had acquired the African legally (by donation, inheritance, exchange, purchase, or other legal means of property transfer) and show that he did not know, and could not have known, that it was an illegal sale: "Paula claims in his defense that he purchased this African from one Agostinho Antonio Leal, and if this is true, he should prove the purchase with a rightful title, and prove further that Agostinho could legally possess this slave."[32] Silveira Martins insisted that the document of manumission was falsified, that there was no record of the master having paid the regular sale tax, and that these facts, together with the testimony of the African, should serve as evidence of the crime. He even accused the chief of police of criminal prevarication, insinuating that he was protecting the captain because he was a person of power and a second-tier elector in Brazil's two-tier electoral system.

Gaspar Silveira Martins had received his law degree from São Paulo in 1856 and had been a municipal judge in Rio de Janeiro since 1859, in addition to being provincial deputy from Rio Grande do Sul. He came from a family of large landowners on the border region with Uruguay, "of the *farroupilha* liberal tradition," and in the late 1860s was involved in the Radical Club of Rio de Janeiro, one of the first republican associations in the country.[33] The young lawyer and deputy, like other radical lawyers and judges, interpreted the 1831 law to mean that Manoel Congo should have been free since landing in Brazil, and therefore Captain José Joaquim de Paula had reduced a free person to slavery. The Ministry of Justice, however, only recognized the right to freedom of Africans rescued at sea or soon after landing on the mainland, thus informally guaranteeing the right to property acquired by smuggling and protecting the holders of illegal slaves from the criminalization of their acts.[34]

A supposed "threat to the public order" was another justification often used to avoid the emancipation of Africans who were being held in illegal

---

[32] Speech by Silveira Martins on September 30, 1862, cited in H. Piccolo, ed., *Coletânea de discursos*, pp. 614–615.

[33] M. Rossato, "Relações de poder," pp. 93–94.   [34] B. Mamigonian, *Africanos livres*.

captivity. In 1868, other Africans from the 1852 Tramandaí landing turned to Luiz Ferreira Maciel Pinheiro, the public prosecutor of Santo Antônio da Patrulha, to plead for freedom. In Conceição do Arroio, an investigation based on the procedures indicated in the Decree of 1832 was led by the judge, who prepared to "liberate a large number of people from slavery." The putative owners intervened and instigated a debate about the value of the victims' testimony. They complained that the Africans in question "had high stakes in the outcome"; therefore, their depositions could not be taken into account. Prosecutor Maciel Pinheiro, in turn, accused "the masters of these and of other Africans" of being criminals who sought to block the actions of the judiciary. But the voice of the putative owners was more powerful than the judicial proceedings, and Pinheiro, under pressure from the provincial president to terminate the case, resigned.[35] A young graduate from Paraíba who was trained in Recife Law School and had been a colleague of the abolitionist poet Castro Alves, Pinheiro was one of the new voices in the legal field who challenged the policy of collusion in cases of illegal enslavement.

RE-ENSLAVEMENT OF FREEDPERSONS

Although it is practically impossible to quantify, there is no doubt that the practice of re-enslaving freedpersons was a frequent occurrence in nineteenth-century Brazil. Several factors contributed to this. First, it was possible until 1871 to legally revert manumission. Although the procedure was complex – the only motive contemplated in the Philippine Code was ingratitude – and the number of cases decreased significantly in the second half of the century, this masters' prerogative might have enabled other ways of retaining dominion over freedpersons. Secondly, conditional manumission was very common and implied a "legal limbo" that put people's freedom in peril. Did the freedperson start to enjoy the benefits of freedom at the time of manumission or when certain conditions were filled? This uncertainty was particularly damaging to freedwomen, since it cast doubt on the status of their children. Finally, the precariousness of life in freedom, which forced freedpersons to seek protection from higher-status patrons and made it difficult for

---

[35] Luiz Ferreira Maciel Pinheiro to Antônio da Costa Pinto e Silva, September 29, 1868; Luiz Ferreira Maciel Pinheiro to Antônio da Costa Pinto e Silva, October 6, 1868. Letters from the Historic Archive of Rio Grande do Sul (AHRS), Justiça, Promotor Público, maço 42 (Sto Antônio da Patrulha). The case was analyzed by P. R. S. Moreira, "Um promotor."

them to differentiate themselves from slaves, also facilitated re-enslavement. In general, those victims who managed to get their cases to the courts did so through civil suits, which were denominated *ações de liberdade* when victims had actually been re-enslaved and *ações de manutenção de liberdade* when they simply ran the risk of re-enslavement. These cases rarely generated criminal proceedings.

The criminal case involving Porfíria in 1849, with which we began this chapter, stands out, shedding light not only on the mechanisms of re-enslavement but also on how the judicial system addressed these crimes. In suits like Porfíria's, the central legal question was the definition of "possession of freedom," and the jurists involved were far from reaching a consensus on the matter.

Manoel Pereira Tavares de Mello e Albuquerque called himself the "master and possessor" of Porfíria and her sons; he sought to demonstrate that she lived under his rule and that she was considered a slave in Porto Alegre, so much so that she had collected alms to pay for her manumission. The procedural discussion and the examination of witnesses revolved around whether Porfíria and her children actually possessed their freedom or not. The police chief, who was also a municipal judge, dismissed the complaint against Albuquerque, having concluded that Porfíria and her children were not in "possession of freedom," which implied that they were not under the protection of Article 179 of the Criminal Code. Moreover, the chief/judge determined that "the right of the mother and her children is not a given," meaning that he doubted their status as free persons, which led him to send Porfíria to a civil court so that her status could be determined before the criminal investigation moved forward.

All of this revealed that even the legal definition of possession was complicated at this time. The variety of meanings conferred on the notion extended back to Portuguese medieval law; until at least the middle of the thirteenth century, the words "possession" and "property" were designated by a single expression, *iur* (from the Latin *ius*), which shows that they were imprecise and confusable terms. In this context, it was possible for a person to obtain ownership of a thing, be it a farm or a person, after possessing it, even if only for a few years. Over time, the concepts of possession and property came to be dissociated, thus increasing the time it took for a possession to be considered property. Yet, even though the right of ownership of some property was contested, possession was still guaranteed to the possessor in the absence of contrary proof, as jurist Correia Telles emphasized in 1846:

Title XIII: Rights and obligations resulting from possession
The possessor is presumed to be master of the thing until it is proven otherwise. If no one else proves that this thing is his own, the possessor is not required to show the title of his possession. If all have the same rights, it is the possessor who has the best condition of all. Any holder or possessor must be protected by Justice against any violence that is intended to be done.[36]

This last sentence illustrates how difficult it was to deal legally with cases based on Article 179. For example, how were the courts to handle cases of conditional freedom – quasi-possession, in legal terms – which was the liminal status of many freedpersons at that time?

Pinho, the public prosecutor in Porfíria's case, thus tried to recast the issue when he appealed the decision to the Municipal Court. Doubting the validity of the documents presented by the defendant and insisting on Porfíria's right to freedom, he directed the legal debate to the moment when manumission took effect. He attached to the records a letter of conditional manumission given to Porfíria and her children by their first master, which had been ignored when they were sold. Pinho claimed that Albuquerque could not "deny them this possession, because freedom is not a material object to be held on to, but rather, it is a right acquired by the person to whom it is transmitted or granted, from the moment in which it is granted." Pinho thus argued that Porfíria and her children possessed civil liberty even though they did not have the material possession of the manumission letter. He reasoned that freedom was granted in the act of manumission and did not depend on the realization of autonomy or the end of the alleged master's domain over Porfíria. In the end, the case was decided against Porfíria, since the judge in charge of the case rejected the prosecutor's appeal.

This question of when a freedperson would be considered legally free occupied multiple jurists and even resulted in a discussion at the Brazilian Bar Institute (Instituto dos Advogados Brasileiros – IAB) in 1857, eight years after Porfíria's case was first opened. As noted earlier, this was a particularly sensitive issue for women, since their status determined that of their children. In the case discussed at the IAB, manumission had been granted in a will, conditional on the provision of services after the death of the master. Jurist Teixeira de Freitas, then presiding the IAB, defended the minority position, according to which the freedperson would be considered free only after fulfilling the conditions, which implied that the children born in the interval between manumission and the fulfillment

---

[36] Proposed legal language from J. C. Telles, *Digesto português*, pp. 86–87.

of the conditions would be born slaves. By contrast, for jurists Caetano Alberto Soares and Agostinho Marques Perdigão Malheiro, freedom was granted in the will, even though the freedperson would only enter into the full benefits of freedom when conditions were fulfilled. Under this interpretation, which was the official position adopted by the IAB, any children that the freedwomen gave birth to in that interval would be free. This decision preserved the principle of seigneurial will, so dear to defenders of property, while simultaneously opening a space for the interpretation of freedom as a natural right and for manumission as the restitution of freedom, principles that would guide gradual emancipation in Brazil.[37]

KIDNAPPING AND THE ENSLAVEMENT OF FREE PEOPLE

The original focus of Article 179 of the 1830 Criminal Code was the enslavement of persons already recognized as free, whose cases would not have raised the same doubts regarding admissibility as did cases involving conditionally manumitted persons or newly arrived Africans. Still, the proceedings reveal the limits to criminalizing the common practice of illegal enslavement, which intensified around 1850 with the closing of the Atlantic slave trade and the rise of the price of slaves.[38]

Although the enslavement of free people has not been systematically investigated, scattered studies give evidence of the profile of the victims, who were most often children or young people of African origin, especially boys, or Afro-descendant women of childbearing age.[39] In Rio Grande do Sul, the border with Uruguay was decisive: most of the victims were kidnapped from "beyond the border," an expression used by Silmei de Sant'Ana Petiz to describe escapes to Uruguay and Argentina in the first half of the century.[40] This geographic detail turned cases of illegal enslavement in the province into diplomatic issues, adding a new layer of complexity to the analysis of how authorities reacted when faced with calls to crack down on these activities.

Although enslaved individuals were being smuggled across borders long before the criminalization of illegal enslavement, the act took on new significance with the independence movements and the gradual

---

[37] L. Nequete, *O escravo na jurisprudência*, pp. 141–163; E. Pena, *Pajens da casa imperial*, pp. 71–144; T. Hoshino, "Entre o espírito da lei," pp. 228–258.

[38] M. Florentino, "Sobre minas"; R. Salles, *E o Vale*.

[39] J. Bieber Freitas, "Slavery and Social Life"; M. Carvalho, *Liberdade*, pp. 242–244; J. Caratti, *O solo da liberdade*, pp. 205–213; A. Pedroza, *Desventuras de Hypolita*.

[40] S. Petiz, *Buscando a liberdade*.

abolition of slavery in the former Spanish colonies of South America, which included the enactment of legislation forbidding the slave trade and declaring freedom of the womb. Illegal kidnappings could then be considered, in fact, an expansion of the frontiers of enslavement, much like that identified by Joseph Miller in Angola, in which people were illegally enslaved outside areas where enslavement, even if not always legal, was accepted by local authorities. The profile of the victims – predominantly children – also coincides with Benjamin Lawrance's characterization of nineteenth-century illegal trafficking in Central and West Africa.[41]

In this context, the border between Uruguay and Brazil constituted a region particularly prone to illegal enslavement. Fully integrated to the agrarian economy of Rio Grande do Sul, it was an area of extensive land holdings and low population density. Most landowners in the north and northeast of Uruguay were Brazilian, and in several of these locations slaves made up one-third of the total population, similar to the figures in Rio Grande do Sul at that time.[42] Especially in the 1840s, the troubled situation in Uruguay and the political instability of the province of Rio Grande do Sul contributed significantly to the increase in the number of people crossing the borders. The Farroupilha Revolution (1835–1845), the Gaucho separatist movement against the Brazilian Empire, and the Guerra Grande (1839–1851), a civil war between the Blancos and Colorados in Uruguay, provoked significant social unrest in the border region, with military incursions on both sides, cattle and horse theft, and the appropriation of slaves to enlist as troops. The tensions in the border area became even more heightened when, desperate for men for its defensive troops, the Colorado government of Montevideo, of which Brazil was an ally, proclaimed the abolition of slavery in 1842. The Blanco government of Cerrito followed with a proclamation in 1846. Aggravated further in the early 1850s with the end of the Atlantic slave trade to Brazil, these factors contributed to a situation which made the Afro-descendants north of the Negro River easy prey to a new form of human trafficking organized on the border of Brazil and Uruguay that lasted from the mid-1840s until at least the early 1870s.[43]

---

[41] J. Miller, *Way of Death*; M. Candido, *An African Slaving Port*; B. Lawrance, *Amistad's Orphans*.

[42] E. Palermo, "Los afro-fronterizos," pp. 190–191; A. Borucki et al., *Esclavitud y trabajo*, pp. 114–163.

[43] R. P. de Lima, *A nefanda pirataria*; J. Caratti, *O solo da liberdade*; E. Palermo, "Secuestros y tráfico"; K. Monsma and V. Fernandes, "Fragile Liberty"; K. Grinberg, "The Two Enslavements of Rufina"; K. Grinberg, "Illegal Enslavement."

It is difficult to ascertain how many of the free people who were victims of kidnapping managed to report the crimes. Probably few. At any rate, unlike the cases of newly arrived Africans and re-enslaved freedpersons, evidence suggests that the Imperial authorities began to seriously address the enslavement of persons recognized as free as of 1850. The problem, clearly not contained to Rio Grande do Sul, was raised in the reports of the Ministry of Foreign Affairs. Indeed, the trafficking of free Uruguayans went all the way to Rio de Janeiro.[44] The frontiers of enslavement also expanded into the Brazilian interior, and in 1869 the minister of justice monitored three cases of illegal enslavement of free persons: two involving minors in Bahia and Pernambuco, the third involving a family of Africans in Minas Gerais.[45]

At a moment when Brazil was suspected of turning a blind eye to the illegal trafficking of slaves, cases involving other countries were taken even more seriously, as the Brazilian government was concerned about negative international repercussions. The abduction of the minor Faustina, analyzed in detail by Jonatas Caratti, is a good example of this situation. In February 1853, the president of the province of Rio Grande do Sul asked the chief of police of the southern city of Pelotas to investigate the whereabouts of Faustina, who "as a free person, was seized by a Brazilian and sold as a slave in that town."[46] A few days later, the Uruguayan authorities demanded the extradition of Faustina, arguing that she was Uruguayan and free. The complaint seems to have had an effect: in an attempt to obtain more information about Faustina, her father, having informed the authorities of her daughter's abduction, was interrogated in Melo, Uruguay; her baptismal record was also located and sent to Brazil. While this was happening, Loureiro, the judge in charge of the case, expedited the order to arrest Manoel Marques Noronha, accused of the crime, on the "presumption of guilt." Noronha was found, arrested, and questioned. The judge concluded that he was in fact guilty, finding that the complaints and documents were sufficient evidence to prove the girl's free status.

Faustina was released and taken home to Uruguay, but the case did not stop there: because of the seriousness of the accusation, the Noronha trial

[44] R. P. de Lima, "Negros uruguaios."
[45] J. Sinimbu, *Relatório da Repartição dos Negócios Estrangeiros* (1860); Brazilian National Archive (AN), "Redução de pessoas livres à escravidão," Relatório da 3a seção [Min. Justiça], April 30, 1870, IJ6 510, fls. 17–17v.
[46] J. Caratti, *O solo da liberdade*, pp. 388 forward.

was brought to a jury, made up of the "good citizens" of Pelotas. Noronha defended himself, arguing that he was suffering political persecution. He further alleged good faith, accusing Maria Duarte Nobre, from whom he had bought Faustina, of being the real culprit. The jury accepted the defendant's arguments and acquitted him, and by September 1854 he was already free from prison. Maria Duarte Nobre was convicted of the crime; however, as she had never been arrested and was not imprisoned during the trial, she remained free. In the end, nobody paid for the crime of Faustina's enslavement. Her release, however, allowed the Brazilian authorities to demonstrate their commitment to suppressing the illegal slave trade and preventing illegal enslavement. Two years later, Manoel Marques Noronha was again accused of kidnapping; this time the victim was twelve-year-old *pardo* Firmino. Of the many cases of kidnapping and illegal enslavement of free people on the border of Brazil and Uruguay, Noronha was the only person convicted. He was condemned and sentenced to three years of prison and the payment of a fine, but, as he brought his case to the Court of Appeals in Rio de Janeiro, it is not known whether he actually ever served his prison sentence.

In this same year, the African Rufina and her four children had a fate similar to Faustina's. Abducted in Tacuarembó, Uruguay in 1854, they were taken to Brazil and sold there. Somehow, Rufina managed to report the crime to the Brazilian police. It became a lawsuit that caught the attention of journalists and the Uruguayan and British consuls in Porto Alegre. At the time, British Foreign Minister Lord Palmerston wrote to Brazil's minister of foreign affairs, Paulino José Soares de Souza, requesting energetic measures against this "new form of trafficking" taking place on Brazilian borders. Rufina was not only freed but also reunited with her family and returned to Uruguay. None of the kidnappers, however, were convicted. They alleged that they were trying to recover escaped slaves and were unaware of the free or freed status of those kidnapped, and the jury acquitted them all.[47]

The conclusion here is somewhat obvious: because of the diplomatic attention they received, cases of enslavement from "beyond the border" reached the courts more frequently than other cases. In the early 1850s, the Brazilian government was forced to take a stand, and it thus pressed the local courts to prosecute captors who imported slaves into Brazilian

[47] Public Archive of the State of Rio Grande do Sul, Processo criminal 3368, maço 88, Bagé, 1855. This case is discussed in J. Caratti, *O solo da Liberdade*; R. P. de Lima, *A nefanda pirataria*; and K. Grinberg, "The Two Enslavements of Rufina."

territory.[48] But already in 1868, during the Paraguayan War, when the Brazilian military depended largely on the mobilization of the Gaucho troops, the minister of justice decreased the pressure on slaveowners on the southern border, stating that the alleged owners of anyone brought from Uruguay to Brazil and illegally enslaved should only be prosecuted under Article 179 if they refused to admit the victim's right to freedom.[49] Nonetheless, the central government did not support the practices of enslavement by masters on the borders in Rio Grande do Sul in the same way or on the same scale, as it overlooked cases involving the illegal enslavement of freedpeople or turned a blind eye to the large-scale enslavement of newly arrived Africans.

CONCLUSION

In late 1851 and early 1852, a major popular revolt against a civil registration law erupted in the backlands of Northeast Brazil. The people who protested against the new law had one recurring concern: to protect their freedom, as they understood that the mandatory civil registration was actually a strategy to enslave free people of African descent after the prohibition of the Atlantic slave trade. They probably feared that civil registration would make official the threats of illegal enslavement they observed in their daily lives.[50] Hardened and cynical from decades of forced military recruitment and severe physical punishment equivalent to that of slaves, they did not trust local authorities to generate vital records or to secure their status.[51]

Although there were no reports of this type of manifestation in southern Brazil, it is plausible that the free population there would have had the same fears. The general picture outlined in this chapter, although preliminary, suggests that the practice of illegal enslavement was recurrent and was met with a variety of legal responses, depending on the victims and the

---

[48] See, for example, "Resolução de 10 de maio de 1856 – A respeito dos escravos que entram no Império, vindos de países estrangeiros," in J. P. J. da Silva Caroatá, ed., *Imperiais Resoluções*, pp. 599–601.

[49] See Brazil, Ministry of Justice, "Notice of the Ministry of Justice to the President of the Province of Rio Grande do Sul, May 6, 1868."

[50] S. Chalhoub, "The Precariousness of Freedom," p. 429; G. Palacios, "Revoltas camponesas"; M. Loveman, "Blinded Like a State."

[51] The mobilization resulted in a reversal of plans by the Imperial government, which canceled the decree of the civil registry and also of the census. M. L. F. Oliveira, "Resistência popular"; M. Loveman, "Blinded Like a State"; S. Chalhoub, *A força da escravidão*, pp. 13–31; P. Beattie, *Punishment in Paradise*.

context. Of the 2,341 criminal cases listed in the catalog of crimes related to slavery in Rio Grande do Sul in the years between 1763 and 1888, sixty-eight, or about 3 percent, were related to reducing free persons to slavery.[52] Thirty-five of those cases refer to illegally enslaved persons, and twenty-nine of those were "beyond the border," confirming that it was the politically and diplomatically charged cases that were most criminalized. Almost all such cases took place in the 1850s and 1860s. Of the sixty-eight cases, the outcome of five was inconclusive (because of trials records with no final verdict, missing pages, etc.). In twelve cases, the decision called for the release of the enslaved victims. None of the defendants in these cases were punished, even though the determination of freedom constituted, in practice, an acknowledgment of the crime. In forty-eight of the cases, the accusation against the slavers was dismissed or they were acquitted. In only three of the sixty-eight cases were the defendants convicted under Article 179 of the Criminal Code, and in two of those it is not known whether they were actually ever imprisoned. In one case, from 1856, the defendant appealed to the Court of Appeals of Rio de Janeiro, and the final verdict is not known; in the other, which occurred in Encruzilhada do Sul in 1878, the defendants were convicted but then released when the guilty verdict was dismissed. Apparently only Joaquim Fernandez Maia, who was prosecuted for beating and enslaving a nine-year-old, João, was sentenced to prison based on Articles 179 and 201 of the Criminal Code. It is important to note that the three cases that led to convictions referred to free or freed people enslaved by a third party.[53]

The early 1870s brought about changes. It had already long been impossible to legally enslave Africans, and after 1871, with the establishment of Free Womb Law, the enslavement of newborn children was prohibited as well. The law of 1871 also created a mandatory slave registry that, for the first time, would generate a record of who was held in slavery and by whom, definitively closing the borders of enslavement. This mechanism, however, also had the role of legalizing the slave status

[52] B. Pessi and G. Souza e Silva, eds., *Documentos*.
[53] The cases are: Pelotas, n. 791, 1856; Cachoeira do Sul, no. 3059, 1860; Encruzilhada do Sul, no. 1644, 1878, all from the Public Archive of Rio Grande do Sul. In Cachoeira do Sul, José Bonifácio Machado, Manoel Peixoto da Silveira, and Joaquim Antonio de Borba Junior were sentenced to imprisonment for the enslavement of Margarida, who had a letter of manumission. Although the conviction rate is quite low in these cases, it is important to note that the number of cases leading to convictions in Imperial Brazil in general was not high. See T. Flory, *Judge and Jury*, p. 125.

of those Africans who had been smuggled into Brazil or otherwise illegally enslaved.[54] It is true that among the stipulations of the Free Womb Law and subsequent decrees was a prohibition on registering as a slave a person who had been conditionally manumitted, which subjected any-one who did so to the penalties provided for in Article 179.[55] Of the twenty-four cases in Rio Grande do Sul between 1763 and 1888 that involved conditionally freed persons, twelve of them were brought to court precisely in this period, in the 1870s and 1880s. Extending protection to conditionally freed persons implied that they counted, at least for the legislators, as free people in possession of their freedom. However, this was not the understanding that prevailed in the courts. Most commentators of the Criminal Code, when discussing the application of Article 179, indicate that by 1860 the possession of freedom had become a mandatory requirement in cases that would be tried by the jury.[56] This indicates that the judiciary came to limit the criminalization of illegal enslavement to only those cases where the victim was undeniably free. This approach had important consequences: as they were not viewed as criminal offenses, cases of illegal enslavement would be brought to court as civil suits (*ações de liberdade*), thus increasing the load on the civil courts. Moreover, the enslavers, even if they lost the slaves, went unpunished.

The existence of court proceedings refutes the conclusion that there was a general collusion between the authorities of the judiciary, legislative, and executive branches – at all levels of power – with illegal enslavement. The cases analyzed here suggest that the prosecutors played an important role in identifying the mechanisms of illegal enslavement and defending the victims. Yet they were overrun by judges who declared the cases inadmissible, by juries that acquitted the defendants, and by superior courts that decided in favor of property even if it was illegally acquired. It is clear that criminals were rarely brought to trial even in the 1880s, when engaged lawyers and judges succeeded in expanding the chances for liberation through freedom lawsuits. In practice, the Brazilian judiciary

---

[54] B. Mamigonian, "O direito de ser africano livre" and "O estado nacional."

[55] See the Law of September 28, 1871, article 8; Decree n. 4835 from December 1, 1871, arts. 33 and 34; Decree n. 5135 from November 13, 1872, art. 87; and the notice from September 22, 1876. Brasil, *Coleção das Leis do Império do Brasil* (1880).

[56] These are recurrently cited in the judgments of the Relação de Rio de Janeiro no. 3446 of September 11, 1860, and no. 3514 of March 12, 1861 (held in Brazil's National Archives), according to which, among the questions for the jury, one should inquire whether the defendant reduced a free person to slavery and whether the victim was in possession of his freedom. See, for example, Filgueiras Júnior (1876, 204) and Luiz Alves Júnior (1883, 87).

allowed for the liberation of individuals through civil cases and made it difficult, if not impossible, to pursue any criminal conviction. After all, the liberation of particular individuals through freedom lawsuits had a impact (albeit limited) on the dynamics of nineteenth-century slavery in Brazil, but this would not be true of criminal offenses. If the enslavers were punished for the crime of illegal enslavement, the potential impact would have been much greater and could even have jeopardized the very survival of master–slave relations, especially after the end of the Atlantic slave trade. Faced with this situation, by guaranteeing impunity to the enslavers at each new phase of the relations among slaves, masters, and the Imperial government, the Brazilian judiciary supported a pact that maintained slavery.

2

"Hellish Nurseries"

Slave Smuggling, Child Trafficking, and Local Complicity in Nineteenth-Century Pernambuco

Marcus J. M. de Carvalho*

INTRODUCTION

The transatlantic slave trade to Brazil became illegal after November 1831. Yet as many as a million African slaves came to the country between 1831 and the early 1850s, when the Eusebio de Queiroz Law finally extinguished the trade. Ineffectiveness did not, however, imply impotence: the 1831 ban still had a profound impact on Brazil's economy, politics, and society. It forced the trade to shift its physical operations from conspicuous ports in the Empire's principal coastal cities to natural harbors and beaches controlled by provincial landowners, many of whom were also the slave trade's avid customers. The trade's new geography and clandestinity spawned important new business opportunities: scores of people were employed in the trade – guiding the slave ships as well as landing, feeding, healing, guarding, and distributing the contraband survivors of the middle passage – and the 1831 law also consolidated the already existing articulation between slave smuggling and cabotage, responsible for a thriving slave trade among Brazil's coastal areas since colonial times. These new economic networks grew embedded in local and provincial politics; in Brazil, as in Africa, the imperatives of Britain's high seas antislavery campaign had to be weighed against the complex internal structures that fortified the slave trade. Multitudes of traders, plantation owners, bureaucrats, and small-time slaveowners depended on slavery and did all within their power to prolong it. The continuous contraband of slaves after 1831 was visible enough to all Brazilians, but the trade's profitability and centrality to national political and economic structures meant that top

* Translation by Marcus Carvalho and Brodwyn Fischer.

governmental officials – including members of several Imperial cabinets – were more than willing to favor power over the letter of the law in the two decades between 1831 and the early 1850s.

Needless to say, the people involved in the contraband of African slaves to Brazil tried to hide their participation. Investigating the process is thus difficult: one must face omissions in the sources and ferret out the secrets kept by those who took part in, condoned, and benefited from an illegal business that involved some of the richest and most powerful men in the country. This chapter will uncover some of those secrets by focusing on the illegal slave trade to the province of Pernambuco between 1831 and the 1850s. This focus is significant for two reasons. First, while there is a wide literature about the Atlantic slave trade to Brazil after 1831, we still know little about how it actually operated – its logistical unraveling on Brazil's remote beaches – or how the adjustments it engendered influenced both the nature of the trade and the evolution of local networks of economic and political power. Second, although Pernambuco's slave trade was in some ways singular, the province was Brazil's third and the Americas' fourth most important destination for enslaved Africans: 854,000, or 8.1 percent of those who came to the Americas between 1501 and 1867, arrived in Pernambuco.[1] Between the sixteenth and nineteenth centuries, the province lagged only behind Rio de Janeiro, Bahia, and Jamaica. Regardless, and surprisingly, what David Eltis and Daniel Domingues da Silva claimed a decade ago still remains true: the slave trade to Pernambuco is less investigated than those to Cuba, Haiti, and the United States, locations that received far fewer African people.[2]

In the following pages I will discuss how Pernambuco's slave trade adapted to the new circumstances created by the 1831 ban. Landing sites shifted to beaches adjacent to plantations. British anti–slave trade squadrons noted the growing use of smaller vessels, which were cheaper, faster, easier to hide, less visible to the British navy, and more capable of entering hidden natural harbors and creeks in both Brazil and Africa. The 1831 law also probably spurred a significant rise in the number of adolescents and children forcibly brought to Pernambuco from West Central Africa. As Herbert Klein has observed, children were usually a distinct minority in the trade before the eighteenth century.[3] This

---

[1] D. Eltis and D. Richardson, *Atlas of the Transatlantic Slave Trade*, pp. 17 and 264.
[2] For the demography of the slave trade to Pernambuco, see D. da Silva and D. Eltis, "The Slave Trade to Pernambuco, 1561–1851."
[3] H. Klein, *The Middle Passage*, pp. 223–224.

changed in the 1800s. Children were frequently forced onto nineteenth-century slave ships;[4] despite slave-dealers' reluctance to trade in them, there was a widespread and significant increase in the importation of people from five to twenty years of age to Brazil between 1810 and 1850.[5] While Klein and others have argued that this transformation reflected changes on the African supply side, the timing and geography of the change suggest it could also have had much to do with the 1831 law. Briefly put, the ban created new logics for profit within the slave trade, especially valorizing agility and subterfuge. Although the slave trade to Pernambuco was less capitalized than that to Rio de Janeiro and Bahia, the trip's short duration drastically reduced the human and monetary risk of voyages undertaken in the tiny, overcrowded vessels that could promise clandestinity. Traders could reap abundant profits if they were willing to use small ships, pack them with the compact bodies of children and adolescents, and forge active partnerships with the complicit plantation owners who controlled the coast, roads, and towns around surrounding Brazil's natural harbors. In encouraging these new and brutal economic logics, the 1831 ban deeply impacted both the social demographics of Pernambucan slavery and the political and economic networks that structured the province.

CAMILO'S STORY AND THE NETWORKS OF THE CLANDESTINE TRADE

The 1831 law presented slave traders with abundant challenges, all of which required strong local networks to overcome. Traders had first to find a proper harbor or beach to land their human merchandise; although the Brazilian coast is gigantic, a slave ship could not stop just anywhere. Once an adequate harbor was found, a human network had to be constructed to facilitate clandestine trade on potentially perilous shores. Systems of signs were devised to communicate with slave ships, including bonfires that were lit at night[6] to guide incoming ships.[7] In Pernambuco, fishermen also used *jangadas*, locally made catamarans, to reach distant slave ships, guide them to the beaches, and help to disembark.[8] At least

[4] D. Eltis, *Economic Growth*, pp. 256–257; P. Lovejoy, "The Children of Slavery," p. 200.
[5] C. Villa and M. Florentino, "Abolicionismo inglês."
[6] L. Bethell, *A abolição*, p. 99; J. Reis, F. Gomes, and M. Carvalho, *O alufá Rufino*, p. 152.
[7] P. Verger, *Fluxo e refluxo*, p. 460.
[8] Consul Edward Watts to Mr. Hamilton, May 9, 1837, 3rd Enclosure to no. 84, in *Parliamentary Papers, Correspondence with Foreign Powers Relating to the Slave Trade, 1837* [Class B], vol. 15, p. 76.

one slave ship was captured off Pernambuco at the moment its captain was riding a *jangada* to the Cabo de Santo Agostinho beach.[9] Once on land, there was need for security, water, and food. Plantation owners, who controlled local lands, roads, and towns, were essential in providing these goods and guaranteeing that the trade would remain an open secret.

It was at a beach adjacent to a sugar plantation that an African boy, who would later be named Camilo, disembarked, enslaved, sometime after 1831. Camilo believed that he was in his forties in 1874, when he filed a civil suit to gain his freedom before the judge of Itambé, Pernambuco.[10] He could not state exactly how long he had been in Brazil: twenty-seven to thirty years, he said. Supposing he was right about his age, the Congolese boy probably disembarked in Pernambuco in the early 1840s. He did not remember the name of the vessel; to him, it would have made little difference. Perhaps the boy was too terrified to pay attention, for he was only "nearly seven years of age" when he faced the middle passage. When he first filed his freedom suit with a notary, Camilo said he did not know the name of the beach where he landed. But when he spoke to the judge later the same day, he claimed to have landed at "Itapuí," probably Atapus, one of the continental beaches surrounding Itamaracá Island near Catuama, an important natural harbor north of Recife frequently used for slave smuggling. He was taken from there – at midnight, he said – to "Major Paulino's" Itapirema plantation, where he was imprisoned for a few days in the *casa de purgar* (the building where the plantation's cane syrup was boiled) along with "ninety" other Africans.[11] We do not know their ages, but they were certainly his *malungos* – that is, fellow captives who were brought to Brazil on the same slave ship.[12]

After a few days, Camilo said, he was bought by a man named Rochedo (later identified as Joaquim de Mattos Alcantilado Rochêdo) and taken to

[9] Vicente Thomas Pires de Figueiredo Camargo to Francisco Antonio de Sá Barreto, August 1, 1837, and November 24, 1837, in the Arquivo Público Jordão Emerenciano (APEJE), Ofícios da Presidência à Prefeitura, Repartição Central de Polícia, pages unnumbered.

[10] The 1871 Free Womb Law expanded the legal mechanisms that allowed slaves to seek freedom in Brazilian courts. One of those mechanisms was to claim that the African-born person had entered the country after the 1831 anti-slave trade law and therefore had been illegally enslaved. See K. Grinberg, "Slavery, Manumission and the Law"; C. Castilho, *Slave Emancipation*.

[11] The full transcription of his freedom suit is in C. Amaral and L. Sette, "Traslado da Ação de Liberdade movida pelo escravo Camilo."

[12] Regarding the notion of *malungo*, see R. Slenes, "Malungu, ngoma vem"; W. Hawthorne, "Being Now, as It Were"; M. de Carvalho, "Malunguinho quilombola."

the house of the "Portuguese" Manoel Gonsalves in Goiana, then the second most important town in the province (smaller only than Recife in terms of population). The boy walked there with four other captives, who had died by the time Camilo filed his freedom suit. The judge asked if the other slaves had remained at Itapirema's *casa de purgar*; Camilo answered that, when he left for Goiana, some others had likewise departed, also in small groups at night, but that half of his fellow captives remained. Once in Goiana, Camilo and his four companions were baptized in the lower room of a *sobrado* (a large townhouse) belonging to Manoel Gonsalves. According to Camilo, the priest (whose name he could not remember) was white and tall. His godfather was "Agostinho de tal" (*de tal* meaning that Camilo did not know the man's last name), whom the clerk described in parentheses as a "natural" son of the *sobrado* owner. It was at this point in his life that the seven-year-old Congolese child became Camilo: the records did not preserve his African name.

After Camilo and his *malungos* Abraham, Manoel, Luis, and Justino were baptized, they were returned to Manoel Gonsalves, the owner of the *sobrado* where the baptism was performed. After a few days' pause for rest and recovery, Camilo, Luis, and Justino were sent to Perory, a sugar plantation in the same county owned by Manoel Gonsalves's legitimate son, Major Henrique Lins de Noronha Farias. Abraham and Manoel stayed in Goiana. Camilo thus came to serve a planter family that lived in the same county he had landed in; when the judge asked him where Agostinho, his godfather, lived, Camilo said he also lived at Perory, "Major" Henrique's plantation. This provides a revealing clue about those plantation owners' family arrangements; as was relatively common in Brazil at the time, members of the same extended family occupied different social classes according to the nature of their parents' relationship. Major Henrique, the legitimate son, owned the plantation, whereas Agostinho, the "natural" son, lived there as a dependent of his half-brother. We do not know if they shared the same skin color, but Agostinho was certainly a free man. Camilo survived his first masters only to serve another generation of the same family; after Major Henrique's death, Camilo told the judge, he was inherited by Belarmino de Noronha Farias, Major Henrique's son and Manoel Gonsalves' grandson.

Camilo's odyssey was repeated by countless African children who were smuggled into Brazil after the 1831 anti–slave trade law. Young people, mostly teenagers but sometimes even children, constituted common cargo on slave ships. That seven-year-old African boy renamed Camilo was one; two others were Maria and Joaquim Congo, who testified in a freedom suit filed by Maria in 1884. Maria and Joaquim were around fifty in 1884, but like Camilo they had been just children when they disembarked in Pernambuco "some forty-something years" earlier, in Joaquim Congo's words. Joaquim's recollections were confirmed by Narciso Congo, an older African, aged fifty-six, who worked as a "water carrier" on the streets of Recife. Narciso Congo and Joaquim Congo were witnesses for Maria in her suit; they were also *malungos*, for they had all arrived on the same ship. Joaquim clearly stated he was no longer a captive at the time he testified and that the claims he had made to be freed could be extended to Maria. He said he was granted freedom "for having proved" that he was illegally smuggled to Brazil after 1831. In 1884, he was a whitewasher (*caiador*) living in Santo Amaro das Salinas, a parish of Recife that was home to many freedmen and women.

Narciso Congo also stated that he was no longer a captive in 1884, and he too had a story to tell. He said he landed with Maria and Joaquim at the beach of Porto de Galinhas. Unlike Maria, Joaquim, or Camilo, Narciso Congo was around sixteen years of age when he arrived in Brazil. He was soon baptized in the town of Cabo, located at a very traditional plantation area south of Recife, where several plantation oligarchies were based, including that of the Baron of Boa Vista, president of the province of Pernambuco between 1837 and 1844. We do not know any more details about the circumstances of Narciso's baptism. But soon thereafter he ran away. Narciso did not talk about his escape route in his statement, except to note that he was "caught in Recife." He was then sent to work at the Arsenal de Marinha, the headquarters of the Brazilian navy in Recife. This is an important detail, because fugitive slaves with known masters were generally sent back to them after capture. The Arsenal, in contrast, was the place "liberated Africans" were taken to and put to work; Narciso's presence there reinforced his claim of free status.[13] Narciso stressed the fact that he was brought to Brazil on

---

[13] When a slave ship was confiscated for disobeying the antitrafficking law of 1831, the captives thus detained were considered "liberated Africans." According to the letter of the law, as well as treaties signed by Brazil, Portugal, and England, liberated Africans were to have their "services" auctioned to suitable people, who could retain the "free" Africans in their custody for up to fourteen years. This limit, however, was rarely adhered to. Most liberated Africans died working for those who had purchased their services or were simply (illegally) enslaved. Still, some remained under the custody of the Brazilian state, working in the arsenals, in public works, and in other governmental installations, including the Imperial Palace. See B. Mamigonian, *Africanos livres*. On liberated Africans in Pernambuco, see C. Oliveira, "Os africanos livres em Pernambuco."

the same slave ship as Maria and confirmed she was just a "girl" (*menina*) when she arrived.[14]

Camilo, in his forties in 1874, and Maria and Joaquim, aged fifty in 1884, had been about the same age when they disembarked in Brazil sometime in the 1840s; they might all have arrived around the same time, perhaps even in the same year, when the Baron of Boa Vista was president of Pernambuco. Nevertheless, they definitely came on different voyages, for Camilo landed on one of the beaches near Goiana, north of Recife, while Maria, Joaquim, and Narciso arrived at Porto de Galinhas, south of Recife. They were all baptized in important towns in plantation counties, which proves that the local clergy condoned the illegal slave trade; one witness even identified the "white and tall" priest who baptized Camilo as one "Father Genuíno." Apart from the teenager Narciso – virtually an adult at age sixteen – the others were just enslaved children who fell from the Congolese slave trade networks into the web of transatlantic smuggling. They should have been freed immediately after reaching Brazilian soil. Or at least that is what the 1831 anti–slave trade law stated. Instead, they were given Portuguese names and remained enslaved.

CHILDREN AND THE MATERIAL CALCULUS OF THE MIDDLE PASSAGE

Louis François de Tollenare, a French cotton merchant who spent a few months in Recife between 1816 and 1817, witnessed one of those slave ships full of boys and girls docking at the port in 1817. The trade of "Congo" captives (those captured south of the equator) to Portuguese America was then still legal. In Tollenare's words, only one-tenth of the slaves in the transatlantic slave trade to Pernambuco were full-grown men. No more than two-tenths were young women between the ages of eighteen and twenty-five. The rest of the human cargo, 70 percent, comprised children of both sexes.[15] Perhaps Tollenare exaggerated when he generalized this particular observation to the transatlantic slave trade as a whole. According to José Francisco de Azevedo Lisboa, a slave trader on the Pernambuco route, a very young cargo was not the most profitable one. In

---

[14] Memorial da Justiça (Recife), Caixa 1161, Fundo: Recife. Ano 1884, Autor Maria (Africana), Réu: Rita Maria da Conceição, pp. 13 e 13 (reverse).

[15] L. Tollenare, *Notas dominicais*, p. 138. According to Mary Karasch, travelers to Rio de Janeiro also observed a large proportion of children on slave ships. See M. Karasch, *A vida dos escravos*, pp. 68–69.

February 1837, Lisboa authoritatively instructed employees at a slave trade *feitoria* (outpost)[16] by the Benin River that it was very important to know how to choose among the slaves offered by the African nobility and middlemen under the suzerainty of the king of Benin. Older people, who were rejected at African fairs, should be rejected by the Portuguese as well, unless they were "women with full breasts" (*negras de peito cheio*). The most valuable merchandise for the "country's taste" (*gosto do país*) were young twelve- to twenty-year-olds.[17] So Narciso, who was sixteen, was more valuable than boys and girls like Camilo, Joaquim, and Maria.

All the same, even if the resale value of children below twelve years of age was lower, they were still good merchandise, and improvements in shipping speeds rendered them a better value still in the nineteenth century. At the pinnacle of the slave trade in the eighteenth century, when the business was still legal, child slaves were assessed lower taxes in the Americas and toddlers were usually exempt. But high mortality rates signaled the frailty of such young human cargo.[18] By the last quarter of the eighteenth century, however, the slave trade moved on faster voyages and resulted in lower mortality rates. It therefore became easier to transport pre-adolescent children, and in the nineteenth century they would become ubiquitous in the transatlantic slave trade. According to Eltis, the child ratio in slave ships steadily increased after 1810.[19]

Captain Henry James Matson had long experience combating the slave trade when he told the British Parliament that the trip from the African coast to Cuba took as long as three months, whereas the route to Brazil was half as long and much simpler, requiring much smaller crews, which meant that old or low-quality vessels could be used. For this reason, Captain Matson asserted, Brazilian smugglers could afford to lose three or even four out of five slave ships and still make a profit, an equation that was impossible for ships heading for Cuba.[20] And of all the slave smuggling destinations in Brazil and the Americas, Pernambuco enjoyed the quickest access from West Central Africa, because of the Benguela current

---

[16] The establishments in Africa where the Atlantic slave traders dealt with the African middlemen and warehoused their trade goods and the slaves to be embarked were called *feitorias*. D. Eltis, *Economic Growth*, p. 56.

[17] Quoted in J. Reis, F. Gomes, and M. Carvalho, *O alufá Rufino*, chapter 10 and passim.

[18] G. Campbell et al., "Children," p. 165. See also H. Klein, *The Middle Passage*, pp. 35, 53, and 162.

[19] D. Eltis, *Economic Growth*, p. 132.

[20] Henry James Matson, June 21, 1849, in House of Commons Parliamentary Papers, Reports from the Select Committee of the House of Lords, 1850, vol. 6, p. 202.

and the Atlantic winds. Inferring from Captain Matson's logic, smugglers
could risk overloading slave ships sailing to Pernambuco, because shorter
voyages meant reduced time for the spread of diseases in the hold or on
deck, as well as fewer deaths from starvation or dehydration. Smaller,
more vulnerable children were especially good merchandise if the trip was
short.

In 1839, the British consul at Recife wrote that the crossing from the
Portuguese possessions in Africa to Pernambuco could take as little as
fifteen days, which led smugglers to overload their vessels.[21] When he
described the slave trade to Pernambuco in 1817, Tollenare said the
journey from Africa was very fast and that he had heard tell of a vessel
that crossed the Atlantic in thirteen days, resulting in a nearly zero
mortality rate.[22] The brief duration of the trip would have made it
possible to bring scores of children in the slave ship that Tollenare
described.

Perhaps the British consul and Tollenare exaggerated. But some
voyages were indeed very fast. The schooner brig *Maria Gertrudes*,
listed in Table 2.1, took no more than twenty days to bring 254 live
captives from Angola to Recife in 1829. The ship was named after the
wife of the slave trader Francisco Antonio de Oliveira, the man who
brought the largest number of African slaves to Pernambuco in the
1820s.[23] Experienced slavers like him were able to cross the Atlantic
very quickly. The *Jovem Marie* took only eighteen days to travel from
Cabo Verde islands to Recife, although we do not know if it brought
any slaves to the province. In 1831, the brig *Oriente Africano* and the
schooner *Novo Despique* sailed only nineteen days from Angola to
Recife.[24] The fastest documented trip after 1831 was the 1840 journey
of the schooner *Formiga*, which sailed from Luanda to Recife in just
seventeen days.[25]

We do not know how many Africans were aboard the *Novo Despique*
and the *Formiga*, but the brig *Oriente Africano* brought fourteen freed

---

[21] Mr. Watts to Palmerston, July 27, 1839, in Great Britain, *House of Commons Parliamentary Papers, Correspondence with British Commissioners and with Foreign Powers Relative to the Slave Trade, 1840* [*Class A and Class B*], vol. 18, p. 391.

[22] L. Tollenare, *Notas dominicais*, p. 139.

[23] For more on the life of Oliveira (the Barão de Beberibe), see A. B. Gomes, "De traficante de escravos." Maria Gertrudes was Ângelo Francisco Carneiro's sister. Ângelo was also a very notorious slave trader, probably the greatest one in the Pernambuco route after 1831. See A. Albuquerque, "Ângelo dos retalhos."

[24] *Diário de Pernambuco*, June 22, 1829, July 6, 1831, and July 31, 1831.

[25] *Diário de Pernambuco*, June 22, 1829, June 6, 1831, July 31, 1831, and March 10, 1840.

TABLE 2.1 *Slave ships that entered Recife's harbor, according to the Diário de Pernambuco, 1827–1831.*

	Year	Ship's Name	Origin	Trip Duration	Alive	Dead	Consignee or Owner of Ship
1	1827	Brigue São Joze Grande	Angola	29	447	45	Antonio Joze Vieira
2	1827	Cutter Conceição Minerva	Molembo	68	102	0	Manoel Alves Guerra
3	1827	Brigue-Escuna Paquete de Pernambuco	Angola	26	284	9	Luis Botelho Pinto de Misquita e Joaquim Antonio de Almeida
4	1827	Brigue-Escuna Neptuno	Angola	39	317	19	Joaquim Pereira da Cunha
5	1827	Brigue Activo	Ambriz	24	342	0	Francisco Antonio de Oliveira
6	1827	Galera Conceição Felis	Molembo	30	255	0	Manoel Antonio Cardozo
7	1827	Brigue Boa União	Angola	25	377	20	Joaquim Avelino Tavares
8	1827	Brigue Maria Thereza	Mozambique	40	260	0	Gil Thomaz dos Santos
9	1829	Brigue-Escuna D. Anna	Angola	29	337	0	José Ramos de Oliveira
10	1829	Brigue S. José Grande	Angola	N/I	507	19	Elias Carvallho de Sintra
11	1829	Brigue-Escuna 04 de Agosto	Angola	22	295	9	Antonio da Silva e Cia.
12	1829	Escuna Borboleta	Molembo	N/I	218	0	Manoel Alves Guerra
13	1829	Brigue-Escuna Maria Gertrudes	Angola	20	254	3	Francisco de Oliveira
14	1829	Galera Tamega	Angola	22	454	0	Antonio José de Amorim
15	1829	Brigue Imperador do Brasil	Angola	26	381	35	Francisco Antonio de Oliveira
16	1829	Escuna Margarida	Ambriz	26	160	7	João Maria Sève
17	1829	Patacho Paquete de Pernambuco	Ambriz	27	231	31	Elias Coelho Sintra
18	1829	Brigue General Silveira	Angola	34	495	11	Elias Coelho Sintra
19	1829	Brigue Trajano	Angola	28	251	4	Antonio Luiz Gonçalves Ferreira
20	1829	Brigue Maria da Glória	Angola	21	60	0	Antonio da Silva e Cia

21	1829	Escuna Maria Gertrudes	Angola	27	285	8	Francisco Antonio de Oliveira
22	1829	Brigue Lião	Angola	22	304	3	José Ignácio Xavier
23	1829	Brigue Triumpho do Brasil	Angola	24	507	20	Gabriel Antonio
24	1829	Brigue Dois Irmãos	Mozambique	57	281	0	Antonio da Silva e Cia
25	1829	Brigue Protetor	Angola	26	120	10	Antonio de Queiroz Monteiro Regadas
26	1830	Escuna Maria Gertrudes	Angola	27	254	4	Francisco Antonio de Oliveira
27	1830	Conceição de Maria	Molembo	53	176	0	Jose Ramos de Oliveira
28	1830	Brigue Sacramento e Prazeres	Angola	34	342	13	Joze Joaquim Jorge Gonçalves
29	1830	Brigue Abismo	Angola	30	191	12	Francisco Ribeiro de Brito
30	1830	Brigue Imperador do Brasil	Angola	21	430	15	Francisco Antonio Oliveira
31	1830	Brigue Paquete de PE	Angola	26	231	26	Elias Coelho Cintra
32	1831	Brigue Sueco Maria	"Da Costa D'África"	28	N/I	N/I	N. Otto Bieber e Cia
33	1831	Patacho Dona Anna	Sierra Leone	33	N/I	N/I	José Ramos de Oliveira.
34	1831	Escuna Jovem Marie	Cape Verde	18	N/I	N/I	Joaquim Joze Soares Miarim
35	1831	Brigue Oriente Africano	Angola	19	22	N/I	Antonio Luiz
36	1831	Brigue Abismo	Angola	23	8	N/I	Francisco Ribeiro de Brito
37	1831	Escuna Margarida	Angola	31	N/I	N/I	Joze Maria Seve
38	1831	Brigue Triunfo do Brasil	Angola	23	N/I	N/I	Gabriel Antonio
39	1831	Escuna Novo Despique	Angola	19	N/I	N/I	João Baptista Cezar
		Totals		1077	9178	323	

Source: *Diário de Pernambuco* (Recife), 1827–1831.

Africans and eight captives owned by the captain himself.[26] The case of the *Formiga* is intriguing, because – although we have no direct evidence of human cargo – the goods within the ship suggested participation in the illegal trade. The *Formiga* arrived in Recife from Luanda in 1840, with only three Portuguese passengers. It was consigned to Pinto da Fonseca e Silva, probably a well-known Rio de Janeiro slave dealer who had contacts in Pernambuco.[27] Apart from its few passengers, the ship carried only palm oil, wax, and mats, which were not nearly valuable enough to justify the trip. This was a very typical cargo for slave ships during the era of the illegal slave trade, when vessels left their more precious human cargo at natural harbors on the coast and proceeded to the major towns of Brazil in order to make repairs and organize subsequent voyages to Africa or elsewhere. The Formiga's seventeen-day journey suggests that Tollenare and the British consul in Recife may not have been too far from reality when they claimed that a slave ship could arrive in fifteen days or less.

Similarly, in their study of the slave trade to Pernambuco, Daniel Domingues da Silva and David Eltis estimated that it was possible to arrive there in less than thirty days. On the basis of large samples for Bahia and Rio de Janeiro but data from only three voyages to Pernambuco, Eltis and Richardson concluded that, between 1776 and 1830, a slave ship took on average 40.9 days to reach Rio de Janeiro, thirty-seven days to Bahia, and only 26.7 days to reach Pernambuco.[28] The sample in Table 2.1, drawn from research in the daily newspaper *Diário de Pernambuco* between 1827 and 1831, shows almost the same average: 26.1 days from Central-West Africa to Recife, although, as we have just seen, it was occasionally possible to make this trip in less than twenty days.

THE ADVANTAGES OF ILLEGAL CHILD TRAFFICKING

Such quick voyages to Pernambuco clearly made the trade of captive adolescents and children from Angola and Congo easier: it is thus unsurprising that it became more common in the nineteenth century. The presence of children entered the vocabulary of the slave trade early on. *Moleques*, *mulecões*, and *mulecotas* recur in slave trade-related sources

---

[26] *Diário de Pernambuco*, August 3, 1831.   [27] *Diário de Pernambuco*, March 10, 1840.
[28] D. da Silva and D. Eltis, "The Slave Trade to Pernambuco, 1561–1851," p. 113; D. Eltis and D. Richardson, *Atlas of the Transatlantic Slave Trade*, p. 185.

and express common Brazilian understandings of age. Yet it is worth highlighting that these words were not originally Portuguese. According to Joseph Miller, their root derives from *muleke*, "dependent" in Kimbundu, one of the major languages of West Central Africa.[29] Assis Júnior translated *mulêKe* as a "young man, boy, servant."[30] In contrast, Valencia Villa and Florentino stated that the expression *moleques*, in the plural, probably originally referred to children of any sex below twelve years of age.[31] These possibilities are not necessarily contradictory. Many captive adolescents and children were male dependents, "servants" in West Central Africa, who were frequently sold in different markets before ending up in the web of the Atlantic slave trade. But other categories of captive children were also frequently sold elsewhere in Atlantic Africa, and the word *moleque* thus gradually lost its conceptual and geographical specificity and came to include young people from the Gulf of Guinea. By 1640, when Portugal separated from Spain, the term had entered the Portuguese language, according to Miller, and it still appears frequently in Brazilian Portuguese.[32]

From the cold-blooded perspective of slave merchants, there were some advantages to buying children. They were relatively defenseless and therefore less able to effectively rebel in the middle passage. They ate and drank less.[33] They abounded at sales points in West Central Africa in the nineteenth century and were less expensive than adults. In Africa, children were more vulnerable than adults, both to *razzias* (slave raids) and natural catastrophe; they could also more easily be kidnapped and were subject to tributary systems and debt relations that eventually justified their enslavement.[34] From the beginning of the slave trade, there were social, economic, and political trapdoors that caught children and threw them into slavery.[35] It is thus little wonder that Captain James Matson, one of the most iconic characters of the British squadron that patrolled the coast of Africa to combat the Atlantic slave trade, said that 1,033 of the 1,683 captives he seized from slave ships were children.[36]

---

[29] J. Miller, *Way of Death*, p. 68.
[30] A. de Assis Júnior, *Dicionário kimbundo-português*.
[31] Valencia Villa and Florentino, "Abolicionismo inglês," p. 7.
[32] J. Miller, *Way of Death*, p. 68.   [33] P. Lovejoy, "The Children of Slavery."
[34] See G. Campbell, "Children and Slavery"; G. Campbell et al., "Children"; P. Lovejoy, "The Children of Slavery"; A. Diptee, "African Children."
[35] A. da Costa e Silva, *A manilha e o libambo*, p. 112.
[36] Matson based his observations in his personal experience between 1832 and 1847. J. Matson, *Remarks on the Slave Trade*, p. 23.

This was further aggravated by the turn of the nineteenth century because the overwhelming volume of the eighteenth-century slave trade put pressure on the supply side of this most lucrative type of business. West Central Africa was much less populated than West Africa, and adults were better able to defend themselves. Soon, new forms of enslavement emerged, endangering children whose parents, close relatives, or lineages could not effectively protect them. Even in places where there were no wars, *razzias*, or kidnappings, defenseless children could still be enslaved. Children could be given as security for debts, and Roquinaldo Ferreira and Mariana Candido have observed that West Central African legal tribunals, backed both by Portuguese authorities and by African middlemen and nobility, often ratified the enslavement of dependent people (servants, retainers, and their children), who could easily fall prey to the Atlantic slave trade networks and end up in one of the slave ships bound for the Americas.[37]

After 1831, when the trade to Brazil became illegal, there was yet another advantage to trading captive children. This was revealed in a letter from Augustus Cowper, the British consul in Pernambuco, to the Count of Clarendon on November 3, 1855, regarding the capture of an unnamed pilot boat at the Barra de Serinhaém (about 80 kilometers south of Recife). This episode embarrassed Brazil's Imperial government, for the ship was seized with enslaved captives aboard five years after the 1850 Eusebio de Queiroz law, which had been passed by the Brazilian government under heavy British pressure in order to put an end to the contraband of African slaves.[38] After 1850, the Brazilian government tasked its navy and local coastal authorities with ending the trade. However, some ships still evaded detection. One of them was the unnamed pilot-boat that came to Serinhaém in 1855, the last one seized in Brazil with captives inside its hold. The boat was only 30 tons but contained 250 captives when it arrived in Santo Aleixo island, facing the beach of Serinhaém – adjacent to Porto de Galinhas – on October 10, 1855. A vessel's tonnage measures volume, not weight. In the early nineteenth century, when the transatlantic slave trade was legal, a slave ship was allowed to carry up to five captives per 2 tons, according to Article 1 of the notorious 1813 *alvará* (decree) that regulated the matter.[39] The British consul in Recife found it

---

[37] R. Ferreira, *Cross-Cultural Exchange*, chapter 3 passim. M. Candido, *An African Slaving Port*, pp. 180, 209.

[38] For the 1855 Sirinhaém episode, see G. Veiga, *O gabinete*.

[39] Alvará de 24 de novembro de 1813 in Brazil, *Colleção das Leis Brasileiras, desde a chegada da corte até a época da Independência – 1811 a 1816*, vol. 2, pp. 292–302.

absurd that so many people could fit inside a 30-ton schooner that, according to the tight rules of the 1813 *alvará*, should have carried only seventy-five slaves. He inferred those captives must have come from some larger vessel far away in the ocean. Indeed, perhaps that was the case; slave traders sometimes used that strategy. But very small slave ships packed with Africans also crossed the ocean toward Pernambuco after 1831. This may very well have been the case here, for the ship was not overloaded with adults. According to the British consul, of the 250 captives thirty were women, and all the rest were just boys. The consul explained that this could have indicated a new strategy that involved bringing only "untattooed boys" to Brazil.[40] The consul may have used the wrong word, for he probably meant that the boys had no scarifications, the diacritical marks of African populations who were subjected to the Atlantic slave trade. Those boys, in other words, were so young they had not been yet initiated in their original African communities. They did not bear what Brazilians called "nation marks" (*marcas de nação*) and could thus easily pass as *crioulos* (Brazilian-born enslaved people, not subject to the 1850 law).

Consul Cowper was probably mistaken when he said that ship was the first one intentionally filled with captives lacking scarifications. Until the Brazilian government decided to fight slave smuggling on the Brazilian mainland in the early 1850s, smugglers were very successful in cheating the British navy and going about their business as usual. That strategy was not new in 1855, for there were children inside slave ships before; kids like Camilo, Maria, or Joaquim were also so young that they were probably unmarked. In this sense Consul Cowper's account is precious, for it explicitly reveals a critical advantage to bringing children to Brazil after the 1831 anti–slave trade law: they could more easily pass as *crioulos* (Brazilian-born slaves) and therefore be sold anywhere in the presence of authorities without suspicion.

This case also shows that, as brutal as it was, bringing children on small vessels was quite normal from the slave traders' perspective. Tiny ships could more easily cheat the British navy, for they were harder to spot. And bringing children as cargo allowed traders to make the most of their limited cargo space. It is even likely that some ships were built with

---

[40] August Cowper to the Earl of Clarendon, November 3, 1855. In Great Britain, *British Parliamentary Papers, Correspondence with British Commissioners and other Representatives Abroad and with Foreign Ministers in England Together with Reports from the Admiralty Relative to the Slave Trade* [Class B], vol. 42, April 1, 1855, to March 31, 1856, pp. 242–243.

precisely that idea in mind. According to Lieutenant R. N. Forbes – the commander of the *Bonetta*, one of the British vessels that patrolled the African coast – nothing was done without reason in the slave trade. In his reports, Lieutenant Forbes praised the beauty of some slave ships, but he also stressed their exiguity, expressed especially in cramped corner spaces that were only 14 to 18 inches high, specifically designed to carry children. According to Forbes, some ships were virtually built for that purpose. In his words, the *Triumfo* (sic), a tiny 18-ton yacht seized in 1842, was one of these "hellish nurseries." In addition to a crew of only five Spanish seamen, the vessel carried a fourteen-year-old girl and 104 children aged between four and nine.[41]

Lt. Forbes' reference to "hellish nurseries" suggests that the British consul may have been mistaken in 1855, when he found it somehow absurd that a small 30-ton vessel could carry 250 people, even if 220 were children so young that they had not been initiated in their original communities. Perhaps Consul Cowper simply could not imagine that the small boat in Serinhaém was just one of those hellish nurseries that Lt. Forbes spoke of, crowded with children from West Central Africa.

The slave ship commander Theodore Canot wrote in his memoirs about a similar episode involving a tiny boat with only two sailors and a pilot, which escaped the British navy and fled to Bahia with a cargo of thirty-three boys. According to him, this grotesque yet successful adventure encouraged other smugglers to repeat it.[42] Pastor Grenfell Hill narrated his journey from Mozambique to Cape Town on a slave ship that carried 447 people, which was seized by the British in 1843; forty-five were women and 189 were men, few more than twenty years old. The rest of the human cargo was composed of 213 boys.[43] According to Manolo Florentino's calculations, the hold where those people were piled up was no bigger than 70 square meters (about 750 square feet).[44] According to Robert Harms, the British had a word for such tight packing of people: "spooning," for it resembled the stacking of spoons.[45]

The brutal way children were confined caused the death of at least sixty of them on a small slave ship that landed in Porto de Galinhas, Pernambuco, in 1844. During its entire voyage from Africa, according

[41] R. N. Forbes, *Six Months' Service*, p. 87.
[42] T. Canot, *Adventures of an African Slaver*, p. 348.
[43] P. Hill, *Cinquenta dias*, pp. 63–64.
[44] Florentino, "Apresentação," in P. Hill, *Cinquenta dias*, p. 15.
[45] R. Harms, *The Diligent*, p. 305.

to British Consul Cowper, 160 of its captives died "from the leaky state of the vessel and other causes." There had been rumors that the thirty-year-old ship was originally bound for Rio de Janeiro, but the ship's sailing master, a near relative of the man who took charge of the surviving slaves in Recife, decided in collusion with the first mate to come to Recife. The second mate – "it is said" – "resisted and was thrown overboard at sea." Consul Cowper did not note the age of the slave trade victims in this episode. He claimed, however, that sixty people, all children, "were drowned or killed by a heavy lurch of the vessel when she first grounded." The 130 survivors, in a "weakly state," were rushed from the ship to be sold in Recife.[46]

Lieutenant Forbes' logic should not be overlooked. Traders did not bring children simply because they had no other choice, either because they lacked capital or because children were the only merchandise available to them on the African coast. Children could fit anywhere, and they were chattel just as adults were, albeit less valuable. Our contemporary notions of infancy did not apply to enslaved children at that time; on the contrary, minors were considered more pliant and flexible workers, and their tiny bodies made it easier to pack them in, just as E. P. Thompson has argued for British mines.[47] If Forbes was right, the vessels themselves were designed to meet the demand for children on the part of buyers who plied the African coast. Those overcrowded ships that came to Brazil may have been full of children so young that they had no scarifications, the diacritical marks of their original ethnic groups in Africa that might otherwise have betrayed them as contraband.

THE DAILY ROUTINES OF CHILD SMUGGLING IN AFRICA AND THE ATLANTIC

Data produced by the British show that, besides schooners and brigs, small yachts were also used in slave smuggling to Pernambuco and other parts of Brazil. The Portuguese consul in Recife – who was not generally very concerned with the slave trade unless it was practiced by Portuguese citizens – confirmed the use of very small ships by Brazilian-born slave dealers. In December 1844, he said that yachts were used to enter West

---

[46] First Enclosure in 266, in Great Britain, *Parliamentary Papers, Correspondence with Foreign Powers Relative to the Slave Trade* [Class B and Class C], n. 28, vol L, February 4, August 9, 1845, p. 414.

[47] E. P. Thompson, *The Making*, pp. 331–332.

African harbors such as Onim, Benin, and Whydah to buy slaves. At least six of them had successfully landed captives in Pernambuco that year.[48] British consular agents did not always report the tonnage of those smaller vessels or note how many people they carried, but they occasionally provided sound information. The yacht *Mariquinhas*, for example, was just a 45-ton boat when its human cargo disembarked in December 1843 near the mouth of the Una River, about 120 kilometers south of Recife, almost at the border with the Province of Alagoas. Based on the regulations of the aforementioned 1813 *alvará* – which specified the brutal terms of the legal slave trade and allowed for very restricted food and water supplies – the *Mariquinhas* should not have held more than 110 to 115 captives. It is hard to imagine how was it possible to fit 203 people into the *Mariquinhas*, unless much – perhaps most – of the human cargo was composed of children like Camilo, Maria, or Joaquim, who also came to Pernambuco in the 1840s. Two people died during the transatlantic crossing of the *Mariquinhas*, and 201 disembarked alive.[49] The voyage of the *São José* had that same scale of brutality. It was an 83-ton vessel and was managed by a crew of thirteen men. It left 340 captives in Catuama in December 1841.[50] Given such crowded conditions, the *Mariquinhas* and the *São José* may well have been two of those "hellish nurseries" Forbes spoke of.

Boys and girls, likely under twelve years of age, also appear in the sources about the slave ships *Camões* and *Veloz*, seized by the British squadron on the Benin River in West Africa, when they were preparing to embark with a load of captives bound for Pernambuco in 1837. The ships belonged to the firm run by José Francisco de Azevedo Lisboa in Recife; the *feitoria* in the Benin River where the two ships operated was one among his many business enterprises. Neither the *Camões* nor the *Veloz* had captives aboard when they were captured by the British schooner *Fair Rosamond*. The slaves were on the beach, waiting to embark. The British officer who apprehended the two slave ships on the river decided to take

[48] Arquivo Nacional da Torre do Tombo (Lisboa): Joaquim Baptista Moreira to the Ministro dos Negócios Estrangeiros, December 10, 1844. *Coleção do Ministério dos Negócios Estrangeiros, Pernambuco*, caixa 3.

[49] First enclosure in n. 265, January 1, 1844, Great Britain, *Parliamentary Papers, Correspondence with Foreign Powers Relative to the Slave Trade* [Class B and Class C], vol. 28, p. 411.

[50] August Cowper to the Earl of Aberdeen, August 4, 1843, *House of Commons Parliamentary Papers, Correspondence with Foreign Powers Relative to the Slave Trade* [Class B and Class C], vol. 26, 1st Enclosure in n. 307, p. 374.

the captives to Sierra Leone at his own risk. Yet at that time, only ships with slaves within their holds were fair game for the British squadron. So the captain of the *Fair Rosamond* decided to load the human cargo inside the *Camões* in order to justify the ship's apprehension and transport to Sierra Leone (the *Veloz* was badly damaged). Of the 138 Africans forced on board, seventy-one were boys and girls. The commander of the *Fair Rosamond* noted that thirty-eight of the boys were healthy when they were embarked, while seven were ill. Twenty-five of the girls were healthy, while one was sick. Of those 138 people, sixty-seven subsequently died, twenty-two during the trip to Sierra Leone and forty-five after landing. This very high mortality rate happened in a ship that had been loaded with slaves by a British commander who was nominally concerned with their fate.[51]

Several employees worked in that *feitoria* by the Benin River. One of them, Antonio Candido da Silva, was in charge of the captives that would be sent to Pernambuco. The appropriate handling of his tasks was crucial to the success of the business. His correspondence with his superiors at the *feitoria* suggests that there were often children among the slaves bought from the African nobility and middlemen. Children were certainly less threatening than adults, but they also demanded a lot from Antonio Candido da Silva, who had to keep them alive, well supervised, and clean. He had to cut their hair, to prevent lice; at least once he ordered his subordinate, a Spanish seaman, to scrape the teeth of the "moleques" to prevent scurvy.[52] Children could also die before embarking, like a poor girl who passed away from diarrhea, whom Antonio Candido described in a note to his manager at the Benin factory, João Baptista Cezar. On occasion, boys tried to escape; Antonio Candido wrote that he had once counted the children twice before lunch, but after the meal he noticed a "moleque" had disappeared. The boy was eventually captured and punished with the help of a local African "queen" (*rainha*).[53]

The presence of enslaved children in the *feitoria* was considered absolutely normal. It is thus not surprising that the captain of the

---

[51] H. W. Macaulay and Walter W. Lewis to Lord Palmerston, January 24, 1838, in *Parliamentary Papers, Correspondence with British Commissioners and Foreign Powers, 1839* [*Class A and Class B*], vol. 16, no. 24 and enclosures, pp. 15–67. See also J. Reis et al., *O alufá Rufino*, chapter 10.

[52] National Archives (London): "Antonio Candido da Silva to Senhor Capitão," Benim, August 5, 1837, in Foreign Office 315/69.

[53] National Archives (London): Antonio Candido da Silva to Senhor Capitão, Bobi, August 17, 1837, in Foreign Office 315/69.

Fair Rosamond, who captured the company's ships, embarked them to Sierra Leone without much concern; the lawsuit at the British and Portuguese Mixed Commission Court in Sierra Leone that eventually resulted from the incident of the *Veloz* and the *Camões* in Sierra Leone did not even mention that it had involved children. Captives were just captives, both for the British and for African and Brazilian slavers – so much so that children were even included among the gifts that the head of operations at the *feitoria*, João Baptista Cezar, intended to send to his family in Recife. Although José Francisco de Azevedo Lisboa was the general manager of the firm, Cezar ran most of the operations on the Benin River, including negotiations with the African nobility over slave purchases. Antonio Candido, the man who took care of the captives, made very clear in his correspondence that Cezar was a strict boss whom Antonio Candido tried hard to please. But two undelivered letters to his wife, seized by the British navy, also indicate that Cezar was a caring and loving husband and father. Writing on successive days, Cezar addressed his wife as "Josephina, cara esposa do meu coração" ("Josephina, dearest wife of my heart") and "Josephina, caro bem da minh'alma" ("Josephina, dearest love of my soul"). In those letters, he wrote that the commander of the *Veloz*, Joaquim Pedro de Sá Faria, had several gifts to deliver to her. In addition to "panos da costa" (the famous Benin cloth), three "esteiras finas" (reed mats), two parrots, and three "dentes de cavalo marinho" (seahorse teeth [sic]), he mentioned that he was also sending gifts to his "filhinhos" (small children): to "Henriquetinha" ("Little Henriqueta"), a "very pretty" "*molequinha*" (a little African girl); to "meu Joãozinho" ("my little João"), a little goat to play with and a "molequinho" (a little African boy). Both those slave children were marked with an "O" on their left arms in order to be easily distinguished among the cargo of captives on the slave ship.[54]

On one occasion, the king of Benin – who sold people to the *feitoria* – decided to send one of his young slaves – whom João Baptista Cezar referred to as a "moleque escravo do rei" ("king's slave boy") – to Pernambuco to learn to "lidar com gente do mar" ("deal with seamen"). He was probably meant to become a cabin boy. Cezar recommended he should be especially well cared for; guaranteeing his safety was very important, because any incident could interfere with the good commercial relationship that Cezar had established with the African nobility who sold

---

[54] National Archives (London): João Batista Cezar to Josephina, September 15, 1837, and João Batista Cezar to Josephina, September 16, 1837, in Foreign Office 315/69.

him slaves.[55] Because of the British Navy's raid against the *feitoria*, we do not know if the "moleque escravo do rei" ever actually made the voyage, though he could have eventually done so on another of the firm's ships.

CONTRABAND AND LOCAL POWER IN PERNAMBUCO

Whatever that particular young African's destiny, other ships came to Pernambuco after 1837; one of them brought Camilo in its hold. His 1874 statement gives us a few other clues about the logic of slave smuggling at the other end of the voyage, on the beaches of Pernambuco. Camilo testified that, after disembarking, he was imprisoned for a few days in a *casa de purgar* with ninety other captives. A few days later, they were sent to Goiana. This part of his statement resembles that of Mohammah Gardo Baquaqua, who also landed in Pernambuco in the 1840s.[56] Once he landed, Baquaqua said that he stayed at a plantation before being resold. The same happened to Camilo, who was taken to the Itapirema plantation and probably sold from there, along with other four captives, to Manoel Gonsalves, whose grandson would eventually become Camilo's last master. It seems that Camilo's and Baquaqua's shared narrative was probably the general rule in the province after 1831: captives disembarked at beaches bordering plantations, where they were kept to recover from the voyage before either being sold or being sent to work on the plantations themselves. One former Brazilian slaver, called before the British Parliament as a witness, said that captives needed about three months to recover from the transatlantic crossing.[57] His experience, however, was with longer routes than the one between Congo/Angola and Pernambuco, and so the time of recovery was thus probably greater than it might have been for other voyages. Investigating reports by Africans who disembarked in Bahia after 1831, historian Ricardo Caíres Silva has shown that many of them stayed several days or sometimes even months near the disembarkation location, during which time they recovered from their journey and learned Portuguese, which increased their price.[58]

[55] National Archives (London): João Batista Cezar to José Francisco de Azevedo Lisboa, September 16, 1837, in Foreign Office 315/69.
[56] According to Robin Law and Paul Lovejoy, he had embarked at some of the ports surrounding Ouidah, probably Little Popo (modern Aného), and traveled from there to Pernambuco. R. Law and P. Lovejoy, eds., *The Biography of Mahommah Gardo Baquaqua*, p. 149.
[57] Joseph Cliffe, excerpted in R. Conrad, *Children of God's Fire*, p. 36.
[58] R. Silva, "Memórias do tráfico ilegal."

It is interesting to note that Baquaqua did not disembark very far from
Atapus, the location where the slave ship that brought Camilo from
Congo arrived. Robin Law and Paul Lovejoy have suggested that
Baquaqua may have hypothetically arrived in 1845. According to the
British consul in Recife, Augustus Cowper, the only ship that came to
Pernambuco in that year landed at a place called "Macaro."[59] Consul
Cowper probably meant the Santo Antonio Macaro parish, on the coast
a few miles north from Catuama and Atapus, according to a map from the
mid-1800s.[60] Camilo and Baquaqua thus came to Brazil through the same
slave smuggling network and perhaps even lived close to each other until
Baquaqua was sold and moved away from the province.

The British consul in Recife virtually repeated Camilo's and Baquaqua's
testimony when he narrated the case of the *Feiticeira*, which landed in Porto
de Galinhas in 1835. That vessel had previously made other slaving voyages
to Pernambuco. In 1835, it brought 300 Africans who were taken from the
beach to the town of Nossa Senhora do Pilar, where they spent the night.
The next morning, they were taken to the Conceição plantation. Finally,
they were "distributed among buyers."[61] In Pernambuco, where the transatlantic voyage was shorter and slave smuggling beaches were located in the
limits of large plantations, the captives did not have to wait long in order to
be sold, for the main market for them was right there on the sugar plantations themselves. The entire operation thus depended on plantation
owners: they were the customers, and the locations where slave ships
disembarked bordered their plantations or towns subjected to their sphere
of influence. For that reason, it was very important for slave ships to arrive
at the exact beach where they were expected. Slave ships that got lost and
ended up at the wrong beach had to pay expensive bribes or risked having
their cargo stolen by landowners who were themselves the authorities in
charge of the local police and the National Guard. The commander of the
ship that brought Baquaqua to Pernambuco had to give eleven slaves as
bribes to local authorities.[62]

[59] R. Law and P. Lovejoy, eds., *The Biography of Mahommah Gardo Baquaqua*, p. 41.
[60] Map archived in the Arquivo Público Estadual Jordão Emerenciano (Recife): V. J. De
Villiers de L'Ile Adam, "Carta Topographica e Administrativa das Províncias do [sic]
Pernambuco, Alagoas e Sergipe," Rio de Janeiro: Didot Irmaos, Belly Le Prieck e Morizot,
1848.
[61] Edward Watts to Lord Palmerston, October 12, 1835, Sub-Enclosure in no. 112, from
Great Britain, *Irish University Press British Parliamentary Papers – Slave Trade*, "Class
B. Correspondence with Foreign Powers Relating to the Slave Trade, 1835," p. 102.
[62] R. Law and P. Lovejoy, eds., *The Biography of Mahommah Gardo Baquaqua*, p. 41.

There was thus a need for a very well-knit articulation between transatlantic traders and plantation owners who controlled the best natural
harbors. In Pernambuco, it is virtually impossible to separate the slave
smuggler from the plantation owner who controlled land access. In his
Corografia Brasílica, originally published in 1817, Aires de Casal wrote
that Pernambuco was perhaps Brazil's best province in terms of distribution of natural harbors, although most could only receive small vessels.[63]
But those harbors were virtually all located in the sugarcane production
region on Pernambuco's coast. Even slave ships that stayed at sea disembarked at beaches on the borders of plantations. Slave smuggling was only
possible with the help of those who controlled the beaches within the
limits of their lands – and thus also the roads and paths that led to other
plantations and to towns in the interior.

Many of Pernambuco's most prominent plantation owners took part in
these transactions. In 1817, Louis François de Tollenare visited the
Salgado plantation near Cabo de Santo Agostinho. According to that
French traveler, Salgado had a harbor that could receive ships of up to
150 tons. Tollenare was curious why the plantation owner, José de
Oliveira Ramos, did not send his sugar directly to Europe. Ramos replied
that the harbor was blocked by ships sunk in the war against the Dutch
(1630–1654). Yet when Tollenare asked around, he found out that this
was not true: the harbor was clear. Because he became friends with
"Mr. Ramos," Tollenare attributed the mistake to the planter's
naiveté.[64] But Mr. Ramos in fact seems to have known very well how to
use his natural harbor. He was a major slave trader, responsible for
bringing at least 5,186 captives to Recife on his slave ships before
1831.[65] We do not know how many more he smuggled directly into his
own plantation.[66] Nearly thirty years later, August Cowper, as British

[63] M. A. de Casal, *Corografia brasílica*, p. 259.
[64] L. Tollenare, *Notas dominicais*, pp. 68–70.
[65] Cited in D. Albuquerque et al., "Financiamento e organização," p. 220.
[66] The records of the 1817 Rebellion investigation contains a "List of traders, manufactur-
ers, farmers, and other wealthy residents of Recife, to whom no contribution is too large
until the amounts noted at the margin are reached" ("Relação dos negociantes,
fabricantes, lavradores e outras pessoas pecuniosas residentes no Recife, e a quem se não
faz pesada qualquer contribuição até as quantias indicadas à margem"). Mr. Ramos, as
Tollenare liked to call him, is at the top of that list, classified as a "money-driven, stubborn
European" ("europeu aferrado à riqueza e teimoso") with a fortune of "around a million
give or take" ("casa de milhão e pouco mais ou menos") in vessels, commercial businesses,
plantations, slave trade businesses, and more than 300,000 *cruzados* in currency.
L. Tollenare, *Notas dominicais*, pp. 218, 225, 228, 231, and 271. See also
J. H. Rodrigues, *Documentos históricos*, vol. cv, pp. 238 and 241.

consul in Pernambuco, became an "intimate friend" (in his words) of
Ramos' son, also named José Ramos de Oliveira, who was then a very
successful businessman and the first president of the Commercial
Association of Pernambuco. The consul paid him a tremendous compli-
ment for the way he managed his 180 captives: "an experience with free
labor," he said. Mr. Cowper also mentioned that the younger Ramos'
father had been a slave merchant.[67] According to the British consul, the
younger Ramos claimed that he had left the trade. However, archival
evidence suggests that the son himself was in fact still involved in illegal
slave trafficking. At least two ships that left Recife to trade in Angola were
consigned to the younger Ramos: the *Leal Portuense* in 1835, and the
Eugenia in 1837 and 1839. The most incriminating evidence, however,
derives from his wife's posthumous inventory, which indicated that the
couple owned the lands that bordered Porto de Galinhas, adjacent to the
Engenho Salgado (Salgado sugar plantation). Several slave ships landed
there after 1831, including the one that brought Narciso, Maria, and
Joaquim from Congo. On the list of slaves of the Engenho Salgado in
1848, there was even one fourteen-year-old Congolese boy, João Baú,
worth 400 mil réis who had not even been born when the trade was
banned in 1831.[68]

   Plantation owners like Mr. Ramos de Oliveira knew very well what
they were doing and made sure they did not leave explicit traces of their
illegal business. But sometimes their names emerge in the sources.
A brother of one of the region's most prominent leaders, the Baron of
Boa Vista – who was president of Pernambuco province when Camilo,
Maria, Joaquim, and Narciso came to Brazil – was himself directly
involved in at least one case of slave trading. The episode was brutal. In
1843, the 381-ton barque *Temerário* set sail from Africa with 913 people
imprisoned in its holds. Only 816 survived the voyage to Catuama,
a natural harbor north of Recife. According to the British consul, the
devastation continued on land, where at least another 300 Africans passed
away from dysentery, four days after they reached shore. According to the
British consul, a relative of the Baron received 10,000 réis for each captive
he harbored in his property before sending them to Recife.[69]

---

[67] National Archives (London): Consul Christopher to Lord Palmerston, May 30, 1850,
pp. 97 and 97 (reverse). Foreign Office, vol. 84/809.
[68] Instituto Arqueológico, Histórico e Geográfico Pernambucano (Recife): Inventário of
Isabel Maria da Costa Ramos, 1849, p. 31.
[69] August Cowper to the Earl of Aberdeen, May 8, 1843, in *Parliamentary Papers,
Correspondence with Foreign Powers Relative to the Slave Trade* [*Class B and Class C*],

CONCLUSION

What, ultimately, became of the children whose stories have helped open a window on Pernambuco's nineteenth-century trade in illegally enslaved children? Maria won her case because her mistress said in court that she considered Maria a freedwoman already. Camilo also won his case in Itambé, thanks to the witnesses. His lawyer argued he could not have come before 1831, simply because he was forty years old in 1874. Therefore, he should be a "liberated African." His master's lawyer, however, argued Camilo had arrived in 1830. One of the witnesses who favored Camilo was Agostinho, the "natural" son to the father of Camilo's first master, Manoel Gonsalves. Agostinho said he was fifty-seven years old in 1874 and just eighteen around the time Camilo arrived at his father's home, which meant that Camilo had been brought around 1834, when the slave trade was already illegal. We don't know if Agostinho acted against the wealthy branch of his family because he resented his condition as a lower, "natural" son, or if he just acted in favor of Camilo because the African was his godson. Maybe both. Camilo's master, however, did not accept the sentence and appealed to a higher court in Rio de Janeiro. I was not able to trace the final outcome of this case.

In Pernambuco, nineteenth-century plantation owners often portrayed themselves as debtors and therefore as victims of slave dealers. However, it was impossible to maintain the slave trade after 1831 without their full participation. They owned the beaches where the Africans were illegally enslaved, and those beaches faced towns dominated by large plantation owners, who controlled the justices of peace, the National Guard, the juries, and all posts at the local town council. They were also the ones in charge of the trade's repression until the 1850 anti–slave trade law gave the Brazilian navy jurisdiction over everyone involved in the contraband, including those who received and harbored slave ships and captives inland. Through their political networks, plantation owners ruled an entire hierarchy of local authorities, and it is thus little surprise that ships were only seized in cases of conflict, most often when a slave vessel mistakenly ended up on a beach controlled by a rival network. But even in those cases, the captives did not become "liberated Africans."[70] They

vol. 26, p. 359; August Cowper to the Earl of Aberdeen, August 4, 1843, in *House of Commons Parliamentary Papers, Correspondence with Foreign Powers Relative to the Slave Trade* [Class B and Class C], vol. 26, p. 364.

[70] For the fate of liberated Africans in Pernambuco, see C. de Oliveira, "Os africanos livres." See also B. Mamigonian, *Africanos livres*.

were simply enslaved by people who originally had no part in the slave ship's voyage. In Pernambuco, plantation owners whose lands bordered the beaches of the province were directly complicit in the contraband trade.

The literature on the slave trade emphasizes how overcrowded slave ships became after 1831. Is seems likely that these overcrowded ships were not packed with adults but rather mostly with small children, who were the only people who could have fit in such numbers inside the tiny ships that plied Pernambuco's coast. We cannot know the precise number of enslaved African *moleques* who arrived in Brazil before the age of twelve. But the evidence suggests that much of Pernambuco's nineteenth-century plantation wealth was generated by a trade in very young people – unmarked children who ate and drank little, rarely rebelled, and were easy to pack like spoons into a slave ship's dank hull. Once they reached Pernambucan shores, such children easily melted into the *crioulo* masses whose enslavement remained the law of the land until 1888.

3

Agrarian Empires, Plantation Communities, and Slave Families in a Nineteenth-Century Brazilian Coffee Zone

Ricardo Salles and Mariana Muaze*

This chapter discusses the existence and reproduction of enslaved families in coffee's "agrarian empires" during Brazil's second slavery.[1] It does so through a case study of the Guaribú *fazenda* (plantation), located in the Vassouras region of Rio de Janeiro's Paraíba Valley, which was at the time the world's most productive coffee region. Guaribú's history allows us to advance three arguments. First, we demonstrate the ways in which the concepts of "agrarian empires," "plantation communities," and "slave neighborhoods" can help us to understand both familial relationships and those that developed between slaves and masters. Second, we show that slave families living on large plantations had better chances than those who lived on smaller estates of remaining together across generations in stable family formations. And finally, we argue that this familial stability enabled Brazil's "mature slavery," during which positive birth rates ensured the preservation of enslaved labor even after the end of the Atlantic slave trade in 1850.[2]

THE PARAÍBA VALLEY IN THE CONTEXT OF SECOND SLAVERY

The Paraíba Valley was the economic center of the Brazilian Empire (1822–1889). At the end of the eighteenth century, the region was virtually

---

* Translated by Brodwyn Fischer and Camila Sotta Elias.
[1] On the concept of second slavery, see D. Tomich, *Through the Prism*.
[2] The concept of mature slavery was coined in Brazil by Ricardo Salles and is explained in R. Salles, *E o vale*.

unexploited by the Portuguese, serving mainly as a transit point to the gold-mining region of Minas Gerais. The valley was home to many Indigenous peoples, and landholders ran subsistence farms and a few *sesmarias* that produced sugar and spirits. Between 1810 and 1840, however, the region's profile changed significantly. Virgin forest was cleared, most of the Indigenous people were decimated or "tamed," and almost all property holders began to cultivate coffee with enslaved Afro-descendant labor. This rapid transformation was a consequence of multiple factors. Increasing international demand fueled rising coffee prices; turbulent politics pushed former coffee-producing areas such as Saint Domingue into steep decline, creating new market openings; the region already enjoyed good access to road and harbor infrastructure first constructed to distribute the products of Brazil's eighteenth-century mining boom; and the valley's extensive virgin forest reserves and proximity to the slave trade operating out of the port of Rio de Janeiro provided raw materials and labor.[3] Thanks to all of this, the Paraíba Valley emerged in the 1830s as the largest coffee exporter in the world, creating tremendous wealth.

The coffee plantations of the Paraíba Valley were characterized by highly concentrated land tenure and by patterns of production that privileged extensive slave ownership, to the detriment of smaller producers. Coffee slavery in the Paraíba Valley was from its origins directed toward mass agricultural production to meet high demand within the European and North American industrial consumer markets. It was what Dale Tomich called "second slavery," differentiated from colonial slavery by its quick pace, high levels of labor exploitation, and close relationship to the international market and industrial capitalism.[4] In Brazil, the same master class that provided the Empire with its dominant source of political, economic, and intellectual support implemented second slavery even as it helped consolidate the Brazilian Imperial State.[5] The backbone of the

---

[3] The turn of the nineteenth century was characterized by the historian Rafael Marquese as a period of expansion for the agricultural export crops in the Americas – especially sugar, cotton, and coffee – due to the substantial changes in the economy and the world connected to the industrialization process in Europe and the slave revolution in Haiti, which started in 1791. The French colony had been responsible for a significant part of the production of those tropical products, and large numbers of slaves were forcibly transferred to new areas of production after Haitian independence. At the same time, the English Industrial Revolution and the new pace of work it entailed encouraged workers to consume more sugar and also increased consumption of stimulants such as coffee. This, along with increasing demand for cotton used in the growing textile industry, made the export of American agricultural products extremely lucrative. See R. Marquese and D. Tomich, "O Vale do Paraíba escravista."

[4] D. Tomich, *Through the Prism*.

[5] On the concept of the master class, see I. Mattos, *O tempo saquarema*.

master class comprised large slaveholding landowners, and especially those who commanded hundreds of slaves in the Paraíba Valley.

Many coffee planters owned several *fazendas*, as well as other related businesses such as commission houses, mule train operators, railroads, and agricultural banks. Furthermore, their power extended to regional and national politics, where the owners' protégés or relatives held positions as city councilors, local police authorities, senators, civil magistrates, chief police officers, members of the National Guard, etc. Large land-and slaveowners forged extra- and intra-class identities, sharing a slavocratic habitus and valuing European patterns of consumption and behavior.[6] The city of Vassouras could itself be said to symbolize the master class. Its luxurious built heritage flaunted the power of the region's leading families; its mansions, like the Big Houses of the coffee *fazendas*, were often designed by foreign architects and decorated with imported European materials.

The hundreds of thousands of slaves whose labor supported this world had been imported in massive numbers from Africa since the beginning of the nineteenth century. The Atlantic slave trade dictated both the dynamics of master–slave relations and the demography of the slave population until 1850, when the trade was definitively abolished. Even though the number of imported African slaves fell considerably after the 1831 law that officially prohibited the Atlantic traffic, the trade was again strengthened – this time illegally – in the late 1830s and 1840s, due to political pressure from large coffee planters from the Paraíba Valley. The 1831 law was never revoked, but the contraband African trade was openly practiced, with the collusion of Imperial authorities. To give some idea of the scale of this illicit traffic, between 1821 and 1831 some 580,000 enslaved Africans were brought to Brazil, and some 65 percent were destined for the Brazilian Southeast, especially the region's burgeoning coffee zones. Between 1831 and 1850, the period in which the trade was illegal but still active, this number grew to some 900,000 Africans, of which 712,000, or 79 percent, were destined for the Southeast.[7] Because of this, the Paraíba Valley would become the Brazilian region with the highest concentration of slaves during the second half of the nineteenth century.

[6] M. Muaze, *As memórias da viscondessa*.
[7] T. Parron, *A política da escravidão*. Data at http://slavevoyages.org/assessment/estimates, consulted on November 30, 2017.

THE CASE OF THE FAZENDA GUARIBÚ

In order to analyze the slave family in the coffee-based agrarian empires of the central Paraíba Valley, this chapter will focus on the Fazenda Guaribú, which belonged to the former Pau Grande *sesmaria*, one of the first to be granted in Rio de Janeiro province's stretch of the Paraíba Valley (see Figure 3.1). Two key factors justify this focus. First, Guaribú is one of the oldest properties of the region, with coffee production dating back to the eighteenth century, when it was still part of the Pau Grande *sesmaria*.[8] Second, the Fazenda Guaribú was officially appraised five times during the nineteenth century: first in the postmortem inventories of Luís Gomes Ribeiro (1841), of his wife Joaquina Mathilde de Assunção (1847), and of their son and heir, Claudio Gomes Ribeiro de Avellar (1863); and then later when Gomes Ribeiro de Avellar's brothers contested their parents' will and Gomes Ribeiro de Avellar's share of the total estate was reassessed in 1874

FIGURE 3.1 Fazenda Guaribú, Vassouras. Picture from the 1970s, INEPAC archive.

[8] M. Muaze, *As memórias da viscondessa.*

and again in 1885.[9] Analysis of this documentation allows us to trace how the slave family, in all of its different forms, changed over time and space within the same plantation structure, from its establishment in the 1840s until the crisis of Brazilian slavery in the 1880s.[10]

The owners of the so-called Casa do Pau Grande were the Portuguese brothers Antônio dos Santos, José Rodrigues da Cruz, and Antônio Ribeiro de Avellar. The property comprised seventeen *sesmarias* – five within Pau Grande, five at Ubá, and seven at Guaribú – and was part of a large business complex that included several *fazendas* in the Valley and outposts in the commercial centers of Rio de Janeiro, Rio Grande do Sul, and Portugal. In 1797, the family company Avellar & Santos was dissolved and the lands were divided. José Rodrigues da Cruz founded the Ubá *fazenda*. The inheritance of Antônio Ribeiro de Avellar, deceased in 1798, was left to his widow Antônia, who kept the *sesmarias* located in Pau Grande. Luís Gomes Ribeiro, António Ribeiro de Avellar's nephew and son-in-law, acquired the lands that had belonged to Antônio dos Santos and José Rodrigues da Cruz in the area known as Guaribú. In 1811, the partnership between Luís Gomes Ribeiro and his mother-in-law Antônia Ribeiro de Avellar ended, and he went to live in Guaribú with his wife Joaquina Mathilde de Assumpção and their two eldest sons.[11]

Luís Gomes Ribeiro began to acquire slaves exactly at this time (in 1811); thirty years later, in 1841, his postmortem inventory listed 411

---

[9] Claudio Gomes Ribeiro de Avellar was unmarried and passed away leaving no acknowledged natural heirs. In his will, he left an inheritance to children he had with the slave Maria das Antas, but he did not acknowledge his parentage. To Manoel Gomes Ribeiro de Avellar and his two brothers, Luís and João, sons of Maria das Antas, all of whom had been born free, he left three of his four *fazendas*: Boa União, Antas, and Encantos, with all of their improvements, lands, and slaves. Guaribú, the fourth and main *fazenda* according to family tradition, was left to his brothers. However, Avellar's will also stipulated that Manoel should select 120 slaves from Guaribú, as part of his and his siblings' inheritance. To Virgínia, sister of the legatees, Claudio left thirty *contos de réis*, which she would receive when he was married or legally emancipated. The legatees, who could not sell or dispose of the properties, were also instructed to provide support to their mother, Maria das Antas, for as long as she lived. As the sons/heirs were underage, a legal representative, or tutor, had to be appointed, and the division of the estate lasted until the 1890s. See Arquivo do Iphan-Vassouras, Testamento de Claudio Gomes Ribeiro de Avellar, 1863; M. Borges and R. Salles, "A morte."

[10] D. Tomich, *Through the Prism*; R. Marquese and D. Tomich, "O vale do Paraíba escravista."

[11] M. Muaze, *As memórias da viscondessa*; R. Moraes, *Os Ribeiro*.

slaves in all his properties. The Fazenda Guaribú alone had 244 slaves, 119,000 coffee trees, two residential homes, one storage shed for coffee, a barn, a kiln to make tiles, and various mills to process sugar, manioc, and coffee. Shortly before drafting his will, in 1829, Luís Gomes Ribeiro, aiming to expand the coffee plantation, acquired the Sítio dos Encantos, a relatively small coffee plantation adjacent to Guaribú.[12] In 1841, Encantos had over 103 slaves, as well as 109,000 coffee trees, a residential house, a barn, a water mill, a fan to dry coffee beans, a mill with pestles, and a mill that ground manioc flour, powered by a water wheel. These properties together formed a large coffee complex – an agrarian empire – that expanded in step with Rio's Paraíba Valley, the world's main coffee producer during second slavery and the accelerated rise of global capitalism. In the 1840s, coffee was already Brazil's most important export, with 100,000 tons exported annually, a figure that doubled in the next decade.[13] During that same period, the number of slaves disembarked in Brazil went from 34,115 captives in 1810 to 52,430 in 1830.[14] The vast majority of these forced laborers were destined for the coffee plantations up the mountains from their ports of entry.[15]

In 1841, when his postmortem inventory was initiated, Luís Gomes Ribeiro's 411 slaves lived in seven *senzalas* (slave quarters), which were "spread out from one another, tiled, with windows and a kitchen."[16] The *senzalas* housed slaves from both Guaribú and Encantos. Although they spoke different languages and belonged to different cultural systems, most of these slaves forged family bonds, networks of kin and fictive kin, and various forms of solidarity in order to survive the grueling experience of captivity. The postmortem inventory lists thirty-five slave couples, thirty comprised of Africans and five comprised of Africans and *crioulos* (Brazilian-born Afro-descendants). The slave families were preserved even after the deaths of Luís Gomes Ribeiro (in 1839) and his wife, Joaquina Mathilde de Assumpção (in 1847). It is interesting to note that the family's strategy for dividing family assets facilitated this preservation: Ribeiro and Assumpção's son, Claudio Gomes Ribeiro de Avellar, who would become Baron of Guaribú, inherited the bulk of slaves from both Guaribú and Encantos, receiving fifty-six from his father and (years later) another seventy from his mother.[17] Such continuity, which the

---

[12] M. Borges and R. Salles, "A morte."   [13] F. Luna and H. Klein, O *escravismo*, p. 105.
[14] F. Luna and H. Klein, O *escravismo*, p. 194.   [15] T. Parron, A *política da escravidão*.
[16] Iphan-Vassouras Archive, Inventory of Luiz Gomes Ribeiro, 1841.
[17] M. Borges and R. Salles, "A morte."

historiography indicates was quite common in plantations, provided great stability for many slave families in the Paraíba Valley.[18] In 1863, when Claudio Gomes Ribeiro de Avellar's postmortem inventory was initiated, forty-eight couples were recognized and listed for Guaribú, seven at Encantos, and forty at the Sítio das Antas and Boa União, which were new properties acquired by Claudio Ribeiro de Avellar. The inventory also listed various descendants of slaves who had inhabited the *fazenda* since 1841.

This evidence shows that the slave family was a reality within the rural settings where most Brazilian slaves lived during the nineteenth century. Moreover, they indicate that the slave family had a significant presence in the large coffee plantations. The meaning of this phenomenon has been contested within Brazilian historiography. In the 1990s, the debate became polarized. One view held that the slave family was the product of resistance, a hard-won achievement that allowed captive Africans and *crioulos* to maintain their social and cultural practices across generations, creating a slave identity that was molded in opposition to the master class.[19] Another view held that the slave family was a concession, an instrument that allowed slave masters to guarantee peace in the slave quarters and exercise greater control over their captives.[20] We argue that any approach that aims to produce a single, unitary view of the slave family's historical meaning may lead to false dichotomies. The slave family could have signified both resistance and coercion. Slave families were nested within broader, extremely unequal configurations of power that disfavored enslaved people; they developed in the midst of structural conditions that facilitated a mode of what we might call slavocratic domination. Yet those families and their meanings varied enormously, depending on a constantly shifting socioeconomic, cultural, and political conjuncture. Broader contexts – such as Brazil's degree of national political stability or instability, the extent to which international actors actively condemned and combatted slavery, or the volume of the Atlantic slave trade – could influence relationships between masters and slaves, thus transforming the signification of the slave family.

More immediately, the economic cycles of Rio's Paraíba Valley – and the point at which any particular plantation found itself in the evolution from initial planting to expansion to greatness and decline – had

---

[18] J. Garavazo, "Relações familiares"; J. Motta, *Corpos escravos*; C. Engemann, "De grande escravaria"; F. Luna and H. Klein, *O escravismo*.
[19] R. Slenes, *Na senzala*.   [20] M. Florentino and J. Goes, *A paz*.

a similar impact on the master–slave relationship.[21] In the end, master–slave relations and the meanings of the slave family came down to the concrete world shaped by a particular master and by the particular people he or she enslaved. But we cannot lose sight of the broader conditions that shaped those actors' lives, even when that context was beyond their immediate understanding.

AGRARIAN EMPIRES IN THE COFFEE-PRODUCING PARAÍBA VALLEY

The postmortem inventories of the municipality of Vassouras during the nineteenth century revealed patterns of slave property-holding at once dispersed and very concentrated. Since the end of the 1990s, new research has deepened our knowledge of the coffee-growing area in the Paraíba Valley. These new findings diverge methodologically from previous historiography, which generally divided slave properties into only three categories: small, medium, and large, with the latter generally described as less important because it was numerically the minority.[22] In Vassouras, a more complex pattern prevailed. There were farmers who owned between one and five slaves, most of whom did not own the land they cultivated and lived together with their captives. Some of those small-time slaveowners had once themselves been captives, before being freed by their former masters. At the other extreme of the pyramid, there were slaveowners with hundreds of slaves, who owned two, three, four, or more plantations. Altogether, our analysis of the collection of 921 postmortem inventories stored in the former Historical Documentation Center of the University Severino Sombra uncovered five categories of owners. Without considering the 2 percent that did not own slaves, the estates can be classified as in Table 3.1.

As we can see in Table 3.1, based on this sample, large and mega owners owned 70 percent of the slaves in Vassouras, which indicates a high concentration of both land and enslaved labor in the region. And these properties determined the conditions in which most captives formed their families.[23] This fact, as we will see, has important consequences

---

[21] For the periodization of coffee cultivation in the Vale do Paraíba, see R. Slenes, "Grandeza ou decadência," and R. Salles, *E o vale.*

[22] In Vassouras, Flávio Gomes identified a fourth category of owners, with over eighty slaves. See F. Gomes, *Histórias de quilombolas.* Ricardo Salles indicated five categories of owners in Vassouras, as will be detailed later (R. Salles, *E o vale*).

[23] R. Salles, *E o vale.*

TABLE 3.1   *Categories of slaveowners.*

Category	Number of Slaves	Percentage in Relation to the Total of Owners	Percentage in Relation to the Total of Slaves in Vassouras
Mini-owners	1–4	16%	1%
Small owners	5–9	39%	11%
Medium owners	20–49	22%	18%
Large owners	50–99	12%	22%
Mega-owners	Over 100	9%	48%

Source: 921 postmortem inventories, Historical Documentation Center, Universidade Severino Sombra.

when it comes to analyzing master–slave relationships in Brazil's most important slave region during the nineteenth century.

Luís Gomes Ribeiro and his son Claudio Gomes Ribeiro de Avellar, Baron of Guaribú, were two of these mega owners. The Baron of Guaribú was in fact the largest of all. With 835 slaves and four farms when he died, in 1863, he built the biggest agrarian empire in the municipality of Vassouras. By agrarian empire, we mean an individual or familial domain – or some combination of both – made up of large landholdings, wherein slaves and land made up more than 60 percent of the proprietors' wealth. The fortunes of mega-owners were unmatched within their municipalities, their provinces, and even the Brazilian Empire as a whole.

Historian William Kauffman Scarborough coined the expression "agrarian empire" when analyzing the slave-owning elite in the US South, based on nineteenth-century agrarian censuses.[24] Scarborough used a minimum of 250 slaves to define an agrarian empire in the antebellum United States. In the context of second slavery, however, the forms of concentrated wealth varied from one slave regime to the next, and we thus resolved to elevate Scarborough's original floor for Rio's Paraíba basin. Based on the profile of seventy-one mega-proprietors whose postmortem inventories were conducted in Vassouras between 1829 and 1885, we established which among them were at the very top of the slaveholding hierarchy, based on the size of their slave holdings. Forty-seven mega-owners owned between 100 and 199 captives, seventeen held

[24] W. Scarborough, *Masters of the Big Houses*, pp. 122–166.

between 200 and 350, and only twelve claimed more than 350.[25] It thus
makes sense, based on the Vassouras inventories, to set the floor for an
agrarian empire in the region at 350, though preliminary studies from
adjacent regions of the Paraíba Valley such as Piraí, Valença, and
Cantagalo suggest that this floor may need to be raised further still. In
general, in this coffee-producing area, ownership of an agrarian empire
indicated an owner's extreme wealth and power. Many were made up of
several large *fazendas*, each with between 100 and 300 slaves.

In Vassouras, the following owners could be said to preside over
agrarian empires: the Baroness of Campo Belo, the Baron of Guanabara,
Ana Joaquina de São José Werneck, Luís Gomes Ribeiro, Manoel
Francisco Xavier, Elisa Constança de Almeida, Anna Joaquina de São
José, Claudio Gomes Ribeiro de Avellar, Francisco Peixoto de Lacerda
Werneck, and the Baron of Capivary. These owners or patriarchs were
true rural potentates, with great power and influence both locally and
across the province of Rio de Janeiro. Although they were mostly dedicated to the administration and control of their domains, they often used
bonds of family, friendship, and political alliance to extend their influence
to the rulers of the Empire. Regardless of whether their partisan political
leanings were conservative or liberal, they supported the monarchical
regime. They formed the core of a dominant class of large slaveholders
and landowners, traders and financiers, who linked their social and economic interests to the Imperial political elite, which in turn governed in
accordance with the planters' interests. Together, the political elite and the
planter class comprised a new Brazilian aristocracy attached to the
Imperial dynasty. Some members of this new aristocracy were granted
nonhereditary noble titles. Through this complex network, the new South
American Empire depicted itself as the representation of European civilization in the New World.[26]

This agrarian civilization was centered in the large rural plantation
houses and their surroundings. Typically, the Big House overlooked
one or more rectangular courtyards, where recently harvested coffee

---

[25] In the 1920s, Eloy de Andrade divided the Vale do Paraíba's rural properties into "fazendas," with up to 120 *alqueires geométricos* of extension and forty to fifty slaves; "large
properties," with 250–600 *alqueires*, on average, and 200 or more slaves; and "latifundia," with over 600 *alqueires* and anywhere from 300 to more than 500 slaves. E. de
Andrade, *O Vale do Paraíba*. According to the *Encyclopedia of Historical Metrology,
Weights and Measures* (v.2, p. 871) each *alqueire geométrico* was about 48,000 square
meters in Rio de Janeiro.

[26] M. Muaze, "Novas considerações"; R. Salles, *E o vale*.

beans were left to dry. Initially those courtyards were simply empty patches of earth, but technological advancements led eventually to stone or macadam pavement. The *senzalas* (slave quarters), usually single-story buildings arranged in lines or squares, were grouped adjacent to the courtyards. The coffee hulling mill, pigsties, animal pens, slave infirmary, and other buildings were also in the so-called functional quadrilateral of the *fazendas*. The whole complex, and especially the Big Houses – which became more and more refined after the mid-nineteenth century – symbolically expressed the master's power.

The configuration and nature of agrarian empires were not always the same. They varied over time, depending on where they found themselves in the cycle of economic establishment, development, and decline; their fortunes also fluctuated according to the regional conjuncture and Brazil's broader economic, social, political, and cultural contexts. Figure 3.2 shows that variation. On a scale of 0 to 900, each dot represents the total number of bondsmen owned by the seventy-one mega-proprietors found in the postmortem inventories of the county of Vassouras during the nineteenth century.

The first mega-proprietor's inventory for our sample appeared at the end of the 1820s. The estate belonged to Felipe Ferreira Goulart, owner of 102 slaves, whose assets were inventoried in 1829, along with those of his wife, Caetana Rosa de Leme. Mega-proprietors started to become more numerous in the 1830s and 1840s, when the first agrarian empires with more than 350 slaves appeared. A good example is the agrarian empire belonging to Manoel Francisco Xavier, whose inventory was completed in 1840 and listed 446 slaves in his four properties. Manoel Francisco's *fazendas* were the site of a famous slave revolt led by Manoel Congo in 1838.[27] The concentration of slave property in mega-estates reached its

[27] Manuel Congo was a slave and the leader of a nineteenth-century slave revolt that broke out in 1838 in the province of Rio de Janeiro, in a place variously known as Quilombo de Manuel Congo, the Quilombo de Santa Catarina, and the Quilombo de Paty do Alferes. He was from Bacongo, in West-Central Africa, and had been brought as a slave to Brazil during the second decade of the nineteenth century. He was baptized in Rio de Janeiro city and sold to work on the Paraíba Valley coffee plantations in Rio de Janeiro province. There, he worked for Manuel Francisco Xavier (who lived from the last quarter of the eighteenth century to 1840), who was master to approximately 500 other slaves. The uprising was a collective escape of hundreds of slaves from two properties belonging to Manuel Francisco Xavier, along with some captives of close farms from other owners, which occurred in November 5, 1838, The fugitives went to a nearby mountain range. They were quickly pursued by local militia troops and were found and defeated after a short but tough confrontation on November 11, with fatalities and injuries on both sides. Most of the rebels were captured, including Manuel Congo. The ones identified as

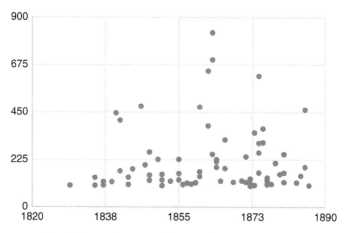

FIGURE 3.2 Distribution of owners of 100+ slaves in Vassouras, according to their number of slaves, 1820–1888. Source: Postmortem inventories, Iphan-Vassouras Archive.

apex during the 1860s, with some estates holding over 600 slaves. Among those, besides Claudio Gomes Ribeiro de Avellar and his 835 slaves inventoried in 1863, we also find Claudio's uncle, Joaquim Ribeiro de Avellar, Baron of Capivary, deceased that same year, who owned the Pau Grande *sesmaria* and 698 slaves. Claudio Avellar's brother-in-law, Francisco Peixoto de Lacerda Werneck (Baron of Paty do Alferes) also counted in this elite group when he died in 1862, holding six *fazendas* in Paty do Alferes and 645 slaves. Such data show that Claudio built his individual holdings within the broader empire of the Ribeiro de Avellar clan, based in Paty do Alferes, where he divided local power with his relatives from the Lacerda Werneck clan.[28] The maximum number of slaves found in postmortem inventories dropped below 400 in the next

leaders were judged and received severe punishments. Manuel Congo was sentenced to death and hanged in early September of the following year. F. Gomes, *Histórias de quilombolas*.

[28] To further demonstrate the power of the Ribeiro de Avellar clan, we can also mention Joaquim Ribeiro de Avellar Jr., son of the Baron of Capivary, who inherited all his father's and aunts' fortunes. Joaquim exploited slave labor up to 1887, when he earned his title (Viscount of Ubá) after promising in an official document to free his slaves in March 1888. However, on August 10, 1886, he registered 349 slaves and 121 sexagenarians under his name at the Collector's Office in Vassouras. National Archive, Fundo Fazenda do Pau Grande, notation 902.

decades, except for the disputed inventory of Claudio Gomes Ribeiro de Avellar.

Inventories are appraisals of assets, carried out at the time of an individual's death. For that reason, it is reasonable to assume that the majority of inventories reflected moments when a person's businesses were already well-established, at a plateau, or even in decline.[29] But this was not always the case. Aside from premature death, which was unusual, an individual's life cycle could diverge from that of their businesses. This is exactly what we can observe in the inventory of Luís Gomes Ribeiro, the first patriarch of the agrarian empire of Guaribú, whose businesses were still on the rise during the 1840s, when coffee was in growing demand on the international market.

In the 1850s, Luís' son Claudio Gomes Ribeiro de Avellar's lands, which were almost contiguous to one another, totalled 3,156 hectares, equivalent to 31.5 million square meters, or 7,795 acres. In comparative terms, his empire was equivalent – both in relation to land area and to number of slaves – to that belonging to John Burnside, Louisiana's biggest sugar producer in 1858. At that time, Burnside's agrarian empire consisted of five contiguous plantations, totaling 7,600 acres of land, with a labor force of 1,000 slaves.[30]

Returning to Figure 3.2, we can see that only four inventories indicated possessions greater than 350 slaves in the 1870s and 1880s. Two of them were the aforementioned reassessments of the Baron of Guaribú's estate, which remained in dispute until the 1890s. His legacy continued to represent the largest concentration of slave property in the region. In 1874, his estate's 621 slaves far exceeded the 353 slaves listed among the properties of Eufrásia Correia e Castro, Baroness of Campo Belo (who died in 1873), and the 372 slaves in the 1875 inventory of José Gonçalves de Oliveira

---

[29] This is, broadly, Renato Leite Marcondes' conclusion in his study about slave accumulation, in which he works with this kind of hypothesis about life cycles. See R. Marcondes, *A arte de acumular*, especially chapter 4 and the appendix, "A hipótese do ciclo de vida."

[30] W. Scarborough, *Masters of the Big Houses*, p. 137. The agrarian empire of Claudio Gomes Ribeiro de Avellar was the largest in Vassouras, at least in number of slaves. But it was not the largest overall. The brothers Joaquim and José de Souza Breves, for example, both owned dozens of *fazendas* and thousands of slaves in Piraí, São João do Príncipe and surrounding areas. They were rivaled only by Antônio Clemente Pinto, Baron of Nova Friburgo, who also had thousands of slaves and dozens of properties in Cantagalo, Nova Friburgo, and São Fidélis. For the Breves brothers, see, among others, T. Pessoa, "A indiscrição." On the Baron of Nova Friburgo, see V. Melnixenco, "Friburgo & Filhos." On the distribution and size of the plantations in the Paraíba Valley, see F. Fridman, "As cidades."

Roxo, Baron of Guanabara. In 1885, the 462 slaves bequeathed by the Baron of Guaribú were still unparalleled. This information matters because it shapes our analysis of the slave family, which was circumscribed within a specific form of property accumulation (involving wealth, land, and labor) that occurred in the southern Paraíba river basin, typified by the region's agrarian empires.

PLANTATION COMMUNITIES

As we have seen, most slaves in the Paraíba Valley lived on large *fazendas* that were part of mega-properties or agrarian empires. On those *fazendas*, a larger number of slaves entailed a greater proportion of enslaved women and a more even gender balance, which made it easier for slaves to pair off and create families. Because so many slaves belonged to the same owner, and because they were often able to establish bonds and lines of communication among contiguous *fazendas*, enslaved people could establish a wide spectrum of social ties, which also made family formation more viable. Furthermore, after the end of the Atlantic slave trade in 1850, an increase in the proportion of enslaved women and the need to produce new laborers within the plantations encouraged masters to strategically promote slave families.

For slave families, the *senzala* was a foundational space. On large *fazendas*, *senzalas* were single-story wattle and daub houses, with thatched roofs that were often converted to tile after 1850, an adjustment that greatly reduced their temperature and humidity. Their floors were mostly beaten earth, though they could sometimes have finished flooring. Most were divided into cubicles of 9–12 meter square. Each cubicle had a door that opened onto the courtyard, and a rare few had windows. Ventilation was generally provided by wooden-barred openings at the juncture of the walls and roof. Each cubicle housed a family or a group of same-sex slaves. In some cases, especially in *fazendas* with numerous slaves, the *senzalas* could themselves form a three- or four-sided enclosure, as was the case on the *fazendas* Santo Antônio do Paiol and Flores do Paraíso, both in Valença.[31] Slave families formed in such spaces, and there they lived, under the daily oversight of foremen, supervisors, and masters.

---

[31] F. Werneck, *Memória sobre a fundação*. *Memória* was published as a book in 1847. For Santo Antônio do Paiol, see the Marc Ferrez photograph, dated 1885, held at the Instituto Moreira Salles. For the Fazenda Flores do Paraíso, see the painting of Nicolau Facchinetti,

Daily conflicts and negotiations between slaves and masters were an inherent and permanent feature of the slave system. As part of this process, enslaved people forged identities and carved out spaces for autonomy, which were sometimes expansive and sometimes more constricted; in these ways, enslaved people left their mark on Brazil's imperial culture and society. Some historians use expressions such as slave communities or *senzala* communities to describe the relationships forged among slaves, their nuclear families, and their extended relatives. This denomination aims to highlight slave autonomy and the sense of common identity that slaves created within captivity, in clear opposition to their masters' domination.[32] According to Flávio dos Santos Gomes, such slave communities communicated with other *senzala* communities, freedpersons, peasants, *mocambos* (runaways), and *quilombolas* (inhabitants of maroon communities) creating what he has designated a "Black countryside."[33]

Yet this focus on autonomy, which was the hallmark of the historiography of Brazilian slavery written in the 1980s and 1990s, should not obscure the fact that these autonomous spaces were forged within structures of power and political, social, economic, and cultural conjunctures that were highly unfavorable to slaves.[34] These structures, which changed considerably over time, set the limits of slave agency. Such boundaries were determined, for example, by the greater or lesser presence of Africans among a given slave population; by the size of the property where slaves lived and worked; or by the manumission practices that were the norm within any given property or region. The class relationships between slaves and owners were thus elastic and turbulent. Without underestimating the importance of the bonds created among slaves or their struggles for autonomy and liberty, we argue that such spaces of agency were circumscribed by the slave regime.

In order to understand the structural asymmetry of master–slave relationships at the local level, we propose in this chapter that the expression

---

from 1875 (*Catálogo da exposição Facchinetti* [Rio de Janeiro: Centro Cultural Banco do Brasil, 2004]).

[32] See F. Gomes, *Histórias de quilombolas*. See also, in the same line of argumentation, R. Slenes, *Na senzala*.

[33] F. Gomes, *Histórias de quilombolas*. About the "Black countryside," see pp. 43–178, 62–63, passim. On the Manuel Congo revolt, see pp. 179–321.

[34] For a critical survey on this historiography in the Brazilian case, see R. Marquese and R. Salles, "Slavery in Nineteenth-Century Brazil." About the relationship between structure and experience, see E. Viotti da Costa, "Estruturas versus experiência."

"plantation community" is more useful than "slave community" or "*senzala* community." In doing so, we not only contest the notion of a community as a harmonious group; we also conceive of slaves' actions as inevitably connected to their masters' dominion. By taking into account only the agency and resistance of the slaves, the "slave community" concept loses some of its analytic capacity. The "plantation community" concept also usefully captures the integration of slaves' workspaces and their living environments. Slaves did not themselves organize the *senzalas*, which were contiguous to the rest of the plantation and ordered according to its larger needs and structure. The formation of plantation communities in the coffee-producing areas of the Paraíba Valley was essential to the process through which any given group of slaves was transformed into a collective labor force, creating a structure of domination that endured for many decades.

In the coffee production zone of the Paraíba Valley, plantation communities were a sine qua non for high productivity and profit. From the toll of the morning bell before sunrise to the final count and slave inspection at the end of a day's toil, the captives' work was mixed with various social activities – meals, rest, chatting, singing, dancing, praying – that could result in new forms of organization, sociability, and family. Enslaved people also usually had Sundays and holidays free, time they spent raising small animals and vegetables to consume or sell to their masters. Work, family, and community were not separated spheres: the result was a dense net of social relations with the slave family at its core. Effectively, the largest slave cohorts – even those recently trafficked from Africa – were never simply groups of people brought together to work. They comprised a plantation community, involving forms of sociability, cultural links, spiritual encouragement, and family life that went well beyond the strict mandates of commodity production. Slave labor could only reach its full productive capacity if it was part of such a plantation community, in which the slave family played a fundamental role. This was true even at the height of the international slave trade, when the high number of men among newly imported Africans produced a significant gender imbalance among slaves. Even under these adverse conditions, the few African and *crioula* women who were present anchored stable relationships and families within the plantations' borders. After 1850, when the international slave trade was abolished, a more equal gender balance among the slaves facilitated family formation.

In short, the concept of a plantation community aims to break the false dichotomy that has dominated the historiography of the slave family in Brazil, which imposes an unnecessary choice between viewing family formation as an act of slave agency and resistance or viewing it as a form of slavocratic oppression. This does not mean that we should for a moment ignore the profound contradictions that placed masters and slaves in opposition, evident in the slaves' many acts of resistance. If slave revolt had not been endemic to the world of slavery, that world would not have been what it was. In situating the slave family as a component of a plantation community, we instead wish to accentuate the slave family's contradictory character and that fact that it was – like other aspects of *fazenda* life, in all their specificity – subject to a constantly shifting balance of power between masters and slaves, both locally and globally.

Nothing demonstrates this asymmetrical balance of power better than the masters' postmortem inventories. These express and expose all of the slave–master relationships' various temporalities and dimensions: the juridico-political norms that consecrated and legitimated slave property; the intimate life of masters and their families; the spiritual and affective realm evident through requests for mass to be said for the souls of family members, godchildren, and slaves; and a material world that included objects, assets, lands, animals, and (inevitably) slaves. Slaves appear in inventories with names, ages, origins, skills, behaviors, family ties, and material appraisals. At one point we might see a reference to an old man, broken and worthless; later we encounter a woman appraised with her newborn baby or child. Further on, we find a note about so-and so, son of such-and-such, appraised individually but listed right below his parents, in implicit recognition of the unity of the slave family. This listing order was common to the majority of inventories and expressed the contradiction inherent in the slave family: enslaved people were joined together by recognized ties, but each was also marked with an individual market value.

The masters' inventories, as snapshots of their time, allow us to perceive gradual mutations and shifts in the slave family, which was shaped by the conditions of each historical period. The Guaribú case is especially valuable in this sense, because it grants us access to so many slave appraisals in a single site. Let us shift, then, to setting the scene of the Guaribú plantation community in the time of Luís Gomes Ribeiro.

THE SLAVE FAMILY IN THE PLANTATION COMMUNITIES OF THE FAZENDA GUARIBÚ

The second patriarch of Guaribú, Claudio Gomes Ribeiro de Avellar, began acquiring slaves even before he inherited the Fazenda Guaribú and the Sítio dos Encantos. In 1831, he was already among the recipients of the assets of his father, Luís Gomes Ribeiro, and he insisted in receiving his payment in lands and slaves, indicating that he was already established as a landowner-capitalist by the time he was around thirty years old. The list of 835 slaves included in his 1863 postmortem inventory indicates that Claudio depended heavily on illegal slave traffic between 1831 and 1850 to expand his businesses; many slaves were from a wide range of African ports, and they were too young to have come before 1831. But that was not enough: the Baron of Guaribú also made heavy use of the internal slave trade to stock his *fazenda* workforce, listing slaves from Bahia (thirty-four), the city of Rio de Janeiro (eleven), Iguaçu (one), and Minas Gerais (three). He also benefitted, of course, from the natural growth allowed by the establishment of stable families during the mature stage of coffee slavery.[35]

Among the 618 slaves whose provenance was listed (75 percent of the total), 52.2 percent were *crioulos* (Brazilian-born) and 47.8 percent were Africans. Among the Africans, 15 percent were women, 32.5 percent of whom were married. Among the 85 percent of Africans who were men, 31.2 percent had spouses. Among *crioulos*, the marriage rate dropped for both men and women; each gender had only five married people. The average age of *crioulos*, however, was much lower than that of Africans, and many were too young to marry. The African women were between forty and seventy-one years old; the African men were between forty-seven and seventy-one. Among *crioulos*, the youngest were one year old, the oldest woman was sixty-one, and the oldest man was fifty-nine. All in all, 24.1 percent of the estate's slaves were married. On the basis of this evidence, we can consider Guaribú a mature plantation community in the early 1860s.

In order to analyze family structures on these properties, we have defined any link that appears on the inventory lists as a familial tie. Our intention was to accommodate the full range of ways in which enslaved people organized their families. Yet it is important not to forget that the number of slave families would be much higher if the inventories had included informal unions, which were unregistered and unsanctioned but quite common in the daily life of plantation communities.

---

[35] On the idea of mature slavery in Brazil, in which agribusiness enterprises and plantation communities were stable but dependent on the existence of slave families that would naturally reproduce the captive population, see R. Salles, *E o vale*.

Among the slaves listed in Luís Gomes Ribeiro's 1841 inventory, 243 lived and worked in the Guaribú property and 168 in the Sítio dos Encantos. Between the 1820s and the 1840s, when the demand for slave labor to structure the coffee economy in the Paraíba Valley was very high, large slaveholders generally preferred African-born slaves between sixteen and forty years of age, who were esteemed for their physical strength and aptitude for work. This created a great imbalance between male and female slaves and led to a very unstable period for slave families. Even so, as was noted earlier, an analysis of slave families on the Fazenda Guaribú under Luís Gomes Ribeiro's administration indicates the existence of thirty-five slave couples, five comprised of African and *crioulo* partners and thirty comprised exclusively of Africans. Among the unions recognized in Ribeiro's inventory, thirteen couples had parented a total of twenty-one *crioulo* children, ranging in age from newborn to eight years of age, which suggests that a policy of encouraging family formation had existed for at least a decade in Guaribú. Such a policy could have taken many forms: masters might have set aside cubicles within the *senzala* for family use, held collective Catholic weddings for slave couples, or simply acknowledged extant stable unions.

One of the *crioulo*–African couples on Luís Gomes Ribeiro's plantation was made up of Francisca, an eighteen-year-old *crioula*, and Custódio, a twenty-four-year-old from Rebolo, who were the parents of three-year-old Brás and three-month-old Cândida. African couples included José Maria from Calabar, forty, and Felizarda from Mozambique, nineteen, who were the parents of seven-year-old Ignês; and Romualdo, thirty-five, and Thereza, twenty, who were both from Mozambique and the parents of five-year-old Philismina and one-year-old Sebastião. The oldest married man was eighty (Francisco from Benguela), and the oldest woman was sixty (Ana, also from Benguela). The youngest married men and women were twenty-four and sixteen respectively, which suggests that enslaved women married at a younger age. It did not seem, however, that the older African men in our sample enjoyed any special privileges when it came to family formation.

On both the Guaribú and the Encantos properties, we found a significant number of African boys and girls with no known family connections. This suggests that they were separated from their families, whether when taken captive in Africa, during the middle passage, or at the point of sale on Brazilian territory. Such were the likely histories of Simplício from Cabinda, ten, and Bernardo from Congo, nine, who were placed at the Sítio dos Encantos, and also of Ninfa from Angola and Aleixo from Congo, both eleven, who worked at the Fazenda Guaribú. Even in these cases, however, a lack of blood relations did not necessarily preclude slave children from forging affective familial ties or other forms of solidarity within the plantation community. Over twenty years later, in 1863, the Baron of Guaribú's slaves were distributed in the following manner: 441 slaves at the Fazenda Guaribú, 315 at the Sítio Antas, seventy-three at the Sítio dos Encantos, and six at Boa União.[36] These numbers, when compared to those found in the inventories of the Baron's parents, suggest that Guaribú and Antas were very productive properties. With regard to slave families, there were eighty families at Guaribú, fifty-two at Antas, seven at Encantos, and none in Boa União in 1863. Much of the family life that these men, women, and children experienced played out in the space of the *senzala*. To shelter the largest concentration of slave labor in the municipality of Vassouras, the Baron had two *senzalas* in Guaribú, one with twenty-five cubicles and another with twenty-four, as well as a separate *senzala* for household slaves; he also had a *senzala* with twenty-two cubicles in Encantos, as well as five *senzalas* in Antas and Boa União, divided into between three and twenty cubicles.

The figures in Table 3.2 indicate that Guaribú, Antas, and Encantos had a stable plantation community, because they show three generations of family members living together. In Guaribú and Antas, the slave family was at the base of this stability, especially if we take into account the large number of slaves who lived amidst relatives and the children who were born in captivity, who were numerous enough to result in a natural increase in Guaribú's enslaved population.

Other features reinforce the impression that these properties functioned as a plantation community. First, families were long-lasting. In the 1863 inventory, there were three families in their third generation, which means that at least twenty-eight children were living with their grandparents in captivity. In the 1874 appraisal, after the Baron of Guaribú had been deceased for more than a decade and the buying of new slaves had almost ceased, there were six third-generation families with fourteen third-generation children. A family's longevity could extend to a fifth generation. Nazário and his *crioulo* son Venceslau, for example, worked on the Sítio dos Encantos. In 1863, Venceslau was married to Fortunata from Monjolo. He was father to Emília, Teolinda, Ventura, and Alexandrina, as well as

[36] Centro de Documentação Histórica (CDH), Vassouras Archive, Inventário Barão do Guaribú, 1863.

TABLE 3.2 *Slave families: Guaribu, Antas, and Encantos plantations.*

Family Types	Guaribú		Antas		Encantos	
	1863	1874	1863	1874	1863	1874
Couples without children	25	19	12	7	1	0
Mothers/grandparents with children/ grandchildren	17	17	8	10	0	2
Fathers/grandparents with children/ grandchildren	0	3	4	4	0	0
Couples with children and/or other relatives	38	14	28	24	6	4
Total families	80	53	52	55	7	6

Source: CDH-Vassouras Archive. Inventário Barão do Guaribú, 1863.[37]

grandfather to Emília's children, Fortunata and Faustino. The family probably lived in one or two of the Encanto *senzala*'s twenty-two cubicles. In 1885, Nazário had died, but his great-granddaughters Fortunata and Alexandrina had already given birth to five free children, Manoel, Cecília, Maximiliano, Felisberta, and Ludovica.

Secondly, family structures varied across time, and slave households often generated new family units. This process reinforces the impression that these were stable families but also suggests that the slave family was a dynamic structure, in constant transformation. Enslaved people recognized the family units among them and sought to ensure their permanence through internal mechanisms of control, such as those that prohibited incest and infanticide or protected orphans. Finally, the advanced age of many of the African-born slaves was a clear sign that the plantation community was well established and had become a stable space where enduring relationships could be forged among slaves, freedpersons, free workers, and masters.

The family of Romualdo and Thereza, both from Mozambique, allows us to explore this dynamic. As was mentioned earlier, Romualdo was

---

[37] We opted not to include the 1885 reassessment in this table, because its lists separated those declared free by virtue of the Free Womb Law from the rest of their families. This new organizational logic, a partial result of the law itself, complicates the comparative analysis of family composition across time. Similarly, the Boa União *fazenda* does not appear in the table, because it had no slave families in 1863. Boa União's 1874 slave families are counted together with those of Antas, since they had been combined in the two other assessments.

thirty-five and Thereza was twenty in 1841, when they were listed as Luís Gomes Ribeiro's property. They had two children, five-year-old Felisbina and one-year-old Sebastião. The family remained together even after Ribeiro's death, as seems to have been common in estates with large concentrations of slave property.[38] Twenty-two years later, in 1863, the couple had had another son, Marcelino, who had been born one year after his brother Sebastião. Romualdo had already died, but his forty-two-year-old widow Thereza was the grandmother of Daniel (eleven), Cândida (nine), Bernardino (nine), and Romualdo (three), who was his grandfather's namesake. Unfortunately, the inventory did not reveal those children's parentage. Nonetheless, it is clear that this family, like many others within that plantation community, remained together for over forty years (1841–1885), having moved from Guaribú to Antas sometime between 1874 and 1885.

The resilience of slave family dynamics in this plantation community emerges when we use postmortem inventories to trace the fates of children who lost their mothers. Anselmo, from Mozambique, remained with his *crioulo* children Helena and Anselmo after the death of his wife. Nazario, also widowed, raised his son Venceslau, who later married Fortunata. They had four children, Alexandrina, Emília, Theodora, and Ventura. When Alexandrina gave birth to Faustino and Fortunata, Nazario's great-grandchildren, a family that had once been reduced to father and son extended to a fourth generation. The estate appraiser's annotations in the Baron of Guaribu's will suggest that the stability of the slave family was understood as an organizing principle, not only among slaves but also among slaveowners and legal representatives: he listed the *crioulos* João (twenty-seven), Idalina (twenty-five), Rosa (twenty-three), and Raphael (twenty-one) as orphans despite the fact that they were adults, in clear recognition that they were siblings who belonged to the same family and ought to be kept together when the estate was partitioned among its heirs.

Significantly, plantation communities within the same agrarian empire were not isolated from one another. The curtailment of free circulation was of course a constitutive element of enslavement and

---

[38] In Florentino and Goes' sample for Rio between 1790 and 1835, three of every four families remained together after the death of the slaveowning patriarch in large plantations. In Garavazo's study of Batatais, São Paulo, the proportion was 86 percent. This did not occur in *fazendas* with smaller numbers of slaves, where they were more susceptible to separation. See M. Florentino and J. Goes, *A paz* and J. Garavazo, "Relações familiares."

an important instrument of control in the hands of slaveowners. But there was still carefully monitored movement among properties that were part of the same coffee complex. Archival documents such as the journal of the Viscountess of Arcozelo, for example, indicated that slaves often moved among properties in order to carry out specific tasks during periods when work rhythms were most intense.[39] Similarly, slaves with specialized skills were sometimes temporarily reassigned to the raw labor of coffee cultivation. Slaves were frequently sent on errands, carrying messages and goods or making purchases; they were also sometimes permitted to date or to attend parties, baptisms, or collective weddings. The Baron of Guaribú's will, drafted on August 26, 1863, a few days before his death, shows us that the movement within a coffee complex could involve an entire family, lending further support to the argument that the family was the basis for labor stability and a sense of common purpose in plantation communities. Claudio Ribeiro de Avellar noted:

The following slaves are now present at the Fazenda Guaribú, although they belong to the Fazenda das Antas and are part of that place: Marçal, a carpenter, with his wife, children and brothers; Faustino Inhambane, a construction worker; Joaquim, a construction worker; Inhambane and his family; Albério Inhambane; Thomas Caseiro; Modesto Caseir; Luiz Inhambane, a muleteer, with his family; Matheus, a muleteer, Messias, a muleteer; Antonio Moçambique, a muleteer; Simão Crioulo; Germano Inhambane, a cook; and Sabino, a muleteer.[40]

Claudio Ribeiro de Avellar's instructions were clear: after finishing their tasks at Guaribú, the slaves should return to their place of residence, the Antas plantation community. Regarding slave mobility, the Baron of Guaribú also included another interesting directive: he asked that his sons Manoel, Luís, and João Gomes Ribeiro de Avellar, heirs of the Antas and Boa União properties, also select 120 slaves from Guaribú as part of their inheritance. In his own words: "I leave to Manoel Gomes Ribeiro de Avellar and his two brothers, Luís and João, one hundred and twenty slaves from the Fazenda Guaribú, which Manuel shall choose at his discretion." The order was carried out, and three Guaribú families were inventoried at the Fazenda das Antas in 1885. The case of Matheus

---

[39] In the Viscountess of Arcozelo's diary, she wrote that on September 12 "Castro sent the folks from Piedade to harvest coffee here: I sent 6 young girls and two cooks to pick coffee." See A. Mauad and M. Mauze, "A escrita da intimidade."

[40] Archive of Iphan-Vassouras, last testament of Claudio Gomes Ribeiro de Avellar, 1863.

Moçambique (fifty-one years old) and Feliciana – parents to Manoel Lino (sixteen), Emerenciana (eleven), the twins Magdalena and Helena (nine), and Feliciana (three) – stands out. In 1885, when he was listed as part of Antas' enslaved property, Matheus was eighty-five, and the siblings Manoel Lino and Helena were the only relatives who were no longer part of the family unit. We cannot say why or at what moment between 1863 and 1885 the family was transferred. But when Matheus was chosen by the Baron's heirs he was certainly very elderly. The will did not require that the heirs respect family units in choosing their 120 slaves. Nevertheless, Matheus was sent along with his family, despite the fact that he was no longer able to work and had virtually no market value, a fact that highlights the importance of the slave family within the plantation community.

Whether they were sent to another *fazenda* to work or to participate in religious celebrations, funerals, or collective slave baptisms, the fact is that captives' spatial experience extended far beyond the boundaries of the plantations where they lived. Even when moves were permanent, like those previously described, the slaves and families we could follow in Gomes Ribeiro de Avellar's inventories were transferred from one community to another but did not go to an entirely unknown or indecipherable space (though this could and did happen in other sales or when slaves ran away). Whether or not their masters recognized it, enslaved people who moved among properties that formed part of the same agrarian empire created webs of solidarity and ties of love and marriage, and they also experienced intrapersonal conflict. In this way, they created every day what Anthony Kaye has referred to as "slave neighborhoods."[41] Yet Kaye's concept of a "slave neighborhood" rejects the prima facie assumption of slave autonomy and harmonious collaboration, seeking also to

---

[41] A. Kaye, *Joining Places*, pp. 4–7. Kaye's introduction analyzes critical debates surrounding the notion of slave community in North America since the 1970s, focusing especially on critiques that equate community with closed, solidarious, harmonious group dynamics without recognizing internal tensions and disputes. The concept of a "slave neighborhood" understands resistance as something that plays out in a spatialized "terrain of struggle," emphasizing the complexity of alliances and expressions of agency therein. In this conception, it would be a mistake to analyze resistance without relating it to seignorial power. Struggles emerged on unexpected grounds and included alliances between slaves and masters as well as alliances among slaves; similarly, conflicts occurred among slaves and among masters as well as between masters and slaves, encompassing a broad spectrum of associations and possibilities. In this chapter, we have elected to use the broad term "plantation community." All the same, Kaye's conceptions of slave neighborhoods and masters' neighborhoods help us to think through the spatial dimensions of agrarian empires.

take into account the slave–master relationship; there is no slave neighborhood without a larger neighborhood largely controlled by masters. Slave neighborhoods were at once individual and collective creations; they were places of work and of leisure, of dispute and of collaboration, of spiritual encouragement and of brutal exploitation, which expanded and contracted depending on both internal and external factors. Slave neighborhoods were home to a wide range of relationships among their social actors, which included field slaves, domestic slaves, masters, free workers, and more. We argue in this chapter that the concept of the slave neighborhood also has an important territorial dimension; its various spatial components – including roads, forest paths, neighboring *fazendas*, nearby cities, escape routes, and ritual spaces – were always interspersed within and enveloped by a master's neighborhood.

CONCLUSION

The analysis of the family ties established by slaves in the Baron of Guaribá's agrarian empire between 1840 and 1880 allows us to reflect more broadly on the importance of the slave family in creating plantation communities in the Paraíba Valley's coffee regions. The profile of the slave family changed significantly with the end of the Atlantic slave trade, when a more even gender balance allowed for considerable growth in the number of slave families. This denser family formation was a fundamental characteristic of "mature slavery" in Brazil, which we define as the point at which plantation structures were well established and stable and when slavery came to be sustained through natural increase without a need for imported slaves. Within plantation communities, slave families – with their forms of sociability, religious beliefs, affective ties, disputes, and quarrels – were fundamental to the process through which slaves became an effective collective labor force. The fact that the same families stayed together on the same plantation over many generations demonstrates their structural importance to the slave system as a whole. What is more, slaves' integrated spatial experiences were not limited to plantation communities; they also participated in Kaye's larger "slave neighborhoods," the fluid boundaries of which extended the unequal symbiosis inherent in the plantation community to broader regional geographies.

4

Motherhood Silenced

Enslaved Wet Nurses in Nineteenth-Century Brazil

Mariana Muaze*

As for the "black mammies," tradition tells us that they held a true place of honor in the bosom of the patriarchal family. When freed, they would almost always round out into enormous negresses. Everyone fulfilled their whims; children asked for their blessing, the slaves treated them as ladies, the coachmen took them out in their carriages. On holidays, anyone who saw them, expansive and presumptuous among the whites of the big house, would have taken them for well-born gentlewomen, never imagining they were slaves from the senzala. . . . It was natural that the *negra* or *mulata* who breastfed the master's son, lulled him to sleep, prepared his food and warm baths, attended to his clothing, told him stories, and at times served as a surrogate mother would have been chosen from the best slaves of the senzala.[1]

In this well-known description, Gilberto Freyre – one of Brazil's most important twentieth-century intellectuals – highlighted Brazilian wet nurses' ability to adapt themselves to the Brazilian patriarchal family. For Freyre, Black culture, characterized as affectionate, creative, and docile, seeped into the intimate domestic relationships of Brazil's plantation houses and urban mansions, helping to forge a master–slave relationship that allowed many Blacks to be seen as part of their masters' family.[2]

Understood in its original context, Freyre's writing constituted a counter-discourse, both opposed to racist theories that were still fashionable in the 1930s and meant to recover and exalt Afro-descendants' role in forging

---

* Translated by Brodwyn Fischer.
[1] G. Freyre, *Casa grande*, 25th edition, p. 352. Translation adapted from Samuel Putnam's (G. Freyre, *The Masters*, pp. 369–370).
[2] R. B. de Araújo, *Guerra e paz*; É. Bastos, "Gilberto Freyre."

Brazilian culture and national identity. In Freyre's view, two decisive forces had shaped Brazilian society: patriarchal domination, which encompassed not only the family but also slaves, lesser masters, and free men; and the scarcity of white women during Brazil's first centuries of colonization, which allowed for high levels of intimate sociability between the dominators and the dominated. Freyre understood the kindness that purportedly characterized Afro-descendants as emblematic of the Brazilian slave–master relationship, a notion that fomented the so-called myth of racial democracy that gained importance in Brazil between 1920 and the 1950s.[3]

Since then, however, historians have repeatedly interrogated and challenged Freyre's notions of docile slavery. In the 1980s, inspired by the women's history movement, Maria Odila Leite Dias and Sandra Lauderdale Graham foregrounded the role of female resistance in the households of nineteenth-century São Paulo and Rio de Janeiro; their work was crucial in placing the relationships between masters and domestic servants – and especially wet nurses – at the center of Brazilian studies of slavery and abolition.[4] In recent years, these topics have received ever more attention.[5] Scholars are unanimous in emphasizing the hierarchical nature of domestic slave labor, and they also stress the place of the wet nurse at the summit of this hierarchy.[6]

All the same, there is still much to be done. This chapter will argue that, while the relationships between masters and slaves in the private sphere did involve affection, dedication, and loyalty, they were also gestated in an environment of abuse, humiliation, and physical and symbolic violence, all of which were essential features of slavery as an institution. Interactions that might be read initially as paradoxical or ambiguous were in fact constitutive of slavery's ideology of domination, experienced and enacted in various ways by both masters and slaves within Brazil's Big Houses and mansions.[7] What is more, the figure of the wet nurse and the practice of relegating breastfeeding to enslaved women – which was generalized among Brazil's dominant classes during the Empire – helped

---

[3] G. R. Andrews, *Blacks and Whites*; J. Needell, "Identity, Race, Gender and Modernity"; L. Schwartz, *O espetáculo*; R. B. de Araújo, *Guerra e paz*; M. Chor Maio, "UNESCO"; É. Bastos, "Gilberto Freyre"; B. Fischer, "Quase pretos"; P. Alberto, *Terms of Inclusion*.
[4] M. O. L. Dias, *Quotidiano e poder*; S. L. Graham, *House and Street* and "O impasse."
[5] M. Matos, "Porta adentro"; M. Carvalho, "De portas adentro"; O. Cunha, "Criadas para servir"; M. Muaze, "O que fará essa gente"; M. Arisa, "Bad Mothers."
[6] M. Muaze, "A descoberta"; M. Ribeiro Carneiro, "Procura-se preta"; B. Martins, "Amas-de-leite"; S. Koutsoukos, "O valor da aparência"; M. H. Machado, "Between Two Beneditos."
[7] L. F. Alencastro, ed., *História da vida privada*, v. II.

to forge a slavocratic habitus, a kind of second nature, in which future masters experienced the social relationships of slavery within their intimate circles and everyday lives from a very tender age.[8] This chapter analyzes these domestic and extremely conflictual interactions as an integral part of the slave system, critical to the symbolic and social reproduction of Brazil's master class.

The study of enslaved wet nurses allows us to explore the limits of a private dynamic that distilled the myriad sentiments that constituted the slave–master relationship in the domestic sphere.[9] A wet nurse was allowed to live and participate in her masters' intimate social world, but without ever overcoming her status as property or escaping the physical and symbolic violence to which every slave was subject. Her body remained commodified: her task was to breastfeed the master's child and care for his or her hygiene and physical education, keeping the child's body healthy until early childhood, when the nurse's nurturing services would no longer be needed. Breastfeeding and childcare were sometimes a wet nurse's only duties, but often wet nurses were often charged with other chores as well. In most cases, wet nursing implied the "silencing" of a woman's own motherhood: enslaved women were forced to give up the feeding of their own children in order to nurture their mistresses' babies. After her infant charge matured, a wet nurse could become an *ama seca* (literally "dry nurse" or nanny), be assigned to another service in the big house, or be returned to the sphere of productive work outside the home (which was especially common when a nurse served her owners' children or relatives). If a wet nurse was rented out – as was frequently the case in urban environments – she would be returned to her master and might never again see the child she had raised.

Contrary to Gilberto Freyre's description, "everyone" did not fulfill the wet nurses' "whims." The intimacy inherent in the nurse's work may have allowed many captives to live a bit better within the system that oppressed them every day; they might have enjoyed better clothing, food, and shelter than field slaves or *escravos de ganho* (those whose services were rented to

---

[8] As defined by Norbert Elias, *habitus* is a reflexive way of feeling and acting, a kind of second nature that gradually, and through self-conditioning, becomes a part of an individual's personality. Based on this notion, I argue that, during the Brazilian Empire, the master class was shaping and being shaped by a profoundly hierarchical and aristocratic structure of feeling, which impacted their views of the world and how they saw themselves in it, therefore establishing a slavocratic habitus. This habitus was shared as a behavioral pattern and an element of identity within and outside of the group, but it was also an element of social distinction. On the concept of habitus, see N. Elias, *A sociedade de corte*; *Mi trayectoria intelectual*; *Processo civilizador*, vols. I and II.

[9] T. Glymph, *Out of the House.*

third parties).[10] But the fact remained that the wet nurse's task necessarily involved the silencing of an enslaved woman's own motherhood; both her owner's will and social customs dictated that she would lose the right to live with her own child, even in the baby's first days of life. In that sense, when we consider enslaved wet nurses' living conditions – and the practices of power that such women were subject to – we can understand how slavery operated at the heart of human nature, seeking to negate an enslaved person's humanity and build a slavocratic habitus that would naturalize the hierarchical relationships that structured Brazilian slavery.[11] And not only that: the slavocratic habitus extended beyond the dominant classes, becoming in a certain sense hegemonic.[12] As newspaper advertisements attest, the use of enslaved wet nurses – along with other dominant practices – became widespread among other social classes, who devised a variety of contractual methods and price points to meet their perceived needs.

In analyzing slave agency through the figure of the wet nurse, this chapter takes a relational approach.[13] After all, the use of enslaved wet nurses – and the broader market that was created for nursing services – depended on slaveowning women's belief that the decision not to nurse one's own children was a form of social distinction. Unlike their North American counterparts, Brazilian historians have largely neglected this inseverable link, shying away from considering the role of white mistresses in the widely disseminated practice of enslaved wet-nursing.[14]

"FOR RENT: A GOOD WET NURSE": THE NEGATION OF MATERNAL BREASTFEEDING AS A SOCIAL PRACTICE IN NINETEENTH-CENTURY BRAZIL

Between the thirteenth and eighteenth centuries, it was common practice among wealthy European women to avoid breastfeeding. For much of this long period, the Catholic Church condemned maternal nursing; this stance was based largely in the philosophy of Saint Augustine, who believed that children were beings crushed by the weight of original sin and saw breastfeeding as a "voluptuous practice" that encouraged vice in

---

[10] M. Carvalho, "De portas adentro."   [11] M. R. Trouillot, *Silencing the Past.*
[12] R. Salles and M. Borges, "A morte do barão."
[13] W. Johnson, *River of Dark Dreams*; T. Glymph, *Out of the House*; S. Jones-Rogers, "She Could Spare."
[14] T. Glymph, *Out of House*; E. Fox-Genovese, *Within the Plantation*; S. Jones-Rogers, "She Could Spare."

newborns and their mothers alike.[15] Although some doctors and theologians exalted breastfeeding, believing it was God's will or nature's calling, their views had scant impact. Thus, from the thirteenth century forward, aristocratic families commonly hired "internal" wet nurses, who lived in until an infant was weaned. Beginning in the seventeenth century, bourgeois families followed suit; by the 1700s, the practice had spread to the middle classes in countries like France, Italy, England, and Portugal, where the women were referred to as *saloias*.[16]

Upper-class women declined to nurse their babies for physical, moral, and sexual reasons: nursing was thought to deform a woman's breasts and body and to be harmful to women's naturally delicate health; the act of breastfeeding signaled a lack of modesty that was beneath the dignity of a lady, stimulating excessive sensuality and desire; and it was thought that sexual activity would contaminate a woman's milk and had to be curtailed for as long as she nursed. Little by little, outsourced breastfeeding, which was originally recommended only in cases where a mother died or was physically incapacitated, came to be understood as a mark of social distinction and a safeguard of feminine morality.[17] Despite some criticism, Brazil's wealthy classes hired women to work in their homes, which allowed them to exercise more control over their children's health and daily life.[18]

In Brazil, this social practice found legal grounding in the Philippine Code (a body of law that structured Brazilian law for more than two centuries after its publication in 1603), which "recognized that some women, because of their rank – that is, their high social status – might not wish to breastfeed their children."[19] And while European wet nurses were generally white, in Portuguese America enslaved Black women generally nurtured their masters' children. The arrival in Rio of the Portuguese Royal Court in 1808 catalyzed this practice, greatly expanding

---

[15] E. Badinter, *O mito*; P. Ariès, *História social*. Until the seventeenth century, some philosophers and theologians showed an actual "fear of childhood." Among them was Saint Augustine, who created a dramatic portrait of children that were in no way differentiated from their parents' sin. Based on this conception, some pedagogical methods emphasized coldness in relation to children. One example is J. L. Vivés' 1542 *Instruction of a Christian Woman*, where he stated: "Pleasures are the things which most debilitate the body, and for this reason, mothers lose their children when they voluptuously breastfeed them" (E. Badinter, *O mito*, p. 57).

[16] C. Heywood, *Uma história*, p. 89; J. Golden, *A Social History*.

[17] The practice of replacing a mother's milk with other forms of nutrition (baby food, flours, milk from animals, etc.) or for mercenary breastfeeding is very old. The Code of Hamurabi already included regulations about wet nurses, as did the codes of Ancient Greece and Rome.

[18] E. Badinter, *O mito*, p. 70.   [19] M. Silva, *Vida privada*, p. 14.

the market for enslaved women who had just given birth. For the nineteenth century, wet nursing by enslaved women is amply documented in
travel narratives, personal letters, lithographs, and photographs, as well
as in countless specialized journal articles and classified advertisements for
the purchase, sale, and rental of wet nurses and their services.[20]

For Sale: a wet nurse with abundant milk of superior quality, with or without her
3-month-old son: may be sold with or without him. A demure and dedicated
housesmaid.

(*Jornal do Commercio*, April 4, 1840)

For Sale: Wet nurse, 640$, one delivery, childless, healthy, good-looking, and
skilled. Inquire at the Beco dos Carmelitas, no. 15.

(*Jornal do Commercio*, August 13, 1840)

For Rent: Wet nurse, at Rua da Cadeia no. 41, a young Black girl with abundant
and very good quality milk, one delivery, childless, a perfect housemaid, very
healthy and with no bad habits.

(*Jornal do Commercio*, October 1, 1845)

For Rent: A Black woman with very good milk, very clean and with no bad habits.
Inquire at Rua Primeiro dos Cajueiros no. 71.

(*Jornal do Commercio*, December 1, 1850)

For Rent: a light-skinned wet nurse, 15, not from Rio, gave birth two months
ago and produces good, abundant milk that can be examined on demand,
guaranteed good conduct: for more information contact Fleuriano & Araujo
Sobrinho at Rua Cortello no. 25, general store.

(*Jornal do Commercio*, May 5, 1878)

In Europe, outsourced breastfeeding was done by peasant women who
did not have to abandon their own babies; in Brazil, by contrast, wet
nurses were generally not allowed to nurture or care for their children.
We can discern this norm in the first advertisement quoted here, which
leaves the purchase of the wet nurse's child to the buyer's discretion, with
no concern for the three-month-old infant's fate should the mother be
sold alone. In the other ads, the enslaved women's children are not even
mentioned; it was quite uncommon for mothers and babies to be obliga-
torily sold together.[21] Research into the *Jornal do Commeércio*'s classified

[20] J. F. Costa, *Ordem médica*; M. Silva, *Vida privada*; M. Ribeiro Carneiro, "Procura-se";
J. S. Jones-Rogers, "She Could Spare."
[21] Among 1,283 advertisements for domestic slaves published in *Jornal do Commercio* in
April, August, and December 1840, only one announced that it was obligatory to purchase a mother and child together. The other ones were silent with regard to the slave's
offspring, who could have died during or after birth or could have been left in the *roda dos*

ads for the months of April, August, and December in 1840, 1850, and
1871 ratifies studies that have already shown that the hiring of wet nurses
was common practice in nineteenth-century Rio de Janeiro and its provincial territories.[22] It was part of the system that reproduced the slavocratic habitus, fomented as much by those who made a business from
reaping wet-nursing profits as by families who hired wet nurses out of
necessity or a desire for social distinction.

Most wet nurses, in both urban and rural homes, were asked to perform
other domestic tasks at the same time that they cared for newborns – thus
the mention in classified ads of nurses who were "skilled" or "perfect
housemaids." In the wealthiest households, wet nurses could dedicate
themselves exclusively to a baby's care, but all the same most sellers
advertised a nurse's other virtues and skills – "devoted in the household
arts," "she knows how to iron, launder, and sew perfectly," "demure,"
"modest," "good at ladies' hairdressing," "a good cook" – in order to
convince buyers that the women would be useful in the household during
and after their period of lactation. In terms of price, a comparison of the
1840s and the 1850s shows that the cost of wet-nursing increased after the
end of the slave trade in 1850, along with the general rise in slave prices
(especially those of enslaved women). In that decade, the quantity of ads
also increased considerably, suggesting that there was a general market
valorization of pregnant or lactating slaves. The sale or rental of enslaved
wet nurses was an important and profitable economic activity in the major
cities of the Brazilian Empire and would remain so in subsequent decades.
In the 1870s, however, the wet-nursing labor force seems to have diversi-
fied considerably, with the entry of free women of color and poor white
women, many of whom were immigrants.[23]

Most wet nurses were hired by families with newborn babies or nursing
children. But nurses were also hired to care for orphans in institutions such
as the *roda dos expostos*, or "baby wheel," which had been founded in
Brazil in the eighteenth century in order to protect abandoned babies and

---

expostos (the place where mothers anonymously gave young babies over to charity) or
   even at the original master's house.
[22] M. Silva, *Vida privada*; M. Muaze, "A descoberta"; B. Martins, "Amas-de-leite e mercado
   de trabalho feminino"; M. Ribeiro Carneiro, "Procura-se"; S. Koutsoukos, *Negros no
   estúdio*; K. Carula, "Perigosas amas"; M. H. Machado, "Between Two Beneditos."
[23] M. Ariza, "Bad Mothers." As a consequence of this diversification, the Brazilian state
   passed a law regulating wet nurses' work in 1878, and different counties followed it with
   their own municipal laws.

save their souls, providing baptism, food, and care until they were old enough to work.[24]

The *roda dos expostos* of the Santa Casa de Misericórdia seeks to rent nurses to feed the children abandoned there: those who wish to offer their services should go to the Rua da Alfândega no. 14.

(Jornal do Commercio, October 12, 1850)

Historian Luiz Carlos Soares has argued that many masters obliged enslaved women to abandon their babies in the *roda dos expostos* because childless women's services fetched a higher price. In doing so, they opted for the certainty of immediate profit, as any earnings that a baby might have produced if he or she survived early childhood were quite uncertain.[25] Historian Maria Elizabeth Ribeiro Carneiro has shown that the overwhelming majority of wet nurses employed by the Casa da Roda (Rio's public "baby wheel") between 1847 and 1888 were enslaved.[26] Their masters – the men who profited from their work – were counselors of state, barons, priests, judges, doctors, and other members of the slaveowning class. Both Soares and Carneiro show that infant abandonment and the selling or rental of wet nurses were interlinked social practices in nineteenth-century Brazilian society. They were rooted in the open social acceptance of the exploitation of women's bodies in the slavocratic Empire.

In intense conversation with their Continental counterparts, Brazilian doctors and educators translated European manuals on early childhood education, seeking to guide families in their choice of wet nurses and advise them on their children's moral and physical instruction.[27] Excerpts from these manuals were published in women's weeklies or "instructional and recreational" magazines, with or without alterations that catered to Brazil's slavocratic reality:

Selecting a wet nurse is such a delicate task that it requires maximum caution and vigilance. She must be perfect. She will not do if she is cross-eyed, or very fat, or very thin. She should be cheerful, and ought to have good manners, good teeth, and good breath. It is important to examine her gums, because any trace of scurvy

---

[24] The *roda dos expostos* was created in Italy and was used throughout the Portuguese Empire. It was brought to Brazil in 1726, first in Bahia and then in several other cities: Rio de Janeiro (1738), Recife (1789), São Paulo (1825), Desterro (1828), and Cuiabá (1833). The wet nurses rented by the *roda dos expostos* would take care of the abandoned children until they were three years old. M. Marcílio, *História social*, p. 59; Venâncio, "Maternidade negada."

[25] L. Soares, O "povo de Cam," chapter 4, "Escravidão doméstica."

[26] M. Ribeiro Carneiro, "Procura-se."

[27] M. Muaze, "A descoberta" and "Garantindo hierarquias."

could be very harmful for a child. Medium-sized breasts are preferable to large ones, and brunettes are preferable to women who are fair, freckled, redheaded or ugly.

(Dr. César Augusto Marques, *Revista Popular*, 4:14 (April 15, 1862))

When it came to choosing wet nurses on the basis of health and hygiene concerns, Brazil's slaveholding upper and middle classes depended to a certain extent on literal translations of European manuals. But their content was resignified in the context of slavery. The enslaved nurse took the place of the European peasant. The appropriation of an enslaved body, justified as an exercise of property rights and a confirmation of the slavocratic habitus, took the place of free labor. A comparison of the imported normative literature with newspaper advertisements shows that this resignification was accomplished quite successfully. The characteristics most valued among wet nurses in Rio de Janeiro's slave markets were: youth (buyers preferred women between the ages of fifteen and thirty); good health; a childbirthing history that included only one delivery; the ability to produce abundant, good-quality milk; demonstrated "good behavior," which meant the woman was modest and home-bound; and possession of a "good temperament," most frequently defined as being calm, affectionate, peaceful, patient, and friendly to children. Beyond this, parents were advised to regulate a wet nurse's diet, consumption of alcoholic spirits, and sexual life in order to guarantee that their children consumed good-quality milk: experts recommended that it be "white and evenly colored, without yellow shadows, with a sweet taste and a substantial consistency."[28] Such recommendations were very close to those detailed in European manuals, but Brazilian classified ads also included descriptions such as *parda*, *crioula*, *preta*, and *preta da nação*, designations of color and status that both clearly marked the border between slavery and freedom and allowed potential buyers to identify which captives they might wish to acquire. Unlike *mucamas* (housemaids) and *pagens* (valets), whose physical beauty was heavily promoted, wet nurses were valued for their health, age, and ability to produce abundant milk.

For Rent: A very good *parda* wet nurse, very affectionate with children, with ample good milk; anyone who would like to have her should go to the Rua da Lapa no. 67.

(*Jornal do Commercio*, August 22, 1840)

---

[28] A. M. de Almeida, *Pensando a família*, p. 131.

For Rent: a *crioula* wet nurse with a great abundance of milk from her first delivery, 18 years old with a good disposition and a way with children, polite; Rua Bom Jardim no. 53.

(Jornal do Commercio, April 16, 1840)

For Rent: a Black African wet nurse, young and modest, with abundant good milk from her first delivery, she is very healthy and affectionate with children: at Rua do Rosário no. 61.

(Jornal do Commercio, December 8, 1840)

Breastfeeding by enslaved wet nurses was a widely disseminated practice among Brazil's wealthy classes until the late nineteenth century. Yet from 1850 forward, the custom attracted increasing criticism. Under the influence of Rousseau's *Emile*, medical and scientific discourse condemned "mercenary" breastfeeding in Europe and Brazil.[29] This emergent vision held that breastfeeding was a mother's highest function. To not perform it was an act against feminine nature, an impediment to the nascent love between a mother and a child, a denial of a woman's most important calling. The only acceptable reasons for a woman to bow out of the full realization of her maternity (which began with breastfeeding) were illness or death. In the new medical discourse, breastfeeding by nurses would only be accepted in order to guarantee a newborn's survival in the event of a mother's absence or incapacitation. This ever-strengthening narrative advocated a new vision of the mother, who was now understood as the central protagonist in the education and instruction of the Empire's future citizens; it also reimagined every role within Brazil's nineteenth-century aristocratic families, placing increasing value on childhood, women's education, and men's patriarchal leadership.[30]

The debate over breastfeeding sparked a war of opinions in the press that extended well past slavery's abolition.[31] Some doctors, such as Antônio Ferreira Pinto, believed that enslaved wet nurses were superior to free ones, because the former lived "in hopes of bettering their condition ... stirred by the expectation of social distinction, friendship, food, compensation or even freedom on the part of their masters or the

---

[29] E. Badinter, *O mito*; E. Shorter, *A formação*; J. L. Flandrin, *Famílias, parentesco*; A. Burguière and F. Lebrun, eds., *Histoire de la famille*; J. Golden, *A Social History*; M. Muaze, "A descoberta"; K. Carula, "Perigosas amas."

[30] M. Muaze, *As memórias.*

[31] Deeper analysis on this confrontation shows that criticism of slave breastfeeding increased during the decades of 1870 and 1880, when other factors such as the abolitionist movement, pressure from the slaves, and moral criticisms of slavery added strength to doctors' concerns about familial hygiene.

parents who rented their services."[32] Such arguments reinforced slavocratic discourse and resonated widely. Yet periodicals such as
O Constitucional and *A Mãe de Família* argued the contrary, summarily
disqualifying enslaved women:

> An infant fed with the mercenary milk of an African woman learns and
> imitates her customs and habits during the first phase of life, the child will
> reach puberty like the inhabitants of central Africa, his speech full of errors,
> with the strangest possible terminology serving as language.
>
> (*O Constitucional*, July 5, 1853)

> African women, stupid, full of had habits, without affection.
>
> (Carlos Costa, "Palestra do medico," *A Mãi de Família*, May 1879)[33]

Notwithstanding the intense battle fought out in the press, in the
medical theses of Brazil's Imperial Academy of Medicine, and in early
childhood education manuals, enslaved wet-nursing endured among
families of the seigneurial class who could continue to afford the costs
of renting or buying nurses even as the slave system entered into crisis in
the 1870s and 1880s. The new familial ideals prescribed that mothers
should bear the greatest responsibility for their children's care and
education, in which breastfeeding played an important role. But in the
private sphere, the slavocratic habitus – regulated by discretionary,
authoritarian, and hierarchical relationships – spoke louder. There,
despite normative medical discourse, white women's exemption from
breastfeeding persisted as a sign of social differentiation and symbolic
reproduction of the dominant class. In debate with strong scientific
criticism, some ads in the *Jornal do Commercio* between 1878 and
1880 offered clients the opportunity to send a nurse's milk for examination before she was hired, thus guaranteeing her cleanliness and
hygiene. In this way, as historian Ilmar Mattos has observed,[34] the
"house" resisted the transformations that the "street" desired, incorporating only those elements that were deemed convenient: a woman's
role as educator, the valorization of childhood, closer parent–child
relationships, the importance of extended family, and the patriarch's
organizing role. Newspaper ads, travellers' accounts, letters exchanged
between relatives, and images of wet nurses preserved in family collections and public and private archives throughout Brazil all bore witness:
the new familial order would not sacrifice the slavocratic habitus.

---

[32] A. F. Pinto, *O médico*, cited in L. F. Alencastro, *História da vida*, pp. 203–207.
[33] Quoted in K. Carula, "Perigosas amas," p. 201.   [34] I. Mattos, *O tempo Saquarema*.

For Love and the Right of Ownership

My Dear daughter,
Like your mother, you were born in Brazil and a slave [Julia Monjola] gave you her milk to drink ... She asked, in tears, as if you could understand, that you never forget the one who held you in her arms and put you to sleep at her bosom every day. And that if some day you became rich, you might buy her so that she would be only yours.
(letter from Charles Expilly to his daughter Martha, Paris, June 1863)[35]

The production of nineteenth-century narratives about wet nurses was quite unequal. Those most easily found by historians were produced by the dominant class, which exercised greater control over the production of discourse. The historian's challenge, then, is to give voice to subaltern groups by way of documents that sought not to erase but rather to silence them.[36] Such is the case of Epilly's letter to his daughter, as well as many other private family documents; such too was the case of the many photographic portraits of enslaved wet nurses commissioned by wealthy Brazilian families during the Empire.

Portraits were the most ubiquitous genre of photography in the nineteenth century. The custom of sitting for and collecting photos spread quickly among the seigneurial class beginning in the 1860s, when the *carte de visite* format arrived in Brazil.[37] Under the reign of the portrait, social groups distinguished themselves from others, constructing their social identity through visual markers. The portrait, which involved choosing the best possible pose for the mise en scène of the photographic studio, signaled the adoption of a particular lifestyle and social standard. In this way, such images enabled the dominant class's self-representation and circulated through mutual exchanges among family and friends. Research in a number of portrait albums indicates that the great majority of portraits (both male and female) were individual.[38] Children, however, could pose alone, in groups, or in pairs, often accompanied only by their wet nurses or nannies. The main motive for any child's trip to the photographer's studio was a desire to

---

[35] C. Expilly, *Mulheres e costumes*, pp. 9–10.   [36] M. R. Trouillot, *Silencing the Past*.

[37] In Brazil, photographs helped to project images and to build self-images in Second Empire society. During this time, photographic production was based on two aesthetic models: the photographic portrait (with sizes varying from the *carte de visite* format, in which a 6 × 9.5 cm photograph was glued on a 6.5 × 10.5 cm card, to the *cabinet size*, in which a 10 × 14 cm photograph was glued on a 16.5 cm card); and the scenic photograph, generally developed on large-scale plates (18 × 24 cm). M. Muaze, *As memórias*.

[38] M. Muaze, *As memórias*; A. Mauad, "O poder."

perpetuate the memory of family and childhood.[39] Yet portraits such as those in Figure 4.1 also had a pedagogical function: the scene aimed to eternalize slavery and its power relations through the figure of the captive nurse, and thus help to construct and perpetuate the slavocratic habitus.

The images in Figure 4.1 reveal the interdependence between the family order and the slave order in nineteenth-century Brazil. They are part of a still-tiny group of photos of enslaved wet nurses that have been located in private and public archives by Brazilian researchers.[40] Captured in

FIGURE 4.1 *Carte cabinet,* Antonio da Silva Lopes Cardozo, National Archives, Bahia, 1868; *carte de visite,* Carneiro e Gaspar, private collection, Roberto Meneses de Moraes, Rio de Janeiro, 1866–1975.

[39] M. Muaze, *As memórias.*
[40] M. E. Leite, *Retratistas e retratados;* S. Koutsoukos, *Negros no estúdio.*

different moments and spaces, the wet nurses are always accompanied by children, who are usually held on the wet nurses' laps. This is how we see the nurse of the young Antonio da Costa Pinto, son of the Baron of Oliveira and Maria Rita Lopes da Costa Pinto, important members of the Bahian sugar aristocracy; and Vitorina, nurse to a girl named Maria Eliza, part of the Pereira da Silva Porto family, which made a living in the 1860s from the exploitation of slaves for hire in Rio but had made its fortune through international slave trafficking until the trade became illegal in the early 1830s.[41] The poses chosen for such portraits were usually similar and resembled those that were standard among free women, reinforcing the nurse's closeness to the children. All the same, it was clear from the photo's slavocratic visual grammar that the women were captives rather than mothers. The women's beautiful garments were part of a Brazilian ethos unveiled by Expilly: "Among the wealthiest families, possessing a wet nurse was a question of honor and self-regard, as well as an indication of the household's prosperity and wealth."[42]

The first image, with its African shawl and turban, ratified the importance of African customs in the care of infants. The second, by contrast, incorporated contemporary medical critiques, instead projecting the ideal of a hygienic and morally elevated nurse: Vitorina's hair was carefully bound, and her well-cut dress framed her décolletage.[43] Both images represent a modest nurse, like those described in so many classified ads. In spite of a medical-scientific discourse that opposed enslaved wet-nursing, the families who ordered these portraits showed the extent to which the practice was entrenched in familial habit – rooted in love, affection, property rights, or a slavocratic habitus that by its own logic was capable of folding all of those things into one. All the same, the photos of nurses and children reveal "a union grounded in love and past violence: a violence that cracked the slave soul, opening an affective space that is being invaded by the child of her master."[44]

---

[41] The Atlantic slave trade was officially outlawed by the Imperial government in 1831, though that law was poorly enforced. Definitive abolition of the trade followed after 1850. On these laws and their consequences, see B. Mamigonian, *Africanos livres*, and K. Grinberg, "Slavery, Manumission and the Law." The historian Ynae Lopes Santos states that the inventory of Vicente Pereira da Silva Porto, from 1865, presented 250 slaves, of whom 234 were intended for profit and the rest for domestic services. Furthermore, he was the owner of two houses and a lot on the Rua dos Arcos, as well as cars, jewelry, and shares from Banco do Brasil, Companhia de Seguro Fidelidade, and Cia de Tabaco, in Portugal. Y. Santos, *Além da senzala*.

[42] M. E. Leite, *Retratistas e retratados*, p. 115.   [43] S. Koutsoukos, *Negros no estúdio*.

[44] L. F. Alencastro, ed., *História da vida privada*, p. 440.

As artifacts, the wet nurse portraits legitimated a slavocratic habitus that placed pedagogical value on the figure of the loyal, dedicated slave, who lived in hope of winning a master's concessions. In exhibiting well-dressed nurses photographed in expensive, award-winning photography studios such as Carneiro & Gaspar or Lopes Cardoso, the portraits also served as a mark of social differentiation within and between classes. Beyond this, they emerged from families' genuine desires to create memories and immortalize affective ties, even as they also separated subjects from one another in ways that visually reproduced the hierarchies inherent to Brazilian slave society.

These photographs only circulated in private and familiar spheres, where they signified the regard a slave had earned within a family. Yet such esteem originated in that same family's claim to own a wet nurse as property. The enslaved woman was thus fixed in a gray space between a family's affection and the violent fact of having been forcibly separated from her child. This ambiguous emotional position was not necessarily understood as contradictory; affection, violence, and loss were constitutive elements in the slavocratic habitus that was shared within so many of Brazil's big houses and mansions. The images immortalized a nurse's favored position in the eyes of her owner, while silencing the real and symbolic violence inherent in separating her from her child and snuffing out her maternal rights.

The "freedom letters" that families sometimes granted to wet nurses – especially powerful documents because they made the dream of freedom concrete – can be read from this same interpretive perspective.[45] Take, for example, the case of a Black woman named Custódia, wife of Pedro, who was manumitted by Antoinio Rodrigues Barbosa "for having (as a slave) raised my son Luis."[46] Or that of all of the nurses who breastfed the children of Florinda Maria da Silva and Caetano Alves de Oliveira, owners of the Barra Limpa and Ribeirão Frio coffee plantations in the part of the Paraíba Valley that sat within the Province of Rio de Janeiro. Their will stated:

I emancipate my slaves Bento (from Congo) and his wife Claudina (*parda*); José Maria (from Benguela); Diogo (from Angola); Vitorino (from Congo) and his wife Feliciana (from Cabinda); Ana (*crioula*), who nursed my son Francisco; Cristina (from Congo), nurse to my daughter Rita; and Joana, the aged nurse of my daughter Joaquina. And as it is my intention to free from slavery all of the nurses

---

[45] R. Slenes, "Senhores e subalternos"; R. Salles, *E o vale.*
[46] Antonio Rodrigues Barbosa's will, October 31, 11839, Piraí. Arquivo Municipal de Piraí.

who cared for my children, who were already divided among some of my heirs, I authorize the executor named below to pay, at fair value, compensation to whichever of my heirs who might have this right, so that they can arrange to grant those slaves letters of freedom, and I beg my heirs to respect my request.[47]

The master clearly delineated who would ascend to the status of free-dperson and why. Among his 683 captives, Caetano Oliveira granted freedom to only twelve, less than 2 percent. Ana (*crioula*), Cristina (from Congo), and Joana (already aged) were explicitly named; the captives Rosa (from Cabinda) and Joaquina (from Benguela), who had been given away as part of the dowry of Caetano's daughters Maria Florinda Alves and Helena Severina de Oliveira Ferraz, had their manumissions paid for by the estate. In all of these cases, freedom letters were granted only after the patriarch's death, in recognition of good service to the family.[48] Thus understood, manumission reinforced the slave system by legitimizing the image of the "good master" and alleviating the internal tensions of a society where the majority was Black and African.[49]

It is important to note that the inherent violence of a system that deprived enslaved women of the right to feed and care for their children was also an explicit part of the patriarchal playbook. Like the children of Caetano and Florinda Alves de Oliveira, the sons and daughters of Mariana and Joaquim Ribeiro de Avellar, Viscountess and Viscount of Ubá, were also cared for by wet nurses. Owners of more than 700 slaves, the couple also loaned lactating captives to close relatives. In 1862, an African woman from Cabinda named Felisberta was sent to care for Maria Izabel, the Viscountess's niece, after having breastfed her mistress's own children, Júlia and Luísa. Four years later, it fell to an African woman from Mozambique named Bernarda to go to Rio de Janeiro to serve the infant Mariana, the second heir of the Viscountess's brother José Maria

---

[47] Caetano Alves de Oliveira's will, April 1, 1844, Piraí. Arquivo Municipal de Piraí.

[48] Nevertheless, it should be remembered that Custódia and the slaves belonging to Caetano Oliveira were freed in the first half of the 1840s, during a period of great expansion of coffee farming in the Paraíba Valley, which drove a steady upward flow in the illicit slave trade and ensured the easy replacement of freed captives (T. Parron, *A política*; R. Salles, *E o vale*). With the end of the transatlantic slave trade after 1850, the price of slaves rose and the number of manumission letters decreased sharply; for two decades they would become scarce benefits, distributed according to the masters' whims. After the Free Womb Law of 1871, manumission letters began to rise again, first timidly and then quickly as slavery entered into its final crisis. This rise was driven not only by enslaved people's post-1871 entitlement to self-purchase (in full or in installations) but also by the expansion of abolitionism, which drove the establishment of emancipation funds and led masters to use conditional manumission as a tool to keep enslaved laborers working on their lands.

[49] R. Salles, *E o vale*, p. 292.

(also called Juca) and his wife Carolina. In a letter to his sister, Juca sent news about the new wet nurse:

Bernarda is fulfilling her duties very well, she is meeting all of our expect-ations and making us very happy. She is very respectful and thanks you with gratitude for all the constant good news that you send to her through me about her son, she thanks you very, very much for all of the care you bestow on Feliciano. If Bernarda continues this way, as I hope, I will be at ease.

Please send us news of our dear friend Felisberta, we never tire of remembering her seriousness and dignity, and the tokens of concern and friendship that she gave us while she was caring for Maria Izabel, what a lovely creature! Please send her our warm regards and tell her that we always remember her with pleasure. . . .

Your brother and sincere friend,
José Maria[50]

Despite Juca's elation about his family's harmonious and cordial relationship with Bernarda and Felisberta, in practice those ties were generated by a situation of extreme violence. From the sequence of letters, based on the birthdates of the children she served, we can calculate that Felisberta had given birth at least four times: in 1857, 1858, 1862, and 1866. In Bernarda's case, given very high rates of infant mortality, the chances that she would reunite with her son Feliciano when she returned to the provinces were very slim. Yet if she had resisted the post of wet nurse that her mistress offered to her, she would have sparked a conflict that could strip her of the hard-won privileges of a "house slave." Her only option was to do Viscountess Mariana's bidding and implore her to look out for the health of the son she had left in the care of other plantation slaves.

In seigneurial discourse, the praise directed at Felisberta and Bernarda wove together notable elements; competence in the tasks they carried out, good behavior, gratitude, a desire to please, subservience, and recognition of the master–slave hierarchy. In exchange, Juca and Mariana engaged in the "politics of favor" instituted by the slavocratic habitus. Cases like Felisberta's and Bernarda's point to the borderlands that existed within the master–slave relationship. Just like the nurses who were manumitted or depicted in family portraits, these women, through long years of intimate coexistence, came to experience affectionate bonds such as those expressed by Juca, Carolina, and Marica Izabel, who even refered

---

[50] Letter from José Maria Velho da Silva to Mariana Velho de Avellar, Rio de Janeiro, August 4, 1866. Roberto Meneses de Moraes private collection.

to Bernarda as *"mãe* [mother] Beta."[51] All the same, those affective ties were constructed through the coercion, oppression, and violence that necessarily grounded all slave–master relationships.[52]

Like Viscountess Mariana, the Viscountess of Arcozelo (Maria Isabel de Lacerda Werneck) – who lived at the Monte Alegre *fazenda* (coffee plantation) and also owned two other *fazendas* in Paty do Alferes (Rio Province) – also received a request for an enslaved wet nurse, this time to serve her granddaughter. In her journal, she explained: "The infant is voracious" (December 21, 1887). In response to the request, she visited her various *senzalas* (slave quarters) in order to find the best nurse. She chose Agostinha, mother of Guilherme, who had been born some six months before on June 25. Viscountess Maria Isabel noted in her diary: "I think she will do" (December 22, 1887). Two days later, before Agostinha left the plantation for Rio de Janeiro, Maria Isabel gave her 42$000 réis as a tip and wrote: "Agostina was pleased." But at the end of the 1880s, when methods of seigneurial control were wearing thin, Maria Isabel was soon frustrated by the news that her plantation administrator, Pedro Celestino, had liberated Agostina and another slave named Inez, in exchange for a payment of 1,326$000. Maria Isabel vented: "I am going to send for Agostinha, who has gone to nurse my little grandchild, and send another nurse in her place. It always shows that Pedro is Black and was once a captive" (December 28, 1887). Her account reveals more than simple dissatisfaction that Agostinha had been manumitted; it was clearly based in the notions of Black inferiority that characterized relations of dominance in Brazilian Imperial society.

Humans participate in history as actors and narrators.[53] This chapter argues that the visual and written narratives of Brazil's master class sought, through multiple practices of power, to construct a vision of the "good wet nurse" and the "generous master" capable of effacing the violence inherent in forcing a woman to nurse another family's baby. In so doing, they sought also to render invisible the violence of slavery itself. The sentiments and affections generated between wet nurses and their white children were a constitutive element of Brazil's slavocratic discourse. Even in a society where slavery was ever more condemned in

---

[51] "From Sabino you will receive a dress that Maria Izabel sends to her mother Beta." Letter from José Maria Velho da Silva to Mariana Velho de Avellar, Rio de Janeiro, March 20, 1867. Roberto Meneses de Moraes private collection.

[52] E. Fox-Genovese, *Within the Plantation*, p. 33.

[53] M. R. Trouillot, *Silencing the Past*, p. 25.

moral terms, enslaved wet-nursing endured because of its critical peda-gogical function in the slavocratic order: it taught future masters to put aside their sentiments in order to exercise control. Affection and violence were thus two complementary faces of a practice that contributed to the construction and reproduction of the slavocratic habitus that was also so precious to the master class as a form of symbolic and social distinction.

Competing with seigneurial discourse, most doctors and educators complained about enslaved wet nursing, alleging that slave women had poor hygiene and that no one could control their inferior temperaments, alimentary habits, and customs, which would inevitably harm a baby's health and moral education. The masters' narrative emphasized the good sentiments that grew from intimate coexistence, thus reviving the figure of the "good master" and seigneurial discourse more generally. Yet the medical narrative was based in a deep suspicion of the enslaved nurse. It cannot, therefore, be said that doctors were opposed to slavery, much less champions of enslaved women. They intended to promote medical know-ledge at the expense of popular curative knowledge, to reassert white women's roles as educators, and to promote maternal breastfeeding for the sake of babies' health and family hygiene.[54] Despite their differences, masters and medical professionals converged in silencing and neutralizing the voices of enslaved women. In various spheres where enslaved women had exercised expertise and influence during the nineteenth century (including healing practices, medicine, childbirth, and child-rearing), Black women's contributions were attacked, criticized, and gradually replaced by occidental medicine and the ideal of the "civilized" white mother.

Enslaved women, however, expressed their suffering through their actions, often quite unexpectedly. This was the case of an enslaved woman studied by Maria Helena Machado, Ambrosina, who suffocated her master's son with a rag doll, killing him. In her deposition, Ambrosina claimed her innocence and revealed that she had been compelled to favor the master's son over her own; both boys were named Benedito. She also endured nights without sleep, suffering from overwork and extreme exhaustion. Her testimony revealed the suffering of a woman divided

[54] J. F. Costa, *Ordem Médica*. Medical manuals researched: F. J. Almeida, *Tratado da educação*; C. Amaral, *Lição para meninos*; L. Barreto, *Tratado de educação*; F. Fénelon, *De l'Éducation*; F. Franco, *Tratado de educação*; F. Froebel, *L'Éducation de L'homme*; J. Imbert, *A infância*; Dr. D. Jaguaribe Filho, *A arte*; V. Jolly, *Tratado de educação*; A. Martin, *Educação das mães*; J. Melo, *Generalidades cerca da educação*; A. J. M. Moraes, *O educador*.

between "two Beneditos," a state that was always denied in the seigneurial discourse.[55] So too was the case of Julia Monjola, who, in saying goodbye to the young Martha Expilly, implored in tears that the girl return to purchase her after she grew up, out of gratitude for the services the nurse had rendered – an appeal, in truth, that was directed more to the adult Expillys, parents to the still-infant child. Julia Monjola sought arguments that might lead to her manumission in the slavocratic primer, finding recourse in the gratitude that the family might have felt during the time she cared for the baby girl. Julia likely feared the fate she might suffer in the hands of another master, but her pleas – like those of thousands of other wet nurses – fell on deaf ears. The boundaries between love and property rights became well drawn, and property rights held the advantage whenever it became necessary to choose between them.

[55] M. H. Machado, "Between Two Beneditos."

5

The Abolition of Slavery and International Relations on the Southern Border of the Brazilian Empire, 1840–1865

Keila Grinberg*

> Ever since the war against the Argentine dictator Rosas ..., the state of Uruguay has become our most sensitive and dangerous foreign policy problem.
>
> Joaquim Nabuco, *O estadista do Império*

Day had hardly broken on August 4, 1864, when José Antonio Saraiva, a Brazilian special envoy in Montevideo, delivered an ultimatum to the Uruguayan government: President Atanasio Aguirre would have six days to heed the requests of Brazilians living in his country, who were demanding compensation for the damage that had been caused to their properties over more than a decade. If he failed to comply, Brazilian troops would attack Uruguay. The response came quickly: the document was returned to Brazil's representative, having been deemed so entirely "inadmissible" that it was unworthy to even "remain in the nation's archives."[1]

In less than three months' time, Brazil would invade northern Uruguay. This Brazilian attack would be crucial in deposing Aguirre, the head of the Blanco government. Venancio Flores, a Colorado, took his place, putting an end of the civil war that had wracked the country for over a year. Nobody might have been aware of it just then, but this would be the beginning of the largest armed conflict in the history of South America. The Paraguayan War, the Guerra Grande, or the War of the Triple Alliance dragged on for nearly six years, leaving hundreds of thousands of civilian and combatant casualties.[2]

---

* Translation by Flora Thomson-DeVeaux.

[1] Acuerdo de 4 de agosto de 1861, Uruguay, *Documentos diplomáticos*, p. 60, note 1.

[2] From here on out, the conflict will be referred to as the Paraguayan War. In December 1864, Paraguay, which had struck an alliance with the Blancos in Uruguay, objected to what it saw as a Brazilian declaration of war and invaded the provinces of Mato

From the start, the Paraguayan War would be the object of intense controversy among politicians, historians, and scholars in general. The first books on the conflict, many containing copies of important diplomatic documents, were published as early as the 1870s. In 1894, José Antonio Saraiva – a Liberal Party member who had pursued a long political career in the Brazilian Empire after the end of his mission in Uruguay – would defend himself publicly against accusations leveled by a Uruguayan colleague, Jose Vasquez Sagastume, that it had been he, Saraiva, who had failed to arrive at a successful deal and thus caused the war. The Brazilian was aided in his defense by fellow party member Joaquim Nabuco, who declared in his masterful book *Um estadista do Império* (1898) that it was thanks to Saraiva that Brazil had been able to secure alliances with Argentina and the Colorados in Uruguay, forming the Triple Alliance, which was to play "the role of a selfless representative of civilization and liberty in South America."[3]

This is an odd statement, coming from one of Brazil's most renowned abolitionists: when the war began, although slavery still remained to a limited extent in Paraguay (it was abolished in 1869), Brazil was the only truly slaveholding country in the region. Over the course of the twentieth and early twenty-first centuries, many interpretations would emerge regarding the causes for the conflict and the motivations of the countries involved (Brazil, Uruguay, Argentina, Paraguay, and, to the eyes of some, England). While not all mention slavery, they hardly corroborate this alleged Brazilian interest in promoting civilization and liberty.

This chapter does not seek to provide a detailed examination of the historiography of the Paraguayan War. Since the 1990s, historians have cast the war as part of the "process of the construction and consolidation of the national states in the Platine region," and that will be the jumping-off point for this analysis. Poorly defined borders, disputed navigational rights along the rivers in the region, the cultivation of yerba mate near the border, Paraguayan access to the Río de la Plata estuary, and cattle smuggling on the Brazil–Uruguay border are seen as the major causes for the start of the conflict, exacerbated by long-harbored expansionist aims and scuffles over local political hegemony.[4]

Grosso in Brazil and Corrientes in Argentina, looking to make it to Montevideo. Brazil and Argentina, longtime allies of the Colorados, joined forces to hold back the Paraguayans. For more on the historical context of the war, see F. Doratioto, *Maldita guerra*.

[3] Resposta do conselheiro José Antonio Saraiva ao dr. Vasquez Sagastume, cited in J. Nabuco, *Um estadista*, pp. 507–508.

[4] F. Doratioto, *Maldita guerra*, p. 18. The historiography of the Paraguayan War is a separate matter altogether. For more, see – in addition to F. Doratioto and R. Salles,

Nevertheless, the reasons that led Brazil to occupy the north of Uruguay in October 1864 have, strangely enough, not been closely examined. Most interpretations tend to attribute the Saraiva mission's failure to avoid the conflict to the impossibility of satisfying the demands of both sides. In broad terms, those demands had to do with attacks on property and the security of Brazilians living in Uruguay, and Brazilians' disrespect for Uruguayan sovereignty and legislation, which was the source of constant friction in the area. But what were Brazilians and Uruguayans complaining about, specifically? And why were those complaints so important that they led Brazilians to invade Uruguayan territory?

In line with a different interpretive strain, I will argue that, for a full understanding of the driving forces behind the complaints lodged by both countries – and, hence, behind the start of the war – we must consider the tensions around the abolition of slavery in Uruguay and the definitive ban of the Atlantic slave trade to Brazil, which took place in the 1840s and 1850, respectively. These tensions were at play in the disputes over the consolidation of local nation-states and are central to an understanding of the historical process that fed into the Paraguayan War.[5]

The abolition of slavery in Uruguay was proclaimed in 1842 and 1846 by the Colorados and the Blancos, respectively, amidst the civil war that was waged from 1839 to 1851. It created a free-soil territory, land on which there were officially no slaves, immediately adjacent to the largest slave territory in South America: the Brazilian Empire.[6] From that time onward, the borders that had once been disputed by the Spanish and Portuguese Empires took on a new meaning, at least in the letter of the law (and the letter of the law carried great weight). Whoever crossed the border from Brazil into Uruguay would no longer be a slave, nor could they be reenslaved if they returned to Brazilian soil, under the terms of that country's 1831 ban on the slave trade.

I hope to make clear that this factor served to heighten the many tensions between Brazilians and Uruguayans in the border region from the late 1840s onward. By the early 1860s they would reach a point of no return, leading to the Brazilian invasion of the north of Uruguay. In making this argument, I will use documents and methods from both

---

Guerra do Paraguai – V. Izecksohn, *Slavery and War*; H. Kraay and T. Whigham, *I Die with My Country*.
[5] Exceptions are the interpretations of F. Doratioto and R. Salles, *Guerra do Paraguai*; M. Maestri, *A intervenção do Brasil*.
[6] S. Peabody and K. Grinberg, "Free Soil."

traditional political history and social history. Beyond the undeniable importance of the acts of the so-called great men, we must reflect on the meanings of the actions of ordinary men and women living in the border region. It is in this sense that I hope to make a contribution to the renewal of the field of the history of international relations. In dialogue with two approaches, working on the border between social history and political history, it strikes me as fundamental that we forge a social history of international relations.[7]

This approach makes it possible to understand the importance of the busy flow of individuals across the border, the flight of enslaved people, violent recruitment for Uruguayan and Brazilian armies and militias, attacks on communities of free and freed Blacks, and above all the vulnerability of Afro-descendant borderland residents, subject as they were to the daily threat of kidnapping and enslavement. It is true that this was not a new development in the 1840s, when slavery was abolished in Uruguay. But the combination of abolition and the fast-approaching end of the Atlantic slave trade to Brazil – where the institution of slavery itself remained unquestioned – created a completely different regional dynamic, catapulting local conflicts and tensions onto the international stage.

SLAVERY ON THE BORDERS OF THE RÍO DE LA PLATA REGION

The political borders of the Platine region were the result of a long process of colonization and disputes between Portugal and Spain over the region of the so-called Continent of Rio Grande and the Plata river basin, dating back to the founding of the Colônia do Santíssimo Sacramento in 1680. The eighteenth century would see Portugal and Spain lodging warring claims, beginning with the Treaty of Madrid in 1750. Diplomatic efforts at the time were ultimately insufficient to avoid the wars that, interspersed with brief periods of calm, were waged through the late 1860s.

Here, as everywhere else in the Americas, colonization brought slavery. In the Platine region in the second half of the eighteenth century, the rising demand for furs and jerky, to be sold on the Andean and Brazilian markets, led to a steady increase in the number of enslaved workers on local ranches. At the same time, slaves were already around 30 percent of the population in the Brazilian captaincy of Rio Grande do Sul. By the last decades of the century, the integration of the Rio Grande do Sul and

---

[7] See R. Sparks, *Where the Negroes*; B. Mamigonian, *Africanos livres*.

Platine economies into Rio de Janeiro's orbit led to more and more enslaved Africans being forcibly brought to the region.[8]

It remains peculiar that the Platine region began to see a greater influx of enslaved Africans precisely in the late eighteenth and early nineteenth centuries, just as the international slave trade was starting to be seriously questioned, due to both British action and burgeoning independence movements in the Spanish colonies.

This phenomenon was even more peculiar in the region that would later become Uruguay, as it was situated in an area that had historically been claimed by both the Portuguese and the Spanish. After all, even after the founding of the city of Montevideo by the Spanish in 1726, the Banda Oriental (so called because it lay on the eastern bank of the Río de la Plata) remained Portuguese until 1777, when the Treaty of San Ildefonso granted Spain the southern half of modern-day Uruguay. By the terms of the treaty, Portugal held onto the north and the lands that would become the provinces of Rio Grande do Sul, Santa Catarina, and Paraná.

The first quarter of the nineteenth century was shaped by struggles between Portugal and Spain over control of the region. In 1801, Portugal agreed to exchange Colônia do Sacramento for the Sete Povos das Missões (or the Misiones Orientales). After the British invasions of Buenos Aires and Montevideo in 1806 and 1807 and the 1808 arrival of the Portuguese Court in Brazil, the Portuguese government decided to take back the left bank of the Río de la Plata just as independence movements in the region were arising – the result being the independence of the United Provinces of the Río de la Plata, led by Buenos Aires. In 1815 Montevideo was part of the territory controlled by the Argentine general Artigas, but in 1816 it passed over to Portugal again and was dubbed the Cisplatine Province. From then on, the area would be at the heart of struggles against Argentina's presence. In 1825, in what would be called the Cisplatine War, Uruguay began the process of breaking away from Brazil – by, among other things, passing a law that put an end to the slave trade and decreeing that slaves' wombs were free. That movement would come to fruition in 1828.[9]

---

[8] From 1788 to 1824, 10,278 slaves entered the province of Rio Grande do Sul; in the Río de la Plata region, between 1777 and 1812, according to research by Alex Borucki, 712 slave-trading voyages were made along the Brazil–Africa–Montevideo route, introducing at least 70,000 more Africans into the region. A. Borucki, "The Slave Trade."

[9] B. Fausto and F. Devoto, *Brasil e Argentina*; G. Palacios and F. Moraga, *La independencia*, vol. I.

There is evidence that, at least as early as the mid-eighteenth century, slaves were crossing the borders between the Portuguese and Spanish Empires in both directions. By that time, the *Reales Cédulas* (Royal Decrees) of 1773 and 1789 had extended the right of asylum in Spanish lands, traditionally limited to the free population (especially Christians and Indigenous peoples), to slaves, granting freedom to those who fled to Spanish soil.[10]

In 1801, the Spanish cartographer and naturalist Félix de Azara referenced these runaway slaves, complaining that the Spanish – who, according to him, treated slaves better than the Portuguese did – should never return them to their owners, "for their flight was a rightful means to achieve liberty, founded in natural law, against which no human convention could stand." Writing a short while later, in 1821, the French traveler Augustin Saint-Hilaire would also reference the slaves fleeing Brazil for the Río de la Plata; he affirmed that "the protection that Artigas granted the slaves who had run away from the captaincy [of Rio Grande do Sul] was the ostensible motive for the outbreak of the war" between the Spanish and Portuguese over the Banda Occidental (Argentina), which had begun in 1811.[11]

The movement of slaves along Brazil's southern border was clearly a source of concern for Portuguese authorities. In 1813, a year after the ban on trading slaves to the United Provinces of the Río de la Plata, the Portuguese government could be found complaining about the decree that granted freedom to "any and all slaves of foreign countries who enter this territory, by virtue of the simple fact of having set foot on it," as we read in the "request from the Portuguese government that slaves having fled from Brazil to the United Provinces of the Río de la Plata be turned over." In it, the Portuguese also expressed their unease about the large numbers of slaves running away from the captaincy of S. Pedro do Rio Grande do Sul

---

[10] E. Isola, *La esclavitud.*
[11] F. Azara, *Memoria sobre el estado.* See also K. Grinberg, "Illegal Enslavement," pp. 31–52; A. Sainte Hilaire, *Viagem ao Rio Grande*, p. 65. Saint-Hilaire referred to the ongoing conflicts between Spanish and Portuguese over control of the Banda Oriental, which had erupted in 1811. Carrying on the independence movement begun in the previous year in Buenos Aires, General José Artigas besieged the city of Montevideo, where the Spanish viceroy had sought shelter. To avoid political strife so near their territory – and fearing that Artigas might move north – the Portuguese, on the pretext of freeing the viceroy, organized a "pacifying army" and invaded the Banda Oriental, starting the so-called Cisplatine Wars, which would only truly come to an end with the independence of the Oriental Republic of Uruguay in 1828. See A. Frega, "Caminos de libertad"; G. Aladrén, "Experiências de liberdade."

toward the territories of the United Provinces; Portugal threatened to go back on the armistice of May 26, 1812, in which it had committed to retreating from the left bank of the Río de la Plata.[12]

The matter had already been the subject of correspondence between Portugal and Lord Strangford, the British ambassador to the Portuguese Court. Strangford had written to the government of the United Provinces of the Río de la Plata, requesting that the runaway slaves be returned immediately and the "disastrous effects" of the decree be undone.[13] In the face of these threats from both governments, Buenos Aires responded by revoking the decree, but not before emphasizing that the declaration of liberty for all slaves brought from foreign territories was an internal order and thus could not "be the cause of any complaint or offense on the part of any foreign government."[14] In February of the following year, the government of Buenos Aires would return to the subject, emphasizing that the decree referred not to slaves who might happen to flee Brazil (such individuals should be returned to their masters) but to those who had been "introduced, by means of trade or sale, in violation of the provisions prohibiting the slave trade."[15]

In the twenty years that followed this discussion, the Atlantic slave trade would be banned in Brazil, as well as in Argentina and Uruguay, but enslaved Africans would continue to be brought illegally into the region. Negotiations between England and the recently created Brazilian Empire (1822) over the end of the slave trade were opened when England set about recognizing Brazil's independence. In 1826, the convention between Brazil and England on the slave trade – shaped by Robert Gordon, the British ambassador to Brazil, and the Marquis of Inhambupe, minister of foreign affairs, and signed by D. Pedro I – stipulated that it be abolished within three years. The anti–slave trafficking agreement between the two countries was already in effect when a Brazilian law was approved on November 7, 1831; in addition

---

[12] "Nota do governo português ao das Províncias Unidas do Rio da Prata," November 30, 1813, in Brasil, *Relatório do Ministerio das Relações Exteriores*, Anexo E, no. 14, p. 40.
[13] "Nota do ministro britânico nesta Corte ao Supremo Governo das Províncias Unidas do Rio da Prata," November 27, 1813, in Brasil, *Relatório do Ministerio das Relações Exteriores*, Anexo E, no. 15, p. 41.
[14] "Nota daquele governo [de Buenos Aires] ao ministro de S. M. Britânica nesta Corte," December 28, 1813, in Brasil, *Relatório do Ministerio das Relações Exteriores* Anexo E, no 16, p. 42.
[15] "Nota do governo das Províncias Unidas do Rio da Prata ao de S. M. Fidelíssima," February 1, 1814, in Brasil, *Relatório do Ministerio das Relações Exteriores*, Anexo E, no. 17, p. 43.

to banning the introduction of further slaves into the country, it freed all Africans brought illegally into Brazil, although it stopped short of considering slave-smuggling to be piracy, as the English had wanted. Even so, the law held traders, ship commanders and other crew members, intermediaries, and purchasers of enslaved Africans all criminally responsible. In keeping with the terms of the convention of 1826, seized slave ships would be subject to the Anglo-Brazilian Mixed Commission Court.

Though it would go down in history as the law "for the English to see" – a Brazilian expression meaning "just for show" – today there is sufficient evidence to demonstrate that, as of 1826, it was commonly believed that the slave trade would be brought to an end in the near future. Hence the rush to enslave Africans and sell them in Brazil, the spike in the price of slaves, and the increase in the number of slave ships landing at ports up and down the coast between 1826 and 1830.[16] The number of Africans brought in as slaves did in fact diminish drastically after the passage of the law, but the trade itself was never interrupted; by the mid-1830s, while it had become contraband, trafficking was again on the rise.

In Uruguay, the slave trade to the Río de la Plata region had been under attack since 1812, when the United Provinces of the Río de la Plata banned it.[17] Nevertheless, Africans continued to be introduced into the territory throughout the Luso-Brazilian occupation of the region, from 1817 to 1828. During the Cisplatine War, the provisional Uruguayan government banned slaves from being imported into the territory in 1825, albeit unsuccessfully; the measure had no effect in Montevideo or Colônia do Sacramento, which were still occupied by the Portuguese and Brazilians. Uruguay's 1830 constitution would ban the slave trade and establish the principle of the liberty of slaves' wombs, following the trend set by other Latin American republics, and from then on, 1812 and 1830 would be considered watersheds in Uruguay's abolition process – even though, in practice, the illegal trade continued at full bore.[18]

In the 1830s, on the eve of the Farroupilha Revolution (1835–1845; the separatist movement that would struggle for ten years to establish Rio Grande do Sul as a republic independent of the Brazilian Empire) and the

[16] L. Bethell, *The Abolition*; K. Grinberg and B. Mamigonian, eds., "Para inglês ver?"; B. Mamigonian, *Africanos livres*.

[17] A. Borucki, "The Slave Trade."

[18] The slave trade would only be banned again in 1839, and that ban was subsequently ratified in an Anglo-Uruguayan treaty in 1842. Even so, the port of Montevideo would be keenly observed by the English through at least the 1850s. A. Borucki, "The 'African'"; A. Borucki et al., *Esclavitud y trabajo*, p. 27; G. Andrews, *Blackness in the White Nation*.

Guerra Grande (1839–1851; the Uruguayan civil war between the Blanco and Colorado parties), the population on the Brazil–Uruguay border was made up of many Brazilians and a large number of enslaved individuals who crossed the border on a daily basis, normally to work, often at the behest of their masters.[19] The so-called Banda Norte region of Uruguay, broadly integrated into the agrarian economy of Rio Grande do Sul, was also an area of sizable territories and low demographic density. Although there were Brazilians among the landowners ranging down as far as Montevideo, the majority lived in northern and northeastern Uruguay, often on farms that straddled the border. In many of these places, such as Tacuarembó, slaves were as much as a third of the local population – the same proportion as in Rio Grande do Sul.[20]

This concentration of Brazilians caused countless diplomatic problems for both countries. The Uruguayan government complained of Brazilian interference in local politics; Brazilians who traded in dried meat pressured the government of Rio Grande, objecting to the presence of farmers who might take cattle over to the Uruguayan side. These complaints led to both an increase in the flow of people across the border and a tightening of the not-always-successful restrictions on cross-border cattle transfer, which also affected the movement of enslaved workers from Rio Grande do Sul to Uruguay.[21] If political instability on both sides of the border was already a significant factor in heightening local tensions, subsequent proclamations of the abolition of slavery in Uruguay would transform the region into one massive powder keg.

THE GUERRA GRANDE AND THE ABOLITION OF SLAVERY IN URUGUAY

The civil war over political control of Uruguay between the Blancos, led by Manuel Oribe, and the Colorados, who followed José Fructuoso Rivera, exacerbated the sense of social disorganization around the border.

---

[19] For more on the Farroupilha Revolution, see S. Pesavento, "Uma certa revolução"; C. Guazzelli, "O horizonte." On the Guerra Grande, see L. R. M. Casas, *Orientales* vol. 1.

[20] Brazilians made up 69.4 percent of the population of Tacuarembó in 1830 and 59.7 percent in 1840. By 1860, 50 percent of local cattle belonged to Brazilians. In the early 1850s, according to a census carried out by the Imperial government, there were 1,181 Brazilian landowners on the Empire's border with Uruguay, with holdings of some 9 million hectares populated with more than a million heads of cattle. The other border districts with a Brazilian presence were Cerro Largo, Minas, and Rocha. E. Palermo, "Los afro-fronterizos," pp. 190–191; A. Borucki et al., *Esclavitud y trabajo*, pp. 162–163, 218.

[21] S. Petiz, *Buscando a liberdade*, p. 41.

There were military incursions in both directions, cattle rustling, and slaves being appropriated right and left to fight on one side or another. In mid-1842, with Rivera retreating and Oribe advancing toward Montevideo, the Colorado government, which had allied with Brazil, soon became desperate for men to shore up its defense. At one point, the Uruguayan government ordered that there be a lottery of slaves to be selected for military service; the masters of selected slaves would be given 300 pesos for each, and the enslaved individuals would immediately be granted manumission, conditioned to the obligation of serving in the army for four years. Perhaps finding this measure insufficient, perhaps due to internal pressures, the Colorado government would ultimately abolish slavery altogether in December 1842.

Masters and slaves, Brazilians among them, were notified straightaway of the new abolition law, which called up all able-bodied men for military service. Since the measure mainly affected Brazilian slaveowners with properties in the Banda Oriental, it provoked a stream of complaints from that quarter; these masters acted to remove their slaves from the country altogether, helped by farmworkers from the province of Rio Grande do Sul and by the Brazilian government, which hid slaves on the Brazilian navy's ships.

Rivera wasn't the only authority to resort to recruiting slaves. As soon as he had consolidated his presence in eastern Uruguay and set up a government in Cerrito, Oribe also began forcibly enlisting slaves to flesh out his army. The 1846 abolition law does not explicitly mention recruitment, but it was designed to that end. A few days after the proclamation, authorities in Cerrito scrambled to incorporate the newly minted freedmen into the Blanco troops before masters could return their slaves to Brazilian soil. The owners were promised compensation "in due time," but in 1847 complaints from Brazilians demanding the return of their slaves began to pile up. Most of these owners never received satisfactory answers from the Cerrito government, which went so far as to refuse to hand over the runaway slaves serving in its army.

In spite of the humanitarian rhetoric of the two abolition proclamations – from the Colorados in 1842 and the Blancos in 1846 – it is impossible to understand them outside the context of war. In both cases, abolition was the only means by which governments at war were able to add more men to their armies' ranks; Uruguayan and Brazilian slaveholders alike stood against the recruitment of slaves, even with promises of compensation. To the eyes of the Brazilian government and Brazilian slaveowners, recruitment provided a clear incentive for slaves to flee from

Rio Grande do Sul. And as if that weren't enough, rumor had it that the
Uruguayan government planned to encourage the British ambassador to
send ships to seize the Brazilian vessels that were concealing slaves. Rumor
or not, the fear that it cast into the heart of Brazil's chargé d'affairs in
Montevideo was undeniable. In December 1842, just after abolition, wary
of "insults" from the English, who were increasingly engaged in repressing
the Atlantic slave trade, and with an eye to saving slaves belonging to
subjects of the Empire, the corvette *Sete de Abril* transported more than
200 slaves to the Brazilian province of Santa Catarina.[22]

The same would happen in 1846. Once again, the Brazilian government
insisted that the Uruguayan decree encouraged slaves to run away. This
was, in fact, the case. The Uruguayan government's proclamation – that
"the negro has been transformed from a thing to a man by those with the
power to change his condition; and he may not return to a state of slavery
unless a great injustice is perpetrated" – was understood perfectly by slaves
on the border, who, having become aware of what arriving in Uruguay
would mean, began running away much more often.[23]

Complaints about runaway slaves from authorities in Rio Grande do
Sul picked up in 1848, when the president of the province requested that
officers of the police in communities near the border calculate the number
of runaways so as to formally request their return by the Uruguayans. The
provincial president's request included several lists of missing slaves,
drawn up using masters' responses to the police inquiry. In 1850, according to official estimates, around 900 slaves were reported as having fled to
Uruguay. Despite vehement complaints, no returns were made. Amidst
the chaos of the Guerra Grande, some of the fugitives apparently joined
Black communities in northern Uruguay, while others volunteered to
serve with the Uruguayan police or military so as to guard against
a forcible return.[24]

The Blancos' abolition decree was especially troubling to Brazilian
slaveowners on the border. Since their properties were situated in the

---

[22] A. Borucki et al., *Esclavitud y trabajo*, p. 221.
[23] A. Borucki et al., *Esclavitud y trabajo*, p. 44.
[24] Arquivo Histórico do Rio Grande do Sul, Correspondência dos Governantes, maço 21,
Relatório da Repartição dos Negócios Estrangeiros apresentado à Assembleia Geral
Legislativa (1850). The original lists are held at the Arquivo Histórico do Itamaraty
(Rio de Janeiro), Missões Diplomáticas Brasileiras, 310/1/1 (1848). These lists, as well
as the precise number of fugitives, have been the subject of careful analysis in the
historiography of slavery in Rio Grande do Sul. See S. Petiz, *Buscando a liberdade*,
pp. 53–54; J. Caratti, *O solo da liberdade*, pp. 100–103; D. Carvalho, "Em solos
fronteiriços," pp. 111–128; and M. Flores, *Crimes de fronteira*.

territories of the Cerrito government, many were unable to keep their slaves from fleeing or being confiscated by the Blanco troops. This state of affairs lasted until at least the end of the civil war and helped to worsen diplomatic relations between Cerrito and the Brazilian Empire, which became increasingly hostile at every fresh report of seized land, cattle, or slaves.[25]

Blanco enmity swelled as Brazilians began interfering in the civil war in favor of the Colorados. Brazilian action was crucial to the eventual Colorado victory in 1851 – and it was likewise decisive in consolidating Brazil's hegemony in the region, as expressed in the five treaties it imposed on Uruguay: the "Treaty of the Perpetual Alliance," which established Brazil's right to intervene in internal Uruguayan conflicts; the "Treaty of Commerce and Navigation," by which Brazil was allowed to navigate along the Uruguay River and its tributaries, and which waived customs fees to Brazil when exporting dried meat and live cattle; the "Treaty of Aid," in which Uruguay recognized its debt to Brazil; and the "Treaty of Bounds," by which Uruguay gave up its territorial claims north of the Quaraí River and gave Brazil the exclusive right of navigation on the Mirim Lagoon and the Jaguarão River, which are natural borders between the two countries. On top of these agreements, there was the treaty by which Uruguay agreed to extradite criminals and runaway slaves.

While the treaties as a whole were broadly rejected by the Uruguayan public – not least because they went into effect without being approved by the legislature – the provision on the return of slaves came in for particularly harsh criticism. The agreement stipulated that enslaved persons who crossed the Brazil–Uruguay border without their masters' consent could be reclaimed by either their masters or the Brazilian government and returned to Brazilian soil.[26] It would even motivate an open complaint from Andrés Lamas, Uruguay's plenipotentiary consul in Brazil, to his friend Paulino José Soares de Souza, the future Viscount of Uruguai. In practice, the treaty amounted to Brazil's flouting Uruguayan abolition laws – which had, precisely in opposition to Brazil, been incorporated into the foundation of Uruguayan nationality.[27]

---

[25] For a general panorama of international politics in the Platine region during this period, as well as diplomatic relations between Argentina, Brazil, Paraguay, and the Blanco and Colorado governments in Uruguay, see G. Ferreira, *O Rio da Prata*.

[26] K. Grinberg, "Slavery, manumission and the law," pp. 401–411.

[27] For more on the relationship between abolition and Uruguayan nationality in the 1840s, see R. Caé, *Escravidão e liberdade*.

Uruguay was not the only power with which Brazil would attempt to strike treaties for the return of runaway slaves. Similar agreements were signed with Peru in 1851 and Argentina in 1857 (likewise not approved by the legislature), and there were additional negotiations with Bolivia, Venezuela, and even Ecuador in the late 1850s and early 1860s. Striving to defend its hegemony in the region, the Brazilian Empire wholeheartedly accepted an "active presence" in diplomatic relations in South America.[28] In all these treaties, the governments of South American republics were called upon to recognize the principle by which slaves belonging to Brazilian subjects who had crossed the border against their masters' wishes had to be returned. Both parties committed to not employing deserters from other countries, precisely to keep slaves or recruited freedmen from running away.[29] Unlike existing slave-extradition treaties between the colonial empires, these were struck between Brazil – a slaveholding nation – and countries that had already abolished slavery. This clearly demarcated a swath of slaveholding territory, standing against the free soil created by its republican neighbors.

The concept of free soil was evidently not a nineteenth-century invention; it has a much longer and more complex history. As Max Weber observed, medieval cities in continental Europe developed customs under which serfs could win their freedom by virtue of the principle *stadtluft macht frei* (city air makes free).[30] Since 1569, slavery had been seen as inconsistent with British law; in the Cartwright case, a serf imported from Russia was judged to be free by the authorities because "England was too pure an aire for slaves to breath in."[31] Cartwright became an important precedent and would be used as an argument in cases concerning slaves brought to England from its colonies in the Caribbean during the eighteenth century. At the end of the century, the discussion over the status of a runaway slave from Jamaica named James Somerset provided a definitive answer to the matter by establishing that, in the absence of

---

[28] See G. Ferreira, *O Rio da Prata*; N. Caldeira, "Cativos asilado," pp. 115–141; L. Santos, *O Império*.

[29] "Tratado entre o Senhor D. Pedro II, Imperador do Brasil, e a Republica Oriental do Uruguay para a entrega reciproca de criminosos, e desertores, e para a devolução de escravos, assignado no Rio de Janeiro em 12 de Outubro de 1851, e ratificado por parte do Brasil em 13 do mesmo mez, e pela da referida Republica em 4 de Novembro do dito anno," articles VI and VII, in *Sistema Consular Integrado – Atos Internacionais – Ministério das Relações Exteriores, Brasil*, Brasil, Rio de Janeiro, Imprensa Nacional, 1851. See http://dai-mre.serpro.gov.br/atos-internacionais/bilaterais/1851/b_26/, consulted October 9, 2013.

[30] M. Weber, *The City*.   [31] L. Higginbotham Jr., *In the Matter of Color*, p. 321.

positive laws regarding slavery, all people who set foot on English soil should be considered free.[32] In seventeenth- and eighteenth-century France, the courts also followed the understanding that "all persons are free in this kingdom; and as soon as a slave has arrived at the borders of this place, being baptized, he is freed."[33] When the Parisian courts found themselves charged with determining the fate of slaves brought by their masters from the French Caribbean, they ultimately freed hundreds of enslaved people as they arrived in the capital.

In the United States, meanwhile, 1857 would see free soil rejected in the Supreme Court decision on the Dred Scott case.[34] Instead of accepting that free states in the Union had created free-soil regions – thus denaturalizing the concept of slavery – the United States chose to institutionalize the concept of race as an essential element of American citizenship. Once tied to race, slavery was cast not as a condition that might be modified but as a characteristic that individuals could not hope to shed. South American interpretations of this principle tended to be quite different. Having recognized the premise that a territory may create rights, the South American republics instituted criteria for citizenship by which citizens were defined by their place of birth, not by attributes such as color or ancestry.

In the specific case of Uruguay, the abolition of slavery and the subsequent definition of its national territory as one of free soil, even in the context of the ongoing civil war, ultimately became defining elements of its national sovereignty, in opposition to what was seen as Brazil's expansionist, slaveholding presence.

BRAZILIAN LANDOWNERS' INTERESTS IN URUGUAY AND THE BAN ON THE SLAVE TRADE TO BRAZIL

The signing of the treaties between Brazil and Uruguay on October 12, 1851, inaugurated a new phase in terms of how slavery was understood by

---

[32] P. Finkelman, *An Imperfect Union*; D. Fehrenbacher, *Slavery, Law, Politics*; J. Oakes, *Slavery and Freedom*.

[33] S. Peabody, *There Are No Slaves*, p. 36.

[34] In this case, the slave Dred Scott asserted his freedom, while living in the slave state of Missouri, by virtue of the fact that he had followed his master to the free states of Illinois and Wisconsin. Though the Missouri court decided in Scott's favor, the Supreme Court concluded that he, as a Black man, was not a citizen of the United States and could neither bring a suit nor stand before an American court. The historiography on the Dred Scott case is massive; a good summary of the case can be found at D. Fehrenbacher, *The Dred Scott Case*.

the two countries. The extradition treaty focused specifically on slaves who had come to Uruguay without their masters' permission. Later that year, even as it continued to recognize Brazilian subjects' claim over runaway slaves and ban the entry of enslaved individuals from Brazil, the Colorado government refused to authorize searches for slaves in its territory, unless they fit the terms of the treaty, as stipulated in this December 6 circular:

> 1st. It is absolutely prohibited to introduce, under any pretext at any place in the Republic, any individual lacking a letter of manumission, until the Legislative Body has met and adopted the resolution it finds most fitting on this score.
>
> 2nd. Runaway slaves who entered the territory of the Republic after November 4 [of the past year] will no longer be returned.
>
> 3rd. Complaints will be seen to when made by the President of the Province of Rio Grande do Sul, for slaves belonging to Brazilian subjects settled in said Province; by the master of the slave; or by the duly authorized representative of said . . . .
>
> 4th. Complaints must be accompanied by titles or documents that, in keeping with the laws of Brazil, prove the ownership so claimed.

A year later, the Uruguayan government was stating that individuals considered fugitive slaves in Brazil who had entered Uruguay before the October 1851 treaty had been ratified should not be considered fugitives. Even if they were, they would not be returned. The same document indicated that masters could no longer invade Uruguayan territory to capture their alleged slaves, whether in person or by sending anyone on their behalf.[35] These insistent reminders of the rules of the treaty are a clear demonstration of how frequent these invasions were – and they would continue throughout the 1850s and into the early 1860s. Not only did Brazilian masters keep on flouting the law, but they were also often aided by the open complicity of the Brazilian authorities, who were given to interpreting the treaty in ways that suited their interests and who could be heard to argue that, if they were to bend to Uruguay's laws, they would be left without any manpower.

Complaints from both sides would lead to an agreement signed by the two governments a few years later. It held that Brazilians could take their former slaves as hired workers into Uruguay, as long as they had letters of manumission (the so-called freedman's certificate). José Maria da Silva

---

[35] Brasil, *Relatório do ano de 1851.*

Paranhos, the Brazilian ambassador in Montevideo, would praise his own work years later and argue that the work contracts used on Uruguayan soil were a brilliant maneuver, for they

sought to ensure that Brazilians might find a legal means to use their slaves to address the dearth of laborers that was felt then and is felt still in the Republic: thus rendering unnecessary the clandestine use of slaves, avoiding the violation of the laws of the Republic, making it possible to attend to the work on the farms in question, and promoting the liberty of many individuals who would have otherwise remained in captivity.[36]

Paranhos' allegedly brilliant solution was ultimately rather inefficient. Questions sent from Brazilian authorities on the border to their superiors are evidence that the legal status of workers in the area was still a matter of confusion – and that attempts to interpret the law in favor of Brazilian masters persisted.

This was the case with the parish inspector in Sant'Anna do Livramento, a small Brazilian town on the border with Uruguay, who sent a letter to Manuel Vieira Tosta, the president of the province of S. Pedro do Rio Grande do Sul and the future Baron of Muritiba. The inspector wanted to know whether slaves who crossed the border "by any chance circumstance" were to be considered free – if, say, they had been chasing down some animal that had strayed into Uruguayan territory. The question also applied to slaves who lived on farms that straddled the border, as well as those who, once hired in Uruguay, were subsequently transferred to the province of Rio Grande do Sul.

Tosta's interpretation was that, given the town's proximity to the border, slaves who crossed the line while carrying out domestic tasks should not be considered freed. Those who tried to take advantage of crossing to claim their freedom would be considered not freedmen but fugitives. In general, the provincial president concluded, slaves might only be freed when forced by their owners to work on the other side of the border, not in cases when they happened to be there momentarily against their master's wishes – these being exceptional circumstances, falling outside the principle that the soil frees the slave that touches it. Tosta also wrote that slaves living on properties that straddled the border were likewise not to be freed: "as in this case, the continuity of territorial property signifies the continuity of a domestic jurisdiction." Only slaves

---

[36] Archivo General de la Nacion (Uruguay), Ministerio de Relaciones Exteriores, Legación del Uruguay en el Brasil, caja 102, carpeta 124, "Nota do governo Imperial Brasileiro a Legação da República Oriental do Uruguai no Brasil," April 27, 1857.

serving as hired laborers or on errands authorized by their masters on the
other side of the border, and who subsequently returned to Brazil, would
be considered free.[37]

In line with the interests of landowners on the border, the provincial
president's interpretation as to the legal status of those crossing the line
between slave soil and free soil was quite simple: when in doubt, keep the
individual a slave; slavery holds out. The problem was that, as everyone in
the south was well aware, in Rio de Janeiro, the capital of the Brazilian
Empire, things were interpreted differently.

This comes through in another letter, this time to the Council of State,
sent by Eusébio de Queiroz, then the chief justice of the Court of Appeals
of Rio de Janeiro. The judge wanted to know "if a slave living in a foreign
country may enter the Empire and be not only maintained in slavery, but
also delivered to his master by the authorities of his country." The query
was in response to the case of a slave who had committed a crime and
whose master lived in Uruguay. The Council of State's opinion, in
a decision which was considered remarkable at the time, drew the following conclusions:

> 1st. That the law of November 7, 1831, did not only seek to do away
> with the trade in new negroes, but also to diminish the number of
> slaves in Brazil, and hence those freed by law as well;
> 2nd. That its disposition would inevitably apply to the case of a slave
> who had, with the consentment of his master, entered a foreign
> country and subsequently reentered the Empire.[38]

The decision was met with vehement criticism from slaveowners in the
province of Rio Grande do Sul. As they saw it, in failing to consider the
characteristics of the border region, the Imperial authorities were setting
a highly dangerous precedent for expropriation. Far away, in Rio de
Janeiro, the members of the Council of State had judged that it was important to confirm the principle accepted in international law by which slaves
setting foot on free soil gained the right to freedom. Despite the protests of
slaveowners and the provincial president, the 1856 decision not only stood
but was reaffirmed in 1858, after a new query was posed by the president of
the province of Rio Grande do Sul to the Council of State.

This time, the case had to do with enslaved persons being taken by their
masters to Uruguayan territory, in particular those slaves who were being

---

[37] Brasil, *Relatório do ano de 1856 apresentado à Assembleia Geral Legislativa.*
[38] Aviso 188 de 20 May 1856, cited in M. Soares, *Campanha jurídica*, p. 7.

used as guarantees against debt in Brazil. To the fury of slaveowners on the border, the opinion, signed by the minister of foreign affairs and approved by the emperor, read as follows:

The slave is ignorant of the transactions of which he is an object; he does not examine them, nor can he; he obeys his master. If the latter should bring him to Uruguay, whatever his obligations may be there, the existence of mortgages notwithstanding, this simple fact confers on the slave his manumission, being a free man in this Republic [Uruguay] and a freedman in Brazil. Both governments are obliged to maintain the right conceded to him; neither may call for his return, nor concede it. This interpretation is so precise that the Imperial government [in a previous case] determined as follows: the slaves who, having traveled as hired workers or on work authorized by their masters in the aforementioned territory and then returned to the province of Rio Grande do Sul must be considered free, inasmuch as the general principle exposed above indicates that the fact of remaining or having remained, with the consent of one's master, in a country where slavery has been abolished, immediately grants the slave the condition of a freedman.[39]

How to understand the stance taken by the authorities of the Brazilian Empire? To judge from these decisions, the Empire not only did not endorse the decisions taken by the president of the province of Rio Grande do Sul but also went so far as to condemn the actions of local proprietors – who, for their part, saw themselves as the defenders of Brazil's southern border. For a better understanding of this apparent paradox, we will have to return to the Brazilian political context in the 1840s and 1850s.

Since the mid-1840s, Brazilian diplomatic rhetoric on the conflicts in the Río de la Plata region had centered on a defense of Uruguay's independence and sovereignty. Once the Cisplatine Province had been lost, it became imperative to ensure that Uruguay would not join the United Provinces of the Río de la Plata. After all, in the eyes of those responsible for shaping Brazilian foreign policy in the region, Brazil had played a crucial role in asserting the independence of both Uruguay and Paraguay in the face of alleged Argentine expansionism.[40]

The problem was that a large part of Uruguay's sovereignty was founded on the principle of freedom, as manifest in its abolition of slavery

---

[39] Arquivo Historico Itamaraty (Rio de Janeiro), Parecer do Conselho de Estado 20 March 1858, Brasil – Uruguai. Extradição de Escravos, 5/58 (1858). In Brasil, Secretaria de Estado dos Negócios do Império e Estrangeiros, *O Conselho de Estado e a política externa do Império*, pp. 31–35.

[40] G. Ferreira, *O Rio da Prata*, p. 226.

in the 1840s – or, rather, founded on the deliberate contrast between
Brazil, the slaveholding empire, and Uruguay, the republic of freedom.
A failure to recognize this would mean agreeing with the accusation
(commonly heard around Montevideo) that the 1851 treaties had
turned Uruguay back into Brazil's Cisplatine Province. In this context,
it hardly seemed wise for Brazil, with its aims of diplomatic dominance
in the Platine region, to officially intervene in the internal matters of
another nation. Andrés Lamas, Uruguay's plenipotentiary consul in Rio
de Janeiro, was well aware that the Brazilian authorities could hardly
keep on criticizing Argentine expansionism if they were also being accused
of expanding the bounds of slavery beyond their geographical borders – especially because, when it came to Brazilian diplomatic relations
in the early 1850s, there was no topic more sensitive than the slave trade.

Although Brazil had been pressured by England to effectively stamp out
the slave trade ever since it had illegally resurfaced in the 1830s, it was
only in 1845, with the Slave Suppression Act (or the Aberdeen Act), by
which the English granted themselves the right to board any ship suspected of transporting enslaved Africans on the Atlantic, that the transatlantic slave trade came under more aggressive control. In 1849, England
transferred a part of its fleet to Brazil. As a result, January 1850 saw the
highest number of seizures of slave ships in Brazil since the policy's
inception. Over the months to come, British warships attacked suspicious
vessels along the northern coast of Rio de Janeiro and near Paranaguá, off
São Paulo's southern coast. In early July, reports arrived in Rio of clashes
between the British, who had torched two ships, and the Brazilians, who,
fearing a search and seizure, opened fire and then sunk their own vessels. It
was said that the British navy wouldn't flinch at attacking the capital itself.
Although a variety of interests contributed to the Brazilian government's
eventual decision to ban the trade in enslaved Africans, it is undeniable
that the unrest provoked by British action in the region played a key role in
obtaining Brazil's September 1850 commitment to abolishing the trade.

This was why the government at Rio de Janeiro needed to demonstrate
respect for and make a point of obeying international agreements – not
only so that Brazil could take on the long-coveted mantle of regional
conflict mediator, but also in order to defend the country's national
sovereignty against England, which was rightfully skeptical of the
Brazilian government's commitment to putting an end to the Atlantic
slave trade. The correspondence between the British and the Brazilians
after the passage of the law of September 4, 1850, shows that the English
were afraid that, just as in 1831, this act would become a dead letter. And

they weren't wrong: at least through 1855, there were still constant attempts to unload Africans in bays and coves along the Brazilian coast.[41]

As the Brazilian authorities were only too well aware, this tense situation only revealed the Empire's international vulnerability. It was impossible, in the context of the international abolition of the Atlantic slave trade and a wave of emancipation proclamations, for a country to aspire to regional hegemony while it continued to meet the demands of its slaveowners (including requests to return fugitive slaves from neighboring nations).

In this light, the Brazilian government seemed to be at a crossroads: on the one hand, there was the need to ensure respect for international treaties and laws, especially in relation to the slave trade, which Brazil was continually accused of disrespecting; on the other hand, it was impossible to forget that the nation's borders in a strategic region were being controlled and protected by precisely the people who were calling for the expansion of slavery beyond those borders.

As if that weren't enough, all this took place in the shadow of the Farroupilha Revolution, in which a significant portion of the population of Rio Grande do Sul had risen up against the Empire and declared the Rio-Grandense Republic in 1836. While the movement was defeated in 1845, dissatisfaction remained among those who were now forcibly reincorporated back into the Brazilian Empire. Since many believed that the Empire wouldn't defend their interests, they felt entitled to take matters into their own hands. In incursions known as *californias*, even major landowners would invade Uruguayan territory in search of lost cattle and slaves.[42]

Uruguay had been a destination for fugitive slaves since its dual emancipation proclamations; in the 1850s it would also be raided by bush captains in search of people to enslave and sell in Rio Grande do Sul. The situation couldn't have been more favorable: the end of the Atlantic slave trade to Brazil in 1850 had driven up slave prices, which had been rising since the 1820s. There was no sign that demand for slaves had dwindled; far from it.[43] A new slaving frontier – this is what Black

---

[41] L. Bethell, *The Abolition*; M. Carvalho, Chapter 2 in this volume.

[42] In 1850, Francisco Pedro Buarque de Abreu, the Baron of Jacuí, organized the largest armed incursion to recover cattle and goods in Uruguay, having recruited and bankrolled a small army of some 300 men. Uruguay, *Reclamaciones*, p. XIII. See also M. Torres, *O visconde*, pp. 79–85; R. Lima, *A nefanda pirataria*; E. Palermo, "Secuestros y tráfico."

[43] M. Florentino, "Sobre minas"; R. Salles, *E o vale*.

communities in northern Uruguay became for slaveholders and slave catchers in the border region.[44]

THE NEW SLAVING FRONTIER

In late 1853, Juan Rosa, his wife Juana Rosa, and their daughter Segundina Marta, who was about four years old, went to the Uruguayan consul in the city of Rio Grande to ask for help and report that they had been kidnapped by Laurindo José da Costa. Laurindo and his accomplices had shown up at Juan Rosa's house, saying that they had orders from the Uruguayan government to "gather up all the men of color and those who were married, with wives and children," which is why they let themselves be tied up and led away. As they traveled, Laurindo continued to kidnap people and murder those who resisted. When they arrived in Pelotas, Juan Rosa, Juana Rosa, and Segundina Marta were sold to a Frenchman, but they were able to flee and make it to the Uruguayan consulate.[45]

A year later, an African woman named Rufina and her four children would suffer a similar fate. They were kidnapped by the same group in Tacuarembó, Uruguay, taken to Brazil, and sold there. Rufina was able to get the attention of the Brazilian police and report the crime, which would be covered and debated by journalists in Porto Alegre and Uruguayan and English consuls. During the process, Paulo José Soares de Souza, then Brazil's minister of foreign relations, received word from his English counterpart, Lord Palmerston, requesting that action be taken against this "new form of trafficking" that was being practiced on Brazil's borders. Rufina was not only let go but also reunited with her family and returned to Uruguay.[46]

Since 1852, people had sought out the Brazilian police, Uruguayan consuls, and even English consular representatives with the same complaint: they had been kidnapped in Uruguay to be sold as slaves in Brazil. According to available documentation, most were women and children. This followed the pattern of illegal enslavement as practiced in other regions over the same period.

[44] The concept of the slaving frontier is used here in the sense formulated by Joseph Miller and widely used in Africanist historiography. See J. Miller, *Way of Death*.

[45] Arquivo Público do Estado do Rio Grande do Sul (APERS) I Vara Cível e Crime, maço 57, processo 2914, 1854.

[46] APERS, I Vara Cível e Crime, maço 88, processo 3368, maço 88, 1855. I analyzed this case in K. Grinberg, "The Two Enslavements," pp. 259–290.

Authorities in Rio Grande do Sul were well aware of this new form of trafficking. Between 1849 and 1853 alone, the provincial justice system would see seven cases of this kind, all reported by Uruguayan consuls.[47] The crimes of the members of Laurindo José da Costa's gang were public knowledge, as we see in an article published in 1854 in the newspaper *O Rio-Grandense* – which, for its part, had copied the report from the *Correio do Sul*. This was the second time that the papers had referenced a crime committed by the group.[48] Andrés Lamas had written to Brazilian minister Limpo de Abreu about the case of Rufina and her children, saying that he hoped that the Brazilian authorities would do their part, in keeping with "international laws and conventions, the law of the Empire, and the particular laws against piracy and the abominable trafficking and importing of slaves."[49]

At the same time as Lamas' complaints were heard in Brazil, the Atlantic slave trade was continuing, illegally, in the province. In April 1852, hundreds of Africans were hastily unloaded on the coast near Tramandaí after the ship on which they had been carried ran aground.[50] Some two years later, Henry Vereker, the English consul in Porto Alegre, would alert the provincial president, João Lins Vieira Cansansão de Sinimbu, that a new load of Africans might have been dropped off along the coast of Rio Grande do Sul. While the latter insisted that it was simply a rumor, the consul seemed unconvinced; Sinimbu then wrote to the minister of foreign affairs, assuring him that nothing of the sort had happened and reiterating that he would stop at nothing "to spare the government the displeasure of seeing this province [Rio Grande do Sul] host to a crime so contrary to Law and Civilization, and which the government itself has striven to punish."[51]

A look at the correspondence between the multiple English consuls in Brazil and the Brazilian authorities in the early 1850s reveals that the issue of slavery was far from settled. As far as the English were concerned, the sale of Africans brought to Brazil after 1831 (reports of which accounted

---

[47] For more on the cases, see the APERS catalog: *Documentos da escravidão: processos crime – o escravo como vítima ou réu.*

[48] *O Rio Grandense*, June 15, 1854. Rafael Peter de Lima also references this article. R. Lima, *A Nefanda Pirataria de Carne Humana*, pp. 145–146.

[49] Archivo General de la Nacion (Uruguay), Fondo Legación, caja 106, no. 70, July 8, 1854.

[50] Provincial officials moved to seize these newly arrived Africans, but most were appropriated by residents living along the coast, and many were taken "over the mountain." See P. Moreira, "Boçais e malungos," pp. 215–235; V. Oliveira, *De Manoel Congo*.

[51] Arquivo Historico do Rio Grande do Sul (AHRS), Ofícios Reservados A2-10, número 3, ofício de 27 de agosto de 1854.

for much of the 1854 correspondence between Howard de Walden, the British consul in Rio de Janeiro, and Limpo de Abreu, the Brazilian minister of foreign affairs), along with the attempted landings of Africans on the Brazilian coast and the kidnappings of Black people along the southern border, all meant one thing: the continuation of the illicit trade in people.[52] It was no coincidence that, later that year, Vereker would write in his annual report to Lord Clarendon, the British minister of foreign affairs:

It should be recognized that the laws of Brazil, in their present state, are completely inadequate to prevent what can be called the illegal domestic slave trade, by which I mean the sale into slavery of Black people who are not slaves according to Brazilian law. To show that this trafficking exists, it would seem necessary only to refer to the fact that, comparatively, few of the Black people brought from Africa since the enactment of Brazilian laws stating that these people should be considered free have actually had their freedom recognized; it is also well known that slaves are often stolen from their owners to be sold; it seems clear that if Brazilian laws were effective in preventing the internal slave trade, the overwhelming majority of Blacks who have been imported into Brazil since 1831 would have obtained their manumission, and the sale of slaves by people who were not their owners ... could not take place, let alone the kidnapping of free people to be sold as slaves.[53]

Diplomatic correspondence and complaints were often reproduced in the Brazilian foreign minister's reports, evidence of the government's care to recognize the existence of these cases and, especially, make their efforts to curb offenses known. In 1859, for example, the minister of foreign relations would allude to Uruguay's complaints of the "theft of people of color in order to be sold" in Rio Grande do Sul. In one of the cases in question, a house was allegedly raided by two Brazilians who carried off a three-year-old child; in another, it was said that "two minors of color were stolen in the region of Aceguá and then sold as slaves in Rio Grande" and that relatives were now demanding "their rescue and return." The minister wrote: "This report was verified in part, and one of the minors, who had been sold under the name Domingos and declared that he was called João Serapio, was judicially deposited in the town of Piratini."[54] In 1860, the report from the minister of foreign relations recounted:

The political head of the department of Salto has informed the government that D. Marcellino Ferreira, a Brazilian subject, has stolen the Black woman Carlota

---

[52] National Archives (London), Foreign Office 84, codices 942, 943, and 944, 1852–1854.

[53] National Archives (London), Foreign Office 84, codex 944, ofício de 30 de junho de 1854, fls. 136 and following.

[54] *Relatório do ano de 1859 apresentado à Assembleia Geral Legislativa*, p. 92.

and four minor children of color born in the Republic, the youngest of which only five months of age, from a residence in the countryside belonging to him, and taken them to Brazil with the objective of selling them as slaves. … Having returned shortly thereafter to the Republic, where he was apprehended by the authorities, he declared that he had indeed taken those people to Brazilian territory with the intention of selling them as slaves and promised to return them within a few days' time … . Rather than fulfilling this promise … Marcellino Ferreira managed to escape on August 29 from the prison where he was held, and evaded the police along his way to the border.[55]

Year after year, as slaveowners and bush captains operated increasingly frequently on the border, the tone of English and Uruguayan complaints became increasingly harsh. As José Vasquez Sagastume, representing the department of Tacuarembó, would write: "[Uruguayan] citizenship is being snuffed out north of the Río Negro: against all that is written in the Constitution of the Republic and established by the liberality of our laws, slavery is a fact in certain areas. … In this, such an important place of the Republic, one may say that there is no more Uruguay: the habits, customs, language, way of life, all is Brazilian: one might say, a continuation of Rio Grande do Sul."[56] Andrés Lamas echoed this sentiment: "At the moment at which, for any reason whatsoever, it so happens that the owner of a person of color conveys that person across the border – and, once across, lets fall the brazen, false disguise with which the laws of the Republic have been flouted – the forsaken victim returns to his public condition as a slave."[57]

Just as with the fugitive slaves, the Brazilian Empire responded to these accusations by doubling down on repression of any attempt to get around the ban on the slave trade. In his 1861 report, the Brazilian foreign minister emphasized that "the Imperial government has called the attention of the president of the province of São Pedro do Rio Grande do Sul to the theft of minors of color in Uruguay, to be sold in Rio Grande as slaves."[58] What's more, he assured, in every case of illegal slaving, "the Brazilian authorities have pursued [accusations] and taken several of the guilty parties to the courts of this country."[59]

This was a half-truth. While officials across a number of municipalities in Rio Grande do Sul had indeed prosecuted certain individuals accused of the crime of "reducing free people to slavery," a look at the sixty-eight

[55] *Relatório do ano de 1860 apresentado à Assembleia Geral Legislativa.*
[56] R. Lima, *A nefanda pirataria,* p. 74.   [57] R. Lima, *A nefanda pirataria,* p. 51.
[58] *Relatório do ano de 1861 apresentado à Assembleia Geral Legislativa,* p. 54.
[59] *Relatório do ano de 1861 apresentado à Assembleia Geral Legislativa,* p. 50.

cases in the Rio Grande do Sul state archives reveals that almost none of the defendants were convicted. By claiming that they were trying to recover runaway slaves, or that they were unaware that the person they had kidnapped was free or a freedman, all but a scant few were absolved by local juries.[60] Moreover, even though in a few cases the British consul Howard was apparently convinced of Brazil's efforts to rein in trafficking and kidnapping, in 1855 he wrote to Clarendon – then the minister of foreign affairs – that it seemed quite unlikely that Brazil's rhetoric had convinced the Uruguayans of the efficacy of their endeavors.[61] In a complaint to the Viscount of Manguarape in 1857 – a long list of reports of incidents over the past three years – the Uruguayan minister didn't flinch at saying that the Brazilian kidnappers were ensconced in their impunity, sure that the authorities would cover up their crimes; for this very reason, he was requesting that the Brazilian government act swiftly to repress this "organized piracy, carried out on a remarkably large scale."[62]

TENSIONS RISE

The years that followed were to bring a gradual rise in the volume of complaints on both sides, now including attacks on the life and property of Brazilians in Uruguay. By the time José Antonio Saraiva arrived in Montevideo in May 1864, the complaints and accusations being tossed back and forth had become positively deafening. In April of the previous year, in opposition to Bernardo Prudencio Berro's Blanco govern-ment, the Colorado general Venancio Flores and allies had landed at Rincón de las Gallinas, a Uruguayan hamlet on the border with Argentina, sparking a new civil war. Although the government in Rio had recommended that Brazilian owners respect their nation's neutral stance, the owners immedi-ately supported Flores and began providing horses, provisions, and money to the rebelling troops. Feeling abandoned by their own government, Brazilian landowners on the border saw the Colorado leader as a chance to free themselves of the Blancos, put an end to the "murders, attacks, and thefts" in the region, and – last but not least – do away with the restrictions on the ways in which they were allowed to use their workers on Uruguayan soil.

---

[60] A more thorough discussion of these numbers can be found in K. Grinberg and B. Mamigonian, Chapter 1 of this volume.
[61] National Archives (London), Foreign Office 84, codice 969, ofício de 30 de junho de 1855.
[62] Ofício de 09 de outubro de 1857, in Uruguay, *Reclamaciones*, anexo 11.

Indeed, since 1861 the number of Brazilian complaints had been on the rise, as registered in the reports from the minister of foreign affairs.[63] The situation had become so drastic that, in November 1863, General Antonio de Souza Neto, a leader in the region since the Farroupilha Revolution, went to Rio de Janeiro to warn the government that it was "not prudent to leave Rio Grande to its own devices," with locals taking it into their own hands to aid their kin. The threat was clear. "The Imperial government must not ignore," Neto went on, "the consequences of an independent stance on the part of the Rio-Grandenses; the rallying cry of some hothead will be enough for thousands of men to take up arms and seek to impress upon the [Uruguayans] the respect due to a powerful neighbor; this will be done, if not in the name of the government, certainly in the name of Brazil."[64]

Neto's speech was soon to echo in the Chamber of Deputies: in the April 5, 1864, session, a number of deputies took the general's complaints to heart and argued that the "Imperial government should take the necessary means to bar the slaughter of Brazilian citizens" in Uruguay.[65] The debate in Rio also resonated in the south: while in Montevideo word had it that D. Pedro II wanted to reannex the former Cisplatine Province, in Rio Grande do Sul landowners believed that the Empire would not ensure its subjects' "security as to a safe and peaceful existence."

It was out of fear of fresh political turmoil in Rio Grande do Sul that the Imperial government decided to send Saraiva to Montevideo on a special mission to negotiate the Brazilian government's demands with the Blancos. The mission, described in Brazil as "entirely peaceful," was accompanied by the distribution of troops along the frontier and the arrival of five warships, anchored in the Río de la Plata basin to "support the negotiations."[66]

In his instructions, Brazil's minister of foreign affairs, João Pedro Dias Vieira, had explained to Saraiva that he ought not to abandon the official neutrality that had so long characterized Brazilian action in the Platine region. He would be charged with defending the life, honor, and property of Brazilians in Uruguay who had suffered the "atrocious, barbaric crimes so incessantly practiced there from 1851 to the present, to say nothing of more distant times."[67]

---

[63] L. Schneider, *A guerra*. The reports may be found at Brazil, *Ministerial Reports (1821–1960): Relações Exteriores.*

[64] L. Schneider, *A guerra*, p. 33.   [65] L. Schneider, *A guerra*, p. 32.

[66] L. Schneider, *A guerra*, p. 34.

[67] Arquivo Histórico do Itamaraty (Rio de Janeiro), Carta de 20 de abril de 1864, *Missão Saraiva*, fls 835–837.

And so Saraiva did, knowing that the Uruguayans in Montevideo would have no sympathy for the Brazilians on the border. Even contemporary accounts openly favorable to Brazilian intervention underscored that lawyers and journalists in the capital were interested in seeing a "democratic levelling," so as to make "these landowners, in their aristocratic isolation, aware that in a republic there can be nothing but the absolute equality of rights."[68] Accordingly, upon his arrival in Uruguay, instead of delivering the latest ultimatum, Saraiva went first to the minister of foreign relations and asked that the Uruguayan government respect the nature of a situation which "the Imperial government cannot foresee, nor may it be able to avoid the aftermath, if the Republic does not move frankly and decisively to remove the causes in question."[69] This was a veiled threat. The letter was accompanied by details of sixty-three formal complaints lodged by the Empire against the Uruguayan government over the previous twelve years. They included attacks on properties, murders, cattle theft, and attempts to force Brazilians into military service.

Juan José Herrera, the Uruguayan minister of foreign relations, reacted sarcastically: with a population of approximately 40,000 Brazilians living in northern Uruguay, what were sixty-three complaints over twelve years? If Brazilians were suffering so terribly in Uruguay, why hadn't they gone back to the Brazilian Empire? Even though he judged them to be equally "inopportune recriminations," he argued that the forty-eight Uruguayan complaints were more relevant, since they had come out of a population of hundreds, not thousands.

As Herrera saw it, the complaints on both sides couldn't justify Brazilians' support for the Colorado invasion led by Venancio Flores, since his supporters didn't live in Uruguay but in Brazil. The reason for the Brazilian "border pirates'" support for Flores had a name: the *californias*, the raids which continued to happen in the north of the country. It was the chance to loot Uruguayan territory that motivated this "barbaric caudillismo," the "heedless lord and master of these territories, the center of a permanent threat to civilization," which evidently had not spared the properties of Brazilians in the region.[70] By defending Neto and his accomplices, Herrera charged, the Brazilian Empire was choosing to abandon its

---

[68] L. Schneider, *A guerra*, p. 25.
[69] "Carta de José Antonio Saraiva ao Ministro das Relações Exteriores do Uruguai, Montevideu, 18 de maio de 1864," in Uruguay, *Documentos diplomáticos*, p. 17.
[70] "Carta de José Antonio Saraiva ao Ministro das Relações Exteriores do Uruguai, Montevideu, 18 de maio de 1864," in Uruguay, *Documentos diplomáticos*, p. 17.

own subjects in Uruguay. At the end of his long letter to Saraiva, Herrera also included a detailed list of the forty-eight Uruguayan complaints against the Empire of Brazil – none of which, he claimed, had been attended to, and some of which had been left entirely unanswered. Of the total, thirty-three concerned the kidnapping of Black people, mostly women and children, to be sold as slaves in Brazil. Between 1853 and 1863, dozens of families were carried off by Brazilian gangs, most of them known to local authorities. Several complaints specifically mentioned Laurindo José da Costa. The Uruguayans described the incidents in detail, naming the cities where the victims had been taken and, in some cases, the buyers' names.[71]

Offended by Herrera's reply, Saraiva wrote a confidential report some days later to the government in Rio de Janeiro, saying that the Uruguayan government had surprised him with "harsh recriminations and inexact characterizations of events, with a dearth of benevolence and tact in the way in which it presented its alleged complaints against the Empire." And he concluded: "It is urgent that we organize and distribute our forces along the border."[72]

We know how the story ended. After a period of negotiations in Buenos Aires in which he sealed the alliance with Argentina and the Colorados, overseen by Edward Thornton, the British government's representative in the Río de la Plata region, Saraiva returned to Montevideo. On August 4, 1864, he gave Herrera the ultimatum that he had been carrying since April, giving Uruguay six days to meet Brazil's demands. At Aguirre's refusal, Saraiva judged his mission complete and left the country. Just over two months later, Brazilian troops would invade northern Uruguay. As Joaquim Nabuco would write a few years later: "from the war with Uruguay came the war with Paraguay, and from the latter came the Triple Alliance."[73]

CONCLUSION: "ONE CANNOT DISCOVER THAT WHICH
IS NOT A SECRET"

I believe I have made the central argument of this chapter clear: namely, it is impossible to fully understand the Brazilian invasion of Uruguay in 1864

---

[71] Of the forty-eight complaints, thirty-three had to do with slavery and ten with other matters, such as military service, murders, and cattle theft. The other five are vaguer complaints about property invasions, including Brazilians', which may have also resulted in illegal enslavement. Uruguay, *Reclamaciones*.

[72] Uruguay, *Documentos diplomáticos*, pp. 25–26.   [73] J. Nabuco, *Um estadista*, p. 508.

and the war that followed without considering the tensions and diplomatic incidents that followed the abolition of slavery in Uruguay. This is not to say, of course, that a conflict of this magnitude can be boiled down to a single cause, nor is it to ignore the friction around taxes on cattle owner-ship, border demarcation, and the larger dispute for political hegemony in the Río de la Plata region. In broad terms, the arguments I have developed here confirm the thesis that the Paraguayan War was motivated by the construction and consolidation of nation-states in the Platine region.

This silence from authorities and in the historiography on the topic is intriguing. José Antonio Saraiva, Brazil's special envoy, was so offended by the list of Uruguayan complaints that he refused to discuss them and failed to even mention them in his correspondence with Rio de Janeiro. The content of the complaints was never repeated directly by Brazilian politicians, not even by those who, like this clerk under Minister of Foreign Affairs João Batista Calógeras, were harshly critical of the con-clusion of the Saraiva mission:

Our policy was wholly wrong-headed from the start. We began by sending a special mission, driven by the threat of a revolution of the Rio-Grandenses who supported Flores .... As for the complaints that we demanded be satisfied, we had ignored them for twelve years, while [Uruguay] had so many other things against us, in what amounted to sheer provocation.[74]

I can hazard a few reasons for the silence around slavery. The first has to do with the formulation of the official narrative about the outbreak of the war, which was written in the immediate wake of events. For the rest of his political career, Saraiva would have to fend off those who called his mission a failure and claimed that he had been unable to avoid the start of the conflict. To this end, two notions would have to be established: first, that it was only thanks to his diplomatic intervention that negotiations with Argentina went successfully, leading to the formation of the Triple Alliance; and second, that the war had actually begun with Paraguay's invasion of Mato Grosso, not Brazil's invasion of Uruguay. By dissociat-ing these conflicts as if they were truly separate, not only Saraiva but the whole of the Brazilian government sought to shrug off responsibility for sparking the catastrophe that was the Paraguayan War.

Only in light of these narrative constructions can we understand Nabuco's affirmation that Brazil played "the role of a selfless representative

---

[74] Antonio Gontijo de Carvalho, *Um ministério visto por dentro*, cited in F. Doratioto, *Maldita guerra*, p. 65.

of civilization and liberty in South America." What's more: to his eyes, Saraiva "was truly the bearer of the new message of peace and goodwill between Brazilians and Argentines. As fate would have it, war ... was the necessary consequence of Paraguay's despotic saber-rattling and would have exploded sooner or later, whenever López's delirium was to manifest itself. ... The origins of the Paraguayan War are, happily enough, beyond doubt."[75]

The political motivations driving Nabuco to frame this version of history are understandable. He was a liberal monarchist and a personal friend of Saraiva's who had helped to build a positive image of the Empire's recent past shortly after the establishment of the Republic (1889), a panorama that included a vision of abolition as the fruit of the abolitionist movement and the Brazilian royal family. It is harder to understand the myopia of Brazilian historiography; many analyses of the period seem uninterested in venturing beyond that nineteenth-century narrative to explore the causes of the conflict between Uruguayans and Brazilians and the rising tensions on the border.

Until recently, historians may have been overly reliant on authors like Luiz Schneider, adviser to the Prussian kaiser and a correspondent for the *Nova Gazeta Prussiana*, as well as the author of *A Guerra da Tríplice Aliança contra o governo da República do Paraguai (1864–1870)*, which was published in 1875 with notes by José Maria da Silva Paranhos Junior, the Baron of Rio Branco. Schneider suggested that no period of prolonged war, such as that which "sprang from the complications involving [Uruguay,] demands such painstaking examination of diplomatic correspondence as this beginning, which was, shall we say, the preamble or pretext for the great struggle which was to follow."[76] There is no mistaking the documentary importance of Brazilian diplomatic correspondence. But if we focus on it exclusively, without examining the letters exchanged between politicians and consular officials from Uruguay, Brazil, and even England, we will only have a partial version of events. To deepen our understanding of events, we must do precisely the opposite: move beyond national narratives.

In the case of Brazil, one of the consequences of the commonly held national narrative is the framing of two fronts of action for the country's foreign policy in the nineteenth century – relations with England and relations with the Río de la Plata region – as completely separate realms. In this telling, the slave trade was the chief issue in the first area; once it

[75] J. Nabuco, *Um estadista*, pp. 507–508.   [76] L. Schneider, *A guerra*, p. 72.

had been overcome, Brazil was able to turn to the second front. Now, as we have seen, nothing could be farther from the truth. Not only did the slave trade remain a sore spot for Brazil and England throughout the 1850s and into the 1860s, but it was also a key element shaping international relations between Brazil and its neighbors in the Río de la Plata region – if not all of South America. The debates over the ban on the trade in Africans and the abolition of slavery do indeed connect these two areas, to the point that one is only comprehensible in light of the other.

However, in order to understand the centrality of slavery in all aspects of Brazilian international relations in the nineteenth century, we must take our investigation beyond the diplomatic correspondence. After all, that which is revealed by diplomatic missives and reports is also that which is hidden. In 1864, diplomatic relations with England having been severed precisely because of over a decade of Brazilian attempts to resist the ban on the international trade in enslaved Africans, Uruguayan reports of the kidnapping of Black people and illegal slaving were not to be mentioned. And, indeed, nobody was mentioning them – not even the Brazilians with some interest in the international public debate, nor the group behind Venancio Flores, the Colorado who rose to power in 1865 with Brazilian aid and helped to construct the official version of the Uruguayan narrative. Indeed, the Uruguayan complaints seem to have gone down with Berro's Blanco government.

But the complicit silence of ministers, ambassadors, and other major figures in international political history cannot withstand the reading of documents produced in the thick of everyday events. As many other Uruguayan and Brazilian historians, many of them hailing from the border region, have shown in recent years, combing through local correspondence between governors, provincial presidents, and consular officials, lists of runaways, baptismal records, newspapers, estate inventories, and criminal proceedings, it is evident that slavery-related issues were so present and so recurrent that they were no secret for anyone living then. After all, "one cannot discover that which is not a secret."[77] By turning our gaze to the everyday lives of women and men on the border between Brazil and Uruguay, we may be only discovering now something that was entirely evident to them.

[77] These words are at the heart of Alberto Mussa's *A hipótese humana*, a mystery novel set in 1854 Rio de Janeiro. While I am using the quote out of context, I do so in the sense that slavery was precisely the secret that was so well known by all those who lived through those years that there was no need to discover it.

From this angle, it is undeniable that the actions of those who fled, resisted kidnappings in the border region, and made themselves heard at police stations and in the courts had a tremendous impact. In that context, their voices would be heard at a great distance, all the more powerful because they articulated the experiences of so many others who were unable to escape enslavement, disappeared without leaving a trace, and would never see their life stories preserved in the archives.

PART II

BOUNDED EMANCIPATIONS

6

Body, Gender, and Identity on the Threshold of Abolition

A Tale Doubly Told by Benedicta Maria da Ilha, a Free Woman, and Ovídia, a Slave

Maria Helena Pereira Toledo Machado*

In the 1880s, a woman known by two names – a "25-year-old *fula*, missing her front teeth" – zigzagged between the coffee regions of the Paraíba Valley and the capital of the Brazilian Empire.[1] Always itinerant, always seeking the freedom to come and go as she pleased, the free Benedicta Maria da Ilha (who was also the enslaved Ovídia) rambled from place to place, hiring out her domestic services and forging bonds with multiple protectors, who would later willingly defend her when she was "unjustly" imprisoned as a fugitive slave. In a peripatetic life that always circled back to the capital city of Rio de Janeiro, Benedicta/Ovídia experienced multiple flights, misadventures, and hairpin shifts in fortune. When she was finally captured and imprisoned at a slave trader's house in a São Paulo coffee town, she presented authorities with a plausible story about her identity as a free, unencumbered young woman who earned her living as a domestic servant in Rio de Janeiro.[2]

An extensive judicial complaint detailed Benedicta/Ovídia's many comings and goings. In it, our protagonist presented a narrative – her own narrative – of an identity built around constant displacement. Yet

---

* Translated by Brodwyn Fischer.

[1] The court records analyzed in this paper contain many references to the color of Afro-descendant people. In general terms, the words *fulo/a*, *cabro/a*, and *pardo/a* alluded to mixed-race people – the first word referred to people with darker skin and the other terms referred to lighter-skinned ones. The words *negro/a* and *preto/a* roughly translate to "Black," but the latter also indicated enslavement. Therefore, it was often complemented with other references to color (i.e., *preta fula*).

[2] Cartório de Terras e Anexos de Taubaté (CTAT). 1880. Processo Crime (Denúncia). A Justiça vs. Capitão Fernando Pinheiro da Silva Moraes e Hermínio José Cardoso.

meticulous subsequent investigations – which privileged the voices of her master, judicial authorities, and medical-legal experts – toppled this constructed identity, concluding that she was indeed Ovídia, a woman enslaved to Captain Fernando Pinheiro, a well-established resident of the Imperial capital.

Even thus unmasked, however, the free woman Beneticta opens an important window, through which we can apprehend the ways in which women on the borders of slavery and freedom constructed their identities during Brazil's age of abolition.

This chapter unravels during the final years of slavery in the 1880s, a time marked by the widespread dislocation of people at various stages of liberation – slaves, fugitives, and the newly free – many of whom abandoned Brazil's plantations en masse, seeking new social and geographic spaces in which to recommence their lives. Yet these processes of physical displacement were highly gendered. Men and women coming out of slavery clearly faced different social challenges. Among women, the path to autonomy had to be continuously negotiated within the private realm of domestic labor and explicit personal dependency.[3]

This chapter builds upon a vast historiography. Over the last few decades, a continuous stream of new research has enriched our understanding of slavery's rapid transformation during the abolition period, especially after the Free Womb Law of 1871 (which, among other things, legitimized slaves' rights to claim freedom in Imperial courts of law). Through careful analysis of freedom suits, criminal records, and other legal documents, this historiography has brought into sharp focus slaves' own agency in acquiring various forms of freedom, ultimately showing how enslaved peoples' legal actions helped to delegitimize slavery itself. Drawing upon this perspective, this chapter seeks to recuperate the social practices, ways of life, and world visions that resided below the surface of the testimonials offered in Benedicta/Ovídia's case.

These reconstructed life narratives – Benedicta's and also Ovídia's – reveal social identities established and divided in the complex borderlands between slavery and freedom. In comparing this young woman's possible lives – as Benedicta and as Ovídia – the commonalities are striking. In cities such as Rio, enslaved and free Afro-descendant women were submitted to the same kinds of labor and social norms. The same commission houses often consigned their services, and even lack of pay did not

---

[3] Among other important works in Brazilian historiography, see S. Chalhoub, *Visões da liberdade*; H. Mattos, *Das cores*; K. Grinberg, *Liberata*.

differentiate them: as "Benedicta" repeatedly noted, even free women often worked without set salaries. Yet the Benedictas and Ovídias of the period diverged in one fundamental respect. Free women enjoyed the privilege of unimpeded displacement, which allowed them to zealously defend more autonomous familiar and affective spaces. Enslaved women, by contrast, felt the full weight of their owners' control in their daily comings and goings. Thus, in the carefully constructed narrative of Benedicta's life as a free woman, she constantly swapped jobs and occupations, always in defense of her autonomy; indeed, constant movement appears to have been the defining mark of a life lived in freedom. Her owner, Captain Pinheiro, reinforced the strategic importance of unimpeded displacement from the opposite perspective, seeking to establish his ownership and authority by affirming his careful control over Ovídia's daily life, even when she was working as a wet nurse or a servant-for-hire.

BENEDICTA'S STORY: A FREE WOMAN FALLS VICTIM TO A "HORRENDOUS CRIME"

On April 15, 1880, Benedicta Maria da Ilha sent an anguished plea to her former employer and protector, Bráulio Muniz Dias da Cruz. Muniz was police delegate in the Paraíba Valley city of São José dos Campos and had previously held the same post in the nearby city of Cachoeira, where he had employed Benedicta as a servant for a few months in 1879.[4] The letter – likely penned by a sympathetic passer-by, as Benedicta was illiterate – was a desperate plea born of desperate circumstances. Benedicta, whom Muniz knew as a free woman, had been taken captive in a slave convoy under the command of Hermínio José Cardoso. The convoy had left Rio de Janeiro in mid-1880 and was now slowly snaking through the Paraíba Valley, displaying its human wares for sale. After a formal salutation, the letter read:

I hope this letter finds your Excellency in perfect health – that is my greatest wish.

On this occasion, I humbly ask to draw upon your help as I did before, when I was imprisoned as a suspected fugitive slave in Cachoeira, today, the same thing has happened, I beg you for your precious protection, as

---

[4] A police "delegado," in the Brazilian context, was roughly equivalent to the chief of a police district; the delegado was responsible for the day-to-day operation of his local police force, for accepting and investigating criminal complaints, and for interactions with higher state and Imperial authorities.

I find myself detained in a house in the city of Taubaté waiting to be sold at 95 Rozário Street.

I ask all the Saints that you might free me from this unjust oppression. Please come, or send my freedom papers so that I can free myself from the hands of these men.

Benedicta Daia [sic]

Taubaté, April 15, 1880[5]

Other letters, always penned and mailed by unknown parties dismayed by the young woman's unjust imprisonment, had already reached Delegate Muniz from Rio de Janeiro, Barra Mansa, and Cachoeira. Muniz had not hesitated in taking action: upon learning of Benedicta's captivity, he wrote directly to the Imperial chief of police and to the police delegates of all the other relevant cities. Muniz demanded immediate investigation and forceful measures against "reducing a free person to bondage, *one of the most horrendous of crimes.*"[6] Upon receipt of the last letter, Muniz went further, travelling to the city of Taubaté determined to do whatever necessary to "*free this unhappy woman from the claws of these vultures.*"[7]

Delegate Muniz's energetic measures added to a chorus of complaints about the illegal enslavement. In her initial deposition, Benedicta testified that her troubles had begun in Rio de Janeiro, when she agreed one day to accompany a clerk to the home of Capitão Fernando Pinheiro da Silva Moraes. Moraes ran a business commissioning the services of slaves and free workers, and Benedicta hoped to claim back wages that he owed her.[8] Instead, she found herself in a terrible predicament. As soon as she entered Pinheiro's home, he asked: "*What is your real name?*"[9] She responded: "Benedicta Maria Albina da Ilha." The Captain did not seem to like her answer, declaring that

this was a very old name and she should change it to Ovídia, because that was one of his daughters' name. When she answered that she would not change her name, Fernandes Pinheiro beat her with a *palmatória* [paddle] until her hands were

---

[5] CTAT: PC. D., 1880, p. 9. Daia is a colloquial contraction of "da Ilha," written as it would be by someone with rudimentary literacy.

[6] That is what public authorities declared several times during the investigation. On the crime in question (illegal enslavement of free people), see "Article 179: Reduzir à escravidão a pessoa livre que se achar em posse da Liberdade," in Carlos Antonio Cordeiro, ed., *Código criminal*, p. 130.

[7] CTAT: PC. D., 1880. The expressions in italics were taken from Bráulio Muniz Dias da Cruz's deposition, pp. 72v.–81.

[8] As will be explained, Benedicta told another witness that the clerk had promised to bring her to meet a sister who lived in another city.

[9] Emphasis from the original.

swollen and told her that if she did not change her name, he would send her to his mother's coffee *fazenda* [plantation] in Valença.[10]

Benedicta was then imprisoned and sent to the slave convoy, which traveled by train to various cities in the Paraíba Valley, displaying its "merchandise" to buyers in private homes. In Taubaté, she had been impounded with other slaves in Manoel Silveira Maciel's house, where she awaited a buyer disposed to spend one *conto* and 200$000 réis on a young housemaid, expert in laundry and ironing, whose race or color was alternately described *as crioula, parda, cabra,* and *fula*.[11]

Benedicta's captors made every imaginable threat and kept her under strict vigilance. All the same, as the many letters to Delegate Muniz attested, she always managed to find strangers willing to help. Even Sabino, a slave-for-hire whom Cardoso had contracted to discipline the slaves in his convoy, ended up allowing her certain liberties, which she used to spread word about her predicament wherever she went. Sabino's hard-hitting deposition suggested that he himself had been convinced by Benedicta's arguments. Identifying himself as thirty-six-year-old unmarried cook, born in the state of Sergipe, Sabino described his first encounter with Benedicta:

He was on Imperatriz Street and saw the girl you see here, held by the collar of her dress by a young man and accompanied by Fernandes Pinheiro. When they arrived at a kiosk at São Joaquim Square, Pinheiro called a nearby slave and told him to help take the girl to Cardoso's house.

Sabino testified that the "girl" always told him that "*she was free and was named Benedicta ... allegations she repeated throughout the journey from Rio de Janeiro to this city.*" In one of the cities where the convoy stopped, Benedicta had encountered some old acquaintances, who found it odd to see her among slaves for sale. It was from them that Benedicta learned Delegate Muniz's whereabouts.[12]

After the initial complaint, Benedicta was transferred to judicial custody and the official inquiry began. All of the witnesses corroborated Benedicta's statements. Delegate Muniz, Benedicta's protector, provided

---

[10] CTAT: PC. D., 1880. Questioning of Benedicta da Ilha, pp. 5 and 5v. The *palmatória* was a perforated paddle often used to punish slaves.

[11] Chalhoub examines several criminal records referring to slaves who, offered for sale in Rio de Janeiro, rebelled and developed resistance strategies. Through these strategies, they sought to prevent their sale to far-away plantations or unknown masters and thus acted as important social agents in the slave trade. S. Chalhoub, *Visões da liberdade*, pp. 29–94.

[12] CTAT: PC. D., 1880, "Deposition of Sabino," pp. 49v.–52v.

especially interesting and influential testimony. Muniz stated that he had first met Benedicta when he was suddenly called to Cachoeira's train station in October or November of 1879. There, he encountered a young woman who had been detained by the local station chief because she had disembarked in Cachoeira (in São Paulo province), even though she held a ticket to Boa Vista (in the Rio de Janeiro district of Resende). For most travelers, this might have been understood as a simple distracted mistake. But Benedicta's appearance rendered her error highly suspicious, and the station chief immediately surmised that she was a slave on the run.

By the 1880s, railroads had considerably expanded the prospects of enslaved runaways: trains themselves facilitated quick escape, and train stations were important spaces to collect information and establish valuable contacts. Vigilance of people who "looked suspicious" intensified accordingly: at times, *capitães do mato* (bounty hunters) lurked in train stations and other public places, on the lookout for those whose manner, color, or social vulnerability might indicate they were fugitives.[13] Benedicta did have at least some money – she had purchased a ticket – and she was respectably dressed in a black dress and shoes (a mark of freedom in much of nine-teenth-century Brazil). Nonetheless, her *parda* skin colour and missing front teeth attracted attention, forcing Benedicta to constantly prove her freedom. Because of her liminal physical appearance, Benedicta was forced to fill in the gaps in her social identity with whatever elements she could attain: a passport, freedom papers, personal references, and personal protection from well-established free families or individuals.[14]

Confronted by the station chief's suspicion in Cachoeira, Delegate Muniz interrogated Benedicta and conducted a thorough investigation in her native region. He concluded that she was free. Still, the relationship he established with her was highly asymmetrical. He came to employ her as a maid but described his payment to her – 9$000 réis that Benedicta herself referred to as salary – as "charitable aid." He also refused to

---

[13] For an extended debate on the limits separating slavery and freedom in 1880s Rio de Janeiro, see S. Chalhoub, *Visões da liberdade*. On the issues of "passing" and changing racial classifications in other slave societies such as the United States, see M. Hodes, *The Sea Captain's Wife*; M. Hodes, ed., *Sex, Love, and Race*; L. Kent, *Woman of Color*; J. Rothman, *Notorious in the Neighborhood*. See also a riveting article by Rebecca Scott, which discusses the limits between slavery and freedom from the viewpoint of the law and explores the agency of an immigrant woman whose indefinite legal status was intertwined with both constant displacement and politics: R. Scott, "She ... Refuses To Deliver."

[14] At that time, Brazilian slave society, and the Paraíba Valley in particular, included a diverse population that included free and enslaved people as well as large contingents of manumitted people.

entrust Benedicta with the documents that supposedly proved her identity as a free woman, giving her only a passport, a document that slaves – but not free people – were required to carry when moving about in public. With seemingly the best of intentions, aimed at shielding a vulnerable person who could easily become the target of all kinds of swindles and abuses, Muniz nonetheless offered Benedicta protection rather than autonomy. As a poor, single woman, lacking family ties and circulating in unfamiliar environments, Benedicta needed to avail herself of personal protection and favors, especially those of men who could offer her safety as she moved about through public space. All women – free, freed, or enslaved – had to tread the path to autonomy with particular care.

For enslaved women – young or not so young – the decade of abolition offered new possibilities, just as it did for other captives. Yet women and their children were a minority among fugitive slaves, rural migrants, and *quilombolas* (maroons). Even in flight, women's space for maneuver was mostly molded in the private sphere of domestic service, which was always understood not as work but rather as an exchange of favors and loving care.[15] For free and enslaved women alike, the paths to autonomy were delimited by restrictive gender norms, which mostly limited poor women's subsistence strategies to the domestic sphere.

Not that Benedicta was indifferent to her juridical status; her entire police complaint illustrates the force, daring, bravery, and cold-bloodedness with which she confronted authorities, slave traffickers, her supposed owner, and all manner of witnesses. In every deposition, she insisted that her real name was Benedicta Maria Albina da Ilha – single, twenty-five years old, born in the city of São José do Príncipe to Albina da Ilha and her legitimate husband Manoel da Ilha (or Manoel Bagre), a fisherman. Her parents were "still alive, and like her aunt, they were never enslaved."[16] She made a living as a domestic servant-for-hire.

These same depositions allow us to retrace Benedicta's life trajectory. She began life on a farmstead called Macundum, in São José do Príncipe, where her family lived and worked as *agregados* (dependents). The owner of the *sítio* (plantation) was Benedicta's godfather, and she was raised in

---

[15] O. Cunha, "Criadas para servir," pp. 377–418. The most thorough study on domestic service in Brazil between the last decades of slavery and the post-abolition moment is S. Graham, *House and Street*. An interesting discussion on the topic of wet nurses and nannies in the US antebellum and postbellum South, focusing on the fact that these work relations were deemed strictly affective instead of professional and monetized, is found in K. Wallace-Sanders, *Mammy*.

[16] CTAT: PC. D. 1880, pp. 91v. and 92.

her godmother's house. Finally, at twelve – that is, in 1867 – she had gone
to Rio de Janeiro, where she began to support herself as a servant-for-hire.
Her life from that point forward was precarious and insecure, as she
zigzagged from one workplace to another. After arriving in Rio, she
hired herself out to D. Elisa, wife of Bento Maria da Cruz; from there,
she passed through six homes, schools, and commission houses before
employing herself in 1876 at the home of Fernando Pinheiro, on the Rua
do Príncipe dos Cajueiros.[17] Pinheiro, however, abused his authority,
renting her out to various other families under the pretense that she was
enslaved. Benedicta testified that she always left such placements – as
a free person she would never permit herself to be treated as a slave –
but Pinheiro never paid her a salary, alleging that he was saving money for
her in a special account. Finally, she and Pinheiro had a falling out; when
she decided to leave, he allegedly told her that "the door was open."

In those circumstances, Benedicta claimed to have left Pinheiro's house,
spending the night in the São Cristóvão railway station on her way to
a "party" near the Boa Vista railway station. Confused, she instead left the
train at Cachoeira, where Delegate Muniz had interrogated her and taken
her in. There she remained for two months, waiting for her freedom
papers. With only a passport and a bit of money, Benedicta then returned
to Rio, where she hired herself out to Fuão Manuel's commissioning
agency, at Rua da Conceição 42. The agency rented her services to
a judicial official, but she soon returned.

In repeatedly seeking out commissioning agencies that rented out the
services of slaves and poor workers, Benedicta reiterated the choices of
many other poor women, free and enslaved, who often resorted to such
firms – intermediaries in the labor markets for wet nurses and other
domestic employees – in the 1870s and 1880s. Increasing attempts to
control "rented" domestic servants – and especially wet nurses –
theoretically assured the moral and hygienic fitness of the wet nurses
and maids who would infiltrate their clients' day-to-day family lives.[18]

In the name of sanitary regulation, Rio's domestic workers increasingly
endured bodily examinations, discriminatory medical-racial classification, and close tracking of their physical movements and employment

---

[17] CTAT: PC. D. 1880, pp. 144, 144v., and 145. Benedicta's depositions reveal the existence
of two lists of jobs in which she engaged. Missing pages in her first deposition, however,
prevent us from comparing the two documents, and Benedicta's deposition itself is not
detailed in terms of the dates of her employment arrangements.

[18] On slaves for rent, see M. Karasch, *Slave Life*, pp. 87–88; L. Soares, O *"povo de Cam,"*
pp. 123–145; M. Ribeiro Carneiro, "Procura-se," pp. 177–215.

arrangements. By contrast, domestic workers created their own social worlds in Rio's streets, tenements, *zungus* (cheap rooming-houses), *casas de fortuna* (centers of fortune telling and other mystical practices), and other oblique spaces. Selling *quitandas* (homemade delicacies), renting out rooms, sharing secrets and religious rites, earning money, experiencing love and flight, raising children or entrusting them to others of their own choosing – these were the key elements of the lives that free, freed, and enslaved women engaged in against the backlight of the whitened, sanitized city imagined by urban authorities and systemized in medical-sanitary discourse. The world of the streets – Carioca Square, Rocio, the Campo de Santana, and so many other spaces inhabited by slaves and other marginalized people in the 1880s – allowed washerwomen, wet nurses, and other impoverished women such as Benedicta Maria da Ilha/Ovídia to survive in the slave city's hostile environment.[19]

Benedicta sometimes chose to work as a laundress, enjoying relative freedom of movement among the city's public fountains and laundry basins; other witnesses would later assert that she also labored occasionally as a wet nurse, an occupation associated with slavery and restricted movement. Regardless, she seems to have developed strategies to preserve some degree of personal autonomy; thus we can understand her constant flights, displacements, and ongoing written and personal recourse to acquaintances, relatives, lovers, and friends.

Yet, as it turned out, Benedicta's strategies could not prolong her freedom indefinitely. After returning to Rio in 1879, Benedicta had her fateful reencounter with Fernando Pinheiro. He then sent a clerk to fetch her, either on the promise of back pay or on the ruse that Benedicta's sister had arrived in Rio and was staying with one of their aunts in Rocio Pequeno 111. But when she arrived at the Largo de Carioca, in central Rio, Pinheiro – aided by his slave Olavo – grabbed her by the collar. And thus began the saga that gave rise to Delegate Muniz's indignant inquiry. In her testimony – given in Pinheiro and Cardoso's presence, with cold-blooded decisiveness – Benedita denied that she had ever had a child or worked as a wet nurse as the captain had declared in his testimony and

---

[19] On urban slavery in Rio de Janeiro, see M. Karasch, *Slave Life*, and L. Soares, *O "povo de Cam."* On the lives of free and enslaved maids and wet nurses outside the employer's house, see S. Graham, *Proteção e obediência*, pp. 73–106. On the sociability of the popular classes in the urban context, see J. Farias et al., *Ciadades negras*, especially the chapter entitled "Nas quitandas, moradias e zungus: fazendo gênero," pp. 83–102; R. Moura, *Tia Ciata*; E. Silva, *Dom Obá*; S. Chalhoub, *Visões da liberdade*, especially chapter 3.

insisted that "she knew Pinheiro as her *amo* [master] but never as her owner, and he only decided to present himself as such a short time ago."[20]

Living by favor in strange lands and strangers' homes, hiring herself out as a domestic servant, jumping constantly from one job to another, lacking a secure hearth or salary, and in constant fear of enslavement, Benedicta's existence might seem provisional and insecure, scarcely distinguishable from urban slavery. Yet even this small degree of provisional freedom was enough for Benedicta to risk everything, incessantly confronting the powerful men who sought to block her path.

There was one last person, however, whom she had yet to confront: Ovídia, a slave woman.

THE SAME STORY IN THE MASTER'S WORDS: "OVÍDIA, A SLAVE I WISH TO SELL, ADROIT BUT PRONE TO RUNNING AWAY"

Accused of criminally enslaving a free person, Captain Fernando Pinheiro da Silva Morais was forced to respond to public authorities in the city of Taubaté under penalty of conviction under the terms of Article 179 of the Imperial Criminal Code.[21] In his deposition, Pinheiro stated that in January 1878 he had purchased a seventeen-year-old slave named Ovídia, a native of São João do Príncipe, from Francisco Picão. As proof, Pinheiro attached a copy of the purchase deed, which in fact attested the purchase of a "17-year-old *crioula*, single and apt for domestic work" for one *conto de réis*.[22] Accordingly, Ovídia/Benedicta was probably twenty-one years old when the case unfolded.

In repeated depositions, Captain Pinheiro stated that, between January 1878 and August 1879, Ovídia had behaved extremely well and was always rented to third parties. After a certain point thereafter, however, she became insubordinate and began to run away incessantly, and Pinheiro decided to sell her away from Rio. What could have suddenly transformed an "adroit," well-behaved young slave into an inveterate runaway, who lied and spurned discipline to the point where her master wished to banish her from the city?

Ovídia's alleged master himself provided a possible explanation. Pinheiro affirmed that for a time Ovídia had been rented out as a wet

---

[20] CTAT: PC. D. 1880, pp. 39, 44.
[21] The quotation in the subheading is drawn from CTAT: PC. D. 1880, p. 56v.
[22] CTAT: PC. D. 1880. Escritura de Compra de Ovídia, pp. 58, 58v.

nurse to a certain "Lucas" and that she had also breastfed one of Pinheiro's own children until white marks on her neck raised suspicions about her health.[23] From then on, Ovídia no longer worked as a wet nurse. Pinheiro said nothing – not a word – about the child that Ovídia must have given birth to; the baby is literally absent from the record. Where might she or he be? Had they been forcibly separated at birth? Was the child stillborn? Had the newborn been given away or placed in the Santa Casa de Misericordia so that Ovídia could work as a wet nurse? The Free Womb Law (1871) would not have permitted the child to be sold as a slave, although there are indications that mothers and *ingênuos* (children born free to slave mothers) were sometimes sold together, on the promise of the services the child might provide as a ward before attaining maturity and full freedom.[24]

As Maria Lúcia Mott and Miriam Moreira Leite have suggested, a history of abandoned enslaved children was the necessary corollary of the demand for wet nursing, which created an impressive rental market for postpartum enslaved women in Brazil until baby bottles came into widespread use in the second half of the nineteenth century.[25] The "baby wheels" of Catholic orphanages frequently received the children who might have been forcibly removed from enslaved wet nurses, whose masters believed that the babies would impede the women's ability to nurse other children.[26] Ironically, those same orphanages themselves employed enslaved women, who – with or without their own babies – had to breastfeed far more abandoned children than their undernourished bodies could sustain.[27] The high mortality rates that decimated such children throughout the nineteenth century would seem to confirm this interpretation.[28] Ovídia and her child may have been part of that history.

[23] CTAT: PC. D. 1880. Interrogation of Fernando Pinheiro de Morais, p. 54.

[24] The designation *ingênuos* applied to the children of enslaved women born after the approval of the Free Womb Law in September 27, 1871. Considering the slave market in the province of São Paulo in the 1880s, José Flávio Motta argues that the sale price of enslaved women was higher if they were sold along with their children. When evaluated separately, these women's sale prices were lower. Ione Celeste de Sousa demonstrates the existence of a monetized labour market involving the *ingênuos* in the province of Bahia even after abolition. J. Motta, "Derradeiras transações," p. 159; I. de Sousa, "Para os educar."

[25] M. L. Mott, "Ser mãe," pp. 21–26; M. Leite, *Livros de viagem*, especially the chapter entitled "O óbvio e o contraditório na roda dos expostos," pp. 143–160.

[26] M. Leite, *Livros de viagem*, p. 145.   [27] M. Ribeiro Carneiro, "Procura-se," pp. 26–52.

[28] M. Leite, *Livros de viagem*, pp. 154–156.

Over the course of the nineteenth century, nascent hygienic discourses increasingly vilified wet nurses as dangerous vectors of contagious disease as well as morally corrupted practitioners of ignorant and barbarous habits. This justified the piecemeal prohibition of wet nursing, which could have occurred in Ovídia's case when Pinheiro began to worry about her health.[29]

If Ovídia was no longer allowed to nurse a white child, could she still have breastfed her own baby? How had the young mother reacted when she was separated from her child? Who was the father? Did the birth or separation explain her constant flights? Did the child live in Rio, and was that why Ovídia always returned there?

The records' opacity in relation to Ovídia's child stands out. Witnesses say nothing, and the authorities display a visible indifference to the motives or consequences of the separation. Not a word indicates the child's fate or even directly acknowledges his or her existence. We only know that Ovídia is a mother because of two indirect clues. First, Pinheiro mentioned that Ovídia served as a wet nurse, though he did not link her change in behavior to the birth of a baby or her separation from the child. Secondly, Benedicta herself denied that she had ever had children, which led Pinheiro to affirm the contrary. This contradiction eventually became a crucial point of evidence in the investigation: to resolve it, two medical specialists submitted Benedicta/Ovídia to a gynecological exam, the results of which confirmed her legal identity. By certifying that the young woman had given birth, the legal-medical procedure put to rest her existence as Benedicta Maria Albina da Ilha.[30]

Despite its unhappy end, Benedicta's biography embodies the ambivalence of her age. In the eyes of her contemporaries – as in ours – the enslaved Ovídia assumed Benedicta's voice to tell a plausible story about

---

[29] There were countless theses produced at medical schools in the provinces of Bahia and Rio de Janeiro dedicated to issues involving breastfeeding and wet nurses – always extolling the former and depreciating the latter. These theses mirrored the rise of medical and scientific knowledge and its experts, men who led campaigns against "retrograde practices" nurtured among Brazilian urban families, such as the adoption of wet nurses, traditional habits of childcare, and the use of uncertified midwives. Nonetheless, one woman had also expressed concerns involving the health of potential wet nurses early on: Mme. Durocher, a famous midwife. From 1834 forward, she carried out clinical examinations on women who applied to work as wet nurses. In 1849, she published a book on the topic and submitted the first project advocating the sanitary inspection of wet nurses to Rio de Janeiro's Municipal Council. Her story reminds us to avoid hasty conclusions about masculine monopolies over medical knowledge and concerns about female health. M. L. Mott, "Parto, parteiras," p. 199.

[30] CTAT: PC. D., 1880, Record of Examination of the Offended Party, pp. 146v.–148.

the border between slavery and freedom. In an era infused with the bitter waning conflicts of slavery and shaped by the webs of dependency and exclusion that enveloped women emerging from captivity, Benedita's credibility swayed on the fine line that separated slavery and freedom.

HALF-SISTERS: BENEDICTA AND OVÍDIA MEET ON THE THRESHOLD OF ABOLITION

Benedicta – variously described as *parda, cabra, fula, crioula,* or *negra* – was so sure in her statements, and witnesses were so decisive in describing their time with her as she lamented her fate on the slave convoy or recounted her story through the bars of her prison cell, that it is difficult for a reader to emerge unconvinced. Yet the investigation undertaken in her native São João do Príncipe unveiled another reality.

As their inquiries deepened, the authorities found another Benedicta – Benedicta do Espirito Santo, a twenty-six-year-old laundress and seam-stress born in Mato-Dentro (a small hamlet on the outskirts of São João do Príncipe) to a man named Manoel Moreno, or Manoel da Ilha, and his wife Albina. This new Benedicta affirmed in a certified letter that her godparents were the same as those whom the other Benedicta had named as her own. She also claimed to know Ovídia: the two had lived together under the roof of José Antonio de Medeiros and his common-law wife, the Benedictas' godmother Maria Benedicta de Sampaio. When Medeiros died, the godmother – Maria Benedicta – inherited the house, but Ovídia was given to their daughter Júlia, an heir to the estate. Júlia married a man named João Baptista Picão, who then moved to Rio and sold Ovídia.

Maria Benedicta, along with the godparents and various plantation owners and residents who still lived in the Vila of São João do Príncipe, provided testimony that finally clarified the mystery of Benedicta's double identities. There was a young woman named Benedicta. But she has never left the Vila.[31]

Was Benedicta Maria Albina da Ilha's story thus just a sham? A fake identity taken on by Ovídia in order to pass as free? How had Ovídia and Benedicta developed a relationship so close that Ovídia could convin-cingly take Benedicta's identity as her own?

Jailed in Taubaté, Benedicta regaled her jailers and passers-by with her story: intent on resolving the intricate mystery, Tabuaté's judge convoked

---

[31] CTAT: PC. D. 1880, pp. 111, 111v.

the jailers as witnesses. One, Ignacio Marcos do Amaral Sobrinho, placed the final piece in the puzzle. He testified that he and Tabuaté's subdelegate happened to be near the jail's barred window one day as a man named Eduardo Rosa conversed with Benedicta/Ovídia. When asked, Rosa stated:

> He had known Benedicta do Espirito Santo ever since she was tiny, and they were always together. ... He had first re-encountered the other young woman [Benedicta/Ovídia] in a convoy belonging to a certain Maciel and asked why she was there. Later, a man named Braulio (along with another named Antonio Floriano) asked Benedicta/Ovídia if she was free or enslaved, to which she replied that she was Maria Benedicta's slave, later passed on to her daughter, whose name he could not remember, who had married João Picão, and sold Benedicta to Pinheiro [... and] that he heard her [Benedicta/Ovídia] say that she was the illegitimate daughter of Manoel da Ilha and Feliciana, who was now enslaved to Possidônio Carapina, who lived across from the railway station in Pindamonhangaba.[32]

Yet in a later conversation through the same jail window, Benedicta/Ovídia offered a different version of the facts; asked the same question, she now responded that she was free, and the child of free parents, and that she had only said she was Ovídia before because she was forced to do so by her false owner.

Benedicta had been born in the region with the greatest concentration of slaves in the Rio de Janeiro portion of the Paraíba Valley: the family Souza Breves alone held an unbelievable 6,000 people. Yet Benedicta/Ovídia emerged in a context of small-scale slave ownership.[33] In that social environment, both Benedicta and Ovídia likely moved in a world where enslaved, freed, and free people intermingled without constraint.

Benedicta and Ovídia shared a father – the poor fisherman Manoel da Ilha, Manoel Moreno or Bagre, or simply Manoel – and to a certain extent a common destiny. They grew up together as dependents in their godparents' house, where their shelter entailed service and favors. Despite their father's poverty, Benedicta do Espírito Santo enjoyed certain advantages: she received her godmother's name and protection, and she could remain in the hamlet where she was born, maintaining the social ties – and the social subordination – she had known since childhood. Ovídia, daughter

---

[32] CTAT: PC. D. 1880, fls. 105, 105v., 106, 106v., 107.

[33] Ricardo Salles elaborated a chart that categorizes levels of wealth among families in an area contiguous to that where Ovídia was born. According to him, slave ownership and high manumission rates prevailed in the area. R. Salles, *E o vale*, pp. 156 and 292, as well as Chapter 3 of this volume.

of the enslaved Feliciana, also bore the burden of growing up in a non-natal household, but it was magnified by the mark of precariousness. When her master died and his heir married, she endured sale and subjection as a slave-for-hire with no certain home, circulating hither and thither, entirely dependent on the needs of others.

Amidst this life of constant displacement, Ovídia conceived a child, whom she could not keep. In her comings and goings, Ovídia tried constantly to find her people. In Boa Vista she sought her mother, who lived nearby; in Rio de Janeiro she said she needed to find her aunt, her niece, or her sister. Above all, despite the risks, Ovídia insisted in going back to the Imperial capital. Even after Muniz granted her a passport, she did not seek out a new path and consolidate her escape as Benedicta Maria Albina da Ilha. Instead she returned to Rio and the risk of re-enslavement. This suggests that, for Ovídia, freedom did not translate into the abstract liberty to come and go as she pleased but rather the chance to maintain and sustain her family and emotional ties. Where were Ovídia's partner and child? It was perhaps to them that she always wished to return.

BENEDICTA AND OVÍDIA: SISTERS IN FREEDOM?

The court records that trace Benedicta/Ovídia's trajectory narrate the final years of slavery in Rio and the Paraíba Valley from the perspective of a young, vulnerable woman. In reading them, a historian is forced to grapple with the many complex scenarios that rendered abolition in the Brazilian Southeast an extremely ambivalent, nebulous, and even disorienting social process. For Benedicta/Ovídia, the decade of abolition did not clarify the frontiers of slavery and freedom; on the contrary, it effaced them, placing the question of freedom on an entirely different plane. The lives of free or freed women tested the limits of an imprecise liberty, which were molded and stretched according to each individual's capacity to mobilize favor and protection. Racialized practices of state sanitary control countervailed, armed with new discourses and policies designed to recreate subservience among the free women who sought to emerge from slavery.

Benedicta do Espírito Santo and Ovídia were sisters, but their fates diverged under slavery – so much so that Benedicta do Espirito Santo, perhaps in defense of her own free status, never once mentioned the intimate ties that bound the two women. But in abolition's wake, their lots would again converge. Women emerging from slavery or its borderlands would negotiate their freedom in the private worlds of kitchens,

wash bins, and backyards, where women – married and single alike –
carried out the endless tasks of domestic labor: nursing and caring for
babies and small children, cooking, telling stories, singing lullabies,
always far from their own sons and daughters. Lodged anywhere they
would fit – in cramped, unhealthy alcoves, pantries, or improvised shacks –
the Benedictas and Ovídias of Brazil's "post-abolition" period remained
almost invisible, both to their contemporaries and to modern historians.

BODY AS IDENTITY: MARKS, FEATURES, DISEASES

From beginning to end, the court records of Benedicta/Ovídia's arrest sought
to establish her true identity. The first question was one of property: who
owned her? Could Benedicta/Ovídia dispose of her own body, moving and
acting freely as an individual? Was her body another person's property? Or
was Benedicta/Ovídia's bodily agency limited, allowing her to act reflexively
while constricting her ability to live as a full social being? The underlying
juridical question takes us to the heart of discussions of slavery and its
ambiguities. Enslaved people's duality – as human beings and as property –
always generated formally irresolvable juridical-philosophical questions,
leaving unsettled the extent to which enslaved people could exercise will,
agency, and consent. Such issues were especially problematic in criminal
cases involving slaves.[34] Brazil's Imperial Criminal Code, from its inception,
crystallized this ambivalence. In defining slaves as potential criminals, capable of free will, the law defined them as "persons." Yet, as legal property,
slaves were by definition entirely subject to the wills of others. This flagrant
contradiction was constitutive of modern slavery, though it rarely impeded
the social relations that upheld Brazilian slavocracy.[35]

The Free Womb Law of 1871, which granted enslaved people the right
to possess savings and negotiate their freedom, fractured slavery's foundations. Throughout the 1880s, challenges to slavery's legitimacy intensified, training a spotlight on the contradictions of rigid juridical definitions.
This, combined with a sharp increase in slave flight and freedpersons'
displacement, evacuated slavery's normative underpinnings, leaving only
a strict and minimalist legal mandate.[36] Thus, in Taubaté, police and

---

[34] W. Johnson, "On Agency," pp. 113–124.

[35] For an excellent discussion on this topic, see S. Hartman, *Scenes of Subjection*, particularly
the chapter "Seduction and the Ruses of Power," pp. 79–114.

[36] On abolition and the attitudes of police and legal authorities toward enslaved people's
insubordination and revolts, see M. H. Machado, *O plano e o pânico*, chapters 1 and 5,

judiciary authorities recognized their obligation to protect any property rights that might have pertained to Benedicta/Ovídia's alleged master, but they also did everything in their power to steer the case in the opposite direction.

Because she was a woman as well as a slave, Benedicta/Ovídia faced distinct social and juridical impediments in her quest to possess and control her own body. As a woman, she shared with her free and freed sisters countless dangers and social restrictions: sexual violence, unwanted pregnancy, the dangers of childbirth, and constant vigilance and constriction. As a slave, however, she bore a burden that distinguished her from the wider circle of women: her race and legal condition rendered her and her body a locus of and justification for sexual transgression.

The nineteenth century imposed a set of norms that controlled – or tried to control – women's social and physical autonomy in order to concentrate and control family property. From the 1860s forward, lawyers and jurists began to formulate their reasoning about sexual crimes in new ways, substituting older notions of patriarchal honor (in which women's virtue was a family possession) with visions centered on women's individual integrity. The belief that women's bodies constituted social capital subject to collective control nonetheless persisted, especially in new medical and hygienist discourses that idealized wifely or motherly domesticity and virtue.[37]

Enslaved women, however, faced a different reality. To start with, the dominant moral codes did not extend to slaves. Reproduction was generally considered desirable (depending of course on economic circumstances, the type of slavery, and the owner's profile). Enslaved women's sexuality did not transgress virginity taboos; it did not result in socially recognized paternal responsibilities; and it did not impact inheritance. From the slaveowners' perspective, enslaved offspring reproduced the workforce and could generate significant profit, even after the Free Womb Law. For masters like Benedicta/Ovídia's, who lucratively leased

and "Teremos grandes desastres." On police authorities' attitudes toward abolitionism, see A. Rosemberg, *De chumbo*, pp. 414–431.

[37] S. Graham, *House and Street*, pp. 90–91. The bibliography on hygienist discourses that regarded domesticity as women's greatest virtue is extensive. It is mostly based on primary sources from the second half of the nineteenth century: doctoral theses produced within Rio de Janeiro's and Bahia's medical schools – particularly those dealing with marriage, breastfeeding, and childrearing – and the Imperial Annals of Medicine.

their slaves as wet nurses in Brazil's nineteenth-century cities, full-term pregnancies were a sine qua non.[38]

If enslaved women sometimes enjoyed more sexual liberty than free women, that liberty was infused with the constant danger of violence – and especially sexual violence. Rapes committed by masters were not considered crimes, because the right of property prevailed over all considerations, regardless of the victim's age, civil status, or physical condition. This same logic, by which a master's right to own and use an enslaved body superseded a slave's right to bodily integrity, applied in cases of prostitution. From the 1870s forward, thanks to a campaign carried out by Rio Judge and Police Delegate José Miguel de Tavares, the practice of slave prostitution was widely recognized as abhorrent. But Rio had no laws or regulations prohibiting prostitution, and no legal impediment prevented owners from sexually exploiting their slaves through prostitution.[39] While humanitarian reform campaigns like Dr. Tavares' – which sought to punish the men and women involved in slave sex trafficking by manumitting the prostituted slaves – had significant social impact, they did not result in jurisprudence that limited seigneurial power over enslaved bodies.

Once more, courts found themselves confronted with a nearly unresolvable contradiction. Consolidated jurisprudence sanctioned property rights over enslaved bodies and their sexuality. But those principles clashed both with laws that protected women from sexual attack and with dominant understandings of honor and morality.[40] To intensify the contradiction, new racial ideas involving Afro-descendant irrationality and impulsivity had begun to slip into debates about slavery's weakening hold. Such ideas were evoked fluidly by lettered observers and manifest in rapidly shifting social norms and practices.[41] Yet in the midst of this flux,

[38] On the wet nurse rental market in the second half on the nineteenth century, see, among others, M. Ribeiro Carneiro, "Procura-se," pp. 177–215. An interesting study on healthcare provided to enslaved men and women in the nineteenth century is A. Porto, "O sistema," pp. 1019–1027. For an excellent analysis of pronatalist policies, gynecological treatment, and pediatric care of enslaved women and their children in the North American context, see M. Schwartz, *Birthing a Slave.*
[39] S. Graham, "Slavery's Impasse," pp. 669–694.
[40] On the theory of seduction discussed in this paper, see S. Hartman, *Scenes of Subjection,* pp. 86–87. In a chapter of another book, Joshua Rothman presents a thorough study on sexual relations between white masters and enslaved women within slaveholding families in the United States (J. Rothman, *Notorious in the Neighborhood,* chapter 4, "The Strongest Passion").
[41] On different concepts of race and their social uses, see M. Hodes, "The Mercurial Nature," pp. 84–118; B. Fields, "Ideology and Race in American History."

observers unanimously held that women – and especially Black and enslaved women – had to be controlled. Thus during the 1880s, when Benedicta/Ovídia confronted jurists, slave dealers, her master, and his witnesses in the courts of law, the freedom she struggled for would still have afforded her only limited bodily autonomy.

The dilemma of Benedicta's legal status – whether she should be classified as free or enslaved – was compounded by the ambiguities of a society that had not yet developed classificatory tools capable of defining juridical personhood more generally. In the 1880s, when slavery still reigned and masses of freed and conditionally liberated people abounded, official social classifications and notarial records could be treacherously fluid and dependent on older forms of social recognition.[42]

Traditional societies did, of course, take a strong interest in controlling their populations. If the notorious case of Martin Guerre awakens us to the incredible feats of an ingenious imposter who successfully impersonated a rich agriculturalist in both business dealings and the matrimonial bed, we must also recall that his deception was entirely undone after three or four months, due largely to a careful investigation of his identity.[43] Still, governments seem to have taken special care in supervising and scrutinizing the mobility of women, whose cold and fluid makeup – according to fashionable Galenic theories – predisposed them to deceit.[44]

In Brazil, private and public strategies of control coexisted through the end of slavery. Faced with the challenge of accurately identifying Benedicta/Ovídia, judicial authorities resorted to divergent identificatory repertoires, blending traditional procedures – which depended on scars, birthmarks, and physical appearance – with modern techniques such as the medical-legal exam.

Just as sanitarist discourses regarding childbirth, childcare, and breast-feeding eventually became the only legitimate source of "rational" healthcare practice, so medical-legal examinations allowed male doctors to appropriate areas of expertise previously dominated by women. Medical-legal examinations, which replaced those traditionally performed by midwives (both medically trained and popular), were highly invasive and permeated by masculine worldviews and scientific

---

[42] For Brazil, see S. Chalhoub, *A força da escravidão* and "Precariedade estrutural"; K. Grinberg, "Reescravização, direitos e justiças" and "Senhores sem escravos." For comparative context, see V. Groebner, "Describing the Person."

[43] N. Davis, *The Return of Martin Guerre.*

[44] V. Groebner, "Describing the Person," p. 19.

racism.[45] By usurping private procedures that women already experienced as shameful, men who carried out gynecological exams and described their findings in impenetrable technical terms demonstrated how medical-juridical practices helped define racialized forms of eugenic knowledge that would shape sanitary discourse at the turn of the twentieth century.

Benedicta/Ovídia's legal-medical examination aimed to determine if she had ever been pregnant and if she had carried a pregnancy to term – which is to say it was yet another attempt to establish her true identity. In the judicial records, amidst the juridical queries and cryptic technical vocabulary, one can discern warnings about the unruly sexual life of a young woman with no name, no family, no master, and no certain home, whose very skin was an emblem of social inferiority.

During the vaginal examinations carried out manually and with a speculum, we observed that the cervix was scarred and dilated, in a semilunar shape, easily accommodating the tip of an index finger. The patient also suffers from a chronic uterine catarrh, with excretions through the cervix. The front lower portion of the abdominal wall (womb) also presents weals characteristic of a woman who has brought a pregnancy to term.[46]

Seen through the eyes of judicial authorities, Benedicta/Ovídia's judicial record depicted a body that reneged both work and proper identification. For an Afro-descendant woman, whose social status oscillated between slavery and social degradation, even fragmentary evidence was sufficient to point toward such a conclusion: sexuality outside of marriage, a pregnancy that failed to produce a family, the marks of diseases transmitted through breastfeeding, a constant, rootless mobility. In laying claim to her own body and its story, Benedicta/Ovídia denied outsiders that interpretive power, even if many dimensions of her life remain obscure.

---

[45] On medical-legal examinations carried out by midwives, see M. L. Mott, "Parto, parteiras," pp. 180–181. An interesting analysis of the relations between sanitarism, the struggle against syphilis, and prostitution is in M. Engel, *Meretrizes e doutores*, pp. 115–116.

[46] CTAT: PC. D., processo crime (denúncia), 1880, pp. 147v.–148; and M. Abreu and S. Caulfield, "50 anos," pp. 15–52.

7

Slavery, Freedom, and the Relational City in Abolition-Era Recife

Brodwyn Fischer*

INTRODUCTION

This chapter tells the stories of three young people, living on the cusp of freedom during Brazil's last decade of slavery. Anísia, thirteen in 1883, was born free to a mother who later married an enslaved man.[1] Guilherme, twenty in 1886, was legal property until Brazil's final abolition but sought his own freedom through negotiation, refusal, and flight.[2] Esperança, fourteen in 1883, was born enslaved and grew up manumitted but unfree, raised and taught letters by the same woman who had sold her mother south.[3]

Anísia, Guilherme, and Esperança all suffered horrific physical and symbolic violence, perpetuated by people who elsewhere donned the mantle of benevolent emancipation. Their stories unveil the malleability of Brazilian slavery in its last gasp but also place in sharp relief the limitations and contradictions of Brazilian freedom.[4] In Recife, as in

* The author wishes to thank everyone who offered critiques and suggestions on this chapter during our two University of Chicago conferences and to specially acknowledge generous comments from Maria Helena Machado and Marcus Carvalho. Thanks as well to participants in the University of Chicago's History and Social Science Workshop, especially Kaneesha Parsard, whose insightful commentary helped open new doors. Emilio Kourí and Keila Grinberg also contributed greatly.
[1] Instituto Arqueológico, Histórico e Geográfico de Pernambuco (IAHGP), Manuel do Valle, 1883 (criminal case).
[2] IAHGP, Pedro Osório de Cerqueira, 1886 (criminal case).
[3] Museu da Justiça of Pernambuco, Herculina Adelaide de Siqueira, 1883 (criminal case).
[4] On the possibilities, limits, and contradictions of freedom in the last years of slavery, see S. Chalhoub, *A força da escravidão*; W. Albuquerque, *O jogo*; W. Filho, *Encruzilhadas*; H. Mattos, *Das cores*; M. Machado, *O plano*.

much of Brazil, the jagged legal border between captivity and manumission marked territory riddled with private power and violence. What did legal emancipation mean when private and corporatist logics contested and controlled the law? How did intimacy structure exploitation, within and outside slavery's bonds? How did dependency open avenues for advancement even as it cemented inequality? How did the stigma of slavery elide with racial subjugation?

Such questions must find answers in the lives of the people for whom they mattered most. Yet they also demand a broader perspective: lives like Anísia's, Guilherme's, and Esperança's cannot be disentangled from their place and time, nor from the broader historical processes they helped to propel. Recife – Brazil's third-largest city and an urban magnet for the Brazilian Northeast – was a striking hybrid in the late nineteenth century: one of a handful of Atlantic cities where radical transformations in global paradigms of urban life overlapped significantly with legal bondage.[5] In Recife – as in Rio, Salvador, Havana, and New Orleans – both slavery and its undoing molded urban modernity, and the cities thus forged call into question many of the central tenets of North Atlantic urban history. Slavery and the struggle for freedom shaped social geographies, the balance between public and private power, the strategies necessary for urban survival and social advancement, the relationship between urbanity and equality, and the nature of urban violence. The resulting urban fabric had a very different relationship with phenomena such as liberalism, citizenship, equality, and the rule of law than idealized formulations of the "sociological modern" might suggest.[6]

As Anísia, Guilherme, and Esperança navigated the juncture of slavery and freedom, their lives, their city, and the historical construction of urbanity were intimately entwined. In this chapter, I probe those linked histories, beginning with Recife's belle-époque self-construction and a few reflections on the sticky normativity of urban historical templates.

---

[5] For an earlier period of Recife's history as a city shaped by slavery, see M. Carvalho, *Liberdade*. For Brazilian comparisons, see M. Karasch, *Slave Life*; L. Algranti, *O feitor ausente*; S. Chalhoub, *Visões da liberdade* and *Cidade febril*; S. Graham, *House and Street*; Z. Frank, *Dutra's World*; J. Reis, *Divining Slavery* and *Rebelião escrava*; R. Graham, *Feeding the City*; M. Nishida, *Slavery and Identity*. For comparative nineteenth-century perspectives, see C. Aguirre, *Agentes*; J. Cañizares et al., *The Black Urban Atlantic*; G. García, *Beyond the Walled City*; R. Johnson, *Slavery's Metropolis*; M. Fuentes, *Dispossessed Lives*; C. Cowling, *Conceiving Freedom*; C. Townsend, *Tales of Two Cities*; L. Harris and D. Berry, *Slavery and Freedom*; K. Mann, *Slavery and the Birth*.
[6] On the sociological modern and its many states of exception, see J. Adams et al., *Remaking Modernity*.

I continue with an analysis of Recife's history as a "slave city," permeated and contoured by the structures, experiences, and struggles of slavery and manumission.[7] I end with Anísia's, Guilherme's, and Esperança's lived experience of that city, illuminated through a close recounting of the three crimes that marked their lives.[8] Throughout, two questions resonate. What kind of city did slavery make? And how did an urbanity shaped by slavery limit the scope of urban freedom?

RECIFE, MODERN CITY

In May 1900, twelve years after abolition, a locally prominent Portuguese-born "merchant and man of letters" named Antônio Joaquim Barbosa Vianna published a historical guide to his adopted city of Recife.[9] There was nothing special about the book. Like countless other literary boosters, Vianna outlined "the history of our capital from its most primitive days" and also "stud[ied] it with much discernment in our own times from a political, aesthetic, religious and commercial perspective."[10] Echoing English chronicler Henry Koster, Vianna introduced Recife as it would have appeared from the deck of a transatlantic steamer, apparently "emerging from the water" as the vessel approached its port.[11] Vianna then condensed four centuries of urban history to a series of legal, military, and technical benchmarks, emphasizing the Dutch engineering that had first rescued Recife – "the American Venice" – from its tidal mudflats; the bridges and landfill that had created continuous terrain from an aquatic archipelago; the erection of churches and monumental buildings; the ways in which foreign observers such as Koster had recognized the city's material

---

[7] The idea of a "slave city" can be usefully juxtaposed with Sidney Chalhoub's notion of the "cidade negra," constituted by Black practices of freedom; the two coexisted in every Brazilian metropolis.

[8] The concept of the "slave city" derives from Ira Berlin's classic iteration of the distinction between a "slave society" and a "society with slaves" (I. Berlin, *Many Thousands Gone*, p. 8). My conceptualization of the "slave city," however, differs in emphasis from Berlin's distinction. A "slave city" is not necessarily a city in which slavery is the inescapable and dominant mode of labor, "at the center of economic production," but it is one in which the nexus of most social, economic, political, and spatial relationships (including those of family and gender) is rooted in the institution of slavery and the processes and struggles of enslavement and manumission that were integral to it in the Brazilian context. This differs from Virginia Meacham Gould's narrower use of the term "slave city" in reference to New Orleans (V. Gould, "Henriette Delille," pp. 271–285). For an interesting discussion of similar issues in a different Latin American context, see S. Bryant, *Rivers of Gold*.

[9] A. J. Barbosa Vianna, *Recife*. [10] Review from the *Jornal Pequeno*, May 4, 1899, p. 2.

[11] A. J. Barbosa Vianna, *Recife*, p. 13; H. Koster, *Travels in Brazil*.

progress; and Recife's nineteenth-century adoption of street pavement, water piping, and port improvements. If there was still much to do, it was "only a matter of time and good will"; Recife would soon be "a great city, hygienic and elegant."[12]

To illustrate, Vianna invited his reader to metaphorically board Recife's "americanos" or "bonds" – the four tramlines that traversed Recife's tiny urban core.[13] Vianna's tour signaled the infrastructure of economic and urban progress: sugar warehouses and ports; rail stations and iron bridges; water, sewer, and gas works.[14] Multiple landmarks embodied modern governance: the governor's palace, the central courthouse, the "magnificent" model prison, military installations, the school inspection board. The sinews of well-regulated economic life extended throughout the central city: banks and commercial associations, fashionable shops, factories, the newly built municipal marketplace, sanitized slaughterhouses. There were public charitable institutions, including hospitals, orphanages, and a beggar's asylum; Recife also boasted multiple pedagogical institutions, from religious and technical schools to selective preparatory schools to institutes of scientific research and one of Brazil's two original law schools. Multisecular Catholic churches had pride of place, but so did a masonic temple and multiple markers of secular associative and cultural life: the stately Santa Isabel Theater; the Institute of Archaeology, History and Geography; the Portuguese Reading Room. There were five newspapers, a telegraph office, a chic "International Club," and an ever-expanding system of parks and plazas suitable for public promenades.

In this initial synoptic excursion, and in the subsequent 200-page *Almanac*, Vianna did not mention slavery. There was no trace of non-European heritage. Indeed, people were scarce, beyond lists of prominent politicians and "men of letters"; it was left to the reader's imagination to fill the streets. In the name of this imaginary urban public, Vianna celebrated Recife's achievements and urged all Recifenses to "come together with the patriotic intention of elevating and strengthening" their beloved city, so that it might achieve the "great, truly great" status it was destined for.[15]

Yet Vianna's sanitized Recife, empty of inhabitants and especially of women and Afro-descendants, was not the only depiction that circulated

[12] A. J. Barbosa Vianna, *Recife*, p. 22.   [13] A. J. Barbosa Vianna, *Recife*, pp. 25–39.
[14] This technique was echoed in a pioneering propaganda film about Recife from the 1920s: Falangola and Cambière (Pernambuco Film), *Veneza Americana* (1925). For a cogent analysis of the film, see L. Araújo, "Os encantos."
[15] A. J. Barbosa Vianna, *Recife*, p. 238

in the belle époque. Recife was a minor destination on the commercial and touristic circuits of the Atlantic world, commemorated in troves of postcards.[16] Some dutifully documented Vianna's progressive wonderland: there were artfully tinted representations of tramlines running past tall, Dutch-style rowhouses, the Santa Isabel Theater abutting a public promenade, the majestic façade of the central railway terminal. But travelers' appetites for picturesque novelty could also prick the boosters' bubble. One missive, mailed in 1904, showed a busy commercial street lined with tall buildings and crosscut with tramlines and electric wires. Among the pedestrians, a lone gentleman in a top hat seems to observe an urban scene to which he does not fully belong: brown- and black-skinned barefoot street vendors, one carrying a basket on his head, crowd the carefully paved street; the only visible vehicles are open-air wagons, propelled by mules. Not a single woman occupies this public place. The scrawled inscription indulgently recounts the inhabitants' recalcitrant relationship with modern times, explaining that, while Recife's city fathers have tried to rename the street after a locally born vice-president of the Republic, "the people" insisted on still calling it the "Rua da Imperatriz," eleven years after the Empire's demise.[17]

Those barefoot Black street vendors, with their stubborn love for a deposed empress, recalled Recife's slavocratic past and had no place in Vianna's city. Neither did the workers in a 1906 postcard image: a row of Afro-descendant washerwomen, dressed in white, beating and scrubbing soiled cloth in the tidal flats of a Recife river.[18] And the inhabitants of Vianna's Recife certainly did not live in the row of mud and palm homes denominated "negerhutten," "negreries," "negroes-houses," or "chouponas dos negros" on another missive.[19] On a final postcard, a top-hatted gentlemen who might have occupied Vianna's public sphere seems displaced on a street, beaten from hard earth and called "the Rua Sete Mocambos" ("Street of Seven Shacks"). He converses in a doorway with a Black woman in a Victorian ankle-length dress; elsewhere, a barefoot man in a straw cap talks with a roughly clad boy, and baby pigs root for food.[20]

It would be easy to dismiss such images as errata, holdovers from another era that still inhabited the margins of a city rapidly evolving

---

[16] The postcards discussed here are archived at the Fundação Joaquim Nabuco (Fundaj), colecção Josebias Bandeira.
[17] Fundaj, colecção Josebias Bandeira, image JB-000917 (1904).
[18] Fundaj, colecção Josebias Bandeira, image JB_000489.
[19] Fundaj, colecção Josebias Bandeira, image JB_001006.
[20] Fundaj, colecção Josebias Bandeira, image JB_000494.

toward Vianna's carefully curated modernity. And yet, during these same years, some of the very pioneering maps and censuses that marked Recife's modernization – the very documents that signaled the city's entry into transnational circuits of urbanity, where places and populations were knowable – indicated that this was far from the case.[21] A 1906 map, prepared by engineer Douglas Fox, showed the bold outlines of urban modernity: rectilinear streets, rail lines, monuments, stone buildings. Yet subsequently annotated copies still preserved in the city's engineering archives mark swampy neighborhoods of "negro" cabins, called *mocambos*, filling in the voids and blank spaces of the original map.[22] In 1905, public health official Octavio de Freitas estimated that the thousands of *mocambos* in Recife were "the main dwellings of the poorer classes."[23] Recife's pioneering 1913 census (the first in Brazil to count informal dwellings) affirmed his point; 66 percent of the city's dwellings were either improvised shacks or auto-constructed wattle and daub homes.[24] While the cinematic tramcar city certainly existed, it was interspersed and overwhelmed by a very different urban and social reality, one in which Black people, the spaces they inhabited and created, and the relationships they forged with the classes who had owned their ancestors shaped the city as surely as did any vision of "modern" progress.[25]

"THE CITY" IN THE URBAN CANON

Vianna's selective urban portrait of Recife was not unique. In the field of urban studies, sage deconstructions of history's grand narratives have been both abundant and relatively futile.[26] Empirically, both scholarship and common sense tell us that cities are enormously heterogeneous, both internally and across time and space. Historians and social scientists have long argued that real cities are forged by geographical accident, socioeconomic contingency, and political expediency, rarely

---

[21] On early censuses of Recife, see B. Fischer, "From the Mocambo."

[22] *Mocambo* is a kimbundu word for self-constructed huts or shacks that was also used in Brazil to mean *quilombo*, or runaway slave community. See J. Lira, "Hidden Meanings," as well as B. Fischer, "A ética" and "From the Mocambo." On the *mocambos* on early maps, see T. Francisco, "Habitação popular," pp. 52–56.

[23] O. Freitas, *O clima*, p. 50.

[24] Estado de Pernambuco, Municipio de Recife, *Recenseamento (1913)*, p. 82.

[25] On race and the *mocambos*, see B. Fischer, "A ética."

[26] J. Robinson, *Ordinary Cities*; J. Ferguson, *Expectations of Modernity*.

tracking the overdetermined narratives that once tethered their emergence to variants of economic, political, or social modernization.
Across many continents, urban novels and ethnographies have dwelled
in the blank spaces of standard mental maps of urbanity, documenting
the emotional, sensorial, extra-official, extralegal relationships, rifts,
and systems that create the stuff, if too seldom the science, of cities.
In the abstract, it seems almost absurd to argue against normative
mirages of urbanity that have already been disrupted and dispersed.

Yet there is a stickiness to the grand urban paradigms, a stubborn,
constant return to the notion that "the city" – as a physical place and an
object of study – is ultimately a site of both rupture with a retrograde
past and normative convergence on an idealized future. Perhaps this is
because so many of the grand modernizing narratives of the North
Atlantic have claimed the city as their stage. Cities have been theorized
as the sites of democracy, citizenship, public law, and state bureau-
cracy; they catalyzed commerce, industry, consumption, and technol-
ogy; they nurtured lettered culture, public spheres, and artistic sea
changes; they produced individualism and anomie but also class consciousness, racial resistance, gendered emancipation, and sexual liberation. Underlying all of this is the notion that cities are exciting because
they are laboratories of forward movement, the sites where the dreary
temporal sequences of human life become "history" through rupture
and transformative change.

Thus, the roads that lead to urbanity might be motley, but their destination – urbanity itself – still announces itself through familiar landmarks.
Physically, "cities" are serviced and sanitized; their streets are paved and
mappable; their safe and solid buildings enjoy access to electricity, water,
and sewage; residents are mobile and connected, whether through telegraph and telephone lines or wireless networks. Legally, cities are legible
and regulated; their expansion is contained by the rule of law, their
cadastral maps are clean, their laws are written to be enforced, their
inspectors and police forces keep order or impose the state's overbearing
gaze. Culturally, cities constitute and broadcast taste, distinction, and
creativity, broadcasting innovation to a global stage, whether in the
form of steel-framed skyscrapers or street art. The idea of the city still
evokes a string of sociocultural forms and values – anonymity, liberal
individualism, egalitarianism, freedom, participation in a vibrant public
sphere. At some abstract level, all of these signs and symbols still converge
on normative hopes for urbanity as the embodiment of progressive transformation – what Mike Davis calls "cities of light, soaring toward

heaven" – even if cracked cement, convoluted politics, and flagrant flouting of urban "norms" evoke continuity, disjunction, or decline.[27]

Historians, especially outside of the North Atlantic, have a peculiar
role in this urban convergence narrative. Individual works of urban history or historical anthropology – Kirstin Mann's *Slavery and the Birth of
an African City*, Partha Chaterjee's *The Politics of the Governed*, or James
Ferguson's *Expectations of Modernity* – pull on the loose strings of urban
convergence, suggesting the ways in which urban futures are also shaped
by threads of continuity with heterogeneous pasts. But in general, even
decades after Dipesh Chakrabarty's call to "provincialize Europe," most
urban histories still adhere to well-circuited scripts and methods.[28]
Particular objects of study periodically glare and fade: historians might
focus on technological modernization or urban planning, city cinema or
hip-hop, bureaucratic rationalization or rights to the city, the formation of
working classes or the ethno-racial dimensions of urban space, consumer-
ism or financialization, gendered emancipation or moral surveillance. But
the overwhelming emphasis is still on the creation and diffusion of historical scripts that circulate across urban borders, emphasize abstract and
idealized forms of urbanity, and are built methodologically from the sorts
of questions, categories, documents, processes, and logics that indicate
rupture and "modernity."[29]

In this process of urban history-making, intense multivalent imperatives are at play. Even in the North Atlantic, but especially outside of it,
scripts of urban rupture and convergence have long held normative power
for policymakers: they shape history on the ground as well as in the
abstract. For a booster like Vianna, living on the perceived edges of
belle-époque globalization, it was vital to construct a version of
Recife's past that pointed toward a modern, Europeanized future –
not only because he shared that urban vision but also because he
believed that his city's fate depended upon its ability to participate
fully in the civilizational and economic circuits of transnational modernity. Intellectuals often find themselves in a similar bind: transnational conversation and the cosmopolitan respect that come with it
involve the deployment of "universal" categories and methods, which
require the translation of local histories into narratives that are recognizable from the perspective of other historical realities. Historians must thus

---

[27] M. Davis, *Planet of Slums*, p. 19.   [28] D. Chakrabarty, *Provincializing Europe.*
[29] On the relationship of modernity and rupture, see E. Clemens, "Logics of History?";
   J. Adams et al., "Social Theory."

play a constant double game, at once describing the historical processes they perceive and linking them to the transnational historical canon.

The urban history that has emerged from this process is substantially incomplete. We understand far more about performative and revolutionary politics than we do about the quiet but vital interactions that structure incremental change. We know much more about the "global city" than we do about vernacular citybuilding.[30] We can trace the urban impact of laws and institutions but remain relatively ignorant about informal networks and orders. We have a vivid imaginary involving the development of the "public" sphere of the lettered city but perceive only fleetingly the circuits of community, politics, and culture that lie beyond its edges. Taken together, these tendencies flatten, blur, and decenter the urban histories of women, people of color, and the urban poor; they also render invisible the ways in which such understudied urban currents shape broader historical processes.

This is especially evident in relation to the urban history of slavery and emancipation, in part because abolition and the movements that lead toward it appear as such significant moments of historical rupture. Cities have been constructed as magnetic spaces of release: when slavery ends, freedom begins, and freedom is heavily associated with the emancipatory currents of urban modernity. Freedpeople mark their liberty by claiming citizenship, entering the public sphere, moving freely, severing the bonds of personal dependence, claiming cultural autonomy and horizontal solidarity – in short, by deconstructing the worlds that slavery made and entering an "urban" space where they act and are acted upon as "modern" subjects. In Brazil, studies of those processes have yielded moving and significant insights into the *cidade negra*, into Black contributions to the making of the Brazilian working classes and the Brazilian public sphere, into Black agency in the forging of Brazilian nationalism and national culture.[31] Yet this approach has its limitations. It is highly gendered, illuminating a public world in which women were largely marginalized; it can also significantly obscure Brazil's urban "afterlives of slavery" and discourage research on the subterranean structures and

---

[30] Though the phrase "global city" can be attributed to Saskia Sassen's book of the same name (1991), the concept has older roots, arguably to the very origins of urban history as a discipline.

[31] See for example F. Fernandes and R. Bastide, *Brancos e negros*; S. Chalhoub, *Visões da liberdade*; R. Rolnik, *A cidade* and "Territórios negros"; Z. Frank, *Dutra's World*; C. Castilho, *Slave Emancipation*; M. MacCord, *Artífices da cidadania*; A. Negro and F. Gomes, "Além de senzalas."

relationships that limited the emancipatory potential of both freedom and urbanity in Brazilian cities.[32]

A few of these urban histories less examined are especially salient if we wish to think more deeply about the urban afterlives of slavery in Brazil, particularly their gendered dimensions. One traces the circuits that continued to bind the rural and urban worlds well beyond slavery. Another emphasizes the intimacy of Brazil's urban inequalities. A third explores relational power (power derived from and structured by personal relationships) and its ability to permeate Brazil's liberal institutions. And a final history highlights urban informality. None of these is in any sense novel in the landscape of Brazilian social thought; the first three have structured iconic iterations of national self-understanding since Euclides da Cunha, Gilberto Freyre, and Sérgio Buarque de Holanda.[33] Yet themes of rural connection, unequal intimacy, and relational power often emerge in Brazilian historiography as features of a temporal, geographic, and normative other – forged in the rural or slavocratic past, symptomatic of stunted development and incomplete modernization, existing in frank opposition to an urbanism forged from liberal modernity. In the case of informality, we see precisely the opposite: it is portrayed as a contemporary urban distortion without a knowable history, unconnected to the deepest currents of Brazil's national evolution.[34]

In the narratives that follow – of the city and of Anísia, Esperança, and Guilherme – I sketch moments lived out in a modernizing city where rural connection, unequal intimacy, relational power, and informality framed and constrained freedom's emancipatory potential; an urban world where *mocambos* and barefoot pedestrians revealed as much about the future as they did about the past. My intention is to dive deeply into the historical junctures where vivid struggles for varying degrees of urban freedom

---

[32] S. Hartman, *Lose Your Mother*. On Caribbean iterations of these limitations, see M. Fuentes, *Dispossessed Lives*. Writing about Bahia, Walter Fraga has brilliantly demonstrated that the ways in which enslaved Brazilians achieved freedom had a deep impact on the social and political strategies they used to occupy it; his work resonates with that of scholars such as Gregory Downs, who has explored the ongoing significance of dependency after US emancipation. Sandra Lauderdale Graham's *House and Street* and Henrique Espada Lima's recent writings on labor and freedom are excellent examples of work exploring the limits of free labor in Brazilian cities: see H. E. Lima, "Freedom, Precariousness," and E. Lima and F. Popinigus, "Maids, Clerks."

[33] E. da Cunha, *Os sertões* (1st edition, 1902); G. Freyre, *Sobrados e mucambos* (2nd edition, 1951) and *Ordem e progresso* (1st edition, 1959); S. Buarque de Holanda, *Raízes do Brasil* (1st edition, 1936).

[34] For development of this theme, see B. Fischer, "A Century."

produced continuity rather than rupture, in hopes of exposing some of the raw historical threads that stretched unbroken from Recife's slave past to its experience of urban modernity. My focus is intensely local and experiential; if Vianna wished us to see the city as it might have appeared to a streetcar tourist in search of Progress in 1900, I aim to recapture something of what Recife might have looked like to an enslaved or Afro-descendant person in search of urban freedom in the 1880s. But my intention is not strictly microhistorical: I highlight the continuity and intersectionality inherent in these urban struggles for freedom not because they were unique but rather because they open windows on global dynamics that shape modern cities far beyond Recife's tidal floodplains.

RECIFE: REEF, ARCHIPELAGO, SLAVE CITY

Recife is, as the name suggests, an aquatic city – less solid land than low-lying archipelago, riddled with swamps and tidal rivers, only rising definitively above sea level several kilometers from the Atlantic shoreline. For nineteenth-century observers, the city had "the appearance of being built on water"; everywhere, the sky and sea stretch uninterrupted to the horizon, broken only by "the coconut palms' fragile grace."[35] Aquaticism could also have a drearier significance: good land was scarce, bad land flooded, with predictable complications for transportation, communication, and even the definition of solid property. In the late nineteenth century, 400 years after initial European colonization, Recife's extensive municipal territory comprised a tiny continuous urbanized core and a web of suburbs, sugar plantations, and hamlets, linked precariously by dirt roads, railways, and rivers.

Recife had evolved as a port city, as a military and bureaucratic bulwark, and as a node of rural power and wealth. Cattle, cotton, slaves, and sugar passed through it; patriarchs and their sons crossed paths and cemented loyalties and enmities in its churches, educational institutions, marketplaces, and government chambers. The streets (and rivers) belonged to a different population: free artisans, freedpersons making ends meet as laborers, dependents, or vendors, and enslaved men and women, feet bare, moving but constrained as slaves *de ganho*, captive free agents.[36] The city's population was sparse – 116,000 in 1872, 146,000 in

---

[35] H. Koster, *Travels*, p. 2; J. Nabuco, "Ramalho Ortigão no Recife," *O Paiz*, November 30, 1887.

[36] On continuities in this picture – and especially rivers – see M. Carvalho, *Liberdade*.

1890 – and many (slave and free, destitute and powerful) still circulated regularly among rural plantations, suburban Big Houses, and urban neighborhoods.[37] Recife was the capital of Pernambuco, larger than São Paulo and the most powerful urban magnet in the Brazilian Northeast. But it was a city deeply entwined with its hinterland and closely integrated in webs of hierarchy and dependency, more the hub of a regional network than a citadel of liberal modernity.

Recife had been built on sugar and slaves, and that fact marked its economy, its population, its social geography, its power structures, and its urban character. From its heights in the early seventeenth century, under a brief period of Dutch occupation, Recife and its sugar economy had ebbed and flowed (but mostly ebbed). The nineteenth century saw considerable expansion in the volume of sugar production, and the 1880s marked something of a resurgence: Imperial subsidies for centralized sugar mills went disproportionately to Pernambuco, and the value of sugar milled in Pernambuco was more than 70 percent higher between 1886 and 1890 than it had been between 1871 and 1875.[38] But problems of supply, transport, and foreign competition ensured that the surge was brief. And even at its height, sugar prosperity was of a very particular kind. It correlated with high slave prices but not with better wages for free labor; it eventually encouraged concentration of landed wealth; it did very little to encourage linkages that might have promoted deeper levels of economic development; it failed to develop transportation and port capacity beyond a scant and dysjunctive railway system; and it required little of its workers beyond raw strength and the specific delicate skills of sugar processing.[39] In the 1880s, sugar was Recife's economic engine and dominated Pernambuco's provincial finances. But the economy thus created showed little dynamism and few opportunities for ascension in a free labor market.

Recife's urban form was thus quite different than that of cities that grew from manufacturing or commerce. Recife's commercial dominance, status as

[37] Population numbers for 1872 and 1890 are confused by the fact that the municipal boundaries changed between the two censuses, making independent municipalities of three of Recife's parishes. The numbers given are for the municipality as it was defined in 1872; if we use the restricted 1890 boundaries, the appropriate population figures are 92,052 for 1872 and 111,556 for 1890. For both censuses, two Brazilian cities were larger: Rio with 275,000 (1872) and 523,000 (1890) and Salvador at 129,000 (1872) and 174,402 (1890). São Paulo was considerably smaller, with 23,000 in 1872 and only 65,000 in 1890. Brazil, Diretoria Geral de Estatística, *Recenseamento de 1872* (v. 9) and *Synopse* (1890), p. 90.
[38] P. Eisenberg, *The Sugar Industry*, p. 15.   [39] P. Eisenberg, *The Sugar Industry*.

the seat of provincial government, and law school all ensured that the Northeast's most powerful families would maintain a strong urban presence. But most of those families were more prominent than rich, and what wealth existed was more effectively controlled than expanded. In 1873, 13 percent of the municipal population was enslaved, working in a wide variety of settings, from the cane plantations of Recife's western expanses to semi-free contract labor in Recife's urban core. That percentage had dropped sharply since mid-century and would drop to around 4 percent before abolition: some able-bodied slaves were being sold south, families ripped apart to feed Brazil's more dynamic coffee economy, and others had been voluntarily freed or promised freedom to encourage loyalty and productivity.[40] Overall, 70 percent of Recife's population was illiterate in 1872. Despite well-publicized initiatives granting tax exemptions to industrial entrepreneurs, only 9 percent of the laboring population was occupied as urban "workers," an expansive category in which factory labor figured lightly. Only 3 percent of Recifenses were "artisans," who tended toward greater skill and political independence.[41] Fewer still belonged to the barely emerging professional and bureaucratic classes. Commerce involved rudimentary basics and imported consumer goods; in both realms, a small class of mostly Portuguese immigrants sat at the top ranks, their dependents and some free Brazilians staffed the middle, and free Afro-descendants dominated street-selling. Most male workers were categorized as undifferentiated day laborers or servants; most women worked in domestic tasks or street-vending.[42] The "free" labor market was constrained in a variety of ways. Vagrancy laws, the threat of military recruitment, and the specter of re-enslavement forced men and women to seek fixed patrons and protectors; the importance of private referrals to the labor market forced all workers to insert themselves into patriarchal hierarchies.[43]

Slavery and the sugar economy also profoundly shaped Recife's demography. By the 1870s, generations of piecemeal manumission – at once a form of labor discipline and a right hard-won by the enslaved and their relatives – had done their work. The free Black population already greatly outnumbered the enslaved, and 59 percent of all Recifenses were Afro-descendant. But "freedom" almost always entailed incorporation into vertical patriarchal networks that greatly restricted effective autonomy,

[40] C. Castilho, *Slave Emancipations*, p. 25; P. Eisenberg, *The Sugar Industry*, pp. 158 and 165.
[41] M. MacCord, *Artífices*.　　[42] M. Silva, "*Domésticas criadas*."
[43] M. Carvalho, *Liberdade*; P. Beattie, *The Tribune*.

and those networks shaped the urban fabric far beyond the edges of slavery. Recife attracted relatively few of the migrants who helped to loosen such structures in other cities; foreigners comprised only 7 percent of the population in 1872, and of those nearly 1 in 10 was born in Africa. But it did attract many migrants from surrounding provinces, sons of provincial patriarchs jockeying for advancement and influence within a dense network of personal and political alliances.

Among aristocratic families and their ranks of slaves and dependents, circulation between the countryside and "the city" was a constant, its circuits etched by personal connections, its rhythm determined by life-stage, health, affective ties, and economic or political exigency. Even within the city, people circulated and moved surprisingly frequently: *sobrados* (aristocratic townhouses) were never static places. Those move-ments hinged on personal and familiar logics and only rarely responded to free markets in land, labor, or housing. Circulation often originated in mortality and sheer need: deadly disease was still a constant, relatively independent of social status; orphans and widows became a malleable and mobile class of domestic dependents; and superstition and sorrow could move even aristocratic families to mobility.[44] Only in the small urban core – the central neighborhoods of Recife, Santo António, and especially São José – did free artisans and workers establish something that more resembled the relatively independent poor workers' neighborhoods of Rio or Buenos Aires.[45]

Recife's topography ensured that its communities were more tentacular than continuous outside of the urban core. But slavery and the vertical patriarchal networks that grew from it created remarkable heterogeneity across the entire archipelago; decades after streetcars and steam railways had made urban social differentiation possible, segregation was rare.[46] In the urban core, some well-to-do families continued to share intimate space with their unequals and to rub shoulders with poorer neighbors, each with its retinue of dependents – slaves, servants, fictive and blood kin, boarders. These unequal intimacies often subsisted within aging *sobrados*

---

[44] One of the most eloquent descriptions of these dynamics can be found in F. Melo and G. Freyre, *Memórias de um Cavalcanti*. The logic of orphan circulation revealed in that work and in the archives of Recife's Santa Casa greatly resembled those discussed by Nara Milanich in Chile (*Children of Fate*) and Ann Blum in Mexico (*Domestic Economies*).

[45] M. MacCord, *Artífices*; S. Chalhoub, *Trabalho lar, Cidade febril*; and *Visões da liberdade*; J. Scobie, *From Plaza to Suburb*; L. Johnson, *Workshop of Revolution*.

[46] This was in sharp contrast to the US experience and to contemporaneous developments in Buenos Aires as described by James Scobie.

(townhouses), where the descendants of once-prosperous rural families hung on to a modicum of aristocracy by taking in paying renters. Outside of the urban core, in the bourgeois neighborhood of Boa Vista or the gentile suburbs of Graça and Madalena, households were larger, but heterogeneity persisted, with slaves, servants, *criados*, and dependents living in the same compounds as lawyers, commercial brokers, and politicians. In Recife's distant outreaches, still more rural than urban, *engenhos* (sugar mills) anchored small communities of intimate unequals. Across the archipelago, wealth, dependency, and bondage moved together, a phenomenon that can be seen in simple statistical correlations as well as anecdotal evidence; again, only the urbanized core showed signs of more significant racial and class differentiation.[47]

Social heterogeneity and the continued importance of vertical social networks had multiple intangible impacts on Recife's urban evolution. In combination with the inconstancy of Recife's social geography, they produced striking degrees of vertical social intimacy and recognition. In Recife's urban archipelago, individual communities were small and interconnected: this was still in some sense a "face-to-face community," where no one was anonymous when they ventured into urban public space.[48] Emblematically, before the early twentieth century, police often failed to ask for specific addresses when interrogating witnesses and defendants, because everyone could be found if need be. And individuals were recognized – seen – as part of a larger, known social network, points in the dense web of vertical social ties that situated every individual and shaped their prospects for sociability, mobility, and advancement. This rarely implied the kind of harmonious coexistence that Gilberto Freyre famously idealized; slavery and weak public institutions ensured that the hierarchies of interdependence were enforced with violence, coercion, and exploitation, whether implied or exercised outright.[49] But poor and marginalized people were not anonymous individuals in Recife, even in the eyes of the wealthy. Everyone was part of someone's network of power and dependency, either immediately recognized as such or sure to make the

---

[47] The most interesting result of a simple correlation of census statistics by neighborhood indicates a very low correlation between whiteness and freedom (indicating that slaves lived with mostly white masters). One of the highest correlations, which reinforces McCord's earlier arguments, is between literacy and artisan status, indicating that artisans tended to know how to read and tended not to live in households with large numbers of illiterate dependents.

[48] I borrow this specific use of the term from S. Dawdy, *Building the Devil's Empire*, p. 23.

[49] For a critique of the conflation of intimacy and harmony in a different context, see S. Hartman, *Scenes of Subjection*.

connection known as soon as they needed to get something done. In the absence of effective public institutions or opportunities for advancement, no one was autonomous. Even in its late-nineteenth-century form, the city was still a space where the lifeblood pulsed from the private sphere, even in ostensibly public contexts.

Against this backdrop, Recife was quickly acquiring the signs and symbols of North Atlantic urban modernity. In the 1860s it became the first city in Brazil (and perhaps the world) to use steam locomotives – *maxambombas* – for municipal transportation. Sewers, running water, pavement, and gas illumination provided creature comforts; new shopping districts, cafes, landscaped parks, theaters, and public buildings came to symbolize the public elegance of the urban core. Law students debated Italian positivist criminology and German legal theory; sugar barons mechanized and modernized; a few factories sprung up; boosters advocated sanitation and slum clearance. After 1870, as slave prices quickly spiked and the 1871 Free Womb Law forecast slavery's institutional expiration, manumissions accelerated and slavery's imprint on the urban landscape began to fade: by 1887, there were only some 2,036 enslaved people in the municipality, down from no fewer than 15,136 in 1872.[50] As Celso Castilho has documented, the politics of abolition and republicanism expanded Recife's public sphere and evoked ideals of citizenship, freedom, and equality that linked Recife to revolutionary spaces across Brazil and the Atlantic world.[51]

For Gilberto Freyre, whose characterizations of nineteenth-century Recife remain iconic, all of this indicated that Recife's heterogeneity was quickly giving way to the ecological succession and social distance predicted by the early Chicago school of sociology.[52] Public spaces were setting the pulse of urban life, no longer simply the channels that linked private worlds but rather powerful arenas of public culture and power. For Freyre, the social world of the *engenho* (sugar plantation) and *sobrado* (townhouse) was disintegrating as freed slaves claimed their independence in nascent shantytowns (*mocambos*) and wage labor markets and commercialism began to cut the bonds of vertical hierarchy, sentiment, and vertical interdependence.[53]

---

[50] Figures from C. Castilho, *Slave Emancipation*, pp. 27 and 147. The 1872 figure may be a low count, because it is based on the census rather than the 1873 slave census.

[51] C. Castilho, *Slave Emancipation*.

[52] See especially G. Freyre, *Mucambos do nordeste*, p. 23, and *Sobrados e mocambos*, p. 783.

[53] G. Freyre, *Sobrados e mocambos* and *Ordem e progresso*.

But there is every reason to think that Freyre lamented prematurely the demise of private, relational power. Recife became linked to a transnational urban ideal in these years, but that ideal's imprint was as inconstant as the city's topography. Slaves walked paved streets with bare feet; tramways passed through swaths of swamp and cane; *quilombos* (maroon settlements) grew strategically near rail stations. Manumission and abolition were achieved on the basis of relational power. Seemingly liberal institutions, as Sergio Buarque de Holanda argued eight decades ago, proved welcoming homes for patriarchal logics.[54] Recife's orphanage favored children with a letter of recommendation for scarce beds; Recife's police delegates, public prosecutors, and judges followed logics of loyalty as well as law.[55]

Even the *mocambos* – the shacks that came to symbolize Recife's informal city, and for Freyre the quintessential symbol of freedmen's desire for independence and the city's increasing social segregation – were from their origins deeply embedded in webs of relational power. *Mocambos* were ubiquitous, part of the city from the start, the majority of urban domestic structures as late as 1913.[56] But they were built not only on resistance but also on sufferance: they occupied ceded land, outside the strictures of the law, at the whim and by the rules of individuals with the material and political resources to create zones of exception in Recife's urban landscape. Already in the nineteenth century, *mocambos* were concentrated heavily in some neighborhoods, especially Afogados and Arraial. But they might appear anywhere; in the backyards of *sobrados*, on the borders of old *engenhos*, on the swampy banks of tidal rivers, in the abandoned interstices of Recife's archipelago. Everywhere, they created zones of private power, where cheap housing came at the price of loyalty, rent, and subordination. It is no accident that many of Recife's poor communities, like many of Rio's favelas, still bear the name of their founder or boss – the Alto Jose do Pinho, the Alto do Pascual, the neighborhood of Mustardinha.[57]

---

[54] S. Buarque de Holanda, *Raízes*.

[55] These conclusions are based on a sample of 165 substantial criminal case records dating from 1859 to 1900 (held in the IAHGP and the Museu da Justiça) as well as two sets of records held in the Arquivo Público Estadual Jordão Emerenciano (APEJE): a complete run of police logbooks between 1872 and 1900, and the Records of the Santa Casa.

[56] Brasil, Pernambuco, *Recenseamento (1913)*.

[57] In this way, Recife's *mocambos* shared much with Rio's early favelas; see B. Fischer, *A Poverty of Rights*, part IV. For a somewhat later journalistic account of these kinds of relationships, see the anonymous article entitled "Mostardinha – senhor feudal de um povoado de lama," from the *Folha do Povo*, Recife, July 23, 1935.

So it was, in general terms, that sugar and slavery imprinted their legacy on Recife, creating dense networks of relational power, altering the meaning of economic and institutional change, forging a distinct urban form in the southern reaches of the Atlantic world. But what did it mean to live in such a place? What did mobility and liberation signify in this urban context? How did their pursuit intersect – or not – with North Atlantic urban ideals such as equality, individuality, citizenship, and public accountability? For historians seeking answers to such questions, a city like Recife presents specific methodological difficulties. Precisely because the city's lettered classes frequently aspired to European forms and ideals, newspapers and literary sources tend to emphasize Recife's intersection with the North Atlantic; likewise, maps, almanacs, censuses, and governmental studies overwhelmingly emphasize normative features of urbanity, obscuring categories and experiences that do not conform. To unearth experiences thus silenced, the remainder of this chapter follows a generation of social and cultural historians to the moldy archives of Recife's criminal justice system, where life stories and sociocultural networks can be painstakingly reassembled and cross-referenced with civil registries and print periodicals. The resulting stories of captivity, freedom, and violence immerse us in the intimate, relational logic of a slave city in its waning days, placing in sharp relief the ways in which legacies of inequality would persist and deepen in the post-emancipation period.

STORIES

Anísia

We begin with a tale about the racial and gendered limits of freedom. Anísia Maria da Conceição was born in 1870 in Boa Vista, an urbane residential and commercial neighborhood that anchored Recife's law school and many prestigious public institutions. Anísia was the *filha natural* (natural daughter) of Antônia Maria da Conceição, a free woman and resident of the parish; no father was listed. Anísia's birth certificate declared her "white," and her godparents were João Rodrigues de Miranda and his sister Francisca Xavier Rodrigues de Miranda, both labeled *solteiros* (single). João would go on to manage the Companhia Telefónica de São Paulo, and their brother became a municipal judge; their father, Francisco, had been a police official, traveled frequently to the south of Brazil, and was remembered in the papers upon his death in 1899 as an "excellent citizen and dedicated father." Whether Francisco or one of his sons, enslaved workers, or servants was Anísia's father we'll never know: whatever protection they promised at her birth had evaporated by her adolescence.

We wouldn't know anything about Anísia if she had not run into trouble at the age of thirteen. She was living at the time with her mother Antônia, who worked as a cook for an English railroad engineer named William Elliot.[58] Antônia lived with her partner, a freedman called Severino, in the neighborhood of Arraial, a still-rural suburb and local transportation hub dotted with small-time farms and *mocambos*. Antônia was illiterate, a single mother, probably a light-skinned Afro-Brazilian. She had clearly managed, through deft manipulation of the narrow opportunities and connections available to her, to find good work and do well enough by her daughter that the girl knew how to read and did not work as a servant. In the slave city of Recife, this signified real social mobility for someone of Antônia and Anísia's racial and social station.

Anísia's good fortune may have changed with adolescence: it certainly went south in July of 1883, when she ran away with Manoel do Valle, an employee of the port works and the adopted son of a prominent lawyer and Liberal Party political activist named Manoel Henrique Cardim.[59] Anísia claimed that Manoel promised to marry her and to set her up in her own house in the nearby neighborhood of Casa Forte. Anísia left her mother's home with Manoel, known as "Neco"; several neighbors – an illiterate washerwoman, a servant, a small-time businessman who referred to Anísia only as a *mulatinha* (a dismissive term for a person of mixed African and European heritage) – testified that they'd recognized him. The servant, who worked with Antônia, said that Anísia's mother had done everything in her power to safeguard her daughter's virtue.

[58] There were two William Elliots who lived in Pernambuco in 1883, father and son. Anísia's mother presumably worked for the father and his wife, who had lived in Pernambuco since 1879 while Mr. Elliot was in charge of constructing a branch of the Great Western of Brazil Railway in Pernambuco. Elliot, whose peripatetic career took him to Russia, India, Argentina, Uruguay, Mexico, and Brazil as well as various European locations, completed the Great Western line and left Pernambuco for Buenos Aires in 1883, shortly after this case began. He would only return to Recife briefly in 1891 to construct one of the city's first large cotton mills, only to die of yellow fever shortly thereafter. See Institution of Civil Engineers (Great Britain), *Minutes*, pp. 371–373.

[59] Do Valle refers to himself as Cardim's *enteado*, and Cardim calls do Valle an orphan for whom he serves as *padrasto* and "tutor," indicating a kind of adoption rather than step-parenthood. Cardim appears in multiple cases stored in Recife's judicial archives, sometimes as an avid defender of freedom suits brought by the enslaved. See, for example, the case brought by the enslaved Elias in 1883, a mere three months before Anísia's case (Museu da Justiça de Pernambuco).

Manoel set Anísia up in the home of one of his neighbors and the two
had sex. Antônia, desperate, scoured the adjoining neighborhoods of
Arraial, Casa Forte, and Poço de Panela for her daughter with the aid of
Mrs. Elliot, finally enlisting the police. Anísia, fearing detection, took
refuge at "Doutor" Cardim's compound, and he personally reunited the
devastated mother and her rebellious daughter at the police station.
Antônia pressed charges against Manoel for kidnapping and deflowerment: Anísia, forced to undergo a gynecological exam, was declared
"semi-white" and definitely not a virgin. The public prosecutor advanced
the charges: it that point, it looked as if Anísia's story might end – as some
deflowerment suits did – with a forced marriage to a higher-status man.[60]

Do Valle was not, however, an average feckless seducer, and the court
system he worked within operated on a highly personalistic logic. In the
months that followed, Dr. Cardim and his lawyer systematically destroyed both the case and the racial and sexual reputations of the women
who had brought it. First, at the trial phase, the police witnesses disappeared or recanted their testimony. A servant in the house where Anísia
briefly stayed went further, claiming that Anísia had actually been raped
by her mother's lover (a former slave!), that another man had gone around
the neighborhood brandishing a bloody shirt and claiming he'd also had
sex with her, and that she (the witness) had only given her original
testimony because the police subdelegate had threatened her. A police
officer who had not testified in the investigative phase of the case repeated
the gossip, adding for good measure that Anísia was now living as
a prostitute. No one was called to defend Anísia – not her mother, not
her mother's employer, not a relative or godparent or protector.

More blows came from Manoel's lawyer and from a former police
delegate and political ally of Dr. Cardim. The lawyer, Luíz Rodrigues
Ferreira de Menezes Vasconcelos de Drummond, penned an elaborate
defense. The whole story was, Drummond claimed, a political intrigue,
manufactured from scratch by the police subdelegate of Arraial (a
Conservative partisan named Joaquim Maximiano Pestana, supposedly
known for his "rash and arbitrary acts").[61] Pestana aimed to damage
Dr. Cardim, who was his political and personal enemy. According to
Drummond, when Dr. Cardim found Anísia in his home, he had fulfilled

---

[60] For comparison, see S. Caulfield, *In Defense*.
[61] Pestana left the *subdelegacia* (subdelegation) of Poço de Panela shortly after, when he was
   appointed first *supplente* (alternate) for the post of local police delegate in the newly
   created district of Apipucos (*Jornal do Recife*, August 31, 1883).

his patriarchal duty, bringing her to the local police station. But Pestana had used his judicial powers as police subdelegate to strike at Dr. Cardim; Pestana allegedly threatened Anísia and her mother with jail, promised to marry Anísia to Manuel, and forced them to "swear on the cross" that Manoel had kidnapped and deflowered Anísia. For good measure, Drummond spent pages applying the minute "science" of hymenology to prove that Anísia had lost her virginity long ago, and he added (as a side note) that police subdelegate Pestana had "satisfied his own sensual pleasures" with Anísia over the course of the inquisition.

In the final phase of the trial, Dr. Cardim personally asked that the judge speak with the former police official of the region, a political ally of Cardim's named João Baptista da Ressurreição. In 1882, Ressurreição claimed, he had heard rumors that Anísia – then twelve – had been beaten and deflowered by her mother's lover, Severino. Ressurreição claimed that Anizia's grandfather had been driven to his death by this rumor, not only because of the beating and deflowerment but also because Severino was a freed slave, and Anísia's sexual union with him was thus an especially devastating dishonor. What's more, Ressurreição was later present at Arraial's public slaughterhouse when a young man named "Augusto something" ("son of Francelina, who lives in Arraial") started bragging that he had had sex with Anizia the night before, brandishing "a shirt with signs of blood and 'nodules' from that same copulation." It was also "public knowledge" in the neighborhood that Anísia's mother had found her in the act of having sex with the "caboclo José de tal," who lived on the lands of "Capitão Vianna," a local notable. In sum, as these facts showed, Anísia's "moral conduct was terrible ... due, no doubt, to the bad education and bad behavior of her mother, who began to be Severino's lover even when he was enslaved, and consented to the concubinage of Anísia's sister with Severino's brother Damião, who was of his same condition."[62]

The judge acquitted Manoel, who went on to live his life unfettered. Joaquim Maximiano Pestana, the police subdelegate who had sparked the inquiry, a Conservative and monarchist as far as the record reaches, continued to provoke strong feelings. A provincial newspaper editor nearly murdered him in 1886, and he took part in an ostentatious ceremony freeing his last slave five days before abolition.[63]

---

[62] For an analysis of the racial dimensions of Anísia's case in the context of other deflowerment suits in late-nineteenth-century Pernambuco, see M. Santos, "Moças honestas."

[63] *Jornal do Recife*, October 19, 1886; *Jornal do Recife*, May 8, 1888.

Dr. Cardim continued his illustrious career, both in Recife's court-rooms and as a prosecutor, orphan protector, and councilman in the nearby hamlet of Bom Jardim. In 1885, when famed abolitionist Joaquim Nabuco finally headed to Parliament after being denied office in two contested and corrupt elections, Cardim was one of hundreds of dignitaries who turned out as Nabuco took an elaborate victory lap by train through Recife's neighboring villages and towns.[64] In the hamlet of Bom Jardim, Nabuco personally pressed freedom papers into the hands of one of Cardim's household slaves as she served them dinner (one assumes the food kept coming).[65] Over the following years, Cardim was ostentatiously fêted as he freed multiple slaves, one of the last (rather conveniently) in February 1888 when the slave in question was being tried for attempted murder.[66]

Anísia and Antônia, meanwhile, disappear from the historical record. One would like to think that Anísia's racial and sexual humiliation was brief; that too much free choice and free movement did not permanently curtail her life as a free person.[67] Maybe she was the same Anísia Maria da Conceição who briefly flashed through the newspapers as orator for a carnival club in 1896 or who married Eustaquio Luiz da Costa in 1899. But she could also have been the Anísia who was arrested as a *gatuna*, or thief, in 1891.[68] The name is too common to tell.

Guilherme

Anísia Maria da Conceição ran against the limits of urban freedom, losing to the relational logic of the courts her sexual honor, her racial status, and the benefit of the law's protection. Guilherme, who had no last name, strained the confines of urban male slavery. On September 25, 1886, Guilherme appeared in the Boa Vista police station, accompanied by the famed abolitionist José Mariano. Guilherme had been whipped terribly, and his unhealed wounds had begun to turn gangrenous. Debates regard-ing the lash raged in 1886, in Recife and across Brazil. Mariano perhaps saw Guilherme's case as capable of opening new paths to freedom; just a few months earlier, Joaquim Nabuco had exposed similar cases of

---

[64] See C. Castilho, *Slave Emancipation*, p. 134 for a description of the celebrations.
[65] *Jornal do Recife*, July 4, 1885.
[66] *Jornal do Recife*, January 18 and February 5, 1888; *Diário de Pernambuco*, May 6, 1888.
[67] On women, movement, free choice, slavery, and freedom, see S. Camp, *Closer to Freedom*; K. McKittrick, *Demonic Grounds*; S. Hartman, "Anarchy of Colored Girls."
[68] *Jornal do Recife*, "Club das Enchadas," March 3, 1896; *A Provincia*, January 8, 1891.

cruelty in the Rio papers in order to advance the abolitionist cause.[69] Mariano's bet at first seemed to pay off: the Liberal police delegate opened an intricate criminal investigation, carried out first in Boa Vista and then in São Lourenço. The story that emerged from the investigation ran as follows.

Guilherme was twenty-one in October of 1886, described as *crioulo* (Brazilian-born), one of the last few thousand slaves in Recife. His mother, Felizarda, may have been freed.[70] Guilherme – young, muscular, and born several years before the Free Womb Law – was sold to a new owner in early 1886. Felizarda lived in Boa Vista, and Guilherme's old master was a merchant in the city. Guilherme's new owner, Tenente Coronel Pedro Ozorio de Cerqueira, was a forty-year-old *senhor de engenho* from the suburban expanse of São Lourenço, part of a small group of ambitious planters aggressively pushing for centralized mills and foreign investment in Pernambuco's cane country.[71] He had recently purchased a plantation called Camorim, and Guilherme – who may not have ever cut cane in his life as an urban slave – was human fuel for that modernizing vision.

It did not prove a good match. Cerqueira showed some ambivalence about the terms of slave ownership; like most of the slaveholding class, he had already freed several people and promised to free the rest if they were loyal for five years. In the flux of Recife's last abolitionist surge, the enslaved could translate ambivalence into bargaining power, and Guilherme only departed for Camorim on the condition that he could visit his mother in central Recife every Sunday. Those visits stretched regularly to two or three days, and even when he was at the *engenho*, Guilherme refused to work. He complained that Cerqueira would not let him rest when he was sick, and he may have told his companions that he would like to break a knife in the belly of the overseer. In June 1886, perhaps having heard rumors of abolitionist clubs, safe houses, and secret routes to the free state of Ceará, Guilherme ran away.[72]

[69] For a summary of debates on the lash in Recife, see C. Castilho, *Slavery Emancipation*, pp. 141–142; in Castilho's doctoral dissertation he references press stories about Guilherme's case (p. 193).

[70] She is described by Guilherme's owner as a "*moradora* [resident] on the Caminho Novo" (the street later known as Conde da Boa Vista); slaveowners generally would not usually use that word (and omit an owner's name) for an enslaved person.

[71] P. Eisenberg, *The Sugar Industry*. The ruralization of urban-born slaves after the end of Brazil's slave trade in the 1850s remains considerably less studied than the interregional trade between the Northeast and the southern coffee regions.

[72] On emancipationist and abolitionist networks in Recife, see C. Castilho, *Slave Emancipation*.

Like many runaways in greater Recife, he didn't go far. For a few months, Guilherme sought refuge in Recife, working odd jobs, some days earning nothing. He eventually fell into the protective network of noted abolitionist José Mariano, who lodged Guilherme and eventually helped him flee to a fiercely secretive runaway community in the "Matas dos Macacos," a jungled expanse that intersected with the Great Western rail line that ran northwest from Recife's city center. The place was likely near the site of the famed Catucá *quilombo*.[73] It was also close to Camorim, where Guilherme had been enslaved, and to a neighboring *engenho* where Guilherme was able to sneak under cover of night and convince two enslaved friends – one male, one female – to join him. All three stayed on in the Matas dos Macacos, working occasionally on plantations owned by abolitionist sympathizers, swearing to kill any outsider who penetrated their territory.[74]

But some slave hunters could pass as captives, and one such small-time *capitão de mata* (bounty hunter) began to frequent the *quilombo* in September.[75] He memorized the runaways' faces and left the *quilombo*, riding from plantation to plantation in search of owners who would pay for information on their runaways. Cerqueira paid, and Guilherme was captured, returned to Camorim, placed in the stocks, and brutally whipped with a five-pronged leather instrument called the *bacalhau*. According to Guilherme, Cerqueira ordered the whipping and watched it, refusing even to give Guilherme water as he bled through his mouth from the violence. Cerqueira denied the story, in testimony and in the newspapers, attributing the beating instead to a subordinate who had disobeyed his orders. Regardless, Guilherme and another slave broke free from the stocks, escaped once more to the Matas dos Macacos, and then found their way to José Mariano and the possibility of judicial protection from slavery's worst brutalities.

It wasn't impossible that things would go Guilherme's way. Just months before, a Recife judge named José Manuel de Freitas had sparked vociferous debate by refusing to apply punishment by the lash.[76] But the public prosecutor assigned to the case was Conservative and ruled that the

[73] On Catucá, see M. Carvalho, "O Quilombo," pp. 5–28; see also M. Carvalho, *Liberdade*, chapter 8.

[74] For a useful summary of contemporary *quilombos*, see F. Gomes and M. H. Machado, "Atrevessado a liberdade."

[75] According to Marcus Carvalho, it was not uncommon for Afro-descendant men to serve as slave catchers in early nineteenth-century Pernambuco (M. Carvalho, *Liberdade*).

[76] C. Castilho, *Slave Emancipation*.

investigation be carried out in São Lourenço. The witnesses were fellow planters, sharecroppers on the Camorim plantation, employees of Cerqueira's, and the *capitão do mato*. Their written testimony repeats, practically word for word, the same far-fetched but exculpatory facts: Cerqueira had gone with his fellow plantation owners to a meeting at the Engenho Central that day and had instructed a worker to simply hit Guilherme with the *palmatoria* (paddle); unable to find the paddle, the employee – not the overseer – had instead whipped Guilherme; the wounds had not been deep, and neither Cerqueira nor his overseer was ever known to hurt his slaves. The wounds, Cerqueira claimed in the papers, had probably been reinflicted by Mariano's associates in order to force Guilherme's freedom. Cerqueira used his connections in Recife to order a new medical exam, which found Guilherme heavily scarred but cured. The police took him from Recife and sent him back to Camorim and to slavery. The prosecutor concluded that there had been no crime.

Another slave from Camorim was tried for attempted murder in 1887 after attacking the same "peaceable" overseer who had allegedly whipped Guilherme.[77] Whether or not Guilherme cheered him on – whether or not Guilherme survived his last years of slavery, whether he finally found work, protection, and freedom in Recife's streets – we'll never know.

Esperança

Esperança was freed in the city but never experienced liberty. Instead, she was confined and brutally murdered in an old *sobrado* on a prominent downtown street, the Rua da Aurora. The likely murderer, Dona Herculina de Siqueira, the daughter of a Liberal rural *coronel*, was probably the woman who had both inherited the girl as a slave and voluntarily freed her. Herculina strangled Esperança with her bare hands after ordering a male slave to suspend the girl from the attic beams as punishment for supposed theft.

The killing happened, it seemed, for no real reason. Esperança, fourteen or fifteen at the time of her death in 1883, had been a favored slave: *parda*, literate, some said spoiled. Dona Herculina had freed her *gratuitamente* (without recompense), though she had also sold Esperança's mother to the south of Brazil. Dona Herculina enslaved a few people – an elderly woman born in Angola named Martha, a younger woman named Luiza, a young man named Vitorino who worked *de ganho* (for

---

[77] *Jornal do Recife*, March 20, 1887.

hire), and his brother, an eighteen-year-old named Felisbino who was, like Esperança, held in high esteem. The enslaved and servants alike lived on the *sobrado*'s attic floor, next to the kitchen; the lower levels were occupied by Herculina, two of her sisters, a few of their slaves and dependents, and three boarders from the nearby law school. It was a crowded place, full of married women whose husbands seemed absent, owned by an aristocratic family but decadent enough that Dona Herculina needed the boarder's rent.

Esperança doesn't seem to have been happy in Herculina's household. She grudgingly completed her household tasks, fought with Felisbino, sometimes spat at passers-by on the street. Herculina and her sisters frequently accused her of stealing, and one of Herculina's in-laws claims to have regularly heard Esperança scream from beatings so terrible that relatives asked the *senhora* to ease up. But Esperança, though free, did not or could not leave, even to join a great aunt who still lived nearby and kept attuned to her welfare: there is, in fact, no record of Esperança ever setting foot outside of the *sobrado*.

So it was that on October 30, 1883, a Tuesday, Herculina's sister complained that Esperança had stolen a bit of cloth. Herculina ordered Felisbino to punish Esperança, as she often did; he dragged her to the attic kicking and biting and suspended her from the crossbeams by her wrists and ankles. She screamed in pain and protest; someone, almost certainly Dona Herculina herself, strangled Esperança to stifle her cries, leaving deep fingernail wounds gashed on her throat. She died within a few hours. The doctor who issued the death certificate – a family friend of Herculina's – said the death had resulted from cholic and labeled Esperança "preta" (literally "Black," but connoting enslavement). Herculina then sent Esperança to be buried in a slave's grave.

That might have been the end of the story, were it not for a chain of not-so-chance encounters on Recife's dark streets. Felisbino, sent to get water from a public fountain, told Esperança's great aunt of the murder. She told a friend, and through connections the story made it to a combative abolitionist police delegate named José Climaco de Espirito Santo. He quickly tracked down Esperança's body at the morgue and verified the signs of her violent death. Luiza confirmed Felisbino's confession, detailing Herculina's orders and her role in the strangling. Herculina and a long string of her friends, relatives, and boarders told different stories, all exculpatory but so contradictory that Climaco refused to believe them. He took the very unusual step of imprisoning both Felisbino and Herculina, accusing both of murder: Herculina, almost uniquely for a woman of her family status, spent more than a month in prison before finally receiving a writ of habeas corpus after a vigorous press campaign. She gained freedom because no free person gave witness to the crime; Felisbino remained in prison largely because he was enslaved.

A judge tried both Felisbino and Herculina and advanced the trial to the final jury phase. But the case against Herculina gradually loosened. She disappeared, first claiming illness, then staying secretly with her sister, then fleeing from Recife in the middle of the night with two men dressed as if they were from the backlands. Rumor had it that Herculina had gone to her family property in Pesqueira. The enslaved Luiza, who had testified against Herculina, also disappeared, and various rumors circulated about her fate. Freed and sent to Ceará? Died of smallpox in the Pedro II Hospital? Spirited to the backlands? Dona Herculina's two other captives equivocated, casting blame on Luiza. The proceedings ground nearly to a halt. Finally, on February 20, 1885, a jury found Felisbino guilty and sentenced him to eighty lashes and four months with an iron around his neck. Herculina, still absent, seems never to have been tried at all.

The verdict sparked fury in the papers. On February 27, an anonymous comment raged at the perceived offense to Recife's honor and the integrity of its justice: who would believe that a brutal whipping could be administered in the "civilized capital of the Empire's second province"? "Can a tribunal be taken seriously when it condemns a machine, an automaton, a blind follower of orders, a miserable *mandatório*, when everyone knows that the audacious authority placed herself far from the law's action, and took refuge in places where justice cannot reach?"[78] Abolitionists – including the famed Ave Libertas society – immediately jumped in to fund Felisbino's appeal and seek his freedom. In that latter aim they failed.[79] But remarkably, on October 26, the judicial appeal succeeded, and the high court upheld the new verdict on December 17, 1887. Felisbino had spent years in prison and was still enslaved, but he would not be whipped and could be released to his owners in the midst of the last throes of abolitionism. The great abolitionist lawyer who achieved this feat? Luiz Drummond – the same man who had, a few short years before, together with his fellow champion of the enslaved Dr. Manoel Henrique Cardim, buried Anísia in racial and sexual dishonor.[80]

---

[78] *Diário de Pernambuco*, "Collaboração," February 27, 1885. According to Celso Castilho, this would have been an early salvo in a cycle of debates about the use of the lash in Pernambuco that stretched through 1886.

[79] On the Ave Libertas, see C. Castilho, *Slave Emancipation*.

[80] *Jornal do Recife*, October 27, 1886.

CONCLUSION: AFTERLIVES OF A SLAVE CITY

What can we learn from Anísia, Guilherme, and Esperança about slavery in the city and about the city that slavery made? In relation to slavery, these cases sound cautions about any easy association of urbanity and full emancipation. Recife was, at least in part, a space of imagined and actual degrees of freedom, where enslaved people could sometimes attain greater control over their work, their time, their homes, and their bodies.[81] In the relative intimacy of homes and small workplaces, manumission seemed more attainable, and many of the enslaved worked autonomously, *de ganho*. Rarely, the brand of slavery itself could fade in the urban crowd, especially among men. All of these hopes and desires were evident in Guilherme's initial foray to freedom or in Antônia and Esperança's life stories.[82] Such hopes surely ratcheted higher during the heyday of Recife's abolitionist movement, amidst a cascade of high-minded speeches, performative emancipations, public homages to prominent abolitionists, emancipationist rallies and cultural events, and steadily expanding channels to freedom. As Celso Castilho and others have shown, activists often elided abolition and citizenship and claimed the public sphere as its amphitheater. It is tempting to grasp at the truly emancipatory strains of those movements and possibilities, to see in abolitionist-era Recife the roots of rupture and convergence on deeper, more egalitarian, and more public freedoms.

Yet our stories strip those hopes away, largely because they occurred in a city where personal power networks permeated the institutions of government and the notion that formal freedom denoted equality, autonomy, or anonymity was almost inconceivable. In Esperança, Guilherme, and Anísia's world, the intimacy of urban work proved deadly, autonomous employment was hard to come by, and runaways didn't stay anonymous for long. Degrees of freedom could be lost as well as won; a single sale transformed an urban slave into a rural one, formal freedom could connote conditions no different than domestic slavery, a string of racial and sexual slurs could turn a white daughter into a mulatta prostitute. Only a strong protector, who by his very presence eroded freedom's meaning, could ward against such fates. Similarly, the performance of emancipationism – or even abolitionism – often had little to do with full freedom, much less equality. One could imagine our protagonists rallying

---

[81] S. Chalhoub, *Visões da liberdade*; F. Filho, *Encruzilhadas*.
[82] For limits on this freedom and doubts about its scope, see M. Carvalho, *Liberdade*.

for José Mariano, or whispering rumors about underground railways, or listening hopefully to the echoes of abolitionist rallies through open windows; we surmise that many like them did just that. But we know for sure that every one of our villains, from Cardim and Drummond to Cerqueira and Dona Herculina, had both personally freed slaves and taken part in the public performance of emancipation – ceremoniously manumitting favored captives to the rapt praise of local journalists, defending powerless slaves in court, denouncing the *barbarie* that slavery inflicted on owners and slaves alike, giving ostentatious speeches on Joaquim Nabuco's selfless dedication to the cause. In Recife, the ethos and logic of inequality encompassed both those who sought freedom and those who believed it was theirs to grant.

The limits of urban emancipation thus underlined freedom's precariousness. But Anísia, Guilherme, and Esperança's stories also reveal the deep and durable logics of an urban form that grew entwined with bondage. In idealized formulations – caricatures, really, but meaningful all the same – cities often represent a stage in a positivistic historical progression: from agriculture to manufacturing, from relational power to liberal governance, from unfree labor and patriarchal dominance to the triumph of market logics and an egalitarian public sphere. But in Recife, as in so many actual cities, – north and south – urbanity meant something quite different. There, the rural and the urban were locked in patterns of symbiotic circulation, and the city derived its power from its ability to serve as a nexus of rural economies and social relations. In Recife, private spaces anchored a discontinuous urban landscape; public space was simply the intersection of the private worlds represented by Dona Herculina's *sobrado*, Cerqueira's *engenho*, and Dr. Cardim's household compound – or even Guilherme's *quilombo* and Antônia's *mocambo*. Within and among those private spaces, everyone – slave and free – was enmeshed in relations of intimate dependency, and nearly everyone's social world was known or discoverable: anonymity was never more than a step or two removed from recognition. Intimacy served as the conduit for information and rumor, within and across social scales; unequal intimacies facilitated urban survival, mobility, and opportunity, just as they regulated passage through degrees of freedom. Relational logics permeated public institutions and shaped the public sphere, limiting liberal visions of egalitarian individualism even when that public sphere was overtaken by the tides of abolition.

What did freedom look like, lived in such a relational city? What did urbanity look like, forged with such unequal freedoms? Did the city that slavery made eventually dissipate, opening space for the liberal, egalitarian, individualistic "city"? Gilberto Freyre, writing between the 1920s and the 1950s, believed regretfully that he was witnessing just such a sea-change.[83] Recife, like many Brazilian cities, spent much of the twentieth century literally and figuratively razing its colonial and slavocratic pasts. *Sobrados* became tenements and then rubble; centenary trees made way for broad avenues; the spaces of wealth and poverty began to disentangle. In our own times, thirteen decades after the events recounted in this chapter, Recife has navigated both modernity and post-modernity: factories have grown and shrunk; boulevards have become thoroughfares; elegant belle époque avenues have fallen into decadence while shiny globalized malls have risen from Recife's mudflats. *Mocambos* have become favelas, Big Houses have become luxury highrises. Recife has protagonized some of the most progressive strains of Brazilian politics, from communism to agrarian reform, liberation theology, the pedagogy of the oppressed, and the right to the city.

But amidst all of the trappings of urban modernity, the building blocks of the slave city are still striking: banal private violence, racialized inequality, unequal intimacy, rural–urban continuums, the discontinuity of public and urbanized space, the powerful logics of relational and private power. These urban continuities – and their utter legibility far beyond Brazil's borders – suggest the need for an alternate modernizing narrative rooted in the slave city and the informal, relational webs that sustained it.

[83] This is most clearly argued in G. Freyre, *Sobrados e Mocambos*.

8

Migrações ao sul

Memories of Land and Work in Brazil's Slaveholding Southeast

Robson Luis Machado Martins and Flávio Gomes[*]

Less than a month after the abolition of slavery on May 13, 1888, Councilor João José de Andrade Pinto – of Brazil's Supremo Tribunal de Justiça (Supreme Court) – received a writ of habeas corpus filed by the attorney Ernesto Ferreira França. He had compiled a vast documentary record of investigations conducted under the direction "of the judges, magistrates and Police Chief of the Municipality of Cantagalo."[1] Their main complaint was as follows: "The former slaves of Fazenda Socorro, in the town of Carmo de Cantagalo ... which belongs to Captain Manoel Pereira Torres, want to leave that plantation; but they are held in unlawful restraint by said Captain." One of the main victims was Sebastião Rufino dos Santos Maranhão, a freedman "to whom the Supreme Court granted habeas corpus, along with his companions," because he had been "perse-cuted, threatened with death and [forced to become a] fugitive."

The counterattack, less than a month later, came from the pen of Jeronymo Mizisur Nogueira Pavido, the planters' lawyer. He had mar-shalled battalions of arguments. On June 9, he told the judge: "I am unaware of the facts that are the subject of said habeas corpus; given that the authorities of the town of Carmo ... will tell me nothing about it, just as the freedmen in question have not made any sort of petition to this tribunal."

[*] The authors wish to acknowledge Brodwyn Fischer and Keila Grinberg for their criticism of and suggestions for the first version of this paper, as well as their support with the English edition. Translation by Sabrina Gledhill and Brodwyn Fischer.
[1] National Archives (Rio de Janeiro), Supremo Tribunal de Justiça, Habeas Corpus, Cantagalo, 1888, Sebastião Rufino dos Santos, HCD, folder 1772, number 2.713.

The crossfire of justifications was just beginning. Witness statements had to be gathered. An immediate decision was made "to hear the former slaveholder; as this is a matter of freedom, he should be summoned to appear in person in order to provide clarifications." However, the first impressions came from the police inquiry. Under the court's order, the local police commissioner of the town of Carmo conducted an investigation. In the following days, he rejected the charges: based on his "reading of the documents" that had been sent, he could "certify that there was no evidence of the violence that those ex-slaves claimed to suffer or the forced constraint that they claimed to be persecuted with." On the orders of police headquarters, a police officer – Lieutenant Francisco da Cunha Telles – was sent out to "visit all the areas where there are large numbers of *fazendas* [coffee plantations] and examine who was doing the work in each place, and also obtain information about how the interests of the freedmen who work on those *fazendas* are being served, and instruct the respective detachments about how to proceed with local authorities in repressing vagrancy and vagabondage, prohibiting illegal procedures with regard to any arrests they might have to make." Various plantations in the municipalities of Sumidouro, Miracema, Muriaé, and Carmo received visits. The result: "it is affirmed that there is nothing new among the freedmen, even on the plantation of Captain Manoel Pereira Torres, they are not constrained, and I inquired in great detail about them."

Interested parties were present at the interrogations of the planter and later of the freedmen. In his statement, Captain Manoel Pereira Torres reportedly said

that after the enactment of the May 13 Law this year, he gathered his former slaves together and declared to them that they were in full enjoyment of their freedom, and that only those who prefer to remain in the *fazenda* [would] stay on, in exchange for their services. And, in effect, none of them is under constraint and they can all go wherever they please at any time.

Most of the freedpersons underwent a group interrogation, though some were dispensed from the summons "to appear at this police station … because they were ill":

The police commissioner posed the following questions to the formerly enslaved people, in the presence of recognized witnesses:

Asked if they were aware of their natural status? They responded yes, they know they are free, due to a Law, from the Princess, which they say dates from May 13.

Asked if, on the Fazenda Socorro, where they were still employed, they were illegally constrained, that is, if they were still treated like slaves and held to be such, thus being prevented, by seigneurial force, from seeking better conditions on other *fazendas*? They replied that since Captain Manoel José Pereira Torres, their former master, declared them free, which took place this past May, they have never found themselves illegally constrained and that if they have not yet left their current employer to this day it is because they are well treated, as the free men they recognize themselves to be, and are paid for their field work, with both men and women receiving a certain amount per month, as well as a housing and sustenance; that they feel themselves to be contracted under such good conditions that they have no wish to leave the house where they work.

Asked whether Sebastião Maranhão, had been denied his *amásia* [concubine] [and] their natural children when he went to fetch them from the Fazenda Socorro? They responded that Torres did not deny Sebastião his *amásia* when he appeared at Fazenda Socorro to take her away, but that they do not know why it was that she did not accompany him. At that moment, one of Sebastião Maranhão's children spoke up and made the following statement: "I, my siblings and my mother, who is not married to my father Sebastião, did not want to accompany our father because we committed ourselves to bringing in the harvest this year and if we entered into those contracts it was because we did not want to leave the *fazenda*, nor did we know where our father was, because he left us two years ago." This is verbatim, and the declarant's name is Ignacio Maranhão.

Asked if they had full liberty to come and go whenever they wanted? They answered that yes, they always went out and if they did not do so more often it was because they did not want to. Asked whether their companions who did not appear at the police station fully enjoyed their rights as the free persons they presently are? They answered yes, that like the respondents they enjoyed their freedom and that they were also content in that house. And since no more questions were asked of them, the police commissioner had this report drafted and after it was read to them and they found it to be accurate, the same police commissioner signed it on their behalf because they could not read or write.

The document described here sheds light on some of the meanings of freedom in the coffee plantation areas in southeastern Brazil during the period immediately after slavery's abolition. Could the freedmen choose where they wanted to live and work? Did they have the autonomy to move freely? What were the expectations of behavior attributed to former masters and former slaves?

These are some of the themes that, in recent decades, have been consolidated in Brazil around the question of post-emancipation. Although the idea is not always stressed, the concept of post emancipation posits that it makes sense to think about Brazil's end of slavery in a plural way. The post-emancipation period – its timelines, periodization, meanings, symbols, issues, theoretical and methodological foundations – is complex. When did it begin? The day after May 13, 1888? When did it end? During the Vargas era in the 1940s, when laws that gave some support to rural workers reverberated with memories of the possibility of true abolition? The concept of post-emancipation demands broader periodization, one that would lead historians to make less use of the idea of "post-abolition" (which refers almost exclusively to the chronological period immediately following the "Golden Law"). This is important because many histories of post-emancipation can be reconstructed from the experiences of thousands of men and women who achieved legal freedom and lived autonomous lives before final abolition, in a nineteenth-century society that was still besieged by slavery. It is thus possible to think of a broadened chronology of post-emancipation – say from 1830 to 1950 – that articulates dimensions of Brazil's rural, urban, and labor history along with aspects of its nation-building projects and social thought. Such a history would place post-emancipation at the very center of contemporary Brazil's historical formation. Researchers from the most varied fields would be challenged to expand the possibilities of addressing Brazil's contemporary history, and especially its labor history, as additional chapters of post-emancipation.

With regard to the histories of slavery and freedom, Brazil went through a long historiographic movement of erasure. We are now assembling another movement, focused on the meaning, resignification, and use of memories and histories of slavery and post-emancipation. In this chapter, we join empirical research with theoretical reflections in order to explore the formation of post-emancipation narratives and memories in Brazil's slaveholding Southeast. It is possible, in that region, to reintegrate the histories of freedom, control, and autonomy in the first decades of the twentieth century. In various archives and other historical sources, we can find inscribed – albeit in multivocal form – important intersections in the histories of land, labor, mobility, migration, control, and power.

ACCESS TO LAND IN THE SHADOW OF SLAVERY

In an original study that combines oral histories and documentary sources, Ana Maria Lugão Rios has demonstrated how an itinerant peasantry was formed in Brazil, particularly in the late nineteenth century and the first decades of the twentieth.[2] This process was grounded in the dynamics of land access: in property that was bequeathed to slaves and freedpersons so that they could engage in subsistence agriculture, in

---

[2] A. M. Lugão Rios, "Família e transição."

occupations opened up by the displacement of Black peasant families in the decades prior to abolition, and even in the formation of Black peasant towns, some of them remnants of *quilombos* (maroon settlements) or linked to them. Rios took an interesting analytical approach in order to deal with the multiplicity of rural universes in which diverse peasant communities – and especially those made up of Black descendants of the enslaved – came into contact. In different regions there were myriad situations. Some areas had open economic frontiers, in others the frontiers had already closed; some had vacant public land, others very little. Some regions were undergoing rapid economic expansion, while others were in decline. Many zones combined plantation agriculture with peasant production, while others were dominated by one or the other. Considering all this diversity, it would be nearly impossible to depict a single reality for the first decades after abolition. The matter would become even more complex if we also considered the earlier period when slavery was still legal and abolitionism was in full ferment.

A national approach to the study of slavery, abolition, and post-abolition – and of post-emancipation in the broader sense – is rife with traps, leading often to overgeneralization, the reinforcement of stigmas, and the silencing of diverse historical experiences. Research is still scarce about the formation of a Black peasantry during slavery and its iterations in widely varying rural settings. In diverse regions, slaves, immigrants, and free workers (many of whom were freedpersons) came together, reproduced, and organized themselves into peasant communities that were rooted in family, territory, or ethnicity and were constantly on the move.

While this movement is difficult to capture in methodological terms, it is not impossible. The flow of land grants to freedpersons in slaveholders' wills does not necessarily have to be quantified or measured by the benchmarks of agricultural production to convey meaning: even singular situations can help explain the expectations of land and work that expanded the meanings of freedom during the last quarter of the nineteenth century and the first decades of the twentieth.

In the slaveholding Southeast – and especially in Rio de Janeiro and Espírito Santo – new rural ventures arose from north to south, often creating tension between coffee, sugar, and food production and the economic frontiers of migration and mobility. For the area of São João da Barra in northern Rio de Janeiro province, for example, several wills reveal narratives containing intersecting sentiments of generosity, expectation, rights, and custom among enslaved people, freedpersons, slaveholders, planters, and heirs.

In 1872, Candido Alves de Azevedo expressly stated in his will: "I hereby leave over one hundred *braças* [fathoms, equivalent to about 6 feet] of land ... including half of the improvements thereon, to Hortência Mariana da Conceição (free) and Prudêncio (baptized as a slave with specific conditions that would lead to his liberty), land that they will enjoy ... after my death and that of my wife." Besides the land, the couple would inherit three slaves. In addition, he left "over one hundred *braças* of land from the same plot as that of the couple, with any improvements thereon, to my slaves Claudino, Felismindo, and Custódio, who will enjoy this bequest after my death and that of my wife." Prudêncio would have to be freed in order to inherit the land, and some other slaves – Norberta, Ana, and Bernarda – would simply be "freed, as if they were born from a free womb."[3]

Domingas Maria de Azevedo's 1873 will was even more detailed. In it, she spelled out the possession, property, and later freedom of "the slave woman named Theodora, who has borne children named Albino, Luiza, Maria, Justina, the first aged sixteen, the second twelve, the third eight, the last three." "To these children," she wrote, "because of the love I came to feel when raising them: I grant Albino his freedom from this date forward, as if he were born from a free womb. To Luiza, Maria and Justina I also grant freedom, but on the condition that they attend to my husband Lúcio Antonio de Azevedo; upon his death they will enjoy full freedom as if born from a free womb." Regarding land, she continued: "I furthermore declare that I leave the said *crias* [children raised in her home] lands 350 *braças* deep, bordering on the front with Dominicano de tal, in the back with José Vieira, on one side with me, and on the other side with Lauriano de tal. I leave these lands to the four aforementioned *crias* and to one more who was born after the Free Womb Law and to any other siblings who might be born in the future."[4]

In 1882, Izabel da Silva Rangel endorsed the manumission of several slaves after her death. We understand more, however, from the words that follow: "I leave half of the lower part of my land to my slave Camilo and his family, because he deserves it by virtue of the good services he has rendered me."[5] In 1883, Domingos Gonçalves da Costa ordered in his will

[3] National Archives (Rio de Janeiro), will of Candido Alves de Azevedo, São João da Barra, Box 700, 1872.

[4] Judiciary Archives (Rio de Janeiro), will of Domingas Maria de Azevedo, São João da Barra, Box 680, 1873.

[5] Judiciary Archives (Rio de Janeiro), will of Izabel da Silva Rangel, São João da Barra, box 695, 1882.

that a house be purchased and granted to some of his slaves, who should also be freed: "Purchase from my assets a house worth up to about four hundred mil reis, for Joana to live in, and for Joaquim, Benedito and Felisminda to live in as long as they are alive, and when they are dead, it should pass to the Santa Casa de Misericórdia [a charity hospital] in this city. I want fifty mil reis given to the Black woman Joana and fifty mil reis given to Felisminda."[6]

The following passage from Antonio Ribeiro de Campos's 1886 will gives us a good idea of the horizon of expectations that slaves might have held when their masters died and their wills and bequests were made public:

I hereby grant unconditional freedom to my slave Maria. I also set free my slaves Geraldo and Rita Ribeira, who are over fifty years of age. I declare that my slave Felipe is obliged to work for two years under the direction of my first executor or either of [his] other two siblings and at the end of said period will be freed. I declare that the Black man Tibúrcio must hire out his services for the time stipulated in the contract he agreed to, the product ... going to benefit my heirs and legatees and those named below.[7] I declare that the slaves Balthasar and Amaro, who belong to Francisco de Sá Junior, find themselves in my service due to a loan I made to the latter, whose slaves will continue to provide services for the benefit of my said legatees until their master's debt is paid unless he pays compensation for the remainder of their services with interest of one percent per month corresponding to the remaining [contract] time.

Regarding land, de Campos mentioned that he was leaving "the small-holding that belonged to Araujo's sons and later to João Brinco to my slave Felipe, and to the freedman Geraldo, with Felipe enjoying in the usufruct of said small holding only after fulfilling the two years of work to which he is obliged, and with both men having only the usufruct of the small holding, usufruct which will pass upon the death of either man to the surviving one, upon whose death it will revert to my heirs and legatees." He left to his slave Rita "a tiny small-holding annexed to the lands of Antonio de Souza de tal, which last belonged to Sebastião Brinco; she may dispose of that land as she wishes." He left other freedpersons farm animals as an inheritance: Rita herself received "an old beast named Maquitola"; "the freedman Geraldo, a dark donkey with damaged

---

[6] Judiciary Archives (Rio de Janeiro), will of Domingos Gonçalves da Costa, São João da Barra, box 717, 1883.

[7] This type of contract – referred to in the document as a *contrato de locação de servir* – was common in late-nineteenth-century Brazil. It generally required enslaved people to hire out their labor and pay a set portion of their earnings to their owners.

hooves formerly owned by the Tram company"; and finally "to the slave Felipe the donkey Quero-Quero, which he can claim in two years."[8]

ITINERANT PEASANTRIES AND ECONOMIC PRACTICES

What did it mean for slaves and freedpersons to sometimes have access to land, by virtue of these kinds of conditional concessions and conquests? In various regions – each with its own sociodemographic specificities – slaves and freedpersons constructed economic practices that gave rise to close interaction among them. In many places, they attended local fairs and markets on Saturdays and Sundays – their customary "free days" – where they would set up *quitandas* (stalls) and sell products from their small farms or gardens. Debate about the meaning of these practices gained strength in Brazilian historiography in 1979 with the publication of a chapter by Ciro Flamarion Cardoso, "The Peasant Breach in the Slaveholding System."[9] Building on the work of Sidney Mintz and Tadeusz Lepkowski (who coined the expression "peasant breach"), Cardoso considered the nature of Brazilian slavocracy, noting the presence of peasant economic activity. He summarized part of the intellectual debate about the Caribbean and elsewhere, stressing the "modalities of the peasant phenomenon under a colonial slaveholding regime." In this conception there were "non-proprietary peasants," "peasant proprietors," "peasant activities of the *quilombolas* [maroons]," and the "slave proto-peasantry." At that time, the debate was fundamentally ideological.[10] The crux of the matter was to find a way to recognize the economic congruity of slaves and peasants without compromising the concept of the "colonial slave mode of production," which was their proposed interpretive foundation.

In 1987, Cardoso would return to the issue, incorporating evidence from new secondary sources and ongoing research and also responding to criticism from Jacob Gorender and Antônio Barros de Castro.[11] He

---

[8] Judiciary Archives (Rio de Janeiro), will of Antonio Ribeiro de Campos, São João da Barra, box 717, 1886.

[9] C. Cardoso, "A brecha camponesa." This article was later published in English as "The Peasant Breach in the Slaveholding System," *Luso-Brazilian Review* 25:1 (1988): 49–57.

[10] Cardoso observes that the first version of this article was written as a presentation for the Second Conference of Historians of Latin America and the Antilles in March 1977 in Caracas. See C. Cardoso, "A brecha camponesa."

[11] C. Cardoso, *Escravo ou camponês?* See also A. B. de Castro, "A economia política, o capitalismo e a escravidão," and J. Gorender, "Questionamentos sobre a teoria econômica do escravismo colonial."

emphasized a wide array of evidence about the practice of granting slaves parcels of land to farm for their own subsistence. This was customary among the Portuguese on the island of São Tomé even before the colonization of Brazil; the practice would eventually become known in many slave regions as the "Brazilian system." There is evidence of it in the Captaincy of Pernambuco as early as 1663. Royal orders and permits from the last decades of the seventeenth century instructed subjects about "rights" to time and land, established so that slaves could provide their own subsistence. In 1701, the well-known chronicler André João Antonil praised the "custom practiced by some masters in Brazil," by which "they give [slaves] a day every week when they can plant and prepare their provisions."[12]

Despite seigneurial prohibitions and complaints, enslaved people sought to build their own economies and thus attain autonomy. In the Caribbean, there are many suggestive examples of slaves who sold produce from their small-holdings and supplied local markets. The Sunday markets that they frequented became spaces for socialization, attracting slaves and freedpersons from multiple plantations, many of whom travelled for miles to get there. The economic circuits created by those who managed to take their produce for sale in nearby towns and cities also allowed information and culture to circulate among slaves in urban and rural areas.[13] Enslaved people's mercantile exchanges with maroons and closer relations with the free poor and freedpersons could also – though not necessarily – lay the ground for indirect attacks on slavery. The actions the maroons took to preserve their communities – veritable Black peasant villages – and the confrontational strategies employed by free people in their struggles for land use and possession helped change the world of those who were still enslaved.[14]

What was going on with the free poor populations who lived on the margins of areas experiencing economic growth or who focused their production on the domestic market? In many parts of the Caribbean, the free Black population enjoyed a reasonable amount of economic autonomy, even during slavery.[15] There are still few studies in Brazil

---

[12] C. Cardoso, *Escravo ou campones?*, pp. 119–120.

[13] D. B. Gaspar, "Slavery, Amelioration and Sunday Markets," and B. Wood, "White Society." See also I. Berlin and P. Morgan, eds., *The Slaves' Economy*, "Introduction," pp. 1–27.

[14] On conflicts in the post-emancipation period, see H. Beckles and K. Watson, "Social Protest," and M. Craton, "Continuity not Change."

[15] Regarding land and expectations during the post-emancipation period in the Caribbean, see J. Besson, "Land Tenure"; H. Johnson, "The Emergence of a Peasantry"; R. Scott and M. Zeuske, "Property in Writing."

that accompany the experiences of freedpersons, documenting their expectations vis-à-vis land during slavery and post-emancipation.[16] A great many small-holdings may have been passed down through generations of families that were enslaved and later freed, resulting after 1888 in conflicts with their former masters.[17] Yet beyond this, studies of Brazilian slave economies have made little progress in empirically demonstrating the circulation of peasant agricultural production among slaves and sectors of the surrounding Black peasantry, including communities of freedpersons and even *quilombolas*.

One archival path that has not been explored is local legislation – which abounded after the mid-nineteenth century – that banned the purchase of products from slaves, as well as the functioning of taverns and like activities. When one accompanies recurrent municipal regulations for the province of Rio de Janeiro, there is a notable concern with commodities, mercantile exchanges, and even the circulation of money involving slaves or the Black population. In the municipality of Rio Bonito in 1876, for example, article 67 of Municipal Regulatory Decree no. 40 imposed fines on those who bought "any object from slaves unless the slaves present written permission from their masters to sell it."[18] Interestingly, an annotation detailed exceptions to this law: "slaves who sell foodstuffs on Sundays and holidays in the streets *quitanda*-style." Even so, it was forbidden for "sellers of beverages to sell spirits to slaves" or even to "open a business after the doors close to buy or sell goods from slaves."

In 1859, the Municipal Regulations for Piraí contained more details along these same lines, imposing a fine or fifteen days in jail on any "person who buys coffee, corn or other agricultural product from slaves if those slaves do not present written permission from their masters or overseers."[19] That same year, the municipality of Paraíba do Sul issued decree no. 1.167 which imposed fines on anyone who "allows slaves to linger in commercial establishments for more time than is reasonably necessary for them to make purchases" or who "negotiate[s] with slaves,

[16] H. Mattos and A. M. Lugão Rios, *Memórias* and "O pós-abolição"; H. Mattos, *Ao sul da história*, "Remanescentes," and "Políticas de reparação."

[17] Regarding slave small-holdings and economies, see B. J. Barickman, "Persistence and Decline"; J. Fragoso and M. G. Florentino, "Marcelino"; M. H. Machado, "Em torno da autonomia escrava," "Vivendo na mais perfeita desordem," and *O plano e o pânico*; and J. Reis and E. Silva, *Negociação e conflito*.

[18] Posturas Municipais do Município de Rio Bonito (1871–1877), *Anais da Assembleia Legislativa Provincial do Rio de Janeiro*, Biblioteca Nacional (RJ).

[19] Posturas Municipais do Município de Piraí (1859), *Anais da Assembleia Legislativa Provincial do Rio de Janeiro*, Biblioteca Nacional (RJ).

buying from them or exchanging any object with them."[20] For the municipality of Barra Mansa, Title IX of the Municipal Regulations established penalties for "any person, whether or not they are a merchant, who buys items of gold or silver, or goods of any other kind (clothes, fabric, tools, coffee, or foodstuffs) from slaves without note or authorization from their masters." Here again, "the provisions of this article do not apply to slaves who might sell foodstuffs on Sundays and holidays in the streets *quitanda*-style." In the municipality of Santa Maria Madalena, the regulations were attentive to weights and measures, stating that that anyone who "buys food from slaves with a value that exceeds 2$ by weight, or 4$ by measure, or any object worth more than 2$, without written permission from those slaves' masters, managers or overseers, will pay a 20$ fine."[21] For the municipality of Capivari, the novelty was a ban on "buying any kind of agricultural products, dead or living animals, birds, or other objects from slaves, without written permission from their masters." Beyond this, in "villages and hamlets" on "festive occasions" it was forbidden to "set up stalls without license from the municipal council to sell goods of any kind." The penalties were "a fine of 20$ for free people, and for slaves eight days in jail."[22] For Itaguaí the prohibitions applied to any "person who buys gold, jewels, fabric, coffee, foodstuffs, or any other objects from slaves without the permission of their masters." In the 1880s in Campos dos Goitacazes the regulations stated that "only *roceiros* [small-holders] and their representatives were permitted to set up market stalls or sell food, crops ... or animal products in the streets, squares or beaches of the city or municipality; they must prove their status as a small-holder to the municipal council with a note from their local justice of the peace." Such attempts to control circulation of goods through municipal regulations open a methodological window through which we can begin to understand the commercial circuits of Rio's Black peasantry.

MOBILITY AND THE "SPECTER OF DISORDER"

Another issue still calls out for further research. Displacement and collective migrations happened before 1888 and were already characteristic

[20] Posturas Municipais do Município de Paraíba do Sul (1859), *Anais da Assembleia Legislativa Provincial do Rio de Janeiro*, Biblioteca Nacional (RJ).
[21] Posturas Municipais do Município de Santa Maria Madalena (1881), *Anais da Assembleia Legislativa Provincial do Rio de Janeiro*, Biblioteca Nacional (RJ).
[22] Posturas Municipais do Município de Capivary (1883), *Anais da Assembleia Legislativa Provincial do Rio de Janeiro*, Biblioteca Nacional (RJ).

experiences among Brazil's itinerant peasantry. The phenomenon was not tardy or isolated, nor was it simply an offshoot of radical abolitionism. What's more, in the last decade before abolition, so-called *retirantes* – freedpeople who had been emancipated collectively – also entered the scene.[23] Meanwhile, in various regions, governmental authorities, planters, and even abolitionists were trying to maintain control over the process of abolition.

In 1887 and 1890, Brazilian newspapers published numerous articles complaining about the abandonment of coffee *fazendas* by fugitive slaves, by freedpeople collectively manumitted before May 13, or by families freed by the Golden Law. After 1888, those complaints appeared in dialogue with others that discussed re-enslavement, vagrancy, and migration. In northern Rio de Janeiro province and the areas bordering on Espírito Santo, local papers were no different. In their very titles, many pieces – published in the crime section, as editorials, and even as letters to the editor – said a great deal about disputed imaginaries involving labor, social control, and conflicting expectations across all sectors of society regarding the immediate post-abolition period. The editors of the *Jornal de Campos* and the *Diário da Manha* received copious correspondence about these issues as early as 1889. One series, entitled "Collaboration – Letters from an Agriculturalist," published a number of complaints about the supposed difficulties in which planters found themselves due to the impact of the May 13 law. One writer, who signed himself J. H., discussed "the adherence of agricultural laborers to new ideas," calling on "companions of class and misfortune ... [who were experiencing] the harshest privations."[24] Under the title "Gold Fever," the following day's column mentioned that "the nation" was "exhausted and disheartened" after May 13.[25]

Complaints, rumors, and expectations reverberated everywhere. Planters and urban residents from northern Rio de Janeiro province, southern Espírito Santo, and the Mata Mineira (a forested zone of Minas Gerais) connected with one another amidst the hopes and misgiving of the freed communities, *quilombos*, and enslaved people that surrounded them.

---

[23] The term *retirantes* is also used in Brazil to refer to refugees from devastating droughts that periodically afflicted Brazilian Northeast; the usage here, although contemporaneous, was distinct.

[24] *Jornal de Campos*, October 20, 1889, p. 1.

[25] *Jornal de Campos*, October 21, 1889, p. 1.

One day later during that same October, also in the *Jornal de Campos*, an article entitled "Assault – Says a Telegram from Leopoldina" reported:

The city was assaulted last night by the freedmen. The City Council was attacked to destroy the [slave] registration records. There was shooting all night long. Families are terrified. There is no public [police] force. The assailants promised to return in greater numbers. It was calculated that there were two hundred of them, all well-armed. We have no protection whatsoever. We ask that measures be taken.[26]

The watchwords in such articles were indemnization, vagrants, vaga-bondage, collective flights, and ruined and abandoned plantations. There was even talk of the need for agricultural aid (both direct invest-ments and loans), and the shortage of "laborers" was a constant motto:

Agriculturalist, we do not perceive the advantages that can come from borrowed money, even at low interest, when we have no workforce to till the land or harvest the crops .... We do not accept the idea that such loans are a favor granted to us by the State, as we were stripped of our legal property by an unpatriotic and violent law .... Where is the person with a keen enough eye to find in this government any indication of good intentions or any proof of patriotism? The chain of emigration has been cut off once and for all! Every day, freedmen are allowed to offer us the most embarrassing examples of vagrancy, drunkenness and theft![27]

Commenting on what was interpreted as utter ruin for agriculture, a report mentioned recent large-scale global economic transformations, which were supposedly characterized "by a fabulous movement of capital" and could result in prosperity. However, in the face of the traumatic experi-ence of abolition, this transformation could actually impede such progress and prosperity in Brazil, causing "backwardness in its industries, vacillation in its commerce, impoverishment in its artisanal activities, and the weaken-ing of agriculture, which will require enormous work to recover from the hard and violent blow it has received from the loss of manpower."[28] Such critiques of the state in which agriculture had been left by the supposed lack of workers were accompanied by proposed solutions: "Without coercive labor laws and the constraint of rigorous penalties for the vagrancy – which is developing among us on a broad and terrifying scale, effectively aided by the goodwill of the laborious population – nothing can be achieved, and agriculture cannot count on those elements of production."[29]

---

[26] *Jornal de Campos*, October 27, 1889, p. 2.
[27] *Jornal de Campos*, October 30, 1889, p. 3.
[28] *Jornal de Campos*, November 1, 1889, p. 1.
[29] *Jornal de Campos*, October 11, 1889, p. 1.

Debates about abolition's ramifications would become entwined with the polemics and expectations of Brazil's republican transformation in 1889. On November 25, ten days after the military coup that "proclaimed" the Republic, the *Jornal de Campos* published an essay by Oliveira Machado in which he expressed serious concerns about debates conducted in such an atmosphere because he figured that most republicans were agriculturalists harmed by the law of May 13 and was very afraid of them.[30] That same day, an essay by Manoel de Paula was also published, glossing the context of debates "about political ideas and institutional reforms":

On the question of the servile element, I was always on the side of those who demanded full, unconditional and immediate liberty for slaves.

Every day for about six long months, I battled in the press, defending the rights of the oppressed, the wretched ones devoid of fortune, without expecting any reward other than the fulfillment of a duty.

At the height of abolitionism, along with the slaves, I had to defend the oppressed who were scattered across the streets and squares of the city.

But it must be said that I have never advised enslaved people to threaten their masters' lives; I never condoned violence or assaults on other people's property, nor did I derive benefit from those unfortunate people's savings with false promises of liberty.[31]

Fears of re-enslavement had even greater repercussions. We still lack studies of the ways in which the political context of the late 1880s and early 1890s created divergent scenarios for different social sectors. Fear of re-enslavement was not just a fiction produced by the monarchists to pit freedpersons against the republicans. The matter took on real and symbolic dimensions, which require further study. In late 1889, several newspapers published a circular that had been issued by Rio de Janeiro's secretary of police on November 27. It read:

As malicious spirits are spreading rumors that the new regime could prejudice the freedom of individuals who acquired it through law no. 3353 of May 13 of last year, I recommend that you make it clear – by posting edicts in all the parishes of your district and by way of the respective police commissioners – that freedmen will continue to enjoy the rights conferred on them by said law, and that in this regard there is no doubt in the intentions of the provisional government of the Republic and of this state.[32]

---

[30] *Jornal de Campos*, November 25, 1889, p. 1.
[31] *Jornal de Campos*, November 25, 1889, p. 3.
[32] *Jornal de Campos*, December 1, 1889, p. 3.

More than just fear and trepidation, there was a real sense that free-dpersons might perceive the change in political regime as an attack on the end of slavery. An article entitled "A Republica e os libertos" (The Republic and the Freedmen) reported that a military detachment had been sent to Cantagalo and Valença, where there had been "significant uprisings of freedmen opposed to the new regime."[33] In July 1890, with the headline "Reescravização" (Re-enslavement), the *Gazeta do Povo* in Campos charged that Alexandre Corrêa, the owner of a small-holding in Vargem Grande, São Fidelis, was privately imprisoning three black freedwomen on his property.[34]

The "specter of disorder" – a hyperbolic and often politically instrumentalized fear of free labor and the transformations it entailed – reared its head in diverse narratives and arguments during the inevitable but at the same time unpredictable end of slavery.[35] Lana Lage's studies of abolitionism in northern Rio de Janeiro were pioneering on this topic, as was Hebe Mattos' research comparing the political and social dynamics of that same region with Minas Gerais. Mattos' work, based in part on local periodicals, also focused on the local repercussions of events in São Paulo, which were often covered in the region's papers. In general, however, Brazilian historiography has analyzed the events of these years through the lens of disputes over the memory of abolition and post-abolition.[36] It is possible to propose an interpretation that goes further, connecting mass desertions, mobile *quilombos*, and especially the movements of newly emancipated slaves to create a history that can supplant the elitist memory of abolition that was constructed in the local press right into the first decades of the twentieth century. Although it was loudly proclaimed by the press, perhaps definitive and unconditional abolition and the transformations of the post-abolition period were not so much faits accompli as they were experiences that converged or diverged across Brazil's heterogeneous regions.

Beyond this, there might have been a dialogic relationship between these happenings and a series of episodes that happened in Western São Paulo, which were widely reported in Rio de Janeiro and may have had an impact in the open borderlands of Rio and Espírito Santo. It is worth emphasizing a series of reports by Arrigo de Zetirry published in the *Jornal do Commercio* in the second half of 1894, which Sheila Faria and

[33] *Jornal de Campos*, December 3, 1889, p. 3.   [34] *Gazeta do Povo*, July 2, 1890, p. 2.
[35] M. H. Machado and F. Gomes, "Eles ficaram 'embatucados.'"
[36] L. da Gama Lima, *Rebeldia Negra e Abolicionismo*; H. Mattos, *Das cores do silêncio*.

Hebe Mattos have already used extensively, regarding "Lavoura no Estado do Rio de Janeiro" (Agriculture in the State of Rio de Janeiro).[37] In addition to Campos, these reports describe several municipalities with open borders in northern Rio de Janeiro state, such as Itaperuna, São João da Barra, and the villages of Carangola and Muriaé. The author, writing both as an observer and analyst, noted that, in "reporting on the current state of work and workers, agricultural labor and its products," he would stress how the freedmen had abandoned the slave quarters and were seeking to negotiate new forms of labor, which included removing their wives and children from the agricultural workforce.[38]

Comparing working conditions in this region with those in São Paulo, where planters made use of an Italian immigrant workforce, Zetirry criticized the freedmen for refusing "family work," predicting that "we will find Black men's wives sitting in the doorway with their hands in their laps, women who are as strong as the men, completely inert." Furthermore, the author added, "It seems that [Brazilian] nationals, especially freedmen, are unaware that the human heart can nurture a desire to change one's life, to improve one's social status."[39] The chronicler also touched on the abandonment of the plantations, the freedmen's lack of ambition, their rejection of plantation labor in favor of their subsistence plots, and the ways in which labor regimes in this region compared with those involving contracted Chinese labor and with those in other parts of northern Rio de Janeiro state. Speaking of the region's Black population, Zetirry observed that "the ranks of freedmen, who are still Itaperuna's main source of labor, have been decimated, whether because other municipalities are attracting them by paying more, or because of high mortality and women's complete abandonment of agricultural toil." Noting that "freedmen generally have a major flaw," he then listed several, among them the supposed fact that "they are content to enjoy the freedom to work or not as they please."[40]

Zetirry also commented on agricultural conditions in the borderlands of northern Rio de Janeiro and southern Espírito Santo, where there was a "relative agricultural expansion" but "in small-holdings rather than large-scale production." In terms of the general panorama, the "large properties that existed during slavery have been completely abandoned for years, or are tended by an extremely limited number of freed laborers,

---

[37] S. de Castro Faria, "Terra e trabalho"; H. Mattos, *Das cores do silêncio.*
[38] *Jornal do Commercio*, June 20, 1894.   [39] *Jornal do Commercio*, July 28, 1894.
[40] *Jornal do Commercio*, June 20, 1894.

who produce a small amount of sugarcane and some grains and also exploit the excellent hardwoods that the remaining forests still possess."[41] Regarding post-emancipation economic landscapes, Zetirry stressed that in northern Rio de Janeiro state, especially in Campos, "despite the lack of hands to cultivate sugarcane and exploit all the land suitable for it – and even though at least half the plantations in the municipality of Campos are completely abandoned and only one-third of the total are being tended with care – despite all of this, the municipality of Campos is not yet one of those in Rio de Janeiro state that has suffered the worst consequences of the law of May 13." According to him, "fortunately those freedmen who are used to working on the sugar plantations have remained loyal."[42]

The chronicler concludes by suggesting the following disheartening situation for large properties and sugar mills: on one hand there were freedpersons, individuals or families, who were either absent or scarce because they were being recruited by other municipalities offering better pay; on the other, there were colonies of freedpersons who entered into partnerships or sharecropping arrangements in order to devote themselves to family farming, thus ruining the sugar economy and nearby sugar mills. Regarding workers on a plantation linked to the Dores Sugar Mill, Zetirry observed: "The freedmen there, like most in this municipality, work as much as is necessary for their subsistence, showing neither interest in improving their status nor any love for saving."[43]

We contend that part of this shortage of freedmen willing to work in regimented and iron-fisted disciplinary regimes – similar to slavery – was either motivated by or emerged from the unfolding of mass flights and the large-scale movement, displacement, and migration of slaves, *retirantes*, and *quilombo* members during the decade of abolition. This would lead to ever-denser migrations and dislocations during the post-abolition period. The Black peasant micro-communities that spread across the region, constantly migrating in search of work and land, were formed through a complex process about which we still know very little.

MEMORY, AUTONOMY, AND MOBILITY

Even beyond expectations regarding land, questions of labor, autonomy, and spatial circulation mobilized the Black population in many parts of

---

[41] *Jornal do Commercio*, October 21, 1894.   [42] *Jornal do Commercio*, July 14, 1894.
[43] *Jornal do Commercio*, August 4, 1894.

Brazil's slaveowning Southeast. These issues could involve widely varying landscapes, characters, and settings. In less than a year, transformations in the worlds of work could bring about profound changes in people's lives and everyday routines. One example – recorded in generational memories – comes from the municipality of Cachoeiro de Itapemirim, in the south of Espírito Santo. Cachoeiro was the area's largest coffee producer, and in the decade of abolition it contained over 50 percent of the region's enslaved workforce, according to registries from 1887.[44] Yet in this period images emerge of plantations deserted both by their owners – many of whom migrated to other towns closer to the center of the province or its capital city Victória, handing over the management of their property to sharecroppers or managers – and by a portion of the Black population, mostly families of freedpersons who took off in search of land, work, and liberty. Phenomena that some newspaper reports characterized as evidence of vagrancy, disorder, laziness, and ingratitude in fact signified chapters in long-standing, multigenerational processes of family migration. For many, running away or abandoning plantations en masse signified total rejection of inadequate wages, limited access to land, lack of autonomy, and subjugation to working conditions analogous to slavery. These were rendered even less tolerable because they were imposed in spaces – real and symbolic – where such families had been enslaved for two or more generations.

These narratives emerge clearly in the memories of descendants of the first generations of Black families that migrated within the region between the end of the nineteenth century and the first decades of the twentieth. Amélia Gonçalves, a granddaughter of former slaves from southern Espírito Santo, described in detail some of the expectations held by her family, the first generation of freedpersons, immediately after May 13, 1888:

[My grandfather] was a slave over there in Ouro Preto [Minas Gerais]. From there he was bought to come here to the Fazenda do Castelo [in the present-day municipality of Guaçuí, former parish of São Miguel do Veado, in the municipality of Cachoeiro de Itapemirim, on Espirito Santo's southern border with Minas Gerais]. He lived on that plantation for many years and ... when slavery was over, everyone had the "free womb" after that, you know ... Well, he was freed there ... So then senhor Roberto [the planter] gave 30,000 reis to my grandfather, 30 *patacas* to my grandfather, and told him, now that slavery is over, no one is

---

[44] According to a report published on April 17, 1887, in *O Cachoeirano*, a newspaper that circulated in southern Espírito Santo, we have found that, of the 12,402 slaves registered with the province by March 30 of that year, 8,043 were working on plantations in two southern municipalities: Cachoeiro de Itapemirim and Itapemirim.

a slave, you will have your children and they will be yours. Then my grandfather bought a piece of land and moved to Guaçuí, to a place called Monte Vidéo, and set up his farm. He lived there for many years until he died, my father's father .... He lived there with the family; my grandfather had a vast amount of land and lived there with his children. It was there that I was born in 1914. My father lived there. He was Evancio Moisés Gonçalves. My uncle Faustino, my uncle Firmino lived there. Aunt Rita. They all lived in that place .... Ah! We used to plant plant cassava, beans, corn, and coffee there – the driving force was coffee.[45]

The wealth of detail in Amélia's statement provides evidence that freedpersons were seeking autonomy – this can be seen in the ways that they exercised family control and spatial mobility to seek better working conditions and access to land. There is also another significant point: Amélia points to the existence of a community of freedpersons made up of members of the same family. Coffee was the only product that the community sold. The other crops they planted – "corn, beans, rice" – "were for our household, for the family itself." She also added:

In the old days, we didn't have this business we have today, people selling everything they harvest. In the old days we stored [enough] beans for the whole year, corn for the whole year. We raised pigs, we raised chickens. My grandfather had grazing land. He had a broodmare, he had a horse, an immense number of streams.

Autonomy over land – a legacy of land access gained through enslaved people's own savings – went hand in hand with the availability of labor and inputs necessary for agricultural work. It seems probable that the owner who acquired that original slave – Amélia's grandfather – also secured other family members, following in the generational logic of an imperfect labor market that was based on the Black family. Desire for family time, land access, and the chance to construct their own economies pervaded the age of emancipation and shaped expectations of freedom from the 1880s to the first decades of the twentieth century. In local memory, there are also indications that freedpersons left the *fazendas* but did not leave the region; this revelation sheds a different light on the images of decadence that are always reproduced in histories of the years immediately after abolition in Brazil's slaveholding Southeast. Local journalistic agendas – which constantly emphasized disorder, desertion, and chaos – greatly influenced historiographical narratives, overshadowing local memory and hiding more complex historical experiences. Images

[45] Interview conducted in Alegre in October 1992 with Amélia Gonçalves, born in 1914 in Guaçuí, ES. She died in 1996.

of the "ruin" that set in months before abolition hid ideologies that sought to control both collective and family-based labor.

Based on a careful dialogic reading of narratives constructed from very different sources and archives – including juridical and print sources, but also local generational memory transmitted through oral history – we have argued here that the characterization of the post-emancipation period as a landscape of catastrophe and total disorganization functioned as part of a dialogue about normative expectations and policies. Euphoria – if it occurred at all – was localized and was the exception rather than the rule; after the celebrations of May 13 were over, at least in the south of Espírito Santo province,[46] freedpeople attempted to reorganize their lives and return to the routine of hard work in the countryside.[47] There, through disputes with a small local agrarian elite, they demarcated their space of autonomy in this new conjuncture. Unlike São Paulo, this was a region where former slaveowners did not have access to a sufficient number of European workers. Beginning 1887, immigrants did arrive to work on the large southern plantations. But they were soon lured by the former province's vast unoccupied territories, either laying direct claim to them or moving to the settlement colonies created by the Espirito Santo government in the center-west. In southern Espírito Santo, the task of reorganizing labor relations in the countryside fell to Brazilian workers, many of whom were freedpersons.

For planters with little capital, or those unwilling to use their capital to pay their workers' salaries, coffee growing through *parceria* (partnership) or *meação* (sharecropping) developed as a feasible way to organize work in rural areas post-abolition.[48] Paulo Vicente Machado, born in 1910 on Fazenda da Presa in the municipality of Alegre (southern Espírito Santo), gives an interesting description of rural arrangements in that context:

And after captivity ended, he [Vicente, Paulo Vicente's father] started farming, that's right … farming, man.

The plantation was on a mountain. He [the planter] divided up the plantation; there were thousands of *alqueires* of land …. So he divided it up for all those folks

---

[46] On this subject, see R. Martins, *Os caminhos da liberdade*.

[47] For some decades now, social historians have been conceptualizing methodologies that seek to reconstruct the past from the stories of ordinary people, who have been "marginalized" in complex social processes such as those experienced in Brazil by the massive number freed from forced labor in the late nineteenth and twentieth centuries. F. Krantz, *History from Below*; J. Sharpe, "History from Below."

[48] H. Mattos, *Das cores do silêncio*; R. Mourão Gontijo, "Parceria e o café"; A. Lugão Rios, *Família e transição*; S de Castro Faria, "Terra e trabalho."

[former slaves], coffee farming. Planting coffee by sharecropping ... each of them got a piece of land to farm.[49]

In fact, the crop was not entirely the worker's, because he had to share half the coffee produced with the landowner. But the fact that the freed-man could work by his own rules seems to have been interpreted as an achievement. In the Mata Mineira zone, in Minas Gerais on the border with southern Espírito Santo, almost all of the municipalities adopted the partnership system after abolition. This labor relationship was attractive to landowners because it kept workers on the property, and it also served as a mechanism to reduce cash payments to the workforce. According to Ana Lúcia Duarte Lanna, the reorganization of work in the Mata Mineira after abolition also depended mainly on Brazilian workers, "a broad category that in our view includes former slaves, who were the workforce that was key to the formation of a free labor market in that region."[50] We suggest that same hypothesis for southern Espírito Santo. In another statement from a descendant of freedpersons, born in 1928 in Córrego do Moinho), we have unearthed some details that suggest that partnership was also the predominant form of labor relations in southern Espírito Santo after captivity's end:

In those days, it was like this: you were a *colono*, you lived on the *fazenda*, the planter gave you the land to farm, and what you planted was yours, you see . . . . The food crops were ours; we ate them and sold them. We only gave [the planter] half the coffee, not the rest of the crops.[51]

Just as Lanna found in the Mata Mineira, fixed workers, whom the planter called *colonos* (settlers), lived on the plantation and tended the crops. In most cases, they could plant grains between the rows of coffee bushes or on land set aside for that purpose, which in general had already been abandoned by large-scale planters. In local memory passed down by freedpersons or their children (first generation), the idea of planting grain is associated with so-called *lavoura branca* ("white farming"), which, in addition to ensuring the worker's subsistence, may even have rendered them better returns, since investment in coffee could take a very long time to produce a profit.

---

[49] Interview conducted in October 1992, in São Gonçalo, RJ, with Paulo Vicente Machado, born on Fazenda da Presa, in the municipality of Alegre, ES, in 1910. An *alqueire* in this region was equivalent to a little more than an acre.
[50] A. L. Lanna, *A transformação*, p. 77.
[51] Interview conducted in October 1994, in Alegre, Espírito Santo, Geraldo Nicomédio dos Santos.

In the Mata Mineira, and quite likely in southern Espírito Santo as well, the big problem that landowners saw in the partnership arrangement was that the colono was more interested in planting grain than coffee.[52] Thus, in addition to the "partners" – who were generally permanent workers, fixed in place – there was also another category of *fazenda* workers: temporary, seasonal migrants who helped to harvest crops the partners had planted and tended. In other words:

the need for temporary workers is imperative because the "partner" guarantees the cultivation of coffee, but not its harvest, which requires more workers. It is also impossible to establish a salaried relationship to carry out all the tasks distributed throughout the year, either because it is impossible to control and regulate the supply of workers, or because the planters lack ready money. Seasonal migration is the option that makes it possible to complete the harvest and carry out production in general . . . . Another advantage of this system is the fact that migrant workers have no other interests except harvesting coffee beans or whatever other specific task might be assigned them. This is not the case with the "colono," who sees the cultivation of grains as yielding the most benefits.[53]

Yet the possibility of migrant labor could cut both ways, especially in less prosperous regions. Analyzing the narratives constructed in Minas Gerais newspapers in the 1890s, Lanna touched on the open appeals of local farmers, who felt disadvantaged by the flow of workers headed to more dynamic coffee-producing municipalities at harvest time:

This emigration of our workforce towards the municipalities of the South, which is reducing our planters almost to despair, still continues at an ever-accelerating rate.
Not a week goes by without seeing large levies leaving us to lend a hand to those who have more resources than we do.[54]

Still little studied, these seasonal migrations flowed toward the coffee-growing regions, in Minas and elsewhere, during harvest season (three or four months in the year). These movements and migrations occurred beyond the boundaries of the coffee-growing municipalities, and they may have had broad and intersecting significance. This was apparent in 1893 in responses given to a questionnaire in the district of São Sebastião do Rio Preto in Minas Gerais. The planters complained that "workers from Minas Novas were going to Espírito Santo."[55] The interesting thing

---

[52] A. L. Lanna, *A transformação*, p. 88.   [53] A. L. Lanna, *A transformação*, pp. 95–96.
[54] *O Serro*, Serro, May 7, 1893, p. 1. In A. L. Lanna, *A transformação*, p. 94.
[55] Responses to the 1893 questionnaire in the district of S. Sebastião do Rio Preto, Conceição municipality, in which there is also the complaint that "the production of food crops has not increased, and prices have increased for about three years, which seems to be caused

about this movement is that it indicates that by this point the coffee economy of southern Espírito Santo was already attracting workers from a neighboring state. This shows that some sectors of the population in parts of Minas Gerais behaved in the same way as their counterparts elsewhere, migrating during harvest season in response to demand for field labor or in order to escape the control, domination, and power of former plantation masters after 1888. This suggests that such movement on the part of freedpeople and Black families can be characterized as a facet of post-abolition.

We wandered and wandered and wandered and finally ended up in Vala de Souza ... yes, in Concórdia, we were there for a long time. But I was born in São Pedro de Itabapoana, in Alcebíades [Espírito Santo] .... I remember, it was on the Fazenda Concórdia, a huge plantation, where dad was a coffee sharecropper and planted lavoura branca. Near a coffee plantation that went on as far as the eye could see .... It belonged to the planter, and he [her father] planted it and gave half to the planter. He kept half, and there they had coffee, they had rice, corn .... They had everything there .... There were a lot of Black people there, yes, still from the time of captivity.[56]

This recollection reveals that – just as we have seen in Minas Gerais – the southern region of Espírito Santo saw a process of generational migration and displacement, an intense mobility practiced by a labor force made up of freedpeople and Black agricultural workers descended from the rural free poor. This is also what emerges from the account of Ana Cândida, the daughter of Gabriel Monteiro dos Santos, a small-holder and seasonal coffee worker. "O Velho" Gabriel managed to buy an *alqueire* of land (a little more than an acre) in Vala de Souza, where the freed family of the formerly enslaved Vicente also owned property; this is where Vicente's son Paulo Vicente Machado and Gabriel's daughter Ana Cândida met and married in 1925.[57] In southern Espírito Santo – an example drawn from oral history accounts – there really was a large concentration of *colonos* who began to cultivate lavoura branca for subsistence after slavery. This seems to have occurred in the former district of Vala de Souza, in the municipality of Alegre, and in the present-day municipality of Jerônimo Monteiro; various accounts refer to areas, places, villages, or small-holdings that were *só de pretos* (only Black). To

---

by the emigration of workers to farms in the riverside forest, other municipalities and districts." In A. L. Lanna, *A transformação*, note 46, p. 95.
[56] Interview with Ana Cândida Vicente Machado, 87.
[57] Paulo Vicente Machado and Ana Cândida Vicente Machado were Robson Martins' maternal grandparents.

this day, there is a Black community there called Sítio dos Crioulos (the farm of the creoles). "O Velho" Gabriel spent a short time in Vala de Souza, where he farmed subsistence crops, which Ana identified as lavoura branca. Gabriel later sold the property and got a job as a sharecropper on a plantation in São João do Muqui, also in the south of the state.

CONCLUSION

Mobility and autonomy allowed rural Afro-descendant people to produce intersecting significations from complex experiences of freedom, work, and access to land. Land grants in wills, villages of free Black peasants, and even itinerant *quilombos* created new rural configurations even during slave times, and these took on new and different meanings in the post-abolition era. For many freedpersons – as was true for a subset of dispossessed free men prior to 1888 – mobility was a facet of their expectations of autonomy, which was also based on family labor and mediated by preexisting or developing personal and family relationships.[58]

More fine-tuned analyses may offer comparisons – or even direct historical connections – with peasant migrations and settlements elsewhere; with Jamaican maroon villages, for example, or with the intense migration of Black communities in Colombia, who eventually reached free areas on the Pacific coast. In other contexts, such as South Carolina, freedpeople organized themselves as communities after emancipation, planning their work with the aim of gaining more control over various forms of agricultural labor. They wanted to guarantee the benefits they had already acquired as slaves, such the right to plant crops for sale and their own subsistence on Sundays and holidays. In that same region, agrarian movements organized by former slaves began to fight for changes in daily work routines, because in their view labor conditions there were a legalized continuation of slavery.[59] They fully understood the meaning of freedom and the entitlements it sanctioned, and they fought to claim their rights.

The same happened in the Brazilian coffee plantation areas we analyzed in this chapter. Even though planters themselves sought to

[58] H. Mattos, *Das cores do silêncio*, p. 361.
[59] J. Saville, "Grassroots Reconstruction"; A. L. Pires et al., *Territórios de gente negra*; J. Besson, *Transformations of Freedom*.

maintain freedpeople on the plantations where they had long worked as slaves, freedpersons' pursuit of autonomy, in the form of control over the rhythms of work and access to land, eventually changed the geography of labor in those areas. In that sense, their experience was common to many societies across the Americas after abolition.

PART III

RACIAL SILENCE AND BLACK INTELLECTUAL SUBJECTIVITIES

9

Breaking the Silence

Racial Subjectivities, Abolitionism, and Public Life in Mid-1870s Recife

Celso Thomas Castilho and Rafaella Valença de Andrade Galvão

Há tempo de calar e há tempo de falar. O tempo de calar passou, começou o tempo de falar.

On these terms, the Afro-Brazilian journalist, educator, and law-school graduate Felipe Neri Collaço (1815–1894) launched the abolitionist newspaper *O Homem*. The opening line, in all its original rhythmic verve, put the northeastern city of Recife on notice: "There is a time to keep silent, and a time to speak up. The time for silence has passed, it is now time to speak up."[1] It conveyed an emboldened and, to many, a dangerously unencumbered Collaço. The well-known sixty-year-old appeared unconstrained by the decades-long relationship he had kept with the ruling Conservative Party. More frightening, perhaps, to the governing class, Collaço's introductory article immediately brought to light the struggles afflicting Recife's "men of color." These ranged from the administration's expunging of prominent Afro-descendants from public posts to the police's dispersal of a meeting where men of color had gathered to sign a petition.[2] In denouncing and linking together what may have otherwise been regarded as separate incidents, and in redefining these events as unconstitutional affronts on Recife's "men of color," Collaço deliberately broke with the entrenched code of keeping silent on race. Indeed, the process of suppressing racial discord in public life had long been integral to the preservation of slavery. *O Homem* thus strove not only to rally Recife's "men of color" around these recent examples of

[1] *O Homem*, January 13, 1876, p. 1.
[2] *O Homem*, January 13, 1876, pp. 1–2; also, *O Homem*, January 27, 1876, p. 2.

exclusion but also to fundamentally render the call for racial solidarity in abolitionist terms. In arguing that slave emancipation was necessary for the fulfillment of racial equality, Collaço effectively sought to transform both the politics of the category "men of color" and the implications of abolitionism. Not surprisingly, a public anti-Black backlash followed. It was neither the first time that Collaço had personally encountered such type of racialized response, nor the last instance where the interracial abolitionist movement would be caricatured in anti-Black tropes. As such, this critical reexamination of *O Homem*'s aims, and of the racialized reactions that the paper elicited, offers a fresh perspective on how the ferment of the abolition debates set in motion important shifts in racial subjectivities.[3]

In probing Collaço's interventions in public life, this chapter also highlights the wider importance that the practices of silencing race held in structuring power in nineteenth-century Brazil. Collaço appears here as illustrative of a subgroup of Brazil's large free population of color that attained notable success.[4] In Recife, as across most cities, free Afro-descendants comprised about 40 percent of the population and gained access to spaces of influence through recognized social practices such as joining religious brotherhoods and civil associations and participating in partisan and professional networks. For the most part, these dynamics transpired in contexts free of legal exclusions based on race. Better yet, a shared cultural understanding prevailed that race was not to be discussed. This silencing of race, then, proved salient to the ordering of a nation that at once held the largest free Black and largest slave populations in Latin America.

Historians agree that official efforts to preclude debates on race were, in fact, critical to the construction and reproduction of racialized hierarchies. In working with parliamentary debates and state memoranda from the early 1820s, Márcia Berbel and Rafael Marquese have

---

[3] The most recent, and certainly the most incisive, study of Collaço's career is R. Andrade Galvão, "Felippe Neri." We know of only two other works touching on *O Homem*: M. Hoffnagel, "*O Homem*," pp. 52–62; and A. Magalhães Pinto, *Imprensa negra*, pp. 53–102. Andrade Galvão noted the following works as containing fragmentary elements of Collaço's biography: A. Xavier, *Letras católicas*, pp. 89–91; A. Blake, *Dicionário bibliográfico*, p. 358; G. Freyre, *Sobrados e Mucambos*, v. 3, p. 477 and *Um engenheiro*, p. 128; O. Montenegro, *Memórias do ginásio*, pp. 52, 53, 170; G. Veiga, *História das ideias*, v. 4, p. 274.

[4] Selected works include E. Silva, *Dom Obá*; E. Azevedo, *Orfeu da carapina*; K. Grinberg, *O fiador*; Z. Frank, *Dutra's World*; M. H. Machado, "From Slave Rebels," pp. 247–274; T. Holloway, "The Defiant Life"; A. Marzano, *Cidade em cena*.

demonstrated that the "absence of race" in the definitions of legal citizenship strategically enabled Brazilian-born Blacks and mulattos to feel invested in a national project dependent on African slavery and the slave trade. Berbel and Marquese maintain that Brazilian political leaders, seeking to prevent any repeat of the dynamics that contributed to the outbreak of the Haitian revolution, worked to minimize racial hostility aimed at free Blacks.[5] Likewise, Sidney Chalhoub's work with the records from the Council of State, an advisory board to the emperor and the ministers, reveals the extent to which the government avoided using racial language to enact race-laden legislation. Chalhoub charts, for instance, the council's deliberations on what to call the newborns of slave mothers who were freed by the gradual emancipation law of 1871, knowing full well that to use the term "freed" would imply a lifetime of social stigma and yet to actually "free" them of this background would also enhance their political rights and significantly increase the Afro-descendant share of the voting population. The state's goal, Chalhoub argues, was to proceed carefully, and with "prudence," recognizing that "the best rule is not to talk about this [racial difference]."[6] Ultimately, Chalhoub contends, political leaders opted for a race-neutral term for the newborns – but then attached a literacy requirement to an electoral law implemented ten years later that, in effect, purged large numbers of Afro-Brazilian males from the voting rolls. Nevertheless, we must also remember that the processes of silencing racial discourse were not exclusively top-down. Hebe Mattos' research shrewdly captures how former slaves purposefully suppressed references to their slave pasts in their interactions with the legal system.[7] This silencing, she argues, should be understood as part of their assertions for autonomy and recognition as equal members of society. For Mattos, this "ethics of silence … reflected the full weight of racialization and racism in Imperial Brazil, rather than its nonexistence."[8]

Taken together, these references offer rich points of entry into the literature on racial silence. Certainly, the works immediately help us better appreciate the extent to which Collaço's opening declaration – "começou o tempo de falar" (it is now time to speak up) – signaled a sharp break with the status quo.[9] In addition, this sampling of the scholarship also permits us to consider how a deeper reckoning with Collaço's *O Homem* can productively spark new questions related to race, abolition, and silencing. For

[5] M. Berbel and R. Marquese, "The Absence of Race," p. 430.
[6] S. Chalhoub, "The Politics of Silence," p. 84.   [7] H. Mattos, *Das cores do silêncio*.
[8] H. Mattos, *Das cores do silêncio*, p. 368.   [9] *O Homem*, January 13, 1876, 1.

example, if historians have mostly, and successfully, explained the policy objectives and consequences of silencing race, there is more to discover about the cultural facets of this process.[10] That is, questions abound about how this code of not talking about race worked publicly, outside of official, legal contexts. For example, how did the crossing, and also the policing, of these lines of "keeping silent" in turn shape the access and representation that Afro-Brazilians had in public life? And, relatedly, how were disputes over public discussions of race, as happened between *O Homem* and other newspapers, linked to ongoing processes of racial and abolitionist formations? It is to these questions that we now turn, beginning in the next section with a detailed analysis of the political and intellectual environment from which Collaço's *O Homem* emerged. In two further sections, we scrutinize what Collaço's "breaking the silence" entailed, both in terms of his racial project for Recife's "men of color" and in relation to the anti-Black backlash that left a lasting imprint on public discourse.

COLLAÇO'S RECIFE, CA. 1876

O Homem burst onto the scene of a dynamic provincial capital. The third-largest city in Imperial Brazil, Recife was the principal port of Pernambuco and home to some 115,000 people. It featured one of the nation's two law schools, several theaters, a bustling press, associations and religious brotherhoods, and distinguished historical and literary institutes. It had been a site of global contact since the beginning of colonization, shaped by native, African, and European traditions. In the mid-seventeenth century, Pernambucan sugar paced world production, fueling both imperial rivalry and the expansion of African slavery. This age of sugar, which sparked the Dutch occupation of the Brazilian northeast (1624–1655), captivated nineteenth-century intellectuals. Specifically, Collaço and an array of playwrights, novelists, and visual artists exalted the multiracial forces that expelled the Dutch and rendered that history as emblematic of Brazil's strong interracial heritage.[11] Effectively, the Pernambucan past stoked the national imaginary, its long history of slavery notwithstanding.

An entrenched seigneurialism also pervaded the rules and customs of Recife, a slaving port since the sixteenth century. Social conventions,

---

[10] The classic study is T. Skidmore, *Black into White*.
[11] Collaço's columns about the "heroes" of the resistance, include: *O Homem*, March 2, 9, and 16, 1876, pages 2, 2, and 3 respectively; *O Homem*, March 23, 1876, p. 2. More broadly, see H. Kraay, *Days of National Festivity*, pp. 220–228.

including the silencing of race, ensured the continuing importance of slavery as an institution that created order, even as the number of people that were actually enslaved decreased over Collaço's lifetime.[12] For example, urban slaves dropped from about 25 percent of the overall population in the late 1840s to approximately 15 percent in the 1870s.[13] This decrease, however, was in line with broader changes in Brazilian slavery, where slave populations were largely reconcentrated in plantation settings from about the 1830s onward.[14] In Pernambuco, if the sugar planters of the late nineteenth century no longer wielded the global might of their seventeenth-century forebears, they still defended slavery and the sugar economy as interrelated matters. They still clung to the slave system, even though so-called free workers were widely available.[15] In the 1870s and 1880s, rural political associations formed to safeguard the "interests" of the sugar economy, which invariably centered on constraining all processes related to emancipation. At this point, the vast majority of the province's slave population toiled in the sugar belt, and virtually half of those laborers (48 percent) were well within prime working age (between sixteen and forty years old).[16] Hardly, then, an institution without deep roots, slavery in Recife and Pernambuco – and across the greater northeastern region, for that matter – held firm on the basis of history, law, and tradition. The fact that announcements for runaway slaves appeared in virtually every major daily in the country up until a handful of newspapers stopped publishing them in the 1880s hints at the cultural ways that slave power was inscribed and reinscribed in public life.

O *Homem*'s publication in 1876 thus emerged in a context where the legitimacy of slavery remained intact; where it was still more honorable to own people than to call that system into question. Altogether, the weekly ran for three months, reaching twelve issues. Its transformative character – its redefining of a "men of color" identity around the principle of abolitionism – becomes more visible when we take into

---

[12] The best book on urban slavery in early-nineteenth-century Recife is M. Carvalho, *Liberdade*. Also on slavery and free people of color in late-nineteenth-century Recife, see M. MacCord, *O Rosário* and *Artífices da cidadania*; F. Cabral and R. Costa, eds., *História da escravidão*; I. Cunha, *Capoeira*; F. Souza, *O eleitorado*; M. E. Vasconcellos dos Santos, "Os significados."

[13] On shifts in the slave population, see M. Carvalho, *Liberdade*, p. 74.

[14] A recent starting point for this literature is R. Marquese and R. Salles, eds., *Escravidão e capitalismo*; see also R. Marquese, T. Parron, and M. Berbel, *Slavery and Politics*.

[15] P. Eisenberg, *The Sugar Industry*, pp. 146–180.

[16] C. Castilho, *Slave Emancipation*, p. 69.

account the state of the abolition debate in the mid-1870s. In Recife, the issue had become debatable among a wider segment of the population about a decade earlier. Prompted by the confluence of different national and international events in the late 1860s – the Paraguayan War, the US Civil War, and the then-recent struggles of liberated Africans – activists took to the press, theater, associations, the courts, and local political bodies to portray slavery as an offense to national ideals.[17] Slaves' pursuits of freedom, through the courts and in conjunction with associational funding-freedom practices, took on new meaning and further politicized the growing civic campaigns. In general terms, then, the movement included Afro-descendants and whites and invented a nationalist narrative of antislavery.

More specifically, abolitionist politics in Recife stemmed in part from local institutions (the law school and the press) and in part from political developments across the country. As in other places, whether it was São Paulo city or Porto Alegre, local abolitionists in Recife imagined their actions on a national scale. However, for most of the 1860s and 1870s, the decentralized form of Brazilian abolitionism remained just that, and most interprovincial and interregional connections were largely symbolic. In the years after O Homem's publication, however, the operation of "underground railroads," the circulation of abolitionist theater troupes, and the more pronounced role of abolitionism in the national capital (Rio de Janeiro) helped fasten ties between local publics. It was also the case that the intensification of Brazil's interprovincial slave trade in the 1870s fueled interprovincial abolitionism.

The abolition debate acquired an intense register rather early in Recife, and activists in São Paulo, Salvador, Fortaleza, and Rio de Janeiro recognized it as an important site of action. In the first comprehensive, national-level study of abolitionist associations, Angela Alonso noted Recife among the places with the largest number of abolitionist events between 1867 and 1871.[18] Also, the provincial assembly of Pernambuco created state emancipation funds in 1869 and 1870. It attributed these measures to intensifying local pressure and to the example of similar funds being created in other provinces. In short, a snapshot of Brazilian abolitionism as it consolidated into a national phenomenon in the late 1860s reveals

---

[17] Several recent works have argued for this longer periodization for the "era of abolition," rooting the beginning of this process in the 1860s, as opposed to the customary 1880s focus. For example, in chronological order of publication, E. Azevedo, O direito; A. Alonso, The Last Abolition; and C. Castilho, Slave Emancipation.

[18] A. Alonso, The Last Abolition, chapter 1.

that Recife occupied as important a place as any city in the national picture. To date, however, we have not found traces of Collaço within this specific milieu, although he had been long active in the press, associations, and the legal arena.

The 1871 Free Womb Law changed the nature of the slavery debate, setting a course for the eventual ending of slavery. Just as important, it galvanized a proslavery reaction. In establishing a "free birth principle," the state ensured that all children born to enslaved mothers after September 28, 1871, would one day (after turning twenty-one) become free. Notably, this law signaled the state's willingness to supersede the owner's authority on how and when to free "someone's property." On the issue of manumission, whereas before the owner had the power to consent (or not) to a slave's request to buy themselves out of bondage, they were now obliged to accept the said person's freedom as long as they provided the requisite compensation. And it was clear that such legal changes immediately resonated among the enslaved, as a woman printed a notice in the *Diário de Pernambuco* asking for a specified sum to buy her freedom.[19] This happened only weeks after the law, illustrating the new ways that the "public" could now participate in this issue. The advertisement, which appeared alongside rows of slave-runaway notices, demonstrated that the points of reference for engaging the abolition debate were changing because of the 1871 law; it also captured the press's role in stretching the political field.

Yet it was not long ago that historians quickly dismissed print culture as a site of critical inquiry, either because Brazilians supposedly did not read or because written culture was considered a domain of the small white elite. Nevertheless, since the early 2000s, a slew of studies about the nineteenth-century press, with most emerging in the Brazilian academy, are changing our view of this phenomenon.[20] These current researchers are not only amassing a more complex view of public life – finding over 140 women's periodicals for the nineteenth century, for example – but

[19] C. Castilho, *Slave Emancipation*, pp. 53–55.
[20] M. Barbosa, *Os donos*; M. Carneiro, ed., *Minorias silenciadas*; M. Morel and M. de Barros, eds., *Palavra*; L. Ribeiro, *Imprensa e espaço*; L. Neves et al., eds., *História e imprensa*; M. Barbosa, *História cultural*; A. Martins and T. de Luca, eds., *História da imprensa*; J. Meirelles, *Imprensa e poder*; M. Balaban, *Poeta do lápis*; C. Mizuta et al., eds., *Império em debate*; P. Knauss et al., eds., *Revistas ilustradas*; B. Santa Anna, *Do Brasil ilustrado*; C. Costa, *A revista*; C. Duarte, *Imprensa Feminina*; A. El Youssef, *Imprensa e escravidão*; R. Godoi, *Um editor*. M. Meyer's *Folhetim* also deserves mention. In English, see H. Kraay, *Days of National Festivity*; A. Silva and S. Vasconcelos, eds., *Books and Periodicals*; Z. Frank, *Reading Rio*.

also revisiting the underlying assumption that only 15 percent of the population was literate. The 15 percent statistic is in fact reflected in the 1872 national census; however, in and of itself, it obscures as much as it reveals when scholars do not sufficiently contextualize it. For Recife, when one calculates the literacy rates for the three most populated and "urban" districts, this number almost triples; for Rio, a similarly closer look at the urban geography puts the city's literacy rate at nearer to 50 percent.[21] The bottom line is that contemporaries recognized the importance of the press, saw in it a space for participating politically, and disseminated information through public collective readings. To brand it a "white" space is to profoundly misunderstand how involved Afro-descendants were as printers, journalists, and readers in the world of print.

Through the press, various constituencies politicized the implications of the 1871 law, essentially reigniting the abolition debates. And it is important to remember that, from the perspective of contemporaries, this law had resolved – that is, settled – the question of abolition. It was not intended as a first step, and the gradualist narrative that has come to define it is mostly the result of later political and historiographical making. Six new, republican abolitionist papers surfaced in the early 1870s. From 1872 to 1875, *A Republica Federativa* and *A Luz* were among the most visible in denouncing slaveowners who continued selling their newborns, despite the prohibitions of the 1871 law. Notably, the papers were rather explicit in this, naming names.[22] Meanwhile, and in response to both the 1871 law and the reemergent abolitionism, Pernambuco's sugar planters launched their own association – the Society to Aid Agriculture in Pernambuco (SAAP) – in 1872. For effect, they organized their inaugural meeting on the first anniversary of the 1871 law. The SAAP was an association of national profile, convening two important congresses in 1878 and 1884. At both, the issue of slavery in general, and the question of how to proceed with the children of the 1871 law in particular, remained a point of anxiety and debate. It was thus upon this immediate context that *O Homem* surfaced: where mobilizations for and against slavery vied for public opinion.

Collaço's appreciation of politics and local power dynamics more generally stemmed from his close contact with the city's important institutional structures. Born into a family with deep roots in Pernambuco – his great-grandfather José Vaz Salgado was considered the richest merchant in the

[21] C. Castilho, *Slave Emancipation*, p. 19. H. F. Machado, *José do Patrocínio*, p. 114.
[22] C. Castilho, *Slave Emancipation*, pp. 59–66.

mid-eighteenth century – he was raised in comfortable surroundings, if not amidst the same levels of wealth that those of earlier generations had enjoyed. His Portuguese-descended father inherited sugar plantations and owned slaves, while his mother was Brazilian, *parda*, and from modest origins. Their marriage, however, left his father estranged from his family. And for Collaço, the fourth of six children, the split from his more affluent family meant a loss of important support.[23]

We know that for almost a decade, beginning in the mid-1840s, Collaço was a copy editor of the *Diário de Pernambuco*. From then until *O Homem* in 1876, he edited a wide range of literary, religious, political, scientific, and women's newspapers. For his role in the print arena, Collaço was recognized as a "dignified representative of Guttenberg" at a national exposition in 1866. In addition, from 1847 through the 1870s, he served as a juror, playing a part in legal matters and showing himself an honorable man of the community. Relatedly, he earned a law degree in 1853, and his knowledge of constitutional matters is on full display in *O Homem*. A devout Catholic, Collaço also belonged to a brotherhood and built extensive ties to church leaders. Still, a significant part of his public profile grew from his role as an educator; for over two decades, Collaço taught at Recife's famed secondary school, the Ginásio Pernambucano. His expertise spanned the subjects of Algebra, Geometry, Philosophy, French, English, and Physics; notably, two of his textbooks were adopted for general use in Pernambuco's education system.[24] These different capacities (he also contracted as a surveyor and an engineer with the municipality) therefore put Collaço at the intersection of powerful entities and influential people. Not surprisingly, a paper he edited in 1859 provided some of the most riveting and detailed coverage of Dom Pedro II's visit to Recife.[25] His place within the patronage networks of the Conservative Party also in part explains his long and successful hold of public posts. In the early 1870s, however, the relationship with Conservatives began to fray, and not long after he was controversially driven from the Ginásio Pernambucano. At that point, through *O Homem*, he railed openly against racial discrimination; and, in joining the abolitionist chorus led by republican newspapers, he posited that only the abolition of slavery could ensure "men of color" the promise of equality enshrined in the constitution.

---

[23] R. Andrade Galvão, "Felippe Neri," pp. 20–28.   [24] D. Collaço, *Aritmética*.
[25] R. Andrade Galvão, "Felippe Neri," pp. 56–57.

OF "MEN OF COLOR" AND ABOLITIONISM

O Homem unfurled its banner of equality on the masthead. The words "liberty, equality, fraternity" encased the full title of the journal: *O Homem: realidade constitucional ou dissolução social*. For emphasis, Collaço affixed quotes from the constitution and the Bible to illustrate these guiding concepts. Below "equality," for example, Collaço inserted two clauses from the famed article 179, which in its entirety reads like a veritable bill of rights. One clause defended all (male) citizens' eligibility for civic, political, and military posts, and a second reiterated that those considerations must rest on "talent and merits alone, irrespective of other differences [read: race]."[26] Interestingly, in analyzing *O Homem*'s constitutionalist language, historian Ana Flávia Magalhães Pinto noted that a Rio de Janeiro Black paper from the 1830s had also used article 179 as a basis for political action.[27] At the very least, this suggests the importance of rights-based discourse to the history of Black political formations. Collaço, meanwhile, also placed a verse from the gospel under "fraternity," which warned about the "darkness that blinds the paths of those who hate their brothers."[28] These referents established the legal, national, and moral foundations of the paper.

O Homem's specific objectives came into focus toward the middle quadrant of the page. Collaço presented them in bullet-point-like fashion, using the first three to articulate his vision for racial solidarity. The first stated that the paper "aimed to promote the unity, education, and moral growth of Pernambuco's men of color." The second stressed that it "would advocate on behalf of the men of color's legitimate and political rights, demanding that the constitution apply equally to everyone." The third promised to "publicize all wrongs committed against us so that the perpetuators would be exposed and feel the same oppression and persecution that their actions bring on others."[29] In these few lines, *O Homem* shattered the long-held custom of not discussing racial problems. It showed, moreover, that this process of "breaking the silence" went hand-in-hand with projecting, if not inventing, a "men of color" subjectivity. It was thus toward this project – of defining the terms of what this category *should* imply – that the paper focused its next several issues. *O Homen*'s abolitionist turn became more explicit later, in what turned out to be the paper's last issues; for reasons still unclear to us, the weekly stopped after

[26] *O Homem*, January 13, 1876, p. 1.   [27] A. Magalães Pinto, *Imprensa negra*, p. 61.
[28] *O Homem*, January 13, 1876, p. 1.   [29] *O Homem*, January 13, 1876, p. 1.

a three-month run. Nevertheless, we note that, from its first numbers, Collaço drew readily from US examples to suggest that Black equality and success could only flourish in a post-emancipation context.

O Homem's project to "unify Pernambuco's men of color" drew on Collaço's vast intellectual repertoire. It featured religious and legal articles on equality, a regular column called "The Illustrious Men of Color" that recovered the life stories of prominent Afro- and Native Brazilians, and a pointed abolitionist platform. Together, these pieces served not only to rebut the string of recent firings of Afro-descendant public officials but also to trouble the code of racial silence. Reviewing the standing context of January 1876, the article explaining the journal's impetus iterated that "in the last year, six men of color have been pushed out from their jobs . . . and that without faith or the rule of law . . . a lasting peace cannot exist."[30] This reality extended a deepening political crisis, as Collaço reminded readers that "men of color" had been excluded from Recife's municipal council for the last twenty-eight years, since the late 1840s.[31] It was thus to religion and science that Collaço turned early in the paper to counter the charges that "society does not want, nor accept, men of color in public posts."[32] Attributing these words to the provincial president, he invokes several "we are created equal" passages from the Bible before seamlessly paraphrasing French naturalists who also argued for humankind's common origins. In confronting – disproving, really – ideas about innate racial differences, Collaço pivoted to the issue of political rights, for the violent dispersal of the public meeting, where notable men of color had gathered to sign and send off a petition to Parliament, illustrated the unequal treatment they endured. The incident encapsulated the disregard for their constitutional rights, he argued, which they had to fight together to reclaim. The incident also revived anxieties over legislation from the year before that placed restrictions on where free and enslaved men of color could hang signs.[33] Collaço believed essential a "unified" response to strengthen the political capital of this "class of people, the most numerous and hardest working in Brazil."[34]

O Homem's process of racial formation required a smoothing over of class and gender distinctions, as it strove to rewrite the political handbook for Pernambuco's "men of color." The newspaper form allowed Collaço a unique means to string together an unending series of "we's" and

---

[30] *O Homem*, January 13, 1876, p. 1.   [31] *O Homem*, February 24, 1876, p. 1.
[32] *O Homem*, January 13, 1876, p. 1.   [33] A. Magalães Pinto, *Imprensa negra*, p. 60.
[34] *O Homem*, January 13, 1876, p. 3.

"our's" when referring to the "men of color" that, when juxtaposed with the "they's" and "them's," gave the impression that oppositional, racial dialectics indeed shaped political dynamics. In fact his trajectory offers a different view of political networks. Though race, of course, shaped social networks of all kinds, the stories of Brazil's prominent Afro-descendants are also stories of interracial collaborations. Furthermore, the "we's" also seemingly glossed salient class differences within a heterogeneous, free, Afro-descendant male population. This "class," in Collaço's words, encompassed carpenters and stonemasons in addition to law-school graduates and influential businessmen.[35] Clearly, the "men of color" invoked in the paper referred to the latter, a small but accomplished and visible group. The gendered nature of the racial category is also explicit in the journal's title. The universalizing form of "man" feeds and reflects extant gendered discourses of power and can be read as part of a discernible nineteenth-century phenomenon of trying to preserve a "masculine" identification with the political arena.[36] For Collaço, who earlier in his career had edited "women's" and "family" newspapers, this contentious entry into public debate required adhering to, and reinscribing, the gendered codes of discussions about political rights.

Historical narratives figured as a source and form of establishing a "men of color" tradition. The recurrent "Illustrious Men of Color" column, for example, accomplished several interrelated objectives. It first provided a context, a "historical" basis from which to establish the legitimacy of the current generation's successes. This tradition of achievement doubtless responded to charges of Afro-descendant inferiority; it used historical biography of past leaders of color to affirm the political rights of the contemporary community. Additionally, the sketching of some figures – like the famed Afro-Bahian jurist Antonio Pereira Rebouças (1798–1880) – also opened the chance to introduce antislavery as a topic that was important to this group. In fact, the paper's first issue carried with it an insert of Rebouças. Collaço extolled Rebouças "for his virtues and service to the *patria* since its beginnings" and reiterated his national standing by pointing to a recent book published in Rio that contained Rebouças' parliamentary speeches from 1830 to 1847.[37]

---

[35] MacCord's books convey well the class spectrum of Recife's free men of color. See M. MacCord, *O Rosário* and *Artífices da cidadania*.

[36] If focused on the United States, an indispensable reference on race and public life is E. Barkley, "Negotiating and Transforming"; on Brazil, see R. Kittleson, "Campaign All"; M. Santos, "On the Importance."

[37] *O Homem*, January 13, 1875, p. 3.

Collaço also emphasized Rebouças' role in presenting a bill to Parliament in 1837 that called for an enforcement of the prohibition on the transatlantic slave trade.[38] Through this specific column, Collaço not only created an antislavery lineage that was important to abolitionist activists in the 1870s writ large; he also made a "man of color" central to this process.

As part of a project of reasserting a historical memory, the "Illustrious Men of Color" articles were instrumental in establishing the key qualities of this group. Whether the biographies focused on known men like Rebouças and Henrique Dias or on lesser-known figures like the musician Elias Lobo, they emphasized personal sacrifice and contributions to the nation. The articles, however, also decried the historical neglect of Afro-descendant achievements, which could have well reflected Collaço's own anxieties about his legacy. These columns also revealed that Indigenous men belonged in Collaço's "of color" category. That is, though the paper's justification stemmed from recent developments involving Afro-descendants, Collaço also wrote about Felipe Camarão, the Indigenous leader who led a native battalion against the seventeenth-century Dutch occupation. Camarão exemplified the national-hero narrative. Collaço also invoked, if in exaggerated fashion, the triumphs of natives across the Americas in order to make the point that "non-white populations enjoyed equal rights in other societies, including in the United States, and in Mexico, Chile, Bolivia, and Peru .... In Mexico, as is well known, a full-blooded Indian [sic] was elected president."[39] These references, including that to Benito Juárez in Mexico, painted Brazil in a comparatively unfavorable light for its inability to consider the talents of the "men of color." This Juárez mention, specifically, foreshadowed a later tendency among Brazilian abolitionists to celebrate the Mexican political leader; an officer of a radical abolitionist association in Ceará, for example, used "Juárez" as his nom de guerre in the early 1880s.[40]

The racial project of *O Homem* acquired a distinctive register when it explicitly embraced abolitionism. The editorial of the fourth issue read: "we want the realization of constitutional equality for all Brazilians ... we want our constitutional rights respected by the rule of law, not granted as an extension of personal favors ... and we want the complete extinction of

[38] For more on Antônio Rebouças's thoughts and deeds on slavery, see K. Grinberg, "Em defesa," pp. 111–146; a sweeping study of his life as it reflects the histories of Brazilian citizenship and state-making is K. Grinberg, *O fiador*.
[39] *O Homem*, March 23, 1876, p. 3.   [40] P. Silva, *História da escravidão*, pp. 191–229.

slavery in Brazil."[41] The racialized "we" here became defined by its call for abolition. In part, Collaço's abolitionism arose from ties maintained with other newspapers in the print milieu. We know that he traded issues with, and reprinted articles from, *A Luz*, the fiery republican abolitionist newspaper printed in Recife in the early 1870s.[42] Antislavery developments abroad also factored into Collaço's thinking. The US context, for example, loomed large. He hailed the enthusiastic reception that *Uncle Tom's Cabin* enjoyed in Europe, whereas in Brazil theatrical adaptations of the story had been all but prohibited up until that point.[43] In the last issue, Collaço most imaginatively created a shared US-Brazilian abolitionist storyline. In an extended two-page article, he invited readers to dream a scenario where the emperor's upcoming trip to Philadelphia, to participate in the US centennial celebrations, would occasion further action in the legislature to end slavery once and for all (with, it should be said, a provision for indemnity). *O Homem* argued that this was a plausible scenario given that the 1871 law had also been passed while Dom Pedro II was out of the country and that, therefore, his presence abroad, especially in the context of this big event in the United States, would allow Brazil to show itself favorably on the world stage. Returning to the domestic context, the article then emphasized that this discussion about abolition was also transpiring in the national capital, via the *O Globo* newspaper. As opposed to *O Homem*, however, the Rio journal was actually adamant in rejecting any and all provisions for slaveowners' compensation. The larger point, *O Homem* stressed, was that the press "worked to bring public opinion around to this perspective" and that in due time the larger dailies across the country would also stoke this debate. "Could this all just be a dream, what we've just described?" asked *O Homem* rhetorically. "Only time will tell," the article closed.[44]

Though it ended rather abruptly, Collaço's newspaper nonetheless calls attention to Afro-descendants' sometimes quite prominent place in public life. Recent research has, in fact, analyzed the relationships between several prominent "men of color," public figures who used newspapers and literature as platforms for also "breaking the silence" on racial matters and on slavery. Historian Ana Flávia Magalhães Pinto, for example, probed and connected the works of José Ferreira de Menezes, Luiz Gama, Machado de Assis, José do Patrocínio, Ignácio de Araújo Lima, Arthur Carlos, and Theophilo Dias de Castro, who in different

---

[41] *O Homem*, February 3, 1876, p. 2.   [42] *O Homem*, January 27, 1876, p. 1.
[43] *O Homem*, March 23, 1876, p. 1.   [44] *O Homem*, March 30, 1876, p. 2.

ways combined forces to make the issues of race, slavery, Black equality, and citizenship all worthy of public discussion.[45] Their concentration in São Paulo and Rio de Janeiro played a part in this recognizable explosion in collaboration and activism. While aware, undoubtedly, of this abolitionist and race-consciousness ferment, Collaço did not align *O Homem* with these contemporaneous developments. His relative isolation may have been because he was historically aligned with men in Conservative networks, while most of these other leaders emerged from Liberal and Republican backgrounds; it may have been because of a generational difference and his lack of contact with this younger cohort of public figures; it may have also been because of his comparatively more recent turn to abolitionism. More work, to be sure, remains to be done on the wider resonance of *O Homem* beyond Recife.

REACTION AND ANTI-BLACK SUBJECTIVITIES

O Homem animated racial subjectivities. However, it was not only Pernambuco's "men of color" that it stirred; it also generated an anti-Black response, showing that racialized discourse indeed played a part in shaping Brazilian power relations. These public airings of anti-Blackness, however, drew on traditions of racial silence instead of deviating from them. In analyzing the policing of these spaces of public discourse, we are able to better understand the contentious terms through which Afro-descendants engaged powerful dimensions of public life, such as the press. José Mariano's daily, *A Provincia*, for example, welcomed the new journal into the public arena. Mariano – the popular, ascendant leader of the Liberal Party – even praised the new organ, lauding its banner of "Liberty, Equality, and Fraternity." Mariano hailed the paper for strengthening Brazil's tradition of a free press and iterated that it would refrain from weighing in on its racial politics until it better understood the paper's objectives. Nevertheless, in its initial observations of the paper, Mariano's *A Provincia* disingenuously questioned whether a public existed for a paper of *O Homem*'s nature and used the ambivalent phrase "mulatos em cena" (mulattos on the scene) to sum up, and spoof, its debut.[46] To be sure, the "mulattos on the scene" phrasing conjures up the mocking and racist spirit of jokes about "uppity" Afro-descendants, jokes that are intended to delegitimize all sorts of broader claims-making.

[45] A. Magalães Pinto, "Fortes laços."   [46] *A Província*, January 14, 1876, p. 1.

The following day, despite its earlier assurances that it would reserve judgment until it saw more from *O Homem*, *A Provincia* unleashed a blistering, front-page attack on the new paper. It called *O Homem* "impolitic" and "unnecessary."[47] And it affirmed that Brazilian citizens already coexisted easily, without distinctions in color and opportunities. Until this point, it mostly repeated the familiar tropes associated with racial silencing; that is, arguing that legal equality already existed for the entire free population. Yet, while deliberately disregarding *O Homem*'s complaints and justifications, *A Provincia* went further and criminalized them. It accused the new paper of fostering racial divisions, of the sort that "would tear the country apart."[48] The portrayal of *O Homem*'s mission as racial, as opposed to political or legal, was itself part of a campaign to delegitimize the paper. This line of attack resonated precisely because of the cultural understanding that it was wrong to discuss racial problems in public. A paper like *O Homem* was simply unprecedented in Recife. Thus, *A Provincia* warned it to "defend the theses and arguments that you wish, but do not call for separate spheres . . . for you are as free and enterprising as those of the *Caucasian* race" (emphasis in original).[49] With some condescension, Mariano tried to reset the framework in which to engage *O Homem*'s claims for broader political rights. Curiously, however, though Mariano was white and Collaço Afro-descendant, Mariano's exploits and reputation up until that moment in 1876 had not matched Collaço's standing. His fame would, of course, far surpass Collaço's in the ensuing decade and in popular memory. As is well-known, Mariano went on to play a prominent role in the national and regional histories of abolitionism. As an elected deputy to parliament in the 1880s, he formed part of, and vigorously defended, the small abolitionist wing of the Liberal Party. He supported measures to halt the interprovincial slave trade and backed an early, radical version of what became the 1885 Sexagenarian Law. He went against the status quo in that latter instance in supporting the immediate and uncompensated freeing of elderly slaves. Because of his abolitionist commitments, however, he lost a reelection bid in 1886. Locally, Mariano allied with the most militant abolitionist societies. After ceremoniously freeing his own slaves in 1882, Mariano acted as an interlocutor for an interracial association that helped enslaved people flee north to the province of Ceará. He was a fiery orator at large, public meetings. And his place in abolitionist lore was enshrined in the popular

[47] *O Homem*, January 27, 1876, p. 1.   [48] *A Província*, January 15, 1876, p. 1.
[49] *A Província*, January 15, 1876, p. 1.

dramatic representation of "May 13," where he was the protagonist that announced news of the abolition law to cheering crowds. Doubtlessly, the charismatic Mariano changed the course of local politics, including how the debates over abolition unfolded.[50]

Yet, from the vantage point of 1876, Mariano's response to *O Homem* showed that an anti-Black rant carried little to no political risks. The rising Liberal in his twenties clearly did not feel intimated by taking on the accomplished Collaço, a man twice his age. The reverse scenario, however – of a younger Afro-descendant challenging a white man as established as Collaço was – is virtually impossible to imagine. Still, the anti-Black response did not register as a "break" with the code of racial silence. Nor, certainly, did it register that this language informed its own process of racial formation, where, if whiteness was not explicitly touted as the ideal, blackness definitely signaled inferiority. Mariano's defense of unified rather than "separate" spheres rested on the belief that indeed all males had equal opportunity to succeed – that what historians have referred to as the "precariousness of Black freedom" did not exist.[51] Nevertheless, it is important to situate Mariano's critique of the "separate spheres" within the context of contemporary abolitionism, for *A Provincia* had also been involved with this discussion since its founding in 1873. Yet the paper operated on a largely partisan basis, mobilizing the abolition issue in order to instrumentally undermine Conservative power. Such was the case, for example, when it denounced slaveowners' abuse of the 1871 Free Womb Law. Like Republican antislavery journals, it publicized instances of owners illegally selling young children; it made an even bigger issue of the province's slow implementation of the national emancipation fund, which was also tied to the 1871 law. Yet in printing runaway slave ads on the back pages of all its issues, and in targeting Conservative rather than Liberal slaveowners, the paper underscored its partisan and contradictory facets. Throughout, its antislavery politics remained bound to an imagined raceless ideal of liberal freedom. In short, the clash between *O Homem* and *A Provincia* demonstrated how their contentious interactions, which at heart rested on who got to determine whether race was silenced in public discourse, played a key part in shaping racial subjectivities. For as much as the "we's" in *O Homem* worked to mold a narrative about what it meant to be "of color," the "we's" in *A Provincia* similarly worked to set the terms for opposition to the presentation of race-specific claims. The terms for the

[50] C. Castilho, *Slave Emancipation*, pp. 120–136; 180–182.
[51] S. Chalhoub, *A força da escravidão*, p. 21.

latter project evolved part and parcel with the sarcastic and insulting references to the "mulattos on the scene."

Notably, another paper, the Catholic journal *A União*, also joined the anti-Collaço chorus. Its editor, however, was a "man of color," which furnished a unique perspective on the tensions surrounding *O Homem*.[52] The argument between the two Afro-descendant editors produced some of the most charged anti-Black discourse seen in the late-nineteenth-century Recife press. Like *A Provincia*, *A União* initially attacked *O Homem* on the grounds "that it was an unnecessary paper because between us, no one pays attention to a man's color; once he displays merits, he is able to ascend the social hierarchy."[53] It silenced race by shifting to a discussion about merit. Thereafter, *A União*'s editor proceeded to ironically and disparagingly invoke Collaço's own trajectory in order to support his position. It stated that *O Homem*'s editor "is proof of what we believe, that despite being *black-skinned* [*sendo de cor preta*], he still holds a degree from the law school; he still holds various public posts, and is currently *enjoying retirement* as a teacher from the secondary school" (italics in original).[54]

This provocative statement stung Collaço on several fronts. First, it brought up Collaço's controversial and racially fraught dismissal from a prestigious secondary school, a circumstance that we will turn to shortly. In so doing, it prompted Collaço to not only refute that characterization of him enjoying a comfortable retired life but also to call his removal an actual "firing." Still clearly reeling from those recent events, Collaço nonetheless warned this now-rival editor that he "could also be displaced from his position, just like I was, given that we are both of the same color, even if you are a little *fulinho* [*lighter-skinned*]" (italics in original).[55] Both men's attacks, then, featured a comment about the other's African heritage. They asserted their power in prying open the other's blackness. Collaço's insult – and it was an insult to highlight someone's African descent in this context – did interestingly hint at a "we" regarding their circumstances: a "we" Collaço forged out of an imagined common struggle as "men of color." This construct lay at the

[52] *O Homem*, January 27, 1876, p. 4. All references to this exchange between *O Homem* and *A União* come from *O Homem*, Collaço's newspaper. We have not had access to *A União*; it is not in the National Library's digital archives. More than ascertaining the actual who-said-what of the back-and-forth, what is important here is to show how *O Homem* framed and responded to *A União*.
[53] *O Homem*, January 27, 1876, p. 4.   [54] *O Homem*, January 27, 1876, p. 4.
[55] *O Homem*, January 27, 1876, p. 4.

heart of *O Homem*'s classed and gendered racial project to unify men of influence. Yet, it was ultimately a fleeting "we," for Collaço reached deeper in order to upset the other man. He followed the comment on his "light skin" by asking "the owner of the *União* if he remembers seeing slaves even lighter than him in the houses he enters," because, Collaço continued, "I can assure you that in the kitchens there are slaves that light, as was the case in my parent's house."[56] Collaço purposely collapsed the socioracial distance that ostensibly differentiated a professional, light-skinned man of color from an enslaved person. Though written to offend, this last matter actually brought out *O Homem*'s larger point that only the abolition of slavery could ensure a meaningful measure of honor and equality for Afro-descendants. Meanwhile, the rather casual reference to the light-skinned slaves Collaço was raised among shows that slaveowners were still not stigmatized at this point in the 1870s. In fact, the allusion to his upbringing – perhaps ironically – lent Collaço a degree of credibility and power with which to debase the other editor.

In contrast to the initial polemic with *A Provincia*, the confrontation with *A União* pointed to and revived Collaço's recent clashes with the provincial government. As everyone knew, those clashes derived from an infamous punch he threw at a colleague during a school function, from the legal battle that ensued, from his subsequent firing, and from the racist overtones that were used to describe the process in the press. In other words, by the time *A União* appeared to take Collaço on, it had been long deemed acceptable to racially slight him. The school incident happened about a year before *O Homem* was published, at a teacher's meeting where a colleague of Collaço's sang the praises of an outgoing administrator. Protesting the glorification, Collaço asked to speak, which prompted the administrator, who was present, to leave the room because he knew the criticism that he awaited. Tensions escalated among the teachers, according to the official account of the afternoon. To resolve matters, the organizers simply ended the meeting. Witnesses reported, however, that the bickering continued, and the speaker told Collaço that his "slandering of the outgoing administrator was as black as his own skin" – in reply to which the accomplished editor, mathematician, and law-school graduate simply decked him on the chin.[57] Collaço was immediately placed under house arrest, and his actions were reported to the provincial

[56] *O Homem*, January 27, 1876, p. 4.
[57] APEJE, Fundo: Instrução Pública, 1875. Documentação administrativa do Ginásio Pernambucano.

president, who ordered a legal investigation. Little question remained that he would be indicted, but – whether because of Collaço's legal acumen or because of the powerful political allies he still preserved – he beat the charges twice, including on appeal.[58] Meanwhile, the partisan press also took up the incident, using the case as a means to defend or support the administration. While it is beyond the scope of this chapter to delve into those details, we can now more clearly appreciate how it was through O Homem that Collaço was finally able to exert his own voice on the situation.

In a most fundamental way, the paper enabled him to make racial discrimination the key problem. And this was not a point that he took for granted. He had endured racial taunts in public for years, long before the incident at the school and despite the norms of racial silencing. The worst, perhaps, happened in 1874, after he returned to the school he taught at from a disputed leave of absence: a note appeared in the city's paper of record, taunting him, asking if "he was ready to obey his superior." Despite this loaded insult, the statement hints at the degree to which Collaço had previously unsettled the so-called order of things. Overall, though, the note surely meant to return him to "his place," a "place" of subordinated blackness. The author signed off, "Vicente, the overseer," so as to leave clear how centrally the reality of slavery shaped the way people exercised racial power.[59] Neither the author, who was presumably tied to the school, nor the editor of the city's most important paper balked at using such language as "overseer" in relation to one of the country's most talented citizens. It was not, then, that race was completely silenced in public discourse. In fact, research on Afro-descendant editors in the Brazilian southeast has shown that they, too, were publicly taunted and referred to as "slave-like."[60]

Such examples iterate that anti-Black language shadowed Collaço's public interventions; that the strategy of turning a political grievance into a discussion about race allowed those in power not only to deflect attention from systemic problems but also to further extend their levels of surveillance over public discourse. The anti-Black responses in effect represented an act of policing public life, an act of constituting racialized normativity. Furthermore, these instances of trying to stigmatize Collaço must be seen as related to ongoing processes of relegating blackness to the

[58] Jornal do Recife, September 6, 1875, p. 2.
[59] Diario de Pernambuco, October 26, 1874, p. 3.
[60] A. Magalhães Pinto, "Fortes laços," pp. 50–52, 99–105, 135–145.

political margins of the nation. And this was not lost on Collaço. He wrote that "the outspokenness against my paper comes from voices interested in preserving the actual state of things."[61] He also went to extraordinary lengths to respond to criticism lobbed against him in equally racialized terms. His was a rare voice that mocked whiteness, referring to those who chided him as "the pretentious descendants of the Caucuses."[62] While the "pretentious" part of the slight probably weighed more than referring to someone as a "descendant of the Caucuses," the conjoining of the two destabilized ingrained assumptions about white superiority. He actually also appropriated the insulting line – "mulattos on the scene" – for the name of a column that he maintained to describe his paper's evolving political stance. In so doing, Collaço signaled the fearlessness that made him appear threatening: "Whatever direction the storm comes from, it no longer scares or bothers us. We are already used to swallowing our pride, calmly and without reacting. This has been the daily bread of our existence."[63]

CONCLUSION

This chapter represents the first in-depth analysis of Collaço and *O Homem* to appear in English. Many more questions than answers remain about Collaço's life, especially about the period following *O Homem*. We have also yet to learn much about his children beyond the reference to them that appeared in his obituary. Still, this initial foray into the newspaper and its editor's biography highlights some salient aspects of the process of slave emancipation: its public nature, the importance of the press, and the racialized political responses that responded to the rise of abolitionism. Clearly, the abolition debates bore upon the practice of politics, and their consequences were felt both immediately in the mid-1870s and in the longer term.

Most uniquely, *O Homem*'s story calls attention to the important nineteenth-century history of racial silencing, which was an ideology and cultural process that shaped power relations. Collaço's paper illuminated the racialized work that this ideology did in suppressing debates on hierarchy and politics and, by extension, slavery. It also helps us better understand how the "breaking of this silence" sparked noticeable shifts in racial subjectivities. *O Homem* argued that patterns of racial

[61] *O Homem*, January 27, 1876, p. 1.   [62] *O Homem*, February 10, 1876, p. 1.
[63] *O Homem*, January 29, 1876, pp. 2–3.

discrimination existed and that the select prominent Afro-Brazilians occupying public posts were being subjected to an extralegal campaign of removal. Collaço's own controversial dismissal from the secondary school doubtlessly drove this perception. These actions, he insisted, violated the constitutional ideal of legal equality and required Pernambuco's "men of color" to respond accordingly and in a coordinated manner.

The newspaper thus represented a bold means of rewriting the racial narrative. Collaço proceeded through a variety of columns on history, the law, religion, science, and contemporary affairs. Notably, he also embraced the abolition of slavery as integral to his project and, for the first time in almost a decade of local abolitionist struggle, linked the debates about abolition to considerations about Black belonging and rights. In so doing, *O Homem* provoked even a publication like *A Provincia* – which was ostensibly on the antislavery side of the political spectrum – to lash out. This racialized response revealed a pervasive ambivalence about blackness, including in circles presumably committed to abolitionism. These contradictory, racist strands of abolitionist discourse endured within the broad reformist coalition. But rather than dismissing this history as exceptional, it is important to situate these anti-Black responses as part of a long and troubling history of anti-Black racialized politics. *A Provincia*'s and *A União*'s interactions with *O Homem*, for example, skirted discussions about power, and in this case public jobs, by generating a polemic around race. These new polemics cleverly and disingenuously changed the focus from racial discrimination and political patronage to whether it was even legitimate for "men of color" to present their grievances in such terms. In a sense, the responses were about a normative construction of an "us" that was strategically portrayed as not being about race, which enabled the perpetuation of Black political exclusion.

In terms of the history of racial silence, then, this chapter points to the public arena as an important site where this ideology operated. It highlights the prevailing discourses used to enforce such "silence," which in the end revealed the rather open nature of racialized language in the press. When one takes into the account the plethora of runaway-slave ads in Brazilian newspapers for most of the nineteenth century, it is clear that both slavery and race were indeed quite regular features of public life. However, the controversies surrounding *O Homem* make it clear that it was not that race could not be discussed but instead that Black empowerment remained too threatening an issue; such discussions endangered not only social relations among the free population but also the slave-based foundation of the national order. The policing of Black political discourse, which we saw practiced by rival white and Afro-descendant editors, also signaled a mechanism through which to constrict how Black politics were articulated and debated. The comparatively small number of avowedly nineteenth-century Black newspapers in Brazil should thus not be seen as reflecting a lower degree of Afro-racial consciousness but perhaps as more a reflection of the dominant modes of public politics.

There remains yet one last consideration to highlight in terms of the effects of anti-Black racialization in political discourse, and that pertains to how former slaveholders in the post-emancipation era depicted the wider abolitionist movement in racialist language to discredit the legitimacy of popular political action. In the months following emancipation, it was not unusual to find articles in the press about "disorderly Black gangs" disrupting procedures on election days or, worse, instigating conflicts to shut down the electoral process altogether.[64] These sentiments, for example, surfaced quite prominently during the last election cycle of the empire (August/September 1889), some eighteen months after the abolition of slavery, and aimed to stoke anti-Black fear and sideline popular, including Black, political participation. Collaço's story, then, especially in terms of *O Homem*, should be understood as connected to this larger period where anti-Black discourse emerged as a response to political contestation. His experience illustrates that within the struggle over abolition, a related, fiercely disputed process unfolded in the press over the place of blackness in public life; that the deep-seated tradition of "silencing race," in effect, set in motion anti-Black racial subjectivities.

---

[64] C. Castilho, *Slave Emancipation*, pp. 182–191.

10

The Life and Times of a Free Black Man in Brazil's Era of Abolition

Teodoro Sampaio, 1855–1937

Wlamyra Albuquerque[*]

In 1955, Gilberto Freyre (1900–1987) published a brief article in the magazine of the Instituto Geográfico e Histórico da Bahia (IGHBa).[1] By then, Freyre's best-known work, *The Masters and the Slaves* (*Casa grande e senzala*), was already an editorial success in Brazil and in the United States, and Freyre was among Brazil's most renowned intellectual interpreters.[2] The IGHBa magazine was celebrating the centenary of engineer Teodoro Sampaio (1855–1937), and Freyre lamented that the occasion had not inspired "any scholar of national questions" to study Sampaio, "that almost forgotten embodiment of a Brazilian from Bahia, who also found a partial place in São Paulo and Rio de Janeiro." Freyre's complaint was justified. Sampaio's essays on topography, fluvial navigation, sanitation, Brazilian history, and Indigenous languages and cultures were (and still are) little known among Brazilian scholars.[3] This lack of interest, Freyre argued, was a sign of the degree to which Brazil's mid-twentieth-century

---

[*] Translation by Brodwyn Fischer. The author would like to thank all colleagues from the research group Slavery and Invention of Freedom – UFba (*Escravidão e Invenção da Liberdade*), as well as the authors of this book and Professor Dain Borges for his comments and suggestions.

[1] G. Freyre, "O centenário." IGHBa is an intellectual institution founded in 1894.

[2] *The Masters and the Slaves* was published in English by A. Knopf in 1946; in 1957, an abridged edition was awarded the Anisfield-Wolf Prize, for the best work about race relations in the world.

[3] The most important works by Teodoro Sampaio are about the history of Bahia, Indigenous cultures and languages, and geography. See, among others, T. Sampaio, *História da fundação*; *O Rio*; *O Tupi*. An exception to the general rule is Stuart Schwartz, who "respectfully dedicated" his 1985 book, *Sugar Plantations in the Formation of Brazilian Society*, to Sampaio and three other "Bahian intellectuals."

intellectuals were depriving themselves of "valuable contributions that would allow them to understand and clarify many shadowy areas of the Brazilian past," which had been expressed in the publications and research notes of the man Freyre called the *eminência parda* of Brazilian letters.[4]

Eminência parda was the term Freyre chose to convince the readers of the IGHBa magazine that the engineer deserved a place among the great interpreters of Brazilian society. Freyre was very careful in his use of this expression, placing it in quotation marks and suffusing it with ambiguity and possible double meanings. In Brazilian Portuguese, *eminência parda* is the most common translation of *éminence grise*, the French term used to describe someone who exercises great and determinate influence over those in power without holding any official position of authority. But the word *parda* was also a category of skin color in Brazil, which meant that *eminência parda* could also be read as "dusky eminence," with all of the ambiguous racial connotations that designation would have carried in early-twentieth-century North America. In using this term, Freyre aimed to highlight Sampaio's position as an influential and lettered *pardo* who had been forgotten by the Brazilian intellectual class.

But this chapter does not spring solely from a desire to explore the gallery of forgotten Brazilian intellectuals. It aims instead to examine the impasses, conflicts, and agreements that shaped Teodoro Sampaio's life trajectory, thus opening an analytic window on the possibilities for social transformation that were available to a man of color during and after the crisis that led to Brazilian abolition. Teodoro Sampaio lived through a time when the dismantling of slavery coincided with a racialization of social status, justified by the postulates of scientific racism. His trajectory thus illuminates how a free, educated son of a freed mother could make his way through a society that was reinventing socioracial hierarchies even as slavery lost its legitimacy. Placing his story in the context of Brazil's broader social history, this chapter aims to elucidate the intricate network of relationships and endeavors engendered by a *pardo*, born on a large slave property, who managed to become an engineer and manumit his three brothers, who were enslaved on the same plantation where Sampaio himself was raised free. Based on Sampaio's autobiographical texts, books, articles, and private correspondence – as well as on what his

---

[4] G. Freyre, "O centenário," p. 11. Freyre was referring specifically to a contribution made by Teodoro Sampaio with notes and information from his research on E. da Cunha's *Os sertões*, a classic masterpiece, published 1902, that detailed the living conditions, ecology, and cultural expressions of people from the *sertão* of Bahia.

contemporaries wrote about him – this chapter will reflect on what we can learn from Teodoro Sampaio's life about what it meant to be a free, lettered *pardo* man during the dismantling of Brazilian slavery.

TEODORO SAMPAIO AND SLAVERY

Sampaio was born on January 7, 1855, at the Engenho Canabrava sugar plantation. The property belonged to Manoel da Costa Pinto, the Viscount de Aramaré. Costa Pinto was an important land- and slaveowner in Santo Amaro, a municipality in the famous Recôncavo Baiano, at the core of the slave-driven economy that then thrived across the Americas. Until the first half of the nineteenth century, the region reliably produced the abundant exports of sugarcane that enriched the slave-owning elite of the Atlantic World.[5] Teodoro Sampaio was born to a freedwoman named Domingas da Paixão do Carmo. His paternity is much disputed. One biographer wrote dramatically that the subject was shrouded by "dense mystery."[6] The most common version of the story attributes Sampaio's paternity to Father Manoel Fernandes Sampaio, who supported Teodoro's schooling and bequeathed his surname. In a brief autobiographical sketch requested by Donald Pierson in 1936, Sampaio claimed to be the son of a modest family. He described his mother as "a Black woman, a person of notable beauty among her race," and he claimed that his father was "a white man, an educated gentleman from a family of agriculturalists, or *senhores de engenho*, from Santo Amaro."[7] One year later, when Sampaio wrote his will, he omitted his father's name, making it clear that he did not want any controversy about the subject.[8] His discretion was understandable, given his ostensible father's clerical status, although Freyre himself had already noted in *The Masters and the Slaves* that such family arrangements were common in the sugarcane regions, where the children of priests were "treated kindly" and raised in "more favorable circumstances than in any other Catholic country."[9] Along these same lines, it was common for men, even if they were priests, to have children with enslaved women; while they might not have been

---

[5] S. Schwartz, *Sugar Plantations.*   [6] R. Silva Júnior, "Vida e obra," p. 30.

[7] IGHB, Autobiographical notes – Teodoro Sampaio, Arquivo TS 06, doc 52; and D. Pierson, *Negroes in Brazil,* p. 353.

[8] Arquivo Público do Estado de Bahia (APEB), Inventory of Teodoro Sampaio, administrator of estate José Teodoro Sampaio, Seção Provincial, 05|2321|2821|13, 1937, p. 5.

[9] G. Freyre, *Casa grande,* 32nd ed., p. 443.

faithful to Church doctrine, they were certainly attentive to Brazilian society's patriarchal logic.

Teodoro Sampaio died on October 15, 1937. In a small departure from his father's discretion, José Teodoro Sampaio (Teodoro Sampaio's son and the executor of his estate) identified Teodoro as *pardo* on his death certificate and named Joaquim Fernandes Sampaio and Domingas Sampaio as Teodoro's parents. In this way, José Sampaio conferred legitimacy on the relationship between Domingas and a certain Joaquim, who was probably a relative of Father Manoel, although I have not been able to find any traces of him in the notarial archives.[10]

There is yet another version of Teodoro's paternity, related by members of the Costa Pinto family, who owned the Engenho Canabrava. In a letter addressed to the biographer Arnaldo Lima in the 1980s, João Gabriel da Costa Pinto said that it was a commonplace in family lore that Teodoro Sampaio was the son of Major Francisco Antônio da Costa Pinto, the Count of Sergimirim and brother of the Viscount of Aramaré; this was a narrative tradition, he claimed, that had "began with his [Sampaio's] birth and was passed down through subsequent generations." Costa Pinto did caution, however, that Sampaio "maintained complete discretion in this regard, perhaps because he was resentful that he had never been recognized by his father, who died a single man." Major Costa Pinto did, in fact, die single in 1863, without recognizing or naming as heirs any natural or illegitimate children.[11] Yet if the major had by chance had children, it would have been relatively uncommon for him – as a well-off nineteenth-century gentleman – to have omitted them. Brazilian historiography is full of studies that show that it was common for men on their deathbeds to recognize their paternity during the time of slavery.[12] Perhaps this supposed kinship was nothing more than a twentieth-century desire on the part of the Costa Pintos, who may not have bequeathed any of their wealth to the son of one of their slaves but wanted nonetheless to inherit his prestige. For even though Freyre was correct in complaining about the general lack of academic interest in Sampaio, the engineer did enjoy fame among some Brazilian intellectual circles for being a son of a slave who had succeeded in the white world. The magazine issue devoted to him by the IGHBa was in this sense emblematic.

---

[10] APEB, Inventory of Teodoro Sampaio, administrator of estate José Theodoro Sampaio, Seção Provincial, 05/2321/2821/13, 1937, p. 4.

[11] A. Lima, "Teodoro Sampaio," pp. 13 and 145.

[12] See, among others, L. Castilho et al., eds., *Barganhas e querelas*.

Regarding Domingas da Paixão, we know that she was a captive and that she worked as a nanny and housekeeper at the Big House and sacristy of the Engenho Canabrava.[13] Although we lack precise information about her manumission, it is reasonable to suppose that her freedom letter resulted from domestic negotiations, in which her dependent position vis-à-vis her former owners would have been evident. Maria Helena Machado's recent research, some of which is included in this volume (see Chapter 6), does much to clarify the customary conditions that delimited freedwomen's autonomy in the 1800s. Sampaio's biographers from the 1950s, in an attempt to construct a romanticized genealogy for a man they termed a "mulato laden with color," described Domingas as a woman of irresistible femininity.[14] She was, wrote Arnaldo Pimenta da Cunha, "graceful and intelligent," the color of "purple cypress or ebony," a woman who "embodied the beauty of those almost regal Black women." "With a truly beautiful face, she had an elegant figure and was very well dressed," demonstrating an "enchantment of posture and elegance" that "attracted and seduced whoever came near" that "daughter of Jeje Africans." Thus Pimenta da Cunha, a biographer and personal friend of Teodoro Sampaio's, went overboard in adhering to the much-contested tendency to rhetorically subsume masters' sexual violence against female slaves in order to celebrate the racial mixture that was – at the end of the day – the supposed legacy of men of Teodoro Sampaio's status. Descriptions such as his were not mere rhetorical devices; it is apparent from the recent historiography that essentialized representations of Black and *mulata* sensuality had broad social and political significance.[15]

Pimenta da Cunha described Father Manoel as a "worshipper of muses"; for that reason he could not keep his vow of chastity. The lapse of this cultured, religious man was justified: he simply could not adhere to the demands of the priesthood in the face of the physical attributes of the *crioula* (Brazilian-born Afro-descendant woman). The daughter of Jeje Africans compelled the priest's sins.[16]

The sexual appetites of the Big House, the masters' desire for the bodies of enslaved women, and the vast numbers of *pardos* who came to populate Brazilian society are all central to Gilberto Freyre's analysis of the formation of Brazilian society and culture. In Freyre's interpretation, "there is no slavery without sexual depravity. Depravity is the essence of such

---

[13] The registration of Domingas' manumission has not been found yet.
[14] R. Da Silva, "Vida e obra," p. 30.   [15] S. Besse, *Restructuring Patriarchy.*
[16] A. Pimenta da Cunha, "Theodoro íntimo."

a regime."[17] From that perspective, the sexual violence carried out by masters entranced by the latent sexuality of African and *crioula* women produced generations of glorious bastards, like the "illegitimate son of the master," who "learned to read and write sooner than did the white lads, leaving them behind as he went on to higher studies. Rural traditions tell us of many such cases ... of *crias* [dependent children raised to serve in families other than their own] who made their way upward, socially and economically, by making good use of the instruction that was given them."[18] In this Freyrean sense, Teodoro Sampaio was indeed an *eminência parda*, the son of a priest gestated in the archaic traditions of Brazil's Northeastern sugar country. Through Freyre's lens, Brazilian society was racially and socially defined by its *mestiço* character, which made the borders between masters and slaves – and whites and Blacks – more plastic, more porous, and less perverse.

This interpretation, which has long been contested in Brazilian academia, was already widespread even before *The Masters and the Slaves* became a bestseller in the 1930s. During the post-abolition period, Sampaio was often exalted by the IGHBa as a successful emblem of miscegenation. Social scientist Thales de Azevedo noted that in 1922 a panel of seventy-nine notable Bahians had been created to commemorate the centennial of Brazilian Independence. One of the most distinguished among them was Teodoro Sampaio, who was by Azevedo's classification a "dark *mulato*."[19]

If Teodoro Sampaio was reserved when referring to his father, the same was not so in relation to the short time that he lived in the Engenho Canabrava. In the autobiographical text that he wrote for Donald Pierson, he boasted about having a grand slave plantation for a cradle. In telling his story, Sampaio took pride in the master's power and the mistress's "generosity":

I was born under the sacred roof of the chapel of Canabrava, an *engenho* that was then owned by a notable agriculturalist and head of an important branch of the Costa Pinto family, in Santo Amaro. I left that place when I was still very small, but I still hold fixed in my memory the image of the *Sinhá* [mistress] who provided me with my first taste of education, taking me in under her roof, as if it were a maternal womb. She was so generously kind, so full of affection, that I will never forget her.[20]

---

[17] G. Freyre, *The Masters and the Slaves*, p. 324.
[18] G. Freyre, *The Masters and the Slaves*, p. 453   [19] T. De Azevedo, *As elites*, p. 162.
[20] IGHB, Teodoro Sampaio, Notas autobiográficas – Teodoro Sampaio, Arquivo TS 06, doc 52.

Though it does not appear among the postmortem inventories of the Recôncavo Baiano's great properties, the Engenho Canabrava, in Bom Jardim, belonged to a wealthy landowner named Manoel da Costa Pinto.[21] The Costa Pinto clan was part of the select group that dominated the social, economic, and political life of Bahia in the nineteenth and even twentieth centuries. According to the historian Eul-Soon Pang, in 1880 the Viscount de Aramaré, a "notable agriculturalist," was a founding partner of the first industrial sugar mill in Bahia, which was located in Bom Jardim.[22] Francisco Antonio de Costa Pinto, Antonio da Costa Pinto Junior, and Manuel Lopes da Costa Pinto comprised the "patriarchy of agrarian modernization in the nineteenth century." A list of their main undertakings includes everything from the founding of Bahia's Imperial Institute of Agriculture (Imperial Instituto Baiano de Agricultura) to their tenacious lobbying of the Imperial and Provincial governments to create the Santo Amaro Railroad Company (Companhia de Estrada de Ferro de Santo Amaro).[23]

The Costa Pinto family was innovative when it came to modernizing sugarcane production but conservative in their politics. They were among the funders of the Society for Agriculture, Commerce and Industry of the Province of Bahia, which mobilized large land- and slaveowners from the Recôncavo Baiano against the abolitionist movement.[24] Freyre visited the Costa Pintos when he was in Bahia in the 1930s and expressed his gratitude to his hosts, whose kitchen served up the "the most delicious flavors from the traditional cuisine of the Big House."[25] Even long after abolition, the sugar aristocracy preserved the flavors of northeastern slave society.

During the time of slavery, Domingas da Paixão occupied herself with the culinary traditions of the Big House at the Engenho Canabrava: it was there that she would have experienced both Teodoro's departure to study in the Imperial capital and the daily plantation routines of her three enslaved sons, Martinho, Ezequiel, and Matias. At the age of ten, father

---

[21] It states in the land registry that Canabrava Mill was 4,356 kilometer square. Registro Eclesiástico de terras, Freguesia de Bom Jardim, Santo Amaro (1859–1863), APEB, Fundo Colonial e Provincial, n. 4669. About properties in the Recôncavo Baiano see: W. Araújo Pinho, *História de um engenho*, p. 323; L. Costa Pinto, *Recôncavo*; M. Brandão, ed., *Recôncavo da Bahia*. In 1880, two new central mills opened in Bahia: Bom Jardim on January 21 and Pojuca on November 18. This might give the impression of a resurgence, but the export figures for the following years continued to demonstrate the severe crisis of sugar production in the Recôncavo Baiano. B. Barickman, "Até a véspera."

[22] E. Pang, *O engenho central*, p. 23.   [23] E. Pang, *O engenho central*, pp. 35–45.

[24] E. Pang, *O engenho central*, p. 28.   [25] G. Freyre, *Casa grande*, 32nd ed., p. xiv.

Manoel arranged for Teodoro Sampaio to leave behind his early education at the *engenho* and attend boarding school at the Colégio São
Salvador, in Rio de Janeiro. The year was 1865, a time when the interprovincial slave traffic was radically reorganizing the regional demography of
Brazilian slavery. The expansion of coffee cultivation in western São Paulo
and southern Rio de Janeiro was absorbing an increasing proportion of
Brazil's enslaved workforce, which had previously been concentrated in
the old plantation zones.[26] Robert Conrad estimates that Bahia's slave
population dropped from 300,000 to 76,838 between 1864 and 1887.[27]
This decrease was substantially impelled by the interprovincial slave
traffic. But Teodoro Sampaio migrated to Rio de Janeiro for other reasons
and with another destiny. After seven years at the Colégio São Salvador,
he enrolled at the Escola Central (the Central School, which would later
become the Escola Politécnica) in December 1871. He claimed to have
been taught by many great men of science, including André Rebouças –
the subject of Hebe Mattos' Chapter 12 in this volume – and the Viscount
of Rio Branco, who were both also from Bahia.[28] José Pereira Rebouças
was part of Sampaio's graduating class in 1876.[29]

During those years the Imperial capital was roiled by debates and
proposals about the so-called servile question. The Viscount of Rio
Branco, Sampaio's sometime teacher and a conservative chief of the
Imperial Cabinet, in fact called the shots in the emancipation process.
The 1871 Free Womb Law, which would grant the incrementally free
status of *ingênuo* to all children born of slave mothers from that point
forward, was in the process of being approved. As the historian Sidney
Chalhoub emphasizes, in the midst of a tense political and judicial debate,
the 1871 law also formally recognized many entitlements that had already
been hard-won in practice by the captive population, such as the right to
accumulate savings to purchase letters of manumission. At the same time,
however, the Rio Branco Law preserved many rituals of subordination; it
remained the masters' prerogative, for example, to personally hand over
a freed person's manumission letter, thus reaffirming freedom as a favor
conceded by the master, which reinforced his or her power over the person
they had once held as property.[30] Even so, large slaveowners such as the

---

[26] R. Slenes, "Malungo, Ngoma vem!"; H. Mattos, *Das cores*.
[27] R. Conrad, *Os últimos anos*, p. 43.
[28] D. Pierson, *Brancos e pretos*, p. 375. André Rebouças was a professor at Escola Central
after being a government employee in 1866. R. Vainfas, ed., *Dicionário do Brasil*, p. 43.
[29] A. Lima, "Teodoro Sampaio," p. 116.   [30] L. Schwarcz, "Dos males."

Costa Pintos still rebelled against what they understood as state interference in their private business and state compromises with those who
yearned for their freedom; in their view, the law ran the risk of compromising the "moral force" that the owners wished to continue to deploy.[31]
Among the most daring Liberal ranks, meanwhile, defenders of the
"slaves' cause" such as André Rebouças acted vigorously to enforce the
captives' rights through the press, the Parliament, and the courts.

When recalling his youth, Teodoro Sampaio commented that "we used
to run from the Polytechnic School to the legislative sessions, trading
a physics class for one in parliamentary oration."[32] In the midst of such
effervescence, however, there is no record of Sampaio's involvement in
either side of the slavery dispute. He did, throughout his five years of
engineering study, maintain regular correspondence with members of the
Costa Pinto family.[33] It seems likely that, in exchange for his frequent
updates about his studies and the life of the Imperial Court, news reached
him about the repercussions of the Free Womb Law in the red-soiled heart
of seigneurial power.[34] When Teodoro Sampaio returned to Bahia in 1877
with his engineering degree, the economic and political scene was highly
unfavorable for the gentlemen of the Recôncavo. Sampaio's visit was brief
and had a single clear objective: to negotiate the manumission of
Martinho, one of his brothers, who was still captive at Canabrava. This
suggests that Sampaio had a plan to manumit all of his brothers,
Domingas' sons. Nearly a year later, Sampaio returned to Bahia to finalize
his purchase of Martinho's manumission letter. Very soon thereafter, he
assumed the post of second-class engineer at the Imperial Hydraulic
Commission, which had been created by the Liberal minister João Lins
Vieira Cansanção de Sinimbu, the Visconde of Sinimbu, in order to study
Brazil's interior ports and navigational conditions.

---

[31] S. Chalhoub, "The Politics of Ambiguity." On agriculture clubs, see, among others,
E. Pang, O engenho central, p. 84, 96–98, 101–102; E. Foner, Nada além; W. Filho,
Encruzilhadas.

[32] T. Sampaio, "Discurso."

[33] There are letters from Teodoro Sampaio addressed to João Ferreira de Moura, Maria
Luísa da Costa, and Antônio Joaquim Ferreira de Moura's son. João Ferreira de Moura
was a member of the Bahian Imperial Institute of Agriculture (Imperial Instituto Baiano de
Agricultura) and vice-president of Bahia province in 1867.

[34] "Informações sobre o estado da lavoura" tells us that in 1874 the 892 existing mills in
Bahia (300 of them powered by steam) were in decay, and the main complaint was lack of
labor. A great number of slaves were taken to the South, to coffee plantations in São Paulo,
and the number of slaves in the province was reduced to 173,639. W. Araújo Pinho,
História de um engenho, p. 323.

It was at that juncture, according to the autobiography that he wrote for Donald Pierson, that Sampaio claimed to have suffered from "race prejudice." In a rare recognition that he had been touched by prejudice, Sampaio broke what Hebe Mattos has termed "the ethic of silence" that surrounded his ambiguous social position. The act of discrimination occurred after he was nominally appointed to the Imperial Hydraulic Commission but then summarily excluded from the official list after an employee of Minister Sinimbu's Cabinet deemed it improvident that a "man of dusky hue" should be among an entourage led by the North American engineer W. Milnor Roberts. "Hence I was excluded and experienced for the first time the sting of prejudice," Sampaio lamented, though he quickly clarified that the incident was rapidly reversed, thanks to the personal mediation of Senator Viriato de Medeiros, who informed Minister Sinimbu of the situation in time for it to be put right.[35]

The attention Sinimbu gave to this incident reveals much about the political alliances that worked in favor of the Costa Pinto family's interests and by extension protected the young engineer. The Viscount de Sinimbu was president of Bahia province between 1856 and 1858, a turbulent period during which he had to confront rebellious multitudes up in arms over the high cost of food and other necessities.[36] Before an attempted assassination that sent him back to Rio de Janeiro in fear for his own life, Sinimbu frequently visited the *engenhos* of the Recôncavo, overseeing provincial public works and planning others that might facilitate the flow of sugarcane production, especially in Santo Amaro. He was an engaged administrator and an enthusiast of projects intended to modernize the sugar sector in the second half of the nineteenth century.[37] It is thus easy to imagine the future Viscounts of Sinimbu and Aramaré, between visits to the cane fields and dinners in the Big House, having opportunity and motive to seal alliances that would end up benefiting Teodoro Sampaio in the 1870s. The clientelistic political culture that structured relationships among the Empire's political leaders would have been useful in undoing the damage done to Sampaio by that "rare" example of "social prejudice" that nearly excluded him from his professional debut on the Hydraulic Commission. The rapid and satisfactory resolution of the problem fit within the paternalistic logic of the day. This "incident," this jabbing "thorn of prejudice," did not even lead Sampaio, in the end, to recognize the existence of any form of

---

[35] D. Pierson, *Negroes in Brazil*, p. 354.
[36] J. Reis and M. Aguiar, "Carne sem osso." See also R. Graham, *Alimentar a cidade*.
[37] E. Pang, *O engenho central*, p. 31.

racial distinction in Brazil. In 1919, analyzing Brazil's slave past, he pondered that "because of their mild ways, Brazilians never experienced the ferocity of [racial] prejudice."[38]

At that point in his life, it was clear that Teodoro Sampaio, like so many intellectuals of his age, tried to downplay Brazilian racism; in his view, it only caused jabs, small discomforts, which did not render professional relationships between Blacks and whites unviable.[39] Because of this, he made use of another strategy of distinction, extolling his own professional capacities and affirming his status as a free and loyal man. In his autobiography he noted that, as soon as he joined the team of North American technicians on the Hydraulic Commission chaired by W. Milnor Roberts, "the cloud of prejudice" was quickly dissipated, thanks to the "value of his work," and Sampaio had "honor of winning their friendship and esteem," which "proved with the passing of the years to be very beneficial and served me well in the profession that I adopted."[40] In this way, the mark of his color was rendered invisible by his excellent engineering attributes. Such was the strategy that Sampaio and so many others chose in order to navigate the minefield that was Brazilian society during the crisis of slavery: it was best to simply snuff out one's racial condition by recourse to exceptional professional talents and skills.

At the same time, Sampaio showered praise on those who showed him "esteem and friendship." One example involved the North American geologist Orville Derby, whom Sampaio met when they worked together at Brazil's Museu Nacional (National Museum) in 1875. Using the racialized vocabulary of the time, Sampaio recognized in the geologist "a sweet and well-grounded soul, with the phlegmatic calm that is characteristic of his race."[41] Thus, even as Sampaio sought to make his own racial condition invisible and to free himself from any "cloud of prejudice," he classified Derby's "sweetness" and "phlegmatic calm" as characteristics of the "race" of the North American man whose admiration Sampaio had earned. Race was not a relevant attribute when Sampaio described himself, but positive racial characteristics were useful when it came to recognizing the condition of whiteness in others.[42]

[38] T. Sampaio, "Discurso." Thales de Azevedo comments on this text in T. de Azevedo, *As elites de cor*, pp. 179–182.
[39] A classical text about the comparison of racial relations in Brazil and in the United States at the time is T. Skidmore, *Black into White*.
[40] D. Pierson, *Negroes in Brazil*, p. 355, translation slightly modified based on the Portuguese original.
[41] R. Silva Júnior, "Vida e obra," p. 36.
[42] For a discussion about identities and racial relations at the time, see W. Albuquerque, *O jogo*; H. Mattos and K. Grinberg, "Antônio Pereira Rebouças."

Even as Teodoro Sampaio grappled with racial identities shaped by the scientific thinking of his day, he strove to realize two great endeavors: the consolidation of his own career and the manumission of all of his brothers. Both tasks required precision and meticulousness, qualities that were also important in his profession, all the more so because he was a man of color who aspired to some form of social distinction. Entangled in a web of favors, protection, and mutual recognition, both Sampaio's employment on the Hydraulic Commission and the purchase of his brother Martinho's manumission letter (finalized in 1878) were woven from threads that linked Sampaio to his family's old masters, the Costa Pinto family. For as long as the Empire endured, Sampaio made use of the family's political connections in order to navigate around his professional obstacles. In truth, recourse to webs of fictive kin and favors was part of the organizing logic of Imperial politics, whether the issues involved were great questions of state or everyday jockeying for employment and prestige among engineers and other professionals, who were extremely dependent on government jobs and resources.[43] For those who depended on governmental decisions to exercise their professions, it was critical to cultivate good relationships with people in positions of power and learn to make effective use of clientelism. For Brazilian engineers in the late nineteenth century, the best opportunities were in grand public works projects such as the expansion of the railway network, the development of the water supply, and the improvement of urban sanitation.

Teodoro Sampaio knew well that without strong relationships, difficulties would emerge. After the Hydraulic Commission's work was finished in 1880, at a time when Brazil's Liberal Party was determined to prevail in the complex internal politics of the Empire, Sampaio lamented:

I have spent six months struggling to find work in my field. I have employed this time teaching Mathematics, History and Philosophy with our friend James Edwin Hewitt. It is worth noting a small injustice on the part of the men who govern us in these times of Liberal rule. The "Hydroelectric Commission" was dissolved in June of last year. All of its members were quickly well placed. My supervisor praised me highly and gave me special recommendations, I had done work that reflected well on me and was praised by the minister himself. All well and good, but when it came time for that same minister, Buarque de Macedo, to offer me a position, he demoted me: he gave me the lowest-ranking engineering job on a railroad line in Pernambuco. I refused this polite favor and have since then been waiting for better days.[44]

[43] R. Graham, "Brazilian Slavery."
[44] IGHB, Teodoro Sampaio, Notas autobiográficas – Teodoro Sampaio, Arquivo TS 06, doc 52.

Researcher Arnaldo do Rosário Lima interpreted this document as evidence of the obstacles imposed upon the engineer by his racial condition.[45] Yet the reasons Sampaio himself gave for his professional annoyances were conjunctural and partisan. His professional difficulties resulted from "injustice on the part of the men who govern us in these times of Liberal rule." The year was 1880. The 1878 cabinet, led by the aforementioned Liberal Viscount of Sinimbu, who was quite close to the emperor, had dissolved because of dissension within the Liberal ranks and the instability provoked by the Vintém revolt in Rio de Janeiro. The political atmosphere was turbulent on the streets and confused in the legislature, and governmental control was hotly disputed among Liberal leaders of various stripes, giving rise to the impasse that hampered Sampaio.

Finally, on March 28, 1880, José Antônio Saraiva, who had been born in Bom Jardim, another district in Santo Amaro, established a new Cabinet, which opened space in the government for two other Liberal Bahians, Conselheiro Manoel Pinto de Sousa Dantas and Rui Barbosa.[46] Ironically, the good times that the engineer so eagerly awaited came with the rise of these Liberals, who had long been committed to the end of slavery and were thus the sworn adversaries of landed elite families such as the Costa Pintos. In this new scenario, Sampaio's employment difficulties were resolved, and he was named to the position of first-class engineer by the provincial government, charged with prolonging the Bahian railway to the São Francisco River Valley region. This new position suited the Costa Pintos as well: they had recently begun operations at the new Bom Jardim sugar mill and were more eager than ever to facilitate the outflow of their sugar production. This was just the opportunity that Sampaio needed to rescue another of his brothers from captivity. In 1882, it was Ezequiel's turn to become a freedman. In a letter addressed to the Viscount of Aramaré, the engineer justified his efforts and appealed to the seigneurial grace of his brother's owner as follows:

I salute Your Excellency and your esteemed family, to whom I commend myself and for whom I wish health and prosperity.

My mother will return [to Engenho Canabrava] today, bearing this letter, in which I once again request Your Honor's protection and friendship.

My promise to free Ezequiel must now be kept, despite the difficulties I now face as I begin to establish my household and family. I thus ask that Your Excellency extend a great favor to your slave, reducing the price of

[45] A. Lima, "Teodoro Sampaio," p. 26.
[46] R. Graham, *Clientelismo e política*; R.Vainfas, *Dicionário do Brasil*, p. 405.

his freedom with the same generosity that you have always proven capable of, especially toward us.

I have some small savings, which I will give up for this end. The loss will not weigh on me, because it is an expenditure that I make with heartfelt goodwill, and I am sure that Divine Providence will not abandon us.

Dr. Teodoro F. Sampaio[47]

After paying his respects and explaining his financial limitations, Dr. Sampaio proceeded to present the Viscount with a choice in forms of payment (cash or bonds), as if he were already certain of a positive response. He made a point of demonstrating that he only had limited savings but that he would willingly make them available, given the importance of the purchase. In such a situation, seigneurial "protection," "friendship," and "generosity" were presented as indispensable. Sampaio was playing with cards from the old paternalistic deck, disregarding the new rules of the game that had been laid down by the abolitionist movement.

After the Free Womb Law of 1871, enslaved people gained the right to buy their freedom, and both they and free abolitionists tenaciously defended that right in the courts and on the streets.[48] As historian Maria Helena Machado has indicated, by the early 1880s the abolitionist movement occupied public plazas to delegitimize slavery in a "turbulent and popular tone." In those years, historian Elciene Azevedo has added, enslaved people's own agency effectively combined with the strategies pursued by lawyers, journalists, and judges who favored "the cause of liberty," amplifying in the courts the growing public dissatisfaction with masters who impeded their slaves' manumission.[49]

The abolitionist wave also advanced among the *senzalas* (slave quarters) of the Recôncavo, in plantations that had held large numbers of slaves since colonial times. The bankruptcy of slavery and the grave crisis of sugar production increasingly preoccupied slave masters, who sought ways to guarantee not only their profits but also their supposed "moral force," which had been viscerally compromised by slavery's delegitimization.[50] In response, they employed strategies such as declaring themselves in favor of abolition or advertising their own supposed benevolence and charity vis-à-vis their slaves. In 1881, the push for freedom gained still more popular support as residents looked forward to the visit

[47] IGHB, Teodoro Sampaio's letter to Viscount de Aramaré, March 13, 1882, Acervo Teodoro Sampaio, caixa 9, doc 75.
[48] S. Chalhoub, *Machado de Assis*. [49] M. H. Machado, *O plano*; E. Azevedo, *O direito*.
[50] The term was analyzed in S. Chalhoub, *A Força*.

of José do Patrocínio, one of abolitionism's most important Black leaders, to the city of Salvador. Patrocínio, who was famous for his intransigent defense of abolition and his passionate speeches, once told the emperor himself: "When this cursed arid soil cracks, after drinking for three centuries the sweat and tears of millions of men, doesn't Your Majesty worry that your throne might be one of the ruins? ... There is only one serious issue in this country: the abolition of slavery."[51] Invited by the *Gazeta da Tarde* to meet with Bahian abolitionists, José de Patrocínio met with a large and attentive audience.[52] Right after his visit, the Sociedade Libertadora Bahiana (Bahian Liberation Society) was founded; it would go on to become the province's most important abolitionist society. Among the most progressive Liberals, the mood was festive. Abolitionist Clubs proliferated in various cities and filled the streets with pamphlets advertising abolitionist rallies and parties to raise funds for "the slave's cause."

Yet despite this ferment, Teodoro Sampaio followed his plans – without politicizing the purchase of his brother's freedom, and without transforming into a right what he could gain from subtly exploiting a wobbly but still pervasive slavocratic logic. In this "game of dissimulation," those involved – and not only Sampaio – showed that they were skilled at negotiating issues of freedom in ways that did much to shape and restrict the place people of color would occupy in a rapidly evolving social order. Elsewhere, I have used the term "game of dissimulation" to describe the interplay of dispute, conciliation, and dissension that surrounded socioracial identities in the context of abolition.[53] The argument is that the flagrant racialization of the actions, political choices, and cultural practices of people of color was integral to the disputes that raged during Brazil's drawn-out emancipation process. Yet the game was never explicit; for Brazil's slaveowning class, it was as important to hide the racial criteria that guided decisions of state as it was to ensure the continuity of social hierarchies inherited from slavery. Teodoro Sampaio, it seems, had mastered the rules of this game.

It was not by chance that the task of delivering the letter negotiating Ezequiel's freedom fell to Sampaio's mother, Domingas. She had once herself been enslaved to the powerful Viscount of Aramaré: because of that, the very act of approaching him with a request saturated with

---

[51] *Gazeta da Tarde*, June 19, 1884, cited in J. Patrocínio, *Campanha*, p. 42.
[52] L. da Fonseca, *A Escravidão*, p. 283; R. Silva, *Caminhos e descaminhos*.
[53] W. Albuquerque, *O jogo*.

reverence and appeals to his seigneurial generosity demonstrated Domingas' respect for the conceptual construction of manumission as a gift. At the same time, she was probably the person to whom Teodoro Sampaio had promised that he would purchase Ezequiel's freedom, spending his savings with "heartfelt goodwill." Because Sampaio had left Canabrava at the age of ten and returned only recently to his birthplace, the freedwoman Domingas would have been the main link between Sampaio and the brothers who had remained on the plantation. Domingas was thus much more than the mere bearer of the letter. According to Robert Slenes, one of Brazil's foremost authorities on the history of the slave family, the purchase of manumission in the nineteenth century was usually a family project engendered by women.[54] By mediating with her ex-master the purchase of her enslaved son by another who had risen to become a *doutor* (doctor), Domingas may have sought to reconstitute in freedom the family ties that slavery had rendered fragile.

In his letter, Teodoro Sampaio noted that he was beginning "to establish" his "household and family." This was his way of noting that he had recently married and begun a new job. On January 18, 1882, only two months before he began to negotiate Ezequiel's freedom, he had married Capitolina Moreira Maia, his cousin, a twenty-four-year-old woman of color[55] – thus the need to establish a household in Alagoinhas, where Sampaio had begun to work on Bahia's railroad line. Not by chance, that same line was used to circulate news about abolitionist agitation across Brazil.[56] Ezequiel's manumission, paid for with Teodoro Sampaio's savings, became reality with little fanfare in 1882; it was, in the end, a negotiation for freedom carried out within the domestic sphere of the Engenho Canabrava. The recent historiography of Brazilian abolition has noted the degree to which manumission became a public spectacle in the 1880s.[57] Yet our engineer closed this chapter of his family saga far from the agitation of the streets, without entering in judicial disputes, distant from the diatribes of abolitionist journals that recounted serial histories involving persistent slaves, engaged lawyers, and slavocratic masters. Sampaio's brother Matias was now the only one whose freedom was yet to be attained.

[54] R. Slenes, *Na senzala*.
[55] IGHB, Teodoro Sampaio's letter to Viscount de Aramaré, March 13, 1882, Acervo Teodoro Sampaio, caixa 9, doc 75; APEB, Inventário of Capitolina Maia Sampaio, inventariante Teodoro Sampaio, 05|2332|2832|o2, May 9, 1932.
[56] R. Souza, *Trabalhadores dos trilhos*.
[57] See, especially, C. Castilho and C. Cowling, "Funding Freedom."

A NEGOTIATED FREEDOM

On June 6, 1884, Manoel Pinto de Souza Dantas, leader of the Liberal Party in Bahia, took office as president of Brazil's Council of Ministers, inaugurating the so-called Dantas Cabinet. On June 15, his son, legislator Rodolfo Dantas, presented an emancipation proposal to the Chamber of Deputies. The bill's most controversial provision was an article that would free all slaves over the age of sixty, with no indemnity to their masters. By the wee hours of the following morning, any demonstration of sympathy for the "slave's cause" was met with harsh criticism. At a party on the grounds of Rio's Polytechnic School, for example, a demonstration of support for the abolitionist movement provoked one conservative deputy and staunch slavocrat to give an inflamed speech in which he railed against the "social anarchy" that had gained resonance in the Dantas project.[58] Councilor Dantas rushed to the tribunal to defend himself and clarify that he was an emancipationist; that is, that he favored the gradual elimination of slavery, carried out under state control, and was not an agitator, a revolutionary, or even an abolitionist. He was a peacemaker, given that "the extinction of the servile element was a national aspiration, in the face of which one cannot retreat, halt, or act precipitously."[59] Yet not even the Parliament was appeased. Historian Jailton Brito has noted that in 1884, the masters' protests against the project were forceful in the Bahian Recôncavo and especially in the Costa Pintos' Santo Amaro stronghold.[60]

The sugarcane aristocracy's first reaction was to fly the abolitionist flag while at the same time declaring themselves averse to "revolutionary agitation."[61] Mindful of the growth of the abolitionist movement, plantation owners sought to reinforce the notion that freedom was a gift, an act of charity on the part of benevolent masters. In presenting themselves as last-minute converts to emancipationism, and in condemning the abolitionists' "revolutionary agitation," the masters exposed the degree to which the crisis of slavery reinforced their desire to racialize freedom. This explains why the Viscount of Aramaré arranged Matias' manumission as soon as the Dantas project came up for discussion on the legislative agenda. In registering the manumission letter of Sampaio's last captive brother, the Viscount wrote:

I present this freedom letter to Matias, my Creole slave, of about 35 years of age, who can enjoy his freedom as if he had been born of a free womb.

---

[58] About Deputy Andrade Figueria's speech, see E. Viotti da Costa, *A Abolição*, p. 80.
[59] Editorial, *Gazeta da Tarde*, July 19, 1884.   [60] J. Brito, *Abolição na Bahia*.
[61] W. Fraga Filho, *Encruzilhadas*, pp. 108–109.

I do this in deference to his relatives' good qualities and receive no indemnity in return.
Engenho Aramaré, September 28, 1884[62]

This time, Teodoro Sampaio had no need to bargain. It would have been misplaced: at that point, with slavery in its death throes, the Viscount of Aramaré was not going to charge him a penny for Matias' freedom. His seigneurial profit would take another form. The viscount thus justified his act with the customary rationale: the freedom letter was payback for or recognition of the "good qualities" of the captive or his relatives. If we follow the Viscount of Aramaré's logic, this act was also an honorable escape from the embarrassment that a captive brother could provoke, not only for a successful engineer like Teodoro but also among the Viscount's allies in the "agricultural and commercial classes" who had recently converted to emancipationist politics. At the same time, Teodoro Sampaio's status as a reputable engineer in charge of the expansion of Bahia's railway line served them as a good example of how seigneurial tutelage was a sure path for men of color.

Matias' manumission was officially registered on September 28, 1884, the anniversary of the 1871 Free Womb Law. There was no more opportune occasion for such an act of lordly charity. During the age of abolition, Brazilian newspapers were full of manumissions that had been sponsored by masters on that same exact date. Their ample distribution of freedom letters was widely publicized by the Bahian press, celebrated in the legislative chambers, and displayed in the public plazas and theaters of various cities. Such performative generosity was part and parcel of the owners' reaction to the Dantas Bill's progress. The masters sought to convince the public that the Free Womb Law was already gradually extinguishing slavery, while the Dantas project only generated social chaos and produced "anarchists." The conservatives' complaints about the project's subversive qualities were exaggerated, but they were still useful, because they reaffirmed the notion that freedpeople could not live in an orderly way if freedom meant escaping from the masters' tutelage. Teodoro Sampaio was also convinced that the 1871 law was the definitive solution to the problem of servitude. In 1916, already quite distant from the orbit of the Costa Pinto family, he wrote:

The [1871] law declared the free status of children born to enslaved women and liberated the sons and daughters of the nation; it even regulated the upbringing and treatment of those minor children and stipulated the annual manumission of

[62] IGHB, Matias' manumission, Acervo Teodoro Sampaio, caixa 5, documento 8.

other slaves. This law was the mature product of the deliberations of our men of State and an integral solution to the servile question; if its action and impact had been realized in the fullness of time, it would in fact have been the greatest trophy among the parliamentary victories that were won in Brazil.[63]

Teodoro Sampaio thus maintained the rationalizations of the sla-veowning class even long after abolition, which demonstrates the political relevance of the defense of the 1871 law. As historian Joseli Mendonça has noted when analyzing the political dynamics of the 1880s, the gradualism laid out in the 1871 law served the cause of "prudent emancipationism," which sought to perpetuate a system of "domestic agreements": the sorts of freedom negotiations – like those undertaken by Teodoro Sampaio – that had been resolved in the living rooms of the Brazil's Big Houses since colonial times.[64] Matias' manumission, like so many across the country, was thus motivated by seigneurial self-preservation and informed by the reigning logic of paternalism.[65] In this way the manumission letter, under-stood as a "gift," simultaneously freed another of Sampaio's brothers, brought one of his life's greatest endeavors to a successful conclusion, fulfilled Domingas' desires, and buoyed the spirits of the Recôncavo's master class.

In the meantime, the defenders of the Dantas project tried to reorganize after the emperor dissolved the Chamber of Deputies on September 3, 1884. On the other side, as soon as the new elections were called the great slaveowners began to envision the survival of the seigneurial world that they so valued. In Bahia, the failure of the Dantas endeavor was already foretold when Rui Barbosa, an import-ant abolitionist, lawyer, and Liberal leader, was defeated in the new elections for the Chamber of Deputies. Bahia's place in the Chamber was occupied instead by Conservative Inocêncio Marques de Araújo Góis Júnior, who had the full support of Santo Amaro's Liga de Lavoura and Commércio (League of Agriculture and Commerce). The League, which counted the Costa Pintos as members, had been created in 1884 with the principal objective of placing a brake on the abolitionist locomotive.

The game had turned in favor of Viscount de Aramaré and his allies. It had been a tough fight, but the slaveowners came away stronger, expounding on the consequences of broad freedom for slaves – even sexagenarian slaves – with heated arguments grounded in scientific

[63] T. Sampaio, "Discurso."   [64] J. Mendonça, *Entre a mão.*
[65] S. Chalhoub, *Machado de Assis.*

racism.[66] On August 10, 1885, Deputy Lacerda Werneck firmly attacked the Dantas project, envisioning the future as follows:

With no sense of justice, with no knowledge of the world, ignorant and incapable of handling themselves, knowing no instincts except those that predominate among their race, incapable of resisting vice, capable of doing anything to satisfy their desire for it; the sexagenarian will be seen by foreigners and by the future historians of emancipation as the most painful evidence of our improvidence.[67]

Incapable, ignorant, stripped of any notion of justice, and governed only by the instincts of his race; such was the freedperson who populated the speeches of the Dantas project's opponents. Thus represented – constructed as beings who would heap shame on the history of emancipation with their vices – Brazil's sexagenarian slaves came to bear not only the weight of their years in captivity but also the burden of racial stigma. The liberty of sexagenarian slaves would encumber them and their nation. There was no shortage of those willing to maintain that, given the vices of their race and the scars of captivity, sexagenarian slaves could not do without the generous protection of their masters. In the end, despite abolitionist efforts to counter this assault, the legislature rejected the Dantas project on the grounds that it provided no state indemnity to slaveowners.

Teodoro Sampaio himself was an apostle of the notion that elderly slaves were best off in benevolent captivity. In "Um Engenho de Cana de Açucar de Santo Amaro," he described thus the "life of elderly slaves" at Canabrava:

Elderly slaves who had given good service earned benevolent references that kept the overseers from bothering them and ensured that they would continue to receive their rations .... This kind of humanity was, truth be told, a general characteristic of Santo Amaro's plantation owners.[68]

And it was in Santo Amaro, this "slave paradise," that he and Domingas must have witnessed the ceremony in which the Viscount of Aramaré presented Matias with his manumission letter. For everyone involved, this was the successful outcome of a plan for freedom. In only six years, Teodoro's family – taking advantage of the political context and the "humanity" of the Big House – fulfilled their collective ambition for

---

[66] On scientific racism, see, for example, L. Schwarcz, *O espetáculo*.

[67] J. Mendonça, *Entre a mão*, p. 75.

[68] IGHB, Teodoro Sampaio, "Um engenho de cana de açúcar de Santo Amaro," Arquivo TS, caixa 1, doc. 15, manuscrito.

liberty. Because she had been a "good-quality" slave, Domingas thus had the chance to reconstitute her family, outside of the gates of the Engenho Canabrava but still within the Costa Pinto family's seigneurial domain. In this she seems to have succeeded: when Matias died on September 11, 1911, he lived in the same house as Teodoro Sampaio, on Misericórdia Street in the Bahian capital of Salvador.[69]

As Domingas began to recreate her family, the abolitionist movement tried to remake itself. And Teodoro Sampaio, for his part, ratcheted up new professional conquests. In 1886, Orville Derby, who was then the director of São Paulo's Geographic and Geological Commission, invited him to lead the team charged with São Paulo province's geological mapping. He recounted for Donald Pearson that, as head engineer, he was once required on short notice to present the visiting Emperor Dom Pedro II with blueprints, sketches, maps, and calculations regarding the navigability of the Parapanema River. During the impromptu audience, the emperor sat Sampaio on his right-hand side and showed much interest, not only in the land-use studies but also in the customs and languages of São Paulo's Indigenous peoples. Pedro II, Sampaio emphasized, was not even uncomfortable with the engineer's field uniform. The emperor's interest convinced Teodoro Sampaio that Pedro II thirsted for knowledge, loved science, and had an "utter lack of class or color prejudice."[70] The emperor's interest and relaxed attitude had redeemed Sampaio from the sting of prejudice that he had experienced at the beginning of his career.

The time of captivity ended on May 13, 1888, when Princess Isabel decreed that, from that day forward, Brazilian slavery would be extinct. The emperor and the monarchy itself quickly gave way as well, after a long reign. Not even the patriarch of the Engenho Canabrava survived those turbulent times. The Viscount of Aramaré passed away from a stroke in 1889, just days after the Republic was proclaimed; an eager proponent of sugar modernization, the Viscount only saw the first rays of the new era that dawned after abolition. In 1905, Teodoro Sampaio commented nostalgically on the end of slavery:

Bahia today is a decadent society, a society in transition, with the sickly aspect of a degenerate people. The cultivated Bahia of times gone by is over. ... It is important to explain that abolition ruined the fortunes of the old inhabitants, destroying the sociability and refinement that had been generated by urbanity. Bahia's decadence dates to abolition. The period that followed was one of remodeling, in which customs and work routines were reformed and life made new

---

[69] A. Lima, "Teodoro Sampaio," p. 27.   [70] D. Pierson, *Negroes in Brazil*, p. 357.

demands of masters and ex-slaves: of the former because they were used to living off the labor of others, and of the latter because they were unprepared for freedom and led by their ignorance and the racial nature to a life of laziness and idleness.[71]

Teodoro Sampaio's complaint echoed those of the Recôncavo's slave-owners at the time of abolition. It was imprudent to have ended slavery without indemnifying the masters; doing so killed all refinement and generated social decadence. At the same time, without the old socioracial rules of deference that Sampaio had manipulated so well, and without any new laws that obligated freedmen to work, the defects of the enslaved race were left exposed. If on the one hand the engineer viewed slavery as a structure that had deformed Bahian customs by making the Big House dependent on captivity, he also believed that the inhabitants of the slave quarters were incapable of navigating freedom without the tutelage of their ex-masters. More importantly still, Sampaio recognized in the "nature" of ex-slaves a tendency toward "laziness and idleness," befitting the race that Sampaio himself bore the mark of.

CONCLUSION

This was the complex character, forged by the crisis of slavery, in whose story Gilberto Freyre recognized the marks of prejudice in 1955. This was why Freyre took such pains to spell out the debt that national memory owed Sampaio, whom he referred to, with clear double entendre, as an *eminência parda*. The debt that Brazilian intellectuals owed to Sampaio was compounded, Freyre emphasized, by the refusal of the Academia de Letras to accept Sampaio's request to become a member. When his candidacy was rejected, Freyre insisted, a "man of letters" who had done "enormous service to Brazil's intellectual life" suffered the "bitter disillusionment of not receiving the glory and recognition he deserved." In Freyre's view, this was another stumble on the part of the Academy, which did not realize the degree to which "that elderly Brazilian of African origin was worthy of representing the Brazilian intelligentsia along with men of letters who were more European in blood and spirit."[72] From a typically Freyrean perspective, in failing to take in a man of letters born of Africa, the Academy had failed to miscegenate the core of Brazilian intellectual life. The Brazilian Academy of Letters had

[71] IGHB, Teodoro Sampaio, "O aspecto da sociedade baiana em 1906," April 5, 1906, Arquivo TS, caixa 5, documento 13.
[72] G. Freyre, "O centenário," p. 12.

shirked the commitment to racial reconciliation that Teodoro Sampaio had believed Brazilian society capable of.

I do not believe that Teodoro Sampaio would have been flattered to be referred to as a "Brazilian of African origin." Yet Freyre's insistence in characterizing him by his racial attributes helps bring to the surface the pitfalls that marked the engineer's life story. The rest of the authors who honored Sampaio in the IHGB's 1955 tribute only briefly mentioned the fact that he was born of slavery before going on to detail Sampaio's intellectual achievements. They portrayed a successful engineer and first-rate intellectual who did honor to the Bahian Institute of Geography and History, thus silencing or minimizing the difficulties he experienced as a Black man in the era of abolition. Judging from his autobiographical writings, Sampaio himself would probably have preferred the script that his IGHBa colleagues adopted. But Freyre managed in only a few pages to suggest another biographical path, portraying an "eminência parda" and a "Brazilian of African origin" who had been frustrated by the refusal of the Brazilian Academy of Letters to seat him and forgotten by Brazil's twentieth-century scientific and academic communities. These two contrasting scripts force us to the abolition-era crossroads where racism and the question of freedom intersected. In this way, Teodoro Sampaio's life trajectory helps us to understand the array of political strategies that could be constructed by a lettered man of color, born on a large plantation, who sought to consolidate his professional career and manumit his siblings even as slavery's demise brought with it a profound racialization of Brazilian social relations.

Political Dissonance in the Name of Freedom

Brazil's Black Organizations in the Age of Abolition

Ana Flávia Magalhães Pinto[*]

On September 23, 1898, Rio de Janeiro's Presidente Barroso Street was graced with the birth of future poet and samba musician Heitor dos Prazeres. Prazeres was the son of Eduardo Alexandre dos Prazeres, a joiner by trade and a clarinetist in the band of Brazil's National Guard. His mother was Celestina Gonçalves Martins, a seamstress. Prazeres' birth alone was enough to make a street of questionable social prestige one of Rio de Janeiro's most important cultural reference points. But the Prazeres family was not alone: in fact, the neighborhood was made up of many other interesting people, brimming with history. The so-called Cidade Nova, centered around the famous Praza Onze in central Rio, was characterized at the end of the nineteenth century by its expressive Black presence. It counted among its residents the well-known *tias Baianas* (literally, "Bahian aunts," Black female migrants from the state of Bahia known for their elaborate dress and protagonistic role in Afro-Brazilian religion, music, and street commerce), as well as their counterparts from Minas Gerais and the province of Rio de Janeiro. They, together with many Black families of freed- and free people who called Cidade Nova home, transformed the region into a *Pequena África* (Little Africa), which eventually extended into the neighborhoods of Saúde, Gamboa, Estácio, and Santo Cristo.[1]

Through their everyday practice, these people found ways to affirm themselves as legitimate residents of the city. On May 13, 1888 – the day of Brazil's final abolition of slavery and ten years before the Prazeres

[*] Translated from Portuguese by Brodwyn Fischer.
[1] See R. Moura, *Tia Ciata*; T. Gomes, "Para além."

family would celebrate Heitor's birth – their neighbors at Presidente
Barroso #36 welcomed a group of twenty-three "residents of the Cidade
Nova and descendants of the Black race who, having already formed an
incipient familial nucleus," discussed the formation of the Sociedade
Familiar de Dança Prazer da Violeta (Violeta's Pleasure Family Dance
Society). The society's inauguration was set for June 29, 1888, the day on
which Princess Isabel – who had signed the abolition decree – would
celebrate her birthday. With this decision, those gentlemen and ladies,
who claimed famed Black abolitionist José do Patrocinio as their "leader
and undefeated liberator," demonstrated "their jubilation in the face of
this brilliant culmination of Brazilian Independence," which allowed
them to "today consider [their] Brazil – with joy, glory, flowers, and
smiles – *confrère* of the great land redeemed by Abraham Lincoln."[2]
The list of signatories, now mostly unknown, included Agostinho José
Alves, Severino de Sousa Júnior, Julio Antonio de Miranda, Guilherme
Ferreira Alves, Afonso Gil da Mata, Adão de Oliveira Costa, Francelino
Satyro de Alcantara, Damasio Ernesto da Fonseca, Alfredo Eloy Cardoso,
Virgilio da Silva Gurgel, Raphael Guillobel, José Joaquim de Oliveira,
Antonio Felix Vieira da Silva, Elisario Luiz dos Santos, Cecilia Maria do
Rosário, Joana Baptista, Augusta d'Oliveira Alves, Lucia Geraldina da
Silva, Anaysa da Conceição, Justina Camila dos Santos, Maria Francisca
Vaz, Antonia Maria da Penha, and Leopoldina Lauriana Rodrigues.
    Cognizant of the moment's significance, these "descendants of the
Black race" – some darker, some lighter, but all free – did not waste the
opportunity to present themselves to society, as soon as possible after
abolition, in terms that they understood as befitting the status of respect-
able citizens. They formed a union of families, they shared an interest in
consolidating a space of healthy recreation for members of their socioracial group, and they showed themselves to be tuned in to the connections
Brazil was establishing with other nations. Against the grain of the racial
stigmas that emerged with new force after slavery's end and tended to limit
freedom's universalization, the Sociedade Familiar de Dança Prazer da
Violeta, from its base in the Cidade Nova, sought to break with a series of
racial stereotypes.[3] At the same time, the Society did not conceal the side

---

[2] *Cidade do Rio*, May 19, 1888, p. 1.
[3] Studies of Black social clubs, as an expression of Black associativism, have achieved notable
advances in recent years. If at the beginning the focus was on *paulista* (São Paulo) experiences from the twentieth century, work is now advancing in various other directions, both
temporal and territorial. The results for Brazil's southern region especially stand out. It is
important to note that the development of this research field owes itself to the articulation

they took in the political dispute surrounding the survival of Brazil's monarchy, distancing themselves from republican partisans and thus – as we shall see – attracting another set of problems.

In this way, despite general goodwill, the group was vulnerable – so much so that, whether due to obstacles created by public security agents, the princess's state of health on her birthday, some internal disarticulation, or subsequent lack of interest on the part of the newspaper, this was the only time that the society's activities appeared in the press.[4] All the same, historians must work with such gaps, and the society's absence from the newspapers should not be taken as proof of the dissolution of the project that had motivated its founding. The practices of sociability that had for decades brought together free people, freedpeople, and the enslaved – practices that continued throughout the region at the time of the society's founding – bear witness to the fact that the Prazer da Violeta was not an isolated phenomenon.[5] The trajectory of Julio Antonio de Miranda (a member of the Prazer da Violeta who had also been secretary of a group of Cucumbi dancers in the 1880s and became a typographer for the abolitionist newspaper *Cidade do Rio* in the 1890s and 1900s) provides just one example of how Black people were involved in a wide variety of associative practices, within and beyond Black organizations.[6]

This rapid snapshot of the activist context that surrounded the publication of the abolitionist daily *Cidade do Rio* invites further attention to the possibilities for action that were then available to free and freed Black people, as well as a re-examination of conceptual categorizations that can be used to legitimize problematic discourses involving the Brazilian racial experience.[7] Along those lines, this chapter is a counterpoint to generalizations established by historian José Murilo de Carvalho and others with regard to the participation of Black and poor populations in the

---

among individuals tied to the clubs, activists in Black social movements, members of the academic community, and governmental agencies. See J. Correia Leite and Cuti, *E disse*; U. de Siqueira, "Clubes recreativos"; F. da Silva, "Os negros."

[4] On the eve of July 29, 1888, the one-month anniversary of the society's founding, "the freedmen of the Lei Áurea of May 13 and the members of the Caixa José do Patrocínio [a mutual aid society]" were frustrated in their intention to greet the "Exalted Princess Redeemer" as a "consequence of a health issue experienced by that august lady" (*Cidade do Rio*, July 26, 1888, and July 28, 1888, p. 3). As Robert Daibert Júnior observes, the association between Princess Isabel's birthday and the abolitionist cause was promoted from the middle of the 1880s. See R. Daibert Júnior, *Isabel*, p. 117.

[5] For a synthesis, see J. Faria et al., *Cidades negras*, pp. 77–152.

[6] *Gazeta de Notícias*, December 30, 1886, p. 3; *Cidade do Rio*, November 30, 1895, p. 2; August 26, 1898, p. 2; December 31, 1901, p. 2; January 29, 1902, p. 2.

[7] See J. Carvalho, *Os bestializados*.

political arena during the last decades of the nineteenth century. Such interpretations – which minimize the political significance of Black associative life – have exercised much influence over the ways in which multiple generations of historians have interpreted the trajectories of free Afro-descendants. On the basis of information uncovered about a group of Black organizations that were active in the immediate post-abolition period in Rio de Janeiro and São Paulo, this chapter aims to analyze anew the articulations among various efforts organized by Afro-descendants in defense of their citizenship and status as free people.[8]

I will meet these objectives by problematizing the similarities and differences that existed among political organizations exemplified by the Liga dos Homens de Cor (League of Colored Men); the Sociedade Cooperativa da Raça Negra (Cooperative Society for the Black Race); the Guarda Negra (Black Guard); and the Club Repúblicano dos Homens de Cor (Black Men's Republican Club); as well as A Pátria – Orgam dos Homens de Cor (a newspaper). All of these operated in Rio and São Paulo between 1887 and 1889 and had significant historical repercussions. Significantly, the name of the Black journalist and abolitionist José do Patrocínio (1853–1905) is a common (if not always sympathetic) reference in documentation related to all of these entities. In general, these organizations did not simply orient themselves around the political controversies that absorbed public attention in their day; their leaders were committed to broader projects such as maintaining Black workers' place in the free labor market, promoting the literacy of their fellow Afro-descendants, and occupying an ever-broader array of social spaces.

It is worth emphasizing that neither these broader projects nor their proponents were elevated to the status of protagonists in the republican political sphere that dominated Brazil after 1889. It is true that Black political projects continued to exist, but they figured as an empirical demonstration of the limitations of democratic possibility in Brazilian society, and their leaders were recognized at most as third-rate supporting players. For this reason, the third section of this chapter returns to a consideration of the impossibility of Black people's equitable participation in Brazil's post-abolition polity.

THE LIGA DOS HOMENS DE COR

In 1887, the majority of Black people was already free or freed and the legality of slavery seemed sure to be broken soon. Given that, a group of

---

[8] A. Negro and F. Gomes. "Além de senzalas."

Black individuals in Rio took the initiative to create the Liga dos Homens de Cor, in order to assure that all could enjoy the conditions necessary to fully exercise their citizenship. With the aim of "raising the moral level of men of color, and endowing them with the cooperation, mutualism and solidarity needed to enter as equals in the elaboration of wealth and the Brazilian future," José do Patrocínio, Antonio Luiz do Espírito Santo Castro, Geraldo José Alexandre das Mercês, Agostinho José Alves, Antonio Honorato de Santa Rosa, Assindino Seveliano José Gomes, and Flávio José de Andrade – among others – assumed the challenge of moving the mission forward.[9] This would not be the first or last time that a good portion of these individuals would involve themselves in associativism. Geraldo das Mercês, the Liga's first secretary, had participated in carnival groups since at least the early 1880s, was on the board of the workers' mutual aid society "Associação de Socorros Mútuos Auxílio Operário" in 1883, and proposed the foundation of the "Sociedade Recreativa e Instrutiva" (an educational and recreational society) in 1896.[10] Assindino Gomes, who took over Geraldo's post in 1889, had been the interim secretary of the Irmandade de Nossa Senhora do Rosário e São Benedito (a Catholic brotherhood) in 1881 and would be part of the board of the Sociedade Cooperativa da Raça Negra, founded in April 1888.[11] As noted earlier, Agostinho Alves, who also acted as Liga secretary, became one of the founders of the Sociedade Familiar de Dança Prazer da Violeta in May 1888.[12] Flávio José de Andrade also participated in the Centro Tipográfico Treze de Maio (a typographer's union named after abolition day) around this same time.[13]

As impressive as these associative connections are for their density and variety, this glimpse of these actors' presence in the aforementioned spaces only captures a small segment of their trajectories. Their lives were full of intricacies, and the influences they absorbed from their presence in spaces of religion, recreation, education, and work were not mutually exclusive. Divergent paths produced distinct individuals with varying profiles. Yet in some ways these men were not so different after all – so much so that, in

---

[9] *Cidade do Rio*, August 2, 1888, p. 3; August 31, 1888, p. 1; *Gazeta de Notícias*, April 22, 1888, p. 4; May 13, 1888, p. 3; May 30, 1889, p. 2; September 1, 1889, p. 5.
[10] *Gazeta de Notícias*, August 8, 1880, p. 3; December 26, 1883, p. 2; *Jornal do Brasil*, March 24, 1896, p. 2.
[11] *Gazeta de Notícias*, July 5, 1881, p. 2; April 11, 1888, p. 2; September 1, 1889, p. 5; *Cidade do Rio*, April 11, 1888, p. 2.
[12] *Cidade do Rio*, May 19, 1888, p. 1.   [13] *Revista Typographica*, July 28, 1888, p. 3.

that historical moment, what brought them together was a shared racial identity. That is, the environment that nurtured class identities was the same one that stimulated the construction of racial identities, to such an extent that they came to underpin political platforms. What is more, this gesture toward politicizing race came as a surprise to no one. So far as I can tell, no one sought out the press because they were surprised by or wished to oppose the existence of these or other Black organizations as they emerged. Slavery was collapsing, but the practices of racialization continued to be naturalized, even as they were re-ordered. By force of habit, individuals and groups oriented themselves by racial categories. It was as simple and as complicated as that.

To a certain extent, there seems to have been support for Black people to speak out in this new context. This stands in contrast with earlier eras, when initiatives of this kind had received no support from authorities. Sidney Chalhoub has recounted the cases of the Sociedade de Beneficência da Nação Conga, the Protetora da Sociedade do Rosário e São Benedito, the Sociedade de Beneficência da Nação Conga Amiga da Consciência, and the Associação Beneficente Socorro Mútuo dos Homens de Cor in the 1860s and 1870s. These, like other Black entities, could exist informally but were condemned by the Imperial Council of State when they sought to legalize their activities, on the grounds that their members sought to organize themselves politically and economically on the basis of race and ethnicity.[14]

In any case, returning to what was distinctive about the Liga dos Homens de Cor: in addition to the men noted earlier, we should also note that the Liga's president – Antonio Luiz do Espírito Santo Castro – resembled José do Patrocinio in his outstanding trajectory. Thanks to a solicitation made by Liberal Party Deputy Sebastião Mascarenhas in August 1888, we know that Espírito Santo Castro enjoyed enough prominence to receive the title of commander (an important Imperial honorific). It so happens, however, that the deputy spoke up not in support of Espírito Santo Castro but rather because he considered the title an absurdity and decided to seek its annulment on the grounds that such an honor did not befit a man who was, by profession, a mere barber.

When he learned of this attack, José do Patrocínio, editor of the *Cidade do Rio*, used one of the journal's premier columns to critically and ironically opine the opposite, presenting details on Espírito Santo Castro's public trajectory. Right at the start, Patrocínio placed Deputy

---

[14] S. Chalhoub, *Machado de Assis*, pp. 240–265.

Mascarenhas' position in check, thus cornering the Liberal Party as a whole. For Patrocínio, there was a "manifest contradiction between [Mascarenhas'] solicitation and the aspirations of his party, which promises us a Democratic Monarchy. Beyond this, the solicitation is also unconstitutional, because the supreme law of the State does not distinguish among citizens except by knowledge, merits, and virtues." Patrocínio then went on to identify Espírito Santo Castro as "Black," reiterate the value of the profession of barber, and again recognize his unjustly maligned colleague as "one of the most important Liberal influencers of the second district of the *freguesia* [parish] of Sacramento." Espírito Santo Castro had always been a parish elector, had been elected a justice of the peace by popular vote in 1879, and was voted the first substitute for justice of the peace in the most recent municipal elections – "despite everything and especially despite his abolitionist views" – eventually assuming the post when the winning candidate resigned. Patrocínio pointed out that Espírito Santo Castro had been president of the Imperial Sociedade dos Artistas Brasileiras for five years; had served as a councilor of the Imperial Sociedade Auxiliadora das Artes Mecânicas e Liberais e Beneficientes for ten years; and was at the time the president of the Liga dos Homens de Cor. Remaining in the sphere of conflictual race relations, Patrocínio emphasized, finally, that "the citizen Espírito Santo Castro only refrained from exercising the functions of *subdelegado* [local police chief] during the Liberal era because he understood that his color might serve as the pretext for painful injustices, and he preferred obscurity to moral suffering brought on by a love of ephemeral positions."[15] Could this slight have been one of the motivations for organizing the Liga? Probably.

Along these same lines, while José do Patrocínio is already well known in studies of nineteenth-century Brazil, he still merits attention here. With the symbolic capital that he accumulated from the press and from abolitionist and republican clashes, he was another founder of the Liga dos Homens de Cor and helped to bring visibility and political relevance to the initiative. It is not unreasonable to deduce that Patrocínio's prestige contributed to the friendly, though discreet, reception given to the Liga by some newspapers. Beyond the backing received from the *Gazeta de Notícias*, which published a series of notes and announcements about the association's activities, the *Diário de Notícias* – which received a copy of

---

[15] *Cidade do Rio*, August 31, 1888, p. 1.

the Liga's statutes along with all of the city's main press outlets in April 1888 – saw fit to praise the initiative:

We received the Statutes of the Liga dos Homens de Cor, a society that aims to morally and intellectually develop the Black and mixed races and restore to them within the Brazilian community the autonomy robbed from them by slavery. The attempt is laudable and without doubt necessary as a complement to the emancipation of the race.[16]

Energy to promote such goals was not lacking among the other Liga participants, above all because they themselves created a context that was favorable to such agitation. In coordination with Patrocínio, Liga members participated in public and private meetings in which they were privileged interlocutors, even in the company of big shots. Admittedly, there are few registers of this activity in the newspapers. All the same, if the opportunity existed to expose their desire to "raise the level of their race through commerce, industry, instruction, and hard work" in an event such as the founding of the Guarda Negra (Black Guard) at the editorial office of the *Cidade do Rio* in September 1888, it is more than probable that they had been present in meetings called to resist the onslaughts of slavocrats and republicans after May 14.[17]

Curiously, José do Patrocínio did not remain in the Liga for long. An acclaimed personality, he was chosen to hand the honorific insignia "Hábito da Rosa" to the Liga's President (Commander Espírito Santo Castro) in October 1888. Yet by the time Espírito Santo Castro died in May of the following year, Patrocínio had resigned because of "growing opposition to him within the Liga."[18] The explanation for this dissention has been lost in speculation involving vanities, uncertainties, and the troubled trajectory of the Guarda Negra itself.

It is important to document that the activities of the Liga dos Homens de Cor were not limited to participation in external events. They also maintained headquarters – open every afternoon – on the Rua do S. Pedro, a street in the Cidade Nova that later gave way to the Avenida Getúlio Vargas in a massive urban renewal campaign. The space was frequently used for debates, as well as for educational and training activities. According to newspaper announcements, the Liga eventually came to

---

[16] *Diário de Notícias*, April 24, 1888, p. 2.

[17] *Cidade do Rio*, September 29, 1888, cited in Rebeca Bergstresser, "The Movement," p. 177. The Guarda Negra was, as we will see, a Black pro-monarchist organization that was the object of racist polemic in the immediate post-abolition period.

[18] *Cidade do Rio*, October 27, 1888, p. 3; *O Carbonário*, May 15, 1889, p. 3.

hold Sunday conferences on "subjects of general interest to our society," in which the associates themselves were charged with taking turns as orators.[19]

With the advent of May 13, this routine was somewhat disrupted, as Liga members were called to meet other demands. They resolved, for example, to accept Deputy Domingos Jaguaribe Filho's suggestion that they lead a public subscription campaign to raise a statue to Freedom. As part of the unfolding of that campaign, the *Diário de Notícias* reported on the formalization of the request on May 15, 1888. Two days later, when a commission representing societies of descendants of the Black race convoked the community to celebrate slavery's end, the Liga dos Homens de Cor would send a message to its associates asking that they report to the headquarters to discuss "urgent business."[20]

Another notable aspect of the experience of the Liga dos Homens de Cor was the way in which it sought to guarantee its existence. As was signaled by the late payment reminders sent out by treasurer Antonio Honorato de Santa Rosa, it was the society's member contributions that allowed it to develop its activities.[21] Consequently, extra incentives were necessary to make sure that such collective collaboration in fact occurred. One strategy deployed in order to reach stragglers was the periodic convening of general assemblies, to which members had to appear armed with their up-to-date passbooks.[22]

Apparently, this insistence met with some success. At the end of July 1888, under a new administration elected after Espírito Santo Castro's death, information circulated about fully functioning night classes, aimed at primary education "for associates and male members of their families." The students could count on classes in Portuguese, arithmetic, and geography. It should not go unnoted, however, that this was a society administered exclusively by men, and the commitment to the advancement of communities "of color" was structured exclusively around male empowerment.[23] Unfortunately, this effort to advance Black men's

---

[19] *Gazeta de Notícias*, April 22, 1888, p. 4; May 6, 1888, p. 4; May 13, 1888, p. 3.
[20] *Diário de Notícias*, May 15, 1888, p. 2; *Cidade do Rio*, May 17, 1888, p. 2; May 20, 1888, p. 3; May 27, 1888, p. 3; *Gazeta Paranaense*, May 23, 1888, p. 2.
[21] *Cidade do Rio*, August 2, 1888, p. 3; August 30, 1889, p. 2.
[22] *Gazeta de Notícias*, August 3, 1888, p. 4; May 30, 1889, p. 2; September 1, 1889, p. 5; *Cidade do Rio*, August 4, 1888, p. 3; May 30, 1889, p. 3; *O Paiz*, August 4, 1889, p. 5.
[23] Some Black women managed to break the fence and even become teachers during the Republic. See M. Müller, *A cor*.

education, which was renewed in the beginning of 1890, was the last action I was able to find connected to the Liga dos Homens de Cor.[24]

THE SOCIEDADE COOPERATIVA DA RAÇA NEGRA AND THE NETWORKS OF BLACK POLITICS

Returning to 1888: even before the Liga's printed statute was ready, the city of Rio de Janeiro received notice of the foundation of the Sociedade Cooperativa da Raça Negra on April 8. Its board of directors included Estevão Roberto da Silva (president), João José Tavares Júnior (vice-president), Lourenço Izidro de Siqueira e Silva (first secretary), Martinho dos Prazeres (second secretary), Manoel Fernandes Tupper (general treasurer). Striving to be a well-structured organization, it also had a council comprising Francisco Paula de Oliveira Veado, Francisco José de Lemos Magalhães, Mizael Gomes da Silva, Jorge Fortunato Martins, Assindino Seveliano José Gomes, João Guedes de Azevedo, Manoel Wenceslau do Valle Porto, Luiz Antonio Ribeiro, Manoel Justiniano de Oliveira, and Manoel Frontino.

The Sociedade emerged with three rigorously defined objectives. Priority number one was to "place the descendants of the African race on the path to work, creating for this purpose *"a register where unemployed people will be listed along with their professions and as much information as can be collected about them."* A second front was opened to "promote primary, commercial, artisanal, and agricultural education." Finally, touching on mutual aid activities, they would found a "beneficent fund and a funeral fund with 15 percent of their income."[25]

The fact that the Sociedade championed employment guarantees and technical capacitation for "descendants of the Black race" immediately stands out. It is also apparent that the Sociedade did not share the belief that Black people, in the abstract, were incapable of acting competently in the autonomous and competitive capitalist labor market. While a lack of education and training was an obstacle for a subset of the group, the constitution of the Sociedade was in itself evidence that another subset suffered unemployment due to deliberate exclusion. Among them were men who could certify defined trades and provide witnesses to attest their qualifications. In other words, even without access to unemployment data

---

[24] *Gazeta de Notícias*, August 3, 1889, p. 4; January 19, 1890, p. 4.
[25] *Cidade do Rio*, April 11, 1888, p. 2; *Gazeta da Tarde*, April 11, 1888, p. 2. Emphasis mine.

disaggregated by race or color, these men met to protest the devaluation of Brazil's Black workers, defend their racial belonging, speak up for their own cause, and oppose white immigration policies that received strong support from Brazil's national elites.

The scenario these men faced had slightly different characteristics than those experienced by free Black men in other eras, who could conceivably diminish their exposure to prejudice by avoiding confusion with the enslaved and distancing themselves from family ties to slavery. In effect, what Hebe Mattos observed in the rural world of southeastern Brazil largely held true for urban spaces as well. As a consequence of slavery's ruin, "sociocultural categories and identities suddenly stopped making sense. Slave owners, slaves, and men who were born free or had become free no longer existed."[26] On the other hand, the targeting of the Sociedade's pedagogical work suggests that it prioritized the aspirations of specific professional categories, such as artisans and those linked to commerce or agriculture, even as it acknowledged the need for general primary instruction. The articulation of mutual aid practices and vocational defense was implicit.[27]

In the face of such details, a simple question seems appropriate: what kinds of experiences inspired these men of color to constitute an organization that was so centered on a commitment to work and technical education? Considering the ideological profile adopted by the Sociedade Cooperativa da Raça Negra, it might be logical to assume that it had some external influence, perhaps from the US Black leader Booker T. Washington, who had become well-known after assuming the direction of the Tuskegee Institute in Alabama, which had a heavy emphasis on industrial education. It so happens, however, that the Afro-American leader would only rise to national fame in the United States after 1895, and his international influence would only become consolidated in the early twentieth century.[28] So that hypothesis must be discarded.

Does the explanation, then, have local origins? Bingo! In search of information about the Sociedade's president, Estevão Roberto da Silva, I found a substantial cache of evidence that explains many of the group's choices. The first indication takes us to the year 1876, an era in which da Silva stood out among the students of the Academia Imperial de Belas Artes (the Imperial Academy of the Arts, Brazil's most prestigious Arts school) and received silver medals for his course performance. Born free in

---

[26] H. Mattos, *Das cores*, p. 309.   [27] See C. Batalha, "Sociedades de trabalhadores."
[28] See B. T. Washington, *Up from Slavery*.

1848, the son of Victor Roberto da Silva, at twenty-eight Estevão was single and an elector of the *freguesia* (parish) of Sacramento. He knew how to read and exercised the trade of painter, earning an annual income of 500 mil reis.[29]

This same man, known as the first Black student to distinguish himself at the Academia Imperial de Belas Artes, eventually became one of the institution's most important representatives and a professor at the Liceu de Artes e Ofícios (Rio's most important vocational high school), noted for his still-life paintings. Writer Artur de Azevedo nicknamed him the "Black Diamond."[30] Yet before this all happened, various episodes defined his trajectory. One of the most impactful ones happened between 1879 and 1880. At the prize ceremony for students who had distinguished themselves in the Academia de Belas Artes' General Exposition, attended by Emperor Pedro II, Estevão da Silva was regarded unofficially by those in the know as the author of the "best work of historical painting." He himself believed that he would be given the gold medal after years of resigning himself to silver or lesser prizes. Yet the medal once again went to another man. Upon seeing himself deprived of the honor he deserved, da Silva protested emphatically.[31] According to the memoirs of his colleague Antonio Parreiras:

We were convinced that the first prize would be given to Estevão Silva. He, trembling and moved, waited. [When another name was read,] his head dropped, his eyes filled with tears. He retreated and went to stand behind all of the others. We were going to protest, but – "Silence! I know what I have to do." So commanding were the words spoken by that sobbing man that we obeyed. One by one, the prize-winners were called. Finally, the name Estevão Silva echoed in the chamber. Calmly, he passed among us. With slow steps, he crossed the room. He approached the Dias, where the Emperor was. Next, it was beautiful! That Black man raised his head haughtily and shouted loudly: "I refuse!"[32]

Unable to claim that Estevão da Silva's work was inferior and did not deserve first place, the professors alleged that they did not award it to him for reasons of seniority. The explanation did not convince those who followed the case. All the same, the faculty did not retreat and, "taking into account as an attenuating circumstance the intellectual poverty of the delinquent student, punished Estevão da Silva with a one-year suspension,

[29] *Diário de Notícias*, May 11, 1876, p. 3; July 26, 1876, p. 2; December 30, 1876, p. 2.
[30] See J. Teixeira Leite, *Pintores negros*; E. Araújo, ed., *A mão afro-brasileira*.
[31] *Gazeta da Noite*, February 1, 1880, p. 1.
[32] Antonio Parreiras, cited in J. Teixeira Leite, *Pintores Negros*, p. 64.

while noting that there had been a desire to expel him immediately."³³ At risk of not completing his education, Estevão da Silva sought out the aid of friends. José do Patrocínio was one of those who responded to the call. In August of that year, he donated his earnings from a public speech to "assist the painter Estevão Roberto da Silva, so that he can go to Europe and complete his studies."³⁴

That voyage, however, never happened: Estevão maintained steady residence at the Rua do General Camara 283 (another Cidade Nova street destroyed by the Avenida Getúlio Vargas) for the entire decade. That address, beyond serving as his home, was also his workshop, where he deployed his skills in carpentry, cabinetry, and portrait and landscape painting. Based at that address, Estevão da Silva was even block inspector for the second district of the freguesia de Sacramento.³⁵ Clearly, the event at Belas Artes did not interrupt his work as an artist and an artisan. Indeed, sometime later he became a professor at the Liceu de Artes e Oficios, an institution that was maintained by the Sociedade Propagadora das Belas Artes (an independent beneficent society frequented by many men from the Academia).³⁶

A dedicated painter, Estevão Roberto da Silva also devoted a great deal of his time to the activities of the city's artisans and workers. In May 1878, he took his place on the board of the Sociedade Beneficente dos Artistas do Arsenal da Marinha da Corte (a beneficent society for artisans employed by Rio's Navy). The following year, he ran for director of the Sociedade dos Artistas Brasileiros Trabalho União e Moralidade, a mutual aid society for artisans that da Silva was affiliated with until his death in 1891.³⁷ In the course of the 1880s, he was part of the board of directors for the União Operária in 1881 and a professor at the free school maintained by the Congresso Operário de Beneficência between 1886 and 1888.³⁸

---

³³ The passage cited here is part of the report prepared by the commission of professors responsible for deliberating on the case. J. Teixeira Leite, *Pintores Negros*, pp. 64–65; *Gazeta da Noite*, March 1, 1880, p. 1.
³⁴ *Gazeta da Tarde*, August 12, 1880, p. 3.
³⁵ *Almanak Administrativo, Mercantil e Industrial*, no. 36, 1879, p. 186; no. 37, 1880, pp. 190, 927, 993; no. 38, 1881, p. 727; no. 39, 1882, p. 715; no. 40, 1883, p. 765; no. 41, 1884, p. 833; no. 42, 1885, p. 812; *Cidade do Rio*, May 24, 1888, p. 1; January 11 1889, p. 1.
³⁶ *Diário do Commércio*, December 2, 1889, p. 1.
³⁷ Even professors at the Escola Nacional de Belas Artes (the Academia was renamed in 1890), which was sent a set of his paintings, lamented his death. *Diário de Notícias*, November 18, 1891, p. 1; December 20, 1891, p. 1.
³⁸ *O Cruzeiro*, May 23, 1878, p. 1; *Gazeta de Notícias*, September 25, 1879, p. 3; October 28, 1881, p. 2; November 25, 1886, p. 2; *Diário de Notícias*, November 7, 1887, p. 1; December 12, 1888, p. 3; *Diário do Commércio*, November 4, 1889, p. 2.

Estevão Roberto da Silva was hard-working and well-connected; he could have continued in this line of associational activism and everything would have worked out relatively well. In his individual and collective tasks, he shared his life with people who were similar to him, either because they faced difficulties linked to their lack of wealth or because they could not help but show their Black skin. All kinds of people were there, Black and white, free and freed, although the proportions varied from case to case. Together they had constructed spaces to defend the rights of the working classes. Yet it so happened that, in the course of this process, slavery's end evidenced – or accentuated – the fragilities that threatened men of color. Added to this, the expectations created around the declaration of civil equality for all Brazilians catalyzed Black and popular political agitation. It matters little that the version of history that later emerged prioritized the abolitionist activity of the elite in the lead-up to abolition. The masses who occupied the streets and appeared in public rallies in those years behaved as protagonists. The moment summoned everyone to take a stand. This is what the men who founded the Sociedade Cooperativa da Raça Negra in April 1888 were doing.

Once the Sociedade came into being, it followed a mold already established in abolitionist activities, seeking adherents through public events, during which the association's basic agenda was presented. On Sunday, April 15, the Sociedade inaugurated a series of talks, in which the orators developed theses about the "necessity and expediency of work and the benefits that result from it" and the "utility of instruction."[39]

Their intentions were certainly not frustrated; with the arrival of May, on the eve of the passage of the Lei Áurea on May 13, the Sociedade had enough backing to take the lead in coordinating Black organizations promoting their own celebrations of the Imperial government's decision. An interesting detail is that they only sought out the city's mainstream newspapers to transmit what had already been decided in their assembly, which leads one to assume that they counted on other communication tools to keep their interlocutors informed. Thus we see a notice that was printed in the *Gazeta de Notícias* and in the *Diário de Notícias*:

At the invitation of the Sociedade Cooperativa da Raça Negra, delegates of various bodies representing descendants of that same race met two days ago to confer about how to thank those who worked for the glorious happening that, honoring our Nation, occurred without any perturbation of public order. They resolved to name an executive commission to coordinate the celebrations, which will present

[39] *Cidade do Rio*, April 14, 1888, p. 3; *Gazeta de Notícias*, April 29, 1888, p. 2.

their full program, including a Te-Deum in the Church of the venerable Nossa
Senhora do Rosário e São Benedito.[40]

For anyone who wished to see it, this was evidently the action of a Black
network that had been publicly established on the basis of the experience
of Black freedom. In historical accounts shaped by the myth of racial
democracy, this network could not even be glimpsed as part of the social
subsoil. Yet for an attentive researcher, every new archival path reveals its
presence, never far from the surface. As difficult as it is to access the
intricacies of these intragroup collaborations among Black activists, we
must take as a starting point their existence and their importance in the
lives of many people. Such acceptance can help us to deconstruct yet again
the arsenal of dogmas that have traditionally shaped our approaches to
the formation of Brazilian social classes. It can also give more consistency
to the innovative perspectives that are currently taking shape in Brazilian
historiography.

THE GUARDA NEGRA

To set the parameters for this intellectual project, it is useful to place
information about Rio's Black networks in conversation with what we
know of Brazil's famous Guarda Negra, which was long portrayed simply
as a horde of mindless thugs manipulated by opportunistic monarchists.
Despite the profusion of individual activists, groups, and public activities
involving the Liga dos Homens de Cor and the Sociedade Cooperativa da
Raça Negra, it was the Guarda Negra that received the most political and
press attention in the nineteenth century. This was also the group that has
been portrayed as the fullest expression of freed and free-born Black
Brazilian activism in the majority of historical narratives about the immediate post-abolition period. In the words of Flávio Gomes: "The racial
question, which had apparently been made invisible during the abolitionist campaign, emerged crystal-clear from the actions of the Guarda
Negra."[41] Except that, instead of emerging as part of a continuum of
popular struggles, the Guarda Negra has often been interpreted as evidence of Black people's inclination to use violence to further their personal
interests and defend those of the Princess Regent and the Empire – none of

[40] *Gazeta de Notícias*, May 14, 1888, p. 2; *Diário de Notícias*, May 14, 1888, p. 3.
[41] F. Gomes, *Negros e Política*, p. 20.

which, of course, signified even a minimal capacity for autonomous thought. As Clícea Maria Miranda has observed:

In the historiography, generally speaking, the study of the Guarda Negra almost always appears in conjunction with the practice of capoeira [a martial art traditionally associated with enslaved and Black resistance] in Rio de Janeiro. This happens, first of all, because historians confuse the actions of gangs [maltas] with those of the Guarda, perhaps because Guarda members were expert practitioners of the game of head-butts and ensnarements.[42]

In the nineteenth century, similar perceptions served both to nurture prejudices about the universalization of freedom and citizenship among all Brazilians and to sell the idea that the installation of a Republic would be the remedy for all of the ills created by the monarchy.[43] As we shall see . . .

The first meeting called to deal with the creation of the Guarda Negra da Redentora (Black Guard of the [Female] Redeemer) took place on July 9, 1888. It was left to the *Cidade do Rio* to inform the public that the encounter would take place in the home of Emilio Rouède and to list the names of the freed Blacks who would be present (unfortunately without reference to their surnames): Hygino, Manoel Antonio, Jason, Aprigio, Gaspar, and Theocrito. The occasion led to the following resolutions:

1. To create an association with the goal of presenting material resistance to any revolutionary movement hostile to the institution that just liberated the country.

2. Only freedpeople who are willing to follow the orders of a Directorship, elected by simple majority in a vote that will be carried out at an opportune moment, can take part.

3. Effective membership is restricted to those who consider the memorable act of May 13 to be a happening worthy of general admiration rather than a motive for declaring war on the humanitarian princess who brought it about.

4. To ask for the support of the Confederação Abolicionista [Abolitionist Confederation] so that its activities have ramifications throughout the Empire.

---

[42] C. Miranda, "Guarda negra," p. 28.
[43] Various arguments against this shallow judgment against the Guarda Negra have been presented in recent years. Outstanding examples include M. Trochim, "The Brazilian Black Guard"; F. Gomes, "No meio"; C. Líbano Soares, *A negregada*; C. Miranda, *Guarda negra*; W. Albuquerque, *O jogo*, ch. 3.

5. To ask the press to promote this sentiment with its valuable cooperation.
6. Finally, to advise in every possible way the freedmen of the interior to only work on the *fazendas* [plantations] of those who have sworn not to make war on the Empire.[44]

The organization's presumed membership would, once again, consist of Black men. Yet this time priority was given to freedmen, leaving no space for those among them who might have republican sympathies. With this announcement made, the second public register of the Guarda Negra's existence appeared when they bestowed the Rosa de Ouro (Gold Rose) on Princess Isabel, in homage to her "liberating action." As multiple historical narratives reiterate, on the night of September 28, the founding of the Guarda Negra was formalized during an editorial meeting of the *Cidade do Rio*, attended by abolitionists such as André Rebouças, João Clapp, Patrocínio himself, and representatives of the Liga dos Homens de Cor.[45] In December, the Guarda Negra returned to press prominence because of the birthday celebrations of the president of the Imperial Council of Ministers, Afonso Celso. The *Diário de Notícias* was one of the papers that reported that the Guarda Negra, "in five streetcars, appeared at the residence of His Excellency, accompanied by musical bands from the Tenth Battalion and from the police force of the Court. Sr. Clarindo Alves orated in his name."[46]

The Guarda Negra became notorious because of a famous melee involving men accused of being part of the Guarda and defenders of the republican cause during a political rally for republican advocate Silva Jardim in the Sociedade Francesa de Ginástica, located near the Praça Tiradentes in central Rio. That event happened on December 30, 1888. But – a curious fact – republicans sought out the pages of papers such as *Novidades*, *O Paíz*, and the *Província de São Paulo* well before that to accuse the Guard of being a "body of thugs" composed of "*capoeiras*" who were "enticed" by the government to secure the princess's throne.[47] Assuming reports are true, this allegation was responsible for contemporary rumors and subsequent memoirs such those of Antônio da Silva Jardim and José Joaquim de Medeiros e Albuquerque, who both had an

[44] *Cidade do Rio*, July 10, 1888, p. 2.
[45] R. Bergstresser, "The Movement," pp. 175–178; R. Magalães Júnior, *A vida turbulenta*, p. 249; and F. Gomes, *Negros e política*, pp. 16–17.
[46] *Diário de Notícias*, December 13, 1889, p. 1.
[47] *Cidade do Rio*, November 31, 1888, p. 1.

interest in defending an image of republican bravery in the face of great risk.[48] A comment in the *Gazeta de Notícias* motivated by the December incident also feeds this suspicion. Lacking any evidence of the Guarda Negra's violent nature, the author, probably the paper's owner Ferreira de Araújo, weaves his comments as though the launch of the Guarda Negra were quite similar to that of the Liga dos Homens de Cor and the Sociedade Cooperativa da Raça Negra:

The aggression suffered by the republicans who came together on December 30 to attend Dr. Silva Jardim's speech is generally attributed to the Guarda Negra. It is not clear exactly what the Guarda Negra is: it is vaguely said that it was constituted by citizens of the recently redeemed Race, inspired by an admirable sentiment of gratitude toward the Redeeming Princess, and with the aim of defending her life.

When the existence of this Guarda and these intentions were first spoken of, no one found it strange; its second sign of life, visible when the Guarda went to the home of the President of the Council to greet him on his birthday, also made little impression; these were manifestations of inoffensive and natural enthusiasm from those who had received such a notable benefit from the Princess and the head of the cabinet.[49]

Indifference, according to the editor of the *Gazeta de Notícias*, best characterized these occurrences. It was thus only after the meeting at the editorial offices of the *Cidade do Rio* that the Guarda Negra began to cause discomfort. It is interesting to note that this process developed in parallel with a series of intrigues surrounding José do Patrocínio. Taking for granted and highlighting Patrocínio's influence on the society of freedmen, these schemes serenely accessed the whole racist catalog to condemn both the man himself and the freedmen's collective action. Patrocínio, as usual, was not intimidated by such outrages and reacted in kind, leveling a volley of insults at republican politicians Quintino Bocaiúva and Rangel Pestana. The following passages capture the tenor of his words:

In order to extend their insult to the entire race to which I am honored to belong, the Praetorians of the oligarchy, the weevils of São Paulo's coffer, say that the Guarda Negra is a gang of paid *capoeiras*.

This is their notion of men whose honesty certainly doesn't suffer in comparison to that of parasites who want to live off the fat of agricultural cultivation and the credulity of simpletons . . . .

[48] A. Jardim, *Memórias e viagens*; J. Medeiros e Albuquerque, *Quando eu era vivo*.
[49] *Gazeta de Notícias*, January 5, 1889, p. 1.

The Guarda Negra as a gang of thugs paid by princes! With good reason this "republic" has not managed to delude the majority of the citizens of May 13 and their blood brothers.

These people believe that Blacks should follow the lawyers who argued against them in the courts of this realm, the philanthropists who beat and sold their brothers, the propagandists who even today characterize as "poor farmers" the gang that, possessing police jurisdiction in the interior, draft to military anyone to whom they owe salary and employ against freedmen the fraternity of powder and bullets.

They declared me a traitor to the Republic and, because they know I am poor and Black, they sold me to the government.[50]

It was no secret that Patrocínio was seen as a reference by many Black men in Rio. What was new was the fear and near panic that emerged with the prospect that such protagonism might be channeled into more incisive interventions or provoke a civil war. Comic or tragic, Brazilian history is full of events forged by the fusion of racism and speculation.

In the last two weeks of December 1888, the tension deepened further still. According to the *Cidade do Rio*, on December 23 "a group of five citizens of black color" who were taking a meal at the hotel Petit-Console were attacked with rocks and gunshots by republican activists because they had shown support for the Crown. According to reports, Clarindo de Almeida, head of the Guarda, sought to dissuade his people from any retaliation, arguing that public disorder was exactly what the neo-republicans wanted. "Our calm is yet another sacrifice made for the government that on May 13 created a homeland large enough to contain both our gratitude and the ignominy of the flunkies of slavocracy who now mascarade as republicans."[51]

Yet even when published in the papers, such words did not impede the grave confrontation that occurred seven days later near the Sociedade Francesa de Ginástica. In an attempt to diminish the racial weight of the conflict, an editorial in the *Cidade do Rio* transmitted a lament that was a bit out of sync with what Patrocínio had written just days before:

Despite the Guarda Negra's abstention, it was impossible to contain yesterday the explosion of popular rage, which has long smoldered at the heart of national character and pride, against propaganda that twice insults our fatherland,

---

[50] The phrase "they sold me to the government" was ironic, a response to the false allegation on the part of certain slavocratic republicans who sought to portray Patrocínio as a monarchist despite undeniable evidence of his critiques of the Imperial regime. *Cidade do Rio*, November 2, 1888, p. 1; January 4, 1888, p. 1.

[51] *Cidade do Rio*, December 31, 1888, p. 1.

demeaning the American ideal and debasing a race that, because of its generous sentiments, has managed to make itself loved to the point that we are a people almost without racial prejudice.

All the same, the tough accusations that weighed ever more heavily on the Guarda continued be guided by the racial origin of its members, a situation that led several of its supporters to go to the papers to defend the group.[52] Apart from José do Patrocínio and Emilio Rouède, Clarindo de Almeida himself would write:

I read yesterday in *Novidades* and in the *Gazeta da Tarde* the tremendous accusation that those papers are making against the Guarda Negra, classifying it as an element of disorder and unrest among the population.
God Almighty, what a mockery!
Is there anyone who can prove everything these papers have said about the Guarda Negra? Is it not patent that the aim is to offend the Guarda simply because it refuses to take part in the disorder? . . .
If the Guarda Negra was a republican corporation, it would be considered the most just and patriotic creation in the world. But since the Guarda Negra is a monarchical corporation, it is considered an affront to the dignity of the Fatherland; it is the Black race that arms itself to kill the white race, making color-based hatred appear in the country, etc., etc. . . . .
I affirm to my country that we do not have the objectives that they attribute to us. We are a corporation that is tied to its fatherland and wants to elevate it to the heights that 300 years of slavery prevented it from reaching.
Our aim is not to make the man of color rise up against the white man, but to restore to the man of color the right to intervene in public affairs that was robbed from him. We don't fight the republicans because they are white, but rather because they are the shame of our nation.[53]

BLACK REPUBLICANS

The existence of the Guarda Negra and the eruption of the December conflict gave impulse to the republican campaign in general, as Maria Tereza Chaves de Mello has observed.[54] But they also gave Black individuals and groups greater political visibility in the anti-monarchist political scene. Beginning in January 1889, the *Gazeta da Tarde* and the *Tribuna Liberal* began to reprint news (mostly from the province of São Paulo) about Black demonstrations in favor of the Republic, which served as a kind of counterweight to the Guarda Negra. This was another route

---

[52] *Cidade do Rio*, January 5, 1889, p. 1; January 16, 1889, p. 1.
[53] *Cidade do Rio*, January 3, 1889, p. 3.   [54] M. Chaves de Mello, "Com o arado."

through which Black subjects made themselves visible in post-abolition political struggles.

One of the first affirmations of this sort to be reproduced in the Rio press documented an agitated gathering that was promoted in São Paulo's capital on January 7, 1888. The document produced at the end of the assembly read:

The men of color resident in this capital, recognizing that the abolition of the servile element in Brazil was done only in virtue of popular efforts, are not disposed to help anyone whatsoever in the plan to divide the country into castes, planting racial hatreds in the soil of our fatherland.

They declare, therefore, that in any emergency they will be on the side of the people.[55]

Days later, as news first printed in the *Tribuna Liberal* resonated in the capital, the press offered more details about another meeting among men of color opposed to the Guarda Negra, which brought together somewhere around 500 people on January 13 in the *quilombo* (maroon community) of Jabaquara, formed in the early 1880s in the vicinity of the port city of Santos, São Paulo, and led by Black abolitionist Quintino de Lacerda.[56] Famous abolitionists from the region were among those present at the 1889 gathering, and Lacerda maintained his leadership role. "The monarchy," he said, "is responsible for the preservation of slavery for three centuries; the monarchy is responsible for the bullets that it ordered shot at some of those present here on the famous Cubatão expedition." Eugênio Wansuit, whom the *Gazeta da Tarde* referred to as "a very intelligent Black man, a military veteran who spent four years in the Paraguay campaign," also gave a speech, in which he opposed the forced military recruitment that the Imperial government had just announced and "incited his comrades to revolt against yet another enslavement." At the end they passed a motion, supported by around 300 signatories, which – beyond reiterating previous points – protested "against those who entice the brothers of our race, forming a true farce that they call the 'Guarda Negra' wherever it is found, because they can see in that infamy the beginnings of a civil war produced by hatred between two races."[57]

---

[55] *Gazeta da Tarde*, January 9, 1889, p. 2.
[56] M. H. Machado, *O plano* and "De rebeldes."
[57] *Tribuna Liberal*, January 15, 1889, p. 2; January 16, 1889, p. 1; *Gazeta da Tarde*, January 16, 1889, p. 2; January 17, 1889, p. 2. On the question of forced recruitment, see A. Nascimento, *A ressaca*.

In February, Black republicans from Mogi-Mirim and Campinas (also in São Paulo Province) took their turn to hold meetings. In Campinas, the gathering occurred during the Festival of São Benedito, right after the mass. The final document also positioned itself against forced recruitment and the creation of the Guarda Negra, speaking out against "racial hatred." Still, according to a notice published in the *Diário de Rio Claro*, one speaker went so far as to state that "those Blacks who belong to the Guarda Negra deserve the stocks, shackles, and the whip."[58]

In June 1889, the Club Republicano dos Homens de Cor (Republican Club of Men of Color) emerged in Rio as part of the scene generated by this dynamic. Its guiding principles were stated as follows:

1. To combat the reigning institutions in every conceivable terrain.
2. To attend all of the political gatherings that take place in this city and fight in their favor.
3. To institute a mutual aid fund and night courses.
4. To recognize as head of state the man elected by the Federal Council.
5. To promote their political cause among the Black race and make this same race believe that they are being victimized by the Crown.[59]

This was, then, a kind of republican version of the Guarda Negra. The founding meeting took place on June 2, 1889, at the residence of José Pedro Ferreira de Souza Coelho, on his initiative and that of his fellow republican proselytizer Deoclesiano Martyr. "Fifty-five men of color" were present, with the common mission to "politically promote republican ideas, in opposition to the reigning institutions."[60] According to the *Gazeta da Tarde*, Augusto Xavier de Mello assumed the presidency of the board; José Martins Pereria assumed the vice-presidency; the office of first secretary was left to Anacleto Alves de Freitas and that of second secretary to Rodolpho Gomes; Sinerio Alves was treasurer; and Francisco Alves de Freitas would be attorney.[61]

The notice in the *Gazeta da Tarde* brought names to the forefront that had previously slipped under the radar in commentary about abolitionists

[58] *Gazeta da Tarde*, February 26, 1889, p. 2; February 21, 1889, p. 1.
[59] *Gazeta da Tarde*, June 3, 1889, p. 1.
[60] *Diário de Notícias*, June 4, 1889, p. 1; *Cidade do Rio*, June 6, 1889, p. 2; *Diário do Commércio*, June 4, 1889, p. 1.
[61] *Gazeta da Tarde*, June 3, 1889, p. 1.

and Black political agitators. It is important to note from the start that I found no evidence that would permit me to state that the two men who hosted the meeting were Black. In truth, the fact that they were not incorporated into the club's board at the end of the meeting and the lack of direct or suggestive comments on the topic lead me to believe that they did not understand themselves to be Black (or were not considered as such). What stands out in the various documents I consulted are the ties both men had to the republican cause. Martyr, what's more, would gain quite a lot of notoriety years later for his intense Jacobin political activism.[62]

The comments on the members of the board, in contrast, pointed in another direction. Aside from the repeated mention of the presence of more than fifty men of color at the reunion, there are documents that inform us of some of their phenotypes. In particular, there is no doubt about Anacleto de Freitas, who in the beginning was first secretary but soon became the Club's principal public representative, eventually assuming the post of president.[63] Evaristo de Moraes, for example, noted that Anacleto de Freitas had been a Black ally to Silva Jardim: "In the heart of the working class, Silva Jardim also had fervent supporters, and the dedication of some men of color from humble backgrounds was especially significant. Accompanying Anacleto de Freitas, they fought in the streets for him against the Guarda Negra."[64]

On the basis of that platform, the Club Republicano dos Homens de Cor would make itself present in Rio's political scene during its first year of existence. Already in the beginning of July, they emitted a call in the *Gazeta da Tarde* directed to "the republican electorate of men of color":

Coreligionaries – the Board of the Club Republicano dos Homens de Cor hereby calls for the republican electorate of men of color to vote for the candidates from the party who were elected by previous acclamation.

We must not retreat before this government, which declared in the Chamber of Deputies that this movement – which today constitutes almost a national aspiration – must be exterminated; it is necessary to show that we are men ready for struggle, whether it be through ballots, through words or by force! . . .

We must not retreat in the face of this uncontrolled thuggery, which is going to appear on the day of the elections to threaten and frighten us so that we do not vote; on that day we must all be there, whether or not we are electors, to repel these villainous disruptors of public order; we must show this government that there are still, in this great Brazilian turf, men who die for a cause! . . .

---

[62] R. Magalhães Júnior, *Machado de Assis*, v. 3, pp. 283–296.
[63] *Diário de Notícias*, July 24, 1890, p. 1.   [64] E. de Moraes, *Da Monarquia*, p. 20.

We must on that day be prepared for everything and not retreat before the *capoeira*'s razor or club, because our patriotic mantra will be – prevail or die!
So, to your stations!
To the ballot boxes!
Forward patriots, and we will win our sainted and just cause![65]

Such mobilization, when reported in São Paulo, received intense support from another society for republican men of color. The crew of the newspaper *A Patria*, São Paulo province's first Black paper, did not spare praise in reaction to their coreligionists from Rio. Taking advantage of the opportunity, Ignácio de Araújo Lima deployed his ink with care to show the proximity of the two experiences:

Could we men of color from the capital of São Paulo receive in silence the news that the São Paulo press has reproduced from the Rio papers, which filled us with such pleasure? No. We who yesterday raised our weak voice against the projected organization of a Guarda Negra here in the capital have long nurtured a hope with the same basis and the same ends as the one that you publicly manifested today. It is also ours, and do you know why? They call us paulistas because we have our cradle in the city of São Paulo, legendary and heroic because of the brilliant accomplishments of her sons. . . . Here in this part of South America we have our cradle, but where is our fatherland? That is the question that we cannot yet answer.[66]

As we can see, the republican side also fostered its network of informational exchange, which advanced both private and general interests related to the recognition of its members' social legitimacy. Seeking to widen their visibility in spaces that brought together men of letters and politics, the Club continued to participate in various public events.

On the hundredth anniversary of the French Republic, on July 14, the Club's members organized themselves both to stage a procession and to give speeches at the commemorative session that took place at the Brazilian Congress, in an event promoted by the Centro Republicano Lopes Trovão. But their interventions were not characterized solely by moderation and restraint. It is practically impossible not to suspect that, on that same day, the Club's members had also been involved in a series of fights that took over the main streets of the city (Ouvidor, Uruguaiana, Gonçalves Dias), which resulted from clashes between monarchists and republicans. Just as had occurred in December, those who narrated the facts were incapable of specifying which group initiated the verbal and physical attacks. Many "long lives" to the monarchy and others to the

[65] *O Paiz*, July 3, 1889, p. 3.   [66] *A Pátria*, August 2, 1889, p. 2.

Republic were heard, soon accompanied by brawls. Among the wounded were at least two men of color: Aristides, *"pardo* [brown], 15 years old, a butler, resident at Formosa Street #13 and wounded in the foot"; and Pedro Justo de Souza, "Brazilian, 24 years of age, single, an employee of the sweet shop on Estácio de Sá Street and resident on the largo de Catumbi #72," who declared that he was a member of the Guarda Negra.[67]

The public recognition of this event cemented still more the end of José do Patrocínio's ties to the Guarda Negra. In a feature article entitled "To Men of Color," Patrocínio (still editor of the *Cidade do Rio*) expressed his disillusion with the paths taken by the group. Showing a somewhat utilitarian understanding of the Guarda Negra's legitimacy, he ended up reproducing various accusations that he had contested over the previous year. The arguments he employed, however, bordered on nonsense. The first established a relationship between the restitution of D. Pedro II's health and the security of the Empire:

The recovery of the Emperor, who took it upon himself to save his dynasty, the political evolution that took place, cooling the hatreds and restoring calm to the political movement, have restored society to its normal state. Since the cause has disappeared, so too must its effects cease.

He thought it strange, for this reason, that the Guarda Negra had continued and, what's more, "been diverted from its noble and generous end by individuals who sought to use it as a ladder for positions." As if this weren't enough, with the aim of explaining the reasons behind this easy distortion, Patrocínio ratified the opinion that freedpeople lacked their "share of education," which left them "more at the mercy of conspiracies that serve the interests of individuals who, calling themselves friends of the Blacks, take advantage of their courage and selflessness." That is to say, there was no vestige here of the erstwhile conscientious citizens of May 13. Finally, Patrocínio called on "men of color with more instruction" to "convince their less fortunate brothers that they would soon be condemned to a form of captivity even worse than yesterday's; that of public hatred."[68]

Once Patrocínio wrote that, it was no use for him to take up the subject again five days later with the pretext of recalling how laudable the initial phase of the Guarda Negra had been.[69] The Guarda was already

---

[67] *Gazeta de Notícias*, July 15, 1889, p. 1; *Gazeta da Tarde*, July 15, 1889, pp. 1–2.
[68] *Cidade do Rio*, July 15, 1889, p. 1.   [69] *Cidade do Rio*, July 20, 1889, p. 1.

condemned in the eyes of the community. This break, in turn, seems also to have been decisive in relation to Patrocínio's ties with other Black organizations with a clearly political character.[70] He was disaffiliated from the Liga dos Homens de Cor in the first half of 1889.

If the good health of D. Pedro II was not enough to cause the dissolution of the Guarda Negra, the proclamation of the Republic was also not understood as a cue for the Club Republicano dos Homens de Cor to disperse. In March 1890, its members appeared at the reception that marked Foreign Relations Minister Quintino Bocaiúva's return to Rio. Their internal affairs also functioned smoothly.[71] At that point, names of new associates beyond the original board members began to appear, such as Thomaz José da Silva, Antônio José Ferreira, Joaquim Euclides de Miranda, Vitor Gustavo da Paixão, and Ezequiel Alves da Silva.[72]

Lamentably, though, in line with the tendency that had been reinaugurated with the 1889 Liberal cabinet of Afonso Celso, the interest that political and media big shots had taken in the actions of both republican and monarchist men of color were in frank decline. Specifically, the republicans who rose to power with the coup of November 15 1889 had no reason to care about what the "Black and *mestiço* [mixed-race] men" who fought against the Guarda Negra and the monarchical government wanted or did not want.

All the same, one month after the first anniversary of the Republic's proclamation, Anacleto de Freitas sought out the *Gazeta da Tarde* to extend an invitation to "all men of color to appear tomorrow, at 4 in the afternoon, in the Largo de Santa Rita, in order to deal with a matter pertaining to your well-being."[73] Something tells me that, clinging to his truer dreams, Anacleto nurtured some hope of seeing his expectations attended to by the First Republic's *donos do poder* (men who controlled power). This must have been what allowed the activity surrounding the Club Republicano dos Homens de Cor to exist for a bit longer, even with the deepening of the marginalization they underwent after 1891. In 1892, for example, Anacleto and other associates of the Club were accused of being involved in a street disturbance motivated by ethnic and racial conflicts.[74]

---

[70] José do Patrocínio continued to maintain ties with the Irmandade de Nossa Senhora do Rosário e São Benedito, as was evidenced during the commemorations of May 13, 1902: *Cidade do Rio*, May 15, 1902, p. 1.

[71] *O Paiz*, March 8 and 10, 1890, p. 1.   [72] *O Paiz*, March 10 and 29, 1890, p. 1.

[73] *Gazeta da Tarde*, December 7, 1890, p. 3.   [74] *O Tempo*, January 10, 1892, p. 1.

After that episode, news about the Club becomes even more sporadic in the papers, even as reports increased of Anacleto de Freitas' imprisonments and involvement in street brawls. He was then accused of being a *capoeira* and of making fun of army battalions, even though he seems himself to have been a military man, having once been identified as a sergeant of the army's First Artillery Battalion.

But even with all of this mess, Anacleto de Freitas would work hard to reactivate the organization in August 1893.[75] Some setback, however, seems to have forced him to change his plans, to the point that he presented a public manifesto breaking politically with the republican government.[76] Unlike other times, Anacleto did not share the Jacobinism that Deocleciano Martyr manifested in his defense of Marechal Floriano (a leader of the republican faction that defended military nationalism). This lack of connection, plus the absence of Silva Jardim as a possible source of support beyond his ties to militarism, severely reduced Anacleto's chances for legitimate participation in that political environment. Here perhaps lies part of the explanation for his ostracism.

In light of this series of mishaps, it was painful to discover evidence of one final act undertaken by the members of the Club Republicano dos Homens de Cor in 1893, when they offered "to their worthy President, citizen Anacleto de Freitas, a gold mechanical pencil in celebration of November 15."[77] I write that it was painful because everything indicates that this event, on the anniversary of the Republic, did not create a glorious reversal of fortunes for the Club. I could not find any further archival trails.

CONCLUSION

It does not seem appropriate to close a chapter that is grounded in the potential of available archival sources with such a sensation of lost perspective. The likely demise of the Club Republicano dos Homens de Cor was not a door that slammed shut. More than representing the end or failure of a general collective experience, the Club's history reinforces the need to perceive voices that, while often stifled in their own times, still produce echoes in the archival documentation. These echoes, if taken seriously, lead us to other Black experiences, daily affirmations of esteem

[75] *O Tempo*, August 23, 1893, p. 1; August 30, 1893, p. 2.
[76] *O Tempo*, September 2, 1893, p. 3.   [77] *O Tempo*, November 18, 1893, p. 2.

for life and desires for a future that was different than the present tense with which they struggled. This attentiveness to the analytic possibilities of echoes and silences is a defining trait of the investigative paths through which the study of freedom and post-abolition has consolidated itself in Brazil. In a country that is still majority Black, investment in the possibility of finding Black people's trajectories in the most varied contexts – far beyond slavery – has spurred a profound renovation in Brazilian historiography and an amplification in its appeal, especially among those who are themselves the subjects of this history.

12

"The East River Reminds Me of the Paraná"

Racism, Subjectivity, and Transnational Political Action in the Life of André Rebouças

Hebe Mattos*

The legalized (!!!) whipping or lynching of Africans in the streets mimics the Yankee Cannibals of Ohio, Mississippi and Missouri.
André Rebouças, Cape Town, South Africa, December 27, 1892

This chapter seeks to illuminate the development of racialized subjectivities as a historical problem in nineteenth-century Brazil. To that end, I will analyze the letters and writings of the Afro-descendant engineer and abolitionist André Rebouças (1838–1898), with special attention to the role of racial silence in Rebouças' personal diary and in the edited papers of his father, lawyer and statesman Antônio Pereira Rebouças (1798–1880).[1]

The Rebouças men were members of the best-known family of Black intellectuals in nineteenth-century Brazil. In personal and political terms, the history of the Rebouças family was shaped by the new opportunities that arose with Brazilian Independence (1822) and the approval of a liberal constitution (1824). The family's first politically prominent member, Antônio Pereira Rebouças, was one of four sons of an Afro-descendant woman and a Portuguese tailor who took part in Independence struggles in the province of Bahia between 1821 and 1823. Brazil's Independence struggles allowed Antônio to attain social and political recognition as a leading expert in civil law. He was decorated

---

* Translated by Brodwyn Fischer.
[1] André Rebouças heavily edited his fathers' papers in order to create the Antônio Pereira Rebouças Collection at the Brazilian National Library. On Antônio Pereira Rebouças' autobiographical manuscripts, see H. Mattos and K. Grinberg, "Lapidário de si."

by the Brazilian emperor, D. Pedro I, was twice elected to the Parliament, was chosen as *conselheiro* (counsel) to Emperor D. Pedro II, and was eventually recognized throughout Brazil for his work as a lawyer. Antônio's brothers also gained prominence in careers formerly prohibited to men "of color": Manoel Maurício Rebouças graduated from medical school and became a member of Imperial Academy of Medicine, and José Pereira Rebouças became a composer and conductor of the Imperial Orchestra.[2] Antônio Pereira Rebouças married Carolina Pinto, the daughter of a wealthy merchant from Salvador. Little is known about her or her family, but according to family memory she was darker in complexion than her husband.[3]

Their sons, Antônio and André Rebouças, enjoyed a first-rate education. They graduated in military engineering from the Praia Vermelha School (Escola de Aplicação da Praia Vermelha) in 1860, and in 1861 Antônio financed a stay in Europe to complement his sons' professional training. Eventually known as the Rebouças brothers, they were among Imperial Brazil's most important engineers, and to this day they maintain a strong presence in Brazil's national memory: streets and public works projects throughout the country bear their names. Antonio Rebouças Filho would die in 1874, already a notable engineer. André would become famous as a social thinker and abolitionist leader.[4] After abolition, André became an increasingly cosmopolitan intellectual who followed with interest not only the technological innovations of the industrial world but also transnational struggles against slavery and other forms of unfree labor "in Europe, the Americas, Asia or Africa," as he wrote in a letter of 1895.[5]

André left behind an extensive diary and many unpublished writings; he also served as editor for the published version of his father's papers. He will be our guide as we reflect on the construction of Black subjectivities in nineteenth-century Brazil. In particular, this chapter aims to understand how and why André Rebouças broke through his previously color-blind

---

[2] K. Grinberg, *A Black Jurist*. See also L. Spitzer, *Lives in Between*; H. Mattos, *Escravidão e cidadania* and "De pai."

[3] Interview by Hebe Mattos and Keila Grinberg with Ana Maria Rebouças, 2006, LABHOI/ UFF.

[4] See, among others, M. A. Rezende Carvalho, *O quinto século*.

[5] "The most effective and energetic way to civilize the barbarous and semi-barborous peoples of Europe, Africa, America and Asia – to emancipate the serfs and the slaves – is to endow them with individual landed property." A. Rebouças, letter of April 23, 1895, to Conselheiro Augusto de Castilho, in J. Verissimo, ed., *Diário e notas*, pp. 428–429.

self-narrative in the letters he wrote during his one and only voyage to the continent of Africa (1891–1893) and in the articles he wrote and published during this period.[6] In exploring this transformation, I also discuss the deep intellectual consequences of André's brief two-week visit to the United States in 1873, which were registered through posts in his personal diary. André Rebouças' transnational experiences, I argue, were directly related to his decision to break the ethic of racial silence that prevailed in his earlier writings.

ON THE ETHIC OF SILENCE

The social historiography of Brazilian slavery, a body of work that inspires many of the chapters in this volume, is centrally concerned with the question of social agency – among captive and freed persons, but also among broader categories of individuals who found themselves in a subaltern social position. The theoretical references for this work, from E. P. Thompson's cultural Marxism to the micro-historical methodologies of Fredrik Barth, emphasize the relational and political meanings of collective identity formation, as well as the relationship between normative structures and social agency. They valorize the role of shared experience and the collective production of hierarchical categories in shaping individual social action and conditioning the impact of individual endeavors on broader historical processes. In this sense, social history research has used individualized trajectories to continuously rewrite the history of slave societies and shed new light on the political and cultural meanings of actions taken by enslaved and freed people and their descendants, as well as the broader significance of the collective processes of identification and classification that have formed them as historical agents.[7]

This historiography does not, however, generally problematize questions of subjectivity and of the processes that condition it. Historians (myself included) have, for good reason, been wary of the anachronism inherent in many attempts at interdisciplinary exchange with the fields of psychology or psychoanalysis. Social history as a field has also generally

---

[6] Fundação Joaquim Nabuco (FUNAJ)/LABHOI-UFF, Coleção André Rebouças: Registro da Correspondência, vol IV (1891–1892); Registro da Correspondência, Vol. V (1892–1893).

[7] See F. Barth, *Ethnic Groups*; E. P. Thompson, *Tradicion, revuelta*; S. Lara, "Blowin' in the Wind"; P. A. Rosenthal, "Construindo o 'macro.'"

tended to turn away from deeper engagement with theoretical work in philosophy or communication studies (influenced by Spinoza and most fully realized in texts by Foucault and Deleuze), even though these works offer broader possibilities for theoretical exchange.[8]

This tendency has, however, been partially modified by the relatively recent consolidation of subfields involving the history of memory (and specifically the memory of Black slavery), which is itself related to the advance of postcolonial studies. This consolidation has paralleled a growing consciousness of the degree to which history – and especially the history of slavery – has constructed the Black subject in the West on the basis of racist frameworks inherent in the received memory of slavery. As Michel Rolph Trouillot postulated in *Silencing the Past*, historical experience is inseparable from historical narrative, especially (though not only) when it comes to the history of slavery.[9] Understanding subaltern social agency should also allow us to problematize subaltern subjects' formation as self-narrators, whose accounts merit careful analysis.

To understand André Rebouças' self narration, and especially the role of racial silence within it, it is useful to begin with broader historical incongruities. In nineteenth-century Brazil, racism and the experience of slavery shaped each other within the contradictory context created by Brazil's political independence (1822) and first constitution (1824). The independent Empire – like the US slave republic or the slave empires of France and Britain – formally committed itself to interrupting the Atlantic slave trade and blocking other forms of new enslavement. Yet slavery was maintained in the name of property rights, supported by an illegal slave trade that operated with tacit Imperial consent. As a constitutional monarchy, Brazil explicitly recognized the civil rights of all Brazilian citizens except slaves, but it excluded freed Africans from the possibility of naturalization.

Despite those limits, the majority of Brazil's new citizenry was comprised of freeborn people of African descent, and the Brazilian Constitution of 1824 rendered unlawful colonial regulations that had barred so-called free people of color from civil and military positions.[10] Article 179 recognized a wide array of civil rights for all Brazilians, banned torture and degrading punishment, and abolished the hereditary privileges of the Portuguese ancien régime.

---

[8] See G. Deleuze, *Spinoza*; M. Foucault, "O sujeito," and "A escrita"; A. F. de Carvalho, "História e subjetividade."

[9] M. Trouillot, *Silencing the Past*.

[10] M. Carneiro, *Preconceito racial*, p. 57; H. Mattos, "'Pretos' and 'Pardos.'"

Political rights were nonetheless restricted, as they were in the contemporary constitutional orders of England, the United States, and France. The 1824 Constitution limited full citizenship on the basis of income and property ownership and excluded African-born former slaves even when they fulfilled these requirements. Brazilian-born freedmen could vote in local elections but could not be elected, even if they met minimum income requirements. Yet their descendants' political rights were in no way blocked, and liberals of the time maintained that Brazilians were divided into only two categories, slaves and citizens. Brazil's new subjects and citizens "of color" pushed the limits of these constitutional contradictions, and their demands for fuller incorporation into Brazil's incipient modern nation became a crucial political issue in the tumultuous early decades of the independent Empire. To some degree, those demands met with political success: an ethic of racial silence established itself in situations of formal equality. Yet denominations of color continued to label Afro-descendants with the stigma of slavery, shaping the experiences of racism among free Afro-Brazilians.[11]

This was the context within which André Rebouças edited his father's handwritten autobiography, based on a manuscript written in 1837/1838 and other personal accounts and published in 1879.[12] In the original, unpublished manuscript, Antonio Pereira Rebouças began the story of his public life with his participation in Bahia's Independence struggles (which ended on July 2, 1823) and recounted many experiences of racial discrimination. Among others, he noted an episode that took place in 1823, after the end of war, as he travelled from Salvador, Bahia, to Rio de Janeiro. Antonio Pereira Rebouças – who wrote about himself in the third person – explained that he was almost "hindered from continuing his journey" and was only authorized to proceed by order of the municipal judge because "they were already familiar with his name and became convinced of his identity when he expressed personal knowledge of [Brazil's] most notable

---

[11] See H. Mattos, *Escravidão e cidadania*; S. Chalhoub, "The Precariousness of Freedom."
[12] A. Rebouças, *Recordações da vida*. The autobiographical documents written by Antônio Pereira Rebouças are part of the Antônio Pereira Rebouças Collection, organized by André Rebouças, held by the National Library of Brazil (BN). They are: "Notas políticas de Antônio Pereira Rebouças" (Rio de Janeiro, December 19, 1868); "Apontamentos biográficos do conselheiro Antônio Pereira Rebouças" (undated, perhaps from the 1860s); "Biografia do advogado conselheiro Antônio Pereira Rebouças" (undated, perhaps from 1837); and "Nota biográfica do conselheiro Antônio Pereira Rebouças" (undated, perhaps from the 1860s).

patriotic episodes and showed professional expertise on juridical legislation."

The autobiography remained unpublished until after the end of Conselheiro Rebouças' life. When André Rebouças finally facilitated its publication in 1879, he edited out all mention of discrimination. André Rebouças' personal diary was shaped by the same preference for color-blind narrative. Those choices reflected the broader ethic of silence that surrounded the question of color throughout nineteenth-century Brazil. The decision to muffle his father's experience of racial discrimination was in keeping with a personal political decision to construct his and his father's self-narratives in a language of universal citizenship.[13]

"THE EAST RIVER LOOKS LIKE THE PARANÁ"

In 1871 – as Brazil enacted the Free Womb Law, the most important legal measure against slavery taken after the end of the Atlantic slave trade – André Rebouças was an established engineer and well-known business-man in the Imperial Court, dedicated, in partnership with his brother Antônio, to modernizing the docks of Rio de Janeiro and building a railroad in the state of Paraná. In 1873, in the midst of a business conflict over the Rio dock project, André Rebouças traveled to Europe and also to the United States to acquaint himself with technological innovations in his field. He spent two weeks in the USA, traveling along the East Coast from New York City, in the midst of Reconstruction (1865–1877) and just a few years after the end of the US Civil War and the abolition of US slavery. The supposed equality of political rights among Blacks and whites in the United States did not prevent Rebouças from experiencing problems at hotels, on trains, and in restaurants "because of his color"; he indicated as much in his diary, though descriptively and without comment.

He depended upon his friends, especially the Brazilian national José Carlos Rodrigues, to facilitate his movement around the country. José Carlos Rodrigues was the editor of O Novo Mundo, "an illustrated periodical of the progress of the era," published monthly between 1870 to 1879 for circulation in Brazil from an office in the New York Times building in New York City. After his trip, André became one of the

---

[13] André Rebouças' original manuscript journal is archived at Fundação Joaquim Nabuco in Recife. I use here its published version, edited by José Veríssimo: A. Rebouças, Diário e notas.

newspaper's regular contributors, as well as a coeditor of the *Revista Industrial*, which was regularly published as an insert in the newspaper. The writings about race and slavery in *O Novo Mundo* offer clues that allow us to understand the ways in which André Rebouças' personal views about these issues changed as a result of his interactions with José Carlos Rodrigues, as well as how this new perception would shape Rebouças' subsequent personal narratives.

One of *O Novo Mundo*'s missions was to "furnish Brazil with detailed news about the political, moral, literary and industrial life of the United States of North America."[14] The paper also sought to offer Brazilian readers news from other parts of the world. The processes through which nations around the globe were emancipating slaves and serfs figured among the paper's topics of interest and were clearly understood as relevant to Brazil's destiny.

An editorial in the paper's first edition, on October 24, 1870, associated Dom Pedro II's famous 1867 speech ("fala do trono") advocating the abolition of Brazilian slavery with the end of American Civil War. The author argued that D. Pedro's declaration that he would take measures to "abolish the subservient element as quickly as possible," made only one year after the conclusion of the American conflict, created the expectation that Brazil would finally accept "the lessons of the US war" and free the slaves. The editorial lamented that Brazil had chosen to become the last in the Americas to reform its labor regime, "trailing even Spain."[15]

The following year, the paper celebrated the ratification of the Free Womb Law on September 28, 1871, albeit with some reservation: "in reality, very little was done here to emancipate the slaves: that little, however, was the most that could be expected of Brazil."[16] Articles in *O Novo Mundo* attempted to demonstrate to Brazilian slaveowners that they needed not fear deeper reforms. The pieces reported good outcomes for Russian agriculture after the emancipation of the serfs and equally favorable prospects for the plantations of the old South after full emancipation in the United States. According to the newspaper, "after Russia freed its serfs, it has taken on a quiet strength, entirely new in its history," without its "nobles" having become "ruined."[17] So it was in the United States as well, where increasing cotton harvests – combined with the "progress of the *negro*," signaled that planters were achieving the best

[14] *O Novo Mundo*, October 24, 1870, p. 14.   [15] *O Novo Mundo*, October 24, 1870, p. 2.
[16] *O Novo Mundo*, December 24, 1871, p. 42, "Os Ganhos de 1871."
[17] *O Novo Mundo*, December 24, 1871, p. 42, "Emancipação na Russia."

of both worlds.[18] The newspaper attempted to convince Brazilian land-owners that even "removing *negras* from the workplace," which had occurred across the American South after the Civil War, had been essentially positive: "emancipation entitled the freedmen to houses, and houses need to be maintained and governed."[19] "Liberals," another article declared, "need not fear freedom."[20]

The March 1872 issue carried a lengthy article about the closure of the Freedmen's Bureau, the US agency that regulated the rights of former slaves, emphasizing its positive achievements. The article recognized the closure's justification as valid: "free men cannot be held under tutelage." But it also lamented the demise of a proposal that had called for each new citizen to receive up to "40 acres of land" in abandoned areas, paying the state 6 percent of the valuation annually in compensation. The article noted with enthusiasm the number of schools established by the Bureau, most of which were being maintained autonomously by the freedmen themselves despite much opposition. According to the newspaper, "racial prejudice" was the worst enemy of universal education among Blacks in the United States. The text noted the role that accusations of misappropriated funds against Bureau director General Oliver Otis Howard had played in hastening the decision to close the Freedmen's Bureau, but it firmly asserted that those allegations were unfounded.[21]

During the early part of the 1870s, optimism and abolitionism continued to color the publication's editorials with regard to the issue of slave emancipation around the world. "Spain and the Slaves" was the title of a January 23, 1873, editorial.[22] "Egyptian Slaves," which lamented the spread of domestic and female slavery in Egypt, appeared in a March 24, 1873, issue.[23] The June 1872 issue returned to Brazil, transcribing an article from the Bahian newspaper *O Abolicionista* that harshly criticized the restrictions of the 1871 Law and concluded:

For the true abolitionists – Conservatives, Liberals or Republicans – there is only one good law: that which brings an end to slavery. How much longer will it take?[24]

---

[18] *O Novo Mundo*, February 23, 1872, p. 75, "Progresso dos Negros."
[19] *O Novo Mundo*, October 24, 1870, p. 11, "Algodão Americano."
[20] *O Novo Mundo*, October 23, 1872, p. 75, "Progresso dos Negros."
[21] *O Novo Mundo*, March 23, 1872, p. 102, "Auxilio do Estado aos Libertos nos Estados Unidos."
[22] *O Novo Mundo*, January 23, 1873, p. 55, "A Hespanha e os Escravos."
[23] *O Novo Mundo*, March 24, 1873, p. 94, "Escravos no Egypto."
[24] *O Novo Mundo*, June 24, 1872, p. 149, "A Lei de 28 Septembro."

Two pages into that same issue, the newspaper published a review of a short story by Bernardo Guimarães, *Uma História de Quilombolas* (A History of Maroons), which had been published in the book *Lendas e Narrativas* (Legends and Narratives). The story was portrayed as a realistic record of the *mocambos* (fugitive slave communities) in the state of Minas Gerais. In conclusion, the editor expressed his hope that the story of the *quilombos* will someday be part of the past: "When will we be able to read *Histórias de Quilombolas* as past histories of a civilization that has already died off?"[25]

But the paper's 1872 run also referred to a series of pessimistic reports published in the *New York Times* about freedmen's labor in the United States. *O Novo Mundo* reported the problems identified by the *Times* but insisted on contextualizing them. According to the paper, vagrancy among freedpeople was a temporary problem brought on by their desire to migrate from the plantations where they had been enslaved. Furthermore, a minority of the freedpeople had clearly improved their lot, and, despite claims to the contrary, Southern landowners were already unanimous in proclaiming the superiority of free labor.[26]

In the July 1873 edition, a month after André Rebouças' US visit, one article noted the results of the most recent US census. According to the article, "one of the principal emblems of the life of a people or race is their spirit of migration .... The search for foreign lands indicates intellectual vigor and wish to seriously shoulder life's hardships." For the writer, the US Black population's demographic growth was an important indicator of the freedmen's "vitality" and "love of free labor." The author further noted the freedmen's preference for cultivating cotton and again praised the expansion of education among former slaves and the removal of freedwomen from the workforce.[27]

José Carlos Rodrigues served as a great interpreter of the United States for André Rebouças, whose brief US sojourn began after more than a year spent traveling through Europe. Upon his arrival in New York on June 9, Rebouças was shocked when several different hotels refused him a room. Only after various failed attempts did he understand that he had been refused hospitality on account of the "color difficulty" (sic).

"I obtained the address for the Brazilian Consulate and headed there in a special carriage," Rebouças wrote in his diary. He was received "very

[25] *O Novo Mundo*, June 24, 1872, p. 154, "Os Quilombolas."
[26] *O Novo Mundo*, October 23, 1872, p. 3, "O Trabalho dos Emancipados."
[27] *O Novo Mundo*, July 23, 1873, p. 163, "Movimento da População Negra."

kindly by the Consul's son," who was also an engineer, and was then able to secure "a room at the Washington Hotel on the condition that [he] take meals in his room rather than in the restaurant." He was initially given a "very dirty little room" on the third floor and was then moved to a bedroom with a sitting room that opened directly to Broadway, which meant that he never had to cross paths with the other guests. According to Rebouças' diary, the establishment – which had "the honor of once welcoming the immortal Washington" – was "in fashion for many years" but had since become "a third-class hotel."[28]

After he finally settled in, André Rebouças returned to the consulate to await José Carlos Rodrigues, with whom he had spent the previous evening visiting the docks, since, according to his diary, "color prejudice impeded [him] from attending the show at the Grand Opera House."[29]

André Rebouças was well-received by engineers of the New York Pacific Railway but spent most of his first days in the United States with José Carlos Rodrigues.[30] As a way to explain the foreigners of the United States to his Brazilian visitor, Rodrigues talked about illustrious non-whites: "the *mulato* [Frederick] Douglass, an old friend of President Grant and very influential in his reelection, had been turned away recently from several hotels in Washington, DC; this fact led to controversy in the newspapers and a motion in the US Senate."[31]

Rebouças had a few other friends in the city, including the Lidgerwood brothers, engineers with whom he met up on June 11. One of the Lidgerwoods agreed to accompany Rebouças on his excursion to various ports along the East Coast "in order to avoid problems of color prejudice."[32] José Carlos Rodrigues saw him off on the steamer *Providence*.

The East River reminded Rebouças of the Paraná River. Always in the company of John Lidgerwood, he visited "magnificent cotton mills" and continued to Boston, eating his meals in public places without any further racial aggravation. On the way to Buffalo, however, when the train stopped for a meal, he was again harassed by a restaurant owner, at which point "John Lidgerwood had to make a point of revealing my nationality, and refer[red] to me constantly as 'Doctor.'"[33] From then on, with each new stop there was a new complaint. Even so, Rebouças marveled at Niagara Falls and the tourism industry that surrounded it,

[28] André Rebouças, *Diário e notas*, p. 245–246.
[29] André Rebouças, *Diário e notas*, p. 246.   [30] André Rebouças, *Diário e notas*, p. 246.
[31] André Rebouças, *Diário e notas*, p, 247.   [32] André Rebouças, *Diário e notas*, p. 248.
[33] André Rebouças, *Diário e notas*, p, 249.

which was like nothing he had seen in Europe. He especially noted the "Yankee audacity" of the ferry and the beauty of the suspension bridge to Canada. In Buffalo, he wrote that all the hotel staff members were "*mulatos* and creoles."[34]

The next day Rebouças visited the "Oil-Creek" oil fields. The progress he observed there astounded him and brought him hope. He firmly shared the optimism of his friend Rodrigues:

> The discovery of oil in "Oil Creek" dates back to 1858; it was during the Civil War that this industry reached maximum production.
>
> In Moses's time, to free the people of Israel, God made water spill from rocks: to free the American slaves, God did even more: he made oil come from the land of Pennsylvania![35]

On Rebouças's return trip, however, the "color prejudice" at the train stops caused him to go two days "without food." All the same, he was impressed, visiting factories, mines, bridges, docks, and shipyards. They traveled by train from Pittsburgh to Philadelphia in a sleeping car, and, as at the hotel, "he was served by *negros* and *mulatos*." When they returned to New York City on June 18, at 11 p.m., there was again no hotel for Rebouças, a problem they finally resolved at the "State House" at 760 Broadway, where he shared a room with John Lidgerwood.[36]

The next day, José Carlos Rodrigues put Rebouças in a room adjacent to his own at French's Hotel, and on June 20 Rebouças received his passport to return home from the Brazilian consulate. Before his departure, Rebouças visited the family home of the Lidgerwood brothers and made additional technical visits to the outskirts of the city. On June 23, two weeks after his arrival in New York, he embarked on the Corvette *Niterói* for his return to Brazil.[37]

Rebouças' journey had been made amidst challenges to his rights as operator of the docks of Rio de Janeiro. The death of his brother Antônio, in 1874, would eventually lead him to abandon his business dreams. In a way, his failure as a businessman would also mark the beginning of his path as an abolition activist.[38] From then on, he became known for his advocacy of social reform projects, which specifically included the abolition of slavery and the democratization of land ownership, both projects clearly inspired by the Yankees.

---

[34] André Rebouças, *Diário e notas*, p. 250.   [35] André Rebouças, *Diário e notas*, p 251.
[36] André Rebouças, *Diário e notas*, p 252–253.
[37] André Rebouças, *Diário e notas*, p 253–256.   [38] A. Trindade, "André Rebouças."

As previously stated, André Rebouças was eventually one of
O Novo Mundo's principal contributors. Among his numerous articles, he wrote his brother's obituary and a tribute to his father,
Counselor Antônio Pereira Rebouças, which was published along
with a full-page portrait on the cover of the February 22, 1875,
edition.[39] It was during this same period that André Rebouças edited
his father's memoirs. The newspaper also published Rebouças' articles
in a special insert called the *Revista Industrial.*[40] These included three
pieces about coffee, cotton, and sugar that made proposals about those
crops' future in Brazil.

The coffee article focused on the prizes that Brazilian beans had
received at the Centennial International Exhibition of 1876, held in
Philadelphia. To maintain the crop's excellence, Rebouças stated, coffee
would have "to undergo a critical progressive evolution from slave to free
labor."[41] For this purpose, his proposal called for the industrialization of
coffee processing and the democratization of agricultural production, to
be achieved by leasing or selling small plots of land to freedmen and
immigrants. That was also the basis for his proposal for sugarcane production: industrialization combined with the democratization of land
tenure and the mechanization of agricultural production, a model he
called "rural democracy."

The article on cotton, however, is especially interesting for the purposes
of this chapter, because it paired proposals for Brazilian agriculture with
an interesting analysis of the US post-emancipation scenario.[42] According
to Rebouças, 1876 was a year of "crisis and decadence in the cotton
culture in this [Brazilian] Empire ... yet one of prosperity and great victory
for cotton in the admirable Anglo-American Republic." The article's
objective was to explain why. For the author, the answer was simple:
"slave labor here, free labor there: an incessant experimental demonstration that constitutes practical proof of the sublime axiom: liberty is the
supreme prerequisite for rational and progressive labor." To prove his
point, he presented figures for the post–Civil War cotton harvest and the
growth of the textile industry in the US South. The harvest of 1875/1876,

[39] *O Novo Mundo*, August 23, 1874, p. 196, "Necrologia – o Engenheiro Antonio
Rebouças"; February 22, 1875, p. 117, "O Sr. Antonio Pereira Rebouças (retrato)" and
p. 122, "O Sr. Conselheiro Rebouças."
[40] *O Novo Mundo*, April 23, 1877, pp. 75–79.
[41] *O Novo Mundo*, April 23, 1877, pp. 75.
[42] Articles originally published in *O Globo* and republished in the April 23, 1877, edition of
O Novo Mundo.

as already been reported in *O Novo Mundo*, had been nearly identical to the largest harvest ever reported during slavery:

Thus, the cotton harvest of 1875–1876 was larger than any from the nefarious period of slavery: it was only 482 bales smaller than the maximum harvest known in the United States.

These figures are irrefutable; it is not freedom; it is God himself teaching us that slavery is not only unfair and unjust, but also fatal to the development of wealth and the prosperity of nations.

And it should also be noted that the 1875–1876 planting season was disturbed by the uprisings of the carpet-baggers; by wretched clashes between freedpeople and their former masters, stirred up by the politicians for electoral purposes.

In the absence of these upheavals, they would have harvested 500 more bales, and the harvest of 1875 to 1876 would have been the largest ever obtained in the United States.

If we go from agriculture to the cotton industry, the results are even more astonishing.[43]

Despite his optimism, Rebouças followed the inclinations of *O Novo Mundo* in being attentive to Southern accusations about the political activities of Northern "adventurers." Those Southern critiques were part and parcel of a strategy to undo Reconstruction and impose racist restrictions on African Americans and would culminate in the fully institutionalized suppression of Black voting rights in the Southern states. But that was still in its early stages in the late 1870s. And André Rebouças, despite his trying experience in the "great Northern republic," as he referred to it, was an optimist when it came to the free movement of goods (which he advocated in the article) and the triumph of free labor around the world.

In addition to closely monitoring the results of the various experiments in emancipation across the Americas, Rebouças was increasingly aware during this period of Black economic activity in Africa, noting:

It is not only in the United States that the slave, purified by freedom, works wonders; it is in Puerto Rico, which is still a colony of Spain; it is in Martinique, which belongs to France; it is in the British colony of Mauritius; it is in the Portuguese colony of Angola, which already sent coffee to Lisbon markets to compete with ours; it is in Liberia, this singular republic of Blacks freed in the United States, already wealthy as a result of oil and palm trade, which now prospers amazingly from the cultivation of the famous Liberian coffee; it is, at last, everywhere in which lawmakers had the wisdom of ordering the unfastening of the hideous chains of slavery.[44]

[43] *O Novo Mundo*, April 23, 1877, p. 78.   [44] *O Novo Mundo*, April 23, 1877, p. 78.

The friendship between André Rebouças and José Carlos Rodrigues would survive the end of *O Novo Mundo*. It would even be maintained when Rebouças decided to accompany the deposed Brazilian emperor into exile in 1889, just as his friend decided to end his own exile in the United States and return to Brazil. These contrary choices both stemmed from the same cause. On May 13, 1888, Brazil's Princess Regent signed the bill that abolished slavery, without compensating slaveowners and after massive flights of the last enslaved workers. A year and a half later, with the full support of discontented slaveowners who came to be known as the "14th of May republicans," a military coup ended the monarchy and instituted Brazil's first Republic.

José Carlos Rodrigues, son of coffee farmers from Cantagalo, was an early republican, who converted to Protestantism and willingly left Brazil to live in exile in the United States, after being accused of corruption by the royalist government while working as a public servant. The republican regime brought Rodrigues back to Brazil, although only for a few years; he would become owner of the *Jornal do Commercio*, one of the most important newspapers in Rio de Janeiro. André Rebouças, as a Liberal monarchist and personal friend of Dom Pedro II, decided to accompany the Imperial family into exile. He was firmly convinced that the republican coup had been fueled by resentment on the part of the old slave-based oligarchies, who feared the implementation of reforms that could lead to a "rural democracy," which, as conceived in Rebouças' articles in the 1870s, would have eliminated large landed estates and complemented the work of abolition. Rebouças never returned to Brazil, but neither did he break his epistolary ties with the friend he had met in the United States.

BREAKING THE SILENCE

In exile, André Rebouças stopped keeping a diary. From that point on, however, he began to save copies of the letters he wrote in his correspondence notebooks. In these letters, written first in Europe and then in Africa, a small revolution took shape in Rebouças' self-narration. It was in a letter to the former owner of *O Novo Mundo*, written as he awaited Dom Pedro II's death in Cannes in October 1891, that Rebouças referred to himself for the first time as "the *negro* André."[45]

---

[45] Fundação Joaquim Nabuco – Recife (FJN)/LABHOI-UFF, Coleção André Rebouças, Registro de Correspondencia, vol. IV, 1891–1892, letter to José Carlos Rodrigues, p. 517, image 1465, Cannes, October 29, 1891.

Judging from his letters, Rebouças' final years in exile were marked by deep melancholy. Leo Spitzer is the only biographer who emphasizes this stage of Rebouças' life, arguing that it underscored the sense of marginality that characterized him.[46] The fact that Rebouças narrated this melancholy as an acute awareness of his African origins, however, suggests that it reflected more than the personal difficulties he confronted.

In Spitzer's reading, Rebouças' anguish at the end of his life is a psychological reflection of the "social anomaly" to which he was condemned as a *mulato* in a white world. From this standpoint, Rebouças' social agency is obscured by an interpretive model that presents racial identities as immutable categories, tragically pitting individual freedom against social structure. Without disregarding the tragic dimension of André Rebouças' trajectory and the richness of certain aspects of Spitzer's analysis, my intention is to capture the dramatic dimension of Rebouças' correspondence. Rebouças' letters dwell significantly on Africa, allowing us to see the sinister edifice produced by European scientific racism and colonialism. His narratives illuminate the multiple actors present in assembling this social drama, including Black diasporic figures like himself.[47]

In fact, much of what André Rebouças wrote about Africa after Brazil's abolition suggests familiarity with the US thinkers whose ideas would later contribute to Pan-Africanism. Rebouças' perception, expressed in his letters from Africa, was that the Atlantic Blacks were also Africans, that they shared the "soul" of their brothers from the "Martyr Continent" and should contribute to the mission of Christianizing and civilizing Africa.[48] Even if US intellectuals did not directly influence Rebouças' thought, it is worth pondering the ways in which the growing importance of race in Western scientific thought after 1870 – and especially after Brazilian abolition – might have led Rebouças to reflect upon the theme in much the same way as Black intellectuals in the United States.

In his self-imposed exile, Rebouças continued to be an active and well-informed intellectual who wrote constantly and published numerous articles in the Brazilian press. His letters discussed a wide array of issues that plagued Brazil and the world. His first article on Africa, *O problema da África* (*The Problem of Africa*), was written on November 7, 1890, while he was still in Lisbon, and published in Brazil's *Revista de*

---

[46] Leo Spitzer articulates this interpretation in *Lives in Between*, particularly chapter 6.
[47] W. Wariboko, "I really cannot."
[48] A. Crummell, *The Future*; E. Blyden, *Liberia's Offering*.

Engenharia the following year.[49] In it, he sought to reflect upon the relationship between slavery and racism:

Africa has always been a continent of slavery ... The color black has always been valued by the exploiters of men as a justification for their inequity ... The color black saved them from a moral struggle ... Because all criminals want to have some justification for their crime.

At that point, Rebouças was still optimistic about the presence of Christianity in Africa, both Protestant and Catholic, and especially about the churches' role in the fight against slavery, which was still thriving on that continent. He praised Cardinal Lavigerie in Algeria (whom he saw as an opponent of Muslim proslavery advocates) and the Black Protestant missionaries in Liberia and Sierra Leone.

Recognizing European and American responsibility for what he referred to as the "African problem," which derived in Rebouças' view entirely from slavery, he counted on the civilizing efforts of Europeans and Americans to repair centuries of African suffering. In the wake of 1888, he firmly believed that Brazil should play a role in a new colonization of the African continent.

Considered from the highest cosmopolitan perspective, Brazil is a great workshop, preparing Humanity for the scientific and industrial conquest of Africa .... Our next steps as Argonauts of this grandiose future, will take us from this beautiful coast to the Continent that faces us from across the Atlantic, so that we can bring to it Civilization, Industry and Progress, and thus pay this great debt of gratitude and recognition that Brazil owes to Africa.

In the best tradition of proto-Pan-Africanism, Rebouças proposed the establishment of a steamer route from Europe to the Pacific, which would pass along the Western coast of Africa and continue to Brazil before rounding the tip of South America. With the death of Pedro II in Paris in early December 1891, Rebouças decided to begin the undertaking himself. He traveled from Cannes to Marseilles in order to seek employment on the Luanda-Ambaca Railroad "or in any company in Africa."[50]

In letters from this period, he described in detail an anticipated expedition to Africa, the primary goal of which was to fight slavery on that continent. He planned to leave on the packet ship *Malange*, "with his friend João Nunes Lisboa," and to visit ports along Africa's East Coast,

---

[49] A. Rebouças. "O problema."
[50] Fundação Joaquim Nabuco – Recife (FJN)/LABHOI-UFF, Coleção André Rebouças, Registro de Correspondencia, vol. IV, 1891–1892, letter to Santinhos (José Américo dos Santos), p. 609/638, images 1564, 1594, Marseille, January 17, 1892.

producing a detailed report of local conditions and possible improvements; he also planned at various points to "take a steamship from Lourenço Marques [the pre-1976 name for Maputo, in present-day Mozambique] to the East Coast," to "set up residence in Ambaca or any other high point along the Railroad," and to "work to develop rail traffic by introducing coffee cultivation to the adjacent areas."[51]

In a long letter to the abolitionist writer Alfredo Taunay, his closest friend and correspondent, he wrote of his desire to be in the "forests of Africa"[52] and his plans to write a book during his time in Africa entitled "Around Africa," of "Tolstoyan" inspiration.[53] In his self-imposed exile, Rebouças openly assumed his Blackness, making reference to his "Portuguese and African grandparents." And he also became a diligent reader of Leo Tolstoy, whom he repeatedly quoted in his letters. Only ten years younger than the novelist, André Rebouças became "Tolstoyan" when the Russian writer was only beginning to gain followers in Europe, advocating a stoic and anti-institutional religiosity, aligned with a new sense of pacifism. For Rebouças, attention to Russia and the United States was part of a larger effort to think about post-slavery societies and their potential for modernization. At the same time, Rebouças sought – "Tolstoy-like," as he liked to say – to morally and intellectually resist the advance of racism in the Western world, an evil that was bolstered by the very "science" in which Western thinkers so believed.

In 1892, André Rebouças finally traveled to the continent of Africa through the Suez Canal. By May he had settled into Lourenço Marques (Maputo). His first impression was one of amazement with the natural landscape and with the new array of languages, religions, and human beings. He felt happy "mingling with all human races; having as enemies only those who monopolized the land and enslaved men."[54] He spent some time there before embarking on the steamship *Tinguá* to South

[51] Fundação Joaquim Nabuco – Recife (FJN)/LABHOI-UFF, Coleção André Rebouças, Registro de Correspondencia, vol. IV, 1891–1892, letter to Antônio Julio de Machado, p. 614, image 1570, Marseille, January 31, 1892.

[52] Fundação Joaquim Nabuco – Recife (FJN)/LABHOI-UFF, Coleção André Rebouças, Registro de Correspondencia, vol. IV, 1891–1892, letter to Taunay, p. 616, image 1572, Marseille, January 31, 1892.

[53] Fundação Joaquim Nabuco – Recife (FJN)/LABHOI-UFF, Coleção André Rebouças, Registro de Correspondencia, vol. IV, 1891–1892, letters to Taunay, p. 616, image 1572, Marseille, January 31, 1892, and p. 617, image 1573, Marseille, February 12, 1892.

[54] Fundação Joaquim Nabuco – Recife (FJN)/LABHOI-UFF, Coleção André Rebouças, Registro de Correspondencia, vol. IV, 1891–1892, letter to Taunay, p. 651, image 1610, Lourenço Marques, May 14, 1892.

Africa. His stay was long enough, however, to change his initial point of view:

I left Cannes on January 8, 1892, with the intent of working on the Luanda to Ambaca Railroad, owned by my friend Antonio Julio Machado. Because of the Portuguese crisis, I was only able to leave on the *Malange* to Lourenço Marques on March 27. There I found revolting slave-ownership in its full debauchery. After twenty days of Herculean effort, I had to seek shelter for my Physical and Moral Health in the Barberton Mountains at an altitude of 1,000 meters.[55]

In finding that slavery continued in Lourenço Marques, and that he was powerless to fight it, Rebouças experienced the first disappointment of his trip. Ongoing slavery was not something he was unaware of before arriving, but its dimensions and intensity rendered his plans to fight it unworkable. But by May 26, he was in South Africa, confident of Britain's capacity to repress slavery and the slave trade.

The stigma of revolting slave-ownership is still very much alive in eastern Africa . . . [but] here in South Africa, the *negro* is already progressing toward rural democracy; they already have houses, cultivated crops.[56]

Rebouças settled in Barberton, which he denominated the "African Petrópolis."[57] He established himself in South Africa as an admirer of the humanitarian sentiment of the British, who were then consolidating the imperialist occupation of the region in the name of "civilization" and the fight against slavery, which had been abolished throughout the British Empire in 1838. The year 1892 was, for Rebouças, one of intense intellectual work. Upon arriving in Barberton, he had "a number of 'idylls' written or ready to write," for which he repeatedly claimed Tolstoyan inspiration.

He sent Taunay a piece entitled "New Propaganda – Dressing 300,000,000 African Negroes," in hopes his friend would facilitate its publication in Brazil.[58] Part of it, – the sixth of his African "Idylls,"

[55] Fundação Joaquim Nabuco – Recife (FJN)/LABHOI-UFF, Coleção André Rebouças, Registro de Correspondencia, vol. V, 1892–1893, letter to Taunay, p. 709, image 1678, Barberton, November 25, 1892.
[56] Fundação Joaquim Nabuco – Recife (FJN)/LABHOI-UFF, Coleção André Rebouças, Registro de Correspondencia, vol. V, 1892–1893, letter to Rangel Costa, p. 673, image 1641, June 14, 1892.
[57] Fundação Joaquim Nabuco – Recife (FJN)/LABHOI-UFF, Coleção André Rebouças, Registro de Correspondencia, vol. IV, 1891–1892, letter to Antonio Julio Machado, p. 668, image 1627, Barberton, May 28, 1892.
[58] Fundação Joaquim Nabuco – Recife (FJN)/LABHOI-UFF, Coleção André Rebouças, Registro de Correspondencia, vol. IV, 1891–1892, letter to Taunay, p. 665, image 1624, Barberton, June 17, 1892.

written in Barberton on May 30, 1892 – was published in the newspaper *A Cidade do Rio*, owned by abolitionist José do Patrocínio, on February 4, 1893. One of the article's central questions foreshadowed W. E. B. Du Bois' seminal *The Souls of Black Folk* (1903):[59]

Why does the African *negro* always laugh, sing and dance?! …
Clad in perpetual mourning, covered in black that is ingrained in his very skin …
Why does the African *negro* always laugh, sing and dance?!
Carrying rough … hard stones, … heavy, cold irons, or dirty and suffocating coal!!! …
Why does the African *negro* always laugh, sing and dance?!! …
When the awful rearguard of the ferocious [Henry Morton] Stanley bought a little Black girl so that they could watch her be eaten alive by the cannibals, they grabbed their Sketchbooks, trained their ears for heartrending screams, and poised their binoculars for emotion scenes … The poor girl raised her eyes towards the Heavens and smilingly allowed them to tear apart her belly …
Why does the African *negro* always laugh, sing and dance?!
When in Campinas a landowner from São Paulo sent an innocent *preto velho* to the gallows in place of his murderous henchman, that poor wretch unconsciously traipsed along the satanic path of the Annas and the Caiaphas: of the corrupt and cynical judges and juries, wrongly sold out to the enslavers of men, usurpers and monopolizers of our national territory … . It was only when the executioner approached him with the rope in hand that the old African *preto* understood how the infernal comedy would end … So he sat down on the steps of the gallows and sang a song that his mother had taught him, here in the Martyr continent of Africa …
Why does the African *negro* always laugh, sing and dance?! …
Do tell, Jesus, Martyr of Martyrs: Do tell, You, for whom there are neither secrets nor martyrdoms in sacrifice and humility; in dedication, in devotion and in self-abnegation …
Do tell: Why does the African *negro* always laugh, sing and dance?!
Blessed be the slaves, the whipped, the insulted, the slandered, the spat upon and beaten.
Blessed be those who suffer injustice and wickedness: abduction and plundering.
Blessed be those who have no land, nor home: nor property, nor family.
Blessed be those who have no homeland: those who are foreigners in their own African continent.

(conceived in Krokodilpoort, May 23, 1892;
written in Barberton, May 30, 1892)

Rebouças spent all of 1892 working diligently on the book he had planned to write while still in Europe. Although he finished the book,

---

[59] For a longer explanation of this passage, see M. Abreu, "O Crioulo Dudu."

entitled *Around Africa 1889–1893: Abolitionist propaganda – Socio-economic life – Anthropology – Botany – Comparison of Brazilian and African Flora – Astronomy, Meteorology, etc.*, the manuscript has not yet been located among Rebouças' papers.[60]

In late May 1892, shortly after arriving in Barberton, Rebouças still felt optimistic about the possibilities of South Africa under British rule. From his standpoint, "the Africans needed to be taught how to read and write ... it should be absolutely clear that the only thing Africans ask for is fundamental justice; equality in payment ..., a bit of land .... To deny this is a diabolical evil."[61]

With the acceleration of the South African gold rush after 1886, however, the Boers from the Republic of Transvaal became a majority. The Republic of Transvaal or South Africa Republic was an independent state until the British defeated it in the Second Boer War (1899–1902). Rebouças was crushed by the racist practices of the Boers and the return of the specter of proslavery sentiments. Abruptly, in a passage that was not foreshadowed in his previous correspondence, he wrote to Nabuco and Taunay:

The fire at the Royal Hotel in Barberton and endless conflicts with slaveowners determined my move to Cape Town, seat of the scarcest slave-ownership on the miserable African continent. The proslavery republicans of the Transvaal say: *To make Money, slavery is necessary.*[62]

Rebouças once again felt powerless in the fight against African slavery. In Cape Town, which remained under British rule, he managed to channel his personal resources from Portugal and Brazil through the Bank of South Africa in order to maintain what he defined as an "anti-slavery and scientific mission."[63] But before long, even his illusions about the British rule in the Cape faded away. Racial discrimination, which was not legalized but was informally tolerated by the British, began to affect him. In

[60] Fundação Joaquim Nabuco – Recife (FJN)/LABHOI-UFF, Coleção André Rebouças, Registro de Correspondencia, vol. V, 1892–1893, letter to Taunay and Nabuco, pp. 716/723, images 1685/1692, Barberton, December 21, 1892.

[61] Fundação Joaquim Nabuco – Recife (FJN)/LABHOI-UFF, Coleção André Rebouças, Registro de Correspondencia, vol. IV, 1891–1892, letter to Antonio Julio Machado, p. 668, image 1627, Barberton, May 28, 1892.

[62] Fundação Joaquim Nabuco – Recife (FJN)/LABHOI-UFF, Coleção André Rebouças, Registro de Correspondencia, vol. V, 1892–1893, letter to Taunay and Nabuco, p. 711, image 1680, Barberton, December 12, 1892. Emphasis in original.

[63] Fundação Joaquim Nabuco – Recife (FJN)/LABHOI-UFF, Coleção André Rebouças, Registro de Correspondencia, vol. V, 1892–1893, letter to the Bank of South Africa, p. 720, image 1689, Cape Town, December 19, 1892.

a dramatic letter to Taunay dated December 19, 1892, he cataloged the list of horrors that British colonialists had allowed or engaged in the once idealized "South Africa."[64] According to him, the British insisted on:

1. Withholding land ownership from the Africans – What a disgrace!? Africans cannot own property on their own continent of Africa!
2. Refusing voting rights to Africans; subjecting them to barbaric laws; judging them in ad hoc courts; using and abusing the atrocious practice of whipping.
3. Employing the brutal Yankee practice of refusing *negros* and *mulatos* hotel rooms, and even making it difficult for clothing stores and toiletry shops to serve them.

All of this was in addition to what happened "in the heinous Republic of the Transvaal, where "former landowners claimed compensation for the formal abolition of slavery by the British," the trading post system "[stole] wages from the African," and settlers practiced violence against entire classes of workers. In 1892, Rebouças witnessed a "horrendous event" that caused him to leave the Granville Hotel in Barberton: the lynching of Africans on the streets, which brought to mind "the Yankee cannibals of Ohio, Mississippi, and Missouri."

Rhetorical references to Europeans and Americans who engaged in actions that were perceived as pure savagery as "cannibals" recurred in Rebouças' writings. Aside from this, his disappointment with British rule in Africa began to diminish his will to fight. For Rebouças, it was becoming increasingly clear that the problem of racism went much further than the Republic of Transvaal. To Rebouças' great disappointment, British colonization of South Africa allowed "the African [to remain] completely naked, unabashed and with no shame, in the company of his family, among the women and his own unmarried sons"; it did not teach Africans "English or Dutch or any other language," because colonists spoke to domestic servants in "a gibberish of Savage, Dutch and Portuguese."[65] He concluded, astonished, by saying that "The London *Graphic* depicted a half-naked African, serving as nanny

---

[64] Fundação Joaquim Nabuco – Recife (FJN)/LABHOI-UFF, Coleção André Rebouças, Registro de Correspondencia, vol. V, 1892–1893, letter to Taunay, p. 734/735/736, images 1703/1704/1705, Cape Town, December 23–27, 1892.

[65] Fundação Joaquim Nabuco – Recife (FJN)/LABHOI-UFF, Coleção André Rebouças, Registro de Correspondencia, vol. V, 1892–1893, letter to Taunay, p. 734/735/736, images 1703/1704/1705, Cape Town, December 23–27, 1892.

in Barberton, carrying a small child and leading the older sister along by the hand!!!!!!"[66]

Rebouças' enthusiasm for the Protestants likewise ended. His Christian mysticism, like that of Tolstoy, held that all religions, without exception, had a nefarious influence on progress and civilization. To him, all missionaries were theocrats who fostered the caste system ("eminently caste-ish"). "The missionaries in Africa teach the Zulu language instead of English or any other civilized language!"[67]

Rebouças' letters, especially those to Taunay, made it clear that he himself was no longer immune to segregationist practices, even in Cape Town. All the same, a few more months had to pass for him to give up on his "scientific and anti-proslavery mission" and decide to leave South Africa. In April 1893, he wrote:

Look, I came to Africa not to hunt lions like a lord, but to fight slavery and territorial monopoly. I disembarked in Port Said on April 2, 1892, and soon engaged in my initial battle. Of course, I do not relate my victories, abhorring the quixotic; but I am happy with myself and not sure if I will die in Africa or in Brazil.[68]

The letters of André Rebouças are a dramatic self-narration, as well as a testament to the contradictions and disillusions of antiracist liberal ideas in the process of European colonization of Africa. According to Paul Gilroy's foundational work (2001), Black critical thought comprised the first "counterculture of modernity," produced by divided subjects defined by a "double consciousness" that at once constituted them as modern and excluded them from modernity because of their race. André Rebouças was, without any doubt, a significant figure in this mold.[69] In his last letter from Cape Town to his friend Taunay, Rebouças narrated his journey in terms of Greek mythology, announcing his departure from Cape Town as a "new chapter in the Odyssey of this miserable African Ulysses."[70]

[66] Fundação Joaquim Nabuco – Recife (FJN)/LABHOI-UFF, Coleção André Rebouças, Registro de Correspondencia, vol. V, 1892–1893, letter to Taunay, p. 734/735/736, images 1703/1704/1705, Cape Town, December 23–27, 1892.

[67] Fundação Joaquim Nabuco – Recife (FJN)/LABHOI-UFF, Coleção André Rebouças, Registro de Correspondencia, vol. V, 1892–1893, letter to Taunay, p. 734/735/736, images 1703/1704/1705, Cape Town, December 23–27, 1892.

[68] Fundação Joaquim Nabuco – Recife (FJN)/LABHOI-UFF, Coleção André Rebouças, Registro de Correspondencia, vol. V, 1892–1893, letter to Taunay, p. 773, image 1744, Cape Town, April 4, 1893.

[69] P. Gilroy, *The Black Atlantic*.

[70] Fundação Joaquim Nabuco – Recife (FJN)/LABHOI-UFF, Coleção André Rebouças, Registro de Correspondencia, vol. V, 1892–1893, letter to Taunay, p. 791, image 1767, Cape Town, June 20, 1893.

In June 1893, André Rebouças considered his book *Em torno D'Africa* "dead," "faced with the impossibility of publishing it in Cape Town." At the same time, "the civil war in Brazil's south" left him with no will to go home.[71] He decided instead to go to Funchal, on the Atlantic Island of Madeira, where some of his Portuguese friends had epistolary contacts. There, he briefly considered the possibility of returning to the "Martyr Continent" so he could experience its Western coast:

> As I wrote in my last letter of 6/20, I arrived on the *Skol* on the 2nd.... Will I wait out the horrors ravaging our miserable Brazil, or will I go to the Western coast of Africa? .... God only knows.[72]

With the historian's magical hindsight, we know that he carried out none of the options. Still in Funchal, Rebouças fell to his death off of an Atlantic cliff in 1898. The self-narratives he left to the posterity are nonetheless powerful testimonies to the significance of transnational politics for universalist Black intellectuals in the nineteenth-century Atlantic World. The arguments set forth in this chapter have sought to illuminate the racialized subjectivization engendered by the stigma of slavery and to portray the ways in which its politicization was shaped by a collective transnational experience.

---

[71] He referred to the Federalist Riograndense Revolution (1893–1895), a civil war in southern Brazil against the centralized power of the Republic. Fundação Joaquim Nabuco – Recife (FJN)/LABHOI-UFF, Coleção André Rebouças, Registro de Correspondencia, vol. V, 1892–1893, letter to Taunay, p. 787, image 1763, Cape Town, June 12, 1893.

[72] Fundação Joaquim Nabuco – Recife (FJN)/LABHOI-UFF, Coleção André Rebouças, Registro de Correspondencia, vol. V, 1892–1893, letter to Barão da Estrela, p. 791, 1777, Madeira Islands, July 4, 1893.

PART IV

AFTERLIVES OF SLAVERY, AFTERWARDS OF ABOLITION

13

The Past Was Black

Modesto Brocos, *The Redemption of Ham*, and Brazilian Slavery

Daryle Williams[*]

The oil painting *Redenção de Cã* (*The Redemption of Ham*, 1895) figures prominently in the life work of the prolific Spanish-born, Brazilian-naturalized artist Modesto Brocos y Gómez (1852–1936).[1]

[*] This is a substantially revised version of a 2013 LASA conference presentation that appeared in print in Portuguese as D. Williams, "Redenção de Cã."

[1] Modesto Brocos y Gómez (Santiago de Compostela, Spain 1852 – Rio de Janeiro, Brazil 1936) came from a Galician family of accomplished artists. Often known by the simplified surname "Brocos," Brocos y Gómez began study at the Escuela de Dibujo de la Real Sociedad Económica de Amigos del País, in Santiago de Compostela, and the Academia de Bellas Artes de La Coruña. In 1871, he set out for Argentina, where he worked as an engraver for the *Los Anales de Agricultura*. In 1872, he moved to Rio, where he introduced the art of illustrated woodcuts into weekly periodicals, including *O Mequetrefe*. In 1875, Brocos entered into the Imperial Academy of Fine Arts (AIBA) as an auditor (*aluno de livre frequência*). Over the next two years, he would study under history painter Vitor Meirelles and sculptor Francisco Manoel Chaves Pinheiro, among others. He transferred to the French École Nationale de Beaux-Arts in 1877. In Paris and Madrid, Brocos studied under Henri Lehmann (1814–1882) and Federico de Madrazo y Kuntz (1815–1894), respectively. Brocos went on to Rome, to study with a fellowship offered by the Coruña Diputación. In 1889, he returned to the Spanish northwest to assume a post at Real Sociedad Económica de Amigos del País. Shortly thereafter, he accepted an invitation to join the reorganized ENBA, in Rio. Arriving in Brazil in early August 1890, he became a naturalized Brazilian citizen the following year. In his art career, Brocos worked in history painting (*La defensa de Lugo*, 1887), sacred art (Life of Saint James triptych, sacristy of the Santiago de Compostela cathedral, 1897–1899), architectural design (Brazilian National Library portico, 1908), decorative arts (*Progresso*, headquarters of the *Jornal do Brasil*, 1908; *A Imaginação* and *A Observação*, Brazilian National Library, ca. 1910), art theory, and fiction. His was a prolific portrait artist. During his formative years of art studies and over the course of a long professional career in Rio, Brocos returned often to landscapes and genre scenes of rustic folk. Brocos self-identified as an *aguafortista* (engraver or etcher), yet his long association with print arts, including a teaching post at Rio's Liceu de Artes e Ofícios (Arts and Trades School), encompassed wood engraving, the illustrated press, and postage stamp design.

Originally exhibited with the title *Redempção de Cham*,[2] the hand-
somely sized (199 × 166 cm), signed and dated oil-on-canvas won the
grand prize at the 1895 Brazilian national salon held at the National
School of Fine Arts (Escola Nacional de Belas Artes, ENBA), where
Brocos held various teaching posts between 1891 and 1934. An instant
success, *Redenção* was acquired by the Brazilian government at the
urging of influential voices in the Brazilian intelligentsia.[3] For the past
seventy-five years, the work has been part of the permanent circuit of
the Brazilian national art museum.[4] In various retrospective exhibits, in
textbooks, and online, *Redenção* commands outsize influence in
Brazil's visual vocabulary, at home and abroad.

A landmark in Brazilian visual culture, the painting has nonetheless
been dismissed for its troubling allegory of race mixture. The notoriety of
Brocos' treatment of an enigmatic Old Testament tale commonly known
as the "Curse of Ham" (Port.: *Maldição de Cã*) conventionally turns on
the troubled history of racial thought in the immediate aftermath of slave
emancipation. In a 2011 popular history piece about the canvas, Brazilian
anthropologist Giralda Seyferth succinctly captures the dominant inter-
pretative framework: "O futuro era branco" (The future was white).[5] In
scholarly literature and in the popular imaginary, *Redenção da Cã* (see
Figure 13.1) serves as the touchstone illustration of the intersection of the
ascendant racial "sciences" of the latter half of the nineteenth century and
an ideology of whitening and Black erasure that informed early twentieth-
century Brazilian thought and social policy. In recent scholarly publications, such as Tatiana Lotierzo's *Contornos do invisível* (2017), and in the
global imaginary, the canvas stands as emblematic of race and racism in
Latin America, notably during the heyday of eugenics.[6]

The burdens of Brazil's racist past (and present) have often confined
readings of *Redenção* to its allegory of a Blackness disappearing into
whiteness. Nonetheless, the painting has been the object of some important reappraisals. Historian Heloisa Selma Fernandes Capel has put the
painting in dialogue with Brocos' theoretical tracts, *A questão do ensino*

---

[2] "Cã" is a Portuguese spelling variant for the name of Noah's youngest son, Ham.
Alternative spellings – "Cam," "Can," and "Cão" – are not to be confused with
"Caim," the Portuguese name for the eldest son of Adam and Eve, Cain.
[3] Arquivo Nacional, Rio de Janeiro, Série Educação (92), IE 7 113, Fls. 19–56, Escola
Nacional de Belas Artes (ENBA) 1895 *Relátorio*, February 21, 1896.
[4] The canvas' most recent appearance in a special exhibition was May–September 2018, in
"Das Galés às Galerias," organized by the Museu Nacional de Belas Artes.
[5] G. Seyferth, "O futuro."   [6] N. Stepan, *The Hour*.

FIGURE 13.1 Modesto Brocos y Gómez, *Redenção de Cã*, 1895. Oil on canvas, 199 × 166 cm, Museu Nacional de Belas Artes, Rio de Janeiro.

de Bellas Artes (1915) and *Retórica dos pintores* (1933), to understand how the piece works in dialogue with the artist's evolving sense of fine art.[7] Art historians Heloisa Lima and Roberto Conduru have discussed the painting in relation to other works about Blacks produced within the ambit of the ENBA and its predecessor, the Academia Imperial de Belas Artes (Imperial Academy of Fine Arts).[8] Brazilian historians Ricardo

---

[7] H. Capel, "Entre o riso."   [8] H. Pires Lima, "A presença"; R. Conduru, *Pérolas.*

Ventura Santos and Marcos Chor Maio grappled with a geneticist's use of the image to "prove" the racial heterogeneity of the Brazilian genotype.[9] In 2013, anthropologists Tatiana Lotierzo and Lilia Schwarcz delved into the gendered visual economy of the canvas, setting *Redenção* within a nineteenth-century white male gaze.[10] The ugly history of anti-Black thought continues to weigh heavily in these alternate analyses, but fresh eyes have chartered approaches to Brocos' most well-known work that may not settle solely on the author's "scientific" appraisal of Brazil's white future.

Paradoxically, *Redenção* remains thinly contextualized in the historical setting of slave emancipation, a process completed a few years prior to Brocos' first rehearsals of the themes later assembled in the notorious allegory. Capel has casually observed that Brocos registered a disdain for enslavement, but how and what Brocos knew of slavery and emancipation have remained largely unexplored in the scholarship. This chapter looks anew at *Redenção*, its author, and their multiple audiences in the temporalities of slavery's final decades in Brazil. Its goal is to resituate the notorious canvas within the complex transitions from bondage to freedom that began in the 1870s and lingered through the 1910s. Arguing that *Redenção* is a painting just as much about a nineteenth-century Black emancipationist past as it is about a twentieth-century post-emancipation whitened future, I will first briefly examine the Biblical story that inspired the canvas, before turning to the painting's reception and circulation. The final third of the chapter situates Brocos and *Redenção* in the interior of Rio de Janeiro state, a physical and social landscape quietly transformed by slave emancipation. Throughout, we probe the history of interpretation that has been reluctant to interrogate what is to be made of the Black characters in the canvas and how Brocos, whose contact with Afro-Brazilians began in the 1870s, during his student years, and intensified after 1890, drew from direct contact with the formerly enslaved to paint his enigmatic portrait of bondage redeemed.

BROCOS AND THE CURSE OF HAM

Redenção de Cã takes direct inspiration from a strange episode in the Book of Genesis, chapter 9. After the Great Flood, Noah gets drunk on

[9] R. Ventura Santos and M. Chor Maio, "Qual 'retrato do Brasil?'" The original article by Sérgio Pena et al. appeared as "Retrato molecular."
[10] T. Lotierzo and L. Schwarcz, "Raça, gênero e projeto."

wine and falls asleep naked in a tent. The patriarch's youngest son Ham reports the scene to his older brothers, Shem and Japheth. The two enter the tent and cover their father, making a deliberate effort to avoid seeing him unclothed. Once awakened from his drunken slumber, Noah – enraged – condemns Ham's son Canaan to servitude. Gen. 9:25 reads "Cursed be Canaan! The lowest of slaves shall he be to his brothers."[11] The following passages describe Canaan's miserable fate and the divine grace extended to the descendants of Shem and Japheth.

The curious episode at Noah's tent invites questions that have challenged theologians, Biblical historians, and the faithful since antiquity. What was the offending nature of Ham's transgression? How could Noah be so intemperate? Why is the seemingly innocent Canaan condemned for the sin of his father, Ham? There have been no clear answers to such questions, but Jewish, Christian, and Islamic theologians of the ancient and medieval worlds found explanations for human bondage in the Hamitic Curse.[12] The idea of servitude gradually came to be attached to black skin, and a scriptural curse of enslavement without explicit reference to skin color evolved into a sacred plan for Black captivity and, more specifically, the subordination of corrupt Africans descended from Black Ham to the righteous non-Blacks who descended from Ham's brothers.[13] In the age of the transatlantic slave trade, the contorted story of Noah, Ham, and Canaan – with occasional admixtures of other figures from Genesis, including Adam and Eve's son Cain and Canaan's eldest brother Cush – figured in numerous tracts on bondage and interracial relations. By the nineteenth century, the Curse had come to serve as a useful agitprop for justifications of Black enslavement and white slaveholding throughout the Atlantic, most notably in the United States South.[14]

Although the transatlantic slave trade to Brazil endured into the 1850s and Black bondage was not abolished until 1888, the Hamitic Curse had a weak uptake in Portuguese America. Nonetheless, variations on the Curse circulated in nineteenth-century Brazil. Castro Alves' poem "Vozes da África" ("Voices of Africa," 1868) and Perdigão Malheiro's monumental tract on slave law *A escravidão no Brasil* (*Slavery in Brazil*,

---

[11] *The New American Bible*, revised edition (2011); King James Version: "Cursed be Canaan; a servant of servants shall he be unto his brethren." A Portuguese-language version contemporary to the painting, appearing in a review by Olavo Bilac, read: "Maldito seja Cham! Seus filhos serão escravos dos escravos dos seus irmãos!" ("Cursed be Ham! His sons will be the slaves of the slaves of his brothers!")
[12] D. Whitford, *The Curse of Ham*; D. Goldenberg, *The Curse of Ham*.
[13] W. Evans, "From the Land."   [14] S. Haynes, *Noah's Curse*.

1866–1867) both reference the sorry fate of Ham and his descendants.[15] Debate on the floor of the Brazilian Parliament and published traveler accounts of the era invoked the Curse as shorthand for Black enslavement.

Brocos' motives for selecting the Curse for his submission to the 1895 salon are thinly sourced. Press coverage registered merely elliptic references to the backstory of the canvas; Brocos did not exert much effort documenting his creative process. There exist, however, some suggestive clues. It's well known that Brocos painted from life models, and he knew people of color to be integral to the fine arts (including the modeling stand) since his days as an art student in the 1870s.[16] His ongoing association with Black models is confirmed by Carlos de Laet, whose write-up of the 1895 Salon includes the snide observation that Brocos was the subject of idle gossip when seen traveling with an aged Black woman who served as his model.[17] Many years later, memorialist Rodrigo Otávio Langgaard de Meneses (1866–1944) wrote that his fair-complexioned son was the model for the child at the center of the composition.[18] The remarks about models from contemporaries establish the context in which Brocos painted and often offer a vantage point onto the social networks that Brocos accessed to construct a pictorial narrative of racial types.

The appeal of whitening was undoubtedly in the air in early Republic, and the newly reorganized national art school, which Brocos joined in its infancy, was in dialogue with the era's scientific and policy debates on race. In early January 1895, Brocos' contemporary Carlo Parlagreco referenced preliminary drawings exhibited in private that might soon develop into "a true work of art that will personify, set within our milieu, one the most incontrovertible principles of American Ethnology."[19] That passage certainly lends credence to the notion that Brocos was familiar with ongoing debates on racial types and mixture, though it does not

[15] C. Ribeyrolles, *Brazil pittoresco*, chapter 3; A. Perdigão Malheiro, *A escravidão*, p. 82. The significance of Ham in the Castro Alves poem is analyzed in A. Bosi, *Dialética da colonização*, chapter 8.
[16] D. Williams, "Peculiar circumstances."
[17] Cosme de Moraes [pseud. Carlos de Laet], "O Salão de 1895," *Jornal do Brasil* (Rio), September 25, 1895. The review contains the not-so-subtle implication that country folk speculated that Brocos and his unnamed model were involved in a sexual relationship.
[18] Rodrigo Otávio Langgaard de Meneses (1866–1944), a memorialist descended from a Danish family, wrote that Brocos had modeled the painting's young child on his fair-complexioned son, born December 8, 1892. Although Otávio Filho would have been about the age of the child in the composition, the claim that he posed for the canvas, written nearly fifty years after *Redenção* was first exhibited, may be apocryphal. R. de Meneses, *Minhas memorias*, p. 289.
[19] C. Parlagreco, "A exposição de Bellas Artes," *Revista Brazileira* 1 (January 1895), p. 50.

speak directly to Brocos' relation to any given strain of racial thought. Galician scholars Fernando Pereira Bueno and José Sousa Jiménez situate the canvas within a wider post-abolition immigration policy that was resolutely anti-Black.[20] Yet the artist's specific attachments to immigration policy remain opaque, and it's difficult to corroborate the implication that the anti-Black undercurrents of Brocos' social utopia novel *Viaje a Marte* (1933) directly inspired a painting completed nearly forty years prior.[21]

Our best clue to the painting's inspiration is its obvious Biblical referent, which can be substantiated in a brief passage in *A questão do ensino* (1915).[22] Sometime during his studies at the Imperial Academy (April 1875–April 1877), Brocos was assigned the theme of Noah's drunkenness for an exercise about canvas composition.[23] That student work (and the Academy records for that period) have been lost, but it can be confirmed that the Hamitic Curse figured directly in Brocos' artistic vocabulary. In a more general sense, there is ample evidence that Brocos took inspiration in Biblical subjects, including his 1883 prize-winning scene of Rebecca and Eliezer at the Well (Genesis 24) and *La adoración de los pastores*, a Nativity scene. A professed admirer of Doré's illustrated Bible of 1866 (a work that contained the plate "Noah Cursing Canaan"), Brocos was conversant with dramatic interpretations of Biblical passages.[24] Although *Redenção* is most often treated as a secular work in dialogue with nineteenth-century "scientific" thought, Biblical characters and themes surely animated the artist.

Biblical inspiration notwithstanding, the work exhibited at the 1895 Salon stepped far outside Scripture, shifting attention from the scene of drunken and angry Noah cursing Canaan to an arresting extratextual allegory of redemption. The drama at the tent is relocated to the threshold of a rustic house bathed in rich illumination and shadows. To the left of the canvas stands an elderly, dark complexioned woman, her bare feet on

---

[20] F. Pereira Bueno and J. Sousa Jiménez, "A *Redención*."

[21] On Brocos' sole work of fiction, see A. Juareguízar, "*Viaje a marte*."

[22] M. Brocos, *A questão*.

[23] "Ao mesmo tempo, ao aproximar-se o termo de ano escolar, [Meirelles] deu-nos um assunto bíblico a pintar 'Noé bêbado.' Aproveitou desse motivo para nos ensinar com toda consciência o processo para se realizar um quadro." M. Brocos, *A questão*, p. 9. A canvas of the same theme by José Maria de Medeiros (1845–1925), a Brocos classmate, was exhibited at the 1878 Exposição Industrial Fluminense.

[24] For the composition *Rebeca Dando de Beber a Eliezer* (1883), the government of La Coruna awarded Brocos a travel prize to Rome, where he was exposed to a wealth of religious art. His respect for Doré's Bible is registered in *Retórica dos pintores*.

unpaved ground. She wears a long-sleeved, dark brown coat with tattered sleeves, a long plain skirt, and a stamped headscarf. Palm fronds gently arch over her head, adding an Orientalist touch to a scene that is non-specific in place and time.

Next to the aged Black woman sits a younger adult female figure, of fine features and brown skin tones, who points with her right hand to the old woman while looking at a child sitting in her lap. A golden wedding band is visible on the younger woman's left hand that emerges from a striped blue shawl draped over a pale pink blouse with tiny polka-dots. The tip of a blue shoe peeks out from under a long, patterned skirt that falls just above the last of the stone pavers. The seated woman gently supports a chubby young child, perhaps one-and-a-half years old, dressed in a stark-white tunic with delicate blue ribbons adorning the sleeves and lacy neckline. The fair-complexioned toddler holds an orange in the left hand, modeling the familiar posture of Christ and the Orb.[25] The young woman and child each motion toward the old Black woman, who raises her hands to the heavens as if in thanks for a gift of divine grace. To the far right, seated and leaning against a wooden doorframe, is an adult male, Mediterranean in facial features and coloration, who looks on dispassionately with a slight smile. Hands clasped over the right knee, the muscular man is dressed in an off-white short-sleeved shirt, checked trousers, and simple leather footwear. In the shadowy background inside of the humble dwelling appear a table and a line of laundry hanging out to dry. Although the home's darkened interior is in sharp contrast to the child's stark white covering, the scene emanates warm luminous gradient tones of sunlight and earth, rough-hewn wood and stone, and weathered sunbaked clay.

Redenção is a fine example of Brocos as colorist, but in its compositional choices the painting might be more readily associated with the painter's lifelong interest in the stages of the human life cycle. Titles such as *Retrato de anciana* (*Portrait of an Aged Women*, 1881), *Retrato de joven* (*Portrait of a Youth*, n.d.), *Niño con piel de cordero* (*Child in a Sheepskin*, n.d.), *El joven violinista* (*The Young Violinist*, n.d.), *Niña cosiendo* (*Girl Sewing*, n.d.), and *Albores* (*Beginnings*, ca. 1888) demonstrate the affinity for capturing subjects of various ages that developed in the years before Brocos took up the Ham canvas. The painter had also

[25] It remains mysterious why Brocos chose an orange, though it may be worth noting that the landscape of the Baixada Fluminense, which Brocos would traverse en route to Guapimirim, was in the early stages of the citrus boom that lasted until the Second World War.

developed an eye for themes of intergenerational dynamics. The prime example (see Figure 13.2) is *Las cuatro edades* (*The Four Ages*, 1888), also known as *Las estaciones* (*The Seasons*). Executed in Rome, two years prior to Brocos' relocation to Rio de Janeiro, *Las cuatro edades* shared with *Redenção* the composition of a humble setting where four rustic individuals of progressively increasing age, from the infant to the elderly, enjoy a moment of domestic intimacy. A similar four-figure composition of unknown dating, *La familia* (*The Family*, n.d.), featured a young child sitting in his finely dressed mother's lap reaching out to another adult female, perhaps a nursemaid, while a bearded male adult in a workman's apron looks on.

FIGURE 13.2 Modesto Brocos y Gómez, *Las cuatro edades* (also known as *Las Estaciones*), 1888. Etching after oil on canvas, *Almanaque Gallego* (Buenos Aires) I (1898): 5.

Engenho de Mandioca (*Manioc Mill*, 1892), Brocos' most significant work of intergenerational relations painted prior to *Redenção*, is in direct dialogue with the 1895 redemption allegory (see Figure 13.3). The 58.6 × 75.8 cm canvas was first exhibited at a break-out show organized at the national fine arts school about two years after Brocos relocated from his native Galicia, Spain, to take up residence in the Brazilian capital. In a remarkable shift in Brocos' aesthetic attentions from the European peasantry to Afro-Brazilian folk people, *Engenho* presents an assembly of young and old Black females seated on an earthen floor in a large tiled-roofed structure familiar to the Brazilian interior. In the background stand more adult women as well as an adult male and a boy of perhaps ten years. The main drama unfolds as these figures peel, grate, press, and cook cassava tubers to make manioc flour. At the work's first public exhibition, Brazilian poet and art critic Adelina Amelia Lopes Vieira favorably noted how the painting included a wide range of figures – the older woman exhausted by work, a proud mother and her nursing infant, a smiling

FIGURE 13.3 Modesto Brocos y Gómez, *Engenho de Mandioca*, 1892. Oil on canvas, 58.6 × 75.8 cm, Museu Nacional de Belas Artes, Rio de Janeiro.

Black woman, a youth at work.[26] *Engenho de Mandioca* was, undoubtedly, an important rehearsal of a major canvas about intergenerational
family relations. In its close attention to a play of light and shadow, the material culture of
rural life (woven baskets, wood furnishings, slip-on footwear, a straw hat),
and the exuberant landscape that surrounded Guanabara Bay (referenced
through the open window on the left), *Manioc Mill* sealed Brocos' standing
as a respected artist of the national fine arts school. The careful detail of the
facial expressions and body positioning of the Afro-Brazilian laborers signaled Brocos' quick study of an adopted homeland and its lifeways of rural
production. The praise of Gonzaga Duque Estrada (1863–1911), an influential critic of the period, was especially important for establishing Brocos as an
interpreter of Brazilian social types. Gonzaga Duque proclaimed Brocos
a "pintor de raça," a subtle word play on the painter's natural-born talents
as well as his innate aptitude to paint "race," an obvious code word for the
Afro-Brazilians who filled *Engenho de Mandioca* and the actual manioc mills
of the late nineteenth-century countryside.[27]

Boosted by accolades from the likes of Gonzaga Duque, Brocos intensified the embrace of themes and tones that prominently featured Afro-
Brazilians. A 1893–1894 trip to Diamantina, a colonial-era town located
in the north-central part of Minas Gerais state, was formative for fixing
a Black Brazilian cast on themes of rural peoples previously rehearsed in
northern Spain and southern Italy. In Diamantina, Brocos experienced the
daily life of a mountainous region deeply rooted in the experiences of people
of color living among spent mining fields. His earlier studies of the Iberian
and Italian peasantry informed new works on Afro-Brazilian countryfolk.
Evocative titles from the trip exhibited at the 1894 salon include *Crioula de
Diamantina* (*Black Woman of Diamantina*), also known as *Mulatinha*
(*Young Mulata*) (see Figure 13.4), and *Garimpeiros* (*Miners*).

In short, Brocos was well rehearsed in a number of the thematic
elements to be assembled in *Redenção* prior to taking up the preparatory
work for the 1895 Salon. In addition to the interplay of age, family, and
agrarian lifeways, he experimented in the tonalities of the soil, flora, and
natural light of the Brazilian countryside. Brocos had acquired the critical

---

[26] A. Lopes Vieira, "Modesto Brocos," *O Tempo*, August 24, 1892.
[27] "Pintor de raça, pintor de fibra, nascido para ser pintor pela fatalidade impulsiva da sua
organização, e, sem dúvida, por influências hereditárias que eu não conheço, mas, é de
supor, existem como estão nos elementos psico-fisilógicos de todos os artistas, ele tomou
lugar bem definido entre os representantes da pintura contemporânea no Brasil."
G. Duque, "Exposição Brocos," *Diário do Commércio*, August 11, 1892, p. 2.

FIGURE 13.4 Modesto Brocos y Gómez, *Crioula de Diamantina* (also known as *Mulatinha*), 1894. Oil on wood, 37 × 27.5 cm.

respect of a "painter of race." The prize-winning canvas of 1895, none-theless, demonstrated important innovations in the strategic choices of subject. Chiefly, *Redenção* elevated the local conditions of an interracial post-emancipation society to the center of artistic expression. The fresh-ness of slave emancipation and the destruction of captivity were the subtext for a composition ostensibly about the "redemption" of the familial order mysteriously violated in Noah's tent.

In this perspective, the Biblical Curse of Ham is wholly upended. In the place of an infuriated Patriarch damning his grandson to bondage, a pitch-black woman stands before a male/female couple and their infant child. The young woman wears a wedding band, underscoring an observation made by various critics of the 1895 salon that the group forms a family.[28]

---

[28] In his brief treatment of *Redenção*, Rafael Cardoso makes a similar point, stressing a physical positioning that evokes a genealogical tree. R. Cardoso, *A arte brasileira*, pp. 102–107.

Rather than Ham crouching in fear of his father's scorn, the adult figure in the center of the canvas – a young woman of color – sits upright and calmly points toward her elderly mother (a figure Azevedo described as "the old African macerated by captivity"), who raises her hands in thanks for the deliverance of a self-evidently sinless grandchild. Noah's enigmatic curse of servitude and the degraded Blackness that came to be attached to it had been redeemed into sacramental interracial marriage and a fortunate, legitimate birth.

RECEPTION, CIRCULATION, AND REPERCUSSIONS

The Rio intelligentsia registered concerns about various technical and thematic elements in *Redenção de Cã* when the painting was first publicly exhibited in 1895. Nonetheless, the canvas was generally well-received by influential voices in Brazilian letters. Playwright Arthur Azevedo (1855–1908) declared *Redenção* a "national painting" (*o seu quadro é um quadro nacional*).[29] Poet Olavo Bilac (1865–1918) declared it to be a "most beautiful grand canvas."[30] Novelist Adolpho Caminha (1867–1897), though underwhelmed by the painting's qualities, conceded that "it has been a long time since a work has received so much praise."[31] The favorable remarks from these influential writers bolstered efforts by Brocos' contemporaries at the ENBA to have the work acquired for the national collection.[32] Such praise also guaranteed that Brocos would not be treated as an artist-traveler but rather as a painter of "national" focus.

In its quick passage from the salon to the national art collection, *Redenção* entered into the wide-ranging conversations about interracial relations in post-emancipation Brazil. That conversation followed two complementary registers. On the first, the central scene was taken to be an illustration of the fortuitous path toward racial "improvement" via miscegenation. Azevedo made the explicit case that an alternative title could be "The Perfection of the Race" (*O Aperfeiçoamento da Raça*).[33] A decade later, Sylvester Baxter, an American newspaper writer from

[29] A. Azevedo, "A Palestra," *O Paíz*, September 1–2, 1895.
[30] "Fantasio na Exposição II, a Redempção de Cham," *Gazeta de Noticias*, September 5, 1895.
[31] "A Exposição de 1895," *O Paíz*, September 14, 1895.
[32] Museu Nacional de Belas Artes, Rio de Janeiro – Arquivo Histórico (hereafter MNBA-AH), Pasta 33, Doc. 10, Rodolfo Bernardelli to Antonio Gonçalves Ferreira, October 22, 1895.
[33] A. Azevedo, "A Palestra," *O Paíz*, September 2, 1895.

Boston passing through Rio, echoed Azevedo, characterizing *Redenção* as a fine allegory of "the development of the Brazilian race."[34] These statements conditioned the long line of interpretation about the painting as an allegory of racial "improvement" through the science of race-mixing.

On the second register, *Redenção* furthered an imaginary of the Black race's disappearance into whiteness. Carlos de Laet characterized the painting as "a genealogy in which by two generations the Ethiopic element becomes white. An old Black woman had a *mulatinha* daughter who shacked up with a rube [*labrego*] and gave birth to a child that exhibits all of the characteristics of the Caucasian race."[35] Adolpho Caminha disputed the implication that whitening might be accomplished in just three generations, but the author of the contemporaneous *Bom crioulo* (*The Black Man and the Cabin Boy*, 1895) manifested confidence that the end product of miscegenation would spell the end to the Black race in Brazil.[36]

Most famously, João Batista de Lacerda (1846–1915), the prominent anthropologist and director of the Museu Nacional, included a reproduction of the Brocos canvas in the French-language print edition of his presentation to the Universal Races Congress held in London in July 1911.[37] Lacerda's paper, "The *Métis*, or Half-Breeds, of Brazil," envisioned the progressive disappearance of the Black race and the victory of civilized whiteness over darkness. Although Lacerda made certain concessions for the positive contributions of mixed-race people, the "science" of his presentation was patently anti-Black. The caption to the accompanying illustration encapsulated the message of Black disappearance, reading: "Black becomes white, in the third generation, through the mixing of races" ("Le nègre passant au blanc, à la troisième génération, par l'effet du croisement des races"). Such a postulation was hotly

---

[34] S. Baxter. "A Continent of Republics," *New Outlook* 894 (1906): 869–875.

[35] "Representa uma genealogia em que por duas alianças o elemento etíope se transforma em branco. Uma preta velha teve filha mulatinha, e esta, consorciada a um labrego, deu a luz um menino em que se exibem todos os caracteres da raça caucasiana." In Brazilian Portuguese, *labrego* can signal a Portuguese immigrant of low education. Cosme de Moraes [pseud. Carlos de Laet], "O Salão de 1895," *Jornal do Brasil*, September 25, 1895.

[36] "There is no doubt that in our American setting the white race tends to absorb the Ethiopic; what I question is that such a thing comes to pass in three generations." Adolpho Caminha, "A Exposição de 1895," *O País*, September 14, 1895.

[37] João Batista de Lacerda, *Sur les métis* (Eng. trans: "The *Metis*"); On the Lacerda paper, see L. Schwarcz, "Previsões." On recent literature on the London Congress, see I. Fletcher, ed., "Forum."

disputed in Brazil, and official census numbers and racial self-identification disproved the argument that the Black race was disappearing into whiteness.[38] Nonetheless, the caption was consistent with the appeals to racial "improvement" through whitening that had circulated since 1895 and framed what was to be made of *Redenção* for later generations.

The Brazilian eugenics movement, and its attendant dim view on the racial health of nonwhites, began to lose luster in the 1930s, a period of great ferment when artists and intellectuals, social thinkers, popular musicians, and politicians turned away from the fantasies of Black erasure.[39] *Redenção*, accordingly, lost much of its relevance and retreated into relative obscurity. Between 1937 and the 1970s, the canvas continued to hang in the National Museum of Fine Arts, but mention in the popular and arts press most often came in relation to *Engenho de Mandioca*, elevated to the status of Brocos' most important work.[40]

When the ideology of "racial democracy," consolidated in the postwar period, faltered in the mid-1970s, *Redemption* grew increasingly discredited as a shameful example of the long history of racial prejudice in Brazil. Brocos himself was generally spared charges of personally harboring racist beliefs, whereas his canvas was singled out as a deeply offensive emblem of white supremacy in a so-called racial democracy. In 1978, Afro-Brazilian activist Abdias do Nascimento (1914–2011) condemned the painting for its "pathological desire, aesthetic and social, of the Brazilian people to become white, imposed by the racist ideology of the dominant elite."[41] The arts world was less openly hostile to the canvas, but in an influential reference work on visual arts published in 1988, José Roberto Teixeira Leite characterized the painting as "one of the most reactionary and prejudiced of the Brazilian School."[42]

North American academics played a central role in fixing the transnational repudiation of *Redenção*. Thomas Skidmore's pioneering *Black*

---

[38] On the controversies surrounding the Lacerda thesis, see T. Skidmore, *Black into White*, pp. 64–69. See also V. de Souza, "Em busca."

[39] The complicated story of the decline of scientific racism and the rise of what would become an ideology of "racial democracy" is told by Thomas Skidmore in *Black into White* and "Racial Ideas."

[40] For example, Fléxa Ribeiro (1914–1991), ENBA professor and future director of Rio's Museu de Arte Moderna, described Redenção as merely a "feliz composição" (happy composition) while devoting an extended discussion to *Engenho*, introduced as "das melhores pintadas no Brasil" ("of the best painted in Brazil"). F. Ribeiro, "Algumas imagens."

[41] A. do Nascimento, *Brazil*, p. 140.   [42] J. Teixeira Leite, "Redenção."

into White (1974) situated the painting as an accessory to Lacerda's 1911 presentation in London. Skidmore's observations were picked up by Brazilian anthropologist Giralda Seyferth and North American historian of science Nancy Leys Stepan, both placing the canvas in the wider history of eugenics and anthropological sciences.[43] Scholarly monographs by Werner Sollors, Teresa Meade, Jennifer Brody, and Darlene Joy Sadlier also touched on the canvas' racist context and content. Several textbooks for the North American higher education market – by E. Bradford Burns, John Chasteen, Theresa Meade, Kristin Lane and Matthew Restall, and Henry Louis Gates – popularized the reading that the painting is an exemplar of the ideology of whitening.[44] Online journalism and most especially social media have extended the work of these academics, repeatedly presenting *Redenção* as an illustration of the persistence of anti-Blackness in Brazilian racial relations.[45] *Redenção* has become shorthand for Brazilian racism.

REDEEMING HAM, ONCE AGAIN: BROCOS
AND THE DESTRUCTION OF SLAVERY

In a 2011 piece of popular history, anthropologist Giralda Seyferth summarized the enduring understanding of *Redenção* as a symbol of scientific racism and whitening: "O futuro era branco" (The future was white). The fair-complexioned child at the center of the canvas – white, young, and innocent – is the primary symbol of that white future. The limitations of such an interpretation include the casual disregard for one of the most self-evident elements of the painting: the *velha preta* (the old Black woman), a figure who evoked a very recent past of slavery's destruction in the largest and most enduring slave society of the Americas, as well as her

[43] G. Seyferth, "A antropologia"; N. Stepan, *The Hour*, pp. 154–158.
[44] W. Sollors, *Neither White*, pp. 102–103; T. Meade, *Civilizing Rio*, p. 30; N. Stepan, *Picturing Tropical Nature*, pp. 141–142; J. Brody, *Impossible Purities*, p. 19; D. Sadlier, *Brazil Imagined*, p. 187. The textbook literature includes E. Burns, *A History*, pp. 317–318; T. Meade, *A Brief History*, p. 103; J. Chasteen, *Born in Blood and Fire*, p. 206; K. Lane and M. Restall, *The Riddle*, pp. 222–223; H. L. Gates, *Black in Latin America*, p. 45.
[45] Take, for example, the online transcript for "Skin Color Still Plays Big Role in Ethnically Diverse Brazil," *All Things Considered*, NPR online, September 19, 2013 (www.npr.org /2013/09/19/224152635/). Like other English-language discussion, this piece mistitles (and misidentifies) the canvas as "The Redemption of Cain." For one of the many examples of social media–driven popular commentary on *Redenção*, see the recurring mention on the blog "Black Women of Brazil," http://blackwomenofbrazil.co.

mulata daughter, a symbol of the experience of the children of slave mothers born in the last decades of the slave regime. In privileging the white future, interpreters place the agency of dynamic change on the male white figure and his even whiter child, leaving the elderly Black woman and her light-skinned daughter to be little more than bit players, objects of the voyeuristic (male) gaze. The prevailing inattention to these women as protagonists of their recently won freedom is striking, as Brocos' biography and artistic output in the 1890s indicate that he held a fascination with the formerly enslaved, especially women.

In this section, I consider how those stand-ins for the descendants of Ham – embodied in the two female characters, one allegorizing the Black African and the other the Brazilian-born *mulata* – are to be read as active agents in the reversal of the Hamitic Curse and the "redemption" of the Brazilian race. I also explore how Brocos acquired the knowledge to situate women of color as the central actors of an image that throws off the shackles of Black captivity.

The approach is informed by two provocations by Brazilian art historian Roberto Conduru. The first departs from the proposition that people of African descent were constituent elements of the progressive stages of modernization in Brazilian fine arts, from the latter decades of the nineteenth century through the 1930s. People of color were artists proper, representing themselves and the experiences of Blackness in a society ridding itself of its slave past.[46] Simultaneously, Conduru asserts, Afro-descendants were the object of study and representation of white artists.[47] Brocos and Redenção fall into the latter category. Linking *Redenção* to other paintings by white artists that feature noble Black subjects (e.g., José Correia de Lima, *Retrato do Intrépido Marinheiro Simão*, ca. 1854; Belmiro de Almeida, *Príncipe Obá*, 1886; Pedro Américo, *Libertação dos Escravos*, 1889; Antonio Parreiras, *Zumbi*, 1927) and well as commonfolk of color (e.g., José de Almeida Junior, *Negra*, 1891; Lucilio de Albuquerque, *Mãe Preta*, 1912), Conduru plots a fine arts tradition that does not conform to the aspirations of unidirectional whiteness and whitening. Conduru comes to no definitive conclusions, but his interventions invite us to look at and to look for the origins of the protagonism of

---

[46] A general overview of this history can be found in N. Aguilar, ed., *Mostra do redescobrimento*.
[47] R. Conduru, "Afromodernidade – representações de afrodescendentes e modernização artística no Brasil," in *Pérolas negras*, pp. 301–313.

Blacks (what he terms "Afro-modernity") in the fine arts (and, implicitly, in multiracial Brazilian society).

The second inspiration draws from Conduru's contextual reading of Brocos' *Mandinga*. First exhibited at the 1892 one-man show organized by the national fine arts school, *Mandinga* (then known as *Feiticeira*, or *Sorceress*) was re-exhibited alongside *Redenção de Cã* at the 1895 salon (see Figure 13.5). The principal subject is a seated dark-skinned sorceress who sits before a serpent, while another woman of olive complexion leans on a table. The eyes of both women appear closed. Conduru asks not merely what is going on in the image but how Brocos might have come to

IMAGE 13.5 Modesto Brocos y Gómez, *Mandinga* (also known as *Feiticeira*), 1895. Oil on canvas, 45 × 34 cm.

know about Afro-Brazilian religion and its practitioners. "Contrary to what one might think, this image could be quite faithful to what the artist would have encountered in the streets of the Federal Capital [Rio] at the time, especially if it is compared alongside the observations of João do Rio [author of *As religiões do Rio* (*The Religions of Rio*), 1906] and Nina Rodrigues [author of *O animismo fetichista dos negros baianos* (*Fetishism among the Blacks from Bahia*), 1896]."[48]

In making a case for a fidelity to the "real" and the documentary, Conduru's method calls for a closer consideration of what Brocos knew of Afro-Brazilian life in the post-emancipation context. He challenges the reader to consider the artist's ideological and visual education in the laboring and spiritual lives of women of color who formed part of urban daily life in Brocos' adopted homeland. Conduru does not discard the notion that the social milieu in which *Mandinga* circulated was rife with anti-Black racism, but he does speculate on the ambiguity of intent and an openness to reading Brocos' other works as products of the artist's direct interactions with laboring people of color who become objects and sub-jects of fine-arts production. Conduru's suggestive thoughts lead us to explore what Brocos knew of slave "redemption" and how that know-ledge informed his artistic output.

The reader is to be reminded that Brocos himself registered precious little about the inspiration for *Redenção*; any argument about his racial thought draws largely from indirect evidence and imputed motivation. Posthumous interpreters, nonetheless, help fill in the gaps. In the intro-ductory essay to the catalog of a 1952 retrospective organized by the Museu Nacional de Belas Artes, J. M. Reis Junior said of the canvas that "[it] raises the issues of an artist concerned with a theme of social import." In 1977, Quirino Campofiorito, another of Brocos' former students, wrote of the painting: "With a certain touch of humor, the fusion of the races in Brazil develops in the passage of four well-placed characters. Both paintings [*Redenção* and *Engenho de Mandioca*] speak to the social conditions that stimulated the artist's sentiments." In an early draft to the preface of the catalog for a 1952 retrospective, MNBA curator Regina Real directly raised the artist's engagement with thorny questions of race and color in Brazil: "[Brocos] approached difficult racial themes [*temas difíceis raciais*] in *Redenção de Cam* and the evolution of age in *Estações* [*Las cuatro edades*]." The catalog's final printed version read slightly

[48] R. Conduru, "*Mandinga*, ciência, e arte – religiões afro-brasileiras em Modesto Brocos, Nina Rodrigues e João do Rio," in *Pérolas negras*, pp. 315–325.

differently: "The Brazilian setting, the landscapes, the racial types, take hold of the artist and he reproduces them with interest and fidelity. We have family portraits of [son] Adriano and [wife] D. Henriqueta, scenes of Soberbo and Teresópolis, and the Blacks and their tribulations of liberty" (*os negros e seus problemas de libertação*).[49] With a certain echo of Duque Estrada's 1892 characterization of the *pintor de raça*, Real's attention to Brocos' relationship to *temas difíceis raciais* and Blacks' *problemas de libertação* pointed to the very proximate but generally overlooked relations to emancipation and freed peoples that the painter knew personally.

That experience began with the Free Womb Law (September 1871), passed eight months before Brocos first arrived in Brazil for a five-year period of study and freelance work as an illustrator. The law had envisioned a slow, largely natural process of abolition that would stretch into the twentieth century. Instead, prolific litigation and radical antislavery mobilizations progressively rendered gradual abolition untenable. Living in Rio just prior to the emergence of popular abolitionism, Brocos accompanied the demographic decline and geographic redistribution that set captivity on an inexorable path to obsolescence. Yet the demise of slavery was hardly sudden, and students including Brocos continued to interact with current and former slaves throughout their daily lives as residents of Brazil's largest slave city. Their professors grappled with disentangling the Academy from a culture of slaveholding that had been part of the institution's foundational years.[50] Outside his formal studies, Brocos worked within a world of print that became deeply engaged with the abolitionist cause, notably in the work of the Italian immigrant Angelo Agostini.[51] In short, Brocos had opportunity to preview the contours of the "tribulations of liberty" that fueled the collapse of Brazilian slavery during Brocos' extended absence from Brazil between 1877 and 1890.

Such contours conditioned the post-emancipation social landscape in all corners of Brazil, including a reorganized national arts school that Brocos joined as teaching faculty in 1891. This acclimation to post-abolition Brazil took place within a social network that linked Brocos' family residence in Rio's Catumbi neighborhood to the Fazenda Barreira do Soberbo, a rural estate located in Guapimirim, a small hamlet in the interior of Rio de Janeiro state, near Magé. Located in the upper reaches of

[49] All quotes taken from catalogs archived by the Arquivo Histórico, Museu Nacional de Belas Artes, Rio de Janeiro.
[50] D. Williams, "Peculiar Circumstances."
[51] On Agostini and the visual culture of Brazilian slavery, see M. Wood, *Black Milk*.

the Guanabara Bay watershed, Guapimirim (1890 population: 3,414) attracted sculptor and director Rodolpho Bernardelli (1852–1931) and his brother, painter Henrique (1857–1936), to make an artists' retreat at the foot of a verdant escarpment leading to the mountainside town of Teresópolis. Shortly after 1891, Brocos joined the Bernardellis as a frequent visitor to Guapimirim (see Figure 13.6).

In the shadow of the towering pinnacles of the Serra dos Órgãos, Brocos shared with the younger Bernardelli and other artists, including the Italian-Brazilian landscape painter Nicolau Antonio Facchinetti (1824–1900), an idyll of temperate air and spectacular scenery. Late in life, Brocos described his retreat on the Soberbo River as a place of great inspiration, where isolation and solitude released a creative spirit often held up by the interruptions of everyday urban life.[52] His artistic output,

FIGURE 13.6 Visitor Center and Museu von Martius (formerly the Fazenda Barreira do Soberbo), Parque Nacional Serra dos Órgãos/Instituto Chico Mendes de Conservação da Biodiversidade. Elizabeth Bravo. Undated.

---

[52] "Foi na Barreira do Soberbo, lugar alto, de ar oxigenado e aguas puríssimas. Onde tive minhas melhores ideais, tanto em arte como em literatura." M. Brocos, *Retórica*, p. 14.

especially in his first decade of residence in Brazil, confirms his later statements about the inspiration drawn from the clean air, light, dramatic landscape, and flora of the Soberbo watershed. An untitled study of the Teresópolis countryside and *Dedo de Deus* (both exhibited 1892), *Paineira* and *Mangueira* (*Silk Floss Tree* and *Mango Tree*, ca. 1900), *Cascata na Barreira do Soberbo* (*Waterfall at Barreira do Soberbo*, 1903), and *Recanto do Soberbo* (*Soberbo Retreat*, ca. 1903) document the inspiration taken from a grand natural landscape located within a half-day's train ride from Rio de Janeiro yet situated far from the bustling city's rapid social and economic modernization.

In Barreira and environs, Brocos also developed an intimate relationship with a human landscape deeply marked by slavery and its recent destruction. In 1895, the painter married Henriqueta Josepha Dias (1859–1941), heir to a large estate adjacent to the Soberbo River established by her father, Henrique José Dias (1819–1904). A one-time model plantation for the cultivation of cinchona (*quina*), an Andean tree used for the manufacture of antimalarials, the 1,500-hectare farm had been battered by declining yields and the unraveling of the slave regime throughout the interior of Rio province.[53] When Brocos first arrived in the vicinity of his future wife's estate, around 1891, cinchona cultivation had given way to manioc and other basic staples of the rural diet that also had markets in urban centers. Black family subsistence labor was at the center of agrarian production in and around the post-emancipation Barreira estate.[54] Brocos was clearly smitten with this laboring landscape turned over to manioc, and his first major work painted in Brazil, *Engenho de Mandioca* (1892), is a testament to his rising attachments.

In the absence of a comprehensive catalog of Brocos' opus, the titles, media, and dating of many of the works produced in this period cannot be treated as definitive, but it is clear that Brocos' visual vocabulary of the Afro-Brazilian post-emancipation rural peasantry sharpened in Soberbo between 1891 and 1895. *Engenho* depicts Black peasant families working manioc in a setting that looked very much like post-emancipation Guapimirim. Registries of titles of contemporaneous works – *Alegria*, *Libertação dos Escravos* (*Happiness, the Liberation of Slaves*) and *Marcolina, Ex-Escrava*

---

[53] In 1868, with the aid of the Imperial Ministry of Agriculture, Brocos' father-in-law had opened a model plantation to cultivate *quina*. With a subvention from the imperial government, the estate had increased to more than 12,000 mature plants under cultivation in 1883. H. Dias, "Cultura da Quina."
[54] A. de Sampaio, "Família escrava."

da Barreira (*Marcolina, Ex-Slave of Barreira*) – prove that Brocos circulated among the former slaves of his father-in-law's estate.[55] The portrait of Marcolina and a contemporaneous work, *Vista da Senzala da Barreira do Soberbo* (*View of the Slave Quarters of Barreira do Soberbo*, 1892), present direct evidence that Brocos came to know the faces of older Black women and the post-emancipation built environment of the daub-and-wattle walls, earthen floors, and open windows featured in *Redenção*. Although these obscure works are now known solely in catalog listings, several of Brocos' contemporaries observed how *Redenção* was exhibited alongside several other works that featured Black female figures. That is, the notorious allegory of a racial future was shown alongside documentary explorations of present Brazilian "reality." The titles, moreover, provide important clues that Brocos developed his work in dialogue with a recent history of Black women's struggles to redefine their legal, family, and work identities in the context of slavery's demise around Barreira.

The demographic history of Magé, the township in which the Fazenda Barreira was located, adds additional context for understanding the realities of rural life that Brocos studied in the early 1890s. Chiefly, Marcolina's counterparts had largely conquered freedom years before final abolition, without miraculous intervention. In the 1872 slave census mandated in the Rio Branco Law, 312,352 slaves were counted in Rio province. That population continued to grow, via the internal trade and natural growth, to 397,456, registered on September 30, 1873. Yet, by the new census completed on March 30, 1886, the number of enslaved in the province had declined by more than half, to 162,421. In Magé, the rate of decline had been much more pronounced. As of September 30, 1873, there were a total of 8,268 slaves (4,658 males and 3,610 females) counted. Between 1873 and 1883, 274 additional males and another 286 additional females had entered the township, whereas 2,481 males and 1,978 females had departed. With the deaths of 658 men and 764 women, and the emancipation of 135 men and 178 women, the municipal slave population on June 30, 1883, stood at 2,941 (1,658 males and 1,283 females). As of March 30, 1887, that figure had continued to drop to 1,244 (651 men and 593 women), about 15 percent the figure for 1873.[56]

[55] In the absence of a comprehensively researched catalog, definitive titles and dates are drawn from period newspapers and the 1952 and 2007 retrospectives organized by the Museu Nacional de Belas Artes.

[56] "Quadro estatístico dos escravos existentes na Província do Rio de Janeiro, matriculados até 30 de Março do corrente anno, em virtude da lei n. 3270 de 28 de setembro de 1885," in Presidencia da Província do Rio de Janeiro, *Relatório* (12 de Setembro 1887).

This precipitous drop in captives – in absolute and relative terms – took place largely in the absence of assistance from the emancipation funds, established under the Free Womb Law of 1871, and other gradualist measures associated with the legalist path to abolition that culminated in the Golden Law of May 13, 1888.

This demographic transition from slavery to freedom also transpired without the presence of white immigrants, who were disinclined to settle among poor rural Blacks. In a 1898 response to a questionnaire submitted by the central government to the municipalities of Rio state, the Municipal Chamber of Magé responded: "The population totals 26,300 inhabitants, almost all nationals (Blacks, whites, and their mixed offspring); there are few foreigners and those that are here are European."[57] Local leaders were undoubtedly open to foreign immigration, informing the state secretary of public works of their fair weather and conditions favorable to white immigrants, preferably from Portugal and Italy. Nonetheless, the southern European immigrant played a minor role in the social formation of the Rio state interior near Guapimirim in the period contemporaneous to the execution and exhibition of *Redenção*.

The absence of white immigration in the agrarian landscape transited by Brocos offers some corrective to the notion of agency that is embedded in a wide strain of interpretation about *Redenção* that presents the painting as a didactic prescription for the "improvement" of the Brazilian race through the reproductive union of immigrant male laborers and Brazilian *mulatas*. Whereas critics like Azevedo and Caminha saw the male figure as the transformative actor, the demographic data tells us that rural slavery in Magé was largely undone without new white arrivals. These demographic indices underscore the fact that the countryside that Brocos came to know after 1890 was populated by agriculturalists who had experienced abolition as a gradual and local process, rather than some abrupt end to an enduring labor system undone by humanitarianism, providential fortune, or foreign arrivals. It was largely a Black story.

The specific resonance of demographic trends in the lives and life arcs of the former slaves and free people of color at Fazenda Barreira shall require close reading of property and civil registries, particularly those found in local archives in Guapimirim.[58] A spectacular find would be the registry of

---

[57] Câmara Municipal de Magé to Hermogenio Pereira da Silva, reprinted in Rio de Janeiro (state), *Relatório* (1898).

[58] After several unsuccessful attempts, Modesto and Henriqueta Brocos and his wife sold the failing estate in 1920. Twenty years later it was seized by the federal government in

Marcolina's manumission and the family dynamics involved in her decision to remain at the Fazenda Barreira, quite possibly to live in the former
slave barracks that Brocos would later paint. But even the more mundane
records of the *meia-siza*, a tax on sale of domestic-born slaves, documents
the lives of slaves engaged in rural work (*escravo de roça*), domestic
service, boating, and skilled trades including tailoring and stone
masonry.[59] The surviving records, corresponding to the years 1863 to
1883, held at the Arquivo Publico do Estado do Rio de Janeiro (AEPRJ),
heavily favor transactions of single Brazilian-born *ladinos* (described as
crioula/o; *de nação*; *natural da província*) matriculated in the slave census
of 1872. However, the APERJ also included records of the sale of slave
mothers accompanied by their children. For example, in 1873 the tax was
levied on the sale Leopoldina, a thirty-five-year-old Black agriculturalist,
unmarried, and her five-year-old son, Belmiro.[60] By the time Brocos came
to know the region of Barreira, Leopoldina would have been in her mid-
fifties, and Belmiro would have been an adult. Both would have been
manumitted for some time, perhaps as long as two decades.
Nonetheless, both would bear with them the experience of slavery and
its often brutal dynamics of sale and dislocation, and also the dynamics of
abolitionism, including the prohibition against the break-up of slave
families imposed in the Free Womb Law of 1871.[61] Such experiences
might have influenced what Brocos came to see and render in the faces
of liberty.

The *meia-siza* records are among the many registries that should yield
further insights into the life experiences of the *caboclinhas, morenas,
mulatinhas, crioulas*, and other racialized and gendered personages in
Brocos' artistic output who, under close scrutiny, bear the marks of
a close, intimate history of the recent slave past. Future research will
yield more granular understandings of the transitions between bondage
and liberty in the rural hinterlands of Guanabara Bay and their translation
into the visual output of Brocos and other artists who ranged far beyond

---

bankruptcy proceedings. The surviving estate records, if any, have not been located. Due
to a series of jurisdictional changes, municipal and ecclesiastical records for Guapimirim
township are dispersed and unsystematized. However, an initial foray into parish records
is found in E. Ribeiro, *A capela*.
[59] Arquivo Público do Estado do Rio de Janeiro (APERJ), Fundo: Presidência da Província
[PP], Pasta 0368, Coletoria de Magé e Parati a Dir. da Fazenda Provincial, Guias de Meia-
siza, 1863–1883.
[60] APERJ-PP, Pasta 0368, Maço 6, Guia de Meia-siza for sale of Leopoldina, July 22, 1873.
[61] Art. 4 § 7.° "Em qualquer caso de alienação ou transmissão de escravos, é proibido, sob
pena de nulidade, separar os cônjuges e os filhos menores de doze anos do pai ou da mãe."

the Academy. Nonetheless, the regional demographic evidence and comparative cases from other regions of Rio province already demonstrate that the children of Ham were "redeemed" from bondage within Black spaces, in Black families, and between Afro-Brazilian women and their children.[62]

CONCLUSION

Close attention to the commonly overlooked conditions under which Brocos conceptualized and then executed *Redenção* offers some tantalizing prospects for documenting the Black agency that remade the countryside allegorized in the canvas. Alongside the unmistakable resonance of *embranquecimento* embraced by a long line of thinkers from Artur Azevedo to João Baptista Lacerda (and critics such as Abdias do Nascimento), we must be attuned to the voices of formerly enslaved peoples who also give meaning to the canvas. The gendered dimensions of these voices are strong, and there is special attention due to rural women of color. The womb as a passage to freedom is an especially important frame for reading an allegory of reproduction; it is directly relevant to a painting completed twenty-four years after the passage of the Free Womb Law – about the same period of time that might be ascribed to the age of the young mother at the center of the canvas.

With these working propositions, we acquire a set of tools to look anew at the Brocos canvas. Black women, rather than white men, help coproduce the "redemption" of the slavish sons of Ham. Although an allegorical appeal to whitening is unmistakable (and well reinforced in a long history of reception), Brocos' vision for the Brazilian race may not be so exclusively white. Without doubt, the elderly Black woman – by far the most imposing and active figure – is not to be easily erased from the post-emancipation order. A 2018 temporary recontextualization of *Redenção*, exhibiting the canvas among dozens of works about and by Afro-Brazilian artists held by the Museu Nacional de Belas Arts, suggestively relocates the female figure deep within a Black milieu that can be read for meanings constructed outside the white and whitening gaze of the historical permanent exhibition (see Figure 13.7).

---

[62] Two of the most influential works on the slave family in the rural southeast are H. Mattos, *Das cores*, and R. Slenes, *Na senzala*. The specifics of the interior of the Guanabara watershed of Rio de Janeiro province are treated in N. Bezerra, *As chaves* and *Escravidão africana*.

FIGURE 13.7 Tomaz Silva/Agência Brasil, "Das Galés às Galerias," 2018.

In a reappraisal of *Redenção* that considers the real alongside the imaginary, the dramatis personae of the story remain largely the same as those seen by the apologists for whitening, but the dynamism of the view shifts from the right of the canvas to the left, from the figure of the largely passive white male toward the elderly Black woman – a former slave, possibly an African. Her posture may have less to do with the awestruck wonder for the birth of a "white" grandchild purportedly fathered by the immigrant son-in-law and more to do with the culmination of a long process of securing the freedom of herself, her offspring, and her race. As we look yet again at the canvas, the dark specter of racial sciences and a whitened future remain, but those "tribulations of liberty" and the *alegria* of slave emancipation that Brocos came to know intimately animate our interest in this enigmatic allegory of history-telling and race-making in Brazil.

14

From *Crias da Casa* to *Filhos de Criação*

Raising Illegitimate Children in the "Big House" in Post-Abolition Brazil

Sueann Caulfield[*]

Historians often scour the judicial archives in search of micro-historical evidence of everyday life and the dynamics of individual relationships, attuned to the possibility that such evidence might challenge normative narratives constructed by previous generations of social scientists. I expected, for example, that a close reading of lawsuits regarding paternity in Brazil would challenge the paradigmatic "traditional Brazilian family" famously constructed by Gilberto Freyre in his 1933 account of hierarchically structured relationships contained within colonial plantation households.[1] According to Freyre, Brazil's national character had been forged through myriad intimate relationships among members of the "Big House," where the master's family resided with various retainers and enslaved domestic servants, and the slave quarters, home to the families of field laborers. In Freyre's account, sexual relationships between Portuguese-descended male patriarchs and Indigenous or African-descended women they held as slaves, together with bonds between white children and their black nannies, or black children and their white mistresses or masters, played crucial roles in the nation's biological and cultural formation. These relationships, Freyre argued, not only produced a variegated population that occupied various rungs of the social ladder but also symbolized the sensual intimacy and affection that underlay the merger of Portuguese,

[*] I am grateful to Paulina Alberto, Hussein Fancy, Susan Juster, Valerie Kivelson, Leslie Pincus, Helmut Puff, Rebecca Scott, Paolo Squatriti, and fellow contributors to this volume, especially Brodie Fischer and Keila Grinberg, for extremely insightful critiques of previous versions of this essay.
[1] G. Freyre, *The Masters*.

African, and Amerindian cultures, moderating the hostility generated by the violence of colonization and slavery.

Already in the 1930s, intellectuals such as historian Sérgio Buarque de Holanda soundly rejected Freyre's nostalgic vision of Brazil's slaveholding households, though without discarding his depiction of the hierarchical kin and patronage-based social organization and cultural values these households nurtured.[2] For Holanda, the "patriarchalism" of colonial society had left a cultural legacy of authoritarianism and patronage that stymied the nation's attempts to modernize and democratize. In the 1950s, sociologist and literary critic Antônio Candido celebrated the demise of the patriarchal family over the preceding 150 years – an uneven process that he attributed to urbanization – while emphasizing core elements of the Freyrean model and insisting that this type of family was the sole source of sexual organization and social identity in colonial Brazil. This patriarchal colonial family, Candido explained, had incorporated all but the "nameless mass of the socially degraded" who "reproduced themselves haphazardly and lived without regular norms of conduct."[3]

Since the early 1980s, Freyre's conclusions regarding racial harmony and national character have been thoroughly discredited by overwhelming scholarly evidence of systematic racism and violence in both Brazil's past and its present. Social historians have also rejected his (and Candido's) monolithic view of colonial society, revealing instead an enormous variety of family and household arrangements throughout Brazil's nearly four centuries of slavery, as well as social networks and norms that tempered patriarchal prerogatives.[4] While rejecting Freyre's romanticism and exaggeration, historians have also refined some of his insight into cultural features and racial and gender dynamics of plantation households. Specifically, they have described the ways violence, patriarchy, and paternalism worked together to structure social and sexual reproduction, producing variegated hierarchies of domination.[5]

---

[2] S. Buarque de Holanda, *Raízes.*   [3] A. Candido, "The Brazilian Family," p. 304.
[4] See M. Corrêa's influential essay "Repensando a família." Elizabeth Anne Kuznesof reviews debates among historians about the weight of patriarchal values throughout colonial society in E. Kuznesof, "Sexuality, Gender." For an updated discussion of research on family and gender under slavery, focusing on the nineteenth century, see S. Caulfield and C. Schettini, "Gender and Sexuality." For discussion of similar themes in English-language historiography, see E. Kuznesof, "The House."
[5] The seminal work is S. Lara, *Campos da violência.* For a review of scholarly assessments of Freyre, see A. Castro, "Gilberto Freyre e Casa-Grande & Senzala: historiografia & recepção," May 16, 2012, https://alexcastro.com.br/gilberto-freyre/, accessed December 13, 2017.

Early-twentieth-century lawsuits by nonmarital children demanding legal recognition of paternity offer a unique ground-level perspective on the legacy of family structures that were shaped by slavery. This type of litigation was prohibited in 1847, then reintroduced by the 1916 civil code. Over the decade that followed, paternity investigations, generally as part of child support or inheritance disputes, became one of the most common types of legally contested civil cases. Most were filed by children, or their mothers or legal guardians in the case of minors, whose alleged fathers occupied a similar or slightly higher social position than their own. In a handful of cases, however, nonmarital children described their upbringing in rural households that bore resemblance to the "traditional" extended family model described by Freyre, in which their alleged fathers sat at the top, and their mothers the bottom, of a multitiered hierarchy. The children themselves held an ill-defined position somewhere in the middle. They usually claimed that their father had at least tacitly acknowledged paternity. They were incorporated into his family not as recognized kin, however, but as *filhos de criação* (literally, "sons/daughters by upbringing").

This chapter recounts the experiences of two such *filhos de criação*, each born to enslaved mothers and raised in the households of white men who were allegedly their fathers at the end of the nineteenth century. Decades later, each of these illegitimate sons sued for the right to paternal recognition and inheritance. A host of individual circumstances and decisions explain the divergent paths that led one of them to impoverishment, alcoholism, and an early death, while the other enjoyed considerable social standing and economic success. Despite their contrasting fates, however, the two illegitimate sons' life histories and experiences in court show striking similarities. Each boy was raised by his alleged father's sister; both women were described as deeply religious and charitable. As their respective aunts' *filhos de criação*, both boys were treated "*like* family," while an unspoken promise of eventual recognition *as* family seemed to dangle elusively before them. When they grew up, the two plaintiffs were burdened by expectations of gratitude and fraught family relationships that reveal the fragility, and suggest the emotional cost, of their relatively privileged position within their households and communities.

FILHOS DE CRIAÇÃO "IN THE TIME OF SLAVERY"

The ubiquity among all social classes of the practice of child circulation – a term that encompasses the variety of ways children are incorporated temporarily or permanently in households not belonging to their biological parents – has been widely documented throughout Brazil's history.[6] In Candido's traditional family model, "the rearing of children of other parents" was commonplace, "a kind of exchange that indicates the broad structure of kinship and perhaps functioned to reinforce it."[7] In the eighteenth and nineteenth centuries, enslavers frequently used the term *crias da casa* or, more frequently, "my *crias*" to refer to enslaved children raised within their homes. Several historians have demonstrated that both female and male enslavers of diverse ethnic and class status commonly expressed special affection toward one or more of their enslaved *crias*. Close relationships between masters and *crias*, including bonds of codependency, were not uncommon, particularly when the social distance between master and enslaved was not great. For example, in her research on wills left by African-born freedwomen whose property included people held as slaves, Sheila Faria finds a common pattern in which, upon their death, these women freed most or all of the enslaved and, in a maternal gesture, selected at least one of the *crias*, almost always female, as a favored heir who would carry on the enslaver's legacy. Testators often freed *crias* while leaving the children's mothers enslaved. The well-documented expectation on the part of enslavers that formerly enslaved workers would remain tied to them for life through a debt of gratitude – an expectation that continued to nurture patron–client relationships well after the abolition of slavery in 1888 – was especially pronounced when the formerly enslaved had been *crias da casa*.[8]

Filhos de criação were usually distinguished from the children of the enslaved. They might be biological kin or other children who shared a similar social status with the household heads, or they might be lower-status dependents or servants. Their relationships to their adoptive parents were rarely legalized. In fact, formal adoption was so uncommon that the author of Brazil's first compendium of family law, published in 1869, remarked that it was pointless to even comment on it; it had "fallen completely out of practice here, as has occurred in all of Europe."[9] This was not entirely accurate, as historian Alessandra Moreno has demonstrated by

---

[6] A. Candido, "The Brazilian Family," p. 301; R. Cardoso, "Creating Kinship"; C. Fonseca, *Caminhos da adoção* and "Patterns of Shared Parenthood"; A. Moreno, *Vivendo em lares*. Child circulation is also a ubiquitous practice throughout Latin America. J. Leinaweaver, "Introduction"; N. Milanich, "Latin American Childhoods."

[7] A. Candido, "The Brazilian Family," p. 301.

[8] S. Faria, "Damas mercadoras" and "Sinhás pretas"; S. Graham, "Being Yoruba." Regarding masters' expectation of gratitude, see M. Abreu, "Slave Mothers"; S. Chalhoub, *A força*.

[9] L. Pereira, *Direitos*, p. 172. Pereira reiterated observations made by several jurisconsults since the seventeenth century. See A. Moreno, *Vivendo em lares*.

uncovering a handful of Portuguese and Brazilian adoption records from the late eighteenth and early nineteenth centuries. The records reveal a complex bureaucratic procedure that included approval by the Supreme Tribunal in Lisbon and written consent of all of the adoptive parent's legal heirs, since adoption could qualify a child for hereditary succession. It was certainly pursued by very few. Instead, adults who cared for *filhos de criação* generally created informal relationships that combined widely varying portions of labor exploitation, education, and loving protection.[10]

As demonstrated in Chapters 4 and 6 in this volume, by Mariana Muaze and Maria Helena Machado respectively, enslaved or free women commonly served as "mothers by upbringing" (*mães de criação*) to the household's children, including both the white offspring of the household head and various others. In the post-abolition period, nostalgic representations of the enslaved wet nurse (*ama de leite*), nanny, "black mother," and "black old lady" (*mãe preta, preta velha*) transformed these figures into romanticized icons of the traditional slaveholding family.[11] Many free poor women also nursed and cared for the children of others, often with the explicit or tacit expectation of compensation, either in cash or through the children's labor once they were old enough to work.

As slavery went into decline in the late nineteenth century, and after it was abolished in 1888, legal guardianship contracts were increasingly pursued by men as a way to acquire child laborers.[12] Guardianship contracts had long been drawn up for children who had been abandoned to the care of religious institutions. These children were frequently placed with families who agreed to provide for their education from age seven and to deposit a monthly stipend in a trust account once they reached the age of twelve, in exchange for their labor. These provisions mirrored laws requiring biological parents to provide for their children (whether legitimate or illegitimate), with mothers specifically charged with early childhood care and fathers responsible for the child's "education" after the age of seven. In either situation, "education" meant socialization, schooling, or professional training appropriate to the child's station.[13]

---

[10] A. Moreno, *Vivendo em lares*; L. Lewin, *Surprise Heirs I*.
[11] Such representations are featured prominently and colorfully in G. Freyre, *The Masters*. In addition to Chapters 4 and 6 in this volume by Muaze and Machado, see P. Alberto, "Of Sentiment"; M. H. Machado, "Entre dois Beneditos."
[12] J. Meznar, "Orphans"; G. Azevedo, "A tutela"; M. Ariza, "Bad Mothers." Henrique Espada Lima points out that employers also incorporated elements of paternalism and tutelage in labor contracts for adults in the post-abolition period. H. Lima, "Sob o domínio."
[13] A. Moreno, *Vivendo em lares*; L. Lewin, *Surprise Heirs II*.

Parents and guardians alike generally expected children under their tutelage to earn their keep and contribute to the household economy. Some, however, contributed more than others. In many cases, informal adoption or formal guardianship bore some similarity to enslavement, as is illustrated by competition for guardianship contracts in the late nineteenth and early twentieth centuries.[14] The continuity between enslavement and tutelage of free children is seen most clearly in the 1871 Free Womb Law, which freed all children born to enslaved mothers from the date of its enactment. As compensation for the expenses of these children's upbringing until they were eight years old, the law gave their mothers' enslavers the right to either profit from the children's labor until they were twenty-one or turn them over to the state in exchange for cash.[15]

In Gilberto Freyre's portrait of the Brazilian "Big House," children born to enslaved mothers and fathered by a member of the slaveowning family invariably counted among the *crias* and *filhos de criação*. Indeed, in Freyre's depiction, polygamy was a central feature of the traditional Brazilian family, a more-or-less open secret. Within their fathers' households, nonmarital children might be singled out for special favor or even treated as a member of the master's family, even if their fathers did not offer legal recognition as true kin or the patrimonial rights that came with this recognition. This was the situation described by Gustavo Nunes Cabral when he filed suit to demand paternal recognition in Rio de Janeiro, in 1917, and by José Assis Bueno, when he did the same in Jaú, São Paulo, in 1929.[16]

FILHO NATURAL OR FILHO DE CRIAÇÃO? EDUCATION, STATUS, AND AFFECTION AS PROOF OF PATERNITY

Gustavo Nunes Cabral

Gustavo Nunes Cabral was born an *ingênuo* (the term used for children born to enslaved mothers after the 1871 Free Womb Law) in 1886, in the

---

[14] J. Meznar, "Orphans"; G. Azevedo, "A tutela" and "De Sebastianas"; C. Fonseca, *Caminhos da adoção*, chapter 2.

[15] Brasil, Lei 2.040 de 28 de setembro de 1871, *Presidência da República, Casa Civil*, www.planalto.gov.br/ccivil_03/leis/lim/LIM2040.htm, accessed December 13, 2017.

[16] Arquivo Nacional, Rio de Janeiro, Corte de Apelação – 20, Apelação civil, Investigação de Paternidade, 1917–1923, apelante, Gustavo Nunes Cabral, apelado, Henrique Gonçalves, n. 3663, maço 413, gal. C (hereafter cited as AN, RJ, Investigação de Paternidade, Gustavo Nunes Cabral); Museu de Jaú, Juizo de Direito da Comarca do Jaú, 2° cartório, Investigação de Paternidade, autor, José de Assis Bueno, réu, Francisco de Assis Bueno, réu, 1929–1931 (hereafter cited as MJ, Investigação de Paternidade, José de Assis Bueno).

rural town of São João do Macaé in the state of Rio de Janeiro. His enslaved mother, Umbelina, was "a young girl of about sixteen and very pretty," according to witnesses. The law prohibited the separation of enslaved parents and their children under twelve years old, but, according to the lawyer who represented Gustavo thirty-one years later, Umbelina rescinded her rights to her baby at the baptismal font. The lawyer called witnesses who testified that Umbelina's surrender of Gustavo was arranged by Dona Teresa Nunes Cabral, a neighboring widow, "because she was certain that her son, Sabino, was Gustavo's father." This certainty also explained why Dona Teresa's daughter, Regina, stood as Gustavo's godmother.[17]

The opposing party in Gustavo's suit claimed that it was not Umbelina but rather her enslaver who had rescinded her rights as per the Free Womb Law. Indeed, grammatical ambiguity in the relevant line on Gustavo's birth certificate permits either reading: "[Gustavo is] the natural son of Umbelina, the slave of Dona Lauriana Rosa da Conceição, who declares that she gives up her rights that the Law confers to her over said *ingênuo*."[18] Both parties agreed that, after Gustavo was given up, Dona Teresa took the baby to her plantation and raised him in the Big House, where her son Sabino also resided. For Gustavo's lawyer, Umbelina consented because she understood that Gustavo would be raised as a *filho família* in his wealthy father's household. The opposing party insisted that Dona Lauriana consented in "an act of generosity," permitting the boy's upbringing by his charitable and childless godmother as a *filho de criação*.[19]

Sabino passed away when Gustavo was five years old. If Sabino had legally recognized Gustavo as his natural son, which the law permitted as long as a child was not incestuous, adulterous, or sacrilegious,[20] Gustavo would have inherited a sizable portion of the family's fortune.[21] Since

[17] AN, RJ, Investigação de Paternidade, Gustavo Nunes Cabral, 24, 314–318v.

[18] AN, RJ, Investigação de Paternidade, Gustavo Nunes Cabral, 24.

[19] AN, RJ, Investigação de Paternidade, Gustavo Nunes Cabral, 247–275, quotation on 267v.

[20] Portuguese ordinances, in place in Brazil until 1916, divided illegitimate birth into two categories: "natural," when there would have been no legal impediments to their parents' marriage; and "spurious," when the parents' union was adulterous, incestuous, or sacrilegious (as when a priest or nun broke their vow of chastity). Although the sacrilegious category was eliminated when marriage was secularized in 1890, the 1916 Civil Code otherwise retained the distinction between natural and "spurious" children, prohibiting parental recognition of the latter.

[21] Sabino had already inherited his portion of his father's estate. If Gustavo had been recognized as his son, he would have inherited Sabino's entire estate as well as half of Sabino's mother's estate (Regina would have inherited the other half).

Gustavo had not been legally recognized, however, the entire estate passed
to Sabino's nearest living heir, his mother. When she died six years later,
her estate passed to her only surviving child, Sabino's sister and Gustavo's
godmother, Regina.

Dona Regina, who was married but childless, took eleven-year-old
Gustavo along with the family estate when her mother died. She raised
him alongside four other *filhos de criação*, an arrangement that was so
commonplace that the question of why the children were not cared for by
their own mothers did not arise in the documents. Commonly, *filhos de
criação* retain a filial relationship to their biological mothers, most typically poor working women who place their children in the care of another
woman whom they believe could better care for them. Anthropologist
Claudia Fonseca describes such arrangements in a poor community in the
south of Brazil in the 1980s, where many people speak of having two or
even more mothers.[22] Likewise, it is clear in Gustavo's case that his *mãe de
criação* did not supplant but rather supplemented his mother's care.

Beyond sending Gustavo to school, Dona Regina seemed to play
a specific role in his "education," one that his mother could not have
fulfilled. As was expected of elite women, Dona Regina nurtured the
family's social network.[23] She used her connections to secure a job for
Gustavo in the city when he was sixteen, then she instructed him how to
behave in order to get ahead. The many letters she wrote to him during the
first six years after he left home (1902–1907), which Gustavo saved for
over a decade and were included as supporting documents in his lawsuit,
reveal her continuing efforts to "educate" him, placing him in a good
working-class job while teaching him proper manners and how to succeed
in a society based on patronage. Her first letter, brimming with joy at the
news that Gustavo had begun work (apparently as a pharmacy assistant),
instructed him to send her warm embrace to her friend, who had secured
the position for him, and asked whether Gustavo had already thanked
him. "If not," she instructed, "do so right away. You should always show
gratitude to Senhor D., as he went to a lot of trouble and sacrifice to place
you."[24]

At first glance, this seems to be an entirely routine command by an elder
to a teenaged boy, the kind of "education" expected of any parent or
guardian in most times and places. In the historical context that shaped

[22] C. Fonseca, *Caminhos da adoção.*   [23] R. Graham, *Patronage and Politics.*
[24] AN, RJ, Investigação de Paternidade, Gustavo Nunes Cabral, 68–86, 88, quotation on 72
(insert).

Regina and Gustavo's relationship, however, everyday "education" in manners potentially carried added weight. In taking Gustavo from his enslaved mother, Regina's mother had also freed Gustavo of his obligations as an *ingênuo*, which would have included providing labor until he reached the age of twenty-one to the woman who held his mother as a slave. Still, his status was akin to that of a freedperson – that is, not unambiguously free. Ordering a freed child to be grateful harkens to the law that permitted former masters to re-enslave freedpersons who failed to display gratitude.[25] As Marcus Carvalho shows in Chapter 2 of this volume, former masters made use of the law to defend their continued right to demand deference, loyalty, and labor of those they had formerly enslaved. Indeed, opponents of the Free Womb Law had argued that it would eliminate freedpeople's gratitude to former masters, thus removing their incentive to work and to respect authority.[26] Regina's letter displays these concerns, exhorting Gustavo to "be very obedient to your boss [*patrão*] and other superiors," while instructing him to remind his boss of his connection to her: "Until I have the pleasure to meet Senhor Moura, and his Excellent wife," she wrote, "be sure to send them my regards." The following year, she praised Gustavo for repaying money he owed to someone, reminding him that "the man who lies and has no credit is worth nothing in society."[27]

These and other letters revealed that Regina believed Gustavo was insufficiently grateful, obedient, and credit-worthy. The letters constantly urged him to "be thrifty" and to nurture his personal relationships, reminding him of her own affection and generosity while relaying news of neighbors and relatives who "always remember you and send remembrances." She frequently scolded Gustavo for not writing back quickly enough, failing to inquire about her health after an illness, or neglecting to send condolences to friends or relatives who had undergone hardship. One letter thanked him for placing flowers on the grave of her "saintly mother" while noting with irritation that he kept ignoring her suggestions. Reiterating this theme in her next letter, she wrote: "If you valued me, you'd follow my advice."[28] Constantly imploring him to "use good judgment," Regina's letters implied that he did not always do so and that her willingness to use her influence in his favor therefore had limits. After an apparent altercation, for example, she wrote that, while she understood

---

[25] Almeida, *Código Filipino*, book 4, title 63, 863.   [26] M. Abreu, "Slave Mothers."
[27] AN, RJ, Investigação de Paternidade, Gustavo Nunes Cabral, 73, 69.
[28] AN, RJ, Investigação de Paternidade, Gustavo Nunes Cabral, 86, 79.

his desire to get a better job and earn more money, "this requires patience and persistence" and that she would not do the favor he asked "for reasons I told you personally." In her angriest letters, she chided Gustavo for having overstepped boundaries during visits home: on one occasion, when Gustavo was eighteen years old, he slaughtered a pig without first consulting her; another time, when he was twenty, he took some shotguns after she had told him not to.[29]

In 1917, about a decade after her final letter to Gustavo, Dona Regina passed away, intestate. Her closest legitimate relative, a cousin, prepared to inherit her estate. Postmortem inventory proceedings were halted, however, by Gustavo's claim that, as her nephew, he was at the front of the line of succession and therefore had the right to inherit the entire estate. The documents do not indicate whether Gustavo had ever previously protested the family's failure to recognize him as an heir, but Regina's death came at the moment when the nation's first civil code made it possible, for the first time since the mid-nineteenth century, for a nonmarital child to demand such recognition in court.

In allowing children such as Gustavo to file paternity suits, the Civil Code of 1916 restored a long-standing legal practice that the Brazilian Parliament had banned in 1847. Medieval Portuguese ordinances had forbidden children of "damnable and punishable unions" (adultery, incest, or sacrilege) to inherit from their parents or be recognized as family members. But Portuguese law granted other children born outside of marriage, known as "natural," the same filial rights as legitimate children. Following Roman law traditions, recognition of maternity was generally presumed, as was the husband's paternity of his wife's children, which could be disputed under very limited circumstances. Paternal recognition of natural children, however, required proof. Judicial investigation of paternity, at the request of natural children, was therefore a commonplace procedure during settlement of a deceased father's estate up until 1847. In lieu of written documentation, authorities accepted a range of evidence, including witness testimony confirming that the alleged father had behaved publicly as such, particularly by giving the child his surname and affection and providing for the child's care and education. These procedures were consistent with the Ordinances' recognition of families formed through consensual unions (often referred to as "marriage as per the Ordinances"), in contradiction to Catholic Tridentine doctrine.[30]

[29] AN, RJ, Investigação de Paternidade, Gustavo Nunes Cabral, 71, 80, 86.
[30] L. Lewin, *Surprise Heirs I*; S. Caulfield, "From Liberalism."

Much more troubling were natural children who demanded recognition from men who did not publicly acknowledge paternity. The widespread practice whereby men from well-to-do families, and generally recognized as white, engaged in sexual relationships and even established households with enslaved or free women of acknowledged African descent produced legions of potential "surprise heirs." Children born to enslaved or poor women seldom had the means to file suit, and it was generally a much better bet for them to accept a tacit or explicit agreement to remain silent in exchange for whatever paternal support the father, or his family, offered voluntarily. Gustavo's upbringing followed a long-standing pattern in which elite fathers, or their families, provided for and "educated" their illegitimate children, sometimes bringing them into their households, without elevating them to the status of family member. Examples abound of fathers whose support permitted their illegitimate children to rise above their mothers' social station. Although many such fathers, as nineteenth-century French traveler Auguste Saint-Hillaire observed, "were cruel enough to leave their own children in slavery," others were inspired by affection, conscience, or the fear of God to free such children at the baptismal font or through their last will and testament, sometimes acknowledging their paternity.[31]

Beginning in the late eighteenth century, various reformers sought to lift the myriad penalties imposed on illegitimate children, arguing that they represented unjust punishment of innocents and promoted the concentration of wealth and power by patriarchs of sprawling clans. After Brazil became an independent empire in 1822, these arguments were revived as part of broader liberal reforms. By the 1830s, however, calls to expand the rights of illegitimate children were increasingly drowned out by cries for the protection of legitimate families from disreputable "surprise heirs," as conservatives warned that a decline of moral authority and expansion of popular access to local courts had produced public scandal in place of justice.[32] Similar debates had raged in revolutionary France and around the Americas, usually resulting in harsher restrictions on illegitimate children.[33] Brazil contributed to the trend in 1847, when Parliament rescinded natural children's right to demand paternal recognition in court. As Linda Lewin explains, the 1847 law reflected the

---

[31] A. Saint-Hilaire, *Segunda viagem*, cited in M. Iansen, "Os senhores"; L. Lewin, *Surprise Heirs II*; C. Lima da Silva, "Senhores e pais."
[32] L. Lewin, *Surprise Heirs II*.
[33] N. Milanich, "To Make," p. 767; R. Fuchs, *Contested Paternity*.

increasing insecurity of white elite families as importation of enslaved laborers continued to rise, revolts multiplied, and, most importantly, the likelihood of abolition in the not-distant future meant that the already large urban free population of color would soon comprise a sizable majority. Although the enslaved could not file paternity suits, freedpersons could. Moreover, in a political and economic climate in which older mechanisms for maintaining social hierarchy came under increasing attack and young men began to experience more autonomy from extended family, the possibility that a husband might acknowledge having fathered children with enslaved or other lower-status women was perceived as a growing threat. The 1847 law protected legitimate families from being forced to accommodate such children, not only by stripping natural children of the right to sue for paternal recognition but also by prohibiting married men from voluntarily recognizing them. Single men could still acknowledge paternity of natural children, but only in writing through a formal legal document.[34]

Arguments over the rights of illegitimate children continued to simmer in late-nineteenth-century legal doctrine and jurisprudence, and disputes over paternal inheritance frequently spilled onto the press. The debate flared up again at the start of the First Republic (1890–1930), reaching its height during the lengthy legislative review that preceded the approval of Brazil's first civil code in 1916. The outcome was a compromise: the code restored natural children's right to sue for paternal recognition if, during the time of conception, the father had had sexual relations, abducted, or "lived in concubinage" with the mother. Liberal jurists lobbied to include a Roman law concept, "possession of status of filiation," as an alternative condition. Citing the Roman legal criteria for determining possession of status (*nomen, tractatus,* and *fama* – the child has been given the father's name, is treated as the father's son/daughter, and is reputed to be the son/daughter), these jurists argued that such social indications of paternity were consistent with both Brazilian traditions and "modern" law, having been incorporated into the civil codes of Portugal and other "civilized" nations. Although conservative legislators struck this provision from the final draft of the code, Brazil's most prominent jurists nonetheless boasted that the code's provisions regarding illegitimate children were among the world's most liberal.[35]

---

[34] L. Lewin, *Surprise Heirs II*, pp. 286–304.
[35] Conservatives also inserted discrimination against adulterous and incestuous children into the code's final draft. S. Caulfield and A. Stern, "Shadows of Doubt," 3.

Filed just a month after the new civil code went into effect, Gustavo's lawsuit provided a testing ground for defining the conditions on which children could now sue. Each party included lengthy discussions of what legislators had meant by "living in concubinage" and the nature of sexual relations between "pretty Black girls" and wealthy white men under the shameful institution of slavery. Yet Gustavo's lawyer rested his arguments primarily on Gustavo's "possession of status." The lawyer emphasized that Sabino and his family had always treated Gustavo as Sabino's son and that this relationship was public knowledge, even though the family did not formally recognize it. As proof, the lawyer brought in five witnesses who had formerly been enslaved by Sabino's family, as well as a woman who had been raised alongside Gustavo as Regina's *filha de criação*. The witnesses corroborated the claim that "everyone on the plantation always knew" that Sabino was his father, that Sabino "never hid this fact," and that Gustavo was raised within the plantation's Big House, where he was differentiated from other *filhos de criação* by the "special affection" of his aunt, his "education" (including enrollment in a private school and the instruction and discipline his aunt imparted at home), and his family name.

The defendant's lawyer countered that Gustavo's mother could not have lived in concubinage with Sabino because the latter resided in the city at the time of Gustavo's birth. Like Gustavo's lawyer, however, the defense attorney focused primarily on disproving Gustavo's alleged "possession of status." Gustavo had never been recognized as a relative by the family, according to witnesses for the defense, but took the family name "just as many former slaves did, out of gratitude." Dona Regina served as Gustavo's godmother and *mãe de criação* out of deep piety and charity, the same motivation that explained why other poor children had been raised "within the family" (*dentro da família*). The undeniable affection she displayed toward Gustavo was explained by her childlessness and generosity of spirit. According to the defense, Gustavo's lack of gratitude and excessive drinking had so disappointed Dona Regina that she had put him out of the house, and she took this disappointment with her to the grave.[36]

According to Gustavo's death certificate,[37] he did drink too much: the document indicated that he died of alcohol-induced pancreatitis in 1920,

---

[36] AN, RJ, Investigação de Paternidade, Gustavo Nunes Cabral, 38, 68, 271–273.
[37] AN, RJ, Investigação de Paternidade, Gustavo Nunes Cabral, 364. This document records Gustavo's color as "white." It is the only indication of Gustavo's color in the case file.

shortly after his lawyer filed a final appeal of the lower court decision. The lower court had decided against Gustavo on technical grounds: when his alleged father died, in 1891, the law did not permit paternity suits; too much time had passed since then; and the estate had passed through too many hands. The appeals court confirmed the sentence, declining to resolve not only whether Sabino was Gustavo's father but also several legal issues brought up by both sides. What was meant by "concubinage," and what form did it customarily take under slavery? Could "possession of status" prove filiation? Were witness testimony and "public knowledge" sufficient to establish possession of status? What kind of treatment or evidence of status distinguished a *filho natural* (natural child) from a *filho de criação*?[38]

José Assis Bueno

Such questions also arose in the paternity suit brought by José Assis Bueno, in 1929. José was born in 1876 in Jaú, a rural municipality in the state of São Paulo. His mother, Dina, was held as a slave by Dona Teresa Assis Bueno, heiress to the coffee fortune of one of the region's wealthiest families. His father, according to the lawsuit, was Dona Teresa's brother, Francisco. In the act of his baptism, Dona Teresa waived her right to José's labor under the Free Womb Law, giving him the birth status of "freed" rather than "ingênuo." Dona Teresa later took charge of the boy's upbringing in the Big House of her plantation, where the alleged father, Franciso, also lived. Dina remained enslaved until slavery was finally abolished, in 1888, selling milk and produce in town while residing in the plantation's slave quarters with her husband, Jonas, with whom she had six additional children.

Dina's marriage to Jonas took place eight days before José's birth, making his civil status, and thus his right to file a paternity suit, much more complex than Gustavo's. According to José, it was a forced marriage, arranged by his father's family to protect their honor and patrimony. To reinforce the legal fiction of Jonas' paternity, one of Francisco's brothers, acting as José's godfather, registered the baby as the "legitimate son of Jonas and his wife Dina."[39]

Fifty years after these events, Dona Teresa passed away, at age seventy-eight. She left a will that named as her heirs "the seven children of Dina,

---

[38] AN, RJ, Investigação de Paternidade, Gustavo Nunes Cabral, 288–297, 390–391.
[39] MJ, Investigação de Paternidade, José de Assis Bueno, vol. 1, quotation on folio 7.

[who is] married to Jonas," including José, while granting the elderly Dina and Jonas usufruct of the shack and farm where they were living at the time. Teresa included special provisions to protect Dina and Jonas' five female children, who were to receive the most stable assets – rental properties in town, rather than farmland – and repeatedly specified that their spouses were not permitted control over any part of their inheritance. One of Teresa's sisters and an assortment of nieces and nephews contested the will, but the executor, another nephew, saw to it that Teresa's wishes were respected. When the estate was settled in 1927, Dina's six adult children (one child, the only other boy besides José, had died) each received properties valued at 250,000 mil reis, a considerable fortune.[40]

In leaving her estate (aside from small bequests to a local chapel and a close female friend) to the children of the woman she had held captive, Teresa's will was certainly unusual, though not unprecedented. Historians have uncovered examples of eighteenth- and nineteenth-century enslavers who left all their property to their *crias*, or children born to enslaved women and raised in their households, although such cases usually involved smallholders, not members of wealthy white families such as Teresa.[41]

The inheritance arrangement in some cases could be characterized as negotiations in which an elderly testator (Teresa was seventy-five when she wrote the will) exchanged a promise of inheritance for continued service and care through death and beyond, as many testators required heirs to attend to their funerals and postmortem care of their souls.[42] Teresa seem to have followed this pattern of codependency with Dina and her daughters. While the postmortem inventory proceedings were held up by Teresa's relatives, Dina's daughters requested a temporary monthly stipend from the estate, stating that they "had always lived in the company of Dona Teresa, who raised them, educated them, and gave them everything they needed, and they now had no means of subsistence."[43] If this was true, we might assume that the daughters, all then in their thirties and

---

[40] Museu de Jaú, Juizo de Direito da Comarca do Jaú, Cartório 1°, Inventário, Teresa de Assis Bueno, 1926, maço 48-A registro 1.7.2.904, folio 5.

[41] R. Slenes, "Brazil."

[42] J. Reis, *Death Is a Festival*; S. Faria, "Sinhás pretas"; S. Graham, "Being Yoruba" and *Caetana Says No*, pt. 2. For discussion of a similar situation of codependency in a matriarchal household in Buenos Aires, see P. Alberto, "*Liberta* by Trade."

[43] Museu de Jaú, Juizo de Direito da Comarca do Jaú, Cartório 1°, Inventário, Teresa de Assis Bueno, 1926, maço 48-A, registro 1.7.2.904, folio 109.

forties, and three of whom had married (two were widowed), had continued living and working on Teresa's estate. Teresa probably provided subsistence in lieu of wages, as the women are not listed among the salaried employees in the inventory (all of the employees listed were *colonos*, or recent European immigrant settlers who had supplemented the former enslaved labor force by the turn of the century).

Teresa's apparent intimacy and reliance on her female dependents, including Dina, who was her own age and had apparently been born on her family's plantation, in addition to her concern to protect Dina's girls from their spouses and her own decision not to marry, may have been influenced by her experience growing up in a patriarchal household with four highly aggressive and unstable brothers. This, at least, was how her family was described in a medical history by physicians who examined her brother Francisco at his wife's request in 1928, declaring him mentally incompetent.[44]

José filed his paternity suit a few weeks after Francisco's wife was granted control of her husband's affairs. He claimed that Francisco had recently promised to formally acknowledge paternity, prompting Francisco's wife's rush to have him declared incompetent and her "hasty and recklessly disposal of Francisco's property" with the intent to "cheat [José] of his rights as Francisco's natural son and sole heir."[45]

José's lawyer opened the suit with an emphasis on Francisco's subjection of Dina to "concubinage," describing the relationship as typical of the abuse suffered by enslaved women. Yet the lawyer was unable to enlist witnesses who had direct knowledge of the relationship. José wanted to call his mother and her husband Jonas to testify. The law prohibited testimony by immediate family members, but the lawyer was able to subpoena Jonas, arguing that he was not a blood relation. Jonas, however, repeatedly failed to appear on designated court dates. José's key witness, according to the lawyer, would have been Dina's "adoptive mother," whom he described as a "near-centenarian ex-slave [who] raised the unfortunate captive, Dina, and knows everything about the sinful

---

[44] MJ, Investigação de Paternidade, José de Assis Bueno, vol. 1, 30–42. The report indicates that Teresa's parents had twelve children, but it discusses only eight. Considering the aggressive and impulsive nature of Teresa's brothers (two had died in armed disputes, and one hung himself) and the mental illness of one of her two sisters (the same sister who, together with the children of the three deceased brothers, tried to obstruct Dina's children's inheritance), the physicians concluded that the whole family suffered from congenital syphilis.

[45] MJ, Investigação de Paternidade, José de Assis Bueno, vol. 1, 3–4.

cohabitation of the defendant and her adoptive daughter." He desisted
from calling this witness, however, because she had been "coached and
bribed by the defendant's ambitious relatives" and then "hidden by her
whites" (*ocultada por seus brancos*).[46]

Unable to establish concubinage, José's lawyer focused on his client's
"possession of status of filiation." The plaintiff's eight witnesses – all men
who had been intimate with the Assis Bueno family for many decades,
including a few of the family's former laborers, an Italian mule driver,
neighboring planters, and childhood friends of both Francisco and José –
presented a consistent story. One of the witnesses, who had been enslaved
"for many, many years" on the Assis Bueno plantation, went so far as to
say that Francisco himself told him he was José's father.[47] He and all the
other witnesses confirmed that "everyone in the Assis Bueno and Almeida
Prado[48] families," "everyone on the *fazenda*, including slaves and *colonos*," and "everyone on the farm and in town" held José to be Francisco's
son.[49] Even the defense witnesses agreed that this was "what everyone
said," although one of them specified that "he never heard anyone of
social distinction say this, although it is correct that this circulates among
lowly people."[50] Witnesses for both parties also agreed that José had been
raised by his aunt Teresa in the Big House, or, as the formerly enslaved
witness explained, "in the house of his whites, not in the slave quarters,"
where Dina and Jonas lived. According to the same witness, Francisco
"did not allow José to keep company with the slaves."[51]

By all accounts, Francisco instead prepared José for the work of "his
whites." After his own father's death, Francisco administered the family
properties, and he remained in the Big House through José's childhood,
along with his wife and his sister Teresa (and in earlier years, his mother
and other siblings). Growing up, José was often seen working alongside
Francisco when he wasn't at school. He drove oxcarts or supervised the
formerly enslaved workers and Italian *colonos* who replaced them. When

[46] MJ, Investigação de Paternidade, José de Assis Bueno, vol. 2, 328–329.
[47] MJ, Investigação de Paternidade, José de Assis Bueno, vol. 1, 98v.
[48] Francisco's mother, as well as his wife (who was also his cousin), along with several other
relatives, belonged to the wealthy Almeida Prado clan. The Assis Buenos and the Almeida
Prados had made their respective fortunes on the coffee frontier, establishing plantations
in Jaú in the 1840s, and then consolidated their economic power through various mar-
riages. See Luiz de Assis Bueno, *O Comércio*, Jahu, August 15, 1953.
[49] MJ, Investigação de Paternidade, José de Assis Bueno, vol. 1, 96–104; vol. 2, 144–173;
vol. 2, 262–263.
[50] MJ, Investigação de Paternidade, José de Assis Bueno, vol. 1, 79v.
[51] MJ, Investigação de Paternidade, José de Assis Bueno, vol. 1, 98v.–99.

José was a young man, Francisco set him up with a business in town. Then, in his early forties (eleven years prior to his lawsuit), José took over the administration of Francisco's property.[52] At that time, he apparently already administered Teresa's estate. His power of attorney, included in the case file, gave him complete autonomy over Francisco's affairs, empowering him to deposit and withdraw funds from his bank accounts, collect rents and evict tenants, enter or revoke contracts (including *colono* labor contracts), oversee coffee production and sales, and conduct other business dealings. He was apparently a skilled businessman and had acquired a few properties of his own. As one witnesses commented, he was already a rich man even before receiving his initial inheritance from Teresa.[53]

Witnesses for both parties also offered consistent descriptions of physical features of the various Assis Buenos. Responding to prompts from José's lawyer, they agreed that whereas José was "a light-skinned mulatto, with somatic features characteristic of the white race," including "straight hair, a fine nose, and blue eyes," Dina, Jonas, and Dina's other children were "very dark negros, with kinky hair, that is, [they were] completely black." Witnesses also generally agreed with the lawyer that "two very dark negros cannot produce a light-skinned mulatto child."[54] A great deal of the litigation centered on José's lawyer's demand for a "comparative physical examination" of José and Francisco, but the defense lawyer successfully obstructed his efforts, first by refusing access to Francisco, then by arguing that the poor state of the science on paternity determination rendered such examinations worthless, and finally (according to José's lawyer) pressuring or bribing the local physicians who had agreed to perform the exam, using photographs of Francisco, to desist, "in order to hide the shame of Francisco's people, rich people."[55] The lawyer finally obtained two medical reports from Brazil's foremost expert on forensic paternity determination, Dr. Flamínio Fávero, of the University of São Paulo. Although Fávero did confirm that race science indicated that "in short time, the black race will completely disappear from Brazil," as two black parents could not produce a mulatto child, he declined to compare José to Francisco or shed any further light on the case.[56]

José's racial classification, professional skills, and economic success set him apart from Dina's five daughters, who had remained entirely

[52] MJ, Investigação de Paternidade, José de Assis Bueno, vol. 2, 436.
[53] MJ, Investigação de Paternidade, José de Assis Bueno, vol. 1, 79.
[54] MJ, Investigação de Paternidade, José de Assis Bueno, vol. 1, 86, 144, 169.
[55] MJ, Investigação de Paternidade, José de Assis Bueno, vol. 2, 262.
[56] MJ, Investigação de Paternidade, José de Assis Bueno, vol. 2, 297–301, 345–351.

dependent on Teresa well into adulthood. It is not clear whether they, too, grew up in the big house. No witnesses say so, and their statement that they had "always lived in the company of Dona Teresa" is ambiguous. Their gender might explain the differences between their and Jose's "education" and subsequent social position, though José's claim that he was differentiated because he was Francisco's son seems entirely credible.[57] Perhaps because of these differences, José's relationship to his half-sisters was conflictual. A year before he filed his paternity suit, his sisters sued him over payment of a small debt (5,000 mil reis).[58]

Notwithstanding overwhelming evidence that José was widely reputed to be Francisco's, not Jonas', son, the judge who decided the case ruled against José on the grounds of "insufficient evidence of possession of status." Although the judge accepted José's comprehensive power of attorney as credible evidence of Francisco's paternity, he discounted most of the other evidence as hearsay. While acknowledging that José had been "treated as a son" by Teresa, the judge insisted that "this has no [evidentiary] value whatsoever" but simply followed "the tradition of the old Brazilian family to hold its good house slaves in high esteem. The black mammy [preta velha], the wet nurse, the so-called black mother [mãe preta], who so amusingly mangled Perrault's marvelous stories, appear in poets' lore and justify a monument."[59] In a split decision, in 1933, the state court of appeals confirmed the sentence, condemning José to pay the considerable court costs accrued over the nearly five years of litigation.[60]

CONCLUSION

The paternity investigations opened by Gustavo Nunes and José Assis Bueno offer rare insight into the internal dynamics of a particular extended

---

[57] The documents do not offer information about Dina's other son, who died prior to these proceedings.

[58] I have not yet located the lawsuit, but it is mentioned in a lawsuit by the lawyer who represented José in the case and complained that José failed to pay him. MJ, Juizo de Direito da Comarca do Jaú, 2° Cartório, Ação de Cobrança, autor, Fausto Guryer Azevedo, réu, José de Assis Bueno, 1928.

[59] MJ, Investigação de Paternidade, José de Assis Bueno, vol. 2, 476–484, 483. The judge might have been referring to the movement underway during these years to create a monument to the mãe preta, or black wet nurse. See P. Alberto, "Of Sentiment, Science and Myth."

[60] "Investigação de Paternidade," Acórdão, n. 19.420, Revista dos Tribunais, vol. 92 (November 1934): 446–450. This publication includes the brief verdict and the dissenting opinion by one of the three appeals judges.

family structure that emerged from plantation slavery, in which lower-status *filhos de criação* were raised to occupy a variety of differentiated social positions within hierarchical extended families. The practice of raising less-privileged *filhos de criação* in the household as family members, but unequal ones, remained a strong social norm, not only for the first generation to emerge from slavery but also for their children and grandchildren through the end of the twentieth century. These children seldom moved into the class status of the legitimate families that headed their households but instead often maintained lifelong, unequal relationships that combined different measures of love, affection, dependence, servitude, and resentment. Among these *filhos de criação*, the unacknowledged "natural children" of elite family members often occupied an elevated position. Yet the cases of Gustavo Nunes and José Assis Bueno suggest that if they tried to translate their elevated position into a legal claim to family rights such as inheritance, they might encounter a thicket of obstacles.

In the case of Gustavo Nunes, Dona Regina's letters reveal the ways these adults "educated" children in manners, including showing gratitude and deference appropriate to their station and crucial for survival. Dona Regina's limitations on the patronage and social connections she was willing to mobilize for Gustavo when he didn't behave according to her wishes, and her decision not to transfer to him a share of the family patrimony upon her death, much less during her life, also illustrate the ways *filhos de criação* were commonly differentiated from *filhos de família*, or legally recognized children, even when they were blood kin. José Assis Bueno's *mãe de criação*, Dona Teresa, followed another well-established, if less common, pattern, in which her *filhas de criação* and their formerly enslaved mother remained by her side, grateful and dependent, most likely working in her household and caring for her until her death, when they finally received a financial reward for their loyalty. The "education" provided to José by his father – again following long-standing patterns that had been solidified by colonial law – together with José's gender and lighter color, placed him in a much higher position, that of trusted administrator with authority over the enslaved and, later, immigrant workforce. This placement (*colocação*), together with José's apparent talent for business, permitted him to achieve considerable economic success but not equal membership in his father's legitimate family. Yet although the courts did not grant either Gustavo or José filial rights, each of the lengthy proceedings (and the split appeals decision in José's case) revealed continuing uncertainty over how to define and enforce paternal responsibility and family membership in the aftermath of slavery.

15

Slave Songs and Racism in the Post-Abolition Americas

Eduardo das Neves and Bert Williams in Comparative Perspective

Martha Abreu[*]

The world of festivities and music has always opened a wide range of possibilities for understanding the Afro-descendant and slave experience in the Americas.[1] *Slave songs* – understood here as songs, dances, movements, and genres developed by the enslaved – were, in Shane and Graham White's felicitous expression, powerful "songs of captivity." "Slave culture," they write, "was made to be heard."[2]

Slave songs profoundly marked the history of conflict and cultural dialogues in slave and post-slavery societies across the Americas. They were part of the repressive disciplinary policies of slaveowners, police, and religious authorities, yet they also proved critical to enslaved people's strategies of resistance, negotiation, and political action. The right to celebrate according to their own customs was – alongside demands for manumission, access to land, and family organization – one of the most important demands of the enslaved in their struggle for autonomy and liberty. The "sounds of captivity" – whether inherited directly from Africa or learned and recreated in the New World – were a constant in the *senzalas* (slave quarters), workplaces, plantations,

---

[*] This chapter is adapted from a deeper discussion in my book M. Abreu, *Da senzala*. Translated from Portuguese by Brodwyn Fischer.
[1] This is evident in works about Black identities and about the continuity of African traditions in the New World, even long after the end of the Atlantic slave trade. Among the classic works, see L. Levine, *Black Culture*. For Brazil, see J. Reis, "Tambores e temores."
[2] S. White and G. White, *The Sounds of Slavery*, p. ix.

cities, meeting places, and religious events of the United States, Brazil, and the Caribbean.[3]

But slave songs also had an impact far beyond the world of enslaved people and their celebrations. Slave songs became spectacles in social and religious events organized by slaveowners, who sought to impress visitors and demonstrate their dominion over slaves. In a depreciative and racist manner – often hovering between the grotesque, the ridiculous, and the sentimental – slave songs appeared in the blackface spectacles of minstrel shows in the United States and Cuba and were also performed by white artists and clowns in Brazilian revues and circuses during the second half of the nineteenth century. *Slave songs* – written here in italics to differentiate them from the songs sung by slaves during captivity – frequently took the form of coon songs, Ethiopian melodies, cakewalks, *lundus*, *jongos*, and *batuques*. These songs, though not necessarily their Black protagonists, enjoyed great success in the promising sheet-music market (see Figures 15.1 and 15.2), as well as in ballrooms, circuses, and theaters. They triggered memories of captivity and of Africa as well as racist images of Black people and cultures. As genres, they competed with waltzes, polkas, *havaneras*, *modinhas*, and recitatives and would eventually enjoy success in the phonographic industry.

This chapter investigates belle époque slave song performance on the stage and in modern cultural circuits throughout Brazil and the United States, exploring its many dimensions and tensions. Focusing on two Black musicians, Eduardo das Neves (1874–1919) and Bert Williams (1874–1922), this chapter will examine these tensions in depth, revealing in the process the Black diaspora's musical connections and links across the Americas and especially south of the equator.

Eduardo Sebastião das Neves was the first Black singer to make records in Brazil's emergent phonographic industry during the first decade of the twentieth century. In previous works I had the opportunity to demonstrate how Neves linked his musical production to crucial political questions such as the valorization of Brazil's republican heroes or Rio de Janeiro's urban problems. His music, published in widely circulating songbooks and recorded in the nascent phonographic industry, represented a noteworthy form of politics. At the same time, Neves' compositions also represented a musical connection to the slave past and the

---

[3] For an overview of Black music and festivities in nineteenth-century Brazil, see M. Abreu and L. Viana, "Festas religiosas." For the United States, see R. Abrahams, *Singing the Master*.

FIGURE 15.1 Sheet music. E.T. Paull, "A Warmin' Up in Dixie," 1899. *Historic American Sheet Music,* Duke University. https://library.duke.edu/digitalcollec tions/hasm_b0158/.

experience of Brazil's post-abolition period, a fact that may have augmented his success. For his repertoire, Neves chose themes involving slavery, the conquest of freedom, the construction of Black identity, and the valorization of *crioulos* (Brazilian-born Afro-descendants) and

FIGURE 15.2 Sheet music. Alberto Nepomuceno. *Suite Brezilienne*. Catálogo de Partituras. DIMAS, Biblioteca Nacional, M786.1 N-IV-59.

mulatas. Eduardo das Neves proudly called himself "the *crioulo* Dudu" and was proud of his talent as a singer of *lundus*, a comical song genre heavily associated with Brazil's Black population.

However, as my research advanced, I realized that an approach limited by national boundaries was increasingly insufficient. Eduardo das Neves was employed by an incipient phonographic industry that was based on multinational capital and had strong roots in and connections with the United States.[4] With that expanded perspective, I came to understand Neves' production as part of the musical field of slave songs, which had established itself as a privileged space of entertainment and business in various cities in the Americas between the end of the nineteenth century and the beginning of the twentieth.[5] I thus soon came to suspect – and suggest – that Eduardo das Neves was not alone. His trajectory paralleled that of many Black musicians from other parts of the Americas. His repertoire and performance style, in turn, echoed a larger set of representations of Blacks and what was understood as "Black music" in the commercial circuits of musical theater and the phonographic industry across the Atlantic World. The circulation of recorded music – that era's most modern cultural product – catalyzed the diffusion of musical genres identified with the Black population.[6]

This chapter aims to deepen our understanding of this history, valorizing the agency of Black musicians in constructing what Paul Gilroy has already celebrated as the "Black Atlantic," in this case south of the equator at the beginning of the twentieth century. Brazil's musical historiography does not usually highlight Black musicians' protagonism in the transformation of the musical field, much less their participation in international cultural circuits before the 1920s. Until very recently, Brazilian histories of music generally argued that Brazilian popular music was above all the space where a disparate nation united; that it constituted the cultural fruit of the intermixing of Portuguese and Black peoples. In interpreting Brazil's twentieth-century musical production, Brazilians have widely employed maxims from the myth of racial democracy.[7]

---

[4] The first recordings in the cylinder and disc formats were made in the United States at the end of the nineteenth century. US and European investors controlled the companies that dominated the market for discs and gramophones such as Victor, Columbia, and Odeon. Eduardo das Neves was under contract with Casa Edison, a Fred Figner company based in Rio de Janeiro. A Czech, Figner had migrated to the United States in the 1880s and discovered the world of phonography in the 1890s. At the end of the nineteenth century, he represented US modernity in Rio de Janeiro and Buenos Aires. At the beginning of the twentieth century, the largest company linked to Fred Figner was Talking Machine Odeon. See H. Franceschi, *A casa*.
[5] In relation to the possibilities of the new invention, see B. Wagner, *Disturbing the Peace*, chapter 4.
[6] See W. Kenney, *Record Music*; P. Archer-Straw, *Negrophilia*; W. Shack, *Harlem in Montmartre*.
[7] See M. Abreu, "Histórias musicais." Black Brazilian musicians' visits to Paris and the presence of jazz, jazz bands, or figures such as Josephine Baker on Brazilian national stages only attracted serious notice from the 1920s forward.

ATLANTIC CONFLICTS AND CONNECTIONS
IN THE POST-ABOLITION PERIOD: BLACK MUSICIANS
AS PROTAGONISTS

Abolition was a political landmark in the nineteenth-century Americas, but it did not substantially alter the paths already followed by slave songs in Brazil and the United States. Slave songs did, however, substantially expand their reach during that time, due to the acceleration of commercial and cultural exchanges in the Atlantic – both north/south and east/west – and the emergence of the phonographic industry.[8] At the turn of the twentieth century, a transnational commercial entertainment network involving circuses, vaudeville, and variety shows stimulated the widespread circulation of styles and people between Europe and the Americas. One result was a magnetic new form of dance music based on genres and rhythms identified with America's Black populations.

Complementarily, slavery's end introduced new elements to the discussion of slave songs' meanings and significance; across the Americas, emancipation opened possibilities for Afro-descendant participation in newly free nations and the extension of the freed population's civil and political rights.[9] Even in the United States, where outsiders had begun to recognize the immense value of spirituals after they were "discovered" by northern progressive folklorists at the end of the Civil War,[10] debates about Afro-descendant musical contributions to national culture and identity became important to the agendas of musicians, intellectuals, and folklorists.[11]

Slave songs did not disappear with abolition, as some hoped and believed would happen. On the contrary, and not by chance, slave songs – renewed in diverse genres such as cakewalk, ragtime, blues and jazz in the United State, rumba and son in Cuba, calypso in the English Caribbean, and *lundu*, tango, *maxixe*, and samba in Brazil – invaded the modern Atlantic circuits of Europe and the Americas in the decades surrounding the turn of the twentieth century.[12] They attracted the attention of erudite musicians and European

---

[8] A. Kusser. "The riddle"; T. Brooks, *Lost Sounds*.

[9] See F. Cooper et al., *Beyond Slavery*.

[10] In relation to the "discovery" of spirituals, see W. Allen et al., *Slave Songs*.

[11] I have analyzed these debates, with reference to W. E. B. Du Bois and Henrique Maximiano Coelho Netto, in M. Abreu, "O legado." See also H. Krehbiel, *Afro-American Folksongs*; L. Sanders, *Howard W. Odum's Folklore Odyssey*, chapter 1.

[12] See R. Moore, "O teatro bufo"; J. Chasteen, *National Rhythms*; B. Wagner, *Disturbing the Peace*, chapters 3, 4.

modernists,[13] as well as that of cosmopolitan businessmen and urban populations across the globe that thirsted for cultural novelties.

However, even as Afro-descendant music and dance achieved success on the world stage, free Afro-descendants' access to venues for artistic expression, citizenship, and society itself were increasingly limited by beliefs about nonwhite inferiority that also circulated throughout the Atlantic world. Scientific racism, which posited the inferiority and degeneration of Africans, would eventually inundate the musical world.

In nineteenth-century Europe and the Americas, Black bodies and their movements came to be interpreted on the basis of racist theories of sex, gender, and culture; resignifications of Africa in the modern artistic field would further reinforce the inequalities of racial representations.[14] Newly valorized representations of slave and Afro-descendant music and dance could still naturalize, rank, and ridicule cultural, musical, and racial identities and differences. Characterizations of Black people and their musical genres – projected in theaters, through song lyrics, on the covers of sheet music, in concerts, on stages, and in musical recordings – helped create and disseminate post-abolition allegories about Afro-descendant inferiority and racial inequality.

The success of slave songs during the decades spanning the turn of the twentieth century cannot be seen in isolation, nor as simply the fruit of French and European modernities, as the Brazilian historiography has often suggested. Nor can the slave songs be considered a "natural" or transparently "national" expression, as many folklorists once argued.[15] The slave songs' popularity certainly did not indicate the existence of a flexible space that facilitated slave descendants' visibility and social mobility. Their success instead needs to be researched through the deeds of the social actors who invested in the struggle for citizenship and visibility in the post-abolition world. The commercial ascension of rhythms, themes, and genres identified in some way with the Black population opened space for Afro-descendants who struggled for liberty and autonomy in order to construct new trajectories or fought successfully for

---

[13] The specialized bibliography usually cites the influence of Black American spirituals and folk songs on US and European modernist composers such as Dvorak, Debussy, Darius Milhaud, and Stravinsky. See R. Radano, *Lying up a Nation*, p. 74.

[14] See A. Lugão Rios and H. Mattos, *Memórias do cativeiro*; M. Seigel, *Uneven Encounters*; K. Butler, "New Negros."

[15] See R. Radano, *Lying up a Nation*; M. Hamilton, *In Search of the Blues*.

inclusion in the modernity of nations that were not willing to fully accept them.[16]

Although the slave songs' Black protagonists did not necessarily accompany the new and modern musical genres as they traveled through global commercial circuits, work opportunities for Black musicians did expand throughout the Americas. And this certainly contributed to subversion in the artistic field of racial hierarchies reconstructed after the end of slavery. In musical productions across the United States and Brazil, Black artists such as Scott Joplin (1868–1917), Marion Cook (1869–1944), Ernest Hogan (1865–1909), Henrique Alves Mesquita (1830–1906), Joaquim Antonio da Silva Callado (1848–1890), Patápio Silva (1880–1907), and Benjamim de Oliveira (1870–1954) moved successfully between the erudite and popular spheres. And their presence made a difference; even if Afro-descendant performers were forced to negotiate the traditional stereotypes of blackface, forms such as ragtime, tangos, cakewalks, and *lundus* gained new dimensions and meanings when they were protagonized by these talented musicians.

Despite racism and commercial profiteering, the musical field also expressed Afro-descendant struggles for equality and cultural valorization. As Paul Gilroy has argued (and Du Bois perceived much earlier), it never stopped being an important channel for the expression and communication of Black political identity across the Americas. Throughout the diaspora, slave songs and their musical legacy were essential to the struggle against racial domination and oppression and opened pathways for social inclusion and citizenship after abolition. It was thus not without reason that the Black leaders of the United States and the Caribbean chose Black music as a symbol of pride, identity, and authenticity in the political struggle against racial oppression.[17]

In my search for the slave songs' Atlantic connections and points of tension, I have chosen to focus comparatively on the Black musicians Eduardo das Neves (1874–1919) and Bert Williams (1874–1922) (see Figures 15.3 and 15.4). This choice deserves some explanation beyond the fact that the two Black singers were contemporaries who left similar archival traces or the existence of a relatively abundant bibliographical

---

[16] For this perspective in the Americas, see J. Chasteen, *National Rhythms*; D. Guss, *The Festive State*; R. Moore, *Nationalizing Blackness*; J. Cowley, *Carnival*; P. Wade, *Music, Race & Nation*.

[17] P. Gilroy, *O Atlântico negro*. See also, W. E. B. Du Bois, *The Souls*, chapter xiv.

FIGURE 15.3 Bert Williams. Library of Congress Prints and Photographs Division Washington, DC, 20540 USA. 1922 January 17. Photo by Samuel Lumiere. cph 3b12509 //hdl.loc.gov/loc.pnp/cph.3b12509.

literature devoted to Bert Williams.[18] Recognized for their *lundus* and cakewalks respectively, each man was a protagonist in the birth of the recording industry in his home country, and both found ways to benefit from slave songs' popularity in the cultural marketplace. Their trajectories demonstrate the degree to which the musical field became an important space for Afro-descendant representation and for the discussion – and subversion – of racial hierarchies.

Histories comparing the construction of racism in Brazil and the United States have generally emphasized specificities and differences, highlighting the role of explicitly oppressive legislation and violent Jim Crow–era exclusion in North America.[19] Without ignoring these unquestionable

[18] In relation to Bert Williams, the following works were consulted, T. Brooks, *Lost Sounds*; R. Martin and M. Hennessey (prod.), *Bert Williams*; L. Chude-Sokei, *The Last*; T. Morgan and W. Barlow, *From Cakewalks*. In relation to Bert Williams, see also A. Chartes, *Nobody*.

[19] The way in which "Jim Crow" came to designate segregationist laws and statutes – as well as the entire segregationist period in US history – provides interesting insight into certain

> EIL-O !

Eduardo das Neves, o famoso e popula-
ríssimo cançonetista e violonista brazi-
leiro, em 'excursão pelos Estados do
Sul, de onde nos enviou esta photo-
graphia com amaveis cumprimentos e
noticias de seus justos successos.

FIGURE 15.4 Eduardo das Neves. *O Malho*, Rio de Janeiro, January 6, 1917.

specificities, I seek here to call attention to important Pan-American commonalities in the experience of racism within in the musical field. Studies of the slave family, of enslaved peoples' visions of freedom, and

aspects of racial domination in the musical field. "Jim Crow" was originally the name of a Black character created for the theater by white actor Thomas Darmouth "Daddy" Rice. The character made his debut on New York stages in the first decades of the nineteenth century, and its enthusiastic reception there and across the United States helped to consolidate the genre of blackface minstrel shows.

of freedpeople's struggles for citizenship have already fruitfully explored Pan-American approximations; adapting this approach to the musical field helps us to better understand not only the actual history of slave songs in the so-called Black Atlantic but also that music's place in national imaginations and the experience of racism after the end of slavery. The musical field in the southern Black Atlantic is a new and fertile field of historical study.

Although they moved in different worlds and genres, Black musicians such as Eduardo das Neves and Bert Williams faced similar obstacles in their quest to find space in the musical universe; they were dogged by racist attitudes throughout their careers; they had to deal with the derogatory images that illustrated the sheet music and playbills of the works they starred in; they had to respond artistically to maxims about the racial inferiority of Africans and their descendants wherever they travelled and performed; and they often had to resist pressure to give up their African cultural inheritance. Although he lived far from the Jim Crow laws, Eduardo das Neves also faced racism during his life and suffered from the numerous limits imposed on men and artists of his color in Brazil.[20] Like Bert Williams, he left perceptible traces of his political activism in the struggle against racial inequalities.

Even though they were in constant dialogue with racist iconography – and even though they often incorporated prejudicial representations of Africa and slavery – Eduardo das Neves and Bert Williams embodied forms of Black identity and musical expression that were no longer imprisoned in the masks of blackface or circus clowns. These artists radically negotiated, resignified, and subverted the powerful canons of blackface. Both men inverted and played with representations of Blacks and with the meanings of the masks of blackface, using their critical artistic sensibility to reinterpret the legacy of slave songs and racist theatrical conventions that identified Afro-descendants with stereotypical propensities for music, joy, naivety, indolence, and easy laughs.[21]

---

[20] The long-standing argument that lynching did not exist in Brazil between the end of the nineteenth century and the beginning of the twentieth is currently being revised. In a recent book, Karl Monsma stated that it was not "true that Brazil was totally free of this type of racial terrorism." In western São Paulo, where Monsma's research is based, the cases are numerically inferior to what occurred in the United States, but the similarities with US lynching rituals and the profound local repercussions are evident. K. Monsma, *A reprodução*, pp. 137, 138.

[21] Louis Chude-Sokei uses the expression "Black-on-black minstrelsy" and notes the existence of other black minstrels who did not necessarily share Bert Williams' political

Eduardo das Neves and Bert Williams were artists who knew how to find humor in difficult racial situations. Neves specialized in *lundus*, a musical genre full of humorous and ironic stories involving *mulatas*, love, and the everyday norms of Black social life. Williams, according to a *New York Times* obituary from March 4, 1922, was not seen as a "great singer," but "he could 'put over' with great effect a song that was really a funny story told to music."[22]

Neves and Williams were born in the same year, 1874, and died not too far apart, in 1919 and 1922 respectively, a little before new genres such as samba, jazz, and blues began to be disseminated as national cultural emblems and celebrated as the musical expression of "Black people." It is unlikely that they met personally, although they could have heard of each other through their managers or through their own exposure to transnational music. Cakewalk was part of the catalogs of the phono-graphic industry and circulated widely in concert halls in the city of Rio de Janeiro.

The two artists also became public successes at the same time, between the end of the nineteenth century and the first decade of the twentieth century. Although the modernities of New York and Rio de Janeiro diverged significantly – and although New York mobilized far more capital for cultural pursuits – both cities epitomized urban culture within their own national contexts. Williams and Neves rose to the top ranks of the recording and theatrical industries and were much applauded in their own time, generally by white audiences; and yet both men fell quickly into oblivion after their deaths.

Neves made his name in the circus and gained recognition through his prowess on the guitar, in theatres, and in musical revues; Williams began as a vaudeville performer. Williams also participated in films, and Neves edited collections of popular songs. Due to their success, they later became stars in the nascent phonographic industry, with an ample and varied repertoire that touched on a wide range of everyday themes but which also always engaged with the question of race.

Williams, it seems, had access to education and was born into a family with some resources. He also received international recognition during his

engagement. L. Chude-Sokei, *The Last*, pp 6, 70. For other works about black artists and racist representations, see P. Alberto, "El negro Raúl"; G. Noiriel, *Chocolat Clown*.

[22] "Bert Williams, Negro Comedian, Dies Here after Collapse on Detroit Stage," *New York Times*, March 4, 1922, quoted in R. Martin and M. Hennessey (prod.), *Bert Williams* (CD3, *His Final Releases*, 1919–1922), p. 7.

visit to England, and after 1910 he was part of the Ziegfeld Follies, one of the most refined musical theatrical companies in New York. Neves never could have dreamed of such applause and recognition beyond the reputation he built from his phonographic recordings. He performed mainly in circuses, in charity balls, in variety shows, and in concert halls in Rio de Janeiro.

Despite these differences, I seek in this chapter to illuminate the parallels between the two men's choices and actions. Their commonalities show how much Black artists across the Americas shared comparable experiences and constructed similar responses to the problems and challenges imposed on Black peoples during the post-abolition period. In a time marked by debates about the possibilities and limits of Afro-descendant citizenship and national belonging, men such as Neves and Williams took advantage of the nascent phonographic industry to expand opportunities for Black artists and widen the scope of theatrical representations of Blackness. No less importantly, their presence and protagonism helped ensure the ascension of their rhythms and tastes in the modern musical market.

BERT WILLIAMS, A BLACK ARTIST ON BROADWAY

Although he was identified as an Afro-American and labeled himself a "colored man,"[23] Bert Williams was born in Nassau, an island in the English Caribbean. He arrived in the United States as a child and began his artistic life in California. From a young age he had been seen as a great artist and imitator, especially of Afro-American customs. He learned to play banjo early on and took part in minstrel shows all over the country, alongside both white and Black artists. After his first successes at the beginning of the twentieth century, Williams moved to New York.

In the 1890s he began to share the stage with George Walker, a young Afro-American from Kansas; their artistic partnership continued until Walker's death in 1910 (see Figure 15.5). The duo toured the United States, presenting Black songs and dances, which were great attractions for

---

[23] B. Williams. "The Comic Side of Trouble," *The American Magazine* 85 (January–June 1918), pp. 33–61, quoted in R. Martin and M. Hennessey (prod.), *Bert Williams* (CD2, *The Middle Years, 1910–1918*), p. 16. In his own text, Williams declared that his father was Danish and his mother the daughter of an African woman who had been enslaved in Spanish dominions; the slave ship that transported her, however, was intercepted by a British frigate, and she had settled as a free woman in the British Caribbean and married a Spanish cooper. Williams' mother was thus half Spanish and half African.

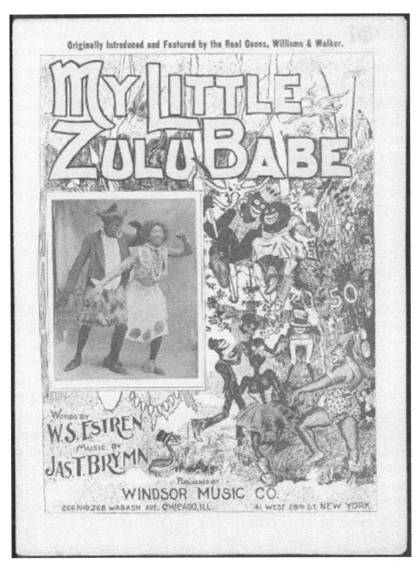

FIGURE 15.5 Williams and Walker. "My Little Zulu Babe." https://digitalcollec
tions-baylor.quartexcollections.com/Documents/Detail/my-little-zulu-babe
/12247.

the minstrel shows' white audiences. In 1900 the two artists were already
recognized as talented comedians and disseminators of the cakewalk, both
in theaters and in the international phonographic industry.

In George Walker's memoir about these early times – published in 1906 by *Colored American Magazine* – he revealed that the duo recognized and discussed all the wounds, persecutions, and prohibitions that plagued the professional life of Black musicians.[24] They were especially concerned with the success of blackface and the tunes known as coon songs. William and Walker made fun of these attempts at imitation, which they considered "unnatural." But when they accepted the moniker "the two real coons," they probably did so with the intention of showcasing Black talent and artistry.[25] When they reached New York, they found their first success with blackface performances in vaudeville and variety shows. Yet they always sought to present and represent – in a multifaceted and polysemic manner – Afro-Americans' "true" and "authentic" artistic and musical abilities. Walker believed that white comedians were ridiculous when they converted themselves into "darkies," painting their lips red and acting out exaggerated mannerisms for ragtime's artificial scenarios.[26]

Williams and Walker both achieved public recognition for their identification with Black musical and theatrical genres, although Williams enjoyed even greater success than his companion. According to a *Washington Post* article from November 10, 1898, Bert Williams "is one of the cleverest delineators of negro characters on the stage, and has no trouble at all in keeping his audience in roars of laughter."[27] This success led the Victor recording label to invite Williams to record his repertoire at the beginning of the twentieth century.

Williams' commercial recordings also had a longer life than Walker's. Tim Brooks attributed Williams' greater success to his unique vocal style.[28] Among the songs located by Martin and Hennessey from the first phase of Williams's musical recordings (1901–1909), the standouts are comic takes on everyday troubles, such as lack of money, and satires of female behavior. Nevertheless, the songs' titles immediately suggest that, when staged, many – some authored by Williams, some not – made what were probably meant to be humorous or ironic references to Africa, the

---

[24] G. Walker, "The Negro on The American Stage," *Colored American Magazine* II, no. 4 (October 1906), quoted in L. Chude-Sokei, *The Last*, pp. 26–28, 165, 271.

[25] L. Chude-Sokei, *The Last*, p. 6.

[26] G. Walker, "The Negro on The American Stage," *Colored American Magazine* II, no. 4 (October 1906), p. 248, quoted in L. Chude-Sokei, *The Last*, pp. 32–33.

[27] Quoted in R. Martin and M. Hennessey (prod.), *Bert Williams* (CD1, *The Early Years, 1901–1909*), p. 11.

[28] T. Brooks, *Lost Sounds*, p. 115.

"racial question," the world of slavery, and the nature of Black men (this last theme was especially prevalent in the "coon song" genre): "My Castle on the River Nile," "African Repatriation," "My Little Zulu Babe," "The Ghost of Coon," "I Don´t Like de Face You Wear," "Skin Lightening," "She's Getting More Like the White Folks," "Where Was Moses When the Light Went Out" (a spiritual from the nineteenth century), and "The Phrenologist Coon."

In the early 1900s, Williams and Walker also managed to produce their first pioneering Broadway musicals, which starred exclusively Black artists, breaking free of the limitations imposed by the ragtime "darky" style.[29] In 1903, *In Dahomey* opened; afterward came *Abyssinia* (1906), in which Bert Williams also participated as a composer and lyricist, and *Bandanna Land* (1908). The songs, librettos, and song lyrics – some of which had already been recorded – were authored by Black composers such as Will Marion Cook, Paul L. Dunbar, J. A. Shipp, and Alex Rogers. All were part of the artistic world of Harlem, where intellectuals, artists and musicians from the United States, the Caribbean, and beyond came together to transform the city of New York into the greatest center of Pan-African arts in the United States.[30] As Walker put it in his memoirs, Harlem was the rendezvous point for artists from "our race."[31]

Although these shows came in for their share of criticism, they were reasonably well-received by the general public. *In Dahomey* even traveled to London and gave a highly praised command performance for King Edward VII. *Bandanna Land* was even more successful: *Theatre Magazine* especially praised the singers' performances and the show's lack of vulgarity.[32]

According to Walker's 1906 memoirs, *In Dahomey* introduced a US audience to the novelty of "purely African" themes. Williams and Walker were, by their own account, pioneers in introducing "Americanized

---

[29] Walker's wife, Ada Overton Walker, also participated in the production with much success. See L. Chude-Sokei, *The Last*, chapter 1. Due to the limits of this chapter, I will not be able to examine in depth the evident gendered dimensions of Bert Williams' and Eduardo das Neves' work.

[30] According to Chude-Sokei, Harlem's Pan-African character, and especially the presence of Black migrants from the Caribbean, allowed Bert Williams to express in his music a modern perspective on transcultural encounters within the heterogeneous Atlantic world. L. Chude-Sokei, *The Last*, pp, 22, 44, 45.

[31] G. Walker, "The Negro on The American Stage," *Colored American Magazine* II, no. 4 (October 1906), pp. 247, quoted in L. Chude-Sokei, *The Last*, p. 26.

[32] R. Martin and M. Hennessey (prod.), *Bert Williams* (CD1, *The Early Years, 1901–1904*), p. 27.

African songs" such as "My Little Zulu Babe," "My Castle on the Nile," and "My Dahomian Queen."[33] However, despite this quest to expand the limits of Black representation, they could not avoid ending the show with a cakewalk, a convention that was considered obligatory for ragtime spectacles featuring "darkies" and "coons." By the early 1900s, despite its subversive origins among nineteenth-century plantation slaves, the cakewalk evoked a certain nostalgia for old Southern plantation life and also guaranteed success to any Broadway show. The duo of Williams and Walker had made their name by performing cakewalks in the 1890s.[34]

In Dahomey and *Abyssinia* showed once again the degree to which Williams and Walker engaged artistically with their era's racial politics. They showed great familiarity with international debates and discussions among Black leaders in the US about the role of Africa and the African past in the history of Blacks across the Americas.[35] In Chude-Sokei's synopsis, *In Dahomey* (1903) was about a dishonest group of Boston investors who proposed a great opportunity in Africa for the oppressed Blacks of the United States.[36] Walker, masquerading as the "Prince of Dahomey," tries to convince hundreds of Floridian Afro-descendants to explore the wonders of his purported homeland. The song "My Castle on the River Nile" musically reinforced these dreams of wealth and power.[37] *Abyssinia*, from 1906, told the story of two friends (Walker and Williams) who, after winning the lottery, resolved to visit the land of their ancestors with some fellow African-American tourists. They had many adventures en route, even coming into conflict with Emperor Menelik II of Ethiopia and being condemned in an

---

[33] R. Martin and M. Hennessey (prod.), *Bert Williams* (CD1, *The Early Years, 1901–1904*), p. 19.
[34] T. Morgan and W. Barlow, *From Cakewalks*, p. 65; L. Chude-Sokei, *The Last*, p. 166.
[35] In relation to disputes among Black leaders in the United States over Africa and its legacy, see S. Capone, *Os Yoruba*. According to Capone, the connection with Africa "was one of the most delicate questions discussed by the first Black nationalist groups" (p. 69). Many activists and intellectuals had reservations about the way in which Williams represented Africa in some of his works. See L. Chude-Sokei, *The Last*, p. 166.
[36] L. Chude-Sokei, *The Last*, pp. 177–178.
[37] The idea of staging *In Dahomey* began after 1893, when natives from Dahomey were exhibited in the Midwinter Fair in San Francisco. Since the native Dahomeans arrived late for the exhibition, African-Americans were hired and exhibited in their place. Williams and Walker were among those hired and subsequently fired shortly after the arrival of the Africans. With free access to the Fair, the pair were able to enter into direct contact with Africans for the first time. Based on that experience Willliams and Walker began to develop plans for a show with a Dahomian theme. About *In Dahomey*, see L. Chude-Sokei, *The Last*, chapter 5, p. 177.

Ethiopian court.[38] Not all the songs from these shows were recorded, but some from *Abyssinia*, such as "Nobody," "Pretty Desdemone," "Let it Alone," and "Here it Comes Again," were eventually distributed by Columbia.[39]

In 1909 George Walker fell ill, and in 1911 he died. Bert Williams, after creating a few other shows with his troop of Black artists, embarked in 1910 for a career in the famous Ziegfeld Follies revue. In this company he worked for almost ten years among white artists, specializing in the original comic sketches that brought him his greatest success. In the Ziegfeld Follies he adopted the clothes that would become his visual trademark: a top hat, high-water trousers, and worn-out shoes. In general, he performed comic roles, poking fun at the misfortunes of taxi drivers, train porters, and poker players. He also touched on subjects of wide popular relevance, such as Prohibition and the question of US participation in the First World War.

During these years, Williams left most material related to Africa behind, but representations of slavery and race relations remained in his comic sketches and in a series of monologues based on folktales from the Afro-American tradition. Bert Williams seems to have continued to be a sui generis "real coon," but he now performed the role solo in an outstanding Broadway company. Among his Columbia recordings from this phase, some dealt with Afro-American questions, such as those that recounted the history of a "trickster" called Sam; told of a slave who had made a pact with the devil ("How? Fried"); parodied the alleged superstition of Blacks ("You Can't Do Nothing till Martin Gets Here"); and portrayed preachers and religious doctrines ("You Will Never Need a Doctor No More").[40] "Nobody," written at the time of *Abyssinia*, continued to be Williams' greatest hit. Among his skits, "Darktown Poker Club" stands out because it allowed him to touch directly on racial stereotypes.

[38] News of Abyssinia, known as Ethiopia, circulated in the newspapers of the Atlantic, including in Brazil, because of Emporer Menelik II's 1896 victory over the Italians. Abyssinia had become an obstacle to imperialist expansion in that region of Africa.

[39] R. Martin and M. Hennessey (prod.), *Bert Williams* (CD1, *The Early Years, 1901–1909*), p. 23. Desdemona was of course the lover of the Moor Othello in Shakespeare's play. "Nobody" became Bert Williams' greatest success. At once ironic and sad, it represented a poetic form of self-denial and devaluation. On the rupture that Williams and Walker's performance represented in relation to the previous paradigms of minstrel shows, see Daphne A. Brooks' important book *Bodies in Dissent*.

[40] R. Martin and M. Hennessey (prod.), *Bert Williams* (CD2, *The Middle Years, 1910–1918*), pp. 8, 20.

In the final phase of his life, between 1919 and 1922, Bert Williams continued to record discs and appear in shows, although he had by then left the Ziegfeld Follies. In his final years, despite widespread recognition and success as a recording artist (he was named a "Columbia Exclusive Artist" a little before the jazz boom), he also left indications of darker moments, due largely to the isolation he appeared to feel in the white artistic world.[41] In an autobiographical text, published in *The American Magazine* in January 1918, Williams reported that he was often asked "if he would not give anything to be white." He had the following response:

> There is many a white man less fortunate and less well equipped than I am. In truth, I have never been able to discover that there was anything disgraceful in being a colored man. But I have often found it inconvenient – in America.[42]

Louis Chude-Sokei's work highlights the fact that Bert Williams' actions were not restricted to his stage successes. He also supported education and community development projects in Harlem, including the creation of the first Black National Guard in 1911 and the projected but never realized "Williams and Walker International and Interracial Ethiopian Theatre in New York City."[43]

Critical response to Bert Williams' musical corpus was not unanimous, and observers have understood his contributions differently over time. Until recently, many observers and scholars criticized Williams for reproducing white stereotypes of Blackness. That interpretation does much to explain Williams' relative obscurity after 1920, when Black intellectuals of the Harlem Renaissance began to embrace another aesthetic that idealized the "new negro," free of the masks of blackface. Other authors, however, argue that Bert Williams pushed the boundaries of prejudice and even transcended his racial condition, becoming a universally recognized comedian on the stages of the United States in defiance of prejudice and racial restrictions.[44]

Williams' Black contemporaries often saw him in a different and more positive light. Leading intellectual and activist Booker T. Washington, for example, wrote that Bert Williams had "done more for the race" than he

---

[41] In his text "The Comic Side of Trouble," Williams reports that when Mr. Ziegfeld set out to hire him, the artists of the company made a "tremendous storm in a teacup," threatening to abandon and boycott the company. R. Martin and M. Hennessey (prod.), *Bert Williams* (CD2, *The Middle Years, 1910–1918*), p. 19. See also T. Brooks, *Lost Sounds*, p. 114; L. Chude-Sokei, *The Last*, p. 23.

[42] B. Williams, "The Comic Side of Trouble," quoted in R. Martin and M. Hennessey, *Bert Williams* (CD2, *The Middle Years, 1910–1918*), p. 16.

[43] L. Chude-Sokei, *The Last*, p. 27.   [44] See T. Brooks, *Lost Sounds*, pp. 111, 117.

had. James Weldon Johnson, a star of the Harlem Renaissance, recognized the global importance of ragtime and cakewalk, because they were Black genres that had conquered the United States, France, and the Americas. According to Johnson, Black artists such as Bert Williams had transformed blackface into the greatest performance genre in the United States. Even W. E. B. Du Bois recognized Williams as a great comedian and a "great Negro."[45]

Most modern scholars view Williams as a pioneering Black star of musical theater on Broadway and one of the most important architects of Afro-American theater. According to his best-known biographer, Louis Chude-Sokei, Williams knew how to transform the blackface space of representation, becoming the most famous "Black blackface."[46] Through this "Black-on-Black minstrelsy," he transformed the meanings of both the mask and the musicals themselves, introducing new themes and forging paths for many other Black musicians and artists such as Josephine Baker.[47]

When worn by Williams, the mask of blackface was layered with other masks. It hid the artist and constructed a composite "negro," divulging often-problematic notions about Blackness and Black identity.[48] But Williams managed to challenge and subvert both white representations of Blackness and Black self-depictions, thus inverting many of their meanings. According to Chude-Sokei, the blackface mask gained unprecedented political dimensions in the hands of powerful artists such as Williams, who played with what were seen as natural markers of Blackness and redefined the field of representation for US Afro-descendants.

A BLACK BRAZILIAN SINGER AT ODEON RECORDS

Eduardo Sebastião das Neves, later known as Eduardo das Neves or simply "Dudu," was born in the city of Rio de Janeiro in 1874.[49] I have

---

[45] L. Chude-Sokei, *The Last*, pp. 51–52, 18, 43–74.
[46] For other analyses of the representations of blackface, see W. Brundage, ed., *Beyond Blackface*; A. Bean et al., eds., *Inside the Minstrel Mask*.
[47] L. Chude-Sokei, *The Last*, pp. 4–6.
[48] Throughout his work, Chude-Sokei traces in depth the sometimes conflictual connections between Bert Williams, US Black leaders of various political stripes (including Booker Washington, Du Bois, and Marcus Garvey), and intellectuals who would emerge as central figures in the Harlem Renaissance during the 1920s (among them James Weldom Johnson, Alain Locke, and Claude MacKay). L. Chude-Sokei, *The Last*, chapter 2.
[49] This data was found on das Neves' death certificate, located in the Archive of Santa Casa de Misericórdia do Rio de Janeiro. In addition to the references cited in the text, the principal bibliographical references for Eduardo das Neves are M. Marcondes,

never managed to locate concrete data about his family background. Only his lyrics and stories allow us to establish some degree of connection to Brazil's slave past and to social struggles such as abolition. Like Williams, Neves was popular among white and Black audiences and was admired by contemporaries,[50] although neither historians and musical memorialists nor leaders of Brazil's Black movement have done much to preserve his memory for posterity.

In one of Neves' first songbooks, he proclaimed himself the *Trovador da Malandragem* ("Trickster Troubadour") and "The Creole Dudu das Neves," which was also the title of one of his compositions.[51] The terrific lyrics of the unrecorded song "O Crioulo" can be read as a type of autobiography, in which Neves inverted the often pejorative meaning of the word *crioulo*, subverting racial stereotypes by confidently affirming his musical abilities and his capacity to attract the attention of *mulatas*, *moreninhas*, and *branquinhas* (all of whom served as muses in his songs).

"Dudu," like various other musically talented Black men from his social background, started working at an early age, finding employment with the Estrada de Ferro Central do Brasil Railroad and Rio's Fire Department. He only dedicated himself fully to an artistic career after he was fired from both workplaces for bad behavior (which included participation in a strike and playing guitar while working). He began in the circus and made his stage debut at the Apolo Theater during the last decade of the nineteenth century.

Neves' trajectory, like Bert Williams', demonstrated considerable entrepreneurialism. He organized collections of popular songs and owned the Circo Brasil (a small circus); he also appeared as a performer at bars, theaters, charity parties, and cinemas.[52] With the title "Crioulo

Enciclopédia da música; P. Maís, *Antologia da serenata*; J. Tinhorão. "Circo brasileiro"; and A. Vasconcelos, *Panorama da música*. Jota Efegê, who consulted the documentation of the Fire Brigade, stated that Dudu was born in 1871 in São Paulo (C. Sandroni, "Música, performance," p. 53).

[50] The obituaries in *Jornal do Brasil* and *Correio da Manhã* on November 12 of that year give a good idea of the extent of the singer's recognition outside of Rio de Janeiro. Nevertheless, Eduardo das Neves, like many musicians of his time, died poor.

[51] E. das Neves, *O Trovador*, p. 64.

[52] He published five songbooks, published in various editions, containing a combination of his own songs and others sung in theaters from the public domain. With the popular publishing house Editora Quaresma do Rio de Janeiro, he published *Cantor das modinhas brasileiras* (probably in 1895), *Trovador da malandragem* (1926, 2nd edition, with songs registered between 1889 and 1902), and *Mistérios do violão* (1905). On the cover of these songbooks, Eduardo das Neves' image is always featured. I also located *O Cancioneiro popular moderno* (10th edition, 1921) and "*O trovador popular moderno*" (16th edition,

Dudu," he cut an elegant figure, according to his sympathizers, in blue tails and a top hat. Many other Black musicians who gained commercial success took similar care with their offstage appearances.

In 1895, Quaresma Publishers released Eduardo das Neves' first song-book, *O cantor de modinhas brasileiras (The Singer of Brazilian Modinhas)*. The book referred to Neves as an "illustrious singer" and included lyrics for his repertoire and that of baritone and Black composer Geraldo Magalhães (who was well known for his *maxixe* performances in Paris). An advertisement for the Circo-Pavilhão Internacional, set up in Rio's well-to-do Botafogo neighborhood at the end of 1897, shows that Neves was already a success in the circus ring, especially with a popular type of syncopated Afro-Brazilian music known as the *lundu*: "The premier Brazilian clown will provide the night's delights with his magnificent songs and *lundus*, accompanied by his plaintive guitar."[53]

Other songbooks followed, and after 1902 Neves began his commercial recording career; he would also perform in many other circuses, revues, cinemas, theaters, and clubs. In the always crowded Parque Fluminense amusement and exhibition hall, he was advertised as the "Popular Singer Eduardo das Neves" alongside tenors, sopranos, and assorted curiosities and variety acts.[54]

Neves' songs, whether published or recorded, were part of a political and aesthetic idiom shared by music producers and the urban public at large. Like other Rio musicians, Neves recorded lovelorn *modinhas*, waltzes, *serestas*, *choros*, *marchas*, *cançonetas*, sambas, *chulas*, comic scenes, and especially *lundus*. He used music to promote republican political campaigns, paying homage to various national heroes. But he also made politics of music, writing songs that dealt humorously and ironically with topics such as the Canudos War, urban social tensions ("Carne Fresca" and "Aumento das Passagens"), obligatory vaccination campaigns, the proliferation of rats that spread bubonic plague, and the popular festivals of Penha.

Neves' choices indicated an unquestionable awareness of the most important national and international topics of his day (he even wrote at one point about the Boer War in South Africa). In various statements, he expressed indignation at white Brazilians' inability to recognize a *crioulo*'s capacity to discuss politics, elections, national customs, urban problems,

1925), which were published by the equally popular C. Teixeira, in São Paulo. All of these books have more than 120 pages.
[53] J. Efegê, *Figuras e coisas*, p. 178.   [54] *Gazeta de Noticias*, September 4 and 11, 1902.

and foreign policy. Neves proudly proclaimed his authorship of many of the songs he published or recorded. But among his successes, none could touch the song he wrote in honor of aviator Santos Dumont upon his arrival in Paris in 1903, when the entire city gave itself over to celebration.[55]

Nevertheless, like Bert Williams, Neves also had the opportunity – and the choice – to articulate and enact slave songs, whose content and lyrics were directly linked to Black history, values, and customs. In the midst of Brazil's national commemorations, Eduardo das Neves affirmed his identity as a Black man – "the *crioulo* Dudu." His songs touched on racial identity and criticized racial inequality, in ways that indicate a desire to affirm the place of Black people and Black experiences in Brazil's musical and theatrical worlds. Although his personal links to the experience of slavery are not clear, Dudu made a point of not forgetting Brazil's slave past, consistently singing, recording, and publishing songs about enslaved people's struggles for manumission, the abolition of slavery, and even the possibility of amorous relationships between Black men and white women. Beyond commemorating national heroes and exploring the everyday quirks and politics of urban life, Neves also touched with great irony and humor on Brazil's Afro-descendant culture and history. Africa was not directly present in his repertoire the way it was in Bert Williams'. But African heritage appeared in recordings of musical forms such as *jongo* or in references to the dialects of African elders important in popular folklore and religion, such as Pai João, Pai Francisco, and Negro Mina. In his musical representations of slaves, Eduardo das Neves often appeared to wear the mask of the *preto velho* (literally the "old negro," a term that could imply a stereotypical subservient slave). But in Afro-descendant religious and popular tradition, *pretos velhos* could also be storytellers, emblems of suffering and resistance, and carriers of African and Afro-descendant memory. And even as Neves mimicked their language and mannerisms, he also proudly broadcasted the musical innovations of their descendants.

Many of Neves' songs touched on race relations in ways that could at once reinforce stereotypes and challenge racist theories or hierarchies of

---

[55] In relation to the political meanings of his songs, see M. Abreu, "O crioulo Dudu." In his publications he sometimes claimed authorship of the songs. Other times, he only comments that the song is from his repertoire. In the recording at Casa Edison, most of the songs sung by Eduardo das Neves are registered without authorship. In the musical archive of Instituto Moreira Sales all the songs of his repertoire can be heard: http://acervo.ims.com.br/.

race and gender: examples include songs that recounted amorous relationships with *iaiás, iaiazinhas,* and *morenas;* the flirtatious provocations of
crioulos; the superiority of the color black; and the cunning and ironic wit
of Pai João (an iconic *preto velho*).[56] The recordings he made at the Casa
Edison often include raucous laughter, shout-outs for *crioulos* and *crioulas,* and joyful banter among the musicians and other colleagues, who
were known as *baianos* or *baianos da guerra.*[57]

Among Neves' songs, some of the most astonishing verses involved
amorous relationships with iaiás (young girls, usually white) and *morenas*
(women of mixed race) or odes to *mulata* enchantments. In Neves' songbooks *Mistérios do violão (Mysteries of the Guitar)* and *Trovador da
malandragem (Trickster Troubadour), mulata* and *morena* muses appear
in "Carmem" and "Albertina."[58] In "Roda Yáyá," a *mulata* enchantress
with links to the devil casts a spell on the protagonist – probably Neves
himself – leaving him "captive and dying" from thirst. In musical
response, Neves – calling himself a *turuna* (a strong, powerful, brave
man, often a practitioner of capoeira) – proclaimed that the *mulata*
would "fall into my net, and never escape from its mesh."[59] As I have
discussed elsewhere, Neves' compositions, like most erudite *lundus,*
deployed the *mulata* as an emblem of beauty and sensuality.[60] But in an
important reversal, Dudu's *mulatas* fall into the nets of cocksure *crioulos*
rather than those of white slaveowners.

The *crioulo*'s flirtatiousness was even more astonishing in the verses
aimed at *sinhazinhas* (young white women on the slave plantations).
Assuming that Neves himself composed these verses, it is remarkable
that a Black musician could depict himself directing seductive versus to
a *sinhazinha.* It could be that such an exchange was considered so absurd
that it was – in and of itself – the heart of Neves' joke: the impossibility or
improbability of such a situation made everyone laugh. At the same time,
when Neves sang such songs, the sexual and racial inversion of the classic
relations of dominance that had always paired white men with Black
women gave such laughter undeniable political significance.

In Eduardo das Neves' Casa Edison period (between 1907 and
1912), many of the *lundus* he recorded for the label revisited the

---

[56] For greater insight, see M. Abreu, "Mulatas, Crioulos and Morenas."
[57] Laughter can also be heard in Bert Williams' recordings, especially in Volume 1 of the
collection organized by R. Martin and M. Hennessy, *Bert Williams* (CD1, *The Early
Years, 1901–1909*).
[58] E. Neves, "Mistérios," pp. 46 and 47, and "O trovador," p. 33.
[59] E. Neves, "Mistérios," p. 28.   [60] M. Abreu, "Mulatas, Crioulos and Morenas."

theme of Black involvement with *sinhazinhas*, though the recording
studio listed the songs' authorship as "unknown." In "Tasty Lundu,"
Neves sung that he would go "to Bahia to see his *sinhá*" and "eat her
dendê oil."[61] The *lundu* "Pai João" paired similar temerity with an
interesting resurrection of the *preto velho*, a literary figure already
familiar in many songs and stories in both Brazil and the United
States. The loyal *preto velho* never ran away – but in Neves' rendering
he also never lost his strength and audacity.[62] Neves' Pai João refused
to open his door to anyone while his wife Caterina was sleeping – not
even to the police chief or his officers. But in a verse about Sundays,
the singer seems to laugh as he sings that "when the master went out"
he (Pai João) "took care of the beautiful *iaiá*."[63]

The preponderance of *lundus* in Eduardo das Neves' recorded repertoire is especially interesting. The *lundu* was a musical genre especially
associated with slave songs, usually performed for laughs in circuses or in
phonograph recordings. But Neves' appropriation of the form can also be
understood as an original and powerful strategy to affirm Black artists and
bring discussion of the racial question to a broader public sphere. It is
important to remember that, during that time, Dudu's comic and ironic
style might have been the only possible way to discuss the Black experience and the problem of racial inequality in Brazil's musical and artistic
sphere. Just like the cakewalks and ragtimes of US blackface, the *lundus*
had earned the affection of white audiences in the nineteenth century; they
were part of a kind of blackface clown repertoire, were printed as sheet
music, and appeared in malicious satirical verses published by refined
authors in respected publications long before the advent of recorded
music.[64] Because the *lundu* was understood as a form of comedy, it
may – like its counterparts in the United States – have created a very
particular way of projecting Black artistry into the field of entertainment,

[61] *Lundu Gostoso*, Odeon, 108673, 1907–1912.
[62] For an approximation between *Pai João* and Uncle Tom in popular song, see Martha
Abreu, *Da senzala ao palco*, chapter 7.
[63] *Pai João*, Odeon, 108075, 1907–1912; *Iaiazinha*, Odeon, 108074, 1907–1912.
Folklorists from the post-abolition period registered many songs in which the protagonist
was Pai João (or some other *Pai*, which, in Brazilian Black religion and oral tradition,
often meant an elder from the times of slavery), and they must have circulated in various
artistic and social circles. M. Abreu, "Outras histórias."
[64] *Lundus*, like ragtime in the United States, were not sung or written only by black artists,
but in general they were associated with the Black and slave population and included
syncopation, comic bits, and *mulata* characters.

eventually constituting the form that came to be accepted and understood as "Black music."

All the same, to extend Paul Gilroy's observations south of the equator, Brazilian Afro-descendants could transform their performances on the stage and in the recording studio into an important form of political action.[65] *Lundus* provided Neves with commercial success and applause, but their intense polysemy also allowed him to invert and subvert the narrow and stereotypical roles traditionally allotted to Blacks. As Chude-Sokei observed about Bert Williams, Eduardo das Neves's *lundu* perform-ances were double-edged. On the one hand, he presented his audiences with visual and sonic images of comic, simple-minded Black slaves; on the other, he enacted clever, cunning, streetwise Black *malandros*, who seduced women of every color and articulated shrewd political and racial critiques. Even though Eduardo das Neves never incorporated the clas-sical disguises of blackface – red lips, bulging eyes – he resembled Bert Williams in his ability to manipulate masks and embody contradictory double-meanings, thus subverting the norms imposed on Black perform-ers who were identified with the cultural heritage of slavery.

Eduardo das Neves' recordings of so-called *gargalhadas* (laughing songs) also had important points of intersection with blackface. Dudu's most successful *gargalhada* was probably "Pega na Chaleira" (literally "Grab the kettle"), which satirized the kinds of political bootlicking and exchange of favors common in Brazil's high society. Raucous, tuneful laughter (literal *gargalhadas*) appeared throughout the song. As it turns out, this genre was probably adapted from "The Laughing Song" and "The Whistling Coon," which were recorded in the United States by George W. Johnson. A formerly enslaved man from Virginia discovered on the streets of New York, Johnson was likely the first Black musician to record for the phonographic industry in the 1890s.[66] Johnson's "The Laughing Song" became a worldwide hit in the 1890s, eventually produ-cing a remarkable 50,000 records that were sold in various parts of Europe and the Americas.[67] Johnson was also the author of a number of other international hits, including "The Whistling Coon," "The Laughing Coon," and "The Whistling Girl." Johnson's recorded laughter appears in a 1902 catalog from Casa Edison in Rio de Janeiro, in a recording entitled "English Laughter."

---

[65] P. Gilroy, *O Atlântico negro*, pp. 189, 245.
[66] B. Wagner, *Disturbing the Peace*, chapter 4.
[67] C. Palombini, "Fonograma 108.077," p. 64. See also T. Brooks, *Lost Sounds*, chapter 3.

According to the musicologist Carlos Palombini, the songs recorded by
George W. Johnson made fun of Black people, just like blackface shows
and "coon songs." The *gargalhadas* recorded by Dudu, which were also
cataloged as *lundus*, might have been inspired by Johnson's style, but they
expanded the satire to include the high politics of Rio de Janeiro.
Regardless, the *gargalhadas* indicate that Eduardo das Neves knew
Johnson's recordings and sought to imitate them.[68] This suggests that he
had heard of Bert Williams and understood the cakewalk's multiple
meanings.[69]

Even after launching a recording career and embarking on very successful tours across Brazil, Neves never distanced himself from the circus. He
achieved success with "singing pantomimes" in a wide variety of theatrical
circus spectacles, showcasing a repertoire of happy, comical, patriotic
ditties, many of which drew from the experience of slavery. Neves was
certainly one of the best performers in this genre, along with Benjamim de
Oliveira, another Black artist who had been born in slavery. Together –
along with Black composer and conductor Paulino Sacramento – they
produced multiple works, including a 1910 farce entitled *A Sentença da
Viúva Alegre* (*The Sentence of the Happy Widow*), which was performed in
the Cinematógrafo Santana. The cinema was located on Santana Street,
near the famed Praça Onze, which was at that time Rio's cultural ground
zero for carnival groups and Black dance associations – Rio's equivalent of
Harlem. The "Sentence" was a parody of the operetta *The Happy Widow*
by Franz Lehár, which had successfully opened in Rio de Janeiro in 1909,
after its 1905 Vienna debut.[70]

According to the music historian José Ramos Tinhorão, both Benjamim
de Oliveira and Dudu used to paint their faces white in order to portray
certain characters. In *The Sentence of the Happy Widow*, they did so while
playing the rich widow's suitors.[71] It would have been difficult for them to
entirely control the audience's reactions to Black men in whiteface, but there
is no doubt that both men intentionally manipulated masks and stereotypical

---

[68] According to William H. Kenney, George W. Johnson produced "an entertainment
commodity that fit the general expectations of minstrel show and coon song traditions
without actually requiring that he sing lyrics that would be humiliating to either himself or
African Americans in general." Eduardo das Neves may also have perceived this meaning
in Johnson's recordings. In this way, Johnson – like Bert Williams and Eduardo das
Neves – may have helped to transform the meaning of the minstrel tradition.
[69] I have found references to Eduardo das Neves dancing the cakewalk in the circus. See
H. Silva, *Circo-Teatro*, pp. 219–220.
[70] H. Silva, *Circo-Teatro*, pp. 219–220, 254.   [71] J. Tinhorão, "Circo brasileiro."

FIGURE 15.6 Benjamim de Oliveira. Sheet music. In Herminia Silva, *Circo-Teatro: Benjamim de Oliveira e a teatralidade circense no Brasil*. Ed. Altana, São Paulo, 2007, p. 241 (foto da autora).

representations of whiteness and Blackness in order to elicit laughter from
their audiences and irreverently invert racial hierarchies. Judging from newspaper advertisements, theirs were the star attractions among the farces and
parodies performed in circuses across the city (see Figure 15.6).

As noted previously, songs protagonized by Pai João (or some other
Pai) probably circulated widely in various post-abolition artistic and
social circles.[72] Such songs were funny and ironic, but they allow us to
perceive a figurative game of hangman in which the slaves' desires (and
possible those of the *iaiás*) became evident even as the slaves' masters and
future employers sought to prevent them from assuming their full shape.
Based on these verses, we can surmise that poets such as Dudu used their
music to explore the meanings of the slave past and the post-abolition
struggle and to redefine race relations and Black identity. Beyond the
artistic world, there are indications that Eduardo das Neves – like Bert
Williams – cared deeply about defending the value of Black people and
their history. He knew pioneering Black political figures of his generation,
such as Federal Deputy Manoel Monteiro Lopes, and during civic commemorations of abolition he participated in events paying tribute to Afro-
descendant abolitionists such as José do Patrocínio.[73] He fought for his
rights when faced with racial prejudice and sought to claim his rightful
place in the public sphere, most directly toward the end of his life when he
sought entry into an important association of performing artists.[74] Neves'
most famous composition was a tribute to Santos Dumont, considered in
Brazil to be "the father of aviation"; when its sheet music was published,
the cover displayed not only the Eiffel Tower but also an image of Neves in
the upper left-hand corner. Although the picture is small, it testifies that
Neves sought to portray himself as a Black man who was modern, elegant,
handsome, and thoroughly Brazilian.

But perhaps Eduardo das Neves' commitment to the history of the
Black population emerges most fully in his recording of the song "A
Canoa Virada" ("The Capsized Canoe").[75] A kind of popular ode to the
abolition of slavery, the song musically commemorated the conquests of
1888, at least twenty years after the fact. The song used strong language
that might have been unsettling for some of Neves' contemporaries: the
time had arrived "for the Black population to *bumbar*," a verb that could

---

[72] M. Abreu, "Outras histórias."   [73] M. Abreu and C. Dantas, *É chegada*, pp. 98–105.
[74] See Arquivo Almirante, Museu da Imagem e do Som, 1965, Eduardo das Neves.
[75] This recording and its implications are examined in greater depth in M. Abreu and
C. Dantas, *É chegada*.

mean both "to celebrate" and "to beat" or "to thrash." Neves referred to May 13, "the day of liberty," as a great moment of real change and dreams of freedom. Slavery was represented as a fragile vessel, a canoe that had literally capsized, ending its long Brazilian journey. The song ironically satirized the "haughty *crioulos*" who would no longer eat cornmeal and beans, and the "Blacks without masters" who were typical of many *lundus* – but it also celebrated the fact that "the day of liberty" had arrived, and there were no more reasons for "the Bahians to cry." Black people, everywhere in Brazil, had longed for – and won – their "day of freedom."

Eduardo das Neves also seemed unintimidated by crude and racist commentaries on his repertoire and personal style, even those written by well-known Rio intellectuals such as João do Rio and José Brito Broca. João do Rio wrote that he had seen Neves in the middle of the stage, in the midst of enthusiastic applause, "sweaty, with a face like pitch, showing all thirty-two of his impressively pure white teeth." In Brito Broca's preju-diced memoirs, the success of the popular Quaresma publishing house, which printed Neves' songbooks, depended a lot on the "inventiveness of that flat-faced negro."[76]

Despite great success in his lifetime and the support of some intellec-tuals concerned with street folklore – including Alexandre Mello Morais Filho, Afonso Arinos, Catullo da Paixão Cearense, and Raul Pederneiras – Eduardo das Neves did not have his work recognized in posterity. Opinions about him, like those about Williams, are far from unanimous. In the Black movements that emerged in Brazil after the 1920s, Neves was scarcely remembered, perhaps due to his complicity with stereotypical representations of slaves and their descendants. Historians of music, in their rush to elevate the supposedly "modern" and "national" genre of samba in the 1920s – granted him no greater role. He was simply seen – or frowned upon – as an interpreter of comical *lundus* and jingoistic songs about republican heroes.

The only exceptions were a few of Neves' contemporary Black intellec-tuals, who seem to have viewed Neves' work and trajectory with admir-ation. For Francisco Guimarães, known as Vagalume, an important journalist and patron of sambas and Black Carnival groups, Neves had honored the "race" to which he was proud to belong. Vagalume called Dudu the "Black Diamond" and considered him to be a "professor"

---

[76] João do Rio, *A alma*, pp. 173–186. B. Broca, *A vida*. According to Brito Broca, the publishing house published inferior writers.

among samba circles.[77] There is also some evidence that Sinhô (1888–1930) and João da Bahiana (1887–1974), who would become samba stars in the 1920s, began their artistic life in Neves' company. João da Bahiana, in an interview with Rio's Museum of Image and Sound, declared that he had worked in Neves' circus, leading the boys who animated his skits. Sinhô, who was anointed the "King of Samba" in the 1920s, accompanied Eduardo das Neves carrying the Brazilian flag during a famous tribute to Santos Dumont in 1903. Later, Eduardo das Neves would record three sambas attributed to Sinhô, before Sinhô was made famous with "Pelo Telephone" ("By Telephone") which is remembered as Brazil's first recorded samba. Neves' final recording, released on April 10, 1919, was "Só por Amizade" ("Just for Friendship"), another samba by Sinhô. It was evident that new generations sought out Neves and that he, like Bert Williams, participated in the formation of future Black musicians.

Thanks to the work of the historian Felipe Rodrigues Boherer on Black territories in the southern Brazilian city of Porto Alegre, we know a little about Neves' tour to that city in 1916. Although he suffered some uncomfortable embarrassments during his stay, Porto Alegre's Black newspaper *O Exemplo* gave Neves a place of honor in its coverage.[78] The newspaper did not hide its pride in the singer, calling him a "countryman" and giving him the title of the "Brazilian nightingale" during his run at the Recreio Ideal Theater and the Sociedade Florista Aurora (a recreational association founded by the city's Black population). Neves was part of a "chic program, featuring the very best of the esteemed artist's repertoire," accompanied by an orchestra and a society band.[79] The day after the opening, the paper announced that the presentation had been much appreciated and that the audience had not held back their "applause for the popular singer and countryman."[80]

In May 1915, during one of his tours through the southern state of Rio Grande do Sul, the "Gazeta Teatral" column in *Gazeta de Noticias* stated that "Eduardo das Neves is an ingenious *crioulo*, the Monteiro Lopes of the guitar, the Cruz Souza of the stage, the Othello of the *modinha*."[81] Like Bert Williams, Eduardo das Neves effectively "conquered" the public

[77] In relation to Vagalume and his importance for the visibility of black songs, sambas, and carnivals, see L. Pereira, "No ritmo." See also M. Pimenta Velloso, *A cultura.*
[78] F. Bohrer, "Inserção social." [79] *O Exemplo*, November 19, 1916, p. 3.
[80] *O Exemplo*, November 26, 1916.
[81] *Gazeta de Notícias*, May 8, 1915, p. 3. Monteiro Lopes was a Black politician; Cruz e Souza was a great Black poet.

with his talent and his performances, leaving his mark on stages throughout Brazil.

CONCLUSION

Black musicians across the Americas may have made enormously varied musical choices. But the life experiences of Bert Williams and Eduardo das Neves indicate that neither the problems they faced nor the paths available to them were so very different. They both experienced profound continuities with the slave past even while surrounded by the novelties of the modern entertainment industry, grappling with old and enduring racist stereotypes about slave songs, Black music, and Black musicians. In seeking to transform both the legacy of the past and their place in post-abolition societies, Williams and Neves (re)created both the meaning of their music and the contemporary musical canon itself. In the midst of sorrow, prejudice, and forgetting, they won applause and recognition. Their very presence on the stage and in phonograph recordings was an important victory. Williams and Neves expanded the spaces available to Black musicians and actors, allowing them to become ever more visible in the circuses, bands, theaters, and recording studios that formed the backbone of the modern commercial entertainment industry.

The musical field thus occupied a fundamental space within the politics of Afro-descendant representation, exclusion, and incorporation (real or imagined) in America's post-abolition societies. Representations of Black people and the meanings attributed to their music – in festivities, through carnivals or costumes, on the covers of musical scores, in sound recordings, or on the stage – could shore up the racial inequalities that reproduced themselves after the end of slavery. Inversely, however, they could also subversively amplify Black struggles for equality and cultural recognition, highlighting the cultural contributions of the descendants of slaves to modern American societies.

Bibliography

SECONDARY SOURCES

Abrahams, Roger D. *Singing the Master: The Emergence of African American Culture in The Plantation South.* New York: Penguin Group, 1992.

Abreu, Martha. *Da senzala ao palco: canções escravas e racismo nas Américas, 1870–1930.* Campinas, SP: Editora UNICAMP, Coleção História Ilustrada, 2017.

"Histórias musicais da Primeira República." *Revista ArtCultura* 13:22 (2011): online.

"Mulatas, Crioulos and Morenas: Racial Hierarchy, Gender Relations and National Identity in Post-Abolition Popular Song: Southeastern Brazil, 1890–1920." In Pamela Scully and Diana Paton, eds., *Gender and Slave Emancipation in the Atlantic World*, pp. 267–288. Durham, NC: Duke University Press, 2005.

"O 'Crioulo Dudu': participação política e identidade negra nas histórias de um músico cantor." *Topoi* 11:20 (2010): 92–113.

"O legado das canções escravas nos Estados Unidos e Brasil: diálogos musicais no pós-abolição." *Revista Brasileira de História* 35:69 (2015): 177–204.

"Outras histórias de Pai João: conflitos raciais, protesto escravo e irreverência sexual na poesia popular (1880–1950)." *Revista Afro-Ásia* 31 (2004): 235–276.

"Slave Mothers and Freed Children: Emancipation and Female Space in Debates on the 'Free Womb' Law, Rio de Janeiro, 1871." *Journal of Latin American Studies* 28:3 (1996): 567–580.

Abreu, Martha, and Sueann Caulfield. "50 anos de virgindade no Rio de Janeiro: as políticas de sexualidade no discurso jurídico e popular, 1890–1940." *Espaço Feminino* 1–2 (1995): 15–52.

Abreu, Martha, and Carolina Vianna Dantas. "*É chegada a hora da negrada bumbar*: comemorações da abolição, música e política na Primeira República." *Varia Historia* 27:45 (2011): 97–120.

Abreu, Martha, and Larissa Viana. "Festas religiosas, cultura e política no Império do Brasil." In Keila Grinberg and Ricardo Salles, eds., *O Brasil Imperial: Vol. III, 1870–1889*, pp. 233–270. Rio de Janeiro: Civilização Brasileira, 2009.

Adams, Julia, Elisabeth Clemens, and Ann Orloff, eds. *Remaking Modernity.* Durham, NC: Duke University Press, 2005.

"Social Theory, Modernity, and the Three Waves of Historical Sociology." In Julia Adams, Elisabeth Clemens, and Ann Shola Orloff, eds., *Remaking Modernity*, pp. 493–515. Durham, NC: Duke University Press, 2005.

Adelman, Jeremy. *Sovereignty and Revolution in the Iberian Atlantic.* Princeton, NJ: Princeton University Press, 2006.

Aguilar, Nelson, ed. *Mostra do redescobrimento: negro de corpo e alma = Black in body and soul.* São Paulo: Fundação Bienal de São Paulo, 2000.

Aguirre, Carlos. *Agentes de su propia libertad: los esclavos de Lima y la disintegración de la esclavitud, 1821–1854.* Lima: PUC Perú, 1993.

Aladrén, Gabriel. "Experiências de liberdade em tempos de guerra: escravos e libertos nas Guerras Cisplatinas (1811–1828)." *Estudos Históricos* 22:44 (2009): 439–458.

Alberto, Paulina L. "El Negro Raúl: Lives and Afterlives of an Afro-Argentine Celebrity, 1886 to the Present." *Hispanic American Historical Review* 96:4 (2016): 669–710.

"Of Sentiment, Science and Myth: Shifting Metaphors of Racial Inclusion in Twentieth-Century Brazil." *Social History* 37:3 (2012): 261–296.

Terms of Inclusion: Black Intellectuals in Twentieth Century Brazil. Chapel Hill: University of North Carolina Press, 2011.

Alberto, Paulina L., and Jesse Hoffnung-Garskof. "'Racial Democracy' and Racial Inclusion: Hemispheric Histories." In Alejandro de la Fuente and George Reid Andrews, eds., *Afro-Latin American Studies: An Introduction*, pp. 264–316. New York, NY: Cambridge University Press, 2018.

Albuquerque, Aline Emanuelle De Biase. "Angelo dos retalhos a Visconde de Loures: a trajetória de um traficante de escravos, 1818–1858." MA thesis in History, Federal University of Pernambuco, 2016.

Albuquerque, Débora de Souza Leão, Flávio Rabelo Versiani, and José Raimundo Oliveira Vergolino. "Financiamento e organização do tráfico de escravos para Pernambuco no século XIX." *Economia* 14:1a (2013): 211–225.

Albuquerque, José Joaquim de Medeiros e. *Quando eu era vivo – memórias (1867–1934).* Rio de Janeiro: Livraria do Globo, 1945.

Albuquerque, Wlamyra R. de. *O jogo da dissimulação – abolição e cidadania negra no Brasil.* São Paulo: Companhia das Letras, 2009.

Alencastro, Luiz Felipe de, ed. *História da vida privada no Brasil.* São Paulo: Companhia das Letras, 1997.

Algranti, Leila Mezan. *O feitor ausente.* Rio de Janeiro: Vozes, 1988.

Allen, William F., Charles P. Ware, and Lucy McKim Garrison. *Slave Songs of the United States: The Classic 1867 Anthology.* New York, NY: Dove Publications, 1995.

Almeida, Angela Mendes de. *Pensando a família no Brasil: da colônia à modernidade.* Rio de Janeiro: Espaço e Tempo/ UFRRJ, 1987.

Almeida, Maria Regina Celestino, and Sara Ortelli, eds. "Atravesando fronteras: circulación de población en los márgenes iberoamericanos, siglos XVI–XIX." Special Dossier of *Nuevo Mundo/Mundos Nuevos*, 2011: online.

Alonso, Angela. *The Last Abolition*. Cambridge: Cambridge University Press, 2022.

Andrade, Eloy de. *O Vale do Paraíba*. Rio de Janeiro: Real Gráfica, 1989.

Andrews, George R. *Blackness in the White Nation: A History of Afro-Uruguay*. Chapel Hill: University of North Carolina Press, 2010.

Blacks and Whites in São Paulo. Madison: University of Wisconsin Press, 1991.

Araújo, Emanoel, ed. *A mão afro-brasileira: significado da contribuição artística e histórica*. São Paulo: Tenege, 1988.

Araújo, Luciana Corrêa de. "Os encantos da Veneza Americana e da propaganda pelo cinema: os filmes financiados pelo governo Sergio Loreto em Pernambuco (1922–1926)." *Estudos Históricos* 26:51 (2013): 94–112.

Araujo, Ricardo Benzaquen de. *Guerra e paz: casa grande e senzala e a obra de Gilberto Freyre nos anos 30*. Rio de Janeiro: Editora 34, 1994.

Archer-Straw, Petrine. *Negrophilia: Avant-Garde Paris and Black Culture in the 1920s*. New York: Thames and Hudson, 2000.

Ariès, Philippe. *História social da criança e da família*, 2nd ed. Rio de Janeiro: Guanabara, 1981.

Ariza, Marília Bueno de Araújo. "Bad Mothers, Labouring Children: Emancipation, Tutelage and Motherhood in São Paulo in the Last Decades of the Nineteenth Century." *Slavery & Abolition* 38:2 (2017): 408–424.

"Mães libertas, filhos escravos: desafios femininos nas últimas décadas da escravidão em São Paulo." *Revista Brasileira de História* 38:79 (2018): 151–171.

Azevedo, Celia. *Onda negra, medo branco: o negro no imaginário das elites – século XIX*. São Paulo: Paz e Terra, 1987.

Azevedo, Elciene. *O direito dos escravos: lutas jurídicas e abolicionismo em São Paulo*. Campinas, São Paulo: Editora da UNICAMP, 2010.

Orfeu da carapina: a trajetória de Luiz Gama na imperial cidade de São Paulo. Campinas, São Paulo: Editora da UNICAMP, 1999.

Azevedo, Gislane Campos. "A tutela e o contrato de soldada: a reinvenção do trabalho compulsório infantil." *História Social* 3 (1996): 11–36.

"De Sebastianas e Geovannis: o universo do menor processos dos juízes de órfãos da cidade de São Paulo (1871–1917)." MA thesis in History, Pontifícia Universidade Católica (São Paulo), 1995.

Azevedo, Thales de. *As elites de cor – um estudo de ascensão social*. São Paulo: Cia. Editora Nacional, 1955.

Badinter, Elisabeth. *Um amor conquistado: o mito do amor materno*, 3rd ed. Rio de Janeiro: Nova Fronteira, 1985.

Balaban, Marcelo. *Poeta do lápis: sátira e política na trajetória de Angelo Agostini no Brasil Imperial, 1864–1888*. Campinas, São Paulo: Editora da UNICAMP, 2009.

Barbosa, Marialva. *História cultural da imprensa, Brasil, 1800–1900*. Rio de Janeiro: Mauad X, 2010.

Os donos do Rio: imprensa, poder e público. Rio de Janeiro: Vício de Leitura, 2000.

Barcellos, Daisy Macedo, et al. *Comunidade negra de Morro Alto: historicidade, identidade e territorialidade*. Porto Alegre: Editora da UFRGS, 2004.

Barickman, Bert. "Até a véspera: o trabalho escravo e a produção de açúcar nos engenhos baianos do Recôncavo Baiano (1850–1881)." *Revista Afro-Ásia* 21–22 (1998–1999): 177–237.

"Persistence and Decline: Slave Labour and Sugar Production in the Bahian Recôncavo, 1850–1888." *Journal of Latin American Studies* 28:3 (1996): 581–633.

Barkley, Elsa Brown. "Negotiating and Transforming the Public Sphere: African American Political Life in the Transition from Slavery to Freedom." *Public Culture* 7:1 (1994): 107–146.

Barreto, João Paulo (João do Rio). *A alma encantadora das ruas*, Rio de Janeiro: Secretaria Municipal de Cultura, Dep. Geral de Documentação e Informação Cultural, 1987.

Barroso, Vera Lucia M., ed. *Raízes de Santo Antônio da Patrulha e Caraá*. Porto Alegre: Est, 2000.

Barth, Frederick. *Ethnic Groups and Boundaries: The Social Organization of Culture Difference*. Boston: Little Brown & Co., 1969.

Bastide, Roger, and Florestan Fernandes. *Brancos e negros em São Paulo*, 4th ed. São Paulo: Global, 2008 (2nd ed., São Paulo: Companhia Editora Nacional, 1959).

Relações raciais entre negros e brancos em São Paulo. São Paulo: Anhembi, 1955.

Bastos, Élide Rugai. "Gilberto Freyre: Casa-grande & Senzala." In Lourenço Dantas Mota, ed., *Introdução ao Brasil I: um banquete no trópico*, 4th ed. São Paulo: Senac, 2004.

Batalha, Cláudio H. M. "Sociedades de trabalhadores no Rio de Janeiro do século XIX: algumas reflexões em torno da formação da classe operária." *Cadernos AEL* 6:10–11 (1999): 41–67.

Bean, Annemarie, James V. Hatch and Brooks MacNamara, eds., *Inside the Minstrel Mask: Readings in Nineteenth-Century Blackface Minstrelsy*. Middletown, CT: Wesleyan University Press, 1996.

Beattie, Peter. *Punishment in Paradise: Race, Slavery, Human Rights, and a Nineteenth Century Brazilian Penal Colony*. Durham, CT: Duke University Press, 2015.

The Tribute of Blood, Durham, CT: Duke University Press, 2001.

Beckles, Hilary, and Karl Watson. "Social Protest and Labour Bargaining: The Changing Nature of Slaves' Responses to Plantation Life in Eighteenth-Century Barbados." *Slavery and Abolition* 8:3 (1987): 272–293.

Berlin, Ira, and Philip D. Morgan. *The Slaves' Economy: Independent Production by Slaves in the Americas*. London: Frank Cass, 1991.

Besson, Jean. "Land Tenure in the Free Villages of Trelawny, Jamaica: A Case Study in the Caribbean Peasant Response to Emancipation." *Slavery and Abolition* 5:1 (1984): 3–23.

Transformations of Freedom in the Land of the Maroons: Creolization in the Cockpits, Jamaica. Kingston: Ian Randle, 2016.

Bieber Freitas, Judy. "Slavery and Social Life: Attempts to Reduce Free People to Slavery in the Sertão Mineiro, Brazil, 1850–1871." *Journal of Latin American Studies* 26:3 (1994): 597–619.

Berbel, Márcia Regina, and Rafael de Bivar Marquese. "The Absence of Race: Slavery, Citizenship, and Pro-Slavery Ideology in the Cortes of Lisbon and the Rio de Janeiro Constituent Assembly, 1821–4." *Social History* 32:4 (November 2007): 415–433.

Bergstresser, Rebeca. "The Movement for the Abolition of Slavery in Rio de Janeiro, Brazil, 1880–1889." PhD dissertation in History, Stanford University, 1973.

Berlin, Ira. *The Long Emancipation: The Demise of Slavery in the United States.* Cambridge, MA: Harvard University Press, 2015.

Many Thousands Gone. Cambridge, MA: Harvard University Press, 1998.

Besse, Susan. *Restructuring Patriarchy: The Modernization of Gender Inequality in Brazil, 1914–1940.* Chapel Hill: University of North Carolina Press, 1996.

Betancur, Arturo, Alex Borucki, and Ana Frega, eds. *Estudios sobre la cultura afro-rioplatense.* Montevideo: Universidad de la República, Facultad de Humanidades y Ciencias de la Educación, 2004.

Bethell, Leslie. *A abolição do comércio brasileiro de escravos.* Brasília: Senado Federal, 2002.

The Abolition of the Brazilian Slave Trade: Britain, Brazil, and the Slave Trade Question. Cambridge: Cambridge University Press, 1970.

Bezerra, Nielson Rosa. *As chaves da liberdade: confluências da escravidão no Recôncavo do Rio de Janeiro, 1833–1888.* Niterói: Editora da UFF, 2008.

Escravidão africana no Recôncavo da Guanabara (séculos XVII-XIX). Niterói: Editora da UFF, 2011.

Bezerra Neto, José Maia. "Por todos os meios legítimos e legais: as lutas contra a escravidão e os limites da abolição (Brasil, Grão Pará: 1850–1888)." PhD dissertation in History, PUC-SP, 2009.

Blake, Augusto Victoriano Alves do Sacramento. *Dicionário bibliográfico brasileiro, vol. 2.* Rio de Janeiro: Conselho Federal de Cultura, 1970.

Blum, Ann. *Domestic Economies.* Lincoln: University of Nebraska Press, 2009.

Bohrer, Felipe Rodrigues. "Inserção social negra através da música: análise dos territórios negros no pós-abolição em Porto Alegre." MA thesis in History, PPGH/ Federal University of Rio Grande do Sul, 2010.

Bonilla-Silva, Eduardo. *Racism without Racists*, 5th ed. Lanham, MD: Rowman and Littlefield, 2017.

Bourdieu, Pierre. *O poder simbólico*, 10th ed. Rio de Janeiro: Bertrand Brasil, 2007.

Borges, Dain. "Puffy, Ugly, Slothful and Inert." *Journal of Latin American Studies* 25:2 (1993): 235–237.

Borges, Magno Fonseca, and Ricardo Salles. "A morte do Barão de Guaribú." In Mariana Muaze and Ricardo Salles, eds., *O Vale do Paraíba e o Império do Brasil nos quadros da segunda escravidão*, pp. 197–241. Rio de Janeiro: 7Letras, 2015. (Also published in *Heera: Revista de História Econômica & Economia Regional Aplicada* 7:13 [2012].)

Borucki, Alex. "The 'African Colonists' of Montevideo: New Light on the Illegal Slave Trade to Rio de Janeiro and the Río de la Plata (1830–42)." *Slavery & Abolition* 30:3 (2009): 427–444.

"The Slave Trade to the Rio de la Plata, 1777–1812: Trans-Imperial Networks and Atlantic Warfare." *Colonial Latin American Review* 20:1 (2011): 81–107.

Borucki, Alex, Karla Chagas, and Natalia Stalla. *Esclavitud y trabajo: un estudio sobre los afrodescendientes en la frontera uruguaya, 1835–1855*, 2nd ed. Montevideo: Mastergraf, 2009.

Bosi, Alfredo. *Dialética da colonização*. São Paulo: Companhia das Letras, 1992.

Braga, Greenhalgh H. Faria, ed. *De Vassouras. Fatos, e gente*. Rio de Janeiro: Ultra-sed, 1978.

Brandão, Maria de Azevedo, ed. *Recôncavo da Bahia: sociedade e economia em transição*. Salvador: Fundação Casa de Jorge Amado, 1998.

Brito, Jailton. *Abolição na Bahia*. Salvador: Edufba, 1997.

Broca, José Brito. *A vida literária no Brasil, 1900*. Rio de Janeiro: José Olympio, 1976.

Brody, Jennifer D. *Impossible Purities: Blackness, Femininity, and Victorian Culture*. Durham, NC: Duke University Press, 1998.

Brooks, Daphne A. *Bodies in Dissent: Spectacular Performances of Race and Freedom, 1850–1910*. Durham, NC: Duke University Press, 2006.

Brooks, Tim. *Lost Sounds: Blacks and The Birth of The Recording Industry, 1890–1919*. Urbana: University of Illinois Press, 2004.

Brundage, W. Fitzhugh, ed. *Beyond Blackface: African Americans and the Creation of American Popular Culture, 1890–1930*. Chapel Hill: University of North Carolina Press, 2003.

Bryant, Sherwin. *Rivers of Gold, Lives of Bondage: Governing through Slavery in Colonial Quito*. Chapel Hill: University of North Carolina Press, 2014.

Bueno, Fernando Pereira and José Sousa Jiménez. "*A Redención de Cam* de Modesto Brocos: ilustración da política migratória brasileira nos inícios da República Velha." *Estudios Migratorios* 9 (2000): 113–127.

Burguière, André, and François Lebrun, eds. *Histoire de la famille: le choc des modernités*. Paris: Armand Colin, 1986.

Burke, Diane Mutti. *On Slavery's Border: Missouri's Small Slaveholding Households 1815–1865*. Athens: University of Georgia Press, 2010.

Burke, Maria Lúcia Garcia Pallares. *Gilberto Freyre: um vitoriano nos trópicos*. São Paulo: Editora UNESP, 2005.

Burke, Maria Lúcia Garcia Pallares, and Peter Burke. *Gilberto Freyre: Social Theory in the Tropics*. Oxford: Peter Lang, 2008.

Burns, E. Bradford. *A History of Brazil*, 3rd ed. New York, NY: Columbia University Press, 1993.

Butler, Kim. "New Negros: negritude e movimentos Pós-Abolição no Brasil e na diáspora africana." In Martha Abreu, Carolina Vianna Dantas, Hebe Mattos, Beatriz Loner, and Karl Monsma, eds., *Histórias do pós-abolição no mundo atlântico*, vol 3., pp. 137–148. Niterói: EdUFF, 2014.

Cabral, Flávio José Gomes, and Robson Costa, eds. *História da escravidão em Pernambuco*. Recife: Editora da UFPE, 2012.

Caé, Rachel da Silveira. "Escravidão e liberdade na construção do Estado Oriental do Uruguai (1830–1860)." MA thesis in History, Universidade Federal do Estado do Rio de Janeiro, 2012.

Caldeira, Newman di Carlo. "Cativos asilado." In Monica Verónica Secreto and Flávio Gomes, eds., *Territórios do sul: escravidão, escritas e fronteiras coloniais e pós coloniais na América*, pp. 115–141. Rio de Janeiro: FAPERJ/7Letras, 2017.

Camp, Stephanie. *Closer to Freedom: Enslaved Women and Everyday Resistance in the Plantation South*. Chapel Hill: University of North Carolina Press, 2004.

Campbell, Gwyn. "Children and Slavery in the New World: A Review." *Slavery and Abolition* 27:2 (2006): 261–285.

Campbell, Gwyn, Suzanne Miers, and Joseph C. Miller. "Children in European Systems of Slavery: Introduction." *Slavery and Abolition* 27:2, 2006: 163–182.

Candido, Antônio. "The Brazilian Family." In T. Lynn Smith and Alexander Marchan, eds., *Brazil, Portrait of Half a Continent*, pp. 291–312. New York: Dryden Press, 1951.

Candido, Mariana. *An African Slaving Port and the Atlantic World: Benguela and its Hinterland*. New York: Cambridge University Press, 2013.

Cañizares-Esguerra, Jorge, Matt D. Childs, and James Sidbury. *The Black Urban Atlantic in the Age of the Slave Trade*. Philadelphia: University of Pennsylvania Press, 2013.

Capel, Heloisa Selma Fernandes. "Entre o riso e o desprezo: Modesto Brocos como crítico na 'Terra do Cruzeiro.'" *19&20* 11:1 (2016): online.

Capone, Stefania. *Os Yoruba do novo mundo: religião, etinicidade e nacionalismo nos Estados Unidos*. Rio de Janeiro: Pallas, 2011.

Caratti, Jonatas. *O solo da liberdade: as trajetórias da preta Faustina e do pardo Anacleto pela fronteira rio-grandense no contexto das leis abolicionistas uruguaias (1842–1862)*. São Leopoldo: Oikos, Editora Unisinos, 2013.

Cardoso, Ciro Flamarion. "A brecha camponesa no sistema escravista." In Ciro Flamarion Cardoso, *Agricultura, escravidão e capitalismo*, pp. 133–154. Petrópolis: Vozes, 1979. (Published in English as "The Peasant Breach in the Slaveholding System." *Luso-Brazilian Review* 25:1, 1988: 49–57.)
   Escravo ou camponês? O protocampesinato negro nas Américas. São Paulo: Brasiliense, 1987.

Cardoso, Fernando Henrique. *Capitalismo e escravidão no Brasil meridional: o negro na sociedade escravocrata do Rio Grande do Sul*. Sao Paulo: Difusao Européia do Livro, 1962.

Cardoso, Rafael. *A arte brasileira em 25 quadros, 1790–1930*. Rio de Janeiro: Record, 2008.

Cardoso, Ruth C. L. "Creating Kinship: The Fostering of Children in Favela Families in Brazil." In Raymond Thomas Smith, ed., *Kinship Ideology and Practice in Latin America*, pp. 196–203. Chapel Hill: University of North Carolina Press, 1984.

Carneiro, Maria Elizabeth Ribeiro. "Procura-se uma 'preta com muito bom leite, prendada e carinhosa': uma cartografia das amas-de-leite na sociedade carioca, 1850–1888." PhD thesis in History, Universidade de Brasília, 2006.

Carneiro, Maria Luiza Tucci, ed. *Minorias silenciadas: história da censura no Brasil*. São Paulo: Edusp/Imprensa Oficial de São Paulo/Fapesp, 2002.

Preconceito racial: Portugal e Brasil-colônia. São Paulo: Brasiliense, 1983.

Carula, Karoline. "Perigosas amas de leite: aleitamento materno, ciência e escravidão em A Mãi de Família." *História, Ciências e Saúde-Manguinhos* 19:sup. 1, 2012: 197–214.

Carvalho, Alexandre Filordi de. "História e subjetividade no pensamento de Michel Foucault." PhD Thesis in Philosophy, University of São Paulo, 2007.

Carvalho, Daniella Vallandro. "Em solos fronteiriços e movediços: fugas cativas em tempos belicosos (Província de São Pedro, século XIX)." In Keila Grinberg, ed., *As fronteiras da escravidão e da liberdade no sul da América*, pp. 111–128. Rio de Janeiro: 7Letras, 2013.

Carvalho, José Murilo de. *A construção da ordem & Teatro de sombras*, 5th ed. Rio de Janeiro: Civilização Brasileira, 2003.

"Federalismo e centralização no Império brasileiro: história e argumento." In José Murilo de Carvalho, *Pontos e bordados: escritos de história e política*, pp. 155–188. Belo Horizonte: Editora da UFMG, 1998.

Os bestializados: o Rio de Janeiro e a república que não foi, 3rd ed. São Paulo: Companhia das Letras, 1987.

Carvalho, Marcus J. M. de. "De portas adentro e de portas afora: trabalho doméstico e escravidão no Recife, 1822–1850." *Afro-Ásia* 29–30 (2003): 41–78.

"Hegemony and Rebellion in Pernambuco, 1821–1835." PhD dissertation in History, University of Illinois, 1987.

Liberdade: rotinas e rupturas do escravismo, Recife, 1822–1850. Recife: Editora da UFPE, 1998.

"Malunguinho quilombola e malunguinho da Jurema: notas sobre as memórias da escravidão em Pernambuco." In Franck Ribard, ed., *Memórias da escravidão em torno do Atlântico*, pp. 51–69. Fortaleza: UFC/CAPES-COFECUB/Expressão Gráfica, 2016.

"O desembarque nas praias: o funcionamento do tráfico de escravos depois de 1831." *Revista de História* 167, 2012: 223–260.

"O quilombo de Catucá em Pernambuco." *Caderno CRH* 15 (1991): 5–28.

Carvalho, Maria Alice Rezende. *O quinto século: André Rebouças e a construção do Brasil*. Rio de Janeiro: IUPERJ/UCAM/Editora Revan, 1998.

Casas, Lincoln R. Maiztegui. *Orientales: una historia política del Uruguay*, vol. 1. Montevideo: Planeta, 2004.

Casey, James. *História da família*. São Paulo: Ática, 1989.

Castilho, Celso Thomas. *Slave Emancipation and Transformations in Brazilian Political Citizenship*. Pittsburgh: University of Pittsburgh Press, 2016.

Castilho, Celso Thomas, and Camillia Cowling. "Funding Freedom, Popularizing Politics: Abolitionism and Local Emancipation Funds in 1880s Brazil." *Luso-Brazilian Review* 47:1 (2010): 89–120.

Castilho, Lisa, Wlamyra Albuquerque, and Gabriela dos Reis Sampaio, eds. *Barganhas e querelas da escravidão- tráfico, alforria e liberdade*. Salvador: EDUFBa, 2014.

Castro, Antônio Barros de. "A economia política, o capitalismo e a escravidão." In José Roberto do Amaral Lapa, ed., *Modos de produção e realidade brasileira*, pp. 67–107. Petrópolis: Vozes, 1980.

Caulfield, Sueann. "From Liberalism to Human Dignity: The Transformation of Marriage and Family Rights in Brazil." In Julia Moses, ed., *Marriage, Law and Modernity: Global Histories*, pp. 27–53. London: Bloomsbury, 2017.

In Defense of Honor. Durham, NC: Duke University Press, 2000.

Caulfield, Sueann, and Cristiana Schettini. "Gender and Sexuality in Brazil since Independence." In William Beezley, ed., *The Oxford Research Encyclopedia of Latin American History*, online. New York: Oxford University Press, 2017.

Caulfield, Sueann, and Alexandra Minna Stern. "Shadows of Doubt: The Uneasy Incorporation of Identification Science into Legal Determination of Paternity in Brazil." *Cadernos de Saúde Pública* 33: Sup 1 (2017): 1–14.

Chakrabarty, Dipesh. *Provincializing Europe.* Princeton, NJ: Princeton University Press, 2007.

Chalhoub, Sidney. *A força da escravidão: ilegalidade e costume no Brasil oitocentista.* São Paulo: Companhia das Letras, 2012.

Cidade febril. São Paulo: Companhia. das Letras, 1996.

Machado de Assis – historiador. São Paulo: Companhia das Letras, 2003.

"The Politics of Ambiguity: Conditional Manumission, Labor Contracts, and Slave Emancipation in Brazil (1850s–1888)." *International Review of Social History* 60:2 (2015): 161–191.

"The Politics of Silence: Race and Citizenship in Nineteenth-Century Brazil." *Slavery and Abolition* 27:1 (2006): 73–87.

"Precariedade estrutural: o problema da liberdade no Brasil escravista (século XIX)." *História Social* 19, 2010: 33–62.

"The Precariousness of Freedom in a Slave Society (Brazil in the Nineteenth Century)." *International Review of Social History* 56:3 (2011): 405–439.

Trabalho, lar e botequim: o cotidiano dos trabalhadores no Rio de Janeiro da Belle Époque. Campinas: UNICAMP, 2012.

Visões da liberdade: uma história das últimas décadas da escravidão na Corte. São Paulo: Companhia das Letras, 1990.

Chasteen, John Charles. *Born in Blood and Fire: A Concise History of Latin America*, 3rd ed. New York: W. W. Norton, 2011.

National Rhythms, African Roots: The Deep History of Latin American Popular Dance. Albuquerque: University of New Mexico Press, 2004.

Chartes, Ann. *Nobody: The Story of Bert Williams.* London: MacMillan, 1970.

Chude-Sokei, Louis. *The Last "Darky": Bert Williams, Black-on-Black Minstrelsy and the African Diaspora.* Durham, NC: Duke University Press, 2006.

Clemens, Elisabeth. "Logics of History? Agency, Multiplicity, and Incoherence in the Explanation of Change." In Julia Adams, Elisabeth Clemens and Ann Orloff, eds., *Remaking Modernity*, pp. 1–72. Durham: Duke University Press, 2005.

Clinton, Catherine. "Caught in the Web of the Big House: Women and Slavery." In Walter Fraser, ed., *The Web of Southern Social Relations: Women, Family and Education*, pp. 19–34. Athens: University of Georgia Press, 1985.

Conduru, Roberto. "Afromodernidade – representações de afrodescendentes e modernização artística no Brasil." In *Pérolas negras: primeiros fios: experiências artísticas e culturais nos fluxos entre África e Brasil.* pp. 301–313. Rio de Janeiro: EdUERJ, 2013.

"*Mandinga*, ciência, e arte – religiões afro-brasileiras em Modesto Brocos, Nina Rodrigues e João do Rio." In *Pérolas negras: primeiros fios: experiências artísticas e culturais nos fluxos entre África e Brasil*, pp. 315–325. Rio de Janeiro: EdUERJ, 2013.

Pérolas negras: primeiros fios: experiências artísticas e culturais nos fluxos entre África e Brasil. Rio de Janeiro: EdUERJ, 2013.

Conrad, Robert. *The Destruction of Brazilian Slavery, 1850–1888.* Berkeley: University of California Press, 1972.

Os últimos anos da escravatura no Brasil. Rio de Janeiro: Civilização Brasileira, 1975.

Cooper, Frederick, Thomas C. Holt, and Rebecca J. Scott. *Beyond Slavery: Explorations of Race, Labor, and Citizenship in Post-Emancipation Societies.* Chapel Hill: University of North Carolina Press, 2000.

Corrêa, Mariza. "Repensando a família patriarcal brasileira." *Cadernos de Pesquisa* 37 (1981): 5–16.

Costa, Carlos. *A revista no Brasil do século XIX: a história da formação das publicações, do leitor e da identidade do brasileiro.* São Paulo: Alameda, 2012.

Costa, Emilia Viotti da. *A abolição.* São Paulo. UNESP, 2008.

Da senzala à colônia. São Paulo: DIFEL, 1966.

"Estruturas versus experiência – novas tendências na história do movimento operário e das classes trabalhadoras na América Latina: o que se perde e o que se ganha." In Emilia Viotti da Costa, *A dialética invertida e outros ensaios.* SP: Unesp, 2014.

Costa, Jurandir Freire. *Ordem médica e norma familiar*, 2nd ed. Rio de Janeiro: Graal, 1983.

Costa, Vivian. "Codificação e formação do Estado-nacional brasileiro: o Código Criminal de 1830 e a positivação das leis no pós-independência." MA thesis in Brazilian Studies, Universidade de São Paulo, 2013.

Costa e Silva, Alberto da. *A manilha e o libambo: a África e a escravidão de 1500 a 1700.* Rio de Janeiro: Nova Fronteira, 2002.

Costa Pinto, Luiz de A. *O negro no Rio de Janeiro: relações raciais numa sociedade em mudança.* São Paulo: Companhia Editora Nacional,1952.

Cowley, John. *Carnival, Canboulay and Calypso, Traditions in the Making.* Cambridge: Cambridge University Press, 1998.

Cota, Luiz Gustavo Santos. "Ave, Libertas: abolicionismos e luta pela liberdade em Minas Gerais na última década da escravidão." PhD Thesis in History, Universidade Federal Fluminense, 2013.

Cowling, Camillia. *Conceiving Freedom: Women of Color, Gender and the Abolition of Slavery in Havana and Rio de Janeiro.* Chapel Hill: University of North Carolina Press, 2013.

Craton, Michael. "Continuity Not Change: The Incidence of Unrest among Ex-slaves in the British West Indies, 1838–1876." *Slavery and Abolition* 9:2 (1988): 144–170.

Cunha, Arnaldo Pimenta da. "Theodoro íntimo." *Revista IGHBa* 69 (1943): 132.

Cunha, Israel Ozanam de Souza. *Capoeira e capoeiras entre a guarda negra e a educação física no Recife.* Recife: Editora da UFPE, 2013.

Cunha, Olívia Maria Gomes da. "Criadas para servir: domesticidade, intimidade e retribuição." In Olívia M. G. da Cunha and Flávio G. dos Santos, eds., *Quase-cidadão: histórias e antropologias da pós-emancipação no Brasil*, pp. 377–418. Rio de Janeiro: Editora Fundação Getúlio Vargas, 2007.

Curtin, Philip. *The Atlantic Slave Trade: A Census.* Madison: University of Wisconsin Press, 1969.

Daibert Júnior, Robert. *Isabel, a "redentora" dos escravos: uma história da princesa entre olhares negro e brancos (1846–1988).* Bauru: EDUSC, 2004.

Dantas, Monica Duarte. "Dos statutes ao código brasileiro de 1830: o levante de escravos como crime de insurreição." *Revista do Instituto Histórico e Geographico Brasileiro* 452 (2011): 273–309.

"Introdução. Revoltas, motins, revoluções: das Ordenações ao Código Criminal." In Monica Duarte Dantas, ed., *Revoltas, motins, revoluções: homens livres pobres e libertos no Brasil do século XIX*, pp. 7–67. São Paulo: Alameda Editorial, 2011: 7–67.

Davis, Mike. *Planet of Slums.* London: Verso, 2005.

Davis, Natalie Zenon. *The Return of Martin Guerre.* Cambridge, MA: Harvard University Press, 1983.

Dawdy, Shannon. *Building the Devil's Empire: French Colonial New Orleans.* Chicago, IL: University of Chicago Press, 2008.

Dean, Warren. *Rio Claro: A Brazilian Plantation System, 1820–1920.* Palo Alto, CA: Stanford University Press, 1976.

With Broadax and Firebrand. Berkeley: University of California Press, 1997.

Degler, Carl. *Neither Black nor White: Slavery and Race Relations in Brazil and the United States.* New York, NY: Macmillan, 1971.

De la Fuente, Alejandro. "From Slaves to Citizens? Tannenbaum and the Debates on Slavery, Emancipation, and Race Relations in Latin America." *International Labor and Working-Class History* 77 (2010): 154–173.

De la Torre, Oscar. *The People of the River: Nature and Identity in Black Amazonia, 1835–1945.* Chapel Hill: University of North Carolina Press, 2018.

Deleuze, Gilles. *Spinoza: filosofia prática.* São Paulo: Escuta, 2002.

Dias, Maria Odila Leite de Silva. "Novas subjetividades na pesquisa histórica feminista: uma hermenêutica das diferenças." *Estudos Feministas* 2:2 (1994): 373–382.

Power and Everyday Life: The Lives of Working Women in Nineteenth-Century Brazil. New Brunswick, NJ: Rutgers University Press, 1995.

Quotidiano e poder em São Paulo no século XIX. São Paulo: Editora Brasiliense, 1984.

Diptee, Audra A. "African Children in the British Slave Trade during the Late Eighteenth Century." *Slavery and Abolition* 27:2 (2006): 183–196.

Donzelot, Jacques. *A polícia das famílias*, 2nd ed. Rio de Janeiro: Graal, 1986.

Doratioto, Francisco. *Maldita guerra: nova história da guerra do Paraguai*. São Paulo: Companhia das Letras, 2002.

Doratioto, Francisco, and Ricardo Salles. *Guerra do Paraguai*. Buenos Aires: Emecé editores, 2008.

Drescher, Seymour, and Pieter Emmer, eds. *Who Abolished Slavery? Slave Revolts and Abolitionism: A Debate with João Pedro Marques*. New York: Berghahn Books, 2010.

Duarte, Constância Lima. *Imprensa feminina e feminista no Brasil, século XIX*. Belo Horizonte: Autêntica, 2016.

Du Bois, W. E. B. *The Souls of Black Folk*. Boston, MA: Bedford Books, 1997.

Efegê, Jota. *Figuras e coisas da música popular brasileira*. Rio de Janeiro: Funarte, 1978.

Eisenberg, Peter. *The Sugar Industry in Pernambuco, 1840–1910: Modernization without Change*. Berkeley: University of California Press, 1974.

Elias, Norbert. *A sociedade de corte*, 2nd ed. Lisbon: Estampa, 1995.

Mi trayectoria intelectual. Barcelona: Ediciones Península, 1984.

Processo civilizador, vols I and II. São Paulo: Jorge Zahar, 1993–1994.

Elkins, Stanley. *Slavery: A Problem in American Institutional and Intellectual Life*. Chicago, IL: University of Chicago Press, 1959.

Eltis, David. *Economic Growth and the Ending of the Transatlantic Slave Trade*. New York, NY: Oxford University Press, 1987.

Eltis, David, and David Richardson. *Atlas of the Transatlantic Slave Trade*. New Haven, CT: Yale University Press, 2010.

eds. *Extending the Frontiers: Essays on the New Transatlantic Slave Trade Database*. New Haven, CT: Yale University Press, 2008.

Engel, Magali. *Meretrizes e doutores: saber médico e prostituição no Rio de Janeiro (1840–1890)*. São Paulo: Editora Brasiliense, 1989.

Engemann, Carlos. "De grande escravaria à comunidade escrava." *Estudos de História: Revista do Programa de Pós-graduação em História* 9:2 (2002): 75–96.

Evans, William McKee. "From the Land of Canaan to the Land of Guinea: The Strange Odyssey of the 'Sons of Ham.'" *American Historical Review* 85:1 (1980): 15–43.

Faoro, Raymundo. *Os donos do poder: formação do patronato politico brasileiro*, 5th ed. São Paulo: Biblioteca Azul, 2012. (First edition: Rio de Janeiro: Editora Globo, 1958.)

Faria, Sheila Siqueira de Castro. "Damas mercadoras: as 'pretas minas' no Rio de Janeiro, século XVIII a 1850." In Mariza de Carvalho Soares, ed., *Rotas atlânticas da diáspora africana: da Baía do Benin ao Rio de Janeiro*, pp. 219–232. Rio de Janeiro: EDUFF, 2006.

"Sinhás pretas: acumulação de pecúlio e transmissão de bens de mulheres forras no sudeste escravista (séculos XVIII e XIX)." In Francisco Carlos Teixeira da Silva, Hebe Maria Mattos de Castro, and João Fragoso, eds., *Ensaios sobre história e educação*, pp. 289–329. Rio de Janeiro: Mauad/ Faperj, 2001.

"Terra e trabalho em Campos dos Goytacazes." MA thesis in History, Universidade Federal Fluminense, 1986.

Farias, Juliana Barreto, Flavio dos Santos Gomes, Carlos Eugênio Líbano Soares, and Carlos Eduardo de Araújo Moreira. *Ciadades negras: africanos, crioulos e espaços urbanos no Brasil escravista do século XIX*. São Paulo: Alameda, 2006.

Fausto, Boris, and Fernando Devoto. *Brasil e Argentina: um ensaio de história comparada (1850–2002)*. São Paulo: Editora 34, 2004.

Feherenbacher, Don E. *The Dred Scott Case: Its Significance in American Law and Politics*. Oxford: Oxford University Press, 1979.

Slavery, Law, Politics: The Dred Scott Case in Historical Perspective. Oxford: University of Oxford Press, 1981.

Fernandes, Florestan. *A integração do negro na sociedade de classes*. São Paulo: Dominus Editora/Universidade de São Paulo, 1965.

O negro no mundo dos brancos, 2nd ed. São Paulo: Global, 2007.

Ferguson, James. *Expectations of Modernity*. Berkeley: University of California Press, 1999.

Ferraro, Marcelo Rosanova. "Capitalism, Slavery and the Making of Brazilian Slaveholding Class: A Theoretical Debate on World-System Perspective." *Almanack* 23 (2019): 151–175.

Ferreira, Gabriela Nunes. *O Rio da Prata e a consolidação do estado imperial*. São Paulo: Hucitec, 2006.

Ferreira, Roquinaldo. *Cross-Cultural Exchange in the Atlantic World: Angola and Brazil During the Era of the Slave Trade*. Cambridge: Cambridge University Press, 2012.

Ferrer, Ada. "Haiti, Free Soil, and Antislavery in the Revolutionary Atlantic." *American Historical Review* 117:1 (2012): 40–66.

Fields, Barbara. "Ideology and Race in American History." In J. Morgan Kousser and James M. McPherson, eds., *Region, Race, and Reconstruction: Essays in Honor of C. Vann Woodward*, pp. 143–177. New York: Oxford University Press, 1982.

Finkelman, Paul. *An Imperfect Union: Slavery, Federalism, and Comity*. Chapel Hill: University of North Carolina Press, 1981.

Fischer, Brodwyn. "A ética do silêncio racial no context urbano: políticas públicas e desigualdade social no Recife, 1900–1940." *Anais do Museu Paulista: História e Cultura Material*, Nova Série 28 (2020): 1–45.

"A Century in the Present Tense." In Brodwyn Fischer, Bryan McCann, and Javier Auyero, eds., *Cities from Scratch: Poverty and Informality in Urban Latin America*, pp. 9–67. Durham, NC: Duke University Press, 2014.

"From the Mocambo to the Favela: Statistics and Social Policy in Brazil's Informal Cities." *Histoire et Mesure* 34:1 (2019): 15–40.

A Poverty of Rights: Citizenship and Inequality in Twentieth-Century Rio de Janeiro. Stanford, CA: Stanford University Press, 2008.

"Quase Pretos de Tão Pobres? Race and Social Discrimination in Rio de Janeiro's Criminal Courts." *Latin American Research Review* 39:1 (2004): 31–59.

Flandrin, Jean-Louis. *Famílias, parentesco, casa e sexualidade na sociedade antiga*. Lisbon: Estampa, 1995.

Fletcher, Ian Christopher, ed. *Forum: New Historical Perspectives on the First Universal Races Congress of 1911. Radical History Review* 92 (2005): 99–152.

Florentino, Manolo. *Em costas negras: uma história do tráfico de escravos entre a África e o Rio de Janeiro.* São Paulo: Companhia das Letras, 1997.

"Sobre minas, crioulos e a liberdade costumeira no Rio de Janeiro, 1789–1871." In Manolo Florentino, ed., *Tráfico, cativeiro e liberdade – Rio de Janeiro, séculos XVII-XIX*, pp. 331–366. Rio de Janeiro: Civilização Brasileira, 2005.

Florentino, Manolo, and José Roberto Pinto de Góes. *A paz das senzalas: famílias escravas e tráfico atlântico, Rio de Janeiro, 1790–1850.* Rio de Janeiro: Civilização Brasileira, 1997.

Flores, Mariana. *Crimes de fronteira: a criminalidade na fronteira meridional do Brasil (1845–1889).* Porto Alegre: Edipucrs, 2014.

Flory, Thomas. *Judge and Jury in Imperial Brazil, 1808–1871: Social Control and Political Stability in the New State.* Austin: University of Texas Press, 1981.

Follett, Richard, Eric Foner, and Walter Johnson. *Slavery's Ghost: The Problem of Freedom in the Age of Emancipation.* Baltimore, MD: Johns Hopkins University Press, 2011.

Foner, Eric. *Nada além da liberdade: a emancipação e seu legado.* Rio de Janeiro: Paz e Terra, 1988.

Fonseca, Claudia. *Caminhos da adoção.* São Paulo: Cortez, 2002.

"Patterns of Shared Parenthood among the Brazilian Poor." *Social Text*, 74 21:1 (2003): 111–127.

Fonseca, Luís Anselmo da. *A escravidão, o clero e o abolicionismo.* Recife: Editora Massangana, 1988.

Foucault, Michel. "A escrita de si." In Michel Foucault, *O que é um autor?*, pp. 129–160. Lisbon: Passagens, 1992.

"O sujeito e o poder." In Paul Rabinow and Hubert Dreyfus, eds., *Foucault, uma trajetória filosófica: Para além do estruturalismo e da hermenêutica*, pp. 231–249. Rio de Janeiro: Forense Universitária, 1995.

Fox-Genovese, Elizabeth. *Within the Plantation Household.* Chapel Hill: University of North Carolina Press, 1988.

Fraga Filho, Walter. *Encruzilhadas da liberdade: historias e trajetórias de escravos libertos na Bahia, 1870–1910.* Campinas: Editora da UNICAMP, 2006.

Fragoso, João Luís Ribeiro, and Manolo Garcia Florentino. "Marcelino, filho de Inocência, Crioula, neto de Joana Cabinda: um estudo sobre famílias escravas em Paraíba do Sul (1835–1872)." *Estudos Econômicos* 17:2 (1987): 151–173.

Franceschi, Humberto. *A Casa Edison e seu tempo.* Rio de Janeiro: Sarapuí, 2002.

Francisco, Thiago Pereira. "Habitação popular, reforma urbana e periferização no Recife, 1920–1945." MA thesis in History, Universidade Federal de Pernambuco, 2013.

Frank, Zephyr. *Dutra's World: Wealth and Family in Nineteenth-Century Rio de Janeiro.* Albuquerque: University of New Mexico Press, 2004.

Reading Rio de Janeiro: Literature and Society in the Nineteenth Century. Stanford, CA: Stanford University Press, 2016.

Frega, Ana. "Caminos de libertad en tiempos de revolución." In Arturo Betancur, Alex Borucki, and Ana Frega, eds., *Estudios sobre la cultura afro-rioplatense,* pp. 45–66. Montevideo: Facultad de Humanidades y Ciencias de la Educación, 2004.

Freire, Maria Martha de Luna. *Mulheres, mães e médicas: o discurso maternalista no Brasil.* Rio de Janeiro: FGV, 2009.

Freitas, Marcos Cezar de, ed. *História social da infância no Brasil.* São Paulo: Cortez, 1997.

Freitas, Marcos Cezar de, and Moysés Kuhlmann Jr., eds. *Os intelectuais na história da infância.* São Paulo: Cortez, 2002.

Freyre, Gilberto. *Casa grande e senzala,* 52nd ed. São Paulo: Global, 2013. (32nd ed., Rio de Janeiro: Record, 1997; 25th ed., São Paulo: José Olympio, 1987; 1st ed., Rio de Janeiro: Maia & Schmidt, 1933.)

The Mansions and the Shanties. New York: Knopf, 1963.

The Masters and the Slaves: A Study in the Development of Brazilian Civilization. Translated by *Samuel Putnam,* 2nd ed. New York: Knopf, 1963.

Mucambos do nordeste, Rio de Janeiro: Ministério da Educação e Saúde, 1937.

Ordem e progresso, 6th ed. São Paulo: Global, 2004. (1st ed., Rio de Janeiro: José Olympio, 1959.)

"O centenário de Teodoro Sampaio." *Revista IGHBa* 79 (1955): 10.

Sobrados e mocambos, 15th ed. São Paulo: Global, 2004. (Also cited: 2a ed. Rio de Janeiro: José Olympio, 1951; 1st ed. São Paulo: Editora Nacional, 1936.)

Um engenheiro francês no Brasil, vol. 1. Rio de Janeiro: José Olympio Editora, 1960.

Fridman, Fania. "As cidades e o café." *Revista Brasileira de Gestão e Desenvolvimento Regional* 4:3 (2008): 27–48.

Fuchs, Rachel G. *Contested Paternity: Constructing Families in Modern France.* Baltimore, MD: Johns Hopkins University Press, 2008.

Fuentes, Marisa. *Dispossessed Lives.* Philadelphia: University of Pennsylvania Press, 2016.

Furtado, Celso. *Formação econômica do Brasil.* São Paulo, Companhia Editora Nacional, 1959.

Galvão, Rafaella Valença de Andrade. "Felippe Neri Collaço: um homem de cor, de letras e de números, Recife, 1815–1894." MA thesis in History, Universidade Federal de Pernambuco, 2016.

Garavazo, Juliana. "Relações familiares e estabilidade da família escrava: Batatais (1850–1888)." In Associação de Pesquisadores em História Económica, *Anais do II Encontro da Pós-Graduação em História Econômica,* no pagination. Rio de Janeiro: Niterói, 2004.

García, Guadalupe. *Beyond the Walled City.* Berkeley: University of California Press, 2016.

Gaspar, David Barry. "Slavery, Amelioration, and Sunday Markets in Antigua, 1823–1831." *Slavery and Abolition* 9:1 (1988): 1–28.

Gates, Henry Louis. *Black in Latin America.* New York: New York University Press, 2011.

Gilroy, Paul. *Atlântico negro: modernidade e dupla consciência.* Rio de Janeiro: Editora 34, 2001.

Glymph, Travolia. *Out of the House of Bondage: The Transformation of the Plantation Household.* Cambridge: Cambridge University Press, 2008.

Godoi, Rodrigo Camargo de. *Um editor no Império: Francisco de Paula Brito, 1809–1861.* São Paulo: Editora da Universidade de São Paulo, 2016.

Golden, Janet Lynne. *A Social History of Wet Nursing in America: From Breast to Bottle.* Cambridge: Cambridge University Press, 1996.

Goldenberg, David M. *The Curse of Ham: Race and Slavery in Early Judaism, Christianity, and Islam.* Princeton, NJ: Princeton University Press, 2003.

Gomes, Amanda Barlavento. "De traficante de escravos a Barão de Beberibe: a trajetória de Francisco Antonio de Oliveira, 1820–1855." MA thesis in History, Universidade Federal de Pernambuco, 2016.

Gomes, Ángela de Castro, ed. *Escrita de si, escrita da história.* Rio de Janeiro: Editora Fundação Getúlio Vargas, 2004.

Gomes, Flávio dos Santos. *Histórias de quilombolas: mocambos e comunidades de senzalas no Rio de Janeiro – século XIX,* revised edition. São Paulo: Companhia das Letras, 2006. (1st ed, Rio de Janeiro: Arquivo Nacional, 1995.)

Nas terras do Cabo Norte: fronteiras, colonização, e escravidão na Guiana brasileira, sécs XVIII/XIX. Belém: UFPA, 1999.

Negros e política (1888–1937). Rio de Janeiro: Jorge Zahar Ed., 2005.

"No meio de águas turvas (racismo e cidadania no alvorecer da República: a Guarda Negra na Corte – 1888–1889)." *Estudos Afro-Asiáticos* 21 (December 1991): 75–96.

"A 'Safe Haven': Runaways Slaves, Mocambos, and Borders in Colonial Amazonia, Brazil." *Hispanic American Historical Review* 82:3 (2002): 469–498.

Gomes, Flávio dos Santos, and Petronio Domingues, eds. *Da nitidez e invisibilidade: legados do pós-emancipação no Brasil.* Belo Horizonte: Fino Traço, 2013.

Experiências da emancipação: biografias, instituições e movimentos sociais no pós-abolição (1890–1980). Rio de Janeiro: Selo Negro, 2011.

Gomes, Flávio dos Santos, and Maria Helena P. T. Machado. "Atravessando a liberdade: deslocamentos, migrações e comunidades volantes na década da abolição (Rio de Janeiro e São Paulo)." In Flávio dos Santos Gomes and Petrônio Domingues, eds., *Políticas da raça,* pp. 69–96. São Paulo: Selo Negro, 2016.

Gomes, Flávio dos Santos, and Rosa Elizabeth Acevedo Marin. "Reconfigurações coloniais: tráfico de indígenas, fugitivos e fronteiras no Grão-Pará e Guiana francesa (sécs. XVII e XVIII)." *Revista de História* 149 (2004): 69–108.

Gomes, Flavio dos Santos, Giovana Xavier, and Juliana Barreto Farias, eds. *Black Women in Brazil in Slavery and Post-Emancipation.* New York: Diasporic Africa Press, 2017.

Gomes, Tiago de Melo. "Para além da casa da Tia Ciata: outras experiências no universo cultural carioca, 1830–1930." *Afro-Ásia,* no. 29–30 (2003): 175–198.

Gontijo, Romilda Mourão. "Parceria e o café na Zona da Mata mineira 1850–1906." MA thesis in Philosophy, Universidade Federal de Minas Gerais, 1992.

Gorender, Jacob. "Questionamentos sobre a teoria econômica do escravismo colonial." *Estudos Econômicos* 1:13 (1983): 7–39.

Gould, Virginia Meacham. "Henriette Delille, Free Women of Color, and Catholicism in Antebellum New Orleans, 1727–1852." In David Gaspar and Darlene Clark Hine, eds., *Beyond Bondage: Free Women of Color in the Americas*, pp. 271–285. Urbana: University of Illinois Press, 2004.

Graham, Sandra Lauderdale. "Being Yoruba in Nineteenth-Century Rio de Janeiro." *Slavery & Abolition* 32:1 (2011): 1–26.

Caetana diz não. São Paulo: Companhia das Letras, 2005.

Caetana Says No: Women's Stories from a Brazilian Slave Society. New York: Cambridge University Press, 2002.

House and Street: The Domestic World of Servants and Masters in Nineteenth Century Rio de Janeiro. Austin: University of Texas Press, 1988.

"O impasse da escravatura: prostitutas escravas, suas senhoras e a lei brasileira de 1871." *Acervo* 9:1–2 (1996): 31–68.

Proteção e obediencia: criadas e seus patrões no Rio do Janeiro, 1860–1910. Translated by Viviana Bosi. São Paulo: Companhia das Letras, 1992.

"Slavery's Impasse: Slave Prostitutes, Small-Time Mistresses, and the Brazilian Law of 1871." *Comparative Studies in Society and History* 33:4 (October 1991): 669–694.

Graham, Richard. *Alimentar a cidade: das vendedoras de rua à reforma líberal (Salvador, 1780–1863).* São Paulo: Companhia das Letras, 2013.

"Another Middle Passage?: The Internal Slave Trade in Brazil." In Walter Johnson, ed., *The Chattel Principle: Internal Slave Trades in the Americas*, pp. 291–324. New Haven, CT: Yale University Press, 2004.

"Brazilian Slavery Re-Examined: A Review." *Journal of Social History* 3:4 (1970): 431–453.

Clientelismo e política no Brasil do século XIX. Rio de Janeiro: Editora UFRJ, 1997.

Feeding the City: From Street Market to Liberal Reform in Salvador, Brazil, 1780–1860. Austin: University of Texas Press, 2010.

Patronage and Politics in Nineteenth-Century Brazil. Stanford, CA: Stanford University Press, 1990.

Grinberg, Keila. *As fronteiras da escravidão e da liberdade no sul da América.* Río de Janeiro: 7Letras, 2013.

A Black Jurist in a Slave Society: Antonio Pereira Rebouças and the Trials of Brazilian Citizenship. Chapel Hill: University of North Carolina Press, 2019.

"Em defesa da propriedade: Antônio Pereira Rebouças e a escravidão." *Afro-Asia* 21–22 (1998, 1999): 111–146.

O fiador dos brasileiros: cidadania, escravidão e direito civil no tempo de Antonio Pereira Rebouças. Rio de Janeiro: Civilização Brasileira, 2002.

"Fronteiras, escravidão e liberdade no sul da América." In Keila Grinberg, ed., *As fronteiras da escravidão e da liberdade no sul da América*, pp. 7–24. Rio de Janeiro: 7Letras, 2013.

Liberata, a lei da ambiguidade: As ações de liberdade da Corte de Apelação do Rio de Janeiro no século XIX. Rio de Janeiro: Relume-Dumará, 1994.

"Illegal Enslavement, International Relations, and International Law on the Southern Border of Brazil." *Law and History Review* 35:1 (2017): 31–52.

"Manumission, Gender, and the Law in Nineteenth-Century Brazil." In Rosemary Brana-Shute and Randy J. Sparks, eds., *Paths to Freedom: Manumission in the Atlantic World*, pp. 219–234. Columbia: University of South Carolina Press, 2009.

"Re-enslavement, Rights and Justice in Nineteenth Century Brazil." *Translating the Americas*, vol. 1, 2013. (First published in Portuguese as "Reescravização, direitos e justiças no Brasil do século XIX." In Silva Hunold Lara and Joseli Maria N. Mendonça, eds., *Direitos e justiças no Brasil: ensaios de história social*. Campinas: Editora da Unicamp/CECULT, 2006: 101–128.)

"Senhores sem escravos: a propósito das ações de escravidão no Brasil Imperial." *Almanack Braziliense* 6 (2007): 4–13.

"Slavery, Manumission and the Law in Nineteenth-Century Brazil: Reflections on the Law of 1831 and the 'Principle of Liberty' on the Southern Frontier of the Brazilian Empire." *European Review of History/Revue Européenne d'Histoire*, 16:3 (2009): 401–411.

"The Two Enslavements of Rufina: Slavery and International Relations on the Southern Border of Nineteenth-Century Brazil." *Hispanic American Historical Review* 96:2 (2016): 259–290.

Grinberg, Keila, and Beatriz Mamigonian, eds. "Dossiê: 'Para inglês ver?': Revisitando a lei de 1831." *Estudos Afro-Asiáticos* 29:1–3 (2007): 87–340.

Grinberg, Keila, and Mariana Muaze. *O 15 de Novembro e a queda da monarquia*. São Paulo: Editora Chão, 2019.

Grinberg, Keila, and Ricardo Salles, eds. *Brasil Imperial*. Río de Janeiro: Civilização Brasileira, 2009.

Groebner, Valentin. "Describing the Person, Reading the Signs in Late Medieval and Renaissance Europe: Identity Papers, Vested Figures, and the Limits of Identification, 1400–1600." In Jane Caplan and John Torpey, eds., *Documenting Individual Identity: The Development of State Practices in the Modern World*, pp. 15–27. Princeton, NJ: Princeton University Press, 2001.

Guazzelli, Cesar. "O horizonte da província: a República Rio-Grandense e os caudilhos do Rio da Prata (1835–1845)." PhD thesis in History, Universidade Federal do Rio de Janeiro, 1998.

Guimarães, Antônio Sérgio A. "A democracia racial revisitada." *Afro-Asia* 60 (2019): 9–44.

"Baianos e paulistas: duas 'escolas' de relações raciais?" *Tempo Social* 11:1 (1999): 75–95.

"Democracia racial: o ideal, o pacto e o mito." *Novos Estudos CEBRAP* 61 (2001): 147–162.

"Preconceito de cor e racismo no Brasil." *Revista de Antropologia* 47:1 (2004): 9–43.

Guss, D. M. *The Festive State: Race, Ethnicity and Nationalism as Cultural Performance*. Berkeley: University of California Press, 2000.

Hamilton, Marybeth. *In Search of the Blues: Black Voices, White Visions*. London: Jonathan Cape, 2007.

Hanchard, Michael. *Orpheus and Power: The Movimento Negro of Rio de Janeiro and São Paulo, Brazil, 1945–1988.* Princeton, NJ: Princeton University Press, 1994.

Harms, Robert. *The Diligent: A Voyage through the Worlds of the Slave Trade.* Oxford: Perseus Press, 2002.

Harris, Leslie, and Diana Berry. *Slavery and Freedom in Savannah.* Athens: University of Georgia Press, 2014.

Hartman, Saidiya. "Anarchy of Colored Girls." *South Atlantic Quarterly* 117:3 (July 2018): 465–490.

Lose Your Mother. New York: Farrar, Straus and Giroux, 2007.

Scenes of Subjection. Terror, Slavery, and Self-Making in Nineteenth-Century America. New York: Oxford University Press, 1997.

Hartog, Hendrik. *Someday All This Will Be Yours: A History of Inheritance and Old Age.* Chicago, IL: University of Chicago Press, 2012.

Hawthorne, Walter. "Being Now, as It Were, One Family: Shipmate Bonding on the Slave Vessel Emilia, in Rio de Janeiro and Throughout the Atlantic World." *Luso-Brazilian Review* 45 (2008): 53–77.

Haynes, Stephen R. *Noah's Curse: The Biblical Justification of American Slavery.* New York: Oxford University Press, 2002.

Hébrard, Jean. "Slavery in Brazil: Brazilian Scholars in the Key Interpretive Debates." In Jean Hébrard, ed., *Brésil: quatre siècles d'esclavage. Nouvelles questions, nouvelles recherches,* pp. 7–61. Paris: Karthala & CIRESC, 2012. (Translated from the French by Thomas Scott-Railton for the University of Michigan's *Translating the Americas* series, 1, 2013.)

Heywood, Colin. *Uma história da infância.* Porto Alegre: Artmed, 2004.

Higginbotham Jr., Leon. *In the Matter of Color: Race and the American Legal Process: The Colonial Period.* Oxford: Oxford University Press, 1978.

Hodes, Martha. "The Mercurial Nature and the Abiding Power of Race: A Transnational Family History." *American Historical Review* 108:1 (2003): 84–118.

The Sea Captain's Wife: A True Story of Love, Race and War in the Nineteenth Century. New York: W. W. Norton & Company, 2006.

ed. *Sex, Love, and Race: Crossing Boundaries in North American History.* New York, NY: New York University Press, 1999.

Hoffnagel, Marc Jay. "'O Homem': raça e preconceito no Recife." *CLIO* 1 (1977): 52–62.

Holanda, Sérgio Buarque de. *Raízes do Brasil.* São Paulo: Companhia das Letras, 2015. (1st edition: Rio de Janeiro: José Olympio, 1936.)

Holloway, Thomas. "The Defiant Life and Forgotten Death of Apulco de Castro: Race, Power, and Historical Memory." *Estudios Interdisciplinarios de América Latina y el Caribe* 19:1 (2007): online.

Hoshino, Thiago de Azevedo Pinheiro. "Entre o *espírito da lei* e o *espírito do século:* a urdidura de uma cultura jurídica da liberdade nas malhas da escravidão (Curitiba, 1868–1888)." MA thesis in Law, Universidade Federal do Paraná, 2013.

Ianni, Octavio. *As metamorfoses do escravo, Apogeu e crise da escravatura no Brasil meridional.* São Paulo: Difusão Européia do Livro, 1962.

Iansen, Martha. "Os senhores que mantinham seus filhos como escravos." Blog *História e Outras Histórias*, July 19, 2011, https://martaiansen.blogspot.com/2 011/07/os-senhores-que-mantinham-seus-filhos.html. Accessed November 2, 2020.

Isola, Ema. *La esclavitud en el Uruguay de sus comienzos hasta su extinción (1743–1852)*. Montevideo: Publicaciones de la Comisión Nacional de Homenaje al Sesquicentenario de los Hechos Históricos de 1825, 1975.

Izecksohn, Vitor. *Slavery and War in the Americas: Race, Citizenship and State Building in the United States and Brazil, 1861–1870*. Charlottesville: University of Virginia Press, 2014.

Johnson, Howard. "The Emergence of a Peasantry in the Bahamas During Slavery." *Slavery and Abolition* 10:2 (1989): 172–186.

Johnson, Lyman. *Workshop of Revolution*. Durham, NC: Duke University Press, 2011.

Johnson, Rashauna. *Slavery's Metropolis*. New York, NY: Cambridge University Press, 2016.

Johnson, Walter. "On Agency." *Journal of Social History* 37:1 (2003): 113–124.
River of Dark Dreams: Slavery and Empire in the Cotton Kingdom. Cambridge, MA: Harvard University Press, 2013.

Jones-Rogers, Stephanie. "'She Could Spare One Ample Breast for the Profit of Her Owner': White Mothers and Enslaved Wet Nurses' Invisible Labor in American Slave Markets." *Slavery and Abolition* 38:2 (2017): 337–355.

Juareguízar, Agustín. "*Viaje a Marte* de Modesto Brocos." *Árbol* 185:740 (2009): 1313–1322.

Karasch, Mary C. *A vida dos escravos no Rio de Janeiro (1808–1850)*. São Paulo: Companhia das Letras, 2000.
Slave Life in Rio de Janeiro, 1808–1850. Princeton, NJ: Princeton University Press, 1987.

Kaye, Anthony. *Joining Places: Slave Neighborhoods in the Old South*. Chapel Hill: University of North Carolina Press, 2009.

Kenney, W. Howland. *Record Music in American Life: The Phonograph and Popular Memory, 1890–1945*. New York, NY: Oxford University Press, 1999.

Kent, Leslie A. *Woman of Color, Daughter of Privilege: Amanda America Dickson, 1849–1893*. Athens: University of Georgia Press, 1995.

Kittleson, Roger. "'Campaign All of Peace and Charity': Gender and the Politics of Abolitionism in Porto Alegre, Brazil, 1879–1888." *Slavery and Abolition* 22:3, 2001: 83–108.

Klein, Herbert S. "A experiência afro-americana numa perspectiva comparada: a situação do debate sobre a escravidão nas Américas." *Afro-Ásia* 45 (2012): 95–121.
The Middle Passage: Comparative Studies in the Atlantic Slave Trade. Princeton, NJ: Princeton University Press, 1978.

Klein, Herbert, and Francisco Vidal Luna. *Slavery in Brazil*. New York: Cambridge University Press, 2009. (Published in Portuguese as Francisco Vidal Luna and Herbert Klein, *O escravismo no Brasil*. SP: Edusp/Imprensa oficial, 2010.)

Klein, Herbert, and João José Reis. "Slavery in Brazil." In José Moya, ed., *The Oxford Handbook of Latin American History*, pp. 181–211. Oxford: Oxford University Press, 2011.

Knauss, Paulo, Marize Malta, Cláudia de Oliveira, and Mônica Pimenta Velloso, eds. *Revistas ilustradas: modos de ler e ver no segundo reinado*. Rio de Janeiro: Maud X/Faperj, 2011.

Koutsoukos, Sandra Sofia Machado. "Amas na fotografia brasileira da segunda metade do século XIX." *Revista Studium – Dossiê Representação Imagética das Africanidades no Brasil*. 2007: online.

Negros no studio fotográfico: Brasil, segunda metade do século XVIII. Campinas: Editora Unicamp, 2010.

"O valor da aparência: nos estúdios fotográficos, negros livres e alforriados criavam uma nova imagem de integração social." *Revista de História* 30, 2008: 84–85.

Kraay, Hendrik. *Days of National Festivity in Rio de Janeiro, Brazil, 1823–1889*. Stanford, CA: Stanford University Press, 2013.

Kraay, Hendrik, and Thomas L. Whigham. *I Die with My Country: Perspectives on the Paraguayan War, 1864–1870*. Lincoln: University of Nebraska Press, 2005.

Krantz, Frederik. *History from Below: Studies in Popular Protest and Popular Ideology in Honour of George Rude*. Montreal: Concordia University, 1986.

Kusser, Astrid. "The Riddle of the Booty: Dancing and the Black Atlantic." *Radical Riddims – Global Ghetto Tech* 10:18 (2011): online.

Kuznesof, Elizabeth Anne. "The House, the Street and the Brothel: Gender in Latin American History." *History of Women in the Americas* 1:1 (2013): 17–31.

"Sexuality, Gender and the Family in Colonial Brazil." *Luso-Brazilian Review* 30:1 (1993): 119–132.

Landers, Jane. "Spanish Sanctuary: Fugitives in Florida, 1687–1790." *Florida Historical Quarterly* 62:3 (1984): 296–313.

Lane, Kris E., and Matthew Restall. *The Riddle of Latin America*. Boston, MA: Wadsworth Cengage Learning, 2012.

Lanna, Ana Lúcia Duarte. *A transformação do trabalho: a passagem para o trabalho livre na Zona da Mata Mineira, 1870-1920*. Campinas: Unicamp/Brasília:CNPq, 1988.

Lara, Silvia Hunold. "'Blowin' in the Wind': E. P. Thompson e a experiência negra no Brasil." *Projeto História* 12 (1995): 43–56.

Campos da violência: escravos e senhores na capitania do Rio de Janeiro, 1750–1808. Rio de Janeiro: Paz e Terra, 1988.

Fragmentos setecentistas: escravidão, cultura e poder na América Portuguesa. São Paulo: Companhia das Letras, 2007.

"O espírito das leis: tradições legais sobre a escravidão e a liberdade no Brasil escravista." *Africana Studia* 14 (2010): 73–92.

Law, Robin, and Paul Lovejoy, eds. *The Biography of Mahommah Gardo Baquaqua: His Passage from Slavery to Freedom in Africa and America*. Princeton, NJ: Marcus Wiener, 2001.

Lawrance, Benjamin. *Amistad's Orphans: An Atlantic Story of Children, Slavery, and Smuggling*. New Haven, CT: Yale University Press, 2015.

Leinaweaver, Jessica. "Introduction: Cultural and Political Economies of Adoption in Latin America." *Journal of Latin American and Caribbean Anthropology* 14:1 (2009): 1–19.

Leite, José Correia, and Cuti. *E disse o velho militante José Correia Leite*. São Paulo: Secretaria Municipal de Cultura, 1992.

Leite, José Roberto Teixeira. *Pintores negros do oitocentos*. São Paulo: Edições K, 1988.

Redenção de Cã: dicionário crítico da pintura no Brasil. Rio de Janeiro: ArtLivre, 1988.

Leite, Marcelo Eduardo. "Retratistas e retratados no Brasil Imperial – um estudo das fotografias carte de visite." PhD dissertation in Multimedia Studies, Unicamp, 2007.

Leite, Miriam Moreira, ed. *A condição feminina no Rio de Janeiro do século XIX*. Rio de Janeiro: Hucitec, 1984.

Livros de viagem. Rio de Janeiro: Editora da UERJ, 1997.

Levine, Lawrence W. *Black Culture and Black Consciousness*. New York, NY: Oxford University Press, 1977.

Lewin, Linda. *Surprise Heirs I: Illegitimacy, Patrimonial Rights, and Legal Nationalism in Luso-Brazilian Inheritance, 1750–1821*. Stanford, CA: Stanford University Press, 2003.

Surprise Heirs II: Illegitimacy, Inheritance Rights, and Public Power in the Formation of Imperial Brazil. Stanford, CA: Stanford University Press, 2003.

Lima, Arnaldo do Rosario. "Teodoro Sampaio: sua vida e sua obra." MA thesis in Social Science, Universidade Federal de Bahia, 1981.

Lima, Heloisa Pires. "A presença negra nas telas: visita às exposições do circuito da Academia Imperial de Belas Artes na década de 1880." *19&20* 3:1 (2008): online.

Lima, Henrique Espada. "Freedom, Precariousness and the Law." *International Review of Social History* 54:3 (2009): 391–416.

"Sob o domínio da precariedade: escravidão e os significados da liberdade de trabalho no século XIX." *Topoi* 6:11 (July–December 2005): 289–326.

Lima, Henrique Espada, and Fabiane Popinigus. "Maids, Clerks, and the Shifting Landscape of Labor." *Luso-Brazilian Review* 62: S2.5, 2017: 45–73.

Lima, Lana Lage da Gama. *Rebeldia negra e abolicionismo*. Rio de Janeiro: Achiamé, 1981.

Lima, Rafael Peter de. "'A nefanda pirataria de carne humana': escravizações ilegais e relações políticas na fronteira do Brasil meridional (1851–1868)." MA thesis in History, Universidade Federal do Rio Grande do Sul, 2010.

"Negros uruguaios na Corte: implicações diplomátias e estratégias de resistência (meados do século XIX)." In *Anais do 5º Encontro Escravidão e Liberdade no Brasil Meridional* (2011): online.

Lira, José Tavares de. "Hidden Meanings: The Mocambo in Recife." *Social Science Information* 38:2 (1999): 297–327.

Lopes, José Reinaldo Lima. *O direito na história*. São Paulo: Atlas, 2011.

Lotierzo, Tatiana H. P., and Lilia K. M. Schwarcz. "Raça, gênero e projeto branqueador: 'a redenção de Cam,' de Modesto Brocos." *Artelogie* 5:5 (2013): online.

Lovejoy, Paul. "The Children of Slavery – The Transatlantic Phase." *Slavery and Abolition* 27:2 (2006): 197–217.

Loveman, Mara. "Blinded Like a State: The Revolt against Civil Registration in Nineteenth-Century Brazil." *Comparative Studies in Society and History* 49:1 (2007): 5–39.

MacCord, Marcelo. *Artífices da cidadania: mutualismo, educação e trabalho no Recife oitocentista*. Campinas: Editora da UNICAMP, 2012.

  O Rosário de D. Antônio: irmandades negras, alianças e conflitos na história social do Recife, 1848–1872. Recife: Editora da UFPE, 2005.

Machado, Humberto Fernandes. *José do Patrocínio e a imprensa abolicionista do Rio de Janeiro*. Rio de Janeiro: Editora da UFF, 2014.

Machado, Maria Helena Pereira Toledo. "Between Two Beneditos: Enslaved Wetnurses Amid Slavery's Decline in Southeast Brazil." *Slavery and Abolition* 38:2 (2017): 320–336.

  "De rebeldes a fura-greves: as duas faces da liberdade dos Quilombolas do Jabaquara na Santos pós-emancipação." In Olívia Maria Gomes da Cunha and Flávio dos Santos Gomes, eds., *Quase-cidadão: histórias e antropologias da pós-emancipação no Brasil*, pp. 241–282. Rio de Janeiro: Editora Fundação Getúlio Vargas, 2007.

  "Em torno da autonomia escrava: uma nova direção para a história social da escravidão." *Revista Brasileira de História* 8:16 (1988): 143–160.

  "Entre dois Beneditos: histórias de amas de leite no ocaso da escravidão." In Giovana Xavier, Juliana Barreto Farias, and Flávio dos Santos Gomes, eds., *Mulheres negras no Brasil escravista e do pós-emancipação*, pp. 199–213. São Paulo: Selo Negro, 2012.

  "From Slave Rebels to Strikebreakers: The Quilombo of Jabaquara and the Problem of Citizenship in Late-Nineteenth-Century Brazil." *Hispanic American Historical Review* 86:2 (2006): 247–274.

  O plano e o pânico: os movimentos sociais na década da abolição. Rio de Janeiro/São Paulo: Editora UFRJ/Editora da Universidade de São Paulo, 1994.

  "Teremos grandes desastres, se não houverem providências enérgicas e imediatas: a rebeldia dos escravos e a abolição da escravidão." In Ricardo Salles and Keila Grinberg, *Brasil Impérial*, vol. 3, pp. 367–400. Rio de Janeiro: Civilização Brasileira, 2009.

  "Vivendo na mais perfeita desordem: os libertos e o modo de vida camponês na província de São Paulo do século XIX." *Estudos Afro-Asiáticos* 25 (1993): 43–72.

Machado, Maria Helena Pereira Toledo, and Celso Castilho, eds. *Tornando-se livre: agentes históricos e lutas sociais no processo de abolição*. São Paulo: Editora da Universidade de São Paulo, 2015.

Machado, Maria Helena Pereira Toledo, and Flávio dos Santos Gomes. "Eles ficaram 'embatucados,' seus escravos sabiam ler: abolicionistas, senhores e cativos no alvorecer da liberdade." In Marcelo MacCord, Carlos Eduardo

Moreira de Araujo, and Flávio dos Santos Gomes, eds., *Rascunhos cativos: educação, escolas e ensino no Brasil Escravista*, pp. 253–283. Rio de Janeiro: 7Letras, 2017.

Machado, Maria Helena Pereira Toledo, Diana Paton, Camillia Cowling, and Emily West. "Mothering Slaves: Motherhood, Childlessness and the Care of Children in Atlantic Slave Societies." Special double issue in *Slavery & Abolition* 28:2 (2017): 223–231; and *Women's History Review* 27:6 (2018).

Maestri, Mario. "A intervenção do Brasil no Uruguai e a Guerra do Paraguai: a missão Saraiva." *Revista Brasileira de História Militar* 5:13 (2014): 6–27.

Magalhães Júnior, Raimundo. *A vida turbulenta de José do Patrocínio*. Rio de Janeiro: Editora Sabiá, 1969.

Machado de Assis – vida e obra, vol. 3 *(maturidade)*, 2nd ed. Rio de Janeiro: Record, 2008.

Maio, Marcos Chor. "O projeto UNESCO e a agenda das ciências sociais no Brasil dos anos 40 e 50." *Revista Brasileira de Ciências Sociais* 14:41 (1999): 141–145.

"UNESCO and the Study of Race Relations in Brazil: Regional or National Issue?" *Latin American Research Review* 36:2 (2001): 118–136.

Maís, Pedro Luís. *Antologia da serenata*. Rio de Janeiro: Simões Editora, 1957.

Maiztegui Casas, Lincoln R. *Orientales: una historia política del Uruguay*, vol. 1. Montevideo: Planeta, 2004.

Mallo, Silvia C., and Ignacio Telesca, eds. *"Negros de la patria": los afrodescendientes en las luchas por la independencia en el antiguo virreinato del Río de la Plata*. Buenos Aires: SB, 2010.

Mamigonian, Beatriz G. *Africanos livres: a abolição do tráfico de escravos no Brasil*. São Paulo: Companhia das Letras, 2017.

"Conflicts Over the Meanings of Freedom: The Liberated Africans' Struggle for Emancipation in Brazil (1840s–1860s)." In Rosemary Brana-Shute and Randy J. Sparks, eds., *Paths to Freedom: Manumission in the Atlantic World*, pp. 235–264. Columbia: University of South Carolina Press, 2009.

"O direito de ser africano livre: os escravos e as interpretações da lei de 1831." In Silvia H. Lara and Joseli M. N. Mendonça, eds., *Direitos e justiças no Brasil: ensaios de história social*, pp. 129–160. Campinas: Editora da Unicamp, 2006.

"O Estado nacional e a instabilidade da propriedade escrava: a lei de 1831 e a matrícula dos escravos de 1872." *Almanack* 2 (2011): 20–37.

Mann, Kristin. *Slavery and the Birth of an African City*. Bloomington: Indiana University Press, 2007.

Marcilio, Maria Luiza. *História social da criança abandonada*. São Paulo: Hucitec, 1998.

Marcondes, Marcos. *Enciclopédia da música brasileira*, 2nd ed. São Paulo: Art Editora, 1998.

Marcondes, Renato Leite. *A arte de acumular na gestação da economia cafeeira: formas de enriquecimento no Vale do Paraíba paulista durante o século XIX*. PhD dissertation in History, Universidade de São Paulo, 1998. (Later published as *A arte de acumular na economia cafeeira: Vale do Paraíba, sec. XIX*. Lorena-SP: Stiliano, 1998.)

Markert, Werner, ed. *Teorias de educação do iluminismo*. Rio de Janeiro: Tempo Brasileiro, 1994.

Marques, João Pedro. "Terão os escravos abolido a escravidão? Considerações a propósito de um livro de Nelly Schmidt." *Africana Studia* 8, 2005: 231–257.

Marques, Leonardo. *The United States and the Transatlantic Slave Trade to the Americas, 1776–1867*. New Haven, CT: Yale University Press, 2016.

Marquese, Rafael. "Capitalism, Slavery and the Brazilian Coffee Economy." In Colin A. Palmer, ed., *The Legacy of Eric Williams: Caribbean Scholar and Statesman*, vol. I, pp. 190–223. Mona: University of the West Indies Press, 2015.

"Estrutura e agência na historiografia da escravidão: a obra de Emília Viotti da Costa." In Tania de Luca, Antonio Celso Ferreira, and Holien Gonçalves Bezerra, eds., *O historiador e seu tempo*, pp. 67–81. São Paulo: Editora Unesp, 2008.

Feitores do corpo, missionários da mente-senhores, letrados e o controle dos escravos nas Américas, 1660-1860. SP: Companhia das Letras, 2004.

Marquese, Rafael, Tâmis Parron, and Márcia Berbel. *Slavery and Politics: Brazil and Cuba, 1790–1850*. Albuquerque: University of New Mexico Press, 2016.

Marquese, Rafael, and Ricardo Salles, eds. *Escravidão e capitalismo histórico no século XIX: Cuba, Brasil e Estados Unidos*. Rio de Janeiro: Civilização Brasileira, 2016.

"Slavery in Nineteenth-Century Brazil: History and Historiography." In Dale Tomich, ed., *Slavery and Historical Capitalism during the Nineteenth Century*, pp. 123–169. Lanham, MD: Lexington Books, 2017.

Marquese, Rafael, and Dale Tomich. "O Vale do Paraíba escravista e a formação do mercado mundial do café no século XIX." In Mariana Muaze and Ricardo Salles, eds., *O Vale do Paraíba e o Império do Brasil nos quadros da segunda escravidão*, pp. 21–56. Rio de Janeiro: Faperj/7Letras, 2015.

Martin, Richard, and Meagan Hennessey (producers). *Bert Williams: The Early Years, 1901–1909, The Middle Years, 1910–1918, His Final Releases, 1919–1922* (liner notes and sound recordings). Champaign, IL: Archeophone Records, 2001-2004.

Martins, Ana Luiza, and Tania Regina de Luca, eds. *História da imprensa no Brasil*. São Paulo: Contexto, 2008.

Martins, Bárbara Canedo R. "Amas-de-leite e mercado de trabalho feminino: descortinando práticas e sujeitos (Rio de Janeiro, 1830–1890)." MA thesis in History, Universidade Federal do Rio de Janeiro, 2006.

Martins, Robson Luís Machado. *Os caminhos da liberdade: abolicionistas, escravos e senhores, na província do Espírito Santo (1884-1888)*. Campinas, SP: UNICAMP/CMU, 2005.

Marzano, Andrea. *Cidade em cena: o ator Vasques, o teatro e o Rio de Janeiro, 1839-1892*. Rio de Janeiro: Folha Seca, 2008.

Matos, Maria Izilda Santos de. "Porta adentro: criados de servir em São Paulo de 1890 a 1930." In Maria Cristina Bruschini and Bila Sorj, eds., *Novos olhares: mulheres e relações de gênero no Brasil*, pp. 193–212. São Paulo: Marco Zero, 1994.

Mattos, Hebe. *Ao sul da história: lavradores pobres na crise do trabalho escravo*, 2nd ed. Rio de Janeiro: Editora Fundação Getúlio Vargas, 2009.

Das cores do silêncio: os significados da liberdade no sudeste escravista. Rio de Janeiro: Arquivo Nacional, 1995.

Das cores do silêncio: os significados da liberdade no sudeste escravista, Brasil, século xix, revised ed. Campinas: Editora UNICAMP, 2013.

"De pai para filho: África, identidade racial e subjetividade nos arquivos privados da família Rebouças (1838–1898)." In Hebe Mattos and Myriam Cottias, eds., *Escravidão e subjetividades no mundo luso brasileiro e francês*. Marseille: Open Edition Press, 2016.

Escravidão e cidadania no Brasil monárquico. Rio de Janeiro: Jorge Zahar, 2001.

"The Madness of Justina and Januário Mina: Rethinking Boundaries between Free and Enslaved labor in Nineteenth-Century Brazil." *Quaderni Storici* 1 (2015): 175–200.

"Políticas de reparação e identidade coletiva no meio rural: Antônio Nascimento Fernandes e o quilombo São José." *Estudos Históricos* 37 (2006): 167–189.

"'Pretos' and 'Pardos' between the Cross and the Sword: Racial Categories in Seventeenth-Century Brazil." *European Review of Latin American and Caribbean Studies* 80 (2006): 43–55.

"'Remanescentes das comunidades dos quilombos': memória do cativeiro e políticas de reparação no Brasil." *Revista USP*, 68 (2006): 104–111.

Mattos, Hebe, and Keila Grinberg. "Antônio Pereira Rebouças e a cidadania sem cor." *Insight Inteligência* 6:20 (2003): 90–96.

"Lapidário de si: Antônio Pereira Rebouças e a escrita de si." In Ângela de Castro Gomes, ed., *Escrita de si, escrita da história*, pp. 27–50. Rio de Janeiro: FGV, 2004.

Mattos, Ilmar Rohloff de. *O tempo saquarema: a formação do estado imperial*. Rio de Janeiro: ACCESS, 1994. (1st ed., 1986.)

Mattoso, Katia de Queiroz. *To Be a Slave in Brazil, 1550–1888*. New Brunswick, NJ: Rutgers University Press, 1986. (1st Portuguese edition, 1982.)

Mauad, Ana Maria, and Mariana Muaze. "A escrita da intimidade: história e memória no diário da Viscondessa do Arcozelo." In Ângela de Castro Gomes, ed., *Escrita de si, escrita da história.*, pp. 197–228. Rio de Janeiro: Editora da Fundação Getúlio Vargas, 2004.

"O poder em foco: fotografia e representação simbólica do poder político republicano do Museu da República." *Cadernos de Memória* 2 (1997): 35–45.

McKittrick, Katherine. *Demonic Grounds: Black Women and the Cartographies of Struggle*, new ed. Minneapolis: University of Minnesota Press, 2006.

Meade, Teresa A. *A Brief History of Brazil*. New York: Facts on File, 2003.

Civilizing Rio: Reform and Resistance in a Brazilian City, 1889–1930. University Park: Pennsylvania State University Press, 1997.

Meirelles, Juliana Gesuelli. *Imprensa e poder na corte joanina: a Gazeta do Rio de Janeiro (1808–1821)*. Rio de Janeiro: Arquivo Nacional, 2008.

Mello, Maria Tereza Chaves de. "Com o arado do pensamento: a cultura democrática e científica da década de 1880 no Rio de Janeiro." PhD thesis in History, Pontifícia Universidade Católica do Rio de Janeiro, 2004.

Melnixenco, Vanessa Cristina. "Friburgo & Filhos: tradições do passado e invenções do futuro (1840–1888)." MA thesis in History, Universidade Federal do Estado do Rio de Janeiro – UNIRIO, 2014.

Mendonça, Joseli Maria Nunes. *Entre a mão e os anéis – a lei dos sexagenários e os caminhos da abolição no Brasil*. Campinas: Editora da UNICAMP, 1999.

"Legislação emancipacionista, 1871 e 1885." In Lilia Schwarcz and Flávio Gomes, eds., *Dicionário da escravidão e liberdade*, pp. 277–284. São Paulo: Companhia das Letras, 2019.

Meyer, Marylse. *Folhetim: uma historia*. São Paulo: Companhia das Letras, 1996.

Meznar, Joan. "Orphans and the Transition from Slave to Free Labor in Northeast Brazil: The Case of Campina Grande, 1850–1888." *Journal of Social History* 27:3 (1994): 499–515.

Milanich, Nara B. *Children of Fate: Childhood, Class, and the State in Chile*. Durham, NC: Duke University Press, 2009.

"Latin American Childhoods and the Concept of Modernity." In Paula Fass ed., *The Routledge History of Childhood in the Western World*, pp. 491–508. New York: Routledge, 2013.

"To Make All Children Equal Is a Change in the Power Structures of Society: The Politics of Family Law in Twentieth-Century Chile and Latin America." *Law and History Review* 33:4 (2015): 767–802.

Miller, Joseph. *Way of Death: Merchant Capitalism and the Angolan Slave Trade, 1730–1830*. Madison: University of Wisconsin Press, 1996.

Miranda, Clícea Maria. "Guarda Negra da Redentora: verso e reverso de uma combativa associação de libertos." MA thesis in History, Universidade do Estado do Rio de Janeiro, 2006.

Mizuta, Celina Midori Murasse, Luciano Mendes de Faria Filho, and Marcília Rosa Perioto, eds. *Império em debate: imprensa e educação no Brasil oitocentista*. Maringá: Eduem, 2010.

Monsma, Karl. *A reprodução do racismo: fazendeiros, negros no oeste paulista, 1880–1914*. São Carlos: EdUFSCAR, 2016.

Monsma, Karl, and Valéria Fernandes. "Fragile Liberty: The Enslavement of Free People in the Borderlands of Brazil and Uruguay, 1846–1866." *Luso-Brazilian Review*, 50:1 (2013): 7–25.

Montenegro, Olívio. *Memórias do Ginásio Pernambucano*. Recife: Assembleia Legislativa de Pernambuco, 1979.

Moore, Robin. *Nationalizing Blackness: Afrocubanismo and Artistic Revolution in Havana, 1920–1940*. Pittsburgh: University of Pittsburgh Press, 1997.

"O teatro bufo: teatro *blackface* cubano." In A. Herculano Lopes, Martha Abreu, Martha Ulhoa, and Mônica Velloso, eds. *Música e história no longo século XIX*, pp. 357–382. Rio de Janeiro: Fundação Casa de Rui Barbosa, 2011.

Moraes, Roberto Menezes de. *Os Ribeiro de Avellar na Fazenda Pau Grande*. Rio de Janeiro: Paty do Alferes, 1994.

Moreira, Paulo Roberto Staudt. "Boçais e malungos em terra de brancos: notícias sobre o último desembarque de escravos no Rio Grande do Sul." In Vera Lúcia M. Barroso, ed., *Raízes de Santo Antônio da Patrulha e Caraá*, pp. 215–235. Porto Alegre: EST, 2000.

"Um promotor fora de lugar: justiça e escravidão no século XIX (Comarca de Santo Antônio da Patrulha, 1868)." *Textura* 10 (2004): 39–47.

Morel, Marco, and Mariana Monteiro de Barros, eds. *Palavra, imagem e poder: o surgimento da imprensa no Brasil do século XIX*. Rio de Janeiro: DP&A, 2003.

Moreno, Alessandra Zorzetto. *Vivendo em lares alheios: filhos de criação e adoção em São Paulo colonial e em Portugal, 1765–1822*. São Paulo: Annablume, 2013.

Morgan, Thomas L., and William Barlow. *From Cakewalks to Concert Halls: An Illustrated History of African American Popular Music, from 1895 to 1930*. Washington, DC: Elliott & Clark Publishing, 1992.

Motta, José Flávio. *Corpos escravos, vontades livres: posse de cativos e família escrava em Bananal, 1801–1828*. São Paulo: FAPESP, 1999.

"Derradeiras transações, O comércio de escravos nos anos de 1880 (Areias, Piracicaba e Casa Branca, Província de São Paulo)." *Almanack Braziliense* 10 (2009): 147–163.

Mott de Mello Souza, Maria Lucia de Barros. "Parto, parteiras e parturientes: Mme. Durocher e sua época." PhD thesis in History, Universidade de São Paulo, 1998.

"Ser mãe: a escrava em face do aborto e do infanticídio." *Revista de História*, 120, 1989: 85–96.

Moura, Roberto. *Tia Ciata e a Pequena África no Rio de Janeiro*, 2nd ed. Rio de Janeiro: Secretaria Municipal de Cultura, 1995.

Muaze, Mariana. "A descoberta da infância: a formação de um habitus civilizado na boa sociedade imperial." MA thesis in History, PUC-RJ, 1999.

As memórias da viscondessa: família e poder no Brasil Império. Rio de Janeiro: Zahar, 2008.

"Garantindo hierarquias: educação e instrução infantil na boa sociedade imperial (1840–1889)." *Dimensões- Revista de História da UFES* 15 (2003): 59–84.

"Novas considerações sobre o Vale do Paraíba e a dinâmica imperial." In Mariana Muaze and Ricardo Salles, eds., *O Vale do Paraíba e o Império do Brasil nos quadros da Segunda Escravidão*, pp. 57–99. Rio de Janeiro: Faperj/7Letras, 2015.

"O que fará essa gente quando for decretada a completa emancipação dos escravos? Serviço doméstico e escravidão nas plantations cafeeiras do vale de Paraíba." *Almanak* 12 (2016): 65–87.

Muaze, Mariana, and Ricardo Salles, eds. *A segunda escravidão e o Império do Brasil em perspectiva histórica*. São Leopoldo, RS: Casa Leiria, 2020.

O Vale do Paraíba e o Império do Brasil nos quadros da segunda escravidão. Rio de Janeiro: Faperj/7Letras, 2015.

Müller, Maria Lúcia Rodrigues. *A cor da escola: imagens da Primeira República*. Cuiabá: Entrelinhas/EdUFMT, 2008.

Mussa, Alberto. *A hipótese humana*. Rio de Janeiro: Record, 2017.

Naro, Nancy. "The 1848 Praieira Revolt in Brazil." PhD dissertation in History. University of Chicago, 1981.

Nascimento, Abdias do. *Brazil Mixture or Massacre? Essays in the Genocide of a Black People*. Dover, MA: Majority Press, 1989.

O genocídio do negro brasileiro: processo de um racism mascarado. Rio de Janeiro: Paz e Terra, 1978.

O negro revoltado. Rio de Janeiro: Nova Fronteira, 1982. (1st edition 1968.)

Nascimento, Álvaro Pereira do. *A ressaca da marujada: recrutamento e disciplina na Armada Imperial*. Rio de Janeiro: Arquivo Nacional, 2001.

Needell, Jeffrey D. "Brazilian Abolitionism: Its Historiography and the Uses of Political History." *Journal of Latin American Studies* 42:2 (2010): 231–261.

"Identity, Race, Gender and Modernity in the Origins of Gilberto Freyre's Oevre." *American Historical Review* 100:1 (1995): 51–77.

The Sacred Cause: The Abolitionist Movement, Afro-Brazilian Mobilization, and Imperial Politics in Rio De Janeiro. Stanford, CA: Stanford University Press, 2020.

Negro, Antonio Luigi, and Flávio Gomes. "Além de senzalas e fábricas." *Tempo Social* 18:1 (2006): 217–240.

Nequete, Lenine. *O escravo na jurisprudência brasileira: magistratura e ideologia no segundo reinado*. Porto Alegre: Tribunal de Justiça do Rio Grande do Sul: 1988.

Neves, Lúcia Maria B. P. das, Marco Morel, and Tânia M. Bessone da C. Ferreira, eds. *História e imprensa: representação culturais e práticas de poder*. Rio de Janeiro: DP&A/FAPERJ, 2007.

Nishida, Mieko. *Slavery and Identity: Ethnicity, Gender and Race in Salvador, Brazil, 1808–1888*. Bloomington: Indiana University Press, 2003.

Noiriel, Gérard. *Chocolat clown nègre: L'histoire oubliée du premier artiste noir de la scène française*. Paris: Bayard Editions, 2012.

Oakes, James. *Slavery and Freedom: An Interpretation of the Old South*. New York: Vintage, 1990.

Oliveira, Cyra Luciana Ribeiro de. "Os Africanos Livres em Pernambuco, 1831–1864." MA thesis in History, Universidade Federal de Pernambuco, 2010.

Oliveira, Maria Luiza Ferreira. "Resistência popular contra o Decreto 798 ou a 'lei do cativeiro': Pernambuco, Paraíba, Sergipe, Ceará, 1851–1852." In Monica Duarte Dantas, ed., *Revoltas, motins, revoluções: homens livres pobres e libertos no Brasil do século XIX*, pp. 391–427. São Paulo: Alameda, 2011.

Oliveira, Vinicius Pereira. *De Manoel Congo a Manoel de Paula: um africano ladino em terras meridionais*. Porto Alegre: EST Edições, 2006.

Osório, Helen. *O império português no sul da América: estancieiros, lavradores e comerciantes*. Porto Alegre: Editora da UFRGS, 2007.

Otovo, Okezi. *Progressive Mothers, Better Babies: Race, Public Health and the State in Brazil (1850–1945)*. Austin: University of Texas Press, 2016.

Pádua, José Augusto. *Um sopro de destruição: pensamento político e crítica ambiental no Brasil escravista (1786–1888)*. Rio de Janeiro: Jorge Zahar, 2002.

Paiva, Eduardo França. "Revendications de droits coutumiers et actions en justice des esclaves dans les Minas Gerais du XVIIIe siècle." *Cahiers du Brésil Contemporain* 53–54 (2004): 11–29.

Palacios, Guillermo. "Revoltas camponesas no Brasil escravista: a 'Guerra dos Marimbondos' (Pernambuco, 1851–1852)." *Almanack Braziliense* 3 (2006): 9–39.
Palacios, Guillermo, and Fabio Moraga. *La independência y el comienzo de los regímenes representativos*, vol. 1. Madrid: Síntesis, 2003.
Palermo, Eduardo. "Los afro-fronterizos del norte uruguayo en la formación del Estado Oriental, 1810–1835." In Silvia C. Mallo and Ignacio Telesca, eds., *"Negros de la Patria": los afrodescendientes en las luchas por la independencia en el antiguo virreinato del Río de la Plata*, pp. 187–210. Buenos Aires: Editorial SB, 2010.
"Secuestros y tráfico de esclavos en la frontera uruguaya: estudio de casos posteriores a 1850." *Revista Tema Livre* 7:13 (2008): online.
Palombini, Carlos. "Fonograma 108.077: o lundu de George W. Johnson." *Per Musi* 23 (2011): 58–70.
Pang, Eul-Soo. *O Engenho Central de Bom Jardim na economia baiana: alguns aspectos da sua história (1875–1891)*. Rio de Janeiro: Arquivo Nacional, 1979.
Parron, Tâmis. *A política da escravidão no Império do Brasil (1826–1865)*. Rio de Janeiro: Civilização Brasileira, 2011.
Peabody, Sue. *There Are No Slaves in France: The Political Culture of Race and Slavery in the Ancien Régime*. Oxford: Oxford University Press, 1996.
Peabody, Sue, and Keila Grinberg, eds. *Free Soil in the Atlantic World*. London: Routledge, 2014.
"Free Soil: The Generation and Circulation of an Atlantic Legal Principle." In Sue Peabody and Keila Grinberg, eds., *Free Soil in the Atlantic World*, pp. 1–10. London: Routledge, 2014.
Slavery, Freedom, and the Law in the Atlantic World: A Brief History with Documents. Boston, MA: Bedford Books, 2007.
Pedroza, Antonia Márcia Nogueira. *Desventuras de Hypolita: luta contra a escravidão ilegal no sertão (Crato e Exu, século XIX)*. Natal: Editora da UFRN, 2018.
Pena, Eduardo Spiller. *Pajens da Casa Imperial: jurisconsultos, escravidão e a lei de 1871*. Campinas: Editora da Unicamp, 2001.
Pereira, Amílcar Araujo, and Verena Alberti. *Histórias do movimento negro no Brasil: depoimentos ao CPDOC*. Rio de Janeiro: Editora Fundação Getúlio Vargas, 2007.
Pereira, Leonardo M. A. "No ritmo do Vagalume: culturas negras, associativismo dançante e nacionalidade na produção de Francisco Guimarães (1904–1933)." *Revista Brasileira de História* 35:69 (2015): 13–23.
Pesavento, Sandra. "Uma certa Revolução Farroupilha." In Keila Grinberg and Ricardo Salles, eds., *Brasil Imperial*, pp. 233–268. Río de Janeiro: Civilização Brasileira, 2009.
Pessoa, Thiago Campos. "A indiscrição como ofício: o complexo cafeeiro revisitado." PhD dissertation in History, Universidade Federal Fluminense, 2015.

Petiz, Silmei de Sant'Ana. *Buscando a liberdade: as fugas de escravos da província de São Pedro para o além-fronteira (1815–1851)*. Passo Fundo: Editora da Universidade de Passo Fundo, 2006.

Pierson, Donald. *Brancos e pretos na Bahia: estudo de contacto racial*. Rio de Janeiro: Companhia Editora Nacional, 1945.

Negroes in Brazil. Chicago, IL: University of Chicago Press, 1942.

Pilotti, Francisco, and Irene Rizzini. *A arte de governar crianças: a história das políticas sociais, da legislação e da assistência à infância no Brasil*. Rio de Janeiro: Amais, 1995.

Pinheiro, Fernanda Domingos. "Em defesa da liberdade: libertos e livres de cor nos tribunais do Antigo Regime português (Mariana e Lisboa, 1720–1819)." PhD dissertation in History, Universidade Estadual de Campinas, 2013.

Libertos ingratos: práticas de redução ao cativeiro na América portuguesa (século XVIII). In Ângela Barreto Xavier and Cristina Nogueira da Silva, eds., *O governo dos outros: poder e diferença no Império Português*, pp. 365–386. Lisbon: Imprensa de Ciências Sociais, 2016.

Pinho, Wanderley Araújo. *História de um engenho do Recôncavo Matoim-Novo Caboto-Freguesia (1552–1944)*. Salvador: Brasiliana, 1982.

Pinto, Ana Flávia Magalhães. "Fortes laços em linhas rotas: literatos negros, racismo e cidadania na segunda metade do século XIX." PhD dissertation in History, UNICAMP, 2014.

Imprensa negra no Brasil do século XIX. São Paulo: Editora Selo Negro, 2010.

Pinto, Luiz de Aguiar Costa. *Recôncavo: laboratório de uma experiência humana*. Rio de Janeiro: CLACSO-UNESCO, 1958.

Pires, Antônio Liberac Cardoso Simões, Axel Rojas, and Flávio dos Santos Gomes, eds. *Territórios de gente negra: processos, transformações e adaptações. Ensaios sobre Colômbia e Brasil*. Belo Horizonte: Selo Negro, 2016.

Porto, Angela. "O sistema de saúde do escravo no século XIX: doenças, instituições e práticas terapêuticas." *História, Ciência e Saúde – Manguinhos* 13:4, 2006: 1019–1027.

Prado Júnior, Caio. *Formação do Brasil contemporâneo*. São Paulo: Martins, 1942.

Priore, Mary del, ed. *História da criança no Brasil*. São Paulo: Contexto, 1991.

Radano, Ronald. *Lying up a Nation: Race and Black Music*. Chicago, IL: University of Chicago Press, 2003,

Reis, João José. *Divining Slavery and Freedom*. New York: Cambridge University Press, 2015.

ed. *Escravidão e invenção da liberdade*. São Paulo: Brasiliense, 1988.

Rebelião escrava. São Paulo: Companhia das Letras, 2004.

"Tambores e temores, a festa negra na Bahia na primeira metade do século XIX." In Maria Clementina Pereira Cunha, ed., *Carnavais e outras festas*, pp. 104–114. Campinas: Unicamp, 2002.

Reis, João José, Flávio dos Santos Gomes, and Marcus J. M. de Carvalho. *O alufá Rufino: tráfico, escravidão e liberdade no Atlântico negro (c.1822–c.1853)*. São Paulo: Companhia das Letras, 2010.

Reis, João José, and Márcia Gabriela D. de Aguiar. "Carne sem osso, farinha sem caroço – o motim de 1858 contra a carestia na Bahia." *Revista da USP* 135 (1996): 133–159.

Reis, João José, and Eduardo Silva. *Negociação e conflito: a resistência negra no Brasil escravista*. São Paulo: Companhia das Letras, 1989.

Ribeiro, Edson Macedo. *A Capela Nossa Senhora da Conceição do Soberbo e o ano que não foi: contribuições à história de Guapimirim*. Magé: Amigos do Patrimônio Cultural, 2012.

Ribeiro, Lavina Madeira. *Imprensa e espaço público: a institucionalização do jornalismo no Brasil, 1808–1964*. Rio de Janeiro: E-papers, 2004.

Rio, João de: see Barreto, João Paulo.

Rios, Ana Lugão, and Hebe Mattos. *Memórias do cativeiro: família, trabalho e cidadania no pós-abolição*. Rio de Janeiro: Civilização Brasileira, 2005.

"O pós-abolição como problema histórico: balanços e perspectivas." *Topoi* 5:8 (2004): 170–198.

Rios, Ana Maria Lugão. "Família e transição – famílias negras em Paraíba do Sul (1872–1920)." MA thesis in History, Universidade Federal Fluminense, 1990.

Rizzini, Irene, ed. *Olhares sobre a criança no Brasil – séculos XIX e XX*. Rio de Janeiro: EDUSU/Amais, 1997.

Robinson, Jennifer. *Ordinary Cities*. New York: Routledge, 2006.

Rodrigues, Jaime. *De costa a costa: escravos, marinheiros e intermediários do tráfico negreiro de Angola ao Rio de Janeiro, 1780-1860*. São Paulo: Companhia das Letras, 2005.

Infame comércio: propostas e experiências no final do tráfico de africanos para o Brasil, 1800-1850. Campinas: Editora da Unicamp, 2000.

Rolnik, Raquel. *A cidade e a lei*. São Paulo: Fapesp/Stúdio Nobel, 1997.

"Territórios negros nas cidades brasileiras." *Estudos Afro-Asiáticos* 17 (1989): 1–17. (Updated version [2013] at https://raquelrolnik.files.wordpress.com/2013/04/territc3b3rios-negros.pdf. Accessed November 2, 2020.)

Rosemberg, André. *De chumbo e de festim: uma história da polícia paulista no final do Império*. São Paulo: Edusp/Fapesp, 2010.

Rosenthal, Paul-Andre. "Construindo o 'macro' pelo 'micro': Fredrik Barth e a 'micro história,'" In J. Revel, *Jogos de escala: a experiência da micro-análise*, pp. 151–172. Rio de Janeiro: Fundação Getúlio Vargas, 1998.

Rossato, Monica. "Relações de poder na região fronteiriça platina: família, trajetória e atuação política de Gaspar Silveira Martins." MA dissertation in History, Universidade Federal de Santa Maria, 2014.

Roth, Cassia. "From Free Womb to Criminalized Woman: Fertility Control in Brazilian Slavery and Freedom." *Slavery & Abolition* 38:2 (2017): 269–286.

Rothman, Joshua D. *Notorious in the Neighborhood: Sex and Families across the Color Line in Virginia, 1787–1861*. Chapel Hill: University of North Carolina Press, 2003.

Russell-Wood, A. J. R. *Escravos e libertos no Brasil colonial*. Rio de Janeiro: Civilização Brasileira, 2005.

Sá, Gabriela Barretto de. "O crime de reduzir pessoa livre à escravidão nas casas de morada da justiça no Rio Grande do Sul (1835–1874)." MA thesis in Law, Universidade Federal de Santa Catarina, 2014.

Sadlier, Darlene Joy. *Brazil Imagined: 1500 to the Present*. Austin: University of Texas Press, 2008.

Salles, Ricardo. "A abolição revisitada: entre continuidades e rupturas." *Revista de História* 176 (2017): 1–11.

E o vale era escravo. *Vassouras, século XIX: senhores e escravos no coração do Império*. Rio de Janeiro: Civilização Brasileira, 2008.

Guerra do Paraguai: memórias e imagens. Rio de Janeiro: Biblioteca Nacional, 2003.

Guerra do Paraguai: escravidão e cidadania na formação do Exército. Río de Janeiro: Paz e Terra, 1990.

"Resistência escrava e abolição na província do Rio de Janeiro: O partido do abolicionismo." In Ivana Stolze Lima, Keila Grinberg and Daniel Aarão Reis, eds., *Instituições nefandas: o fim da escravidão e da servidão no Brasil, nos Estados Unidos e na Rússia*, pp. 266–293. Rio de Janeiro: Fundação Casa Rui Barbosa, 2018.

Salles, Ricardo, and Magno Fonseca Borges. "A morte do Barão de Guaribu, ou o fio da meada." In Mariana Muaze and Ricardo Salles, eds., *O Vale do Paraíba e o Império do Brasil nos quadros da segunda escravidão*, 197–241. Rio de Janeiro: 7Letras/ Faperj, 2015.

Sampaio, Antônio Carlos Jucá de. "Família escrava e a agricultura mercantil de alimentos, Magé 1850–1872." *População e Família* 1:1 (1988): 119–141.

Sanders, Lynn Moss. *Howard W. Odum's Folklore Odyssey*. Athens: University of Georgia Press, 2003.

Sandroni, Carlos. "Música, performance vocal e 'língua de preto' em um lundu interpretado por Eduardo das Neves." In Cláudia N. Matos, F. T. de Medeiros, and L. Davino de Oliveira, eds., *Palavra cantada, estudos transdisciplinares*, pp. 53–77. Rio de Janeiro: Eduerj/ Faperj, 2014.

Sant'Anna, Benedita de Cássia Lima. *Do Brasil Ilustrado á Revista Ilustrada: trajetória da imprensa periódica literária ilustrada fluminense*. Jundiaí, SP: Paco Editorial, 2011.

Santos, Claudia Regina Andrade dos. "O ativismo político da Confederação Abolicionista antes e depois do 13 de maio de 1888." In Ivana Stolze Lima, Keila Grinberg, and Daniel Aarão Reis Filho, eds., *Instituições Nefandas: o fim da escravidão e da servidão no Brasil, nos Estados Unidos e na Russia*, pp. 294–326. Rio de Janeiro, Fundação Casa Rui Barbosa, 2018.

Santos, Luís Cláudio Villafañe Gomes. *O Império e as Repúblicas do Pacífico: as relações do Brasil com Chile, Bolívia, Peru, Equador e Colômbia (1822–1889)*. Curitiba: Editora da UFPR, 2002.

Santos, Maria Emília Vasconcelos dos. "'Moças honestas' ou 'meninas perdidas': um estudo sobre a honra e os usos da justiça pelas mulheres pobres em Pernambuco." MA thesis in History, Universidade Federal de Pernambuco, 2007.

"Os significados dos 13 de maio: a abolição e o imediato pós-abolição para os trabalhadores dos engenhos da Zona da Mata Sul de Pernambuco, 1884–1893." PhD dissertation in Social History, UNICAMP, 2014.

Santos, Martha. "On the Importance of Being Honorable: Masculinity, Survival, and Conflict in the Backlands of Northeast Brazil, Ceará, 1840s–1890." *The Americas*, 64:1 (2007): 35–57.

Santos, Ricardo Ventura, and Marcos Chor Maio. "Qual 'retrato do Brasil'? Raça, biologia, identidades e política na era da genômica." *Mana* 10:1 (2004): 61–95.

"Retrato molecular do Brasil." *Ciência Hoje* 159 (2000): 16–25.

Santos, Wanderley Guilherme dos. *Ordem burguesa e liberalismo político*. São Paulo: Duas Cidades, 1978.

Santos, Ynae Lopes. "Além da senzala: arranjos escravos de moradia no Rio de Janeiro (1800–1850)." MA thesis in History, FFLCH/USP, 2006.

Sassen, Saskia. *The Global City: New York, London, Tokyo*. Princeton, NJ: Princeton University Press, 1991.

Saville, Julie. "Grassroots Reconstruction: Agricultural Labour and Collective Action in South Carolina 1860–1868." *Slavery and Abolition* 12:3 (1991): 172–182.

Scarborough, William Kauffman. *Masters of the Big House: Elite Slaveholders of the Mid-Nineteenth Century South*. Baton Rouge: Louisiana State University Press, 2006.

Schultz, Kirsten. *Tropical Versailles: Empire, Monarchy and the Portuguese Royal Court in Rio de Janeiro, 1808–1821*. New Brunswick, NJ: Routledge, 2001.

Schwarcz, Lilia M. "Dos males da dádiva: sobre as ambiguidades no processo da abolição brasileira." In Olívia Maria Gomes da Cunha and Flávio dos Santos Gomes, eds., *Quase-cidadão: histórias e antropologias da pós-emancipação no Brasil*, pp. 23–54. Rio de Janeiro: Editora Fundação Getúlio Vargas, 2007.

"Previsões são sempre traiçoeiras: João Baptista de Lacerda e seu Brasil branco." *Historia das Ciências e Saúde-Manguinhos* 18:1 (2011): 225–242.

O espetáculo das raças. São Paulo: Companhia das Letras, 2008. (1st edition, 1993.)

Schwartz, Marie Jenkins. *Birthing a Slave: Motherhood and Medicine in the Antebellum South*. Cambridge, MA: Harvard University Press, 2006.

Schwartz, Stuart B. *Slaves, Peasants and Rebels: Reconsidering Brazilian Slavery*. Urbana: University of Illinois Press, 1992.

Sugar Plantations in the Formation of Brazilian Society: Bahia, 1550–1835. Cambridge: Cambridge University Press, 1985.

Scobie, James. *From Plaza to Suburb*. New York: Oxford University Press, 1974.

Scott, Rebecca J. "Paper Thin: Freedom and Re-enslavement in the Diaspora of the Haitian Revolution." *Law and History Review* 29:4 (2011): 1061–1087.

"'She … Refuses to Deliver Up Herself as the Slave of Your Petitioner': Émigrés, Enslavement, and the 1808 Louisiana Digest of the Civil Laws." *Tulane European and Civil Law Forum* 24 (2009): 115–136.

Slave Emancipation in Cuba: The Transition to Free Labor, 1860–1899. Princeton, NJ: Princeton University Press, 1985.

Scott, Rebecca, and Jean Hébrard. *Freedom Papers: An Atlantic Odyssey in the Age of Emancipation*. Cambridge, MA: Harvard University Press, 2012.

Scott, Rebecca, and Michael Zeuske. "Property in Writing, Property on the Ground: Pigs, Horses, Land, and Citizenship in the Aftermath of Slavery, Cuba, 1880–1909." *Comparative Studies in Society and History* 44:4 (2002): 669–699.

Secreto, María Verónica, and Flávio dos Santos Gomes, eds. *Territórios ao sul: escravidão, escritas e fronteiras coloniais e pós-coloniais na América*. Río de Janeiro: 7Letras, 2017.

Seigel, Micol. *Uneven Encounters: Making Race and Nation in Brazil and United States*. Durham, NC: Duke University Press, 2009.

Seyferth, Giralda. "A antropologia e a teoria do branqueamento da raça no Brasil: a tese de João Batista de Lacerda." *Revista do Museu Paulista* 30 (1985): 81–98.

"O futuro era branco." *Revista de História*, June 3, 2011: online.

Shack, William. *Harlem in Montmartre, A Paris Jazz History Between the Great Wars*. Berkeley: California University Press, 2001.

Sharpe, Jim. "History from Below." In Peter Burke, ed., *New Perspectives in Historical Writing*, pp. 24–41. Oxford: Polity Press.

Shorter, Edward. *A formação da família moderna*. Lisbon: Terramar,1975.

Silva, Ana Cláudia Suriani da, and Sandra Guardini Vasconcelos, eds. *Books and Periodicals in Brazil, 1768–1930: A Transatlantic Perspective*. Oxford: Legenda, 2014.

Silva, Cristiano Lima da. "Senhores e pais: reconhecimento de paternidade dos alforriados na pia batismal na Freguesia de Nossa Senhora do Pilar de São João del-Rei (1770-1850)." In Laboratório de História Econômica e Social, *Anais do I Colóquio do LAHES* (Juiz de Fora, June 13–16, 2005): online.

Silva, Cristina Nogueira, and Keila Grinberg. "Soil Free from Slaves: Slave Law in Late Eighteenth and Early Nineteenth Century Portugal." In Sue Peabody and Keila Grinberg, eds., *Free Soil in the Atlantic World*, pp. 101–116. London and New York: Routledge, 2014.

Silva, Daniel Barros Domingues da, and David Eltis. "The Slave Trade to Pernambuco, 1561–1851." In David Eltis and David Richardson, *Extending the Frontiers: Essays on the New Transatlantic Slave Trade Database*, pp. 95–129. New Haven, CT: Yale University Press, 2008.

Silva, Eduardo. *Dom Obá d' África, o príncipe do povo: vida, tempo e pensamento de um homem de cor livre*. São Paulo: Companhia das Letras, 1997.

Silva, Fernanda Oliveira da. "Os negros, a constituição de espaços para os seus e o entrelaçamento desses espaços: associações e identidades negras em Pelotas (1820–1943)." MA thesis in History, Pontifícia Universidade Católica do Rio Grande do Sul, 2011.

Silva, Hermínia. *Circo-teatro: Benjamim de Oliveira e a teatralidade circense no Brasil*. São Paulo: Ed. Altana, 2007.

Silva, Luiz Geraldo. 2001. "Esperança de liberdade: interpretações populares da abolição ilustrada (1733–1774)." *Revista de História* 144 (2001): 107–149.

Silva, Maciel Henrique Carneiro da. "Domésticas criadas entre textos e práticas sociais: Recife e Salvador (1870–1910)." PhD dissertation in History, Universidade Federal da Bahia, 2011.

Silva, Maria Beatriz N. da. *Vida privada e cotidiana no Brasil – na época de D. Maria I e d. João VI*. Lisbon: Estampa, 1993.

Silva, Pedro Alberto de Oliveira. *História da escravidão no Ceará: das origens à extinção*, 2nd ed. Fortaleza: Instituto do Ceará, 2011.

Silva, Ricardo Tadeu Caíres. *Caminhos e descaminhos da abolição: escravos, senhores e direitos nas últimas décadas da escravidão (Bahia, 1850–1888)*. Curitiba: UFPR/SCHLA, 2007.

"Memórias do tráfico ilegal de escravos nas ações de liberdade: Bahia, 1885–1888." *Afro-Ásia* 35 (2007): 50–58.

Silva Júnior, Romão. "Vida e obra do sábio Teodoro Sampaio." *Revista IGHBa* 79 (1955): 27–55.

Sinha, Manisha. *The Slave's Cause: A History of Abolition*. New Haven, CT: Yale University Press, 2016.

Siqueira, Uassyr de. "Clubes recreativos: organização para o lazer." In Elciene Azevedo, ed., *Trabalhadores na cidade: cotidiano e cultura no Rio de Janeiro e em São Paulo, séculos XIX e XX*, pp. 271–312. Campinas: Editora da Unicamp, 2009.

Skidmore, Thomas. *Black into White: Race and Nationality in Brazilian Thought*. Oxford: Oxford University Press, 1974.

"Racial Ideas and Social Policy in Brazil, 1870–1940." In Richard Graham, ed., *The Idea of Race in Latin America, 1870–1940*, pp. 7–36. Austin: University of Texas Press, 1990.

Slenes, Robert W. "Brazil." In Robert Paquette and Mark Smith, eds., *The Oxford Handbook of Slavery in the Americas*, pp. 111–133. Oxford: Oxford University Press, 2010.

"The Demography and Economics of Brazilian Slavery: 1850–1888." PhD dissertation in History, Stanford University, 1976.

"Grandeza ou decadência? O mercado de escravos e a economia cafeeira da província do Rio de Janeiro, 1850-1888." In Iraci Costa, ed., *Brasil: História econômica e demográfica*, pp. 103–155. São Paulo: Instituto de Pesquisas Econômicas, 1986.

"Malungu, ngoma vem: Africa coberta e descoberta do Brasil." *Revista USP*, 12 (1991–1992): 48–67.

Na senzala uma flor, esperanças e recordações na formação da família escrava: Brasil Sudeste, século XIX. São Paulo: Editora da Unicamp, 1999.

"Senhores e subalternos no Oeste Paulista." In Luiz Felipe de Alencastro, ed., *História da Vida Privada no Brasil*, vol. II, pp. 233–290. São Paulo: Companhia das Letras, 1997.

Soares, Antonio Joaquim de Macedo. *Campanha jurídica pela libertação dos escravos (1867–1888)*. Rio de Janeiro: Jose Olympio, 1938.

Soares, Carlos Eugênio Líbano. *A negregada instituição: os capoeiras no Rio de Janeiro*. Rio de Janeiro: Coleção Biblioteca Carioca, 1994.

Soares, Luiz Carlos. *O "Povo de Cam" na capital do Brasil: a escravidão urbana no Rio de Janeiro do século XIX*. Rio de Janeiro: 7Letras, 2007.

Soares, Rodrigo Goyena. "Nem arrancada, nem outorgada: agência, estrutura e os porquês da Lei do Ventre Livre." *Almanack* 9 (2015): 166–175.

Sollors, Werner. *Neither White Nor Black Yet Both: Thematic Explorations of Interracial Literature*. Cambridge, MA: Harvard University Press, 1997.

Sousa, Ione Celeste de. "Para os educar e bem criar – tutelas, soldadas e trabalho compulsório de ingênuos na Bahia -1878–1897." Unpublished paper presented at the XXV Congresso Nacional da ANPUH in the Grupo de Trabalho "A Abolição da Escravidão e a Construção dos Conceitos de Liberdade, Raça e Tutela nas Américas," Fortaleza, Universidade Federal do Ceará, July 2009.

Souza, Flávia Fernandes. "Para casa de família e mais serviços: o trabalho doméstico na cidade do Rio de Janeiro no final do século XIX." MA dissertation in History, UERJ, 2009.

Souza, Felipe Azevedo e. *O eleitorado imperial em reforma*. Recife: FUNDAJ, 2014.
Souza, Robério. *Trabalhadores dos trilhos: imigrantes e nacionais livres, libertos e escravos na construção da primeira ferrovia baiana (1858–1863)*. Campinas: Ed. UNICAMP, 2015.
Souza, Vanderlei Sebastião de. "Em busca do Brasil: Edgard Roquette-Pinto e o retrato antropológico brasileiro (1905–1935)." PhD dissertation in the History of Science, Fundação Oswaldo Cruz, 2011.
Sparks, Randy. *Where the Negroes Are Masters: An African Port in the Era of the Slave Trade*. Cambridge, MA: Harvard University Press, 2014.
Spitzer, Leo. *Lives in Between: Assimilation and Marginality in Austria, Brazil, West Africa, 1780–1945*. Cambridge: Cambridge University Press, 1989.
Stein, Stanley. *Vassouras: A Brazilian Coffee County (1850–1900)*. Cambridge: Harvard University Press, 1957.
Stepan, Nancy. *The Hour of Eugenics: Race, Gender, and Nation in Latin America*. Ithaca, NY: Cornell University Press, 1991.
Picturing Tropical Nature. Ithaca, NY: Cornell University Press, 2001.
Tannenbaum, Frank. *Slave and Citizen*. New York, NY: Beacon Press, 1947.
Thompson, Edward P. *The Making of the English Working Class*. New York: Vintage Books, 1966.
Tradicion, revuelta e consciencia de clase: estudios sobre la crisis de la sociedad preindustrial. Barcelona: Editorial Crítica, 1979.
Tinhorão, José Ramos. "Circo brasileiro, local do universal." In *Cultura popular, temas e questões*. São Paulo: Ed. 34, 2001.
Tomich, Dale W. *Pelo prisma da escravidão: trabalho, capital e economia mundial*. São Paulo: EDUSP, 2011.
Through the Prism of Slavery: Labor, Capital, and World Economy. Lanham, MD: Bowman & Littlefield Publishers, 2004.
Torres, Miguel Gustavo de Paiva. *O Visconde de Uruguai e sua atuação diplomática para a consolidação política externa do Império*. Brasília: Fundação Alexandre de Gusmão, 2011.
Townsend, Camilla. *Tales of Two Cities: Race and Economic Culture in Early Republican North and South America*. Austin: University of Texas Press, 2000.
Trindade, Alexandre Dantas. "André Rebouças: da engenharia civil à engenharia social." PhD thesis in Sociology, UNICAMP, 2004.
Trochim, Michael. "The Brazilian Black Guard: Racial Conflict in Post-Abolition Brazil." *The Americas* 44:3 (1988): 285–300.
Trouillot, Michel Rolpfh. *Silencing the Past: Power and the Production of History*. Boston, MA: Beacon Press, 1997.
Vainfas, Ronaldo, ed. *Dicionário do Brasil Imperial*. Rio de Janeiro: Objetiva, 2002.
Vasconcelos, Ari. *Panorama da música popular brasileira*. Rio de Janeiro: Martins, 1964.
Veiga, Gláucio. *História das idéias da Faculdade de Direito do Recife, vol. 4*. Recife: Editora Universitária, 1981.
O gabinete Olinda e a política pernambucana: o desembarque de Serinhaém. Recife: UFPE, 1977.
Velloso, Mônica Pimenta. *A cultura das ruas no Rio de Janeiro (1900–1930)*. Rio de Janeiro: Casa de Rui Barbosa, 2004.

Venâncio, Renato Pinto. "Maternidade negada." In Mary del Priore and Carla Bassanezi, eds., *História das mulheres no Brasil*, 6th ed., pp. 189–222. São Paulo: Contexto, 2002.

Verger, Pierre. *Fluxo e refluxo do tráfico de escravos entre o Golfo de Benin e a Bahia de Todos os Santos dos séculos XVII a XIX*. São Paulo: Corrupio, 1987.

Villa, Carlos Valencia, and Manolo Florentino. "Abolicionismo inglês e tráfico de crianças escravizadas para o Brasil, 1810–1850." *História* 37 (2016): 1–20.

Wade, Peter. *Music, Race and Nation: Música Tropical in Colombia*. Chicago, IL: University of Chicago Press, 2000.

Wagner, Bryan. *Disturbing the Peace: Black Culture and the Police Power after Slavery*. Cambridge, MA: Harvard University Press, 2009.

Wagley, Charles. *Race and Class in Rural Brazil*. Paris: UNESCO, 1952.

Wallace-Sanders, Kimberly. *Mammy: A Century of Race, Gender, and Southern Memory*. Ann Arbor: University of Michigan Press, 2008.

Wariboko, W. W. "I Really Cannot Make Africa My Home: West Indian Missionaries as 'Outsiders' in the Church Missionary Society Civilizing Mission to Southern Nigeria, 1889–1925." *Journal of African History* 45:2 (2004): 221–236.

Weber, Max. *The City*. New York: Free Press, 1966.

Weinstein, Barbara. "Postcolonial Brazil." In Joseph C. Moya, ed., *The Oxford Handbook of Latin American History*, pp. 212–256. New York and London: Oxford University Press, 2010.

White, Shane, and Graham White. *The Sounds of Slavery: Discovering African American History through Songs, Sermons and Speech*. Boston, MA: Beacon Press, 2005.

Whitford, David M. *The Curse of Ham in the Early Modern Era: The Bible and the Justifications for Slavery*. Farnham: Ashgate, 2009.

Wicks, Nilce Parreira. "Pathways to Freedom: Slavery and Emancipation in Nineteenth Century Ouro Preto, Brazil." PhD dissertation in History, UCLA, 2017.

Williams, Daryle. "'Peculiar Circumstances of the Land': Artists and Models in Nineteenth-Century Brazilian Slave Society." *Art History* 35:4 (2012): 702–727.

"Redimindo Cã mais uma vez: Modesto Brocos, *Redenção de Cã* e o fim da escravidão no Brasil." In Flávio Gomes and Petrônio Domingues, eds., *Políticas da raça: experiências e legados da abolição e da pós-emancipação no Brasil*, pp. 173–194. São Paulo: Selo Negro, 2014.

Williams, Eric. *Capitalism and Slavery*. Chapel Hill: University of North Carolina Press, 1944.

Wood, Betty. "'White Society' and the 'Informal' Slave Economies of Lowcountry Georgia, c. 1763–1830." *Slavery and Abolition* 11:3 (1990): 313–331.

Wood, Marcus. *Black Milk: Imagining Slavery in the Visual Cultures of Brazil and America*. New York: Oxford University Press, 2013.

Xavier, Alfredo. *Letras católicas em Pernambuco*. Rio de Janeiro: Cruzada da Boa Imprensa, 1939.

Xavier, Giovana, ed. *Histórias da escravidão e do pós-abolição para as escolas.* Salvador: Ed. UFRB/Fino Trato, 2016.
Intelectuais negras visíveis. Rio de Janeiro: Malê, 2017.
Yousseff, Alain El. *Imprensa e escravidão: política e tráfico negreiro no Império do Brasil, Rio de Janeiro, 1822–1850.* São Paulo: Editora Intermeios, 2016.

PRIMARY SOURCES

Almeida, Cândido Mendes de. *Código Filipino, ou, Ordenações e Leis do Reino de Portugal: recopiladas por mandado d'el-Rei D. Filipe I.* Facsimile of 14th edition, according to the first from 1603 and the ninth from 1821, with an introduction and commentary by Cândido Mendes de Almeida. Brasília: Senado Federal, Conselho Editorial, 2004.
Almeida, Francisco José. *Tratado da educação physica dos meninos.* Lisbon, Officina da Academia Real das Sciencias, 1791.
Alves Júnior, Thomaz. *Anotações teóricas e práticas ao Código Criminal,* vol. 3. Rio de Janeiro: Garnier, 1883.
Amaral, Carlos Alberto V., and Lara Schechtman Sette (transcription). "Traslado da Ação de Liberdade movida pelo escravo Camilo, por meio de seu curador, datada de 10/06/1874, perante o juizo da Comarca de Itambé, Vila de Pedras de Fogo, Pernambuco." *Revista Documentação e Memória* (Memorial da Justiça-TJPE), 3:5 (2012): online.
Arquivo Público do Rio Grande do Sul (APERGS). *Documentos da escravidão: processos crime-o escravo como vítima ou réu.* Porto Alegre: Companhia Rio-Grandense de Artes Gráficas, 2010.
Assis Júnior, A. de. *Dicionário kimbundo-português.* Luanda: Argente, Santos e Companhia Ltda, no date.
Azara, Félix de, *Memoria sobre el estado rural del Río de la Plata y otros informes.* Madrid: Imprenta de Sánchiz, 1847.
Azevedo, Arthur. "A Palestra." *O País,* September 1–2, 1895.
Barreto, Luiz Carlos Muniz. *Tratado de educação fysica e moral dos meninos de ambos os sexos.* Traduzido do francês. Lisbon: Officina da Real Academia de Sciencias, 1787.
Baxter, Sylvester. "A Continent of Republics." *New Outlook,* 894 (1906): 869–875.
Blyden, Edward W. *Liberia's Offering: Addresses, Sermons, etc.* New York, NY: John A. Gray, 1962.
Brasil. "The Aurea Law: Abolition of Slavery, May 13, 1888." In Sue Peabody and Keila Grinberg, eds., *Slavery, Freedom, and the Law in the Atlantic World: A Brief History with Documents,* pp. 165–166. Boston, MA: Bedford Books, 2007.
Coleção de leis do Império do Brasil. Rio de Janeiro: Imprensa Nacional, 1880.
"Decree of April 12, 1832. Dá regulamento para a execução da Lei de 7 de Novembro de 1831 sobre o trafico de escravos." In Brasil, *Coleção de leis do Império do Brasil – 1832,* vol. 1, part II: 100.
"Law of December 16, 1830. Manda executar o Código Criminal do Império." In Brasil, *Coleção de Leis do Império do Brasil – 1830,* vol 1, part I: 142.

"Law of November 7, 1831." In Brasil. *Coleção de leis do Império do Brasil –* *1831*, vol. 1, part I: 182.

"Law of September 13, 1830. Regula o contrato por escrito sobre prestação de serviços feitos por brasileiro ou estrangeiro dentro ou fora do Império." In Brasil, *Coleção de Leis do Império do Brasil – 1830*, vol 1, part I: 33.

Ministerial Reports (1821–1960): Relações Exteriores. Online: http://brazil .crl.edu/bsd/bsd/u1489/contents.html. Consulted on January 25, 2018.

"Resolução de 10 de maio de 1856 – a respeito dos escravos que entram no Império, vindos de países estrangeiros." In José Próspero Jeovah da Silva Caroatá, ed., *Imperiais resoluções tomadas sobre consultas da seção de justiça do Conselho de Estado*, vol. 1, pp. 599–601. Rio de Janeiro: Garnier, 1884.

Brasil, Diretoria Geral de Estatística. *Recenseamento do Brasil de 1872*, vol. 9. Rio de Janeiro: G. Leuzinger, 1874.

Synopse do Recenseamento de 31 de Dezembro de 1890. Rio de Janeiro: Officina da Estatística, 1898.

Brasil, Ministério da Justiça. "Nota do Ministro da Justiça ao Presidente da Província do Rio Grande do Sul, 6 de maio de 1868." *Revista do Instituto da Ordem dos Advogados Brazileiros* 7:6 (1868): 231–232.

Brasil, Ministério de Relações Exteriores. *Relatório do ano de 1851 apresentado à Assembleia Geral Legislativa*. Rio de Janeiro, Imprensa Nacional, 1852.

Relatório do ano de 1856 apresentado à Assembleia Geral Legislativa. Rio de Janeiro, Imprensa Nacional, 1857.

Relatório do ano de 1859 apresentado à Assembleia Geral Legislativa. Rio de Janeiro: Imprensa Nacional, 1860.

Relatório do ano de 1860 apresentado à Assembleia Geral Legislativa. Rio de Janeiro: Imprensa Nacional, 1861.

Relatório do ano de 1861 apresentado à Assembleia Geral Legislativa. Rio de Janeiro: Imprensa Nacional, 1862.

Relatório do Ministério das Relações Exteriores, Rio de Janeiro: Imprensa Nacional, 1857.

Brasil, Pernambuco (state), Municipio de Recife. *Recenseamento realizado em 12 de Outubro de 1913*. Recife: Colegio Salisiano, 1915.

Brasil, Rio de Janeiro (province), Presidencia da Província do Rio de Janeiro. *Relatorio apresentado à Assembléa Legislativa Provincial do Rio de Janeiro na abertura da segunda sessão da 26ª legislatura em 12 Setembro de 1887 pelo presidente Dr. Antonio da Rocha Fernandes Leão*. Rio de Janeiro: Tipografia Montenegro, 1887.

Brasil, Rio de Janeiro (state). *Relatório da Secretaria das Obras Publicas e Indústrias do Estado do Rio de Janeiro*, vol. 1, 1898.

Brasil, Secretaria de Estado dos Negócios do Império e Estrangeiros. *O Conselho de Estado e a política externa do Império*. Rio de Janeiro, Brasilia; CHDD, Funag, 2005

Brocos, Modesto. *A questão do ensino de Bellas Artes (seguido da crítica sobre a Direcção Bernardelli e justificação do Autor)*. Rio de Janeiro: no publisher named, 1915.

Retórica dos pintores. Rio de Janeiro: Typ. A Indústria do Livro, 1933.

Caminha, Adolpho. "A exposição de 1895." *O Paíz*, September 14, 1895.

Canot, Theodore. *Adventures of an African Slaver: Being a True Account of the Life of Captain Theodore Canot, Trader in Gold, Ivory & Slaves on the Coast of Guinea: His Own Story as Told in the Year 1854 to Brantz Mayer*, edited with an introduction by Malcolm Cowley. New York and London: Cornwell Press, Bonibooks, 1935.

Casal, Manuel Aires de. *Corografia brasílica: Ou, relação histórico-geográfico do Reino do Brasil*. Belo Horizonte: Itatiaia, 1976.

Cliffe, Joseph. "An Ex-Slave Trader's Account of the Enslavement Process in Africa and the Illegal Traffic to Brazil (1848–1849)." In Robert Conrad, *Children of God's Fire: A Documentary History of Black Slavery in Brazil*, pp. 28–36. Princeton, NJ: Princeton University Press, 1983.

Collaço, D'Felipe Nery. *Aritmética prática para uso das escolas primarias de ambos os sexos*, 16th ed. Recife: Livraria Franceza, 1888.

Costa, Carlos. "Palestra do médico." *A Mãi de Família* 1:9 (1979): 65–67.

Cordeiro, Carlos Antônio, ed. *Código Criminal do Império*. Rio de Janeiro: Tip. de Quirino & Irmão, 1861.

Crummell, Alexander. *The Future of Africa: Being Addresses, Sermons, etc. Delivered in the Republic of Liberia*. New York: Scribner, 1862.

Cunha, Euclides da. *Os sertões*. Rio de Janeiro: Laemmert, 1902.

Dias, Henrique José. "Cultura da quina." *Revista Agrícola do Imperial Instituto Fluminense de Agricultura* 4 (1886): 181–185.

Estrada, Gonzaga Duque. "Exposição Brocos." *Diario do Commercio*, August 11, 1892, 2.

Expilly, Charles. *Mulheres e costumes no Brasil*. Paulo: Companhia Editora Nacional, 1935.

Falangola, Ugo, and J. Cambière (Pernambuco Film), *Veneza Americana* (1925).

Fénelon, François. *De l'éducation des filles: fables choisies*. Paris: Librarie Bibliothèque Nationale, 1885.

Filgueiras Júnior, Araújo. *Código criminal do Império do Brasil anotado com os atos dos poderes legislativo, executivo e judiciário que têm alterado e interpretado suas disposições desde que foi publicado, e com o cálculo das penas em todas as suas aplicações*. Rio de Janeiro: Eduardo & Henrique Laemmert, 1876.

Forbes, Lieutenant R.N. *Six Months' Service in the African Blockade, from April to October 1848, in Command of H.M.S. Bonetta*. London: Richard Bentley, New Burlington-Street, 1849.

Franco, Francisco de Mello. *Tratado de educação física dos meninos*. Lisbon: Academia Real das Sciencias de Lisboa, 1790.

Freitas, Octavio de. *O clima e a mortalidade da cidade do Recife*. Recife: Imprensa Industrial, 1905.

Froebel, Frédéric. *L'Éducation de l'homme. Traduit de l'allemand par la Baronne de Crombrugghe*, 2nd ed. Paris: G Fischbacher, 1881.

Graham, Maria. *Diário de uma viagem ao Brasil e de uma estada nesse país durante parte dos anos de 1821, 1822 e 1823*. São Paulo: Companhia Editora Nacional, 1956.

Hill, Pascoe Grenfell. *Cinquenta dias a bordo de um navio negreiro*. Rio de Janeiro: José Olympio, 2008.

Imbert, João Baptista A. *A infância considerada na sua hygiene*. Rio de Janeiro: Typ. Franceza, 1843.

Institution of Civil Engineers (Great Britain). *Minutes of the Proceedings of the Institution of Civil Engineers*, vol. 111. London: Institution of Civil Engineers, 1893.

Jaguaribe Filho, Domingos J. N. *A arte de formar homens de bem*. São Paulo: Typ. do Correio Paulistano, 1880.

Jardim, Antonio da Silva. *Memórias e viagens: campanha de um propagandista (1887–1890)*. Lisbon: Tipografia da Companhia Nacional Editora, 1891.

Jolly, Vallier de Sant. *Tratado de educação fysica e moral dos membros de ambos os sexos*. Lisbon: Academia Real das Sciencias, 1787.

Koster, Henry. *Travels in Brazil*. London: Longman, 1816.

Krehbiel, Henry Edward. *Afro-American Folksongs: A Study in Racial and National Music*. New York, NY: Frederick Ungar Publishing Co., 1971. (First edition New York, NY: G. Schirmer, 1914.)

Lacerda, João Batista de. *Sur les métis au Brésil*. Paris: Devouge, 1911. (English translation: "The *Metis*, or Half-Breeds, of Brazil." In Gustave Spiller, ed., *Papers on Inter-Racial Problems, Communicated to the First Universal Races Congress*, pp. 377–382. London: P.S. King & Son/Boston: The World's Peace Foundation, 1911.)

Livingston, Edward. *A System of Penal Law for the State of Louisiana*. Philadelphia and Pittsburgh: James Kay, Jun. and Co./John I. Kay and Co., 1833.

Luiz, Francisco. *Código Criminal do Império do Brasil teórica e praticamente anotado*. Maceió: Tipografia de T. de Menezes, 1885.

Malheiro, Agostinho Perdigão. *A escravidão no Brasil: ensaio historico-juridico-social*, vol. III. Rio de Janeiro: Typographia Nacional, 1866–1867.

Martin, Louis Aimé. *Educação das mães de família* (traduzido do francês). Rio de Janeiro: 1834.

Matson, James Henry. *Remarks on the Slave Trade and the African Squadron*, 4th ed. London: James Ridgeway, 1848.

Melo, Félix Cavalcanti de Albuquerque, and Gilberto Freyre. *Memórias de um Cavalcanti*. São Paulo: Editora Nacional, 1940.

Melo, Joaquim Pedro de. *Generalidades cerca da educação physica dos meninos*. Rio de Janeiro: Typ Teixeira, 1846.

Meneses, Rodrigo Otávio Langgaard de. *Minhas memórias dos outros*. Rio de Janeiro: Civilização Brasileira, 1979.

Moraes, Alexandre José de Mello. *O educador da mocidade brasileira*. Bahia: Typ. de Epiphanio Pedroza, 1852.

Moraes, Cosme de (pseudonym Carlos de Laet). "O Salão de 1895." *Jornal do Brasil*, September 25, 1895.

Moraes, Evaristo de. *Da Monarquia para a República (1870–1889)*, 2nd ed. Brasília: Editora UnB, 1985.

Nabuco, Joaquim. *Minha formação*. Rio de Janeiro: Garnier, 1900.

O abolicionismo. London: Abraham Kingdon, 1883.

"Ramalho Ortigão no Recife." *O Paiz*, November 30, 1887.

Um estadista do Império: Nabuco de Araújo, sua vida, suas opiniões, sua época, 5th ed. Rio de Janeiro: Topbooks, 1997. (1st edition, 1899.)

Neves, Eduardo das. *Cantor das modinhas brasileiras*. Rio de Janeiro: Livraria Quaresma Editores, 1895.

O cancioneiro popular moderno, 10th ed. São Paulo: C. Teixeira, 1921.

Mistérios do violão. Rio de Janeiro: Livraria Quaresma Editores, 1905.

O trovador da malandragem, 2nd ed. Rio de Janeiro: Livraria Quaresma Editores, 1926.

O trovador popular moderno, 16th ed. São Paulo: C. Teixeira, 1925.

Parlagreco, Carlo. "A exposição de Bellas Artes." *Revista Brazileira* 1 (January 1895): 47–55.

Patrocínio, José do. *Campanha abolicionista – coletânea de artigos*. Rio de Janeiro: Fundação Biblioteca Nacional, 1996.

Pereira, Lafayette Rodrigues. *Direitos de família*. Rio de Janiero: B. L. Garnier, 1869.

Pessi, Bruno Stelmach, and Graziela Souza e Silva, eds. *Documentos da escravidão: processos crime – o escravo como vítima ou réu*. Porto Alegre: Companhia Rio-Grandense de Artes Gráficas (CORAG), 2010.

Piccolo, Helga Iracema Landgraf, ed. *Coletânea de discursos parlamentares da Assembleia Legislativa da Província de São Pedro do Rio Grande do Sul, vol 1. 1835-1889*. Porto Alegre: Assembleia Legislativa do Estado do Rio Grande do Sul, 1998.

Portugal. "Lei de 6 de junho de 1755, Para se restituir aos índios do Pará e Maranhão a liberdade de suas pessoas e bens." In Portugal, *Colleção da Legislação Portuguesa desde a última compilação das Ordenações redigida pelo Desembargador Antonio Delgado da Silva. Legislação de 1750 a 1762*, pp. 369–376. Lisbon: Typografia Maigrense, 1830.

"O Problema da África." *Revista de Engenharia* (1891): 249–251.

Rebouças, Antônio Pereira. *Recordações da vida patriótica do advogado Rebouças*. Rio de Janeiro: Typografia G. Leuzinger & Filhos, 1879.

Ribeiro, Fléxa. "Algumas imagens do Brasil." *Ilustração Brasileira* 23:123 (1945): 20–23.

Ribeyrolles, Charles. *Brazil pittoresco: historia-descripções-viagens-instutuições*, vol. III. Rio de Janeiro: Typographia Nacional, 1859.

Rodrigues, José Honório, ed. *Documentos históricos: Revolução de 1817*. Rio de Janeiro: Biblioteca Nacional, 1953–1955.

Saint-Hilaire, Auguste de. *Segunda viagem a São Paulo e quadro histórico da província de São Paulo*. Brasília: Senado Federal, 2002.

Viagem ao Rio Grande do Sul. Brasília: Senado Federal, 2002.

Sampaio, Teodoro. "Discurso." *Revista IGHBa* 42 (1916).

"Discurso." *Revista IGHBa* 43 (1917).

"Discurso." *Revista IGHBa* 45 (1919).

História da fundação da cidade de Salvador. Salvador: Beneditina, 1949.

O Rio São Francisco e a Chapada Diamantina. São Paulo: Tipografia Salesianos, 1906

O Tupi na geografia nacional. Rio de Janeiro: Cia Editora Nacional, 1987. (1st ed., 1901.)

Saraiva, José Antonio. *Resposta do conselheiro José Antonio Saraiva ao dr. Vasquez Sagastume*. Bahia: Typographia e Encadernação do Diário da Bahia, 1894.

Schlichthorst, Carl. *O Rio de Janeiro como é (1824–1826): uma vez e nunca mais: contribuições de um diário para a história atual, os costumes e especialmente a situação da tropa estrangeira na capital do Brasil.* Brasília: Senado Federal, 2000.

Schneider, Luiz. *A Guerra da Tríplice Aliança contra o governo da República do Paraguai (1864–1870), con notas del Barón de Río Branco.* Río de Janeiro: Typographia Americana, 1875–1876.

Silva, José Bonifácio de Andrada e. *Representação à Assemblea Geral Constituinte e Legislativa do Imperio do Brasil sobre a escravatura (1823).* Paris: Typographia de Firmin Didot, 1825.

Sinimbu, João Lins Vieira Cansação de. *Relatório da Repartição dos Negócios Estrangeiros apresentado por João Lins Vieira Cansansão de Sinimbu,* Anexo Q. Rio de Janeiro: Typographia de Laemmert, 1860.

Tavares, Constantino do Amaral. *Lição para meninos.* Bahia: no press named, 1861.

Telles, José Homem Correia. *Digesto português, ou tratado dos modos de adquirir a propriedade, de a gozar e administrar, e de a transferir por derradeira vontade; para servir de subsídio ao novo código civil.* Coimbra: Imprensa da Universidade, 1846.

Tollenare, Louis F. de. *Notas dominicais tomadas durante uma viagem em Portugal e no Brasil, em 1816, 1817 e 1818.* Salvador: Progresso, 1956.

Uruguay, Ministério de Relaciones Exteriores. *Documentos diplomáticos: Misión Saraiva.* Montevideo: Imprenta de "La Reforma Pacífica," 1864.

Reclamaciones de la República Oriental del Uruguay contra el Gobierno de Brasil. Montevideo: El País, 1864.

Vasconcellos, Bernardo Pereira de. "Projecto do Código Criminal apresentado em sessão de 4 de maio de 1827 pelo deputado Bernardo Pereira de Vasconcellos." In Brasil, *Anais do Parlamento Brasileiro, Câmara dos Deputados,* 1829, vol. 3, pp. 95–109. Rio de Janeiro: Typographia de H. J. Pinto, 1877.

Veríssimo, José, ed., and André Rebouças. *Diário e notas biográficas.* Rio de Janeiro: José Olympio, 1938.

Vianna, A. J. Barbosa. *Recife, capital do estado de Pernambuco.* Recife: Atelier Miranda, 1900.

Vieira, Adelina Amelia Lopes. "Modesto Brocos." *O Tempo,* August 24, 1892.

Walker, George. "The Negro on The American Stage." *Colored American Magazine* 2:4 (1906): 243–248.

Washington, Booker T. *Up from Slavery: An Autobiography.* New York: Dover Publications, 1995.

Werneck, Francisco Peixoto de Lacerda (Barão do Paty do Alferes). *Memória sobre a fundação de uma fazenda na província do Rio de Janeiro.* Brasília: Senado Federal, 1985. (1st ed., 1847.)

Williams, Bert. "The Comic Side of Trouble." *The American Magazine* 85, 1918: 33–61.

Index

Page numbers in *italics* indicate an illustration, and in **bold** indicate a table or chart.

advertisements
  for manumission fees, 247
  for runaway slaves, 245
  for wet nurses, 113
affection, 20, 108–109, 123–125, 126
Africa, 317, 329–337, 404–405
  Angola, 65
  Benin, 74, 76
  Christianity in, 330
  land ownership in, 335
  law and legal systems, 335
  musical representations of, 404, 410
  Pan-Africanism, 329, 330, 403
  Pernambuco, journey to, 64
  racism in, 334, 335
  Republic of Transvaal, 334, 335
  royalty, 76
  slavery in, 332, 334
  South Africa, 332–336
  West Central Africa, 69, 70
African people
  emancipation of, 43
  enslaved, 8, 100, 101
    children and young people, 49, 58–59,
      60–63
    preference for, 101
  "liberated," 43, 44, 62, 81
  possession of freedom, determination of, 41
Afro-descendants
  see Black people.
afterlife of slavery, 2, 26–29, 30, 32, 192
  scholarship of, 2–7
agency, 2, 17
  in abolition, 16
  of Black people, 28, 364, 366–367,
    416–417
  legal, 11, 37, 46, 47, 48, 60–63, 81, 293
  political, 398, 406, 409–411, 413–414
  of enslaved people, 17, 178, 277
  suppression of, 31
  of women, 365, 366
  see also autonomy.
Agostinha (enslaved wet nurse), 125
Agostinho (natural son of Manoel
  Gonsalves), 81
Agostinho de tal, 61
Agostini, Angelo, 360
agriculture
  artistic representation of, 349, 351
  avoura branca ("white farming"), 233
  democratization of, 326

export crops, 84
  by freed people, 230–231, 232–234
  mass production in, 84
  meação (sharecropping), 232–233
  parceira (partnership), 232, 233–234
  post-abolition, 326–327
  in post-emancipation period, 224, 225,
    228–229, 362–363
  small-holdings, 221, 228
  subsistence, 221, 233, 236
Aguirre, President Astanasio, 128, 155
AIBA (Academia Imperial de Belas Artes,
  Imperial Academy of the Arts), 341,
  347, 360
Albuquerque, Manoel Pereira Tavares de
  Mello e, 35, 36, 47
Albuquerque, Wlamyra, 27
Alfredo, João, 15
Almeida, Clarindo de, 305, 306
Almeida, Elisa Constança de, 92
Alonso, Angela, 246
Alves, Agostinho José, 291
Alves, Castro, 345
Alves, Clarindo, 303
Alves, Sinerio, 308
Amazonas, 13
Ambrosina (enslaved wet nurse), 126
Andrada e Silva, José Bonifácio de, 9
Andrade, Flávio José de, 291
Andrews, George Reid, 5
Angola, 65
Anselmo (enslaved person), 104
anti-Black racism, 125, 242, 255–261, 262,
  263
anti-racism, 251–252
Antonil, André João, 221
APERJ (Arquivo Publico do Estado do Rio
  de Janeiro), 365
Aramaré, Viscount de (Costa Pinto, Manoel
  da), 266, 270, 276–277, 280–281, 284
Araújo Filho, José Tomás Nabuco de, 12
archives, 313
  Arquivo Publico do Estado do Rio de
    Janeiro (APERJ), 365
  civil registries, 364
  communities, recorded in, 188
  diaries, 315, 316
  editing of, 319–320
  and historiography, 19
  inventories, post-mortem, 90, 91, 95, 99,
    100

For EU product safety concerns, contact us at Calle de José Abascal, 56–1°,
28003 Madrid, Spain or eugpsr@cambridge.org.

www.ingramcontent.com/pod-product-compliance
Ingram Content Group UK Ltd.
Pitfield, Milton Keynes, MK11 3LW, UK
UKHW010248140625
459647UK00013BA/1724